CURRENT POLITICS:

the way things work in Washington

JOHN F. BIBBY
University of Wisconsin-Milwaukee

ROBERT J. HUCKSHORN
Florida Atlantic University

CURRENT POLITICS:
the way things work in Washington

WINSTON PRESS   •   25 Groveland Terrace, Minneapolis, Minnesota 55403

ACKNOWLEDGMENTS

A special note of thanks is due to Sherry DeMatteo, Randy
Smith, Dolores Snyder, Esther Ward, Dean Ragland, Mary
Klein, and Robert deVilleneuve. Each made a contribution
of time and talent toward the publication of this volume.

Front Cover Design by Ruth Riley
Back Cover Photo by John Goodwin

Preface

This volume was prepared because of our conviction that students and teachers require specific and up-to-date examples and analyses, if the academic study of American politics is to be as meaningful and as interesting as we think it should be. The articles contained herein were first published in the weekly *National Journal*. The *National Journal* is designed to provide political leaders, both inside and outside government, with current, detailed and sophisticated analyses of the political scene in Washington. It is considered required reading in congressional and senatorial offices, at the White House, and in pressure group and political party headquarters. Academic readers of this volume will therefore be using one of the same information sources that policy-makers have used in making their decisions.

The *National Journal* articles selected for inclusion in this book are designed to provide insights into the workings of American political institutions and how these institutions are dealing with critical issues of public policy. The articles originally appeared in the *National Journal* between November 1970 and May 1972. All have been revised and up-dated to reflect changes that have occurred since the original publication.

Milwaukee, Wisconsin   J. F. B.
Boca Raton, Florida   R. J. H.

Contents

Preface   v

1   Political Parties and the Electorate   1

Nixon strategy calls for low-key campaign with strong emphasis on performance – Dom Bonafede   3

O'Brien presses for unity: Democrats prepare for 1972 convention – Jonathan Cottin   14

Pollsters prowl nation as candidates use opinion surveys to plan '72 campaign – Andrew J. Glass   26

Political spending law will have impact on candidates, business, labor – Jonathan Cottin   39

2   Pressure Groups   49

GM gets little mileage from compact, low-powered lobby – Frank V. Fowlkes   51

Labor and industry gear for major battle over bill to curb imports, multinationals – Charles Culhane   71

Common cause seeks to have broad role on issue in 1972 campaign – Andrew J. Glass   85

3   The Congress   101

Mansfield reforms spark quiet revolution in senate – Andrew J. Glass   103

Two money committees wield power differently – Frank V. Fowlkes and Harry Lenhart, Jr.   120

4 The President   157

    Haldeman directs staff as President's alter ego – Dom Bonafede   159

    Ehrlichman acts as policy broker in Nixon's formalized domestic council – Dom Bonafede   169

    Speechwriters play strategic role in conveying, shaping Nixon's policies – Dom Bonafede   183

5 The Administrative Process   195

    The making of the President's budget: politics and influence in a new manner – Dom Bonafede   197

    HEW department, largest federal spender, seeks to funnel more money to the poor – John K. Iglehart   212

    Community development proposal pits President's influence against established lobbies – William Lilley III   229

6 Law and Justice   239

    FBI at end of Hoover era lacking blueprint for transition – Richard S. Frank   240

    Federal strike forces dominate government's war on organized crime – Richard S. Frank   258

    Ponderous, public-oriented American Bar Association has an image crisis – Richard S. Frank   271

7 Public Policy Issues   291

    Defense and Foreign Policy   292

        Senate attempts to limit President's power to make war – John Maffre   293

    The Economy   305

        Beleaguered cost of living council set to focus on major market forces – Andrew J. Glass   306

    Transportation and Communication   317

        Congress plods through complex arguments over transportation regulation – Vera Hirschberg   318

        Broadcasters charge FCC and courts erode media freedom – Bruce E. Throp   332 *viii*   **Health, Education and Welfare**   343

   Legislation could revolutionize federal programs for higher education –
   Joel Havemann   344

The Environment   359

   White House seeks to restrict scope of environment law – Claude E. Barfield and Richard Corrigan   360

1 POLITICAL PARTIES AND THE ELECTORATE

The major functions of a political party are designed to mobilize support behind efforts to capture public office, to carry out party policy, and ultimately, run the government. Even before the electorate can play its role in the selection of the rulers, the political party organization must play its part in structuring the electoral situation. Each party, however, treats its role in a different fashion from the other. The party controlling the presidency will set as its principal national goal the continued occupancy of the White House, while its counterpart will do what it can to oust the incumbent. It is to these ends that Republican President Richard M. Nixon and Democratic National Chairman Lawrence O'Brien have been working since the 1970 congressional elections. Nixon, as undisputed head of his party, and O'Brien, as national chairman of his, are working to mobilize the support necessary to build the electoral pluralities or majorities necessary to win or retain control of the presidency and Congress.

As described in the first selection, the Nixon re-election strategy, directed by former Attorney General John N. Mitchell, was first organized from the offices of the Committee for the Reelection of the President in order to keep the President from being engaged prematurely in blatant election year politics. The constantly shifting tactics of a presidential campaign are described in terms of the decisions made and the individuals whose responsibility it is to make them.

The problems facing Lawrence O'Brien are vastly different from those facing the incumbent President's strategists. Faced with a seemingly insurmountable debt and a multiplicity of Democratic candidates, Mr. O'Brien directed the party's effort largely by persuasion and mediation. His expertise and his wide political experience permitted him to impose his own personal style of politics on the Democratic party as the year progressed. In a very real sense, O'Brien's guidance of the national party organization might eventually determine whether or not the Democrats mount a successful and unified campaign against President Nixon.

Two of the principal ingredients in modern political campaigning—money and opinion polls—are discussed in the final two selections. To help alleviate the vast costs of national campaigns, the Congress in 1972 passed the first new campaign collection and expenditure control law in many years. Addressed particularly to the enormous costs of media campaigning and to limiting levels of contributions, the new law is being carefully watched by professional politicians in both parties to assay its effects on national campaigning. Obvious loopholes in the law will possibly be exploited by the parties

2 and their candidates, but it is a much tighter law than the legislation which it replaced.

The world of politics has changed drastically as a result of the growth of scientific public opinion polling. This history and description of polling techniques explores the role of polls in the campaign strategies of President Nixon and the major Democratic candidates. The cost, technical problems, and public misunderstandings of opinion polls are discussed in this section.

An election year brings all the shadows and images of politics and politicians into sharp focus. The articles in this chapter demonstrate the pervasive influence of personalities, political organizations, campaign money and public pulse-taking in the selection of the leaders who will ultimately run the government.

Nixon strategy calls for low-key campaign with strong emphasis on performance

Dom Bonafede

During a private White House talk with Republican Governors in March, President Nixon said that he intends to follow a "50-state strategy" in his 1972 reelection bid.

As defined by Harry S. Dent, special counsel to the President for political affairs, Mr. Nixon was alluding to the fact that the Republican Party was not taking any state for granted nor writing off any state as hopelessly in the column of the Democratic Party.

"Like the Bible, we are going all the way from Genesis to Revelations and show the President as a man of peace," Dent said.

Thus, unlike 1968 when Mr. Nixon rode to victory behind the so-called "southern strategy," he will seek to make a broad, national appeal to American voters and present himself as President of all the people. And, in contrast to the 1970 midterm elections, Mr. Nixon will eschew divisive politics; less will be heard about law and order, violence and dissent.

Head start: White House staff members, officials of the Committee for the Reelection of the President and other Nixon political operatives, express optimism that the President was in a favorable position in the early stages of the pre-convention campaign.

"We've got a President making a lot of headway in a lot of ways," said Jeb S. Magruder, deputy to former Attorney General (1969-72) John N. Mitchell, who is Mr. Nixon's campaign manager.

Nixon officials quote the polls to support their thesis that Mr. Nixon's popularity is firm and rising. Nonetheless, they say they anticipate a tough race and that fast-breaking domestic developments, the new enemy offensive in Vietnam and a breakdown in the President's new economic policy could have a decisive effect on the fate of the Nixon campaign.

Incumbency question: They also are aware that the advantages traditionally conceded an incumbent President may not hold fast in Mr. Nixon's case because of several reasons: he is a member of a minority party who won in 1968 with only 43 per cent of the vote; much of his domestic legislation has been stymied by a Democratic Congress; he is not a figure who inspires deep personal affection or wide public adulation; and he conceivably could be brushed with a scent of scandal emanating from the International Telephone and Telegraph Corp. case. Also, like all incumbents, he is a sitting target for those who will seek to measure his Administration by its early promises and its eventual performance.

Thomas E. Cronin, a Brookings Institution fellow and Presidential scholar, says that "the Presidential incumbency is a vastly overrated advantage."

He said that during the past century Presidents serving full four-year terms won reelection only six times.

Franklin D. Roosevelt did it three times, William McKinley, Woodrow Wilson and Dwight D. Eisenhower each won reelection once.

"To be sure," Cronin said, "four other Presidents were elected as incumbents (Theodore Roosevelt, Calvin Coolidge, Harry S. Truman and Lyndon B. Johnson) but each ascended to office upon the death of his predecessor and was elected President on his own for the first time. The rather important point to appreciate is that while four Presidents have won reelection as full-term incumbents, the exact same number of Presidents (Grover Cleveland, Benjamin Harrison, William Howard Taft and Herbert C. Hoover) lost their bids for reelection despite the supposed advantage of the Presidential incumbency.

"On the balance, then, it appears that one must examine the context of the times, party strength, the political character of the President and the challenger and perhaps most importantly, the extent to which the President has a successful record."

Ready for takeoff—Today, with less than seven months remaining before the Nov. 7 election, the Nixon reelection forces are fully operational, elaborately organized and, according to indications, psychologically primed for battle.

Vice President Spiro T. Agnew told the Republican National Leadership Conference on March 3: "We have the issues. We have the candidate. We have the organization that will turn out the vote."

Yet, as the President himself

4

1972 campaign will present Mr. Nixon as President of all the people

has said, the issues of today may not be the issues of November.

STRATEGY

With the political winds rapidly shifting, Nixon aides say it would be impractical at this point in the campaign to develop a grand strategy. "You never hear big strategy as such discussed," Dent said. "If there is any, it is in the minds of Nixon and Mitchell."

Nevertheless, there are several verities that prevail in the Nixon camp:

Mr. Nixon will remain aloof from partisan politics and leave the campaigning to trusted surrogates until after the Republican convention in Miami in August.

Emphasis will be on the President's record and performance rather than on his personality.

"The selling of the President" will be less blatant in 1972 than in 1968, with more stress on campaign fundamentals (organizing at

the grass-roots level, promoting voter registration, and getting out the vote) than on media theatrics.

Despite the alleged disaffection among the blacks and the young for the Administration, an intensive effort will be made to convert them to Mr. Nixon's side.

National climate: To a large extent, the shape and strategy of the Nixon campaign (as well as the Democrats' campaign) is being determined by the national political climate.

"Mostly, we react to the people's moods and attitudes," said an official of the President's reelection committee. "The American voter is more intelligent and sophisticated than he is given credit for being. He has a keener sense of the values which affect his life and his family's life than most politicians do.

"The electorate, as a result, largely determines the issues, whether it is peace, school busing or the credibility gap. How the candidate

responds goes a long way in whether he wins or loses. The day when a candidate can simply be merchandised and packaged is over. Take Muskie (Sen. Edmund S. Muskie, D-Maine). He has had a big media campaign but has been flabby on the issues and look what has happened to him."

The campaign official acknowledged that Mr. Nixon's March 16 statement on school busing and quality education was prompted by highly charged public sentiment over the issue. However, he denied that the President's antibusing stance was in any way influenced by the large voter turnout given Alabama Gov. George C. Wallace, D, a vigorous opponent of busing, in the March 14 Florida primary.

"We have been accused of playing politics with the issue," he said. "But the fact is the statement was ready before the Florida primary but the White House decided to delay it until afterwards so it would not look like the President was trying to capitalize politically with it."

The incident, nonetheless, illustrates the weight which a vital public issue carries in the political arena.

Then and now—Since Mr. Nixon first took office almost three-and-a-half years ago, the nation has witnessed several basic developments: the war issue, though not dead, is less of an emotional point of reference; political violence has subsided on the campuses and streets; people are more concerned about jobs, inflation and prices; voters have less confidence in their political representatives and public institutions.

These changes undoubtedly will

Murray M. Chotiner

have a direct relationship with the kind of campaign waged by Mr. Nixon. Essentially, his advisers say, he will not pursue the politics of polarization he unsuccessfully attempted in 1970.

The man—Mr. Nixon's personal evolution as President, plus his style and image, also will have a bearing on his campaign.

He has proved to be more flexible than his critics imagined in foreign policy matters (thereby alienating many hardliners in his own party) and more innovative in the domestic affairs area, particularly in proposals regarding revenue sharing, welfare reform, government reorganization and economic controls. His relations with Congress generally have been disappointing. And while he gives the appearance of being a diligent, hard-working President, he has shown himself to be an exceedingly private person.

One prominent journalist, *Life* columnist Hugh S. Sidey, reported last October, "Nixon the man is not much better understood now than the day he came into office."

Thus, how Mr. Nixon, the man, fits into the political equation cannot easily be gauged.

But it is significant that the Nixon media managers go to extremes to downplay his name and personal characteristics.

His principal political vehicle—the Committee for the Reelection of the President—fails to include his name in its title; nor is it mentioned on the committee's letterhead or campaign buttons. Television spots and newspaper ads promoting his candidacy in the early primary states seldom showed his picture.

Missing person: Above all, Mr. Nixon himself is absent from the campaign. According to Dent, "The President won't actively campaign until after the convention. How he campaigns—whether he will barnstorm, what states he will visit—won't be decided until then." (Also, the current thinking among some White House staff members is that he will not campaign this fall on behalf of Republican candidates for Congress nearly so much as he did in 1970.)

This low-profile approach, his aides say, is being taken to accent the statesman-President image as opposed to the private man. And, unlike some of Mr. Nixon's Democratic rivals, he has no identification problem and could be more hurt than helped by publicity overexposure in which he is cast as a politician wooing votes.

Furthermore, if he so desires, he can monopolize the vast resources of the national media at almost any time he chooses.

Among Mr. Nixon's political counselors, Murray M. Chotiner, for one, is convinced that the

magic attributed to media advertising in a presidential campaign is exaggerated, at least so far as an incumbent is concerned.

"You want to use the media to acquaint people with the performance of your candidate and his program," Chotiner said. "Somehow, the public gets a pretty good idea of what's going on without a lot of carnival and hoopla."

Surrogates—Although the tone of the Nixon campaign is low-keyed, its size in terms of manpower and available facilities is immense. In addition to using the resources of the White House, the Republican National Committee and the reelection committee, the President relies on non-career appointees in the executive branch and Republican Governors, such as New York's Nelson A. Rockefeller and California's Ronald Reagan, to act as his proxy in making political speeches and raising campaign funds.

During the Florida primary, Shirley Spellerberg, a Republican state committeewoman who worked for the candidacy of Rep. John M. Ashbrook, R-Ohio, said of the Nixon campaign, "This talk of a low-keyed campaign for Nixon is ridiculous. They're coming down here in hordes. If this is low-keyed. I'd hate to see what they'd do if it were high-keyed."

Traveling salesmen—The most popular Administration speakers are Cabinet members and White House staff members, including Herbert G. Klein, director of communications for the executive branch; Robert H. Finch, counselor to the President; and Dent. One unexpectedly effective campaigner for the President is his youngest daughter, Julie Nixon Eisenhower. She has made appearances in several states and is scheduled to be used more frequently.

During one recent week, Dent made nine speeches. Besides making speeches, the Nixon evangelists hold news conferences and appear on local radio and television stations.

On two occasions, Presidential surrogates have made national front-page news. On Feb. 3, Secretary of State William P. Rogers said that Sen. Muskie had damaged prospects for a negotiated peace in Vietnam be rejecting the President's latest peace proposals before the enemy formally replied to them. Rogers' accusation was surprising since partisan politics is considered outside the province of the Secretary of State.

Less than a week later, H. R. Haldeman, assistant to the President and White House chief of staff, declared on the "Today" show (NBC-TV) that critics of the President's war policy "are consciously aiding and abetting the enemy." Haldeman's comments were viewed in a political context since most of the Democratic candidates are opposed to the President's war policy.

Dent on the Road—Describing his role as Administration spokesman on the road, Dent, a former aide to Sen. Strom Thurmond, R-S.C., and an architect of the "southern strategy," said: "I go out and sell what the Administration is doing. I localize it, put it in hard, cold political terms and rev them up on the economy, busing world peace, the whole gamut . . . .

"The old conservative Strom Thurmond image which people hang around my neck turns out to be an advantage when you are in the South and running against a guy like Ashbrook. My credentials are good, and can help offset Ashbrook.

"I don't decide what I'm going to say until I get there. I kind of case the joint. In almost every instance, they want the hard line. I put a conservative twist to welfare reform and generally translate what the President is doing in conservative terms to meet demands of conservatives around the country."

Dent, who speaks all over the United States, said, "The farther you get out in the field, the more saleable you are."

He added that in speaking to college students he found that "if you tell the truth, not be a false prophet and don't try to pull the wool over their eyes, they'll give you a good reception even if they don't agree with you philosophically."

Registration project—One of the GOP national committee's major endeavors called "Target '72," is aimed at getting voters registered. So far this year, the project has resulted in almost 100,000 new registrations.

Voter registration is especially essential to the Republicans since the Democrats outnumber them five to three. As Vice President Agnew frequently reminds party workers, Mr. Nixon won in 1968 with a plurality of only 500,000 votes, fewer than three votes per U.S. precinct. While Mr. Nixon's winning vote total was 31 million, 38 million potentially eligible voters did not cast a ballot because they had not registered.

STATE CAMPAIGNING

Mr. Nixon's overwhelming victories over his two Republican challengers, Ashbrook and Rep. Paul N. McCloskey Jr. of California, in New Hampshire and Florida, caused a change in the strategy and direction of the President's reelection campaign. Mr. Nixon received 69 per cent of the Republican vote in New Hampshire and 87 per cent in Florida.

"The voters in the two states gave us a broad hint they approve of the President's programs and policies," said DeVan L. Shumway, director of public affairs for the reelection committee. "As a result, we made a decision to pull back and not spend a great deal of money in Wisconsin and some of the other primaries.

"New Hampshire gave us concern because we didn't have a feel how it would go. Florida, too. Now we feel comfortable."

"Our problem in New Hampshire was apathy; we were concerned about a low turnout. But we went after the apathy problem and turned out the voters. We feel it was a good effort since we didn't have a candidate there. In Florida, it was the same thing.

"The primaries now are not a major factor in our situation since we have little or no opposition. The interest obviously is on the other side. For us, this is a period of consolidation, building up organizational strength in the states, planning for state conventions, working with constituent groups and developing strategies depending on who becomes the Democratic candidate."

CHOTINER: IN THE CAMPAIGN WITH AN 'HONEST-ELECTION' ROLE

Murray M. Chotiner, the controversial Nixon loyalist, once again is working for his political idol.

Chotiner, who often has been accused by his political opponents of engaging in questionable campaign tactics, has been assigned by Nixon-reelection forces to ensure an "honest count" in the 1972 election.

At the direction of John N. Mitchell, former Attorney General (1969-72) now serving as Mr. Nixon's campaign manager, Chotiner has been put in charge of "ballot security."

Job definition—During an interview at his law office, located a block from the White House in the same building as the Committee for the Reelection of the President, Chotiner elaborated on his new campaign role:

"Essentially, it will be my job to see that everyone who has a right to vote has an opportunity to do so and to see that there is an honest count. We're not involved in technical enforcement, but we don't want to see voting by people who are clearly ineligible because of lack of citizenship, or who don't reside in the state or who are resting in graveyards.

"And we want to make certain that voting machines do not have votes registered on machines before the polls open, and that people are not transported across the border from Mexico. I'm not suggesting they (the Democratic opposition) have done so in the past; we just want to make sure they don't in the future.

"Also, we want to be certain that when they count absentee paper ballots, those favorable to the President are not mutilated or discarded. In short, we want to guarantee that the 1972 Presidential election is an honest election."

On call: Chotiner, who has had a role in almost every Nixon campaign since the President first ran for the House in 1946, obviously was delighted to be back in harness. After a short stint in the White House as a political aide, he left in March 1971 to practice law in Washington. In a warm farewell letter, President Nixon told Chotiner that if the need arose he would again "call on you for assistance." Evidently, the need has arisen.

Chotiner said he did not discuss his new assignment with the President and further did not know if Mr. Nixon was consulted regarding it. However, it is inconceivable that the decision would have been made without Mr. Nixon's approval, particularly because of the controversy that has long surrounded Chotiner.

A master campaign technician, Chotiner sometimes has advocated what many consider unorthodox tactics. Chotiner, for example, was responsible for distributing more than a half million "pink sheets" comparing the voting records of Rep. Helen Gahagan Douglas, D-Calif., Mr. Nixon's 1950 opponent for a Senate seat from California, with that of former Rep. Vito Marcantonio, a New York politician often associated with pro-Communist causes.

A practitioner of gut politics,

Chotiner once said, "What is the difference between legitimate attack and smear? ... It is not a smear, if you please, if you point out the record of your opponent ... Of course, it is always a smear when it is directed to our candidate."

Precedent—With a lawyer's precision, Chotiner pointed out that his assignment, while more formally organized and extensive than in the past, is not without precedent. In 1968, he said, Lou Nichols, a former chief aide to FBI Director J. Edgar Hoover, supervised voting surveillance on behalf of the Republican Party. Called "Operation Eagle Eye," it marked the first time that election security was conducted on a national basis.

Chotiner recalled that the Nichols operation was set up because of charges of election fraud in Illinois and Texas following the 1960 election. Both states were won narrowly by John F. Kennedy.

"You'll remember that at the time it was suggested that the ballots in the two states be impounded," Chotiner said. "Nixon, however, decided against it because it would create too much turmoil in the international situation if no one knew who was the President of the United States. He didn't want to be in the position of charging a dishonest election.

"We were determined that it would not happen in 1968. But the Nichols operation, which was not established until September 1968, didn't have enough time or personnel to do a complete job. We'll be better prepared and organized."

Procedures—Chotiner said that he has asked Republican committee chairmen in 26 states so far to set up security units. He also said that members of his law firm (Reeves & Harrison) are studying state election laws to ascertain legal voting requirements and to determine areas of potential violations.

"We intend to inspect each voting machine and see how it operates so we'll know what to look for," he said. "Each state provides by law that you have a poll watcher but the mere fact that you have someone watching is no guarantee. I don't want to suggest that this is necessary in each state; in some states there hasn't been a breath of scandal but we're not taking any chances. Legally, you have a right to inspect voting machines and see no votes are prematurely cast or levers pulled"

Bid to Democrats—Chotiner contended that election surveillance should be a bipartisan objective and that Lawrence F. O'Brien, chairman of the Democratic National Committee, will be invited to participate in a joint effort.

"I can't imagine the opposition objecting or refusing to join in," Chotiner said. "Obviously, they are as interested in an honest election as we are."

He said after the state election laws are well researched, the material probably would be turned over to O'Brien and to Sen. Robert Dole, R-Kan., chairman of the Republican National Committee.

Chotiner said that from time to time he meets with top officials of the Nixon-reelection operation to discuss over-all strategy. "I'll probably continue to do this," he said. "But I haven't the slightest idea what else I'll do other than what I've been assigned thus far."

Swing states—Dent listed the key states for the President as Ohio, Illinois, California and Texas. "Supreme efforts will be made in those places," he said. "Even if they go against us, we can survive. But we have to pick up all the votes we can in the South, Midwest and Northeast.

"I'm not as worried about Texas as some people. John Connally (Treasury Secretary John B. Connally) is a key factor there. The last time he rasied Hubert Humphrey's hand, and then there was George Wallace to drain votes from us, so we lost the state." (Sen. Hubert H. Humphrey, D-Minn., a Democratic Presidential candidate, was his party's nominee for President in 1968.)

Dent said the Republicans "have to do more in California; but I have faith we'll pull it off, it's the President's home state."

Regarding Republican chances in other states, he said, "There is no problem in Indiana. Mitchell is convinced that New York can be taken. Michigan can be taken for no other reason than busing. New Jersey, Pennsylvania and some New England states can also be taken."

On the campaign trail—Connally, the highest-ranking Democrat in the Administration, already has agreed to campaign actively for the President. And in a significant but little-noticed move, Lyn Nofziger, former deputy chairman for communications at the Republican National Committee, has been sent to California to work in the primary there. Nofziger, former press secretary for Ronald Reagan, again is working for the Governor.

Reagan is chairman of the President's reelection committee in California, as Gov. Rockefeller is in New York.

THE WHITE HOUSE

Since last year President Nixon has taken the position that partisan politics and White House business should not be commingled. Of late, however, little effort is made to keep up that separation.

Mr. Nixon continues to avoid any appearance of political involvement or make any political statements. Nevertheless, a White House aide reported, "The really big stuff on the direction of the campaign is decided by Nixon and Mitchell. Decisions are made at the lower levels. Mitchell then goes in and says, 'Mr. Nixon, we've decided to do this or that.' If Nixon doesn't like it, it will be changed."

Staff involvement: Meanwhile, almost all of the President's top aides are to some degree involved in the reelection campaign:

Haldeman is the main conduit to the President and works closely with Mitchell on stragety and items of major political significance.

John D. Ehrlichman, executive director of the Domestic Council, provides information on various domestic issues to the reelection committee, the GOP national committee and other party organizations.

Henry A. Kissinger, assistant to the President for national security affairs, performs the same function in the area of foreign affairs and national security.

Frederic V. Malek, special assistant to the President for personnel, acts as liaison between the White House and the reelection committee and also recruits campaign workers.

Charles W. Colson, special counsel to the President, deals with special-interest groups regarding political and fund-raising activities.

Clark MacGregor, counsel to the President, serves as a link with Congress and keeps Mr. Nixon informed on political and legislative matters.

Herbert G. Klein, executive branch communications director, serves as itinerant speechmaker and supplier of information to the media on Administration activities.

Ronald L. Ziegler, White House press secretary, coordinates news releases with counterparts at the reelection committee and the GOP national committee.

Harry Dent, White House political aide, serves as speechmaker, coordinator with state party leaders and political briefer to the President.

"I can't think of anybody over there (the White House), we don't work with, depending on the activity," said a reelection committee official. "We all know each other and talk to each other."

He said, however, that the payrolls of the White House and the reelection committee are kept separate.

Dent's office since early this

HOW REPUBLICANS SIZE UP THE COMPETITION

Throughout the early primaries, Administration officials have been keeping a close watch on the leading Democratic Presidential candidates and potential candidates. This is how they are rated by White House staff members and officials of the Committee for the Reelection of the President:

Sen. Edmund S. Muskie, D-Maine: A spokesman for the committee said, "If Muskie was the person he was in 1970 he'd be a hell of a candidate. But his appeal has gone way down. He would have been in a good position if he had done well in Wisconsin but now he is just one in the pack."

Sen. George S. McGovern, D-S.D.: The committee spokesman said of McGovern, "He knocked (New York Mayor John V.) Lindsay out of the race and is doing better than anyone expected. If he can pull off a couple more wins and does well in California and Oregon, he's going to be tough.

"Basically, of course, he's got Kennedy (Sen. Edward M. Kennedy, D-Mass.) support. If he can overcome the feeling he's not electable, he could take it all. McGovern has to show he can win."

Sen. Kennedy: Of Kennedy, the committee official said, "It's hard to say. It's a question of whether the public perceives him as Presidential quality. He raises some doubts in people's minds as to his age and record. The public perception in his case is very high. Everybody, of course, still remembers Chappaquiddick."

Sen. Hubert H. Humphrey, D-Minn.: A White House aide said that Humphrey is "well-qualified and more statesmanlike than generally believed. By far, he's their best candidate. He's active and energetic and a good campaigner.

"He should do well in the future primaries, which would give him an edge over Muskie. And the polls show he is gaining. He could put together a fairly good coalition, including labor and blacks."

Gov. George C. Wallace, D-Ala.: Harry S. Dent special counsel to the President for political affairs, said: "Lots of the experts are saying Wallace would cut into Nixon's strength in the South if he runs as a third-party candidate. Actually, he would take more votes from the Democrats in the North.

"He's hurting the Democratic candidates now by making them come to him on the issues and by piling up votes against them, making them look bad.

"We think the President is in good shape from Virginia to Texas and that he could take most of the southern states away from Wallace."

Disarray among Democrats—Another assessment was offered by Murray M. Chotiner, a veteran Nixon campaign adviser.

"It's the field against Mr. Nixon," he said. "To use an old cliche, you can't elect somebody with nobody. They have a multitude of candidates but no leader."

A spokesman for the reelection committee said that the plethora of Democratic candidates and the resulting disarray within the organization's ranks will have repercussions at the party's convention in Miami Beach.

"With Wallace on the right, blacks and the liberals on the left and (Chicago Mayor Richard J.) Daley in the center, there is bound to be chaos. Traditionally, the center is boss-ruled at the Democratic convention. But Daley can't control it and it will be up for grabs.

"As a result, the activists will go for the center as the conservatives did in 1964 for Goldwater. This can only mean trouble for them." (Sen. Barry Goldwater, R-Ariz., was the GOP Presidential nominee in 1964.)

In the meantime, the spokesmen said, the Republicans are building up their credibility with the various voting blocs and ethnic groups.

"Our delegation will be as balanced as theirs, with women, blacks, young people and Mexican-Americans. It will be very representative," he said. "We are pleased with our activities in those areas."

year has been increased from seven to 10 employees, including five professionals.

Each day he signs about 150 memos dealing with political reports for the President.

REELECTION COMMITTEE

On April 13, Mitchell, the President's first Attorney General, 1968 campaign manager, close friend and former law partner, formally took charge of Mr. Nixon's 1972 reelection bid.

For Mitchell, who earlier had resigned from the Justice Department, the transfer simply meant moving out of his law firm into a spacious office long reserved for him at the headquarters of the Committee for the Reelection of the President. Both offices are on the fourth floor of a bank building at 1701 Pennsylvania Ave. NW, a block away from the White House.

Although the distance was short, the move could have a far-reaching effect on Mr. Nixon's political future and ultimately on the history of the country.

Mitchell, in point of fact, had been running the reelection committee from behind the scenes since it was first established last summer.

Now, as the election fever begins to spread, he will orchestrate the multitude of daily activities necessary for conducting a modern presidential campaign.

Assessing Mitchell's role, a White House official said, "He's the next thing to the President. He awes people and his presence over there is vital.

"He is in demand but dull as a public speaker. But in private talks, he is very good."

The committee: When first set up, the reelection committee was composed of fewer than 20 members and occupied a single suite of offices.

Today, it lists about 140 full-time employees, plus a varying number of volunteers. The number of salaried employees will go up to 200 when the committee reaches its full complement at the height of the campaign.

The committee's expansion is further reflected in the fact it now occupies one complete floor of the same bank building and parts of four others.

Activities—The committee's multifaceted operations cover the spectrum of campaign activities, including fund-raising, liaison with constituent blocs, political coordination with state and regional groups, press relations and "in-house task force on advertising."

Among the committee's top officials are: Maurice H. Stans, former Commerce Secretary, director of fund raising operations; Jeb Magruder, who had been in charge of the committee's day-to-day activities, now second in command to Mitchell; Harry S. Flemming, former White House aide, political scientist; Robert C. Odle Jr., office manager; and Herbert L. Porter, in charge of scheduling Administration speakers.

Meanwhile, other committee members are assigned to working with the various voter groups in an effort to solicit their support. They include: Clayton K. Yeutter, agriculture; Paul R. Jones, the black community; Paul W. Kayser, business organizations; Webster B. Todd, the elderly; Alex M. Armen-

NIXON TEAM MORALE: HIGH DESPITE ITT AND OTHER SETBACKS

Nixon Administration officials contend that the public furor over the International Telephone and Telegraph Corp. case should have little or no adverse affect on the President's reelection efforts.

They further maintain that despite reports to the contrary, the young and the blacks are not overwhelmingly in the camp of the Democratic opposition.

ITT case—In reference to published accusations that ITT pledged $200,000 for the Republican national convention in San Diego in return for a favorable ruling by the Justice Department in an antitrust suit, a top official for the Committee for the Reelection of the President said:

"If a reputed scandal ends up in an indictment and directly involves a candidate, it could cause problems. But if there is no conclusion—and I don't think there will be in the ITT case—it won't help us or help them.

"Politically, I don't think it will affect us. However, it does affect public confidence in the whole apparatus of government.

"The President is perceived as a very honest, hard-working guy. It won't affect him personally or politically."

The official said that the polls and the primaries fail to show any impact by the ITT investigation.

"We're in the middle of it (the investigation) and it is not hurting us," he said.

Presidential aide Peter M. Flanigan, whose name has figured in the case, claimed in an interview that the accusations were "politi-cally motivated ... but it won't work."

Murray M. Chotiner, an old political associate of Mr. Nixon's, said:

"People understand and therefore are not excited about the charge that there has been a contribution in fact or contemplated.

"First of all, neither the Republican Party nor the campaign would get the money. It would go to the San Diego convention bureau.

"Second, as the President has pointed out, ITT became a conglomerate during the Kennedy and Johnson Administrations and nothing was done to hold it in line until the Nixon Administration compelled it to divest itself of a number of its acquisitions. If anything, ITT would be more grateful to the Democratic Party than the Republican Party."

Nixon on ITT—During a press conference in his White House office on March 24, Mr. Nixon told reporters:

"It is significant to note—and I would hope that the members of the press would report this, because I have not seen this in many stories—it is significant to note that ITT became the great congolmerate that it was in the two previous Administrations primarily, the Kennedy Administration and the Johnson Administration. It grew and grew and grew, and nothing was done to stop it.

"In this Administration we moved on ITT ... We moved on it effectively. We required the greatest divestiture in the history of the antitrust law ... If we wanted to do a favor for ITT, we could just continue to do what the two previous Administrations had done, and that is nothing: let ITT continue to grow."

Youth vote—According to most political analysts, the great majority of the almost 25 million new voters between 18 and 21 years will cast their ballots for the Democratic ticket.

Not so, Administration officials say.

"Remember, only 5.8 per cent of the new voters are in college," said White House political aide Harry S. Dent. "Most of the others are workers. We think we will do well there.

"I've never yet failed to get a standing ovation preaching Richard Nixon at the colleges. I think the President's opportunity with young people is better than expected. Contrast this Administration with other Administrations on such issues as the war, the draft and fairness—that is, treating all people alike. Young people are idealistic, they want fairness."

During a television interview with four network commentators on Jan. 4, 1971, Mr. Nixon mentioned that 40 per cent of the 18- to 21-year-old voters had no party affiliation. Said the President:

"So this means that the young people of America are a very volatile group, that they are a group that both parties are going to have to go out and have to try to win. I think that we have just as good a shot at them as others do, but we don't have the confidence of

12 young people that some in the other party have, which they have at this time, because we have all of the problems and we are responsible for them.

"But if we can end the war, if we can end the draft, if we can bring jobs and equal opportunity without the cost of war and without the cost of the rise in inflation, I believe that young people as they see our very imaginative programs for reforming government, for the environment and the rest, they will be attracted to our party not as a party, but to our principles beyond party."

On April 15, the White House reported that it was accepting "in whole or in part" almost 60 per cent of the proposals made by the White House Conference on Youth in 1971.

Black vote—In an effort to improve its relations with blacks, the White House has increased its meetings with black organizations and black leaders. Robert J. Brown, a special assistant to the President and a black, acts as liaison for such sessions.

"Bob Brown has used me considerably for such meetings," Dent said.

"We have the potential to make gains with the black vote. Our prospects are twice as good in the South as in the North. Blacks in the South are not so militant; they've experienced desegregation and see better housing.

"Whenever I speak in the South I address the blacks. Nixon has been fair with them; they've more opportunities, more jobs, higher pay, better conditions. He has treated the South like the rest of the country. There is no class, race or sectional warfare."

daris, Spanish-speaking Americans; Kenneth C. Rietz, youth affairs; and Patricia G. Hutar, volunteers.

In recognition of the women's liberation movement and also to "get away from the tea-and-coffee syndrome," the committee decided to integrate women into the various working units rather than set up a separate group. One of the charter members of the committee

and its leading women's advocate is Rita E. Hauser, New York lawyer and U.S. delegate to the United Nations.

Expected to join the committee soon to head up its political section is Robert C. Mardian, assistant attorney general for internal security.

Press-media setup—Assisting Shumway in the public affairs section are Ann Dore and Thomas E.

Girard. They serve as liaison with press officials in each of the state party organizations.

An innovative step taken by the Administration led to the creation of its own advertising agency, headed by Los Angeles advertising executive Peter H. Dailey, a one-time classmate of Haldeman's. The agency, more commonly known within the Administration as the "November Group," is located in

Lyn Nofziger *Robert C. Mardian* *Frederic V. Malek*

New York. It creates all of the Nixon media advertising, subject to approval by Mitchell and other Nixon aides, including Haldeman.

Committee spokesmen, however, are quick to emphasize that Haldeman, a former advertising executive with the J. Walter Thompson agency, does not run the November Group. They further maintain that at this point in the campaign there are no plans for Roger E. Ailes or Harry Treleaven Jr. to join the president's media operation.

The two directed Mr. Nixon's media campaign in 1968.

Polling analysis for the committee is conducted by Robert M. Teeter, head of Market opinion Research Inc., Detroit.

The committee also publishes its own newspaper. *The ReElector.*

Circulation for the first edition published in April totaled 50,000. Plans call for a publication run of 200,000 before the November election.

OUTLOOK

Although buoyant, none of the officials associated with the Nixon reelection campaign are flatly predicting victory in November.

The general feeling was summed up by Chotiner:

"I don't think the election will be based on who the President's opponent is. The question is whether the public wants to reelect Mr. Nixon. An incumbent must have a record of performance, a program, plus the confidence of the voters. The President has the first two; the only one to be established is the third element and the polls say he has that."

In a Gallup poll published April 10, Mr. Nixon led Muskie 46 to 36 per cent and Humphrey, 46 to 35 per cent.

The Nixon forces, however, are aware of the imponderables which could surface before the November election, such as a slippage in the economy, an escalation in the war or the disclosure of a new scandal.

They are also cognizant that Mr. Nixon is a minority President and that any setback in his political appeal could be fatal to his reelection hopes.

"The Democrats have numerical superiority and we'll have to scrape for everything we get," Dent said.

O'Brien presses for unity; Democrats prepare for 1972 convention *Jonathan Cottin*

Not so long ago, Joseph E. Mohbat, press secretary at the Democratic National Committee, noticed that everyone in the office called Chairman Lawrence F. O'Brien "the chairman." Whether it was a switchboard operator or a high-level staff man speaking of or to O'Brien, it was always, "the chairman."

Mohbat decided to launch a campaign against such formality, both in fun and to nip in the bud any cult of personality. "Larry's an informal guy," he told his office colleagues. "Why don't we just call him 'the'?"

For a while, young staff members tried the new title among themselves. But it never caught on.

For, around the DNC, as well as around the country among party leaders, "the chairman" is accorded such firm respect that few feel comfortable being the least bit playful with the man who is rebuilding a party that was in pieces just two years ago.

The most serious criticism any party leader has made to *National Journal* about O'Brien was that "he hasn't been able to wipe out the ($9.3-million) debt of the national committee." But that critic, Neale Chaney, Washington state Democratic chairman, added: "I don't think anybody could."

Down in Arkansas, State Democratic Chairman Joe Purcell said "The chairman is doing a very splendid job. He has put the national committee and the Democratic Party into an organizational unit."

"The chairman is one of the really good political planners around. He more or less wrote the book," said Clif Larson, Iowa Democratic chairman.

O'Brien, whose bosses are the 110 national committeemen and committeewomen who govern the DNC, has not revitalized the party by himself. He has had substantial assistance from Texas millionaire Robert S. Strauss, the party treasurer, who has raised the cash that keeps the national party operational.

But it has been O'Brien's responsibility to keep the half-dozen serious Democratic candidates from feuding openly. To O'Brien, also, has fallen the job of unifying city, state and congressional Democrats. In addition, he has been given the task of setting up the July 10-13 Presidential nominating convention in Miami Beach.

O'Brien's future success will depend on how well his staff functions in the months to come.

CHAIRMAN'S OFFICE

High-ranking officials at the national committee often tell visitors that the headquarters office is loosely knit, with responsibility shared fairly equally. Yet O'Brien's operating inner circle is essentially limited to four men: Stanley L. Greigg, 39, deputy chairman; William B. Welsh, 46, executive director; John G. Stewart, 36, communications director; and Joseph E. Mohbat, 33, press secretary.

Stewart and Mohbat feed O'Brien ideas on issues and on public relations, but are seldom in on the day-to-day operations of the chairman's office. Greigg and Welsh furnish O'Brien with planning, political intelligence and administrative expertise.

Greigg—A former House Member from Iowa (1965-67), Greigg is "my office manager," said O'Brien.

All spending requests from the staff, reports and telephone calls for the chairman go through Greigg.

Some lower-echelon staff members, who requested anonymity, are unhappy with Greigg's administration. "It takes longer to get a piece of paper to and from the chairman," said one staff worker. Greigg, who replaced the late Ira Kapenstein in the deputy position April 21, said the complaints were largely owing to his reluctance to authorize expenditures.

"You operate with that budget in front of you every hour of the goddamned day," he said. Some papers get action more quickly than others because they have higher priority, he said.

Greigg's daily operations involve a good deal of detail work. But, he said, "there's no one here more involved in detail work than Chairman O'Brien."

In addition to his administrative duties, Greigg is O'Brien's representative at the meetings he has set up among staff assistants to the

Presidential hopefuls. Established to work out details on a proper-behavior pact for candidates, agreed to in principle July 14, the working staff group deals with media-spending limits and the possibility of pooling resources to purchase special polls. Greigg also discusses with the candidates' staff the prospect of pooling all their talent after the convention to work for the party's nominee in the general election.

Another of his responsibilities is supervision of the Office of Campaigns and Party Organization, which services local and state organizations with technical advice.

Robert E. Moss, 31, his deputy, has been assigned most of the nuts-and-bolts work in the office, including the preparation and publication of a new voter-registration manual.

Moss has developed plans for a series of regional political workshops. Campaign techniques, use of free radio and television time, polling and voter identification will be discussed at these seminars. O'Brien has committed $50,000 for the programs, scheduled thus far in Boston, Minneapolis, San Francisco and for a Southern city yet to be selected.

Welsh—"The next nominee isn't going to face what happened to Hubert Humphrey in 1968. No nominee deserves that. That's the principal reason I'm here," said Executive Director Welsh.

Primarily a planner, Welsh was responsible for the proposal that the Democratic National Committee issue a preliminary convention call to the states. His main reason was to ensure that the parties would know well in advance that

O'BRIEN'S PENTAGON PAPER

Although Democratic fund raising has been more successful in 1971 than it was in 1970, release of the Pentagon papers in June 1971 caused a temporary reduction in party donations.

Olga B. Gechas, who directs the DNC direct-mail fund-raising effort, said that more than 100 Democrats who had been solicited for their financial support wrote letters critical of the previous Democratic Administration's decision making as revealed in the classified papers.

The objections were so numerous and of such intensity that DNC Chairman Lawrence F. O'Brien was persuaded to sign a form letter to all Pentagon paper critics. The letter, signed by O'Brien July 2, said, in part:

"I do not believe that the partial publication to date should be taken as a full and definitive record of the entire decision-making process. Nor should any total appraisal of these events be made without full reference to the concept of bipartisan-supported national security objectives as developed from the end of World War II to the present."

O'Brien, who, as Postmaster General (1965-68) was a member of the Johnson Cabinet, called for "a complete study and review of government classification policies."

In a closing paragraph, he wrote: "I appreciate having your thoughts on this difficult and important issue."

they must reform their delegate-selection procedures or face a credentials challenge at the national nominating convention. On Feb. 19, and DNC issued that early call, advising the state parties of the requirement to conform with the rules fixed by the Commission on Party Structure and Delegate Selection.

Since that call was issued, many parties have been trying to meet the new guidelines so as to avoid a credentials challenge. "Can't you see the pandemonium around the country if we had waited and issued the first call on Oct. 13?" Welsh asked.

"What I try to do for O'Brien is to try to think of where this whole thing fits together," he said.

Welsh performs missionary work for O'Brien among leaders of the party's historic allies in the labor movement. His major contact is with Alexander E. Barkan, director of the AFL-CIO's Committee on Political Education, the political funding unit of the labor federation.

Welsh also keeps in touch with state party officials.

With labor leaders and party officials, Welsh concentrates on the new reforms. One night, Hawaii party leaders were unnerved by another DNC staff member's warning that the party's delegation in Miami Beach would risk a credentials challenge. Welsh spent more than three hours negotiating with them.

"One cannot assume that the reforms are understood by anybody," he said.

O'Brien—Meanwhile, the chairman, who must lean heavily on his small staff for most of the day-to-day work, has found himself in great demand as a speaker. "I can't be chained to my desk," O'Brien said.

"My biggest problem is the leadership I must provide," he said in an interview. "It involves me in activities at a level I am not in a position to delegate."

As a result, he said, "I'm spread thin as hell."

CANDIDATES' AGREEMENT

State and national Democratic leaders, including staff assistants to the presidential candidates, are nearly unanimous in citing as O'Brien's major achievement the arrangement of a peace pact among the candidates.

The agreement, approved in principle by all of the potential candidates, holds the candidates to a spending ceiling in the primary races and pledges them to avoid frivolous credentials challenges at the convention.

John F. English, chief political strategist for Sen. Edmund S. Muskie, D-Maine, praised O'Brien for his accomplishment. "It's very necessary to have an honest broker," he said.

"He's made a valiant attempt to keep the candidates from cutting themselves and all of us up," said John M. Bailey, a former national chairman (1960-68), who now heads the Connecticut Democratic Party.

"It was what we needed," said Iowa's state chairman Larson.

Idea—O'Brien said the idea of opening up communication among the candidates occurred to him after the 1970 election, as the hopefuls began to make their political soundings around the nation.

Committee strength—"After the November election, the efforts expended in the campaign of the DNC, in areas other than financial, added up to me to what was a reasonable recognition in Democratic Party circles that the committee had functioned quite well," O'Brien said.

"There was an observable improvement in the relationship between the party and various elements; an upbeat mood. We got what we needed: a victory."

O'Brien set about organizing disparate elements of the party. He arranged for the Democratic governors and mayors to meet on legislation with House and Senate leaders. He assigned an office to the state chairmen and another to the Governors at DNC headquarters in the Watergate Office Building in Washington.

Communication—After 1968, the party "was lying around in pieces. The party could be brought

Lawrence F. O'Brien

back as was shown in 1970, and I became the focal point for all that," said O'Brien.

At the same time he was promoting communication and unity among congressional leaders and state Democratic officials. O'Brien said, he decided to test the candidates' willingness to talk about unity.

"In order to communicate, you've got to have some central point where individual elements inside and outside the party can mesh. I decided my role as chairman included providing some leadership to try to help communication between the candidates."

Meetings—Early last winter, O'Brien made contact with each of the candidates individually. He invited them to a dinner party in his apartment at the Sheraton-Park Hotel Feb. 9.

First session—"The first meeting was carefully orchestrated," he said. "I asked each candidate to come and have dinner, without any person knowing the full guest list. It had to be determined if any communication could be started which would lead to some agreement. It was a very sensitive area. It had to be exploratory. This was a social gathering. I did not have an agenda."

Attending the meeting were Sens. Muskie; George S. McGovern, of South Dakota; Hubert H. Humphrey, of Minnesota; Henry M. Jackson, of Washington; Edward M. Kennedy, of Massachusetts; Harold E. Hughes, of Iowa; and Fred R. Harris, of Oklahoma. Sen. Birch E. Bayh, of Indiana, who did not attend, later met with O'Brien and agreed to join the others in subscribing to the informal pact.

DNC PRESS SECRETARY

At a recent St. Louis news conference, Joseph E. Mohbat, press secretary to Democratic National Chairman Lawrence F. O'Brien, noticed a reporter's pencil idle while the chairman was speaking. Mohbat took the newsman's notebook and wrote in it: "O'Brien is very funny—and charming."

Mohbat, 33, a veteran Associated Press correspondent who left to work for O'Brien, believes what he wrote.

"O'Brien has a special touch that nobody else does. He makes things happen," said Mohbat, the DNC's middleman with the media. "The idea of being around excellence, contributing to it, is appealing. It's awful nice to know that if Larry O'Brien's going to do something, you are one of the first people he will see."

A Nieman Fellow (1966-67) who first got to know O'Brien while covering national politics for the wire service, Mohbat is one of four DNC staff men who have instant access to the chairman.

He said he took the press job not only because of the opportunity to work with O'Brien but because he wanted to see President Nixon beaten in 1972.

As O'Brien's principal spokesman, he helps write the chairman's speeches and often travels with him. Mohbat also sets up press conferences in cities where O'Brien is scheduled to make an appearance.

Mohbat said he has attempted to trim the number of inconsequential press releases emanating from his office, in an effort to save the time of political reporters. "We've really tried to cut down on the crap," he said. Most Washington correspondents know when they get an envelope from the DNC press office that "we're saying something," said Mohbat. "They know O'Brien doesn't blow smoke."

Mohbat gets high marks from most Washington political correspondents on his performance. They say he is fair and tells them as much as he can. One national reporter held Mohbat in such high regard that he recently called to sound him out on what he thought would happen to Vice President Spiro T. Agnew at the Republican convention next year.

Another reporter said of Mohbat: "In terms of pure professionalism, I find him vastly superior to the fog factory on Capitol Hill—the Republican National Committee."

Mohbat is married and the father of one son. He lives in Washington.

Also at the meeting were Senate Majority Leader Mike Mansfield, of Montana, and House Speaker Carl Albert, of Oklahoma.

"There was a discussion of the issues, but more in terms of the Administration's failures and of efforts that should be made to spotlight the Administration's record," O'Brien said.

"Harold Hughes made a significant comment. He said, 'I have waited over a year for this kind of thing to happen in my party.' Muskie said, 'Larry, I'm glad we're here.' Then he told the others, 'We must give the chairman all the support we can in his efforts.' Three or four others said we must have more meetings like this.

"I said, 'I want to tell you, I want this meeting to be considered private. I don't want it to inhibit anybody.' They said, 'We think you ought to announce that the meeting took place.' Someone said, 'It's too bad you haven't a photographer.' "

One of O'Brien's staff assistants called Mohbat to ask about a picture. Mohbat remembered that George Tames, a *New York Times* photographer, lived nearby. Tames was notified and came over to take the picture.

Second session—At the second meeting, July 14, O'Brien had an agenda. He forged an agreement among all the candidates except Jackson, who was unable to attend because of a schedule conflict. Jackson's administrative assistant, S. Sterling Munro, in staff meetings with Greigg since the second session, has agreed to the spending limit.

Key element—O'Brien said the "key element" in the agreement was the pledge to limit broadcast spending in each of the primary states to five cents per registered voter—or $2.8 million per candidate in all 23 primary states.

At the second meeting, O'Brien said, "Mansfield and Albert both made a very strong representation that we would be destroyed without this. Albert said, 'It was just vital to the party.' I fully expected some broadening of the base, some alternatives, but there weren't."

Developments— Now, the agreement is being examined in detail by Deputy Chairman Greigg and the candidates' principal staff men.

"The staff is now meeting regularly to develop recommendations for discussion by the principals. I have built some continuity into this agreement," said O'Brien.

Problems: O'Brien conceded that the temptation to break the agreement as the campaigns heat up will increase.

"All you have built into this is a significantly high aspect of public awareness—that's got to inhibit a little bit their making personal attacks on each other. It's a gentlemen's agreement in principle."

"Is it better to have done what we have done than to have done nothing at all?" he asked.

CONVENTION PLANNING

As important as an unsplintered party for the Democrats next year is a well-run, non-violent convention.

To this end, O'Brien has assigned Richard Murphy, 41, a former assistant postmaster general (1961-69) to be convention director.

Murphy assignment: Murphy, signing on to serve O'Brien for the third time in his life (his first was as national coordinator of Young Voters for Kennedy-Johnson in 1960, before becoming O'Brien's deputy in the Post Office) is optimistic about the convention. "I

think the convention is the most exciting thing in the world, although, after 1968, a lot of people wouldn't want this job," he said.

Murphy has been charged with overseeing all aspects of convention preparation—from insuring that each candidate has reasonable work space at the convention hall to negotiating all concession contracts.

"We will build this into a Murphy-managed convention," said O'Brien.

Murphy has been assigned an office in a far corner of the DNC suite. O'Brien said he ordered this to conserve manpower. "I keep Murphy away from the rest of the DNC so you don't have everybody in the office working on the convention," he said.

Agreement—With Treasurer Strauss, Murphy has negotiated and signed all contracts covering use of the convention hall, housing, transportation and other logistical services. The agreements guarantee the DNC $450,000 in cash, plus a number of free services, and the promise of additional revenue of $1 per person per night from the South Florida Hotel and Motel Association. Murphy said this contract might produce another $50,000.

City—The key contract, an agreement signed Sept. 10 with the city of Miami Beach, provides free use of the Miami Beach Convention Center, with the city paying for construction of box seats, temporary buildings and television camera stands.

The city also will provide free:
all necessary electrical power;
air conditioning that will keep the hall 15 degrees cooler than

the outside temperature;
a public address system;
insurance.

The contract also binds the city to maintain bus and taxi fares at preconvention rates. Miami Beach promised to provide shuttle buses at 25 cents a ride. These buses will run between the convention center and "the entire hotel area wherever delegates and alternates to the convention are housed."

Housing—The contract with the Hotel and Motel Association guarantees the DNC 80 per cent of all luxury hotel rooms and 70 per cent of lower-priced hotel accommodations. Rooms can be released by the DNC up to a month before the convention opens.

Those that are not released, but remain unused, will cost the DNC $150 a room for the four-day convention at the more expensive hotels and $50 at the middle-priced ones.

In addition, Murphy said he has found some "very nice, very clean" rooms in older Miami Beach hotels at $12 a night for two persons. He is also talking with officials at the University of Miami about the use of some dormitory rooms, most of them without air conditioning, at rates well below $6 daily per person. "There will be no problem in terms of the abundance of low-cost housing," he said.

Security: Mindful of the violence that marred the 1968 Democratic convention in Chicago, Murphy and the DNC have begun to establish a close relationship with Miami Beach Police Chief Rocky Pomerance and Gov. Reubin Askew, D. In addition, the DNC, which is to assume responsibility for all security inside the

MISSION TO INDEPENDENCE, MO.: A DAY IN THE LIFE OF LAWRENCE O'BRIEN

The black limousine, District of Columbia tag No. 32, pulled up before the TWA terminal in Washington. Out stepped Lawrence Francis O'Brien, 54, Democratic national chairman. He gathered up his briefcase and suit carrier and walked slowly into the building.

The license number on the car from which he emerged has been assigned to the Democratic National Committee since 1932, when Franklin D. Roosevelt brought the Democrats back into the White House.

Now, O'Brien, embarking Sept. 25 on his second trip of the week, was intent on setting the stage for a new Democratic assault on the White House, once again in Republican hands. Scheduled that day was a trip to Independence, Mo., to visit Roosevelt's successor, Harry S. Truman. The visit was to be followed that evening by a fund-raising dinner in St. Louis honoring Truman.

O'Brien, 40 minutes early for his plane, sat in the waiting area, reading *The Washington Post.* "Well, I see Fred is launched," he said, referring to the Presidential candidacy announcement of Sen. Fred R. Harris, D-Okla. He said nothing more on the matter. Harris had preceded O'Brien as chairman.

O'Brien read through the paper quickly, then set it aside. He stood up and paced restlessly for some moments before a young man walked up to him.

"Hi, Larry," the young man said, shaking the chairman's hand. "Remember that dinner in Kansas City? I was the guy with the camera, taking pictures."

O'Brien faces legions of photographers nearly every day. He smiled as if he remembered.

O'Brien, who tolerates the boredom of waiting and travel with good humor, began preparing himself for the day in Missouri as soon as he settled himself in the aircraft.

Study—He first studied his briefing book, a black looseleaf notebook prepared for him by the DNC research office. Occasionally, he would comment on the latest economic statistics in the booklet, which showed unemployment rising and the cost of living up.

His staff had also provided him with several pages of remarks by Mr. Truman. O'Brien would later be able to use them to remind the former President of bygone days.

O'Brien then turned to the speech he would deliver that night. He read in silence for awhile. "It's a real give-em-hell speech," said O'Brien. "But we have to do more than just give Nixon hell. We have to concentrate on alternatives. I'm still looking for a focus."

O'Brien expressed some concern that his role had changed over the years, from the time when he was President Kennedy's campaign manager in 1960. Now that the party was without a Presidential candidate, he was its major spokesman. "It's different now. I didn't have to worry about the speech and the rest when I was with Jack," he said.

In Kansas City, O'Brien was met by his press secretary, Joseph E. Mohbat, and Nick Kostopulos, his advance man. The group walked to the TWA Ambassador's Lounge, reserved for first-class passengers. O'Brien sipped a soft drink while his staff briefed him on the timing of the Truman visit and the press coverage arrangements in Independence.

Truman visit—Half an hour before his scheduled arrival at the Truman home, a short ride from the airport, O'Brien and his party started off in a limousine. Kostopulos, who had timed the trip in advance, advised the driver to go slowly, since he didn't want to be early. Nevertheless, the limousine was five minutes ahead of schedule as it entered Independence. The driver was told to take a detour, around the back of the Truman house. The O'Brien car, exactly on time, pulled up before a small crowd of reporters and cameramen waiting in front of the house.

Bess Truman, 86, greeted O'Brien at the door. He emerged 52 minutes later.

He told reporters he had been given "marching orders" to open the campaign against Mr. Nixon. "We have just kicked off the 1972 Presidential campaign here today in Independence, Mo.," said O'Brien. He also told questioners that Mr. Truman had no favorite among the Democratic hopefuls.

Riding back to the Kansas City airport after his visit, O'Brien was elated with his meeting. "Boy," he said, "I'm glad I wasn't against that fellow 20 or 30 years ago. He must have been really tough then."

(Staff members said later that

O'Brien's enthusiasm was not unusual. Despite his many years in national politics, "he's one of the least cynical people I've run into," said John G. Stewart, DNC communications director.)

Halfway inside the Kansas City air terminal, O'Brien stopped abruptly and headed back outside to the taxi stand. "I forgot to thank the driver," he said, rushing back to do so before the driver departed.

Consideration—(A staff aide said that O'Brien's thoughtfulness about the limousine driver was typical. Press secretary Mohbat recalled that two days before, O'Brien had traveled to Dallas, the city where President Kennedy was murdered. Students from Southern Methodist University, where O'Brien was to speak, had warned Mohbat ahead of time that the only way the chairman could make his engagement without being late was for them to drive him through downtown Dallas. This meant he would have to drive by the Schoolbook Depository Building. It was in front of this structure that President Kennedy was shot in 1963.

(When O'Brien entered the car for the ride to SMU, Mohbat tried to seat him in the rear. But the chairman sat up front with a student from SMU. Asked if he wanted to study his speech enroute, O'Brien declined. All the way to his engagement, O'Brien watched the passing scene, never saying a word, Mohbat said.

(Hours later, when they were flying back to Washington, Mohbat asked O'Brien if he was aware of where he was on the trip to the campus. O'Brien said he had been "but I didn't want to embarrass

the kids," so he had said nothing.)

Press—At the St. Louis airport, O'Brien was called before the cameras by a woman reporter for the local CBS-TV station. She asked him about the party's $9.3-million debt. "We're taking contributions," he replied.

(The chairman's sense of irony is well known. In April 1970, speaking before the predominantly Republican U.S. Chamber of Commerce, many of whose members own firms that are DNC creditors, O'Brien said: "Even though many of you skillfully hide your true political feelings, I know that in your hearts you want the Democrats to win this fall. Because you know that only a Democratic victory will produce the money we need to pay the bills we owe you."

(O'Brien can also turn his wit for the purpose of not-so-gentle personal invective. Such was the case in a September 1970 speech to California Democrats on behalf of Sen. John V. Tunney, then opposing Republican Sen. (1965-71) George Murphy. "I will only say that your Republican Senator may have been there in the Senate chamber—he says he was, and I'll take his word for it—but so was every chair and table in the chamber. And those chairs and tables accomplished about as much for the people of California as George Murphy has.")

O'Brien faced more newsmen at the Chase Park-Plaza Hotel in downtown St. Louis. There, he criticized Mr. Nixon for delaying any action on the economy until Aug. 15. He said the President had been handed "a lot of tools" by the Democratic Congress more than a year ago. Of the wage-price freeze,

he said: "I hope it isn't too late. Every American hopes that."

Later, upstairs in his suite, which, like the limousines at his disposal and all meals for him and his staff, would be paid for by the St. Louis Democratic Committee, O'Brien tried to relax for a half-hour.

Mohbat told him that Missouri Gov. Warren E. Hearnes, D, was reported to be planning an announcement at the Truman dinner concerning his own national political plans. Mohbat said that some reporters he spoke to thought he would announce support for Sen. Edmund S. Muskie, of Maine, and express an interest in the vice presidency. O'Brien said without rancor that such an announcement might "change the lead" on news stories about his visit to Truman and his speech in St. Louis. Instead of the two events capturing the headlines, Hearnes' announcement would preempt him, he said.

The chairman then began to reflect on past vice-presidential moninations at Democratic conventions.

"I'm just thinking out loud now, for the first time on this," he said. "But why shouldn't a man who wants it have to run for vice president as hard as they do for Presidential nomination? Why should it be automatic that the nominee pick his running mate? How democratic is that?"

Speech—Across town, at the Sheraton-Jefferson Hotel, where the fund raiser was held, O'Brien was told that Hearnes had ordered a change in the order of speakers. Although he was slated to follow O'Brien, he would now speak before the chairman. His purpose in doing so was to make his announcement in time for the 10 p.m. TV news. O'Brien accepted the decision without complaint, although he had told his staff he was tired and would like to leave the gathering as soon as possible.

Hearnes, who could not have succeeded himself as Governor, announced that he was leaving politics. O'Brien publicly lamented the decision.

O'Brien was introduced by Sen. Stuart S. Symington. D-Mo., a close friend. "He has a certain characteristic," Symington told the diners in the hot, crowded ballroom. "You never leave this fellow without feeling a bit better than you did before you talked with him."

(Later, O'Brien expressed pleased surprise at the warmth of Symington's remarks. "Did you hear what Stu said?" he asked his staff. "I didn't expect that.")

In his speech, O'Brien coined a new catchword to criticize the Republican Administration—"Nixolution."

"You recognize the Nixolutions," he told the crowd. "The economy staggers along under Nixonomics for two-and-a-half years and the President says he'll do nothing about it—until it's perhaps too late. That's a Nixolution.

"The Democratic Congress passes a law to provide hundreds of thousands of immediate jobs to the unemployed—and the President vetoes it. That's a Nixolution.

"Why, it's simply 'Nix' on this and 'Nix' on that—whenever any hand or voice is raised toward social change and progress and healing in this divided and troubled country of ours."

Reminding his listeners of his years with President Kennedy, he vowed to "wage this 1972 campaign with all the pride and all the fierce determination and all the ardent idealism that a young President taught us to love."

After his speech, O'Brien, who had forsaken the overcooked steak at the fund raiser, quickly departed the hotel through a side exit and joined his staff aides for a long, late dinner in an expensive restaurant.

Relaxing over a drink before his first meal of the day, the chairman was in an expansive mood, exchanging stories with his staff, but telling most of them himself.

(Mohbat described O'Brien as "the authentic American indoorsman. In this sun-worshipping world of ours, he's much more comfortable in a good restaurant with good food and fine wine, being the host.")

By 1 a.m., the O'Brien party was back at his hotel. This time, the chairman remembered to thank the driver before leaving the car.

hall, has been in touch with "high-ranking former or present national officials of recognized police organizations," said Murphy. A private police agency may be hired for inside security, he said.

Disruption—Murphy said "we would not use the same (police) methods used at the 1968 convention." Inside the hall, "there will be the proper allowance for any legitimate type of activity at the convention, but no demonstration should be allowed to disrupt the convention . . . . There will be no overly repressive security system that people would rebel at," he said.

Pomerance—On Sept. 23, when the 44-year-old police offi-

cial was appointed, he said:

"The reputation of our city, state and nation is at stake during this vital American process. Everyone is looking forward to a peaceful convention . . . ."

Murphy said that during the convention, he expected Pomerance to be "a constant companion of ours at all times."

In a telephone interview from Miami Beach, Pomerance declined to say that he would follow the counsel of O'Brien or Murphy. However, he added, in the event of a security crisis, "I expect we will have a mutual approach."

O'Brien said he did not have much concern about security problems at the Miami Beach conven-

tion. "Pomerance's reputation is that he is very good. After very careful checks in all kinds of directions, there are high marks on this guy and I have a comfortable feeling."

COMMUNICATIONS AND RESEARCH

Nothing the DNC does would ever attract public notice without the Research and Communications Offices. While Research develops the party message, Communications is the medium for its public distribution.

Research: David Cooper, 32, director of political research, with a background as a staff assistant with the Mervin Field and Louis Harris polling firms, concentrates most of his time on public-opinion sampling.

Polls—"My basic tool is the telephone," he said. "I'm talking to pollsters, people all around the country. My people are talking to county chairmen and state chairmen." The political intelligence gathered is sent through channels to O'Brien.

Cooper is thinking of "piggybacking" some polls to be taken by major polling organizations in the near future. Through this device, he can have the pollster tack on a question to a regularly scheduled poll. It is far less costly than commissioning a full poll.

Cooper is also sounding out candidates who are buying polls, to determine their willingness to turn over the detailed, tabulated results to the DNC. He is also talking to the pollsters to gain their approval.

Issues—Until recently, Cooper had charge of issues research for the DNC, now in the hands of Communications Director Stewart.

Interviewed before the reshuffling, Cooper said:

"Our role is to develop the tools for the next campaign and, to that end, we are going to have a comprehensive file on what are likely to be the major issues in the campaign; we will also have a fairly complete file of statements made by this Administration.

"We're here to help set the climate ... at this point we are the spokesman for the Democratic Party. We look for weak points in the Administration. Our focus is wholly on the Administration."

A roomful of file drawers includes several boxfuls of statements by Mr. Nixon and top Administration officials. They are cross-referenced and kept up to date, Cooper said.

Communications: Stewart's responsibilities include supervision of the party's public affairs audio news service and preparation of the party's two regular publications as well as special booklets. He is also Mohbat's immediate superior. In addition, Stewart is now breaking in Arden P. Kosatka, an experienced television producer.

Radio—A one-man operation, the DNC's audio project is located in a small room in headquarters. Kosatka, who runs the service, tapes statements from various Democratic officials. Then he calls key radio stations across the country, offering the recorded "actualities" for news programs. Many radio stations, short of stories for their hourly news slots, gladly take the DNC offerings.

Publications—The DNC's two periodicals are *Fact* and *National Democrat*. While *Fact,* published biweekly, pummels the Administration and is sent to 5,000 influential Democratic leaders, the quarterly *National Democrat* is more a "house organ," in Mohbat's words. It goes to 35,000 persons and institutions, including libraries, schools, labor leaders and party leaders. "It's not a rap sheet," said Mohbat.

Fact, while not shrilly partisan, nevertheless sustains an attitude of hostility toward the Nixon Administration. In the Sept. 3 edition, the magazine accused Mr. Nixon of hypocrisy, saying he invoked a wage-price freeze, advocated sacrifice, but then turned around and spent federal money on his own political advancement.

Commenting on the President's late August trip across the nation, *Fact* called it "little more than a pre-campaign, across-country political tour." It said that "Mr. Nixon has no hesitation in sending the bills (for the trip) to the U.S. Treasury instead of the Republican National Committee."

In July, *Fact* disclosed that the Transportation Department had distributed a promotional booklet on behalf of the supersonic transport to about 50,000 school teachers.

The booklet was entitled "Teacher's Guide for the SST ... T ... T (Sound, Sense, Today, Tomorrow, Thereafter)." It included a "fable" about Marita, "the supersonic pussycat." *Fact* reprinted the story about a pussycat riding on an SST to France.

"My mistress took me aboard the biggest plane I have ever seen," the cat wrote. "It looked like a flying hotel with a pointed nose ... We made ourselves comfortable in large roomy seats.

"The ride seemed normal enough at first, but suddenly the pilot announced to all of us that we were cruising at an altitude of 64,000 feet and at a speed of 1800 mph—faster than the speed of sound. Why at this rate, I thought, we'd be in Paris in less than three hours," Marita said. "By the time I had a few slivers of liver (excellent by the way) and watched a short movie, we had arrived."

Fact was highly critical of the Department of Transportation's expenditure of $13,000 for the promotional publication. It called the booklet an "incursion into the minds of grade school children at the taxpayers' expense. We can only hope that in the future DOT is able to clear up the pink fog and get down to the business of unbiased educational materials for children—and stop pussyfooting around in propaganda."

TV—Stewart's most recent staff member is Mel Ferber, 48, a West Coast free-lance television producer. He has a long list of dramatic and public affairs program credits.

Ferber's principal assignment will be the design of a telegenically appealing convention.

"He will try to develop a format and events so the whole production will have the maximum possible impact," said Stewart. "The convention is a mixture of an entertainment show and a news event."

The communications director said the convention will be presented as "a gathering of people trying to solve some very difficult questions—and controversies will arise out of people expressing their beliefs and being taken seriously. It's going to contrast so markedly with what the Republicans will do. We can offer real excitement, which is always more compelling than the phony excitement the Republicans will have.

"A very large number of people will vote for President on the basis of the two conventions. If we can handle the mechanics of the convention well, it will permit us to devote time and energy for more productive things."

Policy council—Stewart is also executive director of the Democratic Policy Council, which de-velops policy papers on a wide variety of subjects—from urban renewal to health care.

In the pre-convention period, the council's subcommittees will hold hearings on domestic problems in various parts of the country. Prominent Democratic leaders will preside. The council's opinions are not binding on the party. It has no formal relationship with the policy-making national committee.

MONEY

Although the national committee has been unable to trim its $9.3-million debt, recent fund-raising efforts have produced money enough to support a $150,000-a-month office operation. Reports on file with the Clerk of the House for the first eight months of 1971 show total receipts of $1,134,766.74 for the DNC, and expenditures of $1,124,343.29.

A revitalized Finance Office, substantial Democratic victories in November 1970, and a growing belief that President Nixon is vulnerable have combined to brighten the party's financial fortunes, said Strauss.

Strauss: The committee's treasurer, known as an aggressive hard bargainer, said that when he took over the party's finances, the first thing he did was to analyze the records and review correspondence between the party and its benefactors.

His finding was that "our contributors, large and small, have suffered from neglect and most of them were irritated with us. They felt neglected just when we needed money."

On March 13, 1970, Strauss wrote the party's big contributors with a frank appeal for help and a warning of impending insolvency.

Letter—"One always imposes on the same friends who usually have earned the right to be left alone," Strauss wrote.

Noting that the DNC's operations even then were costing more than $100,000 monthly, Strauss said he and O'Brien "have not had time to make our own judgment with respect to these expenditures—we may need more; we may need less ... Unfortunately, there is no income to carry on this operation on a day-to-day basis, much less begin to retire the very substantial debt."

Strauss asked the big donors to give $100 a month each for the remaining nine months of 1970.

Result—The appeal produced 400 monthly $100 contributors.

"The letter was so honest and so candid and so forthright that the people were responsive," said Strauss.

He and O'Brien began making periodic reports on the rebuilding of the party. "People started writing back to me. What we really changed was the attitude. We started getting happy letters."

This year, the big givers were contacted again, and asked to be members of a $72-a-Month Sponsors Club. "We were one of the first institutions in America to lower our prices before Nixon froze them," said George Bristol, assistant to Strauss.

Program: Bristol is now after even bigger money, selling advertisements in the national convention program that is being produced by convention director Murphy. The ad solicitations went out to officers in the nation's 1,000 biggest firms. The ads cost $10,000 a page. The DNC is telling potential advertisers that the ads are tax-deductible, since the money will be used to finance the convention.

Praise—Bristol said several other money-making devices are being contemplated, including a cocktail party for the big givers with the candidates before the convention and another with the nominee after the decision is made in the convention center. Yet, said Strauss' assistant, none of the gimmicks by themselves could have rescued the party from its financial plight without the treasurer. "He's the best fund-raiser in or out of the White House I've ever seen," he said. "We've got the money now to plan a year ahead of time. He'll see a guy on the street in Dallas (Strauss' home) and say, by God, give us $72 a month."

Bristol continued: "The big factor is that Strauss hustles. We all hustle. To raise money, you've got to be thinking money all the time."

Direct mail—One of Strauss' biggest disappointments when he arrived in the finance office was the absence of a long list of reliable contributors. He turned to Olga B. Gechas, a direct mail specialist, for help. Miss Gechas, who had operated a successful solicitation program for the United Nations International Children's Emergency Fund, was undaunted by the evidence.

"There was no established base when I got here," she said in an interview. "I found 8,000 or 9,000 names." Miss Gechas declined to speculate about the fate of any other lists before her arrival.

Miss Gechas began buying and exchanging lists of names with mail order houses, magazine companies and groups espousing various causes. Her early test mailings were not, by her own admission, "terribly effective."

Short letter—In early 1970, Miss Gechas tried a short letter, built around opposition to Mr. Nixon, that yielded an unexpected cash harvest that is still coming in—$700,000 that year and $600,000 for the first eight months of 1971.

Signed by O'Brien, the letter says:

"Dear Friend:

"If ever there was a time to help the Democratic Party, it is now.

"I could give you many reasons why you should, but I have answered the Party's call because of mainly two:

"One is President Nixon.

"The other is Vice President Agnew.

Whichever reason you choose, please send us your membership contribution today and strengthen Democrats in this all important election year. The future of Richard Nixon depends on it!

"P.S. To say nothing of the future of all the rest of us."

The slightly revised 1971 version asserts:

"What this country needs to get back on its feet again is a good healthy ex-president like Richard M. Nixon. And a good healthy ex-Vice President like Spiro T. Agnew wouldn't be bad news either."

An enclosed card offers a checkoff box for Republicans.

The card says "I happen to be a Republican so don't send me a Membership Card. I am sending money anyway because I want to do *something!*"

Independents can check a box reading: "I am an independent and do not want to be listed as a member and do not want a card. I am sending money in hopes that *you* will do something."

Commitment—Miss Gechas said she had a commitment from Strauss and O'Brien to spend up to $100,000 on direct mail tests. She said she expected to produce $1 million in 1971. Of that, $500,000 would be profit.

"I have been given almost unlimited funds to pursue research," she said.

Numbers—Miss Gechas now has 65,000 names of contributors on file. She said she has written to five million persons. "By July of 1972, we will have mailed to 10 million people."

With almost another year remaining to test mailing lists before the nominee is chosen, Miss Gechas is hoping to have a new direct-mail piece, built around the convention victor, ready for mailing shortly after the convention closes. She said she wanted to mail to 20 million Americans.

Groups—Miss Gechas is now testing 100 different mailing lists, bought or exchanged with numerous groups and companies. She said the most lucrative producers are lists provided by organizations backing causes. Among these are UNICEF, the United Nations Association, the Congress of Racial Equality, the American Civil Liberties Union, the Committee for a Sane Nuclear Policy and the Committee on Africa.

Problems—Miss Gechas reported that she faces two major problems in raising money through the mail. "Ninety per cent of the resistance is because of the uncertainty over who the candidate will be."

The other reason is that many potential donors "still have visions of Chicago (the 1968 nominating convention site) and that the convention was not responsive."

One non-giver, responding to the direct mail plea, wrote the DNC:

"Please do not have another Chicago . . . 1968-type convention. It almost made me vote for Nixon upon the theory that I would rather support a known scoundrel than a fraud."

A Montana Democrat who gave nothing wrote: "How come no contribution? Because I don't like buying something, sight unseen. If you could just promise me something besides Edward Kennedy and Hubert Humphrey, I might have ventured a few bucks toward the cause . . . ."

Miss Gechas said her mail showed no groundswell of support for any of the Democratic hopefuls. "However," she said, "from the mail I see, I would say (Sen. Henry M.) Jackson is mentioned most negatively."

Assessment—Both Strauss and Bristol declared the biggest thing going for the Democrats is Richard Nixon.

Strauss believes his present efforts will pay off in a "campaign set up for the candidate and a political staff to execute it and enough money in the bank for him to take off a few weeks to do planning and staffing.

"There is an anti-Nixon feeling," he said.

Bristol said the President's vulnerability, as disclosed in some polls, makes the difference.

"If we were 30 points down, we couldn't raise the kind of money that we are. The Republicans got the hell kicked out of them in 1970 and that built the confidence of the Democratic winners and the party."

Pollsters prowl nation as candidates use opinion surveys to plan '72 campaign *Andrew J. Glass*

From the White House to small-town America, the political pollsters are once more on the prowl.

An August 1971 *National Journal* survey of political pollsters and their clients revealed that the business—which, like politics itself, is as much an art as a science—is deeply rooted in the campaign process. It revealed also that many candidates still are reluctant to say publicly how heavily they rely on polls.

Like people who never walk under ladders even though they say they are not superstitious, candidates go on buying the polls. With the approach of the 1972 national elections, spending for political surveys is likely to match or exceed 1968 levels.

In his book, *Financing the 1968 Election* (D.C. Heath and Company, 1971), Herbert E. Alexander estimated that spending for public opinion polls for all candidates at all levels in 1968 came to $6 million.

The estimate, based on 1,200 polls which cost an average of $5,000, is conservative; one comprehensive statewide poll can cost $15,000.

Top to bottom—The White House receives a steady stream of public opinion survey results. Some of them are commissioned, directly or indirectly, by the White House itself; others result from "piggybacking"—adding questions to polls already commissioned by Republican candidates or to polls taken for other purposes.

A campaign task force, working in secrecy, has defined polling needs for Mr. Nixon's 1972 campaign.

In addition, the President requests and receives regular "weathervane" polls that are commissioned for him by friends and admirers, mainly in the business world. Similar polls were taken on a regular basis for Presidents Eisenhower, Kennedy and Johnson.

But the political polling profession does not subsist alone on surveys taken by the White House or by the President's Democratic rivals.

Robert Teeter, the White House liaison man for Detroit-based Market Opinion Research, a Republican-oriented polling firm, said: "One of the big changes we're seeing is the level down to which polling is used.

"It used to be that there were a few sophisticated gubernatorial and senatorial campaigns using it. Now, almost all of them are in it. Many Congressmen use it. And it pops up in state legislatures and in city races."

Oliver A. Quayle III, who has taken polls for most of the Democrats now in the Senate, said: "It's now almost SOP. If you're interested in what people think, this is the best way to find out. People who have never polled before are polling now. It's standard procedure."

The "new breed"—A veteran Democratic campaign manager believes the pollsters' growth is based in part on a new breed of politician. As he put it:

"You're finding more people running for political office with less political experience than ever before. So they really don't have an intuitive base of how well they'll do. They don't have the knowledge of their state that a guy who has been in politics a long time has. But they know enough that they need to know. So the pollsters are all selling."

At its higher rungs, the polling profession remains a tight-knit group. It divides, almost equally, into those who poll only for Republicans, those who poll only for Democrats and those who poll for both.

But, as pollster Michael Rowan said, "we're all one club."

NIXON

In seeking the Presidency in 1968, Richard Nixon spent about $500,000 for the longest, most costly and most complex polling project in campaign history. Although there is no real battle for the nomination in sight, the Nixon White House has budgeted $500,000 for polling research for the 1972 campaign.

Organization: In the White House itself, the gathering of poll information is supervised by H. R. Haldeman, the President's chief of staff, who has a background in advertising and market research.

Campaign planning beyond the White House gates is being handled by Citizens for the Reelection of the President, which is, in effect, a White House political task force; by the Republican National Committee; and by Attorney General John N. Mitchell.

A coordinating committee is shaping the campaign research effort, which will rely heavily on public opinion surveys.

Magruder declined to comment for publication on polling or on any other aspect of White House campaign planning. One official, who asked to be identified only as an Administration spokesman, said: "We don't want to get into even what we're *thinking* about doing . . . . They (the Democrats) know something is going on. Let them find out by working for it."

White House polls: Mr. Nixon has had access to a steady stream of private polling information since he took office. These polls have kept the President abreast of domestic political moods and furnished him with insights into changing trends on such questions as the public attitude toward admission of the People's Republic of China to the United Nations.

An almost continuous polling effort for the White House has been conducted, in secrecy, by Chilton Research Services, of Philadelphia, a division of Chilton Co. An aide to the President said, "The outside pollster (John H. Kofron, Chilton's senior vice president) consults almost always directly with Haldeman, although on a nonsensitive matter he may talk with Strachan or Higby." (Lawrence M. Hibgy is Haldeman's administrative assistant.)

The President and his top staff also have access to other private polls, conducted for Republican senatorial or gubernatorial candi-

GALLUP AND HARRIS: THE PUBLISHED NATIONAL POLLS

George H. Gallup and Louis Harris respectively head the only polling organizations that regularly publish political survey results on a national scale. Both Gallup and Harris maintain extensive private polling operations, which account for the bulk of their revenues. They do not accept political clients.

The Gallup Poll, first published in 1935, now is syndicated and goes twice a week to some 100 U.S. newspaper clients. The *Gallup Opinion Index,* a 32-page booklet that is published monthly, offers detailed breakdowns of Gallup polling data. It has about 1,000 subscribers.

The Harris Survey, syndicated by the *Chicago Tribue,* goes to 125 U.S. newspaper clients. The Harris column first appeared in 1963 and is mailed twice a week to subscribers. Harris also polls for Time Inc. He plans to publish a hardback, 500-page *Harris Survey Yearbook,* which will carry data on which his column is based.

The normal lag between interviews and publication in newspapers for both Harris and Gallup is two to three weeks.

In forecasting Presidential elections, both Gallup and Harris strive to minimize the undecided vote in their interpretations and to base their predictions upon estimates of voter turnout on election day. The two pollsters, however, employ differing methods in dealing with undecided voters and nonvoters. The variations in their techniques, along with sample error, account for the spread between their estimates.

The Gallup Poll samples all adults of voting age and then excludes likely nonvoters. The Harris Survey does not interview people who say they are not registered and excludes them from its sample. A further exclusion of unlikely voters is made later.

The Harris interviews normally last 90 minutes. Persons are asked for their Presidential preference three times in the course of the interview: a direct question at the start, a secret "ballot box" question near the close and another direct question at the close. The Gallup Poll asks one secret "ballot box" question early in the interview.

The Gallup Poll is prepared in Princeton, N.J., by the American Institute of Public Opinion, a firm headed by Gallup.

The Harris Survey is prepared in New York by Louis Harris and Associates Inc. The Harris firm was bought in 1970 by Donaldson, Lukin and Jennerette Inc., a stock brokerage firm which is publicly owned. The sale was for 80,000 shares of voting common stock, worth about $720,000 at current market prices.

A CANDIDATE LOOKS AT HIS POLLS

In an interview with National Journal, *Sen. Hubert H. Humphrey. D-Minn., reflected upon the role that polls played in his unsuccessful 1968 Presidential campaign and in his 1970 Senate campaign:*

In 1968, we were so damned short of money that we didn't use polls as much as I think we should have. Had we used them a little better, I think I might have been a little more effective.

Which is another way of saying, if you're not just looking at how popular you are as a candidate, but rather are using the polls to base your public attitudes on public issues, I think you can become a more effective candidate. You at least have the means of being one.

The polls can also show your areas of weakness. It gives you time, if you take them early enough, to repair those areas if it's at all possible. It also shows your areas of strength that you can be sure of and other areas that you need to buttress and maintain.

It takes time to do polling that's effective. If we had the time and the money, we would have been much better off, particularly where it comes to issues.

For example, I know that in '68 we had some gut reactions on the law-and-order issue. But we didn't have an in-depth understanding of its intensity. Even though I worked at it, I didn't start early enough. I also think we might have been able to detect age-group differences and how each group reacts.

It's all a question of what you ask for. And what you ask for is oftentimes determined not only by what you want but what you can afford.

In order to use polls really ef-fectively, you need to take a series of them—in depth.

The man or the firm that does that kind of polling has to be very sophisticated in terms of the kind of questions which evoke honest, objective answers. You've got to be careful that you don't set up questions that give you answers that you want.

So you really have to deal with professionals in this business that have a great professional reputa-tion at stake.

In 1970, we used polling very effectively. I started early. In fact we had one of our early polls in hand months before I even de-clared. We took it simply to see what the reactions might be and what the issues might be.

In other words, I wanted to know myself: Did I have political strength and where did I have it?

Then, we also had in that first (Oliver A.) Quayle poll a number of issues that we wanted to get a response to.

One of the things that I found in the polls, for example, that al-ways intrigued me was the tremen-dous support we had among young people—running as high as 80 per cent support within this group. I didn't believe at first I could have so much support in the 21-25-year-old group. But it became obvious afterwards that I did.

I noticed that when we'd go into neighborhoods where there were many young married couples how well we would do with them. In the elections, the young married cou-ples stuck with us, so the polls verified themselves.

Also, you would think in a state like mine, in Minnesota, that the agricultural and economic issues might be paramount.

But we found that there were other issues that were much more overriding than merely the eco-nomic issue. Like the law-and-or-der issue, for example. And we acted on that information.

So, I'm a great believer in the use of polls as a tool—providing that you're willing to spend the money to get a first-class job. You must not deal with amateurs in this business.

I think John Kennedy used polls very effectively. When he got a poll that was a plus for him, he used it to build further support.

I think this can be done today.

If a county chairman sees you're ahead in the polls, he tends to say, "Well, he can win." It isn't a question of whether he likes you or not. It builds a bandwagon ef-fect. It creates a political atmos-phere.

Actually, the politics of polls can be most important of all.

If they're favorable to you, or if they show you with a trend—even if you're not ahead—if the trend seems to be coming your way, then it has a tendency to build its own momentum.

It really is almost better than spot announcements (commer-cials) on television. It's a kind of political advertising in its own right.

As Humphrey noted in connection with his 1968 campaign, an impor-tant test of a Presidential campaign is the depth and breadth of its re-search effort—which, to a large de-gree, relies on public opinion surveys. The Senator as yet has not commis-sioned any new polls to test the appeal of his candidacy for President in 1972.

dates as well as by political pressure groups friendly to the Nixon Administration. These polls are supplied without charge: the Chilton surveys are underwritten by the Republican National Committee.

A pollster who declined to be quoted by name said, "A lot of the (White House) work that was done in the past three years was done by individual candidates who were doing it as an accommodation."

The White House intends to repay some of these favors during the 1972 campaign. A Presidential aide, speaking for "background," said: "When Nixon is ready to go into an area, an offer for a 'piggyback' (poll) will be made. I think in almost every case, it will be the Nixon White House that will offer it down rather than its being offered up (to the President)."

Campaign firms—The White House scheduled a series of meetings Aug. 9-11 to review the capabilities of more than a half-dozen Republican-oriented polling firms.

"All of them were approached with the idea of contributing to the campaign as a sole or prime contractor," said a White House political aide. "But it's not inconceivable that Haldeman will decide 'I don't want any one person to know everything, so I'm going to parcel it out and these people can just like it.' He's like that."

Another White House official noted that "the Nixon campaign is being organized on a priority basis and therefore the need for national pollsters is minimized." The emphasis, he said, will be on disregarding those states where there is "no opportunity" and concentrating on the big electoral states

"which will either win or lose the election for us."

Each of the polling concerns which made presentations to the White House was screened in advance by Haldeman. The group includes:

Cambridge Opinion Studies Inc.,

Chilton Research Services,

Decision Making Information Inc.,

Market Opinion Research of Detroit,

Opinion Research Corp. of Princeton, N.J.

David Derge, although a regular White House visitor, did not attend the presentation sessions, which were held in the offices of the "Citizens" group, one block from the White House. Derge is known to be a strong partisan of ORC.

Split verdict—A decision on the allocation of polling resources for the campaign is expected to be submitted to the President for his review and approval by the end of August.

Whether or not a prime polling contractor is chosen, a White House official said that polling arrangements for the 1972 campaign may not emerge in a clear-cut manner.

The official said: "Knowing the President, he never puts all his marbles in one basket .... He will want additional head-to-head and special-issue polling.

"He never even tells anybody about it. But you always have somebody on the side who will do a weathervane sampling after a (Presidential) night on television .... That's just Nixon. All of us get used to that. There's always an

edge."

Another White House official who will be involved in the campaign, also speaking privately, said that, in all probability, some of the more sensitive polling results will go to the President directly, perhaps through Haldeman, without being circulated to the White House political staff.

"There are some things—like how does Agnew affect the ticket—that might be asked that even Mitchell won't get," the official said. (Mr. Nixon's choice of Spiro T. Agnew as his Vice Presidential running mate in 1968 was influenced by ORC polls which showed him running better alone than with any possible "name" in the Republican Party. Mr. Nixon decided to bypass better-known personalities for Agnew, who was then Governor of Maryland.)

Utility—Although White House officials seek to dampen publicity on their polling efforts, they say privately that polling information, while in plentiful supply, does not play a critical role in White House political decision making.

"Nixon has never had much use for polls," a personal friend of the President said. "He only pays attention when they happen to agree with his gut feelings. And he likes situations where the polls do not put him under pressure, such as his Agnew decision of 1968."

A GOP official agreed with this assessment and added: "Most of those people (the White House staff) just look at the head-to-head results—at just two numbers. It's very sad. Most of them just flip to the last page (of the polling report) to see, in summary, how we are doing."

Of Mr. Nixon's potential Democratic opponents in 1972, only Sen. Edmund S. Muskie, of Maine, was the first to engage in polling research.

An initial round of telephone-interview polling for Muskie was completed in late July by Independent Research Associates Inc., a Washington-based firm headed by William R. Hamilton, who has worked mainly for Democrats in the South. Before joining the Muskie staff in January, Miss Anna Navarro worked for Hamilton.

Media—While it is unusual to have a pollster on a campaign staff, Miss Navarro said she felt the arrangement benefited the Senator. She saw her role as the "realist"—the person who must "knock down theories and present unpalatable news."

In that capacity, Miss Navarro has been working closely with Robert D. Squier, 36, head of Communications Co. of Washington, D.C., and Muskie's media consultant.

"Squier is involved in the whole process," Miss Navarro said. "We work as a team and talk about what his data needs are. Polling is moving more toward a media orientation because people are getting their information through the tube."

Meanwhile, she said, "The Senator is always badgering us for information." Muskie plans to receive in-depth surveys from five or six primary states by January 1972. In addition, Muskie requires polling research on such political questions as how closely should he affiliate himself with Chicago Mayor Richard J. Daley, a controversial figure but a potential source of delegate support in Illinois.

THE ETHICAL DILEMMA: POLITICIANS VS. POLLSTERS

In the spring 1963 issue of *Public Opinion Quarterly,* Louis Harris wrote: "The pollster who is knowledgeable about politics will inevitably be invited to sit in on strategy meetings . . . . (He) will more and more be in a position of recommending when and how many polls should be conducted for his client, rather than simply waiting for the political powers-that-be to call him and set the timetable."

Harris was writing from experience. In October 1959, he was one of nine men who met with John F. Kennedy to plan Kennedy's 1960 presidential campaign. (Harris went on to take polls for the Democratic National Committee until he started a newspaper column in 1963.)

Yet, a deep involvement with a candidate's fortunes raises an ethical dilemma for some pollsters, especially those who consider themselves social scientists, seeking to discover what motivates people, rather than campaign consultants, seeking to get their candidate elected.

One pollster, Mervin Field, noted in a 1967 speech before his colleagues that "there is an implicit pressure to use the (polling) research for other than purely objective fact gathering. It is used to convince financial backers, to encourage party workers, to bolster the confidence of the candidate, to freeze out potential opponents and to support existing biases."

In this climate, Field said, a major problem can arise over "the selective use of certain findings to create a misleading impression." Thus, "there are leaks to newsmen for 'background,' and leaks to the opposition to lull them or to steer them in a direction that will help (the client)."

AAPOR: In an effort to minimize unethical conduct, the American Association for Public Opinion Research, founded in 1947, has set standards for reporting poll results.

An AAPOR code of ethics, adopted in 1960, calls upon members to monitor release of the results and to correct promptly any misinterpretation of their findings.

In 1968, AAPOR, which includes both commercial and academic members, issued a standard "which news media can utilize when reporting poll results." Each of these news reports, AAPOR said, should include:

the identity of the survey's sponsors:

a description of the sample, including its size;

an indication of the allowance that should be made for sample error;

a report on which results, if any, are based on only parts of the total sample (For example, some poll results may represent interviews only with those persons who are likely to vote.);

a statement of technique—whether the interviewing was done in person, by telephone, by mail or on street corners;

a statement on the timing of the interviews, putting them in context with relevant events.

The AAPOR code applies both to polls which are prepared for publication and to polls taken for a private client whose results subsequently are publicized.

AAPOR members elect a standards committee, which is charged with investigating complaints of misuse of polls. It is currently studying allegations of irregularities in published polls taken during the Democratic mayoral primary in Philadelphia earlier this year.

No individual ever has been cited by the standards committee for misconduct, although the panel occasionally has met privately with pollsters whose conduct was under question. AAPOR's governing body, an executive council, is empowered to warn by a citation or to expel members, but it has never done so. Sidney Hollander Jr., a member of the AAPOR council and a former chairman of its standards committee, said: "The mood of the organization is chang-

ing and they're in a position to be much tougher."

Irving Crispi, executive vice president of The Gallup Organization and also a former chairman of the AAPOR standards committee, wrote in *Polls, Television and the New Politics* (Chandler Publishing, 1970) that the 1968 code should dampen "the inclination of many journalists to make blanket statements as to 'what the polls are showing' " while encouraging "the reporting of *whose* poll using *which* methods and (obtaining) *what* results."

NCPP: In April 1968, George H. Gallup invited some 25 pollsters to attend an organizational meeting in Santa Barbara, Calif., on the eve of the annual AAPOR conference. The session led to formation of the National Council on Public Polls, which at present has 16 member organizations.

NCPP dues are $100 a year for membership. The group's current president is Robert T. Bower, director of the Bureau of Social Science Research, Washington, D.C. Its trustees are three pollsters—Gallup, Harris and Archibald M. Crossley—and Richard M. Scammon, director of the Election Research Center of the Governmental Affairs Institute.

"As of now," Bower said, "there

is no evidence that a 'bandwagon effect,' induced by polls, influences the result of elections."

The group will issue a quarterly newsletter, starting this fall, aimed at journalists and other users of polls. As yet another way of promoting more sophisticated evaluations, NCPP plans to sponsor seminars for Senate aides, political managers and newsmen, at which polling techniques will be analyzed.

Legislation: There have been a few attempts to enact laws to regulate polling, but none has succeeded.

Rep. Lucien N. Nedzi, D-Mich., is sponsoring a Truth-in-Polling Act (HR 5003), which has been referred to the House Administration Committee.

The provisions of the Nedzi bill parallel those of the AAPOR and NCPP codes. (In one respect, the bill goes further by requiring public filing of the percentage of interviews in the total sample that were completed and the percentage of persons in the sample who refused to be interviewed.)

In March 1963, a bill aimed at rigorous control of the publication of any preelection poll passed both houses of the Texas legislature. It was vetoed by Democratic Gov. (1963-69) John B. Connally, who is now Treasury Secretary.

Telephone—The Hamilton firm uses a "tight screen," seeking to reach only persons who intend to vote in selected 1972 Democratic primaries.

In upholding their telephone-based techniques, Hamilton and Miss Navarro explain how they

attempt to establish a good rapport during the half-hour interviews. The technique also costs about 60 per cent less than field interviews of comparable size—a major consideration in the money-short Muskie campaign.

For the Muskie polls, numbers

are gleaned from telephone directories in the areas to be surveyed and several digits are changed before the call is made. This ensures that unlisted numbers will be represented in the sample. (In Los Angeles, 35 per cent of all residential telephones are unlisted; in

New York, 20 per cent.)

The Hamilton interviewers call back three times if no one answers; they do not always interview the person who answers the phone. They also employ a toll-free "verification number," which most people ask for but which only a minority actually call. This keeps their rejection rate to 5 per cent.

Criticism—In general, pollsters for Democratic candidates have shunned telephone polling, and the Muskie techniques have elicited criticism from established pollsters. They wonder, in private, whether Hamilton, who has been polling since 1963, can "go the distance" in a Muskie Presidential campaign.

"Since when did a 24-year-old kid know something?" said a veteran pollster who works mainly for Democrats, referring to Miss Navarro. "I couldn't handle a Presidential campaign when I was 24. I think it's silly."

Miss Navarro said: "It's too new, and conventional wisdom says it's no good. Yet I have a gut feeling for what I'm after; you have to know how to play with it."

After the round of open-ended telephone questioning, Miss Navarro said she is more convinced than ever that the system works well and will provide the kind of data the Senator needs.

The non-pollers: Other Democrats who are either in or at the edge of the battle for the party's Presidential nomination have not yet commissioned any private polling. The Democratic National Committee, still in debt from the 1968 campaign, has no plans to poll, but David A. Cooper, the DNC's director of research, said

he is prepared to offer technical polling advice to any Democrat seeking office in 1972. (None of the Presidential hopefuls has contacted him.)

McGovern—"We've seen some private polls that other people have done," said Gary W. Hart, campaign director for Sen. George S. McGovern, of South Dakota. "The reason we're not doing it is that, first of all, it's too early and, second, it costs too much money and, thirdly, they won't tell us anything we don't already know . . . .

"My own horseback judgment is that our supporters ought to be able to tell us what's on the minds of people. Also, people are much more nationally oriented; you don't have the kind of Balkanization on issues that you used to have."

Hart nevertheless said that the McGovern forces probably would poll in Wisconsin and Oregon "to find out what issues predominate" there. Hart said, "I think that would be worth the outlay. But that's January or February."

Bayh—Robert J. Keefe, administrative assistant and a top campaign planner for Sen. Birch Bayh,

of Indiana, said the Senator strongly believes in taking polls, but, in light of his "low-recognition profile, there's not much point in taking them now."

Keefe said he had been "picking the brains" of two pollsters, John F. Kraft and Quayle, "both of whom are trying to get our business."

"When we go into (the Florida) primary situation, we will poll three of four months out," Keefe said.

Kennedy—"We have no reason to poll," said Richard C. Drayne, press secretary to Sen. Edward M. Kennedy, of Massachusetts.

"My boss reads polls rather avidly. He's pretty good at interpreting them. But we don't pull our own. There are other people who pull them for you, or maybe send you results, but we've not commissioned any. There's no point in paying $40,000 for a poll just to see whether you were right on an issue."

Humphrey—In the 1968 Presidential campaign, Hubert H. Humphrey, the Democratic nominee, spent $262,000 on polls taken

Tully Plesser   *Robert Teeter*   *Anna Navarro*

by Quayle and five smaller firms.

Now that he is in the Senate, according to Jack McDonald, his press secretary, "There's no activity of any kind . . . . He doesn't have advance men. He doesn't have money men. He doesn't have delegate people. He doesn't have pollsters."

Jackson—A no-polling report also came from the office of Sen. Henry M. Jackson, of Washington, whose supporters are gearing up for a major effort in next March's Florida primary.

S. Sterling Munro Jr., Jackson's administrative assistant, said that "When your investment is zero, your cost-benefit ratio is 100 per cent."

Sharing the burden: At a dinner meeting of Presidential candidates, called by party chairman Lawrence F O'Brien July 14, Muskie proposed undertaking a pooled public opinion survey, utilizing a single pollster, as a means of saving campaign funds.

The Muskie plan will be studied further in staff meetings, but it was not greeted with enthusiasm.

None of the dark-horse candidates—such as Sen. Fred R. Harris, of Oklahoma, and Rep. Wilbur D. Mills, of Arkansas—are having any polling done for them, and they are not interested in paying an equal share of the cost of a joint survey—the formula the Muskie's staff regards as the most equitable.

All pollsters interviewed by *National Journal* opposed the shared-data proposal, although they did not want to say so publicly for fear of offending Muskie, whose business they believe is still up for grabs. One pollster said, "You can't do that any more than you could work for Ford *and* General Motors. It just seems unnatural to me."

TECHNIQUES

The late Elmo Roper, a pioneer pollster, said that the polling business sat on a three-legged stool: sampling, interviewing and interpretation.

This base has remained constant since Roper began polling in the mid-1930s. But the kind of information that sohpisticated politicians are seeking and the kind of techniques that pollsters are using to obtain it for them have changed profoundly.

A Midwestern Senator said, "Quite frankly, the trial heats and the stock question about approval is probably the least valuable, so far as I'm concerned, because there isn't a thing you can do with that kind of information." (The Senator, who is up for reelection in 1972, will be polling heavily, but he does not want his constituents to know about it because "it weakens my posture.")

Utility—William Hamilton, now polling for Muskie, said that private polls can tell candidates what issues are important enough to change voting decisions; whether these issues can be welded into a campaign theme; and how the over-all political climate, including the other candidates in a race, will affect the outcome.

(Pollster Tully Plesser said his polls revealed that a referendum on liquor-by-the-drink was a major factor in the senatorial contest in Texas in 1970, because of the voters who were attracted to the polls by the liquor issue.)

Interest groups who are seeking to affect the outcome of an election may take polls that elicit complex data.

"COPE can buy 10 surveys and deliver them to the candidates," said pollster John Kraft. "It gives them a certain control over the campaign." The Committee on Political Education, the political action arm of the AFL-CIO, has been taking polls since 1958.

Similarly, the American Medical Political Action Committee (AMPAC), through its state organizations, spend more than $400,000 to poll for Republicans between the 1968 and 1970 elections. Vincent P. Barabba, chairman of Decision Making Information Inc., a California-based AMPAC pollster, said: "Those guys (at AMPAC) have done as much to improve the systematic analysis of the political process as any organization in existence today."

In Barabba's view, "A critical ability of a good (polling) firm is to have experience in overcoming the hesitancy on the part of some campaign managers to *really* make use of this information. If you accept a campaign as an economic concept—that is, you are going to attempt to allocate limited resources in the most efficient way—then this information is crucial."

Costs and timing—Thomas W. Benham, vice president of Opinion Research and its liaison man with the White House, said: "If you're running a campaign where you're going to spend $500,000, you better put 10 per cent aside for polling research, because it can make the other 90 percent twice or three times more efficient" . . . .

THE RISE OF THE POLLS: BLOOPERS AMID IMPROVING AIM

Although political polls are commonplace today, the use of scientific surveying techniques is less than 40 years old. Yet, in one way or another, polls have been part of the campaign scene for nearly 150 years.

Straw polls—In 1824, reporters for the *Harrisburg Pennsylvanian* walked the streets of Wilmington, Del., asking people whom they preferred as their Presidential candidate. In that first recorded United States newspaper poll, the *Pennsylvanian* found Andrew Jackson running well ahead of John Quincy Adams. (Although Jackson won a popular plurality, the election was thrown into the House of Representatives, which picked Adams.)

Newspapers took straw polls throughout the rest of the 1800s. The *Farm Journal* became the first national magazine to take one—in 1912. By 1928, newspapers and magazines were conducting six nationwide and 79 state and local straw polls.

By far the most prominent of the magazine straw polls was that of the *Literary Digest,* which began polling in 1916. The *Digest*'s streak of correct Presidential predictions remained unbroken until 1936, when the magazine reported that Alfred M. Landon would win 59.1 per cent of the popular vote and 370 of 531 electoral votes. Actually, Franklin D. Roosevelt won 60.2 per cent of the popular vote and 523 electoral votes.

George H. Gallup, a pioneer scientific pollster, publicly predicted at the time that the *Digest*

would fall on its face; he was meanwhile accurately predicting the results.

As Gallup noted, the *Digest* mailed its more than 10 million sample ballots solely to car owners and telephone subscribers—two groups at the time heavily weighted with high-income people who tended to vote Republican—and still do. The 2,376,523 respondents to the *Digest* poll tended to be the wealthiest and best-educated sub-group in the sample, which biased the results still further. Furthermore, the *Digest* failed to take into account six million new voters, five million of whom voted for Roosevelt. The pool results helped drive the *Literary Digest* out of business as public confidence in the magazine sagged.

Scientific polls—The first scientific poll—based on a representative sample of the population—was taken in July 1935, when *Fortune* reported on public reaction to Roosevelt and his New Deal programs.

The poll was taken by three partners, Paul T. Cherington, Elmo B. Roper Jr. and Richardson K. Wood. They had been conducting private market research and were looking for a dramatic way to prove the degree of accuracy that could be obtained through scientific sampling. The idea was especially attractive to Roper who, according to his son, Burns W. Roper, was fascinated by politics and "always wanted to be a United States Senator."

Gallup's scientific sampling also

was published in 1935, when a group of newspapers agreed to syndicate his findings in a Sunday column. Archibald M. Crossley entered the business in 1936, at the behest of King Features.

For many years, Roper, Gallup and Crossley were "the big three" of the polling business; most of the pollsters active today got their start in their organizations.

The three men also were great friends who bet on which of the three would come closest to predicting the outcome of a Presidential election. Roper won in 1936, 1940 and 1944, each time collecting a case of Scotch from Gallup and Crossley.

Although Roosevelt used private polls informally to discern the public mood, the first major private political poll was taken by Roper for Jacob K. Javits in 1946 when Javits was running on the Liberal Party and Republican lines for a House seat from upper Manhattan.

Disaster—For a time, the pollsters' success in predicting election results gave them oracular status. But the bubble burst in 1948.

In that year, all the major polls picked Thomas E. Dewey to defeat Harry S. Truman by a landslide. Roper stopped polling in mid-September, certain that Dewey would win.

After the election, the Social Science Research Council, a private group, named a committee to inquire into the pollsters' methods.

The panel found that the sampling method they used was a valid one, but that the pollsters, in their overconfidence, ignored both undecided voters and others who had switched from Dewey to Truman late in the campaign. They had also underestimated the turnout; this made Dewey look better than he should have.

Through post-election polling, the committee found that one voter in seven decided how he would cast his ballot during the last two weeks of the campaign and that 75 per cent of this group voted for Truman.

Controversy—In 1968, a dispute arose shortly before the Republican National Convention that many pollsters now feel damaged public trust in the business.

At the time, Gov. Nelson Rockefeller of New York was basing much of his campaign for the presidential nomination on the ground that polls showed he would be a stronger candidate than Mr Nixon when pitted against the eventual Democratic nominee.

Rockefeller and Nixon aides were circulating private polls with conflicting results on various "trial heats." Then a Gallup Poll, taken July 19-21, showed Mr. Nixon as the stronger candidate. Three days later on July 30, a Harris Survey was published, with data collected July 25-29, which showed Rocke-

feller more likely to defeat Hubert H. Humphrey or Eugene J. McCarthy.

On Aug. 1, George H. Gallup Jr. and Louis Harris issued an unprecedented joint statement that Rockefeller had "now moved to an open lead" over the two Democrats. The statement was widely interpreted as a public retraction by the Gallup organization, but none of the principals has discussed the incident publicly. When the campaign got under way, the pollsters accurately measured the Humphrey surge in October and the decline in support for George C. Wallace, the third-party candidate.

"You might want to do a 'base study' early in the campaign year. This could be an interview that lasts 45 minutes to an hour and it's a big, expensive undertaking. But, from that, we can do selective studies. We can check out changing issues.

"And then we can do a small-scale telephone effort, re-interviewing certain people (a technique known as panelback), to see if they have changed their minds. You can develop a sophisticated tool and it can still have good economy to it."

Costs of seemingly comparable surveys can vary as much as 30 per cent, depending on the procedures, the overhead and the profit margin.

Senatorial and gubernatorial candidates commonly budget $30,000 for polling research over the course of a campaign. One statewide poll in a big state may cost $10,000 to $15,000; a survey

of a congressional district can cost up to $10,000. (The techniques of conducting both polls are essentially the same; the only major saving is in travel.)

"People are beginning to see that this kind of data is much more valuable if you can establish a trend," said Teeter of Detroit Market Opinion Research. This, of course, entails multiple interviews; in the field, interviewers are paid $2 an hour or more, plus expenses.

DMI's Barabba said: "The difficulty you have in measuring costs between companies is knowing whether you're measuring apples and apples or apples and oranges. There are a lot of ways to cut costs in this kind of research. Unfortunately, there is a direct relationship between costs and quality."

The product—John Kraft, who has 18 years' experience working for both Democratic and Republican candidates, said he normally prepares a written report, about 40

pages in length, of which three-fourths is interpretation. "I'll also supply the (computer) printouts when I'm asked to, but I've had only two such requests."

Kraft, like most other pollsters, prefers to discuss results and their meaning with the candidate and his staff. "In many cases, it's best to talk it out," he said.

Unfavorable reports can bring complications.

Teeter recalled: "I had one guy several years ago who had been working hard for two or three months and got a bad poll and just sat in a hotel room and drank for about four days. We couldn't move him; he was in shock because the poll still showed him 10-15 points behind. He eventually won . . . . Now, we talk a lot about how to lay bad ones on people before we do it. It's a very tricky thing."

Developments—Most pollsters interviewed by *National Jour-*

nal said they recently have started making more exhaustive studies of sub-groups and analyzing the response to various issues. "There's particular interest in the young voters in '72," Quayle said.

Quayle also reported that he is asking more media-related questions. "It's the sort of question I don't like to ask, because I don't think people really know how they get their information. I'm amazed at how little the television people know sometimes (about the makeup of their audiences) in a given market. But we're learning to work better together."

ORC's Benham said his firm had been able to shorten substantially the time period from "problem to data" by using more telephone interviews. "We've also learned how to weigh them better."

William M. Longman, president of Central Surveys Inc., said in a telephone interview from Shenandoah, Iowa, that his firm now was able to provide overnight results to political clients through arrangements for the use of computers at the interview sites.

Robert K. McMillan of Chilton Research Services, a proponent of telephone interviewing, said: "In a day, you can do here what it would take you four weeks to do if you had to mail out questionnaires (to interviewers). I also think we get higher cooperation rates around the country than is possible in face-to-face interviews. In some areas, you can't get people to go in at all."

Cleavage—Telephone survey research for politicians has mushroomed with the widespread use of bulk-rate long-distance (WATS) lines and computerized random generation of telephone numbers. But some members of the political polling fraternity remain opposed to telephone surveys.

Charles W. Roll Jr., president of Political Surveys and Analysis Inc. (PS&A), which has done most of the polling commissioned by Nelson Rockefeller, said: "If I were buying surveys for a political campaign that I felt was terribly important, and there was enough money, I wouldn't touch a telephone survey. I have reason to believe (from Rockefeller campaigns) that some people are far less critical of individuals when asked about them over the phone, and that, of course, creates a different result.

"If I were involved in a Presidential campaign, I would throw the telephone away, unless there was an extremely urgent time factor involved."

(Roll is an employee of George H. Gallup, who bought PS&A from its founder, Archibald M. Crossley, in 1970; PS&A uses Gallup's sampling, interviewing and tabulating facilities, which are based solely on field interviews.)

DMI's Barabba said: "You can get more about a person at the door than on the telephone. The telephone's great strength is that you get wider distribution of your sample and interview clusters."

Don M. Muchmore, chairman of Opinion Research of California, who has done comparative studies of telephone and field interview polls, said the field work produces superior results and should be used, except in high-urgency polls of national scope. "With no eye-to-eye contact, there's no trust," Muchmore said.

Sample methods—Political pollsters also divide over whether to use quota or probability samples.

Quayle said: "Nobody does probability samples, strictly speaking. And if you did, it would be obscene, because you'd be charging a guy an arm and a leg for a greater degree of accuracy than he needs . . . .

"None of the private pollsters do complete probability sampling because of the prohibitive expense. (Quayle noted that this was not the case for the Gallup Poll and the Harris Survey, "because their necks are on the line.")

"You pick up a point to a point-and-a-half of margin with probability samples. I've done them when I've had to, when I knew I was in a different ball game."

John Kraft and his wife, Fran Farrell Kraft, who is also a well-known pollster, agreed with Quayle. "There is no significant difference in the result," Kraft said.

Several pollsters disagreed, however. One was PS&A's Roll, who said: "The respectability of quota samples went out in 1948, with the Truman-Dewey election. You don't know what your sample error is. Luck is with them. But it's certainly not enough to hang your hat on, I would think."

ORC's Benham said his firm used only probability samples. However, he said: "In many situations, you can use the best scientific probability sample or a mediocre quota sample and get the same results—because there's no critical element that would make an essential difference."

ASSESSMENT

Pollsters and politicians coexist uneasily, needing each other and yet aware of each other's limitations.

Both are victims of a vicious circle in politics: the degree of media exposure affects poll results; poll results affect the amount of campaign funds that can be raised; campaign funds affect media exposure.

Drawer syndrome — Muchmore thinks campaign managers, more than candidates, are responsible for poor relationships. "We give them a battle plan, and many times they don't want to use it because they have a feeling it's going to go a different way. Sometimes they're right; sometimes they're wrong. But, more often, they're wrong."

Another Californian, Vincent Barabba, said: "We see an awful lot of what we refer to as the righthand drawer syndrome. You give a guy a survey—you make a fancy presentation—and he says, 'Gee, that's great!' And he opens up the right-hand drawer of his desk and puts it in there, and that's the last time it's used.

"Then, if someone asks what are you basing all those decisions on, he opens up the drawer and says, 'Well, we got a survey.' "

MOR's Teeter believes the worst is over. "Two or three years ago," he said, "we had a real problem with guys who were using it for the first time and thought they had just bought themselves magic buttons. With some people, it became a narcotic. If they didn't know what to do, they had another poll taken."

Getting more: From the client's side, a Democratic Senator said privately: "I don't know of anyone around here who is having polling done and who wouldn't like to get more than he's getting out of it. But I know it's simply a matter of dollars. They have a product to sell; they have costs."

If finances are often a central problem to the pollster, they are even more of one to the politician. A Republican Senator from the Northeast said: "There isn't any question that I couldn't solve if I wanted to spend $25,000 for a survey."

But the difficulties range beyond insufficient funds. A campaign manager who has worked with pollsters for many years said privately:

"I think there's room in this business for someone who really wants to drive it wide open. He could drive all these guys out. For example, why not add an entire demographic package with sample electoral analysis and priority ranking of states, congressional districts and counties, with crossdata by issues. It's possible with computer analysis. That's a service I could really use."

In 1968, the National Republican Congressional (Campaign) Committee and its Senate counterpart bought a $400,000 survey through Datamatics Inc., a subsidiary of Spencer-Roberts and Associates, a California-based campaign consulting firm. Datamatics is now dissolved; at the time, it was headed by Vincent Barabba.

Neither the House nor the Senate committee is scheduling any polling projects for 1972. Paul A. Theis, director of public relations for the House group, said: "We got committed to doing the (1968) thing without assessing as much as we should have in advance."

Pressure points — In a profession linked closely to the academic community, but with no entry standards, salesmanship remains a persistent problem. "It's the gut problem in the business," said Albert H. Cantril, a Washington-based polling consultant. Cantril is the author, with Charles Roll, of *Hopes and Fears of the American People* (Universe Books, 1971), which is based on Gallup research.

Said Cantril: "The only way you can seek new business is to tear down the other guy's methods and try to show politicians that they are not getting anything too useful. There are no teaching materials you can use unless you break the confidence of a private (political) client."

Political pollsters also are encountering fresh problems in seeking to assemble valid public opinion data. An executive at Chilton Research Services in Philadelphia said: "There's no use kidding anybody; the cooperative rate is decreasing every year. It used to be 20 years ago if we got a 3-per cent refusal rate we were concerned about it; today, they are running 10 and 12 per cent.

"It's all part of the misuse of research techniques. People today are just more suspicious. You know, a salesman calling up and saying he's making a survey and the next thing he's knocking at your door."

Dangers—Private polls can cause complications in campaigns that are not always readily apparent. For example, Sen. Jacob K.

Javits, R-N.Y., received a poll from Tully Plesser in 1968 that showed Javits leading his Democratic opponent, Paul O'Dwyer, 48-16.

Javits' advisers were hesitant about releasing the poll, despite the strong lead, for fear it would not be believed and would raise a "credibility issue." Yet another consideration was fear that it would be harder to raise money if potential backers thought Javits could not lose.

The poll was nevertheless "leaked" to *The New York Times* for its "band-wagon" effect and because it showed Javits to be the strongest Republican politician in New York state at the time.

The release of the poll led to a charge by O'Dwyer that it was a deliberate attempt to influence the *New York Daily News* Poll, which was scheduled to commence canvassing just after the GOP poll was released.

While the Javits "leak" was a deliberate one, candidates often insist that a pollster report directly to them in an effort to control access to private polls on the campaign staff.

Pollsters and politicians are coming increasingly to agree that there is a limit to what surveys can accomplish. MOR's Teeter said: "You can't go and say to some guy, 'Look, if you go out and take this stand, you'll increase your support 4 per cent.' That's crazy"

Progress—If political pollsters are still searching for a firmer foundation, there are nevertheless signs of progress.

Quayle said: "A couple of years ago, everybody was trying to get into the act. And that's not hap-pening anymore. A lot of commercial firms—the guys who were researching soap and so forth—began to dabble in politics, looking at it as a new market. But you've got to know something about politics in this business. It's an art as well as a science."

Roll believes that what is needed is better liaison between the campaign and the pollsters— "politically sensitive men inside the campaign organization who are at the same time highly sophisticated about the use of polling techniques."

"It's a funny business," another well-known pollster said. "When you get all this stuff done, the candidates look at it and if it doesn't really agree with them, they're very suspicious. But if it agrees with them, it's the best poll in America."

Political spending law will have impact on candidates, business, labor   *Jonathan Cottin*

In the wood-paneled den overlooking his snow-blanketed estate in Locust Valley, N.Y., Leonard W. Hall was reliving his political career. Behind him sat a row of tiny elephants, carved from an elephant's tusk and symbolizing the Republican Party, to which Hall has devoted much of his life.

Hall rose to national prominence in 1952, when he helped Dwight D. Eisenhower win the Presidency, in an election that ended 20 years of Democratic rule. In 1956, he ran Eisenhower's campaign. In one corner of his living room are photographs of the late President bearing warm personal messages; in another corner, expressions of gratitude adorn a photo of Richard M. Nixon, taken when he was Vice President.

Hall, 71, was talking nostalgically about the fading glory of the old campaign techniques, of the days back in 1952 when a coast-to-coast whistlestop tour was a feature of any national campaign.

"I'm sorry the old trains are out," he said.

"When you got on the back of that platform, and you went out before a crowd, you got a reaction. In 1952, you knew Ike was going to win by watching those crowds."

But, as Hall fully realizes, that tradition is over. Modern candidates watch polls, not crowds. And instead of boarding a train for a whistlestop campaign, they talk to the voters on television—and reach more of them in a nimute than they could hope to meet in a week on the rails.

HIGH-FLYING CREDIT

Hotels, telephone companies and a host of small businesses have found out the hard way that Presidential campaigning is expensive business—but no single identifiable category of companies has suffered more than the airlines.

In the summer of 1971, the major airlines submitted to the Civil Aeronautics Board an accounting of debts outstanding accumulated by candidates and political parties. Sen. Hugh Scott, R-Pa., who was seeking tight regulations on unsecured credit used by candidates, included the data, showing unpaid bills of more than $2 million, in the July 23, 1971, *Congressional Record:*

American Airlines Inc.	
Organization	**Debt**
Republican National Finance Committee	$ 151,871.00
Richard M. Nixon	69,386.00
Democratic National Committee	426,833.00
Robert F. Kennedy	415,120.00
Hubert H. Humphrey	138,762.00
McCarthy for President	135,872.00
	$1,337,844.00

Eastern Air Lines Inc.	
Democratic National Committee	$ 208,876.12
Republican National Committee	112,823.44
	$ 321,690.56

Trans World Airlines Inc.	
United Democrats for Humphrey	$ 221,519.55
Humphrey Charter	25,091.04
Republican National Committee	13,196.95
	$ 259,807.54

United Airlines Inc.	
Nixon-Agnew Campaign	$ 75,107.55
Humphrey-Muskie Campaign	79,083.65
Democratic National Committee (Robert F. Kennedy)	12,651.97
	$ 166,843.17

As the sophisticated techniques of campaigning replace the devices Leonard Hall used in his prime, election costs have soared, bringing with them the fear that only the rich or those beholden to wealthy special interests can be elected to office.

Calls for spending ceilings and public demands for a complete accounting of where the money comes from also have accompanied the rapid growth in campaign costs.

Law—On Jan. 19, Congress responded, after years of controversy, by passing a law (86 Stat 3) designed to curb campaign spending in the media, force complete reporting of all political contributions and make it easier for the less affluent to buy broadcast time in the quest for elective office. President Nixon signed it Feb. 7.

The law will affect airlines, labor unions, telephone companies, radio and television stations, eight entities of the federal government, candidates—and the voters.

And while it is as yet untested, many are already worried by some of the requirements. Network officials and labor leaders, for example, are saying the law may cause more trouble than it will do good.

Officials in both the Democratic and Republican Parties are also worried by certain sections of the law, as are candidates and their fund raisers.

The cumulative evidence suggests that the legislation is likely to change markedly the way in which campaigns for federal office are run and financed in the United States, beginning in 1972.

CANDIDATES, PARTIES

The law was drawn primarily to regulate candidates for federal office and their political parties, and the targeted groups have begun to measure its effect.

The law ends the practice under which big contributors who wished to remain anonymous have been able to do so by funneling their money to candidates through political committees set up in the District of Columbia, where laws do not require identification of the committees' sources of funds. Political fund raisers concede the full disclosure required for all contributors giving more than $100 may make it harder to attract money.

Democrats complain that tightened airline credit regulations may hurt them.

And all sides say that the so-called "television blitz," in which wealthy men purchase huge amounts of broadcast time to advance their candidacies, is a thing of the past.

Disclosure: Experienced political money men concede the full disclosure provisions of the law may inhibit both givers and their candidates.

Problems—In the case of Sen. Edmund S. Muskie, D-Maine, the new provision is welcome in some respects, since its absence has caused him some unique political and financial problems in the past.

As Muskie explained to a "Meet The Press" panel (NBC) Jan. 16, he made full disclosure in 1970 of funds received for his successful Senate reelection campaign and also identified those who gave to his "national political operation."

As it turned out, the unilateral release of names of his backers hurt Muskie. "People ... whose names I reported, were then used as a target," by fund raisers for other candidates, he said.

The presidential candidate told his questioners:

"The willingness of people to contribute—and it may be nothing more than the problem of reconciling their action with the views of their employers, or with neighbors, or what have you, the fact they are subject to an unequal requirement inhibits them, whether for good reasons or bad, whether for corrupt reasons or noncorrupt reasons. You just can't set this kind of standard unilaterally."

Givers—On the other hand, Muskie's dilemma may become more complicated with the advent of full disclosure. Richard A. Kline, national finance adminis-

trator for the Muskie campaign, said public identification of givers could cut off the flow of Republican donations to Muskie.

Noting that a Feb. 4 Gallup Poll showed Muskie's support among Republicans at 13 per cent, Kline said the campaign was "getting more money from Republicans. Where these Republicans will be scared silly of the Republican Administration, disclosure inhibits them."

Kline said many Democrats have "given to several Democratic candidates ... some are giving to us, while pledging fealty to Hubert (Sen. Hubert H. Humphrey, D-Minn.)." Moreover, he added, the disclosure provision may affect wealthy persons with a preference for anonymity. "There are a lot of people who simply don't want their names made public."

Despite that, Kline said, he was "not really too concerned. We have a very, very broad base ... of contributors."

At Humphrey's headquarters, S. Harrison Dogole, a major fund raiser for the Senator, expected few reductions in cash gifts because of the identification requirement. "You may eliminate a few, but I don't think it will be a substantial number of givers." Dogole said the provision may do much to "clear up the mystique" about fund raising.

S. Sterling Munro Jr., administrative assistant to Sen. Henry M. Jackson, D-Wash., another Presidential candidate, said the section would be an "inhibiting factor for some people who do not want to be identified." As an example, he cited "a guy who didn't want another candidate to know that he's working for more than one."

A spokesman for Sen. George S. McGovern, D-S.D., a Presidential candidate, said the disclosure section will have no impact on that campaign, since McGovern has pledged to identify all his financial backers whether or not it is required by law.

A spokesman for the Republican National Committee said the disclosure section may have "some negative effect" on would-be contributors. However, he added, "we'll live with it."

Receivers—Candidates for the presidency this year are nearly unanimous in claiming that they have always been wary and that the law will do little to make them more careful about the sources of campaign contributions.

The issue of refusing gifts does not even arise at McGovern headquarters, suggests one of the Senator's aides: "people who are embarassing for us" do not offer contributions, she claimed.

"We're very careful," said Kline, Muskie's money man. However, he continued, "You never know, if you're raising money, where every nickel is coming from." Kline said all incoming money is diligently scrutinized. "We have refused to accept money that is a least little bit tainted. Why destroy our whole campaign theme (Trust Muskie) for a few thousand dollars?"

Dogole, Humphrey's fund raiser, like the others, said his candidate has "always been careful." Contributions are returned to anyone who "has problems, or is doing something not consistent with the integrity of the candidate."

A Republican spokesman said it was "conceivable" that the provision could force the return of donations that might embarass President Nixon. But, he added, "time will tell."

Russell D. Hemenway, director of the National Committee for an Effective Congress, a principal strategist in the successful effort to pass the campaign financing bill, said the disclosure section cannot help but serve as a built-in psychological inhibitor.

"It's going to make the giver more sensitive, significantly inhibit a giver who wants to remain undisclosed. And candidates who don't want to be subjected to subsequent blackmail will have to think very carefully about not reporting all gifts."

Howard J. Samuels, the wealthy unsuccessful candidate for the 1970 Democratic gubernatorial nomination in New York, sided with Hemenway, saying the law means that candidates "will be scared to death."

Early money: Hemenway, who described his scheme for passing the bill through a reluctant House as one of "keeping it moving without educating the Members," said many candidates are using the period before the law becomes effective April 7, to raise money.

Noting that the House put off final action on the measure until the Christmas recess, Hemenway said:

"The only reason the House didn't act before the recess is so that the Members could go home and raise all the dough they need."

Since the identity of financial backers is much easier to hide under the old Corrupt Practices Act (43 Stat 1070) than it will be under

the new law, candidates may ask for early money and offer a guarantee of anonymity, Hemenway said. "I personally know candidates in New York and elsewhere using this argument." Would-be candidates with "rich families," who will be forbidden from investing large sums on their own behalf once the law is operative, were also building their political war chests in the interim, said Hemenway. He declined to identify them.

One House Member planning to fund his 1972 campaign before the law goes into force is Rep. John B. Anderson, R-Ill., who was the Republican floor manager of the spending limit bill. He said that a $25-a-plate dinner, providing the bulk of his reelection campaign funds, is to be held in mid-February, well in advance of the new law's effective date.

Television — The reform-minded Hemenway said the sections of the new law affording candidates the right to purchase broadcast time at lowest unit rates and setting spending ceilings for all advertising will have the greatest impact.

"There will be no more TV blitzes" because of the spending ceiling, said Hemenway, who was the chief acrhitect of an earlier television spending-limit bill, which was passed by Congress but vetoed by President Nixon in 1970.

"It's certainly going to control media spending," said Anderson. As a result, he said, "you may find people giving more to direct mail," which is not covered in the law.

Looking ahead to the 1972 Presidential election, former (1953-57) Republican National Chairman Hall said the basic problem in the "powerful" medium of television was to insure equal access.

"This may be heresy, but I think both candidates should have the same amount of money to spend on TV. It's healthy," said Hall.

Hall believes that "intelligent advertising men," taking care to protect their candidate from over-exposure, will make sure that time purchases are "equalized."

Family money—One section of the law certain to affect future campaigns provides that a candidate and his immediate family may not spend more than $50,000 of their own money on his campaign.

One wealthy politician who welcomes the ceiling is Howard Samuels, who now is president of New York's Off Track Betting Corp. He said the limitation should avoid instances such as this one:

"The other day I had a call from someone asking me to run for Mayor because I could afford it." Pacing behind his desk at OTB headquarters in midtown New York, Samuels said: "That's a hell of a way to run someone for Mayor." (The law only applies to federal elections, but Samuels would like it to apply at local levels.)

Samuels said the provision could limit the political operations of wealthy men like Gov. Nelson A. Rockefeller, R, if it was applied to statewide races. "I watched Nelson Rockefeller buy the governorship of New York with family money for 12 years and buy the Republican Party as well," said Samuels.

If the law had been in effect in

MAJOR PROVISIONS OF CAMPAIGN LAW

The Federal Election Campaign Act (86 Stat 3) applies to all primary and general elections for federal office. It repeals the Corrupt Practices Act (43 Stat 1070) which in theory imposed a limit of $5,000 on contributions by any individual to a single candidate. Major provisions follow:

Media

Rates—Broadcast and print media must charge candidates their "lowest unit rate" in the 45-day pre-primary period and for 60 days before each general election.

Limits—No candidate may spend more on media than 10 cents multiplied by the voting-age population in the geographical area where he is seeking election, or $50,000, whichever is larger. Only 60 per cent of the total media expenditure may be made for purchase of broadcast time.

Permission—No media spending by any candidate-approved organization or individual on behalf of a candidate may be accepted unless the candidate certifies in writing that the expenditure will not put him over the limit. However, committees promoting a candidate without his authorization may operate as long as all their ads say they are unauthorized.

Access—Broadcast stations may have their licenses revoked if they fail to sell "reasonable amounts of time" to candidates.

Penalty—Violation can result in a $5,000 fine and a five-year sentence.

Contributions

Promise—No candidate may promise a contributor any legislation, job, compensation or contract in exchange for support. Violation is punishable by a $1,000 fine and a year in jail.

Contractors and companies—Any business organization which is negotiating or performing a government contract and which contributes to a candidate is liable for a $5,000 fine and five years in jail, as is any candidate who accepts such a contribution.

Ceilings—No candidate and his immediate family may give in the aggregate to him or committees supporting him more than $25,000 if he is running for the House, $35,000 if he is running for the Senate, or $50,000 if he is running for President or Vice President. Violation is punishable by a $1,000 fine and one year in jail.

Disclosure

Committees—Every political committee spending or receiving $1,000 or more a year must report four times a year the name, address, occupation and place of business of each person lending, giving or receiving more than $100; and the date of each gift.

Individuals—Anyone giving more than $100 for the election of a candidate other than to the candidate or a committee must report it.

Reports—Disclosure must be made to the House Clerk for House Races; the Senate Secretary for Senate contests; and the Comptroller General in presidential elections, as well as to the Secretary of State in each state applicable. These authorities must make the data available immediately and publish an annual cumulative summary of all reports. Any person believing a violation has occurred may complain to the appropriate officer who "shall expeditiously make an investigation . . . ." The Attorney General may seek civil action against violators.

Transfers—"No person shall make a contribution in the name of another person, and no person shall knowingly accept a contribution made by one person in the name of another person."

Penalty—Conviction for violating any of the disclosure provisions may bring up to a $1,000 fine and one year in jail.

Unsecured Credit

Regulations—The Civil Aeronautics Board, Federal Communications Commission and Interstate Commerce Commission must each draw regulations regarding the extension of credit by industries they regulate to candidates and persons supporting such candidates.

1968, it could have seriously hampered Rockefeller's abortive second campaign for the Republican presidential nomination. Herbert E. Alexander, in *Financing the 1968 Election* (D.C. Heath and Co., 1971), reported that Rockefeller spent $356,000 in his short-lived pre-nomination bid.

Credit—From the standpoint of the Democratic National Committee, the most troublesome aspect of the bill is a directive to the Interstate Commerce Commission, Federal Communications Commission and Civil Aeronautics Board to draw regulations regarding the use of unsecured credit by candidates.

DNC Treasurer, Robert S. Strauss, whose party still owes creditors, including those regulated by FCC and CAB, more than $9 million from the 1968 campaign, said "the industries don't like" the regulation requirement.

Strauss said the proposal was pushed through by Sen. Hugh Scott, R-Pa., the Senate minority leader, in an attempt to hurt the Democrats. "I happen to know Scott's out to make it tough on us," said Strauss.

Scott called a meeting on Jan. 31 in his office with the chairmen of the three regulatory agencies to outline his views on what the regulations should contain. He told the agency officials they should require candidates to make "firm declarations on intent to pay, within a period, certain percentages" of their bills, said Kenneth Davis, Scott's legislative assistant. He also suggested that the regulated companies make periodic public reports of candidates' outstanding debts, Davis said. The agency chairmen "wanted to cooperate as much as possible," said Davis.

Strauss called the meeting "highly inappropriate."

He said, "Scott and the Republican National Committee have forgotten 1960, when John Kennedy defeated Richard Nixon and the Republican Party stayed in debt to the phone company and airlines for four long years."

"I'd like to have an opportunity to have some input when they start drafting those regulations because we know what the parties can live with," Strauss added.

As for the Democrats' present financial status, he said "we have been highly prudent in the use of credit and highly diligent in paying current bills." As for the old balance, "we are paying it when we can," he said.

At the Republican National Committee, Robert P. Odell Jr.,

executive director of the RNC's Finance Committee, said he thought the agencies should forbid an airline or a phone company to serve any candidate whose unpaid bill exceeds $50,000.

Rep. Morris K. Udall, D-Ariz., Democratic floor manager of the bill, said the $50,000 figure sounded "too low" to him.

The agencies must promulgate their regulations 90 days after Mr. Nixon signed the bill. Agency officials said normal rule-making procedures would be followed, including, if needed, public hearings.

Evasion: Although experienced fund raisers acknowledge that the law is tight, most maintain it can still be bypassed.

"Anyone who wants to circumvent it can do so," said Rep. H. Allen Smith, R-Calif.

Thomas McCoy, a fund raiser for former Sen. (1959-69) Eugene J. McCarthy, D-Minn., when he ran for President in 1968, said that he "can't believe" that "a convicted tax evader couldn't find seven guys to give money to his candidate," thus preserving his own anonymity.

"Anybody who wants to give money will still give it," agrees the DNC's Strauss.

Former GOP Chairman Hall said good legal minds will find loopholes. "The lawyers are going to be looking at this law and asking, how are we going to do what we always did?"

GOVERNMENT

Eight separate government units are responsible for implementation of the law: the Senate Secretary, House Clerk, General Accounting Office, Secretary of Commerce, Secretary of Labor, Civil Aeronautics Board, Interstate Commerce Commission, and Federal Communications Commission.

Labor and Commerce: The easiest jobs fall to the Labor and Commerce Departments, which will merely provide data used by the FCC in computing broadcast spending limits.

Labor will notify the FCC and General Accounting Office of the consumer price index, a statistic it compiles anyhow. The figure will help both to decide whether a cost-of-living increase should be allowed above the 10-cent-per-voter media limit.

Commerce will provide the agencies with the other necessary figure in the computation: the number of voting-age people in the country.

Congress—The Senate Secretary and House Clerk will receive the detailed campaign donation and spending reports of Members in their respective bodies. They are required to make the data available for mechanical duplication or hand copying as soon as it is received. Candidates must file the data four times a year.

FCC: The Federal Communications Commission has a more difficult set of tasks. It must draw rules for the use of unsecured credit by candidates using telephones, and establish what candidates must pay for broadcast media at "lowest unit rate." Since almost every radio station and television outlet in the nation has a different rate system, and some have no organized charge structure at all, the job will be difficult. The FCC, as it has in the past, also will compile from the stations a record of candidates' time purchases.

Howard L. Kitzmiller, a member of the commission's legislative liaison staff, said the forthcoming unsecured credit regulations "will give the telephone company a chance to push the candidate (to pay) a little bit, where it might not have been politic to do so before."

As for a definition of lowest unit rate, said Kitzmiller, "ultimately, that will be our responsibility. It will give the candidate the benefit of volume discounts" granted to big advertisers.

CAB and ICC: The Interstate Commerce Commission also must draw rules on the use of unsecured credit by candidates, but the impact will be limited, since candidates rarely run up big bills for trains and other carriers regulated by the commission.

More important to the candidates will be the CAB's credit regulations. The Democrats still owe the airlines about $2 million from 1968.

T. William Swinford, a CAB press officer, said Secor D. Browne, the Republican CAB chairman who met Jan. 31 with Sen. Scott, "will meet with anyone who wants to meet with him . . . he would be happy to talk with Democratic candidates and other Republican candidates."

GAO: The General Accounting Office has the biggest share of the administrative workload, and even before the law was signed it had assembled an informal interagency staff to plan implementation of the measure. Under the provisions of the law, the GAO must:

draw up reporting forms for

presidential and vice presidential candidates and their party organizations (to achieve uniformity in Senate and House spending report forms, officials from Congress are invited to staff sessions);

distribute reporting forms to every political group that might work in presidential campaigns;

determine what lowest unit rate will mean for non-broadcast media, including newspapers and magazines, and police adherence to the limits.

L. Fred Thompson, legislative attorney at GAO who heads the agency's task force, said candidates and other political officials are "going to have problems understanding what their responsibilities are."

In the case of political committees which have kept their financial books in a "slipshod manner" previously, the stringent disclosure requirements will mean they will have to do "considerable work to get their books in order."

As planning goes ahead, said Thompson, the GAO will be forced to divert some of its staff members to the job of compiling necessary data, preparatory to implementation of the law. These staff members later may be used to compile the presidential campaign spending reports, which must be filed with the agency according to the law.

Identification of all political committees involved in presidential campaigns may be the hardest task, Thompson said. "There is no precedent; no scientific way to go about it. We will identify as many as we can ... we plan to work with the national parties, political action committees, state political

committees. Hopefully, we can get quite a boost from the news media, which could build public interest in this."

REGULATED INDUSTRIES

Airlines and the telephone companies, which have lost large sums by extending credit to candidates, have expressed relief that the government will force them to be more circumspect on billing. This is so even though the companies did little to force the issue in Congress.

At the same time, broadcasters find little in the bill that causes them to cheer.

Planes, phones—Davis, Sen. Scott's campaign spending expert, said neither the telephone nor the airline industry pressed for an unsecured credit amendment. "They didn't do anything. They just weren't going to get involved in something like this," he said.

James M. Mundis, news services director for the American Telephone & Telegraph Co. in Washington, agreed that the firm was inactive. To the question of what A T & T did to lobby for the bill, Mundis said he was authorized to reply: "Nothing—absolutely nothing."

Spokesmen for two major airlines likewise said their companies had done little to advance the bill. John Coris, assistant to the vice president for public relations at Trans World Airlines Inc., said the carrier "advised when asked for our views" that it favored the unsecured credit provision. American Airlines Inc. vice president Cyrus S. Collins said, "I'm sure we told anyone who asked us that we fa-

vored it."

As for the kind of regulations American Airlines would like, Collins was explicit: "To sum it up, we'd like to get cash." Failing that, a bond for 50 per cent of the credit limit allowed a candidate would be desirable, he said. Whatever the rule is, it should require someone to guarantee payment. "Somehow or other, we want someone on the hook," said Collins.

As to why the industries did not push for the regulation even though they wanted it, one industry official conceded that none wanted to be identified as asking the government to make the going hard for a candidate who might one day be President. A T & T's Mundis said: "It's awkward."

Broadcasters: Broadcast media opposition to some sections of the law is motivated primarily by economic considerations. While it has lobbied for campaign spending reform and limits, the industry has opposed consistently the lowest unit rate provision, as well as the mandate that a candidate limit his broadcast spending to 60 per cent of his over-all advertising budget.

NAB: Speaking for the industry, Vincent T. Wasilewski, president of the National Association of Broadcasters, summed up arguments against the two sections in a futile last-ditch attempt to strike them from the bill. In letters to each House Member Jan. 5, two weeks before the House voted final passage, the NAB official called the proposals "discriminatory."

He said the law allowed print media to charge candidates rates comparable to those charged other advertisers but forced broadcasters to sell candidates time at lowest unit rates.

At the same time, a candidate is unable under the law to disburse his full media spending limit "in whatever media he prefers," said Wasilewski.

Local stations—The spending limit and rate imposed by the law are troubling small station managers around the country.

One television station official in a Tennessee city, who declined to be identified, said some marginally profitable broadcast operations count on political advertising, formerly purchased at regular rates, to keep them going.

Another broadcaster in Nebraska, who declined to be identified, said his station might go under. Campaign advertising keeps his business afloat, he said. "I have a feeling that without the limit on campaign spending, we would be in the black this year," he said. "Slowly but surely they're driving people out of the broadcast business."

James D. Johnson, general manager of KHOL-TV, a small station in Holdridge, Neb., said the spending limit "will affect us quite a bit."

Johnson predicted that the media spending limits would force presidential candidates to avoid outlays for television advertising in less populous areas.

"Presidential campaign money will go into the 50 major markets. This will penalize us," said Johnson.

Networks—While all three major television networks support the NAB position on the discriminatory nature of the two broadcast spending sections, there is little concern that they will cut profits.

"We don't think it will have any impact," said a spokesman for American Broadcasting Co. Similar views were voiced by officials at National Broadcasting Co.

The networks were less concerned with the financing sections of the legislation than with provisions designed to regulate access to nationwide air time for candidates.

In particular, the networks tried, unsuccessfully, to persuade Congress to repeal the equal-time requirement imposed by Section 315 of the Communications Act (48 Stat 1064).

NBC President Julian Goodman told congressional committees that repeal of the requirement would allow the networks to improve their campaign coverage by presenting debates between major candidates without having to include minor party aspirants. It thus would have offered national candidates an inexpensive way to obtain national exposure, he said.

Richard W. Jencks, president of the CBS Broadcast Group, sided with Goodman on the equal-time issue.

If the campaign-spending law had done nothing more than "repeal ... 315, it would have been public enlightenment," Jencks said in an interview. "Without it, I think it's just an experiment."

Jencks said he also envisioned trouble for broadcasters from another section of the bill requiring them for the first time to sell time to candidates. He said he knew of instances when stations in the CBS family had refused to sell time.

He said the CBS television outlet in New York, which reaches an audience in about 40 congressional districts, would probably be "very hesitant" to sell time to a House candidate, since his message would be of decidedly limited interest to almost everyone in the viewing area.

Another example of potential conflict cited by Jencks: "I don't think that an all-news station, at least in prime listening time, will want to sell a half hour of time to a candidate."

The entire provision, said Jencks, "creates all sorts of confusion."

LABOR

The American labor movement feels as badly treated by the bill as the broadcasters.

Labor's political strategists are concerned by two of the new law's provisions which, they say, will limit the ability of unions to provide manpower for candidates—traditionally a greater source of political credit than unions' relatively small campaign contributions.

Labor leaders say that limits on political participation by union rank and file would constitute a serious setback. They fear that labor's allies in Congress, unable to count on the same degree of help from union members in their campaigns, would prove to be less sympathetic to labor's legislative demands.

Phone banks—The United Auto Workers Union and the AFL-CIO, which rely heavily on their memberships to mount election-time telephone canvasses, see a threat to the practice in a section that includes the use of telephone equipment and paid telephonists in the general limits on media spending.

To illustrate the problem, one labor official who declined to be identified cited a hypothetical example involving a pro-labor candidate. If the candidate has only a few thousand dollars left to spend up to his limit, he must choose between buying time on television or authorizing the installation of a telephone bank, to be manned by union volunteers. Should the candidate spend up to his limit by purchasing television time rather than telephone equipment, labor's ability to provide manpower will be of no use, the union official suggested.

Thomas E. Harris, associate general counsel to the AFL-CIO, said unions might avoid the problem by encouraging volunteers to canvass from their home telephones, thus saving the candidate the cost of the equipment and maintaining the union's political power.

However, William Dodds, political director of community action for the UAW, said the home telephone idea is flawed from the start.

"They'll make 10 times as many calls if they're all together. It will be more fun," said Dodds.

Registration—Even more disturbing to some unions, notably the International Brotherhood of Teamsters, is the requirement that union registration money can no longer be used for area-wide registration efforts, as it has in the past. Union officials believe the law permits labor money that has been earmarked by union dues payers for registration to be used only in registration among union members

TELEVISION ADVERTISING: A SKEPTIC'S VIEW

The three major candidates for President spent about $21 million on advertising—mostly in television—in 1968. But, says a man who should know, the spending was only "marginally effective."

Allan D. Gardner, who was Hubert H. Humphrey's advertising coordinator in 1968, says President Nixon's 43 per cent popular vote "was identical to his showing in the public opinion polls the previous May," before he spent most of his $12-million advertising budget on television.

Writing in *The Wall Street Journal* Feb. 1, Gardner contended:

"If wealth, good looks and sophisticated advertising could turn the trick, Nelson Rockefeller would have been in the White House long ago . . . but on the presidential trail, he has been humbled on successive occasions by the sons of an Arizona haberdasher and a gas station owner from California."

Gardner, vice president of David, Oksner & Mitchneck Inc., a New York advertising firm, says "the political marketplace has done nothing more than borrow the imprecise research techniques developed in the packaged goods world; and it is still impossible to isolate quantitatively the effectiveness of most consumer advertising."

Growing reliance on broadcast advertising is partly a consequence of the emergence of a new breed of campaign manager, Gardner explains. Since "today's young, tough campaign manager did his apprenticeship in media politics . . . he knows more about television and charisma than canvassing or precinct captains, and once the campaign gets serious, he calls in a television expert." By that time, says Gardner, the candidate, "depressed by the endemic confusion, is ready to believe the advertising can play a crucial role
. . .

Even more influential in a candidate's decision to spend heavily on television, Gardner writes, is his "predisposition to believe that television has some special magic."

Gardner himself does not share this belief:

"Sooner or later either you must assume that the media men can manipulate the electorate, or you can take solace in the voters' ultimate intelligence. Most conventional wisdon holds with the manipulation theory, but it overlooks the distinction between advertising's pervasiveness and its power. I prefer to believe that in presidential elections the voters wisely and instinctively reject most issue-related appeals (they've been burned too often) and make a conscious visceral decision on the basis of trust."

48 and their immediate families.

"That narrows the greatest impact we're going to have—to encourage the greatest participation in an election," said an official in DRIVE, the Teamsters' political action organization.

Dodds said in a town such as Janesville, Wis., where community leaders diligently seek to register every eligible citizen, the UAW local there would be forbidden from providing money for a community-wide registration drive. "We could not use union money to join with the public effort," said Dodds. "I seriously question the constitutionality of that."

Paul Minarchenko, director of legislation for the American Federation of State, County and Municipal Employees (AFL-CIO), said the law will definitely have the effect of forcing labor "to think through a lot more carefully how it does things."

ASSESSMENT

Some are cynical about the new law's effectiveness. Others express disappointment that it is not stronger. But those who worked for its passage believe it will begin to sweep away doubts and misgivings about the role of money in American politics.

"The political system is so filthy that they have not cleaned it up with this law," said New Yorker Samuels.

Rep. Anderson of Illinois admitted that there are problems.

"You can't write a foolproof law," he said.

"I am not blind to the fact that if you are going to be crafty, you can always find some stratagem to go around it. But it reduces the chance of venality and expands by a quantum leap the amount of information available. It's a deterrent. It will make those think twice or even three times. There will always be a little fear."

NCEC's Hemenway is more definite. With the law in force, "you're really going to know where the money came from," he said.

But a veteran Republican politician who declined to be identified said he will still be able to get any amount he wants to give to the candidate of his choice without being identified publicly.

He said he would do it through gifts to friends who would in turn list themselves as the contributors.

"There's room for Mickey Mouse here," agreed Udall of Arizona. "I suspect after this election, we will be back, seeking amendments."

2   PRESSURE GROUPS

Along with political parties, organized pressure groups provide the citizen with his principal access to government policy-makers. In general terms, pressure organizations have been defined as organized groups of citizens having shared attitudes and making claims upon society. Those groups which make claims upon or work through government are called "political" pressure groups. Such groups include not only broadly based organizations designed to implement a program of action in behalf of their memberships (AFL-CIO), but also corporations seeking assistance or making demands upon government (General Motors), as well as groups of citizens who pressure government in behalf of goals which they consider to be for the good of society as a whole (Common Cause).

Most pressure group activities are carried out through: (1) grassroots campaigns engineered by the national leadership of the group, and/or (2) lobbying efforts directed toward legislators, administrators or other governmental deci-

sion-makers.

Virtually all groups are characterized by minority or oligarchic leadership. Most group members are apathetic, thus permitting small leadership cadres to exercise nearly absolute control. There are several reasons for this tendency to oligarchy, the most important of which is that access to the decision-makers is a prerequisite to the group's success. Maintenance of such channels of access normally depends upon a small number of experienced and established group leaders. This is not always the case, however, the General Motors Washington staff enjoys a relatively short period of tenure.

Styles of group action differ widely. In the selections that follow, the efforts of General Motors, the AFL-CIO, and Common Cause are examined, revealing the variety of lobbying and grassroots techniques used by pressure groups in Washington. General Motors, believed to have a generally ineffective lobbying operation, has failed to develop the sophisticated lobby techniques that have been used

effectively by other groups. GM's access to congressmen is sporadic and limited, and their choice of techniques has often been unproductive. Nevertheless, as noted, the one major effort made by GM activists did prove to be an effective piece of lobbying.

The AFL-CIO is almost universally recognized as an effective organization in pressuring legislative and administrative officials. Its access to congressmen is guaranteed by the use of campaign contributions in the form of grassroots organization and voter registration drives. Combined with a highly regarded research operation and an effective and hard-hitting lobby organization, the AFL-CIO is the epitome of pressure group capability. The efforts of the group in support of the Foreign Trade and Investment Act (Hartke-Burke bill) curbing imports are described and analyzed in the second article in this section.

One of the newest Washington based pressure groups, Common Cause, has worked throughout its brief existence to develop efficient grassroots pressure in behalf of a variety of "citizen's" issues. More successful than originally anticipated, Common Cause has begun to face internal cohesion problems that often beset newly organized pressure groups once they have made their initial impact.

The activities that go to make up pressure politics are guaranteed by the First Amendment to the United States Constitution. As is evident from these articles, much more is involved in the use of free speech to petition Congress than mere desire. Organizational effort, issue sophistication, political involvement and understanding, and money are all ingredients which go to make up successful pressure politics.

GM gets little mileage from compact, low-powered lobby

Frank V. Fowlkes

General Motors Corp., which takes pride in the power it packs under its hoods, has a Washington lobby that sometimes is unable to make it up Capitol Hill, even in low gear.

So far, that seems to be exactly the way the world's largest industrial complex wants it.

GM has nearly 800,000 employees, worldwide; more than 100 plants scattered around the United States; and dealerships in every congressional district. It is the nation's biggest taxpayer. In 1969, it took in more money than the government spent on the Vietnam war—$24,295,141,357.

Yet, an excise tax on automobiles, which GM badly wants repealed, still is on the books 38 years after its enactment.

An attempt to head off federal safety regulation of automobiles in 1966 failed miserably, and the government's grip on auto standards gets tighter every year.

This year, GM is on the verge of losing big on tighter air pollution controls, the most important legislative challenge the company has ever faced.

And the chief lobbyist for the Ford Motor Co. maintains that the GM lobby is so underpowered that it often has had what amounts to a free tow on issues from Ford and other automobile lobbies.

The seeming paradox of GM in Washington is caused by several factors, some historic:

General Motors never has considered the federal government important to its prime considerations of producing autos and profits. As Peter Drucker pointed out in a July, 1961, *Fortune* magazine review of the book, *My Years With General Motors,* by Alfred P. Sloan, former GM chairman (1946-56): "(There is) not one word about the role and function of government."

GM's size often is more handicap than help. For reasons of image and fear of antitrust action, GM avoids using muscle. Like a prize fighter whose fists are registered weapons, GM has chosen to walk away from a number of federal fights.

GM's lobby is handicapped by a credibility gap among key staff members and legislators on Capitol Hill—a gap resulting from its past positions on safety and pollution controls. "It's one of the crosses we have to bear," said GM lobbyist William C. Chapman.

GM's most important federal battles in recent years have involved air pollution and safety and, in a public relations sense, the corporation has been on the wrong side of both. "It's an awkward environment in which to lobby," said Jay G. Hall, head of GM's Washington office. "No matter how reasonable our arguments are, we always come out looking like we are against motherhood."

Although GM shored up its Washington lobbying staff last year, its approach to influencing federal policy-makers remains the same.

The strong point in GM's Washington operation is the presentation of engineering data to regulatory agencies or evidence to courts. In forums such as the National Highway Safety Bureau, where decisions are swung by facts, the factual approach is relatively successful. In Congress, where politics and pressure from the home district weigh heavily in decisions, the approach is not.

Nor is the future likely to grow any brighter for GM.

The growth of organized and sophisticated lobbying by consumer and environmental groups is having an impact on Capitol Hill.

Whether GM will continue its low-pressure, low-profile approach to government depends on how it sees these new consumer issues affecting its corporate life. In one recent case, involving vehicle recall legislation, GM demonstrated it can count votes in a conference committee with the best of them.

It is clear that GM's leadership has come to the conclusion that automotive decisions are not made exclusively in Detroit.

It is not clear whether GM could change any of the pending major automobile legislation even if it had Washington's strongest lobby.

Ford, after all, although possessing a smoother Hill operation, has had no better luck than GM in fending off stricter controls over safety and pollution.

WASHINGTON OUTPOST

By the standard of other major corporations, GM maintains a

modest lobbying operation in Washington.

From an office at 1660 L St., NW, six professionals monitor the activities of the federal government for GM and present the company's position on federal actions affecting the industry.

Of the six, only three are registered lobbyists; of those, only one has been stationed in Washington for more than 18 months.

Even this small operation is substantially bigger than GM saw fit to support until last year. Previously, GM kept only one registered lobbyist in Washington, Ernest L. Barcella, a former United Press International correspondent and member of the prestigious Gridiron Club of Washington. Barcella presided over a staff which never exceeded six men and which was responsible both for government relations and for public relations.

GM's assessment of the relative importance of the two responsibilities was reflected in the fact that Barcella reported to Anthony G. DeLorenzo, Detroit-based vice president in charge of public relations.

Barcella was well-liked on Capitol Hill, but he had to spread himself too thin to provide the representation one might expect for a corporation of GM's size and stake in federal activities, and he knew it. According to an official in GM's Detroit office, who asked not to be identified by name, Barcella often and vainly asked for more manpower to beef up the Washington operation.

Detroit's traditional method was to try sending Detroit people to the capital to deal with specific problems as they arose.

For years, GM had a registered lobbyist based in Detroit who would fly to Washington as needed. The last of these flying lobbyists was Hall, who was transferred to Washington on April 1, 1969, as part of a general reshuffling of the GM lobbying operation.

Chain of command—On that same date, responsibility for industry-government relations, which had been diffused throughout the company, was gathered under a newly created Detroit office called Executive in Charge of Industry-Government Relations.

The office is headed by Robert R. Magill, former head of the GM tax division.

Magill's appointment represented a philosophic as well as an organizational break with GM tradition.

Magill's company ties and background are in GM's finance division. Under his direction, recommendations of the Washington office no longer are routed through the public relations division. Instead, they are fed directly into the powerful and influential finance division.

Hall reports to Magill who reports to Oscar A. Lundin, executive vice president for finance. Lundin, in turn, reports to Richard C. Gerstenberg, former executive vice president for finance and current vice chairman of the company, who is responsible only to President Edward N. Cole and Chairman James M. Roche. Lundin, Gerstenberg, Cole and Roche all sit on the company's finance committee, GM's senior policy group.

David L. Lewis, who worked in GM public relations from 1959 to 1965 and who is now a professor of business history at the University of Michigan's Graduate School of Business Administration, said the "financial people regard themselves as the heart of the company, and they are. They have encroached on the other staffs. It must have been a blow to DeLorenzo that the Washington industry-government operation was taken away from him, but it will have much more clout and be considerably more effective under finance."

Staff—When Hall was transferred to Washington, he assumed direction of industry-government relations, leaving Barcella with responsibility for public relations.

Barcella has two staff members. Hall has five: James M. Morris, Chapman, Albert D. Bourland, William D. Thompson and Bernard E. (Gene) Ritzinger. Only Hall, Morris and Chapman are registered as lobbyists, but Hall has a request pending in Detroit to register Bourland and Thompson as well. Lundin told *National Journal* he did not know when GM would grant the request because it depended on congressional action in the areas for which Bourland and Thompson are responsible. Already this year, Congress has taken major action in trade policy, one of Thompson's areas of responsibility.

Functions—Lundin said the office expansion resulted from increased federal regulation of the automotive industry and meant no change in office functions.

Reading from an internal memorandum written by Chairman Roche, Lundin described for *Na-*

tional Journal the purpose of the Washington office as follows:

The first and clearly most important job of the office is to provide thorough reporting on Washington developments. "We need good intelligence input," Lundin said. "In our view this is number one on the list of functions."

The operation's next most important function is to analyze developments in the government. "In order to make decisions, we have to know what needs to be done and what it involves," said Lundin.

The last function, which Lundin described as "far down the list," is lobbying. "Our main concern in this respect is how an action of the government will affect us competitively. If we feel that Congress or an agency doesn't have the facts, then we try to provide them."

GM STYLE

The low priority which GM assigns to lobbying at least partially explains some otherwise curious characteristics of the company's Washington office.

Corporate rank: Whereas Ford and many other major corporations keep vice presidents in Washington to head their lobbying operations, GM does not. Hall is not a vice president and neither is Magill, to whom Hall reports in Detroit, although Lundin says Magill's rank is equivalent to vice president.

Rodney W. Markley, head of the Ford Washington office and vice president of the company, said Ford made the decision to have a vice president in Washington because management felt his rank would make him a more ef-

fective representative. Based on three years of experience, Markley said, "I think they were right."

James Morris in GM's Washington office agrees that having a vice president in charge would be an advantage. "There is no question that we need someone at the vice presidential level in Washington," said Morris. "Markley at Ford can open a door faster than Jay Hall or even Bob Magill." Markley agreed that this was probably the case.

An additional benefit to having a high-ranking corporate executive in Washington could be that he would more likely be plugged into the corporate decision-making process. "Ford's Washington office has always had the ear of Detroit much more than has GM's," *National Journal* was told by a veteran auto lobbyist familiar with both companies, who asked not to be quoted by name. Markley sees this advantage.

"Frequently on a legislative problem, you have to make a quick decision," he said. "Being an officer of the company, I can get in the mainstream of this decision-making and call Henry Ford directly when necessary." Markley said he often talks to Ford.

Hall said there is nothing to prevent his calling Roche directly and that he has done so, but that he usually goes through channels to get the views of Magill and others.

Hill experience—Traditionally, the committees and offices of the House and Senate have served as training grounds for lobbyists. Hill staff members, wise in the workings of Congress and sometimes fortuitously allied with key

members or committees, offer the richest single pool of potential lobbying talent in Washington.

Ford, like other corporations and trade associations, has dipped into this pool for several lobbyists. One, Robert W. Smith, is a former aide to Rep. Paul Rogers, D-Fla., chief sponsor of the House version of the pending Clean Air Amendments, which are important to the future of the auto industry. Another, Wayne H. Smithy, is a former staff member of the Senate Judiciary Committee, whose Antitrust Subcommittee has been among the most active in investigating the automobile industry.

GM has ignored the Hill staffs in recruiting. None of the six professionals on its Washington industry-government staff has ever worked on Capitol Hill, where (by legal definition) the GM men must do all of their lobbying. Moreover, of the six, only Hall and Morris have extensive Washington experience in other capacities. Both Bourland and Thompson said that when they came to Washington slightly over a year ago they were largely unfamiliar with the legislative process.

National Journal asked Lundin why GM had not sought men with congressional experience for its Washington office. His answer was the same he had given for not having a vice president in Washington: that GM attached little importance to lobbying and therefore did not feel the necessity.

Ford does feel the necessity. Markley told *National Journal* that it is easier to take someone familiar with Washington and teach him about a company than to take someone who is familiar with a company and teach him about Washington.

Hall's politics— Lundin's claim that GM attaches little importance to its diplomatic presence and lobbying in Washington is confirmed by the politics of Jay Hall. Hall is known on Capitol Hill as a Goldwater conservative, a longtime friend and booster of the Senator.

Although Hall says he does not regard himself as conservative on social matters, he is identified in the minds of committee staff members with Goldwater's views on federal regulation of industry, views generally antithetical to those of the Democratically inclined staff members of committees important to the auto industry.

National Journal asked one staff member who has had prime responsibility for auto legislation whether Hall's political views affected him.

"Sure," he said, "You tend to be skeptical of what you're told if you know it's coming from an ideologue."

National Journal asked Lundin whether GM had taken Hall's political inclinations into account when it sent him to Washington. He said it had not and again pointed out that Hall's politics were no impediment to performance of his main functions: information-gathering and analysis. "We don't have a bunch of handshake people in Washington," Lundin said.

Antitrust—Some congressional figures see an antitrust rationale behind the low emphasis which GM puts on its lobbying in Washington.

"GM is highly fearful of antitrust action," a Michigan congressman who is close to the company told *National Journal.* "As a result, they tend to use a feather touch, preferring to let legislation go against them rather than attract attention with a tough lobbying campaign."

GM spokesmen in the Washington office would only hint that the company's size and antitrust problems are a factor restraining its lobbying. Hall told *National Journal* that it is GM's style to be low pressure in all its dealings, even those with suppliers.

"It would be highly unwise for GM to get into the pressure area," Hall said. Barcella supported this view. "If you're the big guy, and you try to flex your muscles, you don't gain anything by it," he said.

OUTSIDE HELP

For Washington dealings, GM has resources other than the Washington office at its disposal.

To press its views in Congress, it has the Automobile Manufacturers Association, the industry trade association to which GM is the major financial contributor. It has experienced Washington lawyer-lobbyists on retainer. And it has its own top executives who can come to plead their case directly with Congress.

AMA: The Automobile Manufacturers Association, with offices in Detroit and Washington, serves as a clearing house through which manufacturers can formulate legislative positions and map strategy on bills affecting the industry.

If, from time to time, the different manufacturers seem to be saying the same thing on an issue, it probably represents a consensus view arrived at through the good offices of the association.

Drafting positions—When the association sets out to issue a statement, the first step is for the staff to prepare a draft. This might be done by AMA President Thomas C. Mann, former Assistant Secretary of State for Inter-American Affairs (1965-65), or by one of his assistants. The draft is then submitted to the individual companies for comments and general approval. When these are received, a final version is drafted and sent to the appropriate audience: the press, Congress, or the federal agencies. Mann personally writes the final draft of every statement that bears his signature.

If the statement contains a legislative position, it has been taken in a meeting of representatives of the companies. These meetings are held in Detroit generally, in Washington sometimes.

GM representative in such a meeting might be Hall, Morris, Chapman, or all three, plus, in some cases, one or more technical experts from the Detroit office. There is no formal voting procedure to determine the association position, according to Mann and Chapman. Issues are simply discussed until it becomes apparent where the areas of disagreement are. The association position is then drafted to contain those points on which all companies agree. Individual companies are left to go their own way where they hold differing views. Unlike some trade associations, such as the American Bankers Association, the Automobile Manufacturers

Association does not take positions which favor some parts of its membership at the expense of others.

The process means that when Congress is pressing for automotive innovation, as it is now, the association positions tend to reflect the technological capabilities of its slowest member. Both Markley at Ford and Chapman at GM conceded that AMA positions are the lowest common denominator of the individual manufacturers' positions.

When association members are meeting on legislative position or legislative strategy, association lawyers are present to ensure that the discussion adheres strictly to the subject and does not stray into the competitive area where the companies could be charged with violation of the antitrust laws. A consent decree accepted by the industry this year limits the areas of permissible discussion in the competitive area to information already in the public domain.

Coordinating lobbyists: When a major legislative fight is in progress, meetings may be held frequently to coordinate lobbying. Standard practice on a big bill is for lobbyists of the different companies to divide up key committees to make certain that somebody sees every Member and that four lobbyists do not show up outside the same Member's door at the same time. The lobbyists generally are assigned to Members they know or Members who have one of the company's plants in their state or district.

There is no schedule for association-sponsored meetings. They may be called by Mann or by

GM'S WASHINGTON LOBBYISTS

GM's Washington staff includes six professionals assigned full time to industry-government relations.

The GM Detroit office contends that legislative experience and political compatibility with congressional leaders were not considered in their selection.

Only one of the six is a lawyer; none of the six had ever worked on Capitol Hill, for either a committee or a Member of Congress; and the head of the office is a Goldwater Republican whose political kinship to the Arizona Senator is well-known.

In manner, GM's six representatives reflect their Detroit backgrounds and orientation. They have neither the backslapping joviality of the stereotyped lobbyist nor the close-mouthed, backroom air of veteran political operatives. They are organization men assigned to Washington.

Jay G. Hall, 59, is manager of the Washington industry-government relations office and the ranking GM representative in Washington. Hall is a long-time personal friend of Sen. Barry Goldwater and frequently helped him with speeches before Goldwater ran for the Presidency in 1964.

Mild, almost benign in manner, Hall has a doctorate in history from the University of Chicago and is a student of Greek and Roman history.

His background, however, is not all academic. He began his career during the depression working on the assembly line of a Ford Motor Company plant in Canada.

Hall began his career with General Motors in 1942 with a job on the business research staff, which handled Detroit-based lobbying before creation of the industry-government relations division. By the time he went to Washington in 1969 he had become director of industry relations on the business research staff. Hall is registered to lobby and has general rather than specific responsibilities.

James M. Morris, 44, also is a registered lobbyist with general responsibilities. He has been with GM since he graduated in political science from Indiana University in 1951. At one time a lecturer with GM's road show, "Parade of Progress," Morris has spent virtually his entire career in GM public relations. He was transferred to the Washington public relations office in March 1966 and joined the Washington industry-government relations department when it was created as a separate unit in 1969.

Morris' manner is straightforward and candid. He is well-liked by congressional staff members with whom he deals.

William C. Chapman, 49, is the third of GM's registered lobbyists. A former soccer and lacrosse player at the Naval Academy and a retired Navy officer, Chapman was formerly assigned to GM's Detroit engineering liaison staff. On technical matters he is the best-informed member of the Washington staff; he has specific responsibility in the areas of auto pollution and safety.

Chapman earned a master's degree in international relations from George Washington University in 1964, and is a candidate for a doctorate in Russian studies at Georgetown University.

Albert D. Bourland, 43, is the only lawyer on the Washington staff. A graduate of Louisiana Tech University and South Texas College of Law, Bourland has worked for GM since 1950. An admitted neophyte in regard to the legislative process when he came to the Washington office a little over a year ago, Bourland was given specific responsibility for the areas of auto insurance, repairs and warranties. However, as much as 80 per cent of his time is consumed by the business administration of the office. Bourland is not registered to lobby.

William D. Thompson, 44, also is not registered and is in a position similar to Bourland's. Thompson's specialties are the areas of trade, labor, defense and accounting. His background includes a master's degree from the University of Maryland, and 17 years with General Motors.

G. E. (Gene) Ritzinger, 39, joined the Washington industry-government relations staff Sept. 1, 1970. His job is reporting to Detroit on government developments affecting the industry. A former *Wall Street Journal* reporter, Ritzinger has been with GM since 1964.

---

association lobbyist John R. MacKenzie; or they may be requested by a lobbyist for one of the individual companies. The meetings are not the only contact the different company lobbyists have among themselves. Their jobs take them to the same places. They call each other to compare notes and discuss developments.

Cutler—In addition to coordinating the industry's legislative efforts, the Automobile Manufacturers Association gives GM and the other manufacturers access to the services of one of Washington's most able lawyer-lobbyists, Lloyd Cutler of the firm of Wilmer, Cutler and Pickering.

It was Cutler, a late entry in the 1966 safety fight, who won a round for the auto industry by persuading Congress not to write criminal penalties into the bill; not to set design standards instead of performance standards; and to acknowledge in the Senate report on the bill that the question of cost should be considered in determining what the manufacturers might be required to add in the way of safety devices.

One former Justice Department lawyer who tangled with Cutler several years ago on a major suit against the Automobile Manufacturers Association called him "hands down, the best lobbyist in Washington." Thomas Mann called him "one of the ablest lawyers I have ever run into in my lifetime."

Cutler's competence has not gone unobserved by GM; but the company cannot retain him as a lobbyist, because to work for both GM and the association would create a conflict of interest, in Mann's opinion. The company has retained Cutler's firm as legal counsel for about five years.

Hollabaugh—The line between legal help and lobbying can be a fine one under the ambiguous lobbying laws. For instance, GM retains another Washington firm, Hollabaugh, Jacobs and Ward, in a legal capacity.

Marcus Hollabaugh, a partner in the firm, was one of several GM representatives who this year successfully lobbied against a proposal to give the Highway Safety Bureau authority to issue a mandatory recall without a full evidentiary hearing. Hollabaugh was not a registered lobbyist. But Hall said he accompanied Hollabaugh on his visits to Capitol Hill, and, therefore, the lawyer was covered by his registration.

Visiting brass: GM will occasionally supplement other lobbying by sending the company brass to town.

In past years, at least three chairmen of the board have made the trek. This year, top GM officials have lobbied Congress on at least two occasions: once when Assistant General Counsel Fraser Hilder came to fight the mandatory recall provision; and, most recently, when GM President Cole came to press for relaxation of standards in the Senate version of the pending Clean Air Amendments.

GM, however, uses its executives in this manner far less than

Ford does. A staff member of the Senate Antitrust Subcommittee told *National Journal* that Ford would send two vice presidents to Washington "at the flap of a hat" just to answer a question the subcommittee had asked.

Markley said he purposely asks for frequent executive support from Detroit because he feels it is effective. "My job is to make the best possible impression in order to sell the concept. I'm competing for people's minds. I have found that bringing an officer back to talk to staff members adds another string to my bow, and I will continue to use it."

CORPORATE PERSONALITY

GM's approach to its dealings with the federal government reflects the cumulative effect of its past relationships with government as well as GM's own corporate personality.

For most of GM's history, its contacts with the federal government have been primarily in the areas of tax and antitrust. Neither relationship is of the kind to inspire love. And both left GM executives with a strong impression that the less General Motors had to do with the federal government the better off the company would be.

Since 1936, the Antitrust Division of the Justice Department has initiated at least 17 antitrust actions involving GM. Since 1966, the division has been sitting on the draft of a suit, prepared by a special task force, which would attempt to force the breakup of GM. GM is aware of the draft's existence, but neither the Antitrust Di-

A GM LOBBYIST'S DAY

A GM lobbyist has no set routine. His job is to react. He is a combination commentator and counter-puncher. His day is shaped by others.

For GM lobbyists James M. Morris, William C. Chapman and Jay G. Hall, the day begins before 8:00 a.m. with its one predictable activity—reading. To keep abreast of Congress and the various agencies affecting GM, they scan the day's news for schedules of committee hearings, upcoming floor actions and proposed rule-making.

Two of three hours are spent each day in reading. The reading list includes *The Washington Post, The New York Times, National Journal, Congressional Quarterly, The Bureau of National Affairs Daily Executive Report, The Federal Register* and relevant items from the previous day's *Congressional Record*.

By 9:30, the GM lobbyists are in the office with enough of the day's reading behind them so that the day's assignments can be made. Depending on what Congress is doing, this might include attending committee hearings, observing floor debate, going to a chamber of commerce or business association meeting or simply visiting with a key legislator or staff member to ensure that the lines of communication are kept open.

For Morris, this means spending at least 50 per cent of his time out of the office. For Chapman, who is assigned to the controversial safety and pollution issues, it means spending even more time away from the office. Chapman also makes frequent trips to Detroit to report in person on developments in his areas of responsibility.

The burgeoning of government activity affecting automobiles has restricted the free time GM representatives have to make calls on Capitol Hill, according to Morris. "It would be highly desirable to visit more often with legislators and staffs, but we are limited by the small staff and the demands on our time."

For William D. Thompson and Albert D. Bourland, who are not yet registered to lobby, the year since they came to the Washington office has been spent largely in acquainting themselves with the people and the workings of the government.

Bourland's duties as manager of the office limit the time he has to get acquainted on the Hill. He estimated the office management chores take up to 80 per cent of his day.

For B. E. (Gene) Ritzinger, who has been in Washington for less than two months, and who is not registered to lobby, work in the Washington office is not unlike the reporting he once did for *The Wall Street Journal*. He is assigned to cover congressional hearings and occasionally to write reports based on information fed to him by Morris and Ch̲ nan. These reports are sent on to Detroit.

While Congress is in session, the lobbyist's day does not end until 6 or 6:30 p.m., and often he is required to attend meetings in the evening. When an important bill affecting the industry is under consideration by Congress—as is the case with the Clean Air Amendment—these evening meetings can run often and late.

vision nor the suit's principal draftsman, Eugene Metzger—who has since left the department—would discuss it with *National Journal.*

Avoiding government—A factor in GM's distaste for dealing with the federal government is that for 28 of the past 40 years Washington has been in the hands of Democrats. GM is strongly Republican, a persuasion reinforced by the running battle between big labor and big business in the Michigan legislature. This has followed party lines, with the United Auto Workers backing Democrats.

Even the tenure of former GM President Charles E. Wilson as Secretary of Defense (1953-57) under the Eisenhower Administration did not appreciably improve GM's relationship with the government. The Wilson experience was not something which pleased GM, according to Professor Lewis.

"They found his presence in Washington disadvantageous on two counts," Lewis said. "They gave up a good man and the government had to bend over backwards not to show favoritism to GM in procurement. They figure they lost contracts as a result. I don't think they'll ever let a top man go to the government again."

GM's reluctance to involve itself with the federal government was evidenced after the 1967 riots in Detroit. Federal funds for job

training were offered to GM and to the other auto manufacturers and were accepted by Chrysler. GM declined the offer, choosing to run its own program with its own funds. "We wanted our freedom to do it our way," recalled Lundin. "We felt we could do it better the way we wanted to do it."

GM's executives: While regulation, antitrust and politics have helped keep GM and the federal government at a distance, these factors do not distinguish GM from many other large corporations. What does set GM apart and ensure a detached attitude are its hiring policies and the backgrounds of the men in top executive slots.

When it comes to management, GM policy is to grow its own. Rarely does it bring in top executives from the outside, and when it does they are likely, as in the case of John Z. DeLorean, the flamboyant head of Chevrolet, to be conspicuously different from the stereotype.

What is the stereotype? By the time a man reaches high office in GM he is apt to have been with the company for 30 or more years. He is likely to be from Michigan, and it is not unusual for him to have had no education beyond high school, except what GM gave him. He comes to work early and stays late; works hard; and has little time left for activities outside his

job. He loves GM and hankers after nothing more.

"We have a job of work to get done," said Oscar Lundin, explaining why GM does not worry itself to the extent Ford does over relations with Washington.

Men of this sort set GM apart from other companies. Semon Knudson, former executive vice president of GM and former president of Ford, maintains that it also accounts for GM's tendency to ignore Washington while Ford does not.

"At GM, the top executives historically have come up through one of the divisions and may not have been exposed to what is going on in Washington," Knudson told *National Journal.* "Ford, on the other hand, has brought in many of their top executives, some of whom have had academic backgrounds. Ford executives, such as (Henry) Ford himself, (Robert S.) McNamara and (Arjay) Miller, are figures in their own right. They were not completely auto-oriented. Their outlook was broader."

A review of the backgrounds of GM's three top executives illustrates the point:

James M. Roche, chairman of the board, born in Elgin, Ill., did not attend college. He began work with GM in 1927 as a statistician with the Cadillac Motor Car Division Chicago sales and service branch.

Edward N. Cole, president, born in Marne, Mich., attended Grand Rapids Junior College and the General Motors Institute, graduating from neither. He began working for GM in 1930 on a special engineering project at Cadillac.

Richard C. Gerstenberg, vice chairman of the board, born in Mohawk, N.Y., graduated from the University of Michigan. He began work with GM in 1932 as a timekeeper in the Frigidaire Division.

By contrast the top executives of Ford have more varied backgrounds and shorter tenure:

Henry Ford II, chairman of the board, born in Detroit, attended, but did not complete, Yale University. He did not start working for Ford until 1940, but has been a director since 1938.

Lee A. Iacocca, executive vice president, born in Allentown, Pa., holds a bachelor of science degree from Lehigh University and master's degree in mechanical engineering from Princeton University. He joined Ford in 1946 as a trainee.

Robert J. Hampson, executive vice president, born in Riverside, Calif., received bachelor of science and master of business administration degrees from Harvard. He joined Ford in the finance department in 1947.

Robert Stevenson, executive vice president, born in Bloomfield Hills, Mich., graduated from the University of Michigan. He joined Ford in 1934 as a draftsman-designer.

Political education: As important as the background of GM executives has been in shaping the company's attitude toward the federal government, it need not have resulted in aloofness from Washington affairs if GM had done more to educate its executives in the workings of Washington while they were climbing the corporate ladder.

"The training of GM executives involves, or has involved until very recently, very little in the way of Washington experience," *National Journal* was told by a legal adviser to the corporation who asked not to be identified by name. "They have hardly been aware of Washington. An executive gets thrown into the presidency of the company, and he has to learn from scratch how to deal with Washington. By the time he has been president for five years and has learned, it is time for him to retire and for someone else to go through the process."

Today, more GM executives than ever before are coming to Washington to see the various federal officials who deal with the auto industry. "I think you will see quite a change in the experience of GM executives with Congress and the regulatory agencies," the legal adviser said.

The increased Washington activity of GM officers has been more the product of necessity than of a change in attitude. The growth of regulation, particularly by the Highway Safety Bureau and the National Air Pollution Control Administration, has meant that GM has many more bases to touch than in the past. "It has become very difficult for an executive to filter his way to the top without coming in contact with the federal government," Lundin told *National Journal.*

Contact with the federal government, while more frequent, is still on a when-necessary basis. There is no formal training program within GM on the workings of government and, according to Lundin, no necessity for one.

In more than two dozen interviews with Members of Congress and their staffs, *National Journal* found nobody willing to bestow on GM's lobbying effort a mark of excellence; in many cases not even a mark of adequacy.

Bad marks: The harshest judgment came from one Michigan Member, who asked not to be identified by name:

"GM probably has the worst lobby on Capitol Hill. It ranks at the bottom in terms of effectiveness. Its Washington operation is the most inept and ineffectual I've seen here.

"It's not the fault of the guys in the Washington office. It's just that management has this disdain for relations in Washington. Central management views the Washington office as a stepchild and doesn't put its heart into it.

"GM is constantly getting hit in the back of the head because they don't pay enough attention to Washington. They get more bad surprises than any other major firm in the nation, and it doesn't have to be that way."

Another Michigan Member, who also asked not to be quoted by name, said:

"They send a guy up here to talk to a committee chairman or a Member, thinking that is the best way to do it. It isn't. A call from the district from someone you know who will be affected by a bill is far more effective.

"The auto industry could take a real lesson from the educators. What do they do? They contact the superintendents and the teachers association back home. The environmental people have wised up to this. If the auto industry is going to compete, they are going to have to use those tactics, too."

Contrast with Ford: One Senate staff member, who deals frequently with the auto companies, says he goes to Ford for industry information whenever he has a choice.

"Ford is faster to respond," said the staff member, who asked not to be identified, "and its answers to questions are far more complete, giving background to the issue and all the ramifications. GM will give you a very specific answer, and it will take time to get it."

"Ford's answers are also realistic," the staff member said. "If you ask them about a defect, they will admit to it, say they are worried about it and are trying to fix it. Often they will send two vice presidents to deliver the answer.

"GM is less quick to send a vice president from Detroit. Their responses read as though they were written on Madison Avenue. They pat themselves first on one shoulder and then on the other, and they stick strictly to the question asked."

Michael Pertschuck, counsel to the Senate Commerce Committee, recalled an incident which he said illustrates the difference between the Ford and GM lobbies.

"Ford called up one day back in 1967 to say that Arjay Miller (then Ford's president) was in town and would like to talk to the staff about servicing and warranties," he said. "He came in and sat down with us in the office, and we talked it over. It was goddamned impressive. Very shrewd. GM would never

think of doing that."

Ford's Markley said that increasing GM's Washington staff has not made the operation more effective.

"It has not done the whole job," he said. "I would rather see highly effective representation at GM. In the past, there were a lot of areas where we worked and they did not. They were frequently the beneficiaries of our and others' efforts."

Safety legislation: The area in which GM's aloofness from Washington has most damaged the company's case is safety.

In 1965, Sen. Abraham A. Ribicoff, D-Conn., asked GM to testify on automobile safety before his Government Operations Subcommittee on Executive Reorganization. The subcommittee was seriously concerned with the problem of injuries caused by auto collisions, and it told GM it would want to hear testimony on what the company was doing about safety research and how much money it was spending.

GM totally misread the mood of the subcommittee. Company witnesses indicated to the subcommittee that GM was satisfied with its progress in safety and said they were unable to provide figures on what was being spent on safety research.

"We went about preparing our testimony in the most ham-handed way," recalled Lewis, to whom part of the job of preparing testimony fell. "We dragged out all the same old tired positions. Ford, on the other hand, set up task forces to prepare new positions."

The subcommittee's reaction to GM's self-satisfied attitude was markedly hostile. It set the mood

for the strong safety legislation of the following year.

When the Senate Commerce Committee began hearings on the Traffic Safety Bill in 1966, the lesson of the previous year had apparently been forgotten. With the committee prepared to write a strong bill, GM and the other manufacturers made what in retrospect they say was an ill-advised plea for self-regulation instead of federal standards.

The action all but destroyed the committee's confidence in the industry's good faith. Markley at Ford recalled the incident as a disaster and as the first major step towards the credibility problem from which the auto manufacturers still suffer on Capitol Hill.

After the industry's do-it-ourselves plea, a tough bill was assured. Only the astute lobbying of Cutler prevented it from being stronger than it was.

Arm's length: The safety legislation experience made GM even more aloof from the Members of Congress.

When two subcommittees of the Select Committee on Small Business held hearings, in July 1968, on planning, regulation and competition in the automobile industry, GM declined to testify even though the hearings dealt almost exclusively with the company.

GM explained that it did not want to testify because the discussion might affect the outcome of the suit which Ralph Nader had filed against GM for having him investigated by private detectives.

Between GM and the staffs of Hill committees there exists a virtual adversary relationship which does not exist with other firms.

The attitude of Leon Billings, Senate Public Works Committee staff member and the key staff man on the pending Clean Air Amendments, is illustrative.

Billings told *National Journal* that GM executives with whom he has dealt "were considerably more arrogant" than those from other companies. He said also he had the impression that GM witnesses before the committee this year had not told the whole truth.

Unions: GM, and other automobile manufacturers as well, have failed to enlist the support of the United Auto Workers in many of their legislative battles.

The normal relationship in which the union supports the manufacturer on legislation affecting the industry never has existed between the auto makers and the UAW.

"We will support them if we think they are right," said Nat Weinberg, director of special projects and chief economist for the UAW. "They have approached us a number of times, but we have felt that their narrow interests were not in the public interest."

One legislative fight in which the union did support the manufacturers was the battle in 1965 for repeal of the auto excise tax. Even then, the UAW made its support conditional on the manufacturers' agreeing to pass on the full savings from the tax reduction to the general public through a combination of improved health and safety features to be built into the cars and through direct price reductions.

Weinberg recalled that the manufacturers were not happy with these conditions and conceded that the lack of a united front could have been a factor in Congress' refusal to remove the tax totally. The tax was reduced in 1965 and a schedule for phasing it out was set up; but the phase-out has been deferred each year.

Dealers: Another potential grass roots lobbying resource which GM and the auto manufacturers have largely ignored is their dealers. The American Bankers Association has what it calls contact bankers in every congressional district and uses them to generate mail to Capitol Hill when banking legislation is being considered. GM could use its dealers in the same way, but it doesn't. *National Journal* asked Robert Magill why.

Magill said some dealers had been contacted during the 1965 excise tax fight and some had been contacted during the current battle over the clean air bill. In general, however, Magill said he felt that letters flowing in from all 14,000 GM dealerships would appear artificial and could prove self-defeating.

Enlisting dealer support might not be easy, in any case. In recent years, relations between GM and its dealers have been flawed by squabbles over reimbursement for warranty repairs, sales performance and dealer profits on fleet sales. *National Journal* called six GM dealers in Maryland and Virginia to find out what, if any, contact they have had with the company on legislative matters. Only one reported being asked by GM to write to a Member of Congress.

WASHINGTON MOOD

Even with the most astute lobbying, GM would find it difficult to be effective on Capitol Hill today.

The major issues affecting the auto industry are issues in which the public relations cards are stacked in favor of the industry's adversaries. Moreover, the industry's past performance has weakened its credibility with the men who make decisions on the Hill.

Issues: Since 1965, GM's two biggest legislative fights have been on the safety and pollution issues. In both cases, GM had to walk a thin line between seeking what it felt was reasonable legislation and appearing to be callous toward the dangers of highway deaths and dirty air. At times, it has seemed to frustrated industry lobbyists that the line was disappearing beneath their feet.

GM lobbyists Morris and Chapman said that the emotionally charged nature of the safety and pollution questions is their number-one problem in trying to argue GM's case in Congress effectively.

Credibility: Compounding this problem is the fact that many Hill staff members simply no longer believe what auto industry lobbyists tell them.

The attitude which GM took in the 1965 and 1966 safety hearings; the contradiction between what the company has said was possible and what it has been able to do in the pollution field under pressure; the apparent suppression of the Chrysler clean air package—all have raised doubts about the good faith of the industry in the minds of many in Congress.

"Unless you are venal, the only lobbyist who is effective is one whose information is impeccably accurate," said staff member Billings. "The industry's statements

62

before this committee as to what they are capable of doing, and their performance in California in claiming that the state standards could not be met, have made us skeptical of what they say."

Although Billings' skepticism embraces the entire industry, GM, he said, is more culpable than the others. In the clean air hearings, he heard all four manufacturers claim that the technology to meet the Senate standards did not exist.

"Listening to GM's witnesses, I never got the impression, as I did from the others, that they couldn't do it. They sounded like they were saying it for the benefit of the other companies."

The lobbyists are well aware that what they say is discounted on the Hill.

"The credibility gap is there," Chapman told *National Journal.* "We honestly don't think we can meet the Senate standards (for emissions), but who knows what breakthroughs there might be in the next couple of years."

Markely at Ford is also troubled by the problem. "It has been extremely frustrating to encounter the credibility problem on the Clean Air bill. I have worked for 20 years to build up our credibility. To face this now has been traumatic."

LOBBYING DIARY

The most serious legislative threat ever faced by the auto industry is posed by the pending Clean Air Amendments of 1970.

The stakes are high because the bill, in the form in which it passed the Senate, would require the industry to eliminate by 1975 90 per

THE AUTO AIR POLLUTION CONTROVERSY: SLOW PROGRESS AGAINST A HEALTH HAZARD

The internal combustion engine is responsible for between 50 and 60 per cent of all air pollution. It is a serious problem which has been badly handled by the auto industry.

The automobile engine has been recognized as a health hazard at least since the early 1950s, but little was done about it until 1965, except in California.

Slow pace—Industry critics have charged that GM and other auto makers have not made vigorous efforts to curb polluting exhaust emissions.

They note that although Chrysler announced in 1962 the development of a clean-air package that would meet proposed California emission standards, none of the manufacturers installed it until the state certified four devices made by independent producers and required that these or comparable devices be installed in cars sold in the state starting in 1966. The entry of the independent manufacturers forced the hands of the big auto companies. Instead of buying one of the independents' devices, GM and the other manufacturers turned to the Chrysler system, which they had previously said would not be ready until 1967.

Conspiracy charge: In 1953, the auto makers entered into an informal agreement to share pollution control technology. In 1955, the understanding was formalized with a cross-licensing agreement, which made the sharing contractual.

The industry explained the agreement as an attempt to speed development of emission control by pooling resources. Critics charged, however, that the result was just the opposite: that the agreement destroyed any incentive to innovate by removing any economic penalty for falling behind. There is no need to spend money on development if you can borrow the work of your competitor, the critics pointed out.

In 1965, the Justice Department began a civil investigation of collusion among the auto companies in the antipollution area. In June 1966, a grand jury was convened in Los Angeles to hear evidence. On the basis of the hearings Samuel Flatow, the Justice Department attorney who headed the investigation, recommended a criminal suit against the manufacturers and the Automobile Manufacturers Association.

The case was reviewed at the department in Washington on a number of levels, and, in December 1967, it was decided not to prosecute the big four and the AMA.

The next question was whether there would be a civil suit. That question was not resolved for more than a year. The files were reviewed and industry lawyers again made their arguments: General Counsel Ross Malone for GM, and Lloyd Cutler for the association.

On Jan. 10, 1970, the Justice Department filed a civil antitrust action, and nine months later the government's case was closed when the industry agreed to a consent decree. In so doing, it acknowledged no violation, but agreed to terminate the cross-licensing agreement and to accept certain limitations on the types of information which could be exchanged.

The argument which the industry used, and which persuaded the Justice Department, was interesting in view of the modest progress made in controlling emissions up to 1965.

The industry argued that antipollution devices added cost to a car and reduced its performance; their installation, therefore, would reduce the sales of any company which installed them while the others did not. Thus, the industry said, the only way to get one company to move forward on pollution control was to let them all move together.

1965 Act: About the time Justice was initiating its investigation of collusion, Congress passed the 1965 Clean Air Act Amendments (79 Stat 992), which required the HEW Secretary to set rules and regulations for auto emissions and to forbid the sale of nonconforming new cars.

Standards—Pursuant to this order, the Secretary in 1966 set standards to become effective for 1968 models. In 1968, these standards were modified for application to the 1970 models.

On November 9, 1970, HEW's National Air Pollution Control Administration announced new standards to go into effect in 1972. While more stringent than the 1970 standards, the new standards were not as stiff as those which NAPCA had proposed in July 1970, over industry protests.

Weaknesses—Although the federal emission standards have been in effect for three years and autos have been certified under them, the effectiveness of the program has been limited by procedural weaknesses inherent in the 1965 language.

The first weakness is that tests which new models must pass in order to be certified are not made on production line vehicles, but on prototypes. These prototypes are pampered and pre-tuned by company engineers to ensure that they are on their best behavior when tested. If they fail, they are tinkered with until they pass. A maximum of four prototypes are tested for each engine size, and the results are averaged.

In addition, while the NAPCA tests the vehicles for emissions at 4,000 miles, it projects rather than measures the level of emissions at 50,000 miles. In this computation, the level of emissions at 4,000 miles is multiplied by a "deterioration factor" supplied by the manufacturer. The product of the calculation is accepted by NAPCA as evidence of the car's emissions at 50,000 miles.

Considering what is tested and how it is tested, it is not cent of the pollutants now emitted by its new cars.

The Senate bill would force enormous expenditures to clean up the internal combustion engine. It could force the industry to abandon this engine, for which its builders claim there is no economically-feasible alternative.

Prelude—On June 10, the House passed its version of the Clean Air bill, which Chapman said GM felt was a "pretty tough" bill until it saw the Senate version.

Although the auto lobbyists had visited all members of the House Interstate and Foreign Commerce Committee while it worked on the bill, the lobbying was not particularly intense.

Initial maneuvering in the Senate began in late winter 1969, as the committee staff began preparing for hearings.

Ford had asked to be the first industry witness. GM had asked not to be first.

Accordingly, Ford preceded GM's director of research, Paul F. Chenea, to the stand when the companies made their presentations March 25.

Thereafter, the record of GM's contacts with the Senate and with other auto makers is as follows:

July 8—GM's Chapman and Morris met with Sen. Hugh Scott, R-Pa., to ask him not to propose an amendment to the Senate bill giving states the authority to set tougher emission standards than those set by the federal government. Under present law, federal standards override all others except those of California.

Chapman and Morris were not certain that Scott intended to introduce this kind of amendment.

surprising that when NAPCA in 1968 and 1969 decided to test certified vehicles in the field, it found that between 13 per cent and 71 per cent of the models tested were in violation of the standard for which their prototype had been certified. Many of the cars had been driven less than 3,500 miles.

Pending bills: Legislation now before Congress would correct some weaknesses in the 1965 law. On June 10, 1970, the House passed a bill (HR 17255) tightening up testing procedures by authorizing tests of cars as they leave the assembly line.

The House bill also requires that each auto tested meet the HEW standards; auto makers would no longer be permitted to average the results of tests. Since cars coming off the same assembly line vary in emissions, this legislation would require manufacturers to engineer their equipment to even tighter standards than the law would require. Failure to pass could result in loss of certification for the entire line.

On Sept. 22, the Senate passed an even tougher bill (S 4358). While including the basic changes of the House bill, the Senate bill directs the HEW Secretary to write standards for 1975 which would cut permissible new car emissions by 90 per cent from the 1970 levels.

The Senate bill also attacks the problem of deterioration by requiring that manufacturers warrant autos to continue to meet emission standards up to 50,000 miles.

Alternative power: One of the areas in which skepticism about the industry's claims is highest is the feasibility of building an alternative to the internal combustion engine.

A number of other propulsion systems, including, steam, turbine and electric engines, would operate more cleanly than the internal combustion engine.

Both Ralph Nader and Robert U. Ayres, vice president of International Research and Technology Corp., who has testified before Congress on alternative power sources, contend that the industry is not trying as hard as it could to develop another engine.

"Their strategy all along has been to delay, linger and wait," Ayres told *National Journal.* "The industry wants to solve the problem, but not at the expense of major change."

GM, However, is traveling both roads. Its engineers, while they work on cleaning up the internal combustion engine, are also investigating other engines. The front-runner is the gas turbine.

GM will have "no hesitation in using a power source other than the internal combustion engine if it will solve the automobile's part of the pollution problem and meet the needs of our customers at a price they can afford to pay," GM President Edward N. Cole said in a speech to the Society of Automotive Engineers Jan. 14.

They went to see him because federal preemption was an issue in Pennsylvania's gubernatorial campaign. Lt. Gov. Raymond J. Broderick had asked Rep. John P. Saylor, R-Pa., to introduce such an amendment in the House, and the amendment had lost. Morris and Chapman were concerned that Broderick's next move would be to ask Scott to do the same.

Chapman and Morris recall that the Senator was noncommittal. To the best of their knowledge, he never pushed the amendment.

July 24—Chapman met with an aide to Sen. Jennings Randolph, D-W.Va., chairman of the Public Works Committee, to inquire about the committee's intentions. Chapman recalls that the aide, Richard Grundy, told him not to worry about the House bill because the Senate committee was planning to start from scratch in writing its own.

July 28—Auto makers met at the Automobile Manufacturers Association offices in Detroit to discuss what was anticipated from the Senate subcommittee. Attending for GM was Chapman from the Washington office.

Aug. 3—Morris, Chapman and representatives of the other manufacturers met in room 4200 of the New Senate Office Building with subcommittee staff member Billings. At the meeting, which had been set up by Ford, industry representatives were shown copies of a draft bill. The copies were numbered. No one was permitted to keep one or to take notes. The draft contained no mention of either a deadline or standards. Chapman remembers that the draft said "technological feasibility" would be considered in holding the auto makers to whatever standards were set. The draft also contained a 75,000-mile warranty provision. Billings discovered after the meeting that one of the draft bills was missing. Phone calls to industry representatives failed to solve the mystery.

Aug. 3—Sen. Gaylord Nelson, D-Wis., introduced a bill which would outlaw the internal combustion engine by 1975. The bill prompted Chapman to begin trying to set up a meeting between Nelson and GM President Cole.

Aug. 14—Cole went to Washington to meet with Nelson. They met after lunch, and Cole talked about what progress GM already had made toward cleaning up the internal combustion engine. Then, at the suggestion of the Washington office, Cole went to see Public Works Committee Chairman Randolph.

Randolph suggested that Cole also see Air and Water Pollution Subcommittee Chairman Edmund S. Muskie, D-Maine, and agreed to set up a meeting. Muskie, in turn, suggested to GM that, if he were to see Cole, he might as well see the other company presidents at the same time. Plans were set in motion for a multilateral meeting.

While Cole was meeting with Randolph, Nelson called the GM Washington office to ask if Cole could come back to his office for another meeting to go over the same ground with the Senator's staff present. Cole complied.

Aug. 21—The staff of the subcommittee dropped a bomb. Billings and other staff members met with industry representatives to give them an incomplete version of Committee Print No. 1, which contained the provision for a 90-per cent reduction by 1975. Company representatives were told that subcommittee approval was expected by Aug. 25; that full committee approval should come by Aug. 27; and that the bill was likely to go to the floor Sept. 1.

Chapman and Morris said that Committee Print No. 1 was their first inkling of the 90-per cent provision. They protested that they had been given no opportunity to testify to the point in hearings. The American Motors representative, according to Chapman, declared outright on seeing the provision that it would require the company to liquidate. "It was a little tense," recalled Billings.

Billings said, however, that if the 90-per cent provision came as a shock to the lobbyists, it could only have been because they had not been doing their homework. On Aug. 11, Sen. Muskie, during public questioning of Russell Train, chairman of the Council on Environmental Quality, had indicated that the committee was considering writing standards and a deadline into the bill. Every member of the subcommittee was aware of the contents of the bill, which had been largely finished in executive session Aug. 19. And *The Wall Street Journal* had printed the gist of the bill's contents in the edition available the morning of Aug. 21.

Ironically, at noon on Aug. 21, GM was laying on lunch for about 30 congressional staff members at the Carroll Arms Restaurant, across the street from the New Senate Office Building. The subject was GM's activities in transportation development, including, according to the invitation, "the environmental and socio-economic aspects." The first speaker on the program was Robert Magill.

After receiving Committee Print No. 1, Chapman made several frustrating attempts to reach high HEW officials to find out what data the department could have given the Public Works Committee to lead it to write the standards. (Under the 1965 law, HEW is charged with oversight and administration of federal auto emission standards.) He found that Secretary Elliot Richardson was in Europe; that Dr. John T. Middleton (head of the National Air Pollution Control Administration) was in Venezuela; and that Under Secretary John G. Veneman was out of town and could not be reached.

Aug. 25—Billings and other staff members met with industry representatives in a hearing room of the Senate Appropriations Committee. This time the GM Washington representatives brought along the company's chief emissions expert, Fred W. Bowditch, who, according to Chapman, "acquainted the committee staff with the problems the Senate bill would cause."

After the meeting with the staff, Chapman, Hall, Bowditch and the company's assistant general counsel, Fraser Hilder, retired to the Automobile Manufacturer Association offices on Massachusetts Avenue to confer with other industry representatives in a meeting which ran late into the night. Subject of the meeting was alternative language the companies hoped to substitute.

Also on Aug. 25, GM president

Cole arrived in Washington for the meeting with Muskie and, according to the plan of Aug. 14, was accompanied by Lee A. Iacocca from Ford, President John J. Riccardo of Chrysler, and Vice President G. C. Meyers of American Motors. The meeting was in Muskie's office in the New Senate Office Building. The subject of the discussion with Muskie was the effect the proposed Senate standards would have on the various companies. Thomas Mann, president of the Automobile Manufacturers Association, who also attended the meeting, said it was the first discussion he had heard on the state of emissions technology in the different companies as the representatives who attended association-sponsored meetings were not permitted to discuss matters of a competitive nature.

While in Washington, Cole also met with Sens. J. Caleb Boggs, R-Del.; Howard H. Baker, R-Tenn.; and Birch Bayh, D-Ind., to whom GM had been assigned by the manufacturers association. Cole also saw Michigan Sens. Robert P. Griffin, R, and Philip A. Hart, D. Hall and Magill accompanied him on most of these visits. According to Chapman, Cole also intended to see Sen. Thomas F. Eagleton, D-Mo., but ran short of time and did not.

Aug. 27—Washington representatives of the auto companies, accompanied by technical experts and by Cutler, met again with the committee staff. The purpose was to present the alternative language they had prepared. Most of the talking for the industry was done by Hilder and by Cutler, who both sought to explain the proposals.

Billings, who told *National Journal* that the industry was essentially asking the subcommittee to undo everything it had done, recalls that he became annoyed and that the meeting was "acrimonious." Chapman also recalls that the discussion was heated and that debate focused on whether it was technologically possible for the companies to meet the proposed 1975 standards.

On the same day, the AMA's Mann wrote a letter to HEW Secretary Richardson saying that the manufacturers could not meet the standards by 1975 and charging that they were based on "technical information supplied by HEW staff which has not received the rigorous technical scrutiny customary in HEW."

Sept. 1—The manufacturers association held another strategy session in Washington. According to Chapman, meetings and informal contacts were so frequent during this period it is difficult for him to separate them. Morris, however, recalls that the Sept. 1 meeting was held to review the alternative proposals which already had been reviewed and modified in the Detroit office.

Sept. 2—Chapman, Mann and Markley met with Dr. Gordon J. F. MacDonald, a member of the Council on Environmental Quality, in one of a series of meetings with relevant agencies in the Executive Branch. The purpose of the meetings was twofold, said Chapman: to acquaint the agencies with what the Senate bill would mean to the industry, and to get their reaction. "Their reaction was generally very bland," Chapman told *National Journal*. At the Office of Management and Budget, where

the industry representatives talked with Deputy Director Caspar W. Weinberger, they found that the Administration had no formal position on the bill. "Weinberger listened, but he didn't commit himself," Chapman said. The lobbyists also talked to the Departments of Justice, Labor, Commerce and the Office of Science and Technology.

Sept. 3—Another meeting was held in the manufacturers association's Washington office. Industry representatives reported what they had found out in their conversations, and further refined their alternative proposals. This alternative language was constantly being "massaged," said Chapman.

Sept. 17—Slightly more than a week after returning from a Sept. 2-8 recess, the Senate Public Works Committee reported a bill (S 4358), after approving a Cooper-Baker amendment giving the industry the right to go to court for a one-year extension of the 1975 deadline if the necessary technological breakthrough was not made by Jan. 1, 1973.

The same day, GM President Cole wrote to Muskie to "emphasize as strongly as possible that General Motors does not have the technological capability to make 1975 *production* vehicles that would achieve emission levels the legislation requires." (Emphasis is GM's.)

The letter was simultaneously sent under a cover letter by Jay Hall to all members of the Senate, to the House conferees; to the Michigan delegation; to selected people in the Administration; and to the press.

Sept. 21—The Senate began debating the bill. By this time, the

GM AS CONTRIBUTOR: 'STINGY'

Among political campaign treasurers, General Motors has a reputation much like that of baseball players among restaurant waiters—stingy.

National Journal interviewed GM employees past and present, state politicians in Michigan and Michigan Members of Congress in Washington, to determine the flow of GM campaign funds, the amounts and recipients.

The interviews support the following conclusions:

GM campaign financing is done entirely through employee donations.

The donations are clearly marked as originating from GM.

The vast majority of the funds go to Republican candidates.

In the past, GM has pressured employees to donate to Republicans.

The total flow of funds is small in relation to the cost of modern political campaigning.

Solicitations—David L. Lewis, former GM public relations employee (1959-65) and now a professor of business history at the University of Michigan's Graduate School of Business Administration, described the following contribution pattern:

From 1959 to 1961, all GM employees on the senior bonus roll (those eligible for bonuses in addition to salaries) received cards asking them to write checks for specified amounts to the Republican party of Michigan.

"If you insisted on giving to the Democrats," Lewis recalled, "you were expected to give at least an equal amount to the Republicans. Those who wrote checks (according to Lewis, he was the only man in the public relations division who refused) sent them not to the party but to the business manager of his GM department. The checks were then presented to the party and GM—not the donors—got the thanks."

It was possible not to give, but it was difficult, said Lewis. "When I refused to write the check, the business manager came around and told me that, as a friend, he advised me to do it. I asked him if he was telling me I was jeopardizing my job, and he said no. I then asked him if he was telling me I was jeopardizing my future with the company, and he told me I could use my own discretion."

Republican bias—After 1961, cards used in the solicitation program were modified by replacing "Republican" with "party of your choice." But it was made clear, Lewis said, that the party of your choice was to be the Republican party.

The Republican bias of GM's employee contributions to the Michigan .parties was confirmed by Stuart E. Hertzberg, treasurer of Michigan's Democratic party. "GM had no bipartisan contribution program until 1968, when we talked them into it. We didn't get a dime out of GM until then."

Since 1968, Hertzberg estimated, GM employees have given about $2,000 a year to the Democratic party of Michigan; and, based on state filings, between $100,000 and $200,000 a year to the state's Republican party.

National Journal asked Harold McClure, the Republican state finance chairman in Michigan, how much money his party received from GM employee contributions. "It's not a subject to be talked about," McClure said. "I'd tell you as much about that as I would about my wife's bank account."

Bipartisan plan—The bipartisan plan to which Hertzberg referred is designed to ensure the privacy of employee contributions. Salaried employees (as opposed to hourly wage earners from whom GM does not solicit) are given two envelopes and a contribution card. They are urged to write a check and put it and the card in the smaller envelope and to address it to the party or candidate of their choice. The smaller envelope is then put into the larger, and the package is given to the individual's supervisor to be sent to Haskins and Sells, the company's accounting firm.

This procedure, the literature which accompanies the envelopes explains, ensures that donations are made on a "completely confidential basis."

It ensures two other things as well. Since the company name is prominently displayed on both the card and the interior envelope, it ensures that the recipient knows the contribution came from GM. And, since the envelopes are collected by supervisors, the company is able to keep tabs on who has contributed.

Recipients—Republican congressmen from Michigan whom *National Journal* contacted said they had received little money from GM.

Guy A. Vander Jagt, R-Mich.,

said he had heard at political breakfasts that a Michigan candidate could not win without auto backing, but that he had never seen the color of the industry's money.

Even James Harvey, R-Mich.,

who has a large GM constituency and who acknowledges getting some GM money from his yearly $25 breakfasts, called GM a "very poor contributor."

---

alternative language the industry had been working on consisted of the following six requests:

the right to appeal earlier than 1973 for extension of the deadline;

federal preemption, which would keep states from setting tougher standards than those set by the federal government;

a warranty provision that would require a defect warranty rather than a performance warranty for pollution control devices;

assurance that the tests used to check compliance under the warranty provision were comparable to the original factory tests;

deletion of any section permitting citizen suits against the HEW Secretary for failing to enforce the law,

permission for the manufacturers to disregard the standards on cars made for export.

According to Morris, all members of the Senate committee had been approached by GM and the other manufacturers about introducing these proposals. No one did, however.

"The atmosphere was such that offering amendments seemed hopeless," Morris told *National Journal*. "It might also have been self-defeating." Morris explained that a heavy "nay" vote against an amendment would probably be interpreted by the conferees as a mandate not to change the provision in question.

As for lobbying the Senate at large, the nature of the issue in the public mind—the industry vs. clear air—made this approach useless. "We did nothing about the bill in the full Senate," said Morris. "I wouldn't think of asking anybody to vote against that bill."

Sept. 22—The Senate completed debate on the bill and passed it, 73-0, without amendment.

The lobbyists turned their attentions to the House and Senate conferees, who will decide the ultimate shape of the legislation. Morris and Chapman told *National Journal* they had talked to both the members and their staffs, but that it had been difficult to get the attention of House conferees who were peering down the gunbarrel of election.

Oct. 8—House and Senate conferees met for the first session of a conference to reconcile differences between the two bills. After the meeting, Muskie announced that the House conferees had agreed to accept the 1975 deadline. Just how firm that acceptance is was not clear. Billings said he thinks the conferees believe the decision is final. GM, however, does not regard it as final.

When the lame duck session begins, the conferees are scheduled to meet Nov. 18. Time will be short, and GM lobbyists conceded that they have no rabbits in their

hats. They will again approach the conferees; tell them that the industry cannot meet the standards; and hope someone believes.

"With the first meeting on the 18th, we will have to work fast," said Morris. "But it is possible that the conferees could become bogged down."

HIGHWAY SAFETY BUREAU

GM's relations with the federal government only begin in Congress. The continuing relationship is with the agency Congress charges with administering its laws.

Until the recent and rapid growth of concern over air pollution, industry and government had most often locked horns over auto safety. The administrative arena for those confrontations was the National Highway Safety Bureau.

Although it is not technically considered lobbying when a corporation presses its view on a regulatory agency—within limits they are invited to do so—the effect can be the same as lobbying if the activity limits the use of legislated powers.

The bureau has two functions: to set safety standards for auto manufacturers, and to require manufacturers to notify owners of any vehicle which is found to have a safety defect. In almost every case, manufacturers—when forced to make notification of a safety defect—have also recalled and repaired the faulty vehicles.

Showing the Flag

GM does not offer low-rate auto leases to legislators, as Ford did until recently. Yet it manages to keep the corporate flag flying on Capitol Hill and around the government with direct leases to the executive departments, the House and the Senate.

Forty-one GM automobiles are now on lease for use by top government officials, 33 of them limousines. The list of users is impressive: every member of the Cabinet, the Chief Justice, the UN Ambassador, the Speaker of the House and the Minority and Majority Leaders of the House and Senate. The rental charge is $1,000 a year for a limousine, $100 a year for a car.

The charge for leasing a limousine quoted *National Journal* by Manhattan Leasing in New York City was $375 a month on a minimum 26-month contract.

GM advantage: The procedures by which industry-bureau dealings are conducted work to GM's advantage. No standard is set, nor is any notification required without meetings and technical hearings in which the industry is given a chance to present its case.

GM excels at these presentations. "GM has superb engineers," said Highway Safety Bureau Director Douglas W. Toms. "From an engineering standpoint, they make more impressive presentations than the other manufacturers."

"GM really puts on a produc-tion," said Frank Armstrong, director of the Office of Compliance for the bureau. "Better than Ford and much better than Chrysler and American Motors."

Man for man and dollar for dollar, GM has the bureau overmatched in both engineering competence and facilities. In proceedings where points are won and lost on the basis of what engineers may or may not be able to demonstrate, this advantage can be telling.

The disparity between the bureau and the manufacturers in the technical area is illustrated by two incidents.

Several years ago, one of the manufacturers wrote to the Bureau suggesting that it send 300 engineers to Detroit for a briefing. The invitation arrived at a time when the bureau had only nine engineers on its entire staff.

A key part of the bureau's responsibility is to determine the effect of a crash on an auto occupant. In 1968, a year in which there were about 500 different models on the market, the bureau had money enough to test-crash only seven cars. For the rest of its data, the bureau had to rely on manufacturers' tests.

Bureau authority: The 1966 Traffic Safety Act (80 Stat 718) provides only that the manufacturer may be required to notify owners of safety defects at the direction of the bureau. The bureau does not have the power to force the manufacturers to recall vehicles or to pay for repair of the defect.

Until 1969, this lack of power was largely academic because notification had always been followed by voluntary recall and repair on the part of the manufacturers.

But in 1969, the bureau's engineers, following up a claim by Ralph Nader, filed two technical reports in which they reported that the three-piece disc wheels used by General Motors on 200,000 three-quarter-ton trucks from 1960 to 1965 were dangerously weak.

It was the opinion of the bureau's engineers that the wheels presented a safety hazard on all 200,000 of the trucks. GM did not see it that way. GM contended that the hazard existed only when the trucks were carrying campers or other special bodies. Although the bureau's technical staff continued to dispute the GM contention, Francis C. Turner, head of the Federal Highway Administration, announced on Oct. 9 that the investigation was being closed and that GM had agreed to recall and repair trucks fitted with campers or special bodies, about 50,000 in all.

The incident pointed up the weakness in the bureau's charter. Faced with a manufacturer who refused to accept the bureau's judgment, and who was under no obligation to recall any vehicles at all, the best the bureau could do was negotiate.

In fact, there was nothing unusual about the way the wheel recall was negotiated. Because it lacks mandatory authority, the bureau negotiates all recalls. The difference this time was that someone challenged the result.

On March 31, Ralph Nader filed a civil suit in U.S. District Court for the District of Columbia, charging Transportation Secretary John A. Volpe, Turner and Toms with misleading the owners of the outstanding GM trucks by approving the selective recall.

On June 26, Judge Joseph C. Waddy ruled that the Transportation Department's original announcement of the recall had misstated the findings of the bureau engineers by making no mention of hazards to owners of trucks without sepcial bodies.

The court ordered the bureau to resume the wheel investigation. On Nov. 4, after further study, the Department of Transportation directed GM to issue notices of defect for all 200,000 trucks. The company simultaneously filed suit in U.S. District Court for the District of Delaware to block the government action. On Nov. 9, the court in Delaware rejected GM's suit.

Mandatory authority: To prevent the sort of situation which has developed over the GM truck wheels, the bureau has asked Congress for authority to require manufacturers to recall and repair as well as to notify.

Mandatory authority would take away the industry's leverage with the bureau. The industry's power not to recall gives it the trump card in negotiating the size of a notification. Toms described as a game of cat and mouse the way in which the bureau must try to parlay its notification authority into the most beneficial mix of notification and recall it can obtain.

Congressional action: An attempt to provide the bureau with mandatory recall authority was made in the 91st Congress. In the Senate, an amendment granting

the authority was added to HR 10105, the bill extending the 1966 Traffic Safety Act.

Senate staff members recall that initially the industry protested the provision. Eventually, however, all the manufacturers except GM agreed not to oppose it. "I guess because of the wheel case, GM saw a problem in mandatory recall which the other manufacturers did not," said James Morris.

In the lobbying campaign which GM mounted, it sought a full evidentiary hearing before recall as quid pro quo for dropping opposition to mandatory authority.

"There was nothing sneaky about it," recalled Lawrence R. Schneider, acting general counsel at the bureau. "GM told us exactly what they were going to do."

What GM did was to visit all the conferees from the House and Senate. In the task, GM's regular Washington lobbyists were helped out by GM assistant general counsel Hilder and by Hollabaugh.

GM got a break too, in the form of fortuitous changing of the guard in the Senate Interstate and Foreign Commerce Committee. With the bill in mid-passage, the committee's counsel, William Meserve, who had been the bill's chief shepherd, left to join a Boston law firm. His replacement, Michael Pertschuck, now concedes that neither he nor the other staff members realized how much progress the lobbyists had made. "We simply did not recognize the seriousness of the GM effort," he told *National Journal.*

In the end, GM won. The House conferees, two of whom

(James Harvey, D-Mich., and Harley O. Staggers, D-W.Va.) had GM plants in their districts, refused to take mandator recall without writing the hearings procedure into the bill. The Senate conferees, headed by Sen. Vance Hartke, D-Ind., refused to accept the hearings, which both they and the bureau felt would give the manufacturers a tool with which to delay recalls. Accordingly, both provisions were dropped. The fight to contain the bureau was won.

OUTLOOK

Writing in the Aug. 27, 1967, issue of *The New York Times Magazine,* Daniel Patrick Moynihan, now counselor to President Nixon and then director of the Joint Center for Urban Studies of M.I.T. and Harvard University, said that federal safety regulation was imposed in 1966 as a result of a series of "swift and decisive" moves that occurred almost without public notice.

When the moves had been made, he wrote, "The largest manufacturing complex on earth, which into the sixth decade of the 20th century had persisted as an utterly unregulated private enterprise, was of a sudden subjected to detailed and permanent government regulation."

The safety regulations brought fundamental changes in the world in which GM executives operate.

For GM's Washington lobby, the changes meant a long, uphill pull—in any gear.

Labor and industry gear for major battle over bill to curb imports, multinationals
Charles Culhane

Organized labor is moving into high gear to push sweeping legislation designed to limit imports and discourage foreign investments by U.S. corporations.

The bill, with support fueled by high unemployment, has set the labor movement at loggerheads with the Nixon Administration on foreign trade and investment.

The proposal also has sharpened divisions between labor and large U.S. corporations, which have $78.1 billion invested in plants and equipment.

Sponsors of the legislation are Sen. Vance Hartke, D-Ind., a Presidential candidate, and Rep. James A. Burke, D-Mass. Both are high-ranking members of the congressional committees having jurisdiction over the legislation.

The Hartke-Burke bill signals the AFL-CIO's final break with its historic free-trade position. The major provisions would:

sharply increase the taxes on corporate profits from foreign operations;

require the federal government to speed up the process through which it determines whether imports are injuring U.S. companies and workers;

empower the President to regulate U.S. international capital transactions if he determines that they are reducing domestic employment;

establish a new agency with strong powers to regulate imports.

Labor leaders launched an aggressive lobbying campaign for the legislation in October. They plan to step up the tempo this year in an effort to get hearings and pave the way for passage of some of the bill's key provisions.

LABOR-INDUSTRY CONFLICT

The bill provides a focal point for the intensifying debate between labor and industry concerning international trade, particularly the role of multinational corporations.

The controversy takes on particular significance in a presidential election year.

One union official said that if high unemployment continues, the Hartke-Burke bill "might be *the* issue of the election campaigns."

A congressional aide who witnessed a rally held by the AFL-CIO to drum up support for the bill said: "I have never seen a more angry union meeting in my life. It sounded like a meeting in the 1930s . . . ."

Industry, for its part, is not taking labor's offensive lightly.

An official of the National Association of Manufacturers said that the NAM is "going to put a lot of money, manpower and resources" into meeting labor on the issue.

Lee L. Morgan, executive vice president of the Caterpillar Tractor Co., said in a Nov. 16 speech that the Hartke-Burke bill poses "the most serious legislative challenge international corporations have ever confronted."

Morgan heads a task force on multinationals for the Chamber of Commerce of the U.S.

Labor spokesmen argue that U.S. multinationals are exporting jobs as they expand their foreign operations. They say that the quest for cheap foreign labor is a prime reason for the growth of multinationals.

They also contend that the free movement of U.S. inventions and technical innovations across national boundaries, through licensing and royalty agreements, is hurting employment here.

Industry spokesmen generally deny labor's contentions. They say that profits from overseas investments help boost domestic employment and improve the U.S. balance of payments.

They tend to minimize low-wage labor as a factor in their foreign investments. They say that a larger factor is industry's need to save transportation costs and to move around foreign-trade barriers to sell goods in overseas markets.

Industry groups plan to begin a systematic lobbying effort against the bills shortly.

Industry split—Meanwhile, the legislation is gaining some support from industry segments that believe imports have seriously damaged their sales. If business support grows, labor could succeed in dividing the strongest opposition to the bill.

Administration—The Nixon Administration strongly opposes the Hartke-Burke legislation. Spokesmen argue that President Nixon's new economic policy pro-

Vance Hartke

James A. Burke

vides the best long-range solutions to the problems of high unemployment and the U.S. trade deficit.

The deficit for 1971—the first since 1893—is estimated at $2 billion by Peter G. Peterson, assistant to the President for international economic affairs.

Peterson says that devaluation of the dollar and realignment of currency-exchange values of the leading industrial nations will make U.S. goods more competitive in world markets.

"We certainly are sympathetic and understanding about labor's concern for jobs," Peterson said in an interview, "but the approach they are supporting would result in reduced trade. The idea that you can block imports without immediately blocking exports is unrealistic. Reducing exports would end up reducing jobs."

He said Administration economists estimate that increased exports could create 500,000 to 750,000 jobs in the next two years.

Peterson said that the Administration may submit some major legislative proposals for international trade and investment policies this year.

Some officials fear that supporters of the Hartke-Burke bill may try to attach portions of it as riders to any Administration proposals.

GENESIS OF LEGISLATION

Organized labor moved toward its present position on international trade and investment in slow stages as jobs declined in some smaller industries, imports increased and direct foreign investment by major U.S. corporations soared.

The pace of labor's turnabout quickened as unemployment deepened while the Nixon Administration tried to dampen inflation by revising its monetary and fiscal policies.

AFL-CIO: The 35-man AFL-CIO executive council, representing an estimated 13.5 million U.S. workers, meeting May 12 in Atlanta, adopted a detailed statement urging new trade and investment legislation.

The federation singled out international operations of corporations for special criticism.

"Multinational firms and banks," the statement said, "usually U.S.-based and sometimes in tandem with foreign-based multinationals, now have global operations which benefit from the policies of every country but which are beyond the reach of present U.S. law or the laws of any single nation."

The statement included a nine-point program that the AFL-CIO leadership recommended for new trade and investment legislation. The points summarized the major provisions later spelled out in detail in the Hartke-Burke proposal, the Foreign Trade and Investment Act (HR 10914, S 2592).

The statement drew heavily on "A Labor View of Foreign Investment and Trade Issues," a paper prepared in September 1970 by Nathaniel Goldfinger, AFL-CIO research director.

Meany testimony—The importance that the AFL-CIO attached to its position became clear May 18 when George Meany, president of the federation, testified before the Senate Finance Subcommittee on International Trade.

The decline in the U.S. position in world trade, Meany said, is hurting jobs of steelworkers, machinists, electrical workers, clothing, garment, textile, shoe, glass, pottery, shipyard and maritime workers.

This country, Meany said, has become a net importer of steel, autos, trucks and parts, clothing, footwear, glass, consumer electrical goods and machinery.

Meany claimed that tens of thousands of workers are losing jobs and suffering a lower standard of living as a result of the government's policies.

"The AFL-CIO intends to pursue this issue," he said, "and intends to fight for international trade and investment policies that will end these hardships."

Ruttenberg report—The AFL-CIO's rationale is summed up in a report prepared by Stanley H. Ruttenberg & Associates, a Washington consulting firm. Ruttenberg is a former assistant secretary of Labor (1966-69) who once worked as an economist for the AFL-CIO.

The 128-page report, "Needed: A Constructive Foreign Trade Policy," is laced with detailed statistics on imports and exports and is sharply critical of multinational corporations.

The heart of the report is a claim, buttressed with statistics from the Labor Department's Bureau of Labor Statistics, that from 1966 to 1969 U.S. foreign trade cost the economy a net loss of 500,000 jobs.

The report was published in October by the AFL-CIO's Industrial Union Department and widely distributed among labor leaders. The department's officials include the leaders of some of the largest industrial unions.

Jacob Clayman, administrative director of the IUD, said the department commissioned the report last spring. Ruttenberg's firm completed most of it before President Nixon announced his new economic policy in mid-August.

However, the introduction to the report, written after Mr. Nixon's announcements, said that the President's new policy would provide only a short-range approach to the nation's international trade problems.

"A new set of exchange relationships for the world's currencies will not provide the necessary level of adjustment that is needed to safeguard the jobs and living standards of America's workers," the report said.

"That can be done only by a program which will prevent foreign producers, many of whom are U.S. multinational corporations, from once again reestablishing, and capitalizing on, the unfair competitive advantage that their low wage rates provide."

Legislative groundwork: After the AFL-CIO spelled out its new policy last spring, one of its experienced lobbyists began laying the groundwork for legislation to carry out the recommendations.

Ray Denison, an AFL-CIO legislative representative who specializes in tax, tariff and trade legislation, talked to Sen. Hartke and Rep. Burke about the proposals.

Hartke is the third-ranking Democratic member of the Senate Finance Committee, which has jurisdiction over foreign-trade legislation. The AFL-CIO's Committee on Political Education supported him in his hard-fought 1970 campaign for reelection.

Burke is the third-ranking Democratic member of the House Ways and Means Committee which, under the Constitution, has original jurisdiction over all revenue-raising measures. COPE also supported Burke's campaign for reelection in 1970.

Hartke—"It is an open secret that much of the impetus for this legislation came from organized labor," said Thomas J. Brunner, a former legislative assistant to Hartke. "The bill was drafted under the auspices of the AFL-CIO." (Brunner resigned from Hartke's staff in late December to accept a job as an assistant to Rep. William D. Hathaway, D-Maine.)

Brunner said that Denison approached Hartke early last summer and asked him if he would be interested in supporting the AFL-CIO's proposals.

"Ray said, 'We are thinking of this type of legislation. Don't think of it as protectionist and dismiss it out of hand. It will be comprehensive, definitive and well-drafted.' "

Hartke's Indiana constituency includes steel manufacturers and steel-workers who have become increasingly alarmed in recent years at the inroads of steel imports. The Senator has sponsored quota legislation for steel imports in the past.

Brunner noted that the Admiral Corp. announced in October that it would close down a plant in Orleans, Ind., and lay off 600 employees.

"The workers were told that one reason was imports of television sets but the company was not willing to say that some of those imports were coming from an Admiral plant in the Far East," Brunner said.

Burke—John J. King, executive assistant to Rep. Burke, said that Denison also urged Burke to support the legislation. "He said they would supply us with statistics, facts and figures, and would help us with the leg work," King said.

He said that the final draft of

THE BILL: CONTROVERSIAL BLUEPRINT FOR TRADE-POLICY OVERHAUL

The Foreign Trade and Investment Act (HR 10914, S 2592), sponsored by Sen. Vance Hartke, D-Ind., and Rep. James A. Burke, D-Mass., proposes drastic changes in foreign trade and investment policies.

The bill would increase the taxes of companies investing in foreign countries, impose percentage quotas on nearly all imports and establish a powerful new agency to regulate imports.

Tax changes—The bill would amend the Internal Revenue Code (26 USC 1) to eliminate a wide range of tax advantages for companies producing goods in foreign countries.

One major provision involves the foreign-tax credit. Under present law, companies can claim taxes paid to foreign countries as full credits against their U.S. taxes. The bill would repeal the credit and make foreign taxes merely deductible from foreign source income, sharply increasing the U.S. tax bill.

Other provisions of the tax section would impose stricter depreciation rules for foreign investment and require taxes on income received by U.S. companies for licensing and transferring patents to foreign corporations. The bill also would require reporting of earnings and profits from foreign investment for the year in which they were earned and eliminate tax exemptions for U.S. citizens living and working in foreign countries. One effect of the tax provisions would be to discourage corporate managers from living in foreign

countries. Tax experts for many major corporations doing business overseas are analyzing the tax proposals to determine the impact on corporate profits.

New agency—The bill would create a Foreign Trade and Investment Commission with three members, one each representing labor, industry and the public. The commission would have strong powers to regulate imports and would take over some of the chief functions of the six-member U.S. Tariff Commission.

Import quotas—The bill would place a ceiling on almost all imports. The quotas for 1972 would be based on the average annual quantity of goods imported from 1965 to 1969.

The limits for subsequent years would be the 1972 levels, increased or decreased by the amounts that the commission estimated as necessary to maintain the same ratio between imports and domestic production that existed in the 1965-1969 base period.

A quota could exceed the maximum limits if the commission found that the imports were necessary for production in the U.S. and the imports would not inhibit domestic production.

The quota section also includes several exemptions. For example, the commission would not apply additional quotas on goods already subject to quotas under voluntary agreements between governments.

Dumping—The bill would transfer administration of the 1921 Antidumping Act (42 Stat 11) and

other operations from the Tariff Commission and the Treasury Department to the Foreign Trade and Investment Commission.

The Act provides for penalties against foreign exporters who injure U.S. firms by selling here at prices lower than the prevailing prices in their home markets. The Hartke-Burke bill also would set a deadline of four months for resolution of dumping complaints.

Escape clause—Under the so-called Escape Clause of the 1962 Trade Expansion Act (76 Stat 872), an industry, company or group of workers can apply to the Tariff Commission and the President for import restrictions and financial assistance when they contend that imports are injuring them and that the injury resulted "in major part" from tariff concessions.

The bill would relax the criteria for assistance. The bill would empower the Foreign Trade and Investment Commission to provide assistance in cases where imports "contribute substantially" to the injury of domestic production or employment.

Capital exports—The bill would establish a new law giving the President the power to regulate capital transfers across national boundaries if he determined that the effect of the transaction would be to decrease domestic employment.

Sponsors of the bill argue that there is precedent for this provision under an order (ExecOrder 11387) signed Jan. 1, 1968, by former President Johnson. The order was designed to limit direct foreign investment to help correct balance of payments deficits.

Patents and licenses—The proposal would empower the President to prohibit any holder of a domestic patent from producing the patented product abroad or from licensing someone else to produce it overseas if he determined that such prohibition would increase domestic employment.

The penalty for violation of this section would be to make the patent unenforceable in U.S. courts. The effect of this section, the bill's sponsors contend, would be to protect U.S. jobs and technology.

Tariff code—The bill would repeal provisions (19 USC 1202, Items 806.30 and 807.00) of the U.S. Tariff Schedule that permit U.S. companies to establish plants in low-wage countries—particularly Mexico—to assemble U.S.-made components into finished products to be exported back to the U.S. at reduced duties.

Other—The bill also would require the Export-Import Bank, the Agency for International Development and the Bureau of Labor Statistics to collect more data on exports, imports and employment. Another provision would insist on more visible labeling on the origin of foreign-made goods and products with components made overseas. Advertising for such goods also would have to indicate clearly the countries of origin.

---

the bill was a joint effort of Burke's staff, Hartke's staff and the AFL-CIO. He said that Elizabeth R. Jager, an international economist on the AFL-CIO staff, provided much of the information for the drafting of the bill.

"I think it is significant that a lot of the work on this bill did originate with the AFL-CIO," King said, "because it indicates how seriously the AFL-CIO regards this problem.

"It is not just one Congressman's thinking. It did not come out of some economics professor's ideas. I am convinced from working with the AFL-CIO on this legislation that they mean business."

King said that Burke represents not only his own Massachusetts congressional district on the Ways and Means Committee but also the interests of all the Democratic Members of the House from the six New England states.

He pointed out that shoe and textile workers throughout New England have become increasingly alarmed at declining jobs and rising imports in these industries. Since 1962, he said, more than 100

shoe factories have closed in New England.

Jobs conference—The AFL-CIO sponsored a national Conference on Jobs in July in Washington with 600 labor delegates from across the nation.

Speakers stepped up the drumfire of criticism of U.S. trade policies and rising imports. They included Rep. Burke, Meany, I. W. Abel, president of the United Steelworkers of America, and Paul Jennings, president of the International Union of Electrical, Radio and Machine Workers.

THE BILL

Sen. Hartke and Rep. Burke introduced the legislation, the Foreign Trade and Investment Act of 1972, almost simultaneously on Sept. 28.

House—"American jobs are being exported," Burke said in remarks inserted in the *Congressional Record* on that day, "as huge amounts of money are shipped abroad to build plants and make goods for sale in the United States.

"American jobs are being lost

because that foreign production often takes the place of possible U.S. exports. Products as varied as airplane parts and shoes, clothing and automobiles, all kinds of jobs are at stake."

Burke said the bill he introduced is neither free-trade nor protectionist. He said the legislation substitutes modern trade regulations for outmoded policies designed for another period of history.

"The bill recognizes that a world with computers and global banks and multinational firms needs new legislation designed to give Americans who live in our cities and towns across the nation realistic solutions to their problems," Burke said.

King said that the bill would not cut off imports but would limit them to certain percentages of the domestic market and provide for orderly growth of domestic production.

"The multinational people come in here and tell us, 'You are ignorant. Are you aware of the tremendous returns to our balance of payments from this overseas investment?' We say this ultimately is giving jobs to foreign workers and taking jobs from American workers.

"What we are going after is the jugular vein that makes foreign investment so attractive: The foreign investment tax credit. We feel there is no reason to treat firms operating overseas more equitably than we do domestic firms."

Senate—Hartke, in remarks in the *Congressional Record* on Sept. 28, said that his bill is aimed at protecting the best interests of the nation against the worst practices of international corporations.

Hartke spoke of the provision that allows a U.S. company with foreign factories to receive credit for tax payments to foreign governments.

"But that same corporation cannot take credit against its U.S. taxes for the state taxes it pays. This bill would end that loophole and make it equally advantageous to invest in Indiana as it is to invest in Ireland," Hartke said.

Brunner, Sen. Hartke's former legislative assistant, said, "We don't have any precise reading of the impact of the tax provisions on the multinational corporations. It is our impression that the companies could absorb this kind of tax disincentive.

"They could continue to operate as domestic industries and be more responsive to the government than they are now. We are not saying that multinational corporations are not a good thing. We are not saying that they do not have a great potential for good. But their impact must be more clearly understood before any value judgment can be made."

Brunner said that Hartke's first objective will be discovering how the multinational corporations operate, what their aims are, how responsive they are—and should be—to the social and economic objectives of the government.

He said the Senator believes present tax laws encourage corporations to invest overseas. "Would it not be better if the tax code encouraged these companies to invest a greater amount of capital in this country and create jobs? Should they not more accurately report their capital gains abroad?

"We are concerned whether the export of jobs in consumer electric goods, textiles and shoes is atypical. Our impression is that it is not. Will we not have these situations repeated in other industries which can get lower wage rates in foreign countries?"

Brunner said that since Hartke introduced the bill, the Senator's staff has received more than 100 telephone calls from law firms and corporations requesting copies of the legislation.

Support—By early January, the bill had 65 cosponsors in the House and two cosponsors in the Senate.

King, Burke's executive assistant, said, "The action on this bill will have to originate in the House so we are very interested in getting as many cosponsors there as possible."

LABOR LOBBYING

The spearhead of labor's lobbying campaign for the Foreign Trade and Investment Act is the AFL-CIO's Industrial Union Department, which represents 59 unions with about six million members.

Abel, president of the Steelworkers Union, heads the IUD. The IUD Committee on International Trade is coordinating the drive. Jennings, president of the International Union of Electrical Workers, is chairman of the 11-man committee.

Convention: The IUD held a one-day rally Oct. 4 to urge congressional support for the legislation. The meeting was a prelude to the department's biennial convention Oct. 5-6 at Washington's Shoreham Hotel.

"The committee suggested we have a rally before the convention," said IUD Director Clayman. "We set it up with a minimum of time and preparation.

"I had anticipated about 2,000 people attending. We had 2,400 seats. After they arrived we estimated there were about 4,000 delegates from all over the country."

Hartke and Burke spoke to the delegates in the morning. In the afternoon, chartered buses carried the labor delegates to Capitol Hill. Some 15 to 20 Washington lobbyists for internationl unions accompanied them.

King said that Burke handed the first printed copy of the bill to Abel at the rally.

"We rushed to put this legislation together in time to present it to the AFL-CIO when they had their meeting," King said.

Lobbying—The largest delegations at the rally came from Massachusetts, Pennsylvania, Maryland, Ohio, New Jersey and New York.

Labor leaders arranged for these groups to meet with their

Comparison of U.S., Foreign Wage Rates

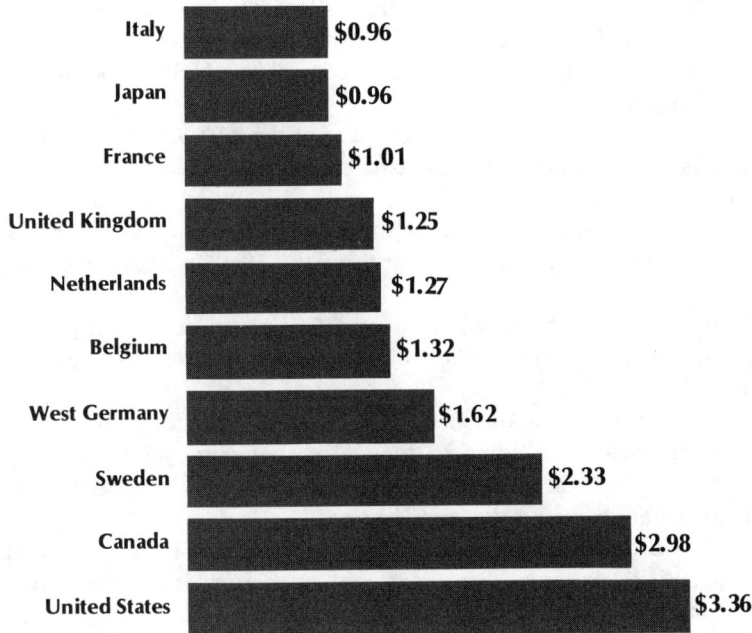

Country	Wage
Italy	$0.96
Japan	$0.96
France	$1.01
United Kingdom	$1.25
Netherlands	$1.27
Belgium	$1.32
West Germany	$1.62
Sweden	$2.33
Canada	$2.98
United States	$3.36

The graph shows the 1970 average hourly earnings of wage workers in factories in the United States and nine other leading manufacturing nations.

SOURCE: Council on International Economic Policy

congressional delegations in large committee rooms on Capitol Hill.

"How many Members were changed, it is difficult to know," said Clayman. "We got a good number of comments from Congressmen and Senators who said they were impressed with the turnout of workers and the intensity of the concern. I think it intensified the Members' awareness of the issue and prepared them for more serious thought on the need for a new national policy on foreign trade."

King said of the opening session of the rally, "I have never seen a more angry union meeting in my life. It sounded like a meeting in the 1930s. We heard that some congressmen were very shaky after the meetings on the Hill."

During the IUD convention itself, labor leaders hammered at import problems and multinational corporations. They urged the delegates to build grass-roots pressure for the Hartke-Burke legislation.

Pennsylvania delegation— One example of the impact of the intensive lobbying effort came from the 27-member Pennsylvania delegation in the House. An esti-

mated 500 labor delegates from the state met with the Pennsylvania Members.

On Oct. 18, two weeks after the meeting, Rep. Thomas E. Morgan, D-Pa., chairman of the Pennsylvania Congressional Delegation Steering Committee, wrote to President Nixon, Sen. Russell B. Long, D-La., chairman of the Senate Finance Committee, and Rep. Wilbur D. Mills, D-Ark., chairman of the House Ways and Means Committee.

Morgan, as chairman of the House Foreign Affairs Committee, is a power in the House.

In his letter, he told President Nixon of the meeting with the labor delegates. He said that U.S. trade policies and the multinational corporations are "undermining the American economy and unfairly eliminating the jobs of American workers."

He urged the President to conduct a vigorous reassessment of foreign trade policy. "Any delay in coming to grips with this serious problem will weaken our domestic industry and further imperil the jobs of American workers," Morgan wrote.

Hearings—The letters to Long and Mills urged them to schedule immediate hearings on the Foreign Trade and Investment Act.

Figures from the Bureau of Labor Statistics indicate that "some 700,000 U.S. workers lost their jobs between 1966 and 1969 because of imports and sales by foreign subsidiaries of American firms competing with U.S.-made products," Morgan wrote. The claim went considerably beyond labor's earlier contention that 500,000 jobs were lost because of imports.

Computer system: Another technique that the AFL-CIO plans to use in its efforts to push the legislation is an expanded computer program.

Clayman said the department plans to upgrade its computer operations to gather information on the problems of imports and foreign investment.

E. F. Shelley & Co. Inc., a computer technology firm with offices in Washington and New York, is developing the system.

The program will be designed to collect data on plants that have gone out of business because of competition from imported goods, companies that have moved into foreign operations and multinational corporations that have bought into foreign corporations.

"This detailed evidence will be used to support our fight against the flood of imported goods which is damaging not only to our members but to the entire U.S. economy," Clayman said.

UAW: The 1.3-million member United Auto Workers Union has not taken position on the legislation.

However, UAW leaders are alarmed at the growing imports of automobiles and parts.

The union also is concerned about the overseas operations of auto companies that provide employment for most of its members.

The UAW maintains a full-time international staff in Washington, which works closely with union leaders in foreign countries.

Leonard Woodcock, president, and John H. Beidler, legislative director of the UAW's Washington office, visited Hartke in mid-

THE AFL-CIO'S TURNABOUT ON FREE TRADE

The AFL-CIO has shifted gradually from its traditional free-trade position to one where it now advocates quotas on most imports and tighter government control of U.S. corporations' international operations.

Factors—Jacob Clayman, director of the AFL-CIO's Industrial Union Department, said that two major factors led to the transition:

increasing pressure from the members of large industrial unions contending that surges of imports in the 1960s were threatening their jobs;

the spectacular growth of direct foreign investment by U.S. companies—from $32 billion in 1960 to $78 billion at the end of 1970.

"Some of our unions have been complaining for years about what imports were doing to their jobs, but these were relatively small unions," Clayman said. They included workers in the shoe, glass, ceramics and pottery industries.

Trade expansion—Delegates to the 1961 AFL-CIO national convention overrode some scattered opposition and voted overwhelmingly to endorse legislation to reduce tariffs and expand foreign trade.

In 1962, the federation's lobbyists worked hard to help pass the Kennedy Administration's Trade Expansion Act (76 Stat 872).

By the late 1960s, some of the federation's largest blocs of workers began to complain about the incursions of imports into their industries—clothing, textiles, steel, rubber, electronics.

The AFL-CIO, responding to membership pressure, urged the Johnson Administration in 1967 to negotiate international agreements to stem the tide of imports.

"We cannot ignore the fact that rising imports have disrupted some domestic markets and resulted in adverse impacts on some industries," the federation said. "These developments have imposed severe hardships on thousands of workers."

Turning point—Clayman said that when the industrial union department was meeting at a convention in 1969, "imports became a front-burner issue. The delegates talked longer and with more passion about this than on any other subject."

I. W. Abel, president of the United Steelworkers of America, pointed up labor's new thrust at a conference in March 1970 in Washington. "A substantial change in U.S. trade policy is needed," he said.

Nathaniel Goldfinger, director of research for the AFL-CIO, speaking at the same meeting, assailed multinational corporations, blaming them for the export of tens of thousands of U.S. jobs.

> **Outcome**—By 1971, the AFL-CIO was ready to translate its new policies into far-reaching legislative proposals. These are embodied in legislation introduced by Sen. Vance Hartke, D-Ind., and Rep. James A. Burke, D-Mass.
>
> "The multinational corporations do not pay full taxes on their profits coming back from operations abroad," Clayman said. "The Hartke-Burke bill would hit the multinationals in their tax breadbasket—and that is their vulnerable spot."

October to discuss other legislation.

Brunner, the Senator's former legislative assistant, said that Hartke mentioned the foreign-trade legislation to Woodcock and urged Woodcock to support it. "Woodcock said he had some problems about supporting the legislation," Brunner said.

Beidler said in an interview that the UAW historically has supported freer trade and opposed legislation to set quotas on imports. "I think we could supoort every part of that bill except the quota provisions," he said.

"My belief is that we ought to support this bill. I am concerned about moving some legislation off the dime that deals with these problems. I think this is the bill that has the best chance."

Political issue—Opponents are apprehensive that labor may make the foreign-trade bill a campaign issue.

George Collins, assistant to the president of the International Union of Electrical Workers, indicated that the fears are well founded.

"This bill will be a touchstone issue for our support of candidates," Collins said. "If unemployment continues, it might be *the* issue of the election campaigns."

Hartke announced Jan. 3 that he will be a presidential candidate in the New Hampshire primary election March 7. His presidential campaign could provide a national forum for publicity on the bill.

A staff member said the Senator already has received telegrams and letters from some labor leaders pledging to support his candidacy on the basis of his trade bill.

Industry allies—Clayman said the AFL-CIO would welcome support from business interests alarmed at competition from imports.

Clayman pointed out that the Steelworkers Union and the steel industry joined in 1968 to press for voluntary steel quotas.

One example of the scattered business support for the bill came from a small steel company in Pennsylvania.

Gene E. McDonald, general counsel and secretary of the Latrobe Steel Co., Latrobe, Pa., said he favors the bill.

"The specialty steel industry has been hurt badly by imports of specialty steel," McDonald said. "We think the only way to solve this problem is through government-imposed quotas."

He said that in 1969 his company had gross sales of $53 million and employed about 2,100 work-

ers. In 1971, he said the company's gross sales were about $43 million and employment was down to about 1,400 persons. McDonald said the decline in sales and employment was a result of the combined effects of the economic downturn and import competition.

Latrobe makes steel alloys which require a higher ratio of manpower to produce than basic steel.

INDUSTRY COUNTERATTACK

Organizations representing industry have been drawing plans for a systematic counterattack against the AFL-CIO's drive for the legislation.

The business groups most active in fighting the legislation include the National Association of Manufacturers, the Chamber of Commerce of the U.S., the Emergency Committee for American Trade and the American Importers Association.

NAM: The National Association of Manufacturers represents 14,000 companies that account for 75 per cent of the industrial output of the nation. The association is planning a strong campaign against the bill.

"The NAM does not take a position on foreign trade," said William R. Pollert, New York-based director of international economic affairs for the NAM. "But we think the major issue in this legislation is the political control of direct foreign investment."

He said that blocking the labor-backed bill will be one of the association's top priorities of 1972.

"The NAM is putting together a very systematic and planned-out campaign to meet organized labor on this issue. We are going to put a lot of money, manpower and resources into this."

Study—One weapon the association will use in the campaign is a heavily documented 92-page report: "Multinational Corporation: The Issue and Policy Alternatives."

Pollert began working on the study last August and completed it in early December.

The NAM's committee on international affairs met Dec. 16 in New York and voted unanimously to distribute the study among Members of Congress, industry officials, key federal policy-makers and communications media.

The study devotes much space to a detailed rebuttal of charges that organized labor has made against the multinational firms, particularly the claim that the companies are exporting jobs that could be performed by American workers.

"The argument that the U.S. multinational corporations displace U.S. jobs by utilizing 'cheap foreign labor' and exporting to the U.S. is not supported by available statistics," says one key portion of the study.

"During the last 10 years, over 65 per cent of U.S. direct investment has been in relatively high wage areas, in Europe and Canada .... Rather than displacing U.S. exports, there is evidence that U.S. foreign direct investment supports and stimulates U.S. exports, thereby creating jobs for American workers."

Implications—"The implications of this bill to U.S. multinational corporations, as well as to non-international firms, are tremendous," the NAM report said.

If enacted, it said, the bill would:

"politicize international investment decisions of the private sector;

"ultimately cost the United States billions of dollars in lost royalties and fees;

"delay foreign direct investments to a point where they would no longer be timely;

"increase the price of domestic products;

"reduce the demand for supplier parts;

"in general, increase rather than reduce unemployment."

Strategy—Pollert says the NAM also plans to generate a grass-roots effort among business people urging them to write letters to Members of Congress and to visit them in Washington "to let them know how business feels about this issue."

One important tool in the campaign, he said, is a computer system which can feed information into the association's New York office.

"With this system, we can segment our membership by congressional district and, within 24 hours, be able to get 10,000 letters out urging our members to take a certain position."

Panel discussion—One sign of the NAM's increasing concern about the escalating debate on the multinational corporation was a panel discussion at a November meeting of the association in Washington.

One of the panelists, Antonie T. Knoppers, president of Merck & Co. Inc., noted that direct foreign investment from U.S. companies increased from $32 billion in 1960 to $71 billion in 1969.

"Today, direct investments by U.S. companies bring back $6 billion yearly into the American economy not counting close to $2 billion from licenses and royalties," Knoppers said.

He conceded that overseas investments and imports have caused some unemployment and plant closures.

"But it is equally true that jobs in the United States depend directly on the extensive activity of U.S. companies overseas," Knoppers said.

ECAT: The Emergency Committee for American Trade represents about 50 of the largest multinational corporations. It was organized in 1967 when protectionist sentiment was rising in some segments of industry and in Congress.

(Peterson was an ECAT member until he joined the White House staff in 1971. For six years, Peterson had been board chairman of Bell & Howell Co., which had 1970 sales of $297.8 million and ranked 339th on *Fortune* magazine's list of the top 500 U.S. corporations.)

Raymond Garcia, program director, said that ECAT strongly opposes the bill.

"We think the bill is based on faulty premises," Garcia said. "Labor says that if the multinational corporations are restructured it will lead to the creation of thousands of jobs in the U.S. economy. We feel that just the opposite would happen—thousands of jobs would be lost."

Garcia said the ECAT is conducting a study of the relationship

MAKING THE CASE FOR MULTINATIONALS

The coordinator of the National Association of Manufacturers' counterattack to organized labor's offensive against multinational corporations is one of the new breed of business representatives—combining high academic credentials with a capacity for research.

William R. Pollert, 28, is the director of international economic affairs for the association. He is based at NAM headquarters in New York.

"If business tries to go to Capitol Hill without any facts, we are going to kill our legitimacy," Pollert said in an interview.

One weapon in the industry campaign is a 92-page study of the multinational corporation that Pollert began to research in August and completed in early December 1971 with the help of the NAM's committee on international affairs.

Pollert, a native of Southold, L.I., N.Y., joined the NAM staff in July 1969. He holds a bachelor of arts degree from Lehigh University in Bethlehem, Pa., a master of business administration degree from Columbia University in New York and a Ph.D. in business administration and management from the University of Florida.

He is a member of the graduate faculty of the University of Connecticut and has written articles for several business journals. He recently was appointed to President Nixon's White House Conference on Children.

---

between foreign trade and jobs and expects to complete it by late January or early February.

"The allegation labor makes is that U.S. corporations close plants here, open plants overseas, and ship the goods back here. Our study will show that this is hogwash. About 85 per cent of the sales of overseas affiliates went to overseas markets."

Garcia said ECAT will distribute its study to Members of Congress and communications media and will "give it to the AFL-CIO if they want it."

Lobbying—Garcia said that ECAT is urging individual companies to analyze the Hartke-Burke legislation to determine how it would affect their operations.

"It is one thing to go to Congress and talk about aggregates. It is another thing to talk about the ABC Company in the fourth congressional district and how this bill could hurt," Garcia said.

"Management people are going to have to get off their duffs, get to Washington and talk. Workers come down here in droves."

Garcia said he believes industry should be more sensitive to the needs of workers. Management, he said, should give more advance notice of plant closures, help workers in relocating other jobs and retrain them in new skills for other jobs if massive shifts occur.

Opening salvo—The first burst in ECAT's lobbying campaign resulted in at least one misfire.

The organization sent letters signed by Donald M. Kendall, chairman of ECAT and president of Pepsi Co. Inc., to Members of Congress. Kendall is a close friend of President Nixon.

"In recent months," the letter said, "there has been an organized and orchestrated attack on American companies with international operations."

The letter also said that the charges against the companies and the legislation sponsored by Burke and Hartke "are directed at destroying the overseas operations of many American companies."

One of the letters assailing the bill went to Burke.

Chamber of Commerce: Donald J. Musch, a staff executive of the Chamber of Commerce Task Force on the Multinational Enterprise, said that the chamber has not taken a specific position opposing the legislation.

However, he said that the chamber has policy positions that would justify opposition to most of the provisions.

"We think it would have dire consequences," he said. "At worst, it could result in bankruptcies for a substantial number of businesses."

Musch contends that "a substantial portion of labor's argument for the bill is based on a very cavalier treatment of statistics and little attempt to look at a broad range of statistics."

He said that the chamber sent questionnaires last year to 600 companies that are among the largest in the nation. One purpose of the survey is to learn why companies locate plants overseas. The chamber staff is analyzing the results.

Musch said that the chamber is working now on a legislative strategy.

"Labor is mounting a pretty big campaign and business feels that this issue merits a lot of interest," he said.

Importers' association: The American Importers Association, headquartered in New York, represents more than 900 companies with an interest in foreign trade. They include customs brokers, law firms, steamship lines, banks and insurance companies.

On Oct. 13, Kurt Orban, president, wrote to the members soliciting money to fight the labor-backed bill and to push for an early end to the 10-per cent surcharge on imports that President Nixon imposed last August and lifted on Dec. 20.

"If organized labor has its way there will be quotas on all imports on a category-by-category, country-by-country basis equal to the average imports for 1965-1969," Orban wrote.

"AIA has begun a vigorous campaign on behalf of all its members to oppose this bill now before Congress and to seek immediate termination of the surcharge. But AIA's actions are limited by the amount of money collected so far."

The organization enclosed a suggested scale of contributions and urged its members to use it as a guide for their minimum donations.

The suggestions ranged from $150 for importers with less than $1 million a year in imports to $2,550 for those with more than $80 million a year. The association

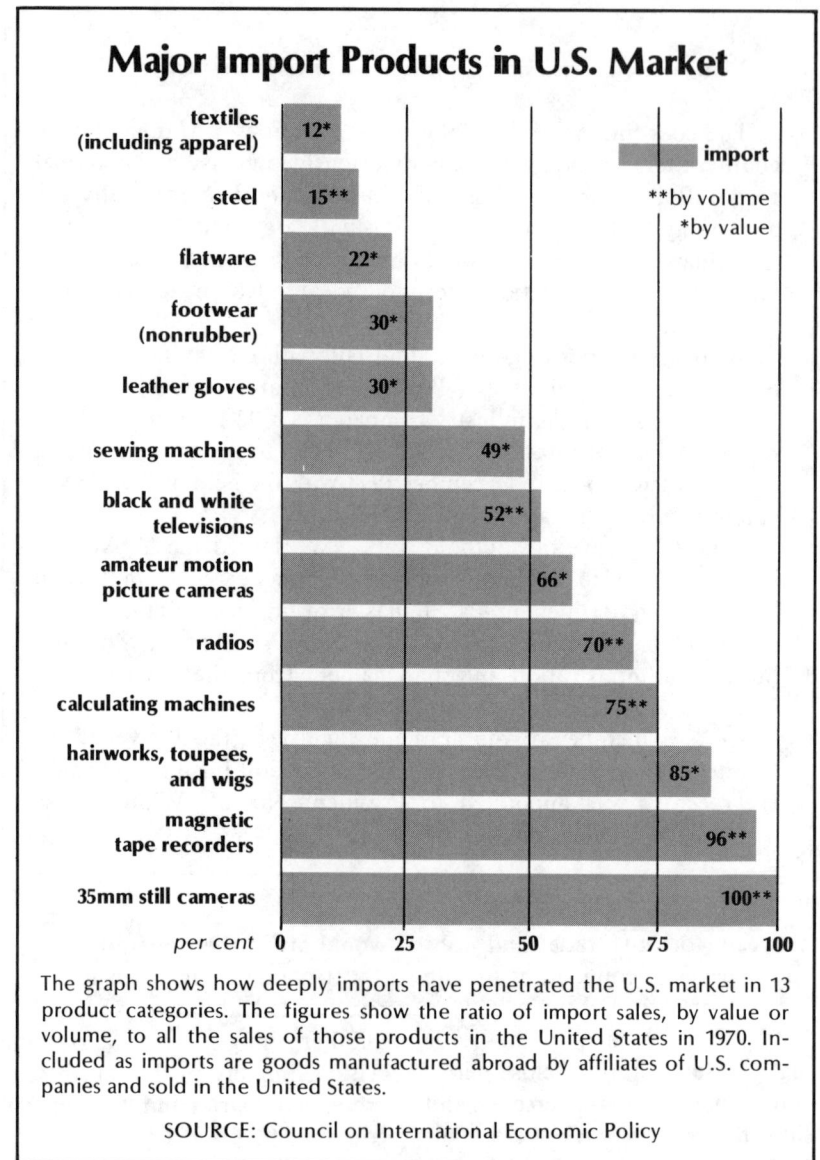

Major Import Products in U.S. Market

Product	Import (per cent)
textiles (including apparel)	12*
steel	15**
flatware	22*
footwear (nonrubber)	30*
leather gloves	30*
sewing machines	49*
black and white televisions	52**
amateur motion picture cameras	66*
radios	70**
calculating machines	75**
hairworks, toupees, and wigs	85*
magnetic tape recorders	96**
35mm still cameras	100**

■ import
**by volume
*by value

per cent 0   25   50   75   100

The graph shows how deeply imports have penetrated the U.S. market in 13 product categories. The figures show the ratio of import sales, by value or volume, to all the sales of those products in the United States in 1970. Included as imports are goods manufactured abroad by affiliates of U.S. companies and sold in the United States.

SOURCE: Council on International Economic Policy

also suggested a flat contribution of $1,000 for banks, steamship lines and insurance companies.

NIXON ADMINISTRATION

Administration officials are united in their opposition to the Foreign Trade and Investment Act.

Some fear that if congressional support for the proposal continues to grow, supporters may try to attach sections of the bill as riders to any foreign-trade legislation that the Administration proposes this year.

White House: "What they are proposing is not compatible with the President's position," said Peterson, who also is executive director of the President's Council on International Economic Policy.

Particular concerns—Peterson said that the Administration opposes especially the import quotas, tax provisions and sections discouraging technology exports.

Peterson said that the White House is considering the possibility of introducing some major legislation in 1972 in the area of foreign trade and investment. The proposals the Administration is studying, he said, include programs to promote exports, expand East-West trade and to change foreign investment policy.

Peterson report—On Dec. 29, Peterson made public a 51-page study he prepared on international trade problems.

While the study did not recommend any specific legislation, it hinted at some of the options the Administration is considering.

It suggested that, in some cases, temporary import restrictions might be necessary to help domestic industries and workers harmed by surges of imports.

The report also said that the growth of multinational corporations poses new challenges that require new policies.

Without naming the AFL-CIO, the report sharply criticized the proposals the federation is advocating.

"We could choose the route advocated by some of erecting a variety of new restrictions," Peterson wrote. "However, I believe this to be a prescription for defeat and the admission of failure."

State: The State Department has prepared a 15-page preliminary analysis giving detailed reasons for its strong opposition to the labor-backed legislation.

"This is a real bad bill," said Joseph E. O'Mahony, chief of special trade activities and commercial treaties.

"It would take us farther away from freer trade policies than we have ever been.

"We would be quick to acknowledge that it is a response to a very serious situation that exists.

"The inrush of imports was symptomatic of problems but it was not the cause. The last thing we want to do is leave the basic problems unattended and deal only with the symptoms."

He said that some of the causes of foreign-trade problems included the fast-moving rate of domestic inflation and imbalances in world currency-exchange rates.

"Domestic producers had problems of not being able to compete in world markets because their costs were going up with inflation." The President's new economic policy, he said, is designed to strike at that type of basic problem.

O'Mahony said that imports in 1970 amounted to $39.8 billion. The Foreign Trade and Investment Act would roll them back to the 1965-1969 average of $28.5 billion—a reduction of $16.9 billion or 37 per cent.

One probable effect, he said, would be a massive trade war as foreign countries, responding to pressures from their export industries, adopt measures to block U.S. exports.

O'Mahony said he believes chances are remote that the bill will pass in its present form.

"I think the prospects are that at least they will get hearings on the bill and I don't think we should be apprehensive about that."

"But very dangerous things could happen," he said. "I think the biggest problem is the possibility that they might pull it apart and tie it onto other legislation here and there."

Commerce Department: Jack E. Butler, executive assistant for domestic and international business in the Commerce Department, said that the tax provisions in the Foreign Trade and Investment Act would seriously damage corporations doing 'business in world markets.

"The majority of U.S. corporations simply could not compete in the international marketplace with that kind of tax load," Butler said. "That kind of legislation could force companies to go out of business. This bill basically says we will ignore the international arena and move out of world trade. I don't think we can afford to take that kind of policy position."

Butler said government studies indicate that only 8 per cent of goods manufactured overseas by U.S. companies returns to this country while 78 per cent is sold in the country where it is produced and 14 per cent goes to third-country markets.

Treasury: Charles E. Walker, under secretary of the Treasury, said in an interview that "the basic thrust of the Hartke-Burke bill is 180 degrees in opposition to the Nixon Administration's international economic policy."

"We are in favor of fair trade but protectionism is not the answer to our trade problems," he said. "The thrust of the international aspects of the President's new economic policy is to defuse the strong grass-roots support for protectionist legislation and move the country toward a constructive,

84 liberal trading position."

Bureau of Labor Statistics—The keystone of the AFL-CIO's argument on the job impact of foreign imports is a set of figures included in a study the Labor Department's Bureau of Labor Statistics submitted in May 1970 to the House Ways and Means Committee.

The Ruttenberg report for the AFL-CIO said that the BLS figures indicated that from 1966 to 1969, jobs related to exports increased from 2.5 million to 2.7 million, a gain of 200,000 jobs. The report said that during the same period the domestic jobs that would have been required to produce the imports moving into this country rose from 1.8 million to 2.5 million, an increase of 700,000.

Subtracting the 200,000 gain in export-related jobs, the Ruttenberg report concluded that U.S. foreign trade produced the equivalent of a net loss of 500,000 U.S. jobs.

However, John Chandler, chief of the division of foreign labor statistics and trade for the BLS, said the relationships between domestic employment and import levels are complex.

"These figures (on jobs and imports) are so hypothetical that any conclusion drawn from them can be misleading or erroneous," Chandler said. "The BLS was reluctant to go into this area from the first because it involves a volatile policy issue. At best, these figures give extremely qualified support to the AFL-CIO."

Chandler was equally critical of a recent industry study aimed at labor's arguments on the employment impact of foreign trade.

The National Foreign Trade Council Inc., New York, an organization of 600 American companies engaged in foreign trade and investment, issued a 34-page report in November based on a survey of 150 of its members.

"There is no cause-and-effect evidence," the study said, "to support the view that foreign production has reduced U.S. exports and domestic employment in companies investing abroad."

Chandler said that the study relied on questionnaires circulated to exporters and multinational corporations. "It paints a very rosy picture but much of it is based on examples rather than on statistically verifiable data."

OUTLOOK

AFL-CIO leader Clayman said that the Hartke-Burke bill will be one of the top half-dozen legislative priorities for the federation in 1972.

Jobs factor—The labor backers of the bill and its major industry opponents agree that high unemployment is gaining support for the legislation.

The Labor Department's Bureau of Labor Statistics announced Jan. 7 that unemployment in December was 6.1 per cent. Average unemployment in 1971 was 5.9 per cent, the highest annual average in 10 years.

"I assume that if the economy changes sufficiently to provide many more jobs for the unemployed, the pressure for this bill would lessen," Clayman said.

"I don't think this is going to happen. Our people are not interested in the ideology of foreign trade. They are interested in jobs and the conditions that are affecting them."

ECAT's program director Garcia agreed on the importance of unemployment.

"The only real solution is for the President's new economic policy to work," he said. "Political pressure would lessen if you got unemployment back down to 4 per cent."

Mills' attitude—Another key factor is the attitude of Rep. Mills, who will strongly influence any trade legislation that emerges from the House Ways and Means Committee.

Mills said in a speech Oct. 28, 1971, to the World Affairs Council in Los Angeles:

"While I cannot agree with the recommendations of some of those who are concerned with the lessening of job opportunities in the United States, I believe we must recognize that the trends (in foreign trade) . . . do pose a threat for the American worker which is not being met."

King, Rep. Burke's executive assistant, said, "What everybody in the multinational corporations better start hoping is that trade figures start going up, the unemployment figures start going down and that trade-adjustment assistance becomes a functioning program."

Mills, King said, "is by no means an enthusiastic supporter of this bill. But some trade matters will come up in the committee this year and any member of the committee can attach a rider to these bills."

Three other members of the Ways and Means Committee have joined Burke as cosponsors of the bill. King predicted the number of House cosponsors, now 65, soon will reach 100.

Common Cause seeks to have broad role on issues in 1972 campaign   *Andrew J. Glass*

CITIZENS LOBBY

Common Cause, the citizens lobby which has just celebrated its first birthday and enrolled its 200,000th member, intends to have an important role in shaping the issues of the 1972 presidential campaign.

John W. Gardner, who created Common Cause as a nonpartisan third force in public life, said its future growth may depend on whom the Democrats and Republicans select to lead them next year. "If we have two candidates that turn a lot of people off, we'll get more members," Gardner predicted.

In Common Cause, Gardner has clearly tapped a vein of discontent in society. Attracting a cadre of top professionals to his side, he has sought, by waging a kind of establishment populism, to hasten the end of American military involvement in Vietnam and to open the elective and governing process to broader participation.

But, as Common Cause has grown beyond his expectations, he has aimed to keep its focus narrow—both as a lobby and as a movement—and to keep its goals within achievable range.

"It's perfectly clear that our efforts to end the war have put about as much pressure on President Nixon as they have on Congress," Gardner said in an interview. "Any major effort spills over and affects him."

Taking a Partner—Gardner's movement was strengthened in March when Jack T. Conway, who has roots in the industrial union movement, joined him as president.

"We had a long series of discussions about what we really believed," Conway recalled. "And I concluded he was for real."

Conway said he wanted from Gardner "a commitment to organize around issues that could be serious enough to pull the house down. When you commit yourself to a battle, do you begin to check as soon as you see what the consequences are?

"I wanted to make sure that I wasn't going to be getting into a powder-puff atmosphere where a call from the White House or a call from somebody turns things off. I have lived in that environment on other occasions and I don't have any interest in that."

Gardner and Conway have seen other citizens movements atrophy; as they won the issues they were fighting for, they faded from the scene. Both men are determined that will not happen to Common Cause.

Conway said Common Cause now is considering whether it should develop a set of "candidate standards" and whether, as a further step, it should endorse candidates who meet those standards.

"We may be forced to move in this direction, or we may move out of choice," Conway said.

Gardner said, "We cannot endorse candidates; that's just out. But obviously, when you come out for legislation, you are by implica-tion setting a standard against which your members may judge a candidate."

Special Rules—Yet, amid all the good works, there is a hint of unconscious arrogance. There is a feeling that because their cause is manifestly just, it need not stand the kind of rigorous ethical test that Common Cause would be the first to apply in an effort to expose pursuits more selfish and ignoble than their own. For example:

Last year, Common Cause hired M. Carl Holman, president of the Urban Coalition, which Gardner had headed, as a $7,200-a-year part-time consultant. Holman advised Gardner on how to improve relations with the black community—advice that often went unheeded. But the arrangement with Holman was not reported in quarterly filings with the Clerk of the House, required under the 1946 Federal Regulation of Lobbying Act (60 Stat 839). ("As a matter of propriety, he should have been listed," said the executive director of Common Cause.) Holman dropped his consulting role last month.

Gardner declined to disclose the sources of his income. It was pointed out to him that his refusal appeared inconsistent with his stand against financial secrecy in lobbying operations and exposed him to conflict-of-interest suspicions.

He then prepared a statement which reviewed his income in broad terms. But he did not disclose his stock holdings, other than

86 to report that dividends account for a sixth of his income.

Gardner takes no salary. Roughly half his income, he said, comes from writing and from speaking.

ORGANIZATION

In its first year, Common Cause for the most part looked inward. It built its name, its membership rolls and its staff expertise.

Now, Common Cause is beginning to push outward. It is opening its policy board to elected newcomers. And it is creating a national field organization.

The election, which is currently under way, and the field campaign, which is just starting to take form, also should give Gardner and his top staff a better idea of who belongs to Common Cause, why they have joined and in what direction they seek to move.

Membership: Conway characterizes the membership as "highly intelligent, highly educated, highly professional, highly white, highly suburban or small town."

Other Common Cause staffers who have dealt directly with members offer similar descriptions. Mitchell Rogovin of the Washington law firm of Arnold & Porter, who is the counsel to Common Cause, said the membership is "white, middle-class, intelligent and educatable."

"This isn't a race-and-poverty group. It doesn't have a groundswell. And it doesn't have muscle in terms of presidential elections," he said.

Conway, who is ultimately responsible for the organizing drive, put it this way:

"These are people who, no matter what their circumstances, feel that they have a stake in the system, and they are worried about it. They want to do what they can, through some personal organization or activity, to get ahold of it again and make it work.

"They are not radical, but they are concerned enough to support anything that's reasonable, that will produce results. . . .

"You'll find that this is not a membership that has other organizations that theoretically also represent them. You don't find people who are union members as activists in Common Cause, any more than you find representatives of farm groups or so on. You find individuals who may be union members but who don't look to their union anymore."

Conway's analysis is currently being supplemented by a scientific canvass of the membership. The purpose is to seek members' views on issues and to be able to project what the second-year renewal rate will be. The telephone survey is being conducted by the New York-based polling firm of Daniel Yankelovich Inc.

Governing Board: The 40-member Common Cause governing board, for the most part hand-picked by Gardner, is in the midst of reconstituting itself. (Because of deaths and resignations, 38 directors serve on the board at present; 19 of them are members of the executive committee.)

Election—About 193,000 ballots were mailed to members of record as of Aug. 1; they must be returned by Sept. 10 to be counted.

After consultations, a nominating committee chose 30 names from which the membership may pick new directors. A folder that accompanies the ballot said: "Although the list includes some prominent Americans, national eminence was not a criterion. Rather, the committee sought evidence that the nominee was an active, effective leader, dedicated to citizen action."

The committee's choices included Elly M. Peterson, the Republican national committeewoman for Michigan and a former assistant chairman of the Republican National Committee (1963-64; 1969-71); Betty Furness, former chairman of the New York State Consumer Protection Board (1970-71); Josiah A. Spaulding, a Massachusetts attorney who ran unsuccessfully for the Senate in 1970 as a Republican against Sen. Edward M. Kennedy; Walter A. Haas Jr., chairman of Levi Strauss and Co., and a trustee of the Ford Foundation; Raymond A. Lamontagne, president of the Washington-based Development Technologies Inc., and a former counsel to John D. Rockefeller III (1964-68); Wilbur J. Cohen, dean of the school of education at the University of Michigan, who succeeded Gardner as HEW Secretary (1968-69); and Gardner.

In addition to the 30 official nominees, the ballot lists 42 candidates who were nominated by petitions signed by at least 10 Common Cause members.

Of the 72 nominees, the 20 receiving the most votes will be elected to three-year terms. Each year, another 20 directors will be picked by the board to serve one-year terms.

Thus, for the first year of the

election plan, the elected directors will constitute a minority on the board. But Conway envisions the time when "our organization will reflect the leadership inputs of these new people."

Control—As matters stand, Gardner, Conway and the inner circle of policy-making aides retain a relatively free hand in their operations. The board has yet to set aside a major policy decision taken by Gardner and his staff.

Rogovin recalled a board meeting at which Vernon E. Jordan Jr., executive director of the United Negro College Fund Inc., questioned the wisdom of intervening against Treasury plans to revise depreciation allowances. Jordan thought the drive would sap strength from another prime Common Cause concern, passage of welfare-reform legislation (HR 1).

As the controversy continued, Gardner sat silently. "John was letting the board argue it out," Rogovin said. "But I got very nervous."

Finally, Leonard Woodcock, president of the United Auto Workers, told Jordan that "the $4 billion they want to give away is your appropriations." That settled the argument.

Afterwards, when Rogovin asked Gardner why he didn't intervene, Gardner said: "Every board likes to wrestle with an issue once in a while. I knew how it would come out.

Field Activities: Conway said: "When I got here (in late March), we had 100,000 members and no notions about what to do"—aside from an already functioning lobbying effort on Capitol Hill.

The Problem—Conway observed that the task of relating a professional lobbying organization to a field constituency has defied almost all groups. He said:

"There's always a jealous separation between the political work of an organization and the legislative work. Invariably, the legislative guy is moaning and groaning because the guy he has carefully developed and nurtured for his specialized reasons doesn't sit well with the people out in the district because he's a rotten old son-of-a-bitch who does the wrong things on most other issues. The fact that he's right on the narrow issues makes the legislative guy very protective.

"The problem is how to put together an articulate constituency which is issue-oriented with a legislative operation in Washington which is, by its very nature, only able to take on a certain number of battles."

Solution—"What I did is to cut through all of the differences of opinion on how to organize by simply saying that, in any event, we couldn't afford to do what everyone was suggesting.

"The only thing we could afford to do was to take our first mission—which is to be a citizens lobby on the Hill in Washington—and to take three or four issues that we are working on and work out some 'target' districts."

The primary intent is to create what Conway calls "a legislative response mechanism" that will reinforce lobbying efforts on Capitol Hill. Conway said the 100 "target" districts were chosen without following any over-all plan.

But, he said, they do reflect such things as whether the Member is on a committee with jurisdiction over an issue that Common Cause wants to pursue; whether the district is politically marginal; whether the Member is especially intelligent or influenceable, and whether the Member is a potential leader in the House.

The field network, based in many districts on a telephone chain, will be organized without the issuance of any formal charters or the formation of any regional, state or local chapters. "Since we're not issuing charters, we don't have any charters to revoke," Conway said.

The new structure is being put together by a veteran Washington lobbyist, David Cohen, who was named in July as director of field organization for Common Cause.

Small field offices already have been opened in San Francisco, Denver, New York and Boston. Cohen said Common Cause plans to open four more offices soon—one each for the industrial Midwest, the Plains states, the South and the Border states.

Special Projects—In the meantime, Common Cause is conducting two programs to gain further experience in how it should organize in the field.

One program, known as the voting rights project, is aimed at identifying obstacles to registration and devising means to overcome them on a state-by-state basis.

The task force assembling the voting rights project is headed by Mrs. Anne Wexler, 1968 organizer for former Sen. (1959-71) Eugene J. McCarthy, D-Minn., and campaign manager for Joseph D. Duffey a Democrat who ran unsuccessfully for the Senate from Con-

88 necticut in 1970.

The drive headed by Mrs. Wexler is directed specifically against restricted registration periods and hours, early filing deadlines, lengthy residence requirements and closed delegate-selection processes for political nominating conventions.

The other program, known as the Colorado project, is aimed at promoting basic changes in the mechanics of state legislature, which, Cohen said, "are now shrouded in secrecy." The project is headed by David Mixner, a 1968 McCarthy organizer and a member of the Democratic Party's Commission on Party Structure and Delegate Selection.

Mixner lobbied for two "right to know" bills in the state legislature. One required lobbyists to register with a state official and to disclose expenses, companies and interests they represent, as well as the legislation in which they are interested.

The other bill required state legislators, elected officials and judges to file periodic statements disclosing their financial interests.

Despite an extensive lobbying campaign, in which many of the 3,475 members of Common Cause who live in Colorado were contacted, the legislature failed to vote on either of the bills.

Assessment—"I had no idea that we could operate in the states as easily as we have," Gardner said. "We've found it's quite possible to lobby there because there hasn't been very much citizen lobbying in the states up to now, and the legislators are quite struck with the citizen voice suddenly appearing."

FINANCES

In early September, Common Cause is going back to its members to ask them to sign on for another year.

"On the first time around, a 50-per cent renewal would be very satisfactory," said Robert Meier, secretary-treasurer of Common Cause. "Anything more than 50 per cent would be great. Anything less than that would range from disappointing to (raising) a question over whether we are responding to what our members really feel like."

The first-year membership drive well exceeded original targets set by Gardner and his staff. The initial goal, 100,000 members by the end of the first year, was reached in 23 weeks. On Sept. 1, membership passed 200,000, with about 5,000 new members being enrolled each week.

Receipts: All operations are funded by membership dues or through contributions. Dues currently account for 77 per cent of total income. (An initial $10,000 loan from the United California Bank was repaid in nine months; Common Cause is now debt-free.)

Dues and contributions are not

MAJOR CONTRIBUTORS

The following persons and corporations have contributed $6,000 or more to Common Cause since July 1, 1970:

Arlen Properties Inc. (now Arlen Realty and Development Corp.), Long Island City, N.Y.; $35,000 ($10,000 of which was a personal contribution by Arthur N. Levien, then president of Arlen Properties, currently chairman of Arlen Realty)

Helen W. Buckner, New York, N.Y.; $7,500

Joseph W. Drown, Bel Air, Calif.; self-employed (real estate and oil); $10,000

Ford Motor Co., Dearborn, Mich.; $10,000

Walter A. Haas Jr., San Francisco, Calif.; president, Levi Strauss and Co., and his cousin,

Madeleine Haas Russell, $6,000 each

Arthur A. Houghton Jr., New York; director, Corning Glass Works; $10,000

Andre Meyer, New York, N.Y.; senior partner, Lazard Freres and Co.; $10,000

Max Palevsky, Los Angeles, Calif.; chairman, Xerox Data Systems, director, Xerox Corp.; $21,000

John D. Rockefeller III, New York, N.Y.; chairman, Rockefeller Foundation; $25,000

Norton Simon, Los Angeles, Calif.; president, Norton Simon Foundation; $6,280.42

Iphigene Ochs Sulzberger, New York, N.Y.; director, The New York Times Co.; $11,000

GARDNER ON GARDNER: CUTTING CLOSE TO THE BONE

In an interview with National Journal, *John W. Gardner, chairman of Common Cause, spoke of the role a public-interest lobby plays and the reasons Common Cause was founded:*

We are going more and more into the kind of issue that isn't going to be settled easily.

When you're talking about the gut questions of who holds power and how deep are the defenses that prevent somebody else from getting power, you are talking about final questions over which people will fight to the death.

Matters like seniority, lobbying controls, campaign spending, exposure of conflict of interest get right to the heart of how the power structure maintains itself. . . .

No President has really tackled these questions—questions that deal with how power is distributed. They do not intervene in these arrangements. They make their accommodations in the course of campaigning with the interests that would have no change.

I believe we're working in a territory that no politician can work. They can't afford to. It's too close to the bone. This campaign spending business, you know, is right at the heart of politics. Some of the things we are going to be saying about money and secrecy in the next few months are things that no politician can say. . . .

If Common Cause continues to exhibit vitality through the Administrations of three or four Presidents, I think we will be unpopular with every one of them. You don't tee off on a President and spend a lot of time at White House dinners. It just doesn't work that way. . . .

I've been concerned about institutional change for the last 20 years, and I don't think there was a time when I thought less about it than when I was Secretary (of Health, Education and Welfare). I had to try to gain yards in terms of the way the game is played. I couldn't think about some other way of doing it. I had to get my appropriations. I had to get my bills passed—and fight, fight, fight. . . .

You have to understand that for a public-interest lobby, the most important weapon is public information. It isn't like a special-interest lobby, which wants to keep most things quiet. The public-interest lobby wants to tell the story and tell it big. With (congressional) seniority, for example, we got the story out and into the papers. That affects the President and the executive branch as much as it does Congress. And it affects the people back home. . . . We succeeded in bringing the issue to public notice, which nobody believed we could do. . . .

Ninety-five per cent of the people are being victimized—not 5 per cent, not 10 per cent, not just the poverty level.

I am paying more for products, I am paying more for services, I am paying more for my utilities—all as a result of inadequate regulation of our public bodies—than I ought to be paying.

If there is anything I have learned in the past year, it is that this discontent—this sense of being "had"—runs right through the American people. The sense of being dispossessed and separated from the decisions governing your own lives is not limited to the black, the poor and the young. It's the average American. It's even the upper-middle-class American. We want to clean up the courts because any average American who gets in there just gets driven crazy.

But there is hardly an issue where a malfunction of government occurs that doesn't hit the poor harder. You know, if it isn't working, the poor get it in the neck quicker. So just in the normal course of events, we're serving the poor. If the courts are clogged, the affluent can follow alternative routes. They can hire an expensive lawyer. . . .

The weight of officialdom lies much more heavily on the poor. First, there is the number of times they must deal with an official in the course of their lives. Second, there is the extent to which that official can control what they do. And, third, there is a lack of alternative routes and resources. . . .

I don't see where John (D.) Rockefeller (III) is going to benefit if and when the society goes down. Do you really believe he's going to benefit by the society disintegrating? And, you know, we didn't pick up 200,000 John Rockefellers.

There's a rather small percentage of any segment of the population or of any group that's committed to the public interest. Maybe 5 per cent. And I don't know that it varies with whatever group you're talking about.

Doctors? Most of them (are) not at all conscious of community needs. But a certain percentage of doctors are just absolutely clear that if the medical profession doesn't serve the community, it's in trouble. . . .

It's exactly the same with businessmen. Most businessmen are selfishly motivated, but there's a percentage that just naturally sees it another way. I think it's some- thing in their character and personal upbringing that makes them see the larger community. So I think the (Tom) Watsons and the Rockefellers are caught in that.

tax-deductible because Common Cause lobbies, but the organization itself is tax-exempt under section 501 (C)(4) of the Internal Revenue Code.

During its first 12 months, Common Cause raised $3,217,297, of which $2,442,832 was in dues and $774,465 was in contributions.

Gifts—Gardner originally planned to raise $500,000 in "start-up" capital that would be used until dues could begin to carry Common Cause expenses. As it turned out, by the time $250,000 was raised, the membership campaign had secured financial stability.

Most of the larger contributors were approached directly by Gardner. Many of them are men and women with whom Gardner has worked in his career as a foundation executive and with whom he worked later as chairman of the Urban Coalition and its Action Council.

In the first year, 5.6 per cent of the total income was raised through gifts of $1,000 or more. Only one contributor in this class serves on the Common Cause governing board. He is Andrew Heiskell, board chairman of Time Inc., and a long-time Gardner friend, who gave $10,000.

Common Cause soon will receive its first foundation grant—

COMMON CAUSE INNER CIRCLE

The following persons play major roles in shaping policy at Common Cause as members of John W. Gardner's staff:

Jack T. Conway, 53, became President of Common Cause in March, stepping into a newly created position. He is a Democrat.

Conway is a tough-minded administrator with broad experience both in government and in pressure groups that affect federal policy. Yet he shares with Gardner a deep idealistic streak.

During part of World War II, Conway worked at a General Motors plant in Melrose Park, Ill., and later in the war he served in the U.S. Merchant Marine. He bristles at any suggestion that Common Cause is an elitist organization.

In 1946, Conway became administrative assistant to the late Walter P. Reuther, then president of the United Auto Workers. He held the position until 1961 when he was named deputy administrator of the Housing and Home Finance Agency, which later became the HUD Department.

In 1963, he resigned to become executive director of the Industrial Union Department of the AFL-CIO, then a Reuther stronghold in the labor movement. He left for a year to serve as deputy director of the Office of Economic Opportunity.

In 1968, Conway resigned from the IUD and founded the Center for Community Change, a tax-exempt organization aimed at bolstering community groups composed of the poor. It is funded largely by the Ford Foundation.

Lowell R. Beck, 37, served as executive director of the Urban Coalition Action Council from its inception in 1968 and retains the same title in Common Cause. Beck said he strongly favored Conway's appointment over him and probably would have resigned had Conway not taken the job. Beck is a Republican.

From 1959 to 1968, Beck worked for the American Bar Association. He served as associate director of ABA's Washington office (primarily, a lobbying job on Capitol Hill) and as director of public service activities at the ABA headquarters in Chicago.

Tom Mathews, 50, is special assistant to Gardner for public relations. A veteran San Francisco newspaperman, Mathews helped organize the Peace Corps and became its first director of public information. In 1968, he ran the Washington press office for the Presidential campaign of Sen. Robert F. Kennedy (D-N.Y., 1965-68).

After Kennedy's death, Mathews worked in public relations in New York on such projects as the Lincoln Center for the Performing Arts. Gardner brought Mathews into the National Urban Coalition as his spokesman. Mathews followed Gardner to Common Cause.

David Cohen, 34, was named in July as director of field organization. He is well known and highly regarded on Capitol Hill as a former lobbyist for the Americans for Democratic Action and for the Industrial Union Department of the AFL-CIO. In 1968, Conway hired Cohen as associate director for field operations, where he continued his lobbying role. He remains a vice-chairman of ADA.

Robert E. Gallamore, 30, director of policy development, joined the National Urban Coalition in 1970 after working for the Bureau of the Budget and the Department of Transportation. He has a doctorate in economics and political science from Harvard.

John Lagomarcino, 35, director of legislation, was a lawyer in Arizona and Iowa until 1966, when he joined the Department of Health, Education, and Welfare to work in the Civil Rights Division of the general counsel's office. He was formerly deputy executive director of the Urban Coalition Action Council.

Robert Meier, 55, secretary-treasurer, served as an assistant to the HEW Secretary from 1962 to 1968 after previous service as a personnel officer and finance administrator in federal and local government.

Georgianna F. Rathbun, 50, edits the monthly *Report from Washington.* She was legislative editor of *Congressional Quarterly* for 15 years and joined the Urban Coalition Action Council in 1968.

$40,000 from the Stern Family Fund—which will be earmarked, under terms of the grant, for the voting rights campaign.

Dues—An initial test mailing in August 1970 placed some membership cards at $10 a year and some at $15. The $15 mailing, surprisingly, drew not only more money but more members as well. Consequently, dues were pegged at $15.

Carl Holman initially argued against the flat $15 rate.

Holman recalled: "I predicted that it would be relatively easy to get a lot of people to pay their $15, but that it was almost automatically going to cant the organization in such a direction that it would be very difficult for them to get some of the very people Gardner was most interested in—the black, the young, the poor."

In a recent interview, Gardner defended his decision to set dues at $15. "You know what the average dues are for the (National Welfare Rights Organization)?" he asked. "Thirteen bucks. You're not going to run a national organization on just nothing. Look at the unions. Look at dues generally."

Nevertheless, Meier reported that Common Cause is considering a reduced student rate. Currently, students and others who send less than $15 are still enrolled if they assert they cannot afford more. But this policy is not publicized.

Membership Drive: Of each $1 raised, Common Cause now plows back about 35 cents to seek new members.

About two thirds of all expenses in the membership hunt go into the direct-mail campaign. Since the initial test mailing a year ago, Common Cause has sent out 6.5 million direct solicitations. (The 6.5 million included what Meier called "an unfortunate number" of duplications.)

About 110,000 persons, or 1.7 per cent of the total mailing, responded by joining up—a rate that professional mailers regard as above average.

"It costs about $6.50 to sign up a new member," Meier said. "That's why we're so much looking forward to renewals, where the cost is at most $2."

Gardner's four-page "Dear Friend" solicitation letters, much of which he composes himself, are viewed as unorthodox by profesionals, who prefer shorter and punchier formulas in their direct-mail campaigns.

Guy Yoltan—The second of three direct-mail specialists who have been successively hired by Common Cause in its first year last July told *Advertising & Sales Promotion* that "Gardner has hit a responsive chord in one helluva lot of people, and all the professional dressing in the world would probably not have done any better."

For the most part, Common Cause buys its mailing lists from list brokers. But Common Cause will not sell its own list, although it will swap lists with other organizations when they are available.

After being widely criticized for one such swap with the Democratic National Committee last March, Common Cause instituted a policy of not exchanging lists with political parties or campaign groups.

Spending: The success of the direct-mail campaign, and of the companion advertising campaign, has enabled Common Cause to accumulate a cash reserve of about $400,000.

First year operations cost $2.8 million, of which $1.2 million was earmarked for the membership drive. Another $1.2 million was spent on "program operations" and $400,000 on such special projects as a half-hour television show on the war in Vietnam ($120,000), filmed by Guggenheim Productions Inc.; the successful attempt to put the 18-year-old vote through 38 state legislatures as a constitutional amendment; and the current voting rights project.

Of total expenses in the first year, about 21 per cent went for salaries; 25 per cent for lobbying activities; 25 per cent for mailings, including a handsomely printed monthly *Report From Washington;* 15 per cent for rent and office expenses; and 15 per cent for field organization.

After the wall-to-wall carpets and other furnishings in the Common Cause offices had been described in several articles, Tom Mathews, Gardner's public relations aide, became concerned. Subsequently, there has been an effort, in the words of one staff member, to "deposh the place." The current atmosphere is comfortable but somewhat informal.

Gardner has an expense account but draws no salary. Conway earns $45,000 a year. Four top professional staff members receive between $30,000 and $35,000, and most of the remaining professionals on the 60-member staff make about $20,000. The average staff salary is $10,000.

Common Cause is operating under a second-year budget of $3.8 million, an increase of 36 per cent over the first year. In the new budget, program operations have been doubled, to $2.5 million.

Another $1.3 million will be spent soliciting new members. Meier said the budget would work if membership rose to 250,000 over the year.

RELATIONSHIPS

The credibility of Common Cause as a bipartisan organization is one of the most sensitive issues facing the citizens lobby today.

Conway, a lifelong Democrat, said: "When I got into the boat, it rocked, there's no doubt about it. I was very conscious of this. That's one of the reasons why I didn't arrive with any particular splash."

GOP Attacks: A week after Conway arrived at Common Cause, *Monday,* the weekly house organ of the Republican National Committee, published an article entitled, "Just How Nonpartisan Is the 'Nonpartisan' Common Cause."

The article included a *Monday* poll of Common Cause's executive committee, which showed Democrats outnumbering Republicans 11-6. One director said she was an independent, and the remaining director was not reached.

Gardner was described in the article as "a nominal Republican (who) . . . has become a purveyor of the radical Democratic line on virtually every issue."

Democratic Consultant—In resuming the assault against Common Cause in May, *Monday* complained that Matt Reese and Associates, a Washington-based political consulting firm, had been hired by Common Cause to aid in its campaign for a U.S. withdrawal from Indochina by the end of 1971.

Reese is a former director of operations for the Democratic National Committee (1961-65). His firm received $19,867.11 to set up a telephone network for the antiwar campaign, according to records filed with the clerk of the House.

Dole Charges—Sen. Robert Dole, of Kansas, the Republican national chairman, on Feb. 24 labeled Gardner's criticism of President Nixon's Vietnam policies "political efforts to gain headlines" and called them "bitterly divisive."

Asked about the series of attacks on Gardner and Common Cause, a top-ranking GOP official said privately: "Things are strained with Mr. Gardner because while he alleges to support us in some areas, he has been less than kind in other areas, such as Vietnam, the national defense and SST. And, in the process, he has made some rather snide remarks about the President."

Response—Gardner has not sought a meeting with the President since Mr. Nixon took office; neither has the White House moved on its own initiative to invite Gardner over.

Nevertheless, in an interview, Gardner said that he has "far better relations with *parts* of the Administration than have ever come out. Referring to his "right-wing critics," Gardner said:

"It would hurt their case if they were honest and said that I work very closely with Elliot Richardson; that we collaborated intimately on Nixon's welfare-reform measures; that I've worked very closely with George Shultz on the Philadelphia Plan and that I was very helpful to him then, and that I testified more recently on federal reorganization and that he felt it was very helpful as well.

"They don't mention that I've worked very closely with Len Garment and Pete Peterson and that George Romney is an old friend and that I've worked with him."

(Elliot L. Richardson is Secretary of Health, Education and Welfare; George P. Shultz, director of the Office of Management and Budget, served previously as Secretary of Labor, where he supported the Philadelphia Plan as a means of hiring more minority group construction workers; Leonard Garment is a special consultant to the President; Peter G. Peterson is an assistant to the President (international economic af-

UNCOMMON NAMES

The following 22 prominent persons are among the 200,000 Americans who have joined Common Cause in its first year:

Gardner Ackley, professor of political economy, University of Michigan, Ann Arbor; U.S. Ambassador to Italy, 1968-69; member, Council of Economic Advisors, 1962-68, and its chairman, 1964-68.

Joseph A. Califano Jr., member, law firm of Williams, Connolly and Califano, Washington; special assistant to President Johnson, 1965-69

Ramsey Clark, member, law firm of Paul, Weiss, Goldberg, Rifkind, Wharton, and Garrison, New York; U.S. Attorney General, 1967-69

Thomas G. Corcoran, member, law firm of Corcoran, Foley, Youngman and Rowe, Washington; assistant to U.S. Attorney General, 1933-40

Lloyd N. Cutler, member, law firm of Wilmer, Cutler and Pickering, Washington; executive director, Commission on Causes and Prevention of Violence, 1968-69

S. I. Hayakawa, president, San Francisco State College, San Francisco

Barbara Laird, wife of Defense Secretary Melvin R. Laird, Washington

Sol M. Linowitz, chairman, National Urban Coalition, Washington; U.S. Ambassador to Organization of American States, 1966-69; chairman, Xerox Corp., 1966

Robert S. McNamara, president, World Bank, Washington; Secretary of Defense, 1961-67

David Packard, deputy secretary of defense, Washington

Gov. Nelson A. Rockefeller, R, of New York

John D. Rockefeller III, chairman, Rockefeller Foundation, New York

Gov. Francis W. Sargent, R, of Massachusetts

Gloria Steinem, journalist, member, policy council, National Women's Political Caucus, New York

Stewart L. Udall, board chairman, Overview Corp., Washington; Secretary of the Interior, 1961-69

Thomas J. Watson Jr., chairman, International Business Machines Corp., Armonk, N.Y.

Winthrop W. Aldrich, U.S. Ambassador to Great Britain, 1953-57; chairman, Chase Manhattan Bank, New York, 1934-53

Herbert Brownell, member, law firm of Lord, Day and Lord, New York; U.S. Attorney General, 1953-57

Henry Steele Commager, author, professor of history, Amherst College, Amherst, Mass.

Richard E. Neustadt, political scientist, John F. Kennedy School of Government, and director, Institute of Politics, Harvard University, Cambridge; consultant to President Kennedy, 1961-63

Jonas E. Salk, developer, poliomyelitis vaccine; director, Salk Institute for Biological Studies, San Diego

Jack J. Valenti, president, Motion Picture Association of America, Washington; special assistant to President Johnson, 1963-66

fairs); George W. Romney is Secretary of Housing and Urban Development.)

"These things just kind of get left out. But we feel it is essential that we not develop a habit of anti-Administration action. We want to work with any part of this Administration we can when they're go-

A FIRST-YEAR AGENDA ON CAPITOL HILL

In its first year of operation, Common Cause has focused its attention on the following issues:

Campaign Spending—Common Cause has lobbied on behalf of the campaign spending bill (S 382) that passed the Senate Aug. 5 by an 88-2 vote. It will make a major effort in the House to seek enactment of a companion reform bill.

Common Cause also filed suit Jan. 11 in the U.S. District Court for the District of Columbia to enjoin the Democratic, Republican and Conservative Parties from violating campaign contribution laws. The major purpose of the suit is to force political parties to observe the spirit of existing restrictions on campaign contributions and spending.

Lloyd N. Cutler, a partner in the Washington law firm of Wilmer, Cutler and Pickering, is acting as Common Cause's attorney in the suit.

Joseph A. Califano Jr., counsel to the Democratic National Committee, is serving as chief defense lawyer for the Democrats. Califano, a one-time special assistant to President Lyndon B. Johnson (1965-69), is a member of Com-

mon Cause.

On Aug. 23, Judge Barrington J. Parker denied motions to dismiss the suit, ruling that the court had jurisdiction to consider the case and that Common Cause held legal standing to bring the action.

Congressional Reform —When Congress convened in January, Common Cause mounted its first major campaign—directed against the seniority system which prevails in the House.

It also endorsed a Senate move to enable itself to choke off filibusters by liberalizing Rule XXII. The Senate move was unsuccessful.

The organization lobbied for automatic open votes in the selection of House committee chairmen; for the removal of three committee chairmen, Reps. William M. Colmer, D-Miss. (Rules); W. R. Poage, D-Tex. (Agriculture); and John L. McMillan, D-S.C. (District of Columbia); and for stripping seniority from the five members of the Mississippi delegation in the House.

None of these proposals were approved.

Equal Employment—Common Cause supports legislation to

grant the Equal Employment Opportunities Commission wider powers to curb job discrimination against minority groups and women.

A floor fight is expected in the House this month over a bill (HR 1746) to increase the EEOC's powers. The main point of contention deals with granting EEOC power to issue cease-and-desist orders.

Job Creation — Common Cause lobbied for legislation to establish a policy of public-service employment. A compromise bill was signed into law July 12 (85 Stat 146).

OEO Extension — Common Cause has testified on behalf of retention of the Office of Economic Opportunity and against efforts by the Administration to strip the antipoverty agency of some of its functions (HR 40 and S 397).

SST—Common Cause joined with conservation groups in the successful effort to end federal subsidies for a supersonic commercial transport (HR 8190).

The organization, acting independently of the Coalition Against the SST, focused on 80 "target" congressional districts and 17 "target" states for action by its membership. It claimed success in 49 districts and 11 states.

Tax Rules—Common Cause has joined in a legal challenge to the Treasury Department's proposed regulations that would liberalize depreciation rates.

In testifying at a departmental hearing, it argued that the new regulations would have the effect of granting tax write-offs of $3 billion to $5 billion to a segment of industry without congressional approval.

Vietnam War—The principal activity of Common Cause on Capitol Hill has been to generate support for a complete withdrawal of U.S. forces from Indochina by the end of 1971 (S 376 and HR 4100). It has concentrated its efforts in the House.

In the spring, Common Cause mounted a campaign to induce House Members to sign either of two "statements of purpose," pledging themselves to strive for withdrawal from Vietnam by the end of the year. A Republican version, circulated by Rep. Charles A. Mosher, Ohio, received 21 signatures by June 16, and a Democratic statement, circulated by Rep. Thomas P. O'Neill Jr., Mass., received 121 signatures by the same date.

On June 17, the House rejected, on a recorded teller vote of 158-254, an amendment by Reps. Lucien N. Nedzi, D-Mich., and Charles W. Whalen Jr., R-Ohio, to bar use of any funds authorized by the fiscal 1972 military procurement bill (HR 8687) for use in Indochina after Dec. 31, 1971, or some other date during fiscal 1972 that the President might recommend.

Only 23 Republicans supported the amendment. But Fred M. Wertheimer, currently the chief Common Cause lobbyist against the war, said that "very significant advances did take place ... among more conservative members of both parties."

Wertheimer's main assignment when Congress resumes work Sept. 8 will be an effort in behalf of the Mansfield antiwar amendment to the selective service bill (HR 6531).

Voting Rights — Common Cause lobbied for congressional approval and ratification by state legislatures of the 26th Amendment, which permits persons between 18 and 21 to vote in all elections.

Welfare Reform—The welfare reform bill (HR 1) that passed the House June 22 was backed by Common Cause. The group's chairman, John W. Gardner, worked with HEW Secretary Elliot L. Richardson on the measure.

Common Cause will seek two changes in the Senate. One would prevent states from paying less to welfare recipients than they now pay. The other would provide larger benefits.

ing in our direction. ... The distances have arisen because there are some policies we just can't accept."

Lowell Beck, who is also a Republican, raised the same theme. He said: "We certainly are not anti-Nixon. But the Administration makes it awfully difficult for us. For one thing, you never know whom to deal with in the Administration. ... And you never know where the next holdup is going to be."

Objectives—Conway is determined to preserve as much of a bipartisan image as possible. As he puts it: "I've tried in everything that I've done here to either maintain a bipartisan balance where it existed or to achieve one where it hasn't. This is a conscious policy. And any structures that we build in the congressional districts and the states, the same thing holds true."

During Gardner's recent trips outside Washington, the small advance team that goes in ahead of his visits has made appointments for him with leading Democratic and Republican figures in the state.

But the credibility problem remains unsettled—even within the Common Cause staff. One staff member, Pamela Curtis, a former aide to Mrs. Peterson at the Republican National Committee, said: "Some of their attacks are justified. If you are setting up to be bipartisan, you have to really do it. There are a lot of people here who have very strong Democratic credentials."

White House: The Nixon staff does not berate Common Cause quite as sharply as Dole and his aides do. However, within the White House, Common Cause is widely regarded as a hostile force.

One aide to the President, who asked not to be quoted by name, said: "They are going to find it very difficult to maintain that nonpartisan image because they have nearly always come down against us.

"Would it have been that difficult for them to pick an issue on

Common Cause: Organization, Money and Impact

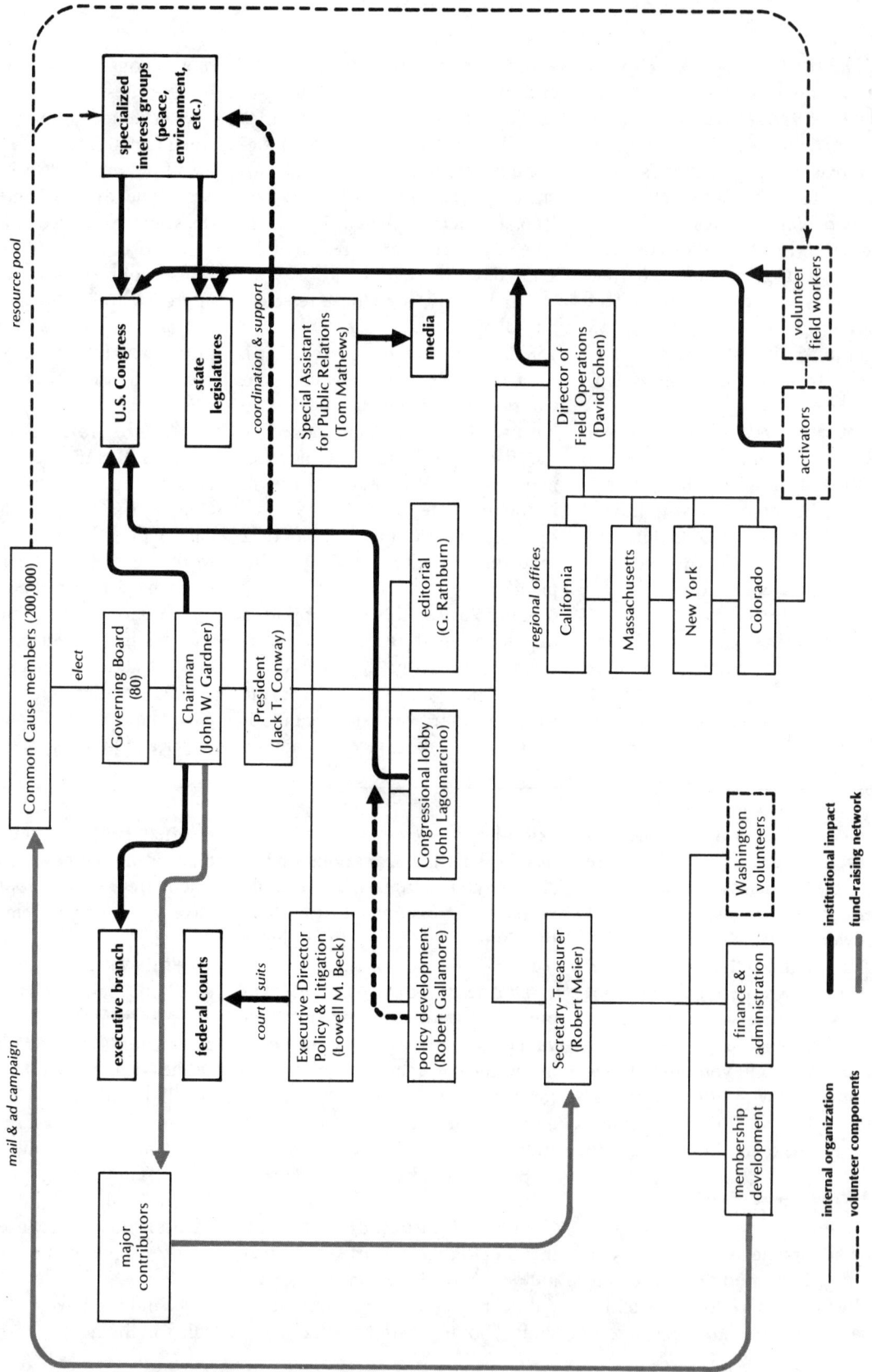

Figure labels:

- specialized interest groups (peace, environment, etc.)
- resource pool
- U.S. Congress
- state legislatures
- coordination & support
- Special Assistant for Public Relations (Tom Mathews)
- media
- Director of Field Operations (David Cohen)
- volunteer field workers
- activators
- Common Cause members (200,000)
- elect
- Governing Board (80)
- Chairman (John W. Gardner)
- President (Jack T. Conway)
- editorial (G. Rathburn)
- Congressional lobby (John Lagomarcino)
- regional offices: California, Massachusetts, New York, Colorado
- mail & ad campaign
- executive branch
- federal courts
- court suits
- Executive Director Policy & Litigation (Lowell M. Beck)
- policy development (Robert Gallamore)
- Secretary-Treasurer (Robert Meier)
- Washington volunteers
- finance & administration
- membership development
- major contributors
- institutional impact
- fund-raising network
- internal organization
- volunteer components

which they could have supported us? For instance, what about revenue sharing? They are no factor there whatsoever. But I suppose it would have cost them something to go in heavily. It would cost them with the powers in their left-of-center group."

Another White House aide grudgingly gave Common Cause high marks for the way in which the lobby organized on the antiwar issue in the House. The aide, who asked not to be quoted by name, said:

"They employed some tactics that were interesting from a lobbying standpoint. And because they were new, they weren't easily detected by House Members and their staffs.

"You have to remember that contact on the district level is new for most of these guys. They are dealing in the field with third- and fourth-level congressional assistants who, whenever they get a dozen calls a day on the same subject, are apt to put in a panic call to Washington.

"By the time it reaches the Hill office, it gets to be 50 calls instead of 12. By the time it gets to the Congressman, it's even more. And the next thing you knov, he's walking around the House floor telling everybody that he's had 100 calls.

"On the war issue, they were probably responsible for turning 20 to 25 House votes—or at least partly responsible. On SST, they may have been a marginal factor in what was, after all, an awfully close vote. On welfare reform, they have been very ineffectual and only half-heartedly into it."

Democrats: Ties between Democratic Party officials in Washington and Common Cause, while not close, are far less hostile than with their Republican counterparts.

"I think quite a lot of people around here are members of Common Cause," a top aide at the Democratic National Committee said. "I think there's a feeling around here that so far they haven't done anything particularly. But they are obviously into an important political strain that affects the two parties."

The official also said that the party's current efforts at internal reform reflect in part pressures raised by Common Cause. Regarding legislation, he said: "At least 90 per cent of the time when they are active on Capitol Hill, they are working for things that we would be for also."

Congress: Of the nine Senators who belong to Common Cause, only two are Republicans: Jacob K. Javits, N.Y., and Charles H. Percy, Ill.

The Democratic members are Sens. Birch Bayh, Ind., Lawton Chiles, Fla., Edward Kennedy, Mass., Edmund S. Muskie, Maine, Claiborne Pell, R.I., Adlai E. Stevenson III, Ill., and John V. Tunney, Calif.

There are also 24 House Members who belong to Common Cause, 19 Democrats and five Republicans.

Although Common Cause has concentrated its efforts on the House in its first year of operation, it has not established effective links with either House Speaker Carl Albert, Okla., or Majority Leader Hale Boggs, La.

(The No. 3 man in the House Democratic hierarchy, Rep. Tho-mas P. O'Neill Jr., Mass., was the chief Democratic sponsor of an antiwar "statement of purpose" pushed last spring by Common Cause.)

Gary G. Hymel, administrative assistant to Boggs, said:

"I remember during the 18-year-old vote—that's the first one they cooked up—some girl kept calling here and asking if she could write a speech. He (Boggs) was for it anyhow. Of course we didn't use it.

"They didn't work on it with the leadership. They seem to be working from underneath rather than from the top. We never have contacted them to get mobilized to help us as we do with labor or with the NAACP."

Lobbyists: Common Cause strives to work in tandem with specialized lobbying groups whenever their interests coincide.

"I'm glad they're here," said Marvin Caplan, legislative representative for the industrial union department of the AFL-CIO. "Often, our objectives differ from theirs. But, at times, they are quite complementary."

The alliances forged by Common Cause are sometimes unplanned. Thus, on the SST battle, Common Cause intervened only after the Washington office received a tide of mail and telephone calls urging action against the appropriation.

Beck reported: "At that point, Friends of the Earth came to see us. We asked how we could be most helpful. We took their list of Congressmen and made calls."

On the antiwar issue, Common Cause took a different tack. It opened an office near the Capitol

98

"WHAT . . . IS THAT GUY DOING?"

A Democratic Party official eased back in his chair, chuckled quietly and said: "John Gardner is a Republican. But he has the Arthur Goldberg view of politics, which is that they should be elected to high office by acclamation. Unfortunately, it never works that way."

A half-mile away, and a day later, Gardner, in shirtsleeves, leaned forward on the edge of his chair and replied to the allegation that he is seeking to build in Common Cause a base to run for the Presidency—or perhaps a base to run someone else.

"It's easier to believe that I have no political ambitions if you understand the potential of what I'm doing here," he said. "If you don't understand that, then it's a mystery. What in Heaven's name is that guy doing, they must be asking themselves. . . .

"But if you take my point of view, I believe we are at something much deeper and much more fundamental than anything that could possibly happen in the 1972 Presidential elections."

Criticism—Gardner has come under attack from both ends of the political spectrum.

An unsigned article in the July 10 issue of *Human Events* said: "Gardner's Common Cause has a sweetheart contract with corporate liberalism—and the diminution of establishment power can never take place so long as the establishment's 'house rebel' is leading the rebellion."

An Oct. 20, 1969, column by Nicholas von Hoffman in the *Washington Post* begins: "People say, 'Don't write anything bad about John Gardner. He's on our side. Leave him alone and stick to attacking the baddies.'" Nonetheless, von Hoffman concludes that Gardner is "a scared man in a world incomprehensibly falling away from him and his social order."

Career—John William Gardner, 59, was born in Los Angeles. He earned his bachelor's and master's degrees at Stanford University and a doctorate in psychology at the University of California. Before World War II, Gardner came East to teach at the Connecticut College for Women and then at Mount Holyoke College.

In 1943, Gardner joined the Marines. He served in Washington, Italy and Austria as an officer in the Office of Strategic Services—the forerunner of the Central Intelligence Agency.

In 1946, Gardner joined the Carnegie Corporation, a philanthropic foundation established by steelmaker Andrew Carnegie. He became its president in 1955.

President Johnson named Gardner Secretary of Health, Education and Welfare in July 1965. He served for 32 months (*Human Events* described him as the "Good German" in the Johnson Cabinet) until a dispute over HEW funding caused him to resign.

Gardner became chairman of the National Urban Coalition. The coalition was formed in response to the black urban riots of the 1960s and was largely funded at the national level by the Ford Foundation. The concept called for bringing together leaders in business, government, labor and the minority community to seek social and economic reforms.

But Gardner found the coalition a limited tool. Seeking to circumvent the federal income tax laws, which bar the coalition from lobbying, Gardner formed the Urban Coalition Action Council, which lobbied, among other things, against the confirmation of G. Harrold Carswell to the Supreme Court and for minority hiring quotas in government construction contracts.

In August 1970, Gardner converted the action council into Common Cause. The key change was his bid for a membership base—and the potential of broad financing that the new base represented.

Several business leaders on the Action Council declined to go along. Among those who resigned from the reconstituted board were James M. Roche, chairman of General Motors Corp.; H. I. Romnes, chairman of American Telephone & Telegraph Co.; David Rockefeller, chairman of the Chase Manhattan Bank; Ben W. Heineman, president of Northwest Industries Inc., parent company of the Chicago and North Western Railway Co.; and Edgar F. Kaiser, chairman of Kaiser Industries Corp.

George Meany, president of the AFL-CIO, who had opposed

Gardner's stand on minority hiring in construction, and Richard J. Daley, mayor of Chicago, also left. But such stalwart supporters as John V. Lindsay, mayor of New York, remained on Gardner's board.

Income—Gardner now earns about $50,000 a year, with speaking fees and royalties accounting for half the total. Harper & Row published *Excellence* (1961), *Self-Renewal,* (1964), and *No Easy Victories* (1970). W. W. Norton published *The Recovery of Confidence* (1970).

Gardner said about a third of his income comes from consulting fees, "now chiefly" from Carnegie and the Mellon Foundation. He plans to resign at the end of the year as a director of American Airlines and Time Inc.

Assessment—"I don't think anybody is a close friend of John Gardner," said David M. Thompson, secretary-treasurer of the National Urban Coalition. "In many ways, he's very aloof. But in other ways, he can be quite warm. I visited 375 corporations last year, mostly at the chief executive officer level. In practically every case, the first question was: 'How is John?' They spoke eloquently many times about how much they admire the man. They spoke of how much they disagreed with him in terms of his position but they ended up by saying, 'Thank God, we've got a John Gardner in this society.'"

Thompson said Gardner's ability as an administrator "is probably the most common concern people have." But he called Gardner "probably the most intelligent man I've ever dealt with."

A foundation official who has known Gardner for many years took a more restrained view.

"He's a complex man, difficult to explain," the official said. "There are those who admire him as a man of the Second Coming. But there are others who, without contesting his charisma, remain concerned about what he really accomplishes."

---

that ultimately served as a base for some 100 peace groups during the height of the campaign that followed the U.S. military intervention in Laos.

"That's where we put our chips," Beck recalled. "We gave the peace groups a logistical base to work with. But we did not attempt to manage the peace movement. That would have been absolute folly."

Not all relationships with similiar-minded lobbies are as smooth as Common Cause would like them to be. For example, Gardner is aware of private criticism by Ralph Nader that Gardner has "pulled his punches" and declined to make an all-out effort on such issues as the protection of the environment and unfair dealings by industry to consumers. Gardner rejects the charge and, in effect, turns the other cheek.

As he put it in a recent interview: "I think what we're at is so big that we're not only going to need all the organizations we have, we're going to need a lot more. . . .

"Look at the thing on environment. We're immensely interested in environment. But how much are we going to be able to do on environment when we're working on the war, on campaign spending and on a lot of other things?

"It is tragic that the environment groups fight each other. The fact that they exist means that when we go on an SST issue we're working with a lot of allies. They know the subject better than we do. And we take their orders."

Money: Until Common Cause came on the Washington scene, most of the effective lobbying that was done on Capitol Hill was related—implicitly or directly—to the promise of future campaign contributions (or the threat of withholding contributions).

Gardner is seeking to prove that a general-purpose lobbying organization can be effective without at the same time providing a direct financial payoff at election time.

Common Cause has stirred the animosity and jealousy of other lobbying groups with similar interests.

The main reason for the resentment is that Common Cause, to keep growing, has had to show results to members and prospective members. And, in publicizing its accomplishments, Common Cause often has neglected to acknowledge that its lobbying role on such issues as the SST and campaign spending was either peripheral or late in coming.

APPROACH

After a year of rapid growth, Common Cause has found its own individual style as a citizens' movement.

The Common Cause agenda has been well refined. It calls for waging limited warfare on selected battlefields—both in Washington and, where the targets are tempting, throughout the country. Gardner is comfortable with this approach and, so far as anyone can tell, so is his constituency.

"We aren't going to be effective if we take only the problems of the blacks and minorities," said Lowell Beck, executive director of Common Cause.

Target Areas: "We have to keep our target areas small. The main issues will continue to be the war, opening up the system and making it honest, and tax reform. The 'B' issues will be health, environment and no-fault insurance. But we will not speak out on everything. We have been silent, for example, on education and housing."

The continued silence of Common Cause on some issues and the familiar, easy relationship between John Gardner and his movement and the upper-middle class have led to a polarization with more radical forces in the society.

"They are just not prepared to lead a broader constituency," said a former consultant to Common Cause, who asked that his name not be used. "They could have transformed Common Cause into an antiwar organization. It might have ended the war, but it would have hurt the organization. It would have been an interesting tradeoff."

Militants **—** Black militants have been equally put off by Common Cause.

While Gardner was forging his new lobby, he attended several meetings in New York, arranged by Carl Holman, with black leaders. Gardner's main purpose was to discuss why Common Cause would make a fight on the seniority issue in the House.

But the blacks thought the main purpose should be to tell Gardner how he could make his lobby more relevant to them and the poor inner-city blacks whom they sought to represent.

Tom Mathews, Gardner's press aide, recalled that "Gardner argued it verv forcibly and argued it against the kind of put-down that you get from angry, intelligent, minority members. It was a reverse kind of education; it was *they* who were being educated by Gardner."

There was no follow-through with the black leadership. But, Mathews said, "We didn't want their follow-through. We just wanted them to think about what this meant to them."

Later in the year, Gardner set up a private meeting between HEW Secretary Richardson and leaders of welfare groups throughout the country to discuss the pending welfare reform legislation—the Administration's family assistance plan.

But George A. Wiley, executive director of the National Welfare Rights Organization, insisted that a large group of welfare mothers, whom he had called to Washington at the same time, also be allowed to attend the meeting with Richardson.

Again, Mathews recalled what happened:

"We offered them up to a dozen slots. Wiley said no dice. The meeting was then canceled (by Richardson and Gardner).

"Wiley was both angry and chagrined because what happened was that he blew the meeting.

"But we took the blame; we didn't lay it on him.

"If you are on their side of the fence, it is timidity or sellout or worse. But you can't be all things to all people and our credibility is better maintained by common sense and restraint than it is by going down some side street with a wild ally."

In working to reform the system, there has never been any question as to what side of the fence Common Cause is on.

3 THE CONGRESS

Congress is a focal point in the ongoing struggle over the future of America. Ultimately all who would influence American public policy—both foreign and domestic—must confront the Congress. Even Presidents have found that the success of their policies depends heavily on congressional support, support that has not always been forthcoming. Congress is an autonomous power center in the American political system. It is influenced by the President and by other forces in American life, but at the same time it is separate from other governing institutions.

One of the bases of congressional autonomy aside from constitutional guarantees, is its membership stability. In both the House and Senate, over 80 per cent of the incumbents normally win reelection—irrespective of the electoral trends nationally or at the state level. This membership continuity is in sharp contrast with the turnover of personnel which characterizes the Presidency and executive agencies. Chairman Wilbur Mills (D-Ark.) of the House Ways and Means Committee, for example, has worked with four different Presidents during his tenure as a committee chairman.

The Congress is a stable and highly institutionalized organization with a finely developed system of rules, procedures, and customs. It represents a peculiar blend of decentralized and hierarchical power. The two articles in this section illuminate the impact of the distribution of power on policy-making in Congress by focusing on two of its most important institutions, the political party organizations and the standing committees.

The standing committee system provides for a division of labor among the membership. It also fragments power by creating semi-independent centers of authority in both chambers. Each committee exercises extensive control over policy within its particular jurisdiction. But while the committee system fragments power, another institution cuts across the lines of committee jurisdiction in an inclusive manner that seeks to centralize power. This institution is the congressional party. The respective Democratic and Republican parties seek to coordinate policy among their diverse members and among the standing committees.

However, as is illustrated in the study of Senator Mike Mansfield (D-Mont.) the Senate Majority Leader, political parties are weak agents of centralization. Yet how they operate and how they are led have a profound effect on policy. No two legislative leaders adopt exactly the same leadership style or role. For example, Mansfield's predecessor, Lyndon B. Johnson was an aggressive man always seeking additional levers of power. Through intense efforts to be both politically and substantively the best informed member of the Senate, and because of unusual skills in bargaining and coalition building, Johnson played a dominant role in Senate policy-making. His influence on the Senate was enhanced by the fact that he served as majority leader while the Republican Party under Dwight D. Eisenhower controlled the Presidency. Johnson was therefore in a position to be highly flexible in the strategies he followed because he was free of any partisan responsibility for steering the President's program through the Senate. In addition, Eisenhower did not play an active role in congressional leadership. Mansfield, by contrast, has served during the administrations of more activist Presidents—Kennedy, Johnson, and Nixon. During his first five years in the leadership post, a fellow Democrat occupied the Presidency and Mansfield therefore had responsibility for helping Democratic Presidents enact their legislative programs. His personality is the antithesis of Johnson's and he has not sought to put his brand on the Senate. In addition, he has also been confronted with activist members of his own party who had become restive under Johnson's firm rein. The result is a pattern of Senate operation which gives maximum leeway to individual Senators and greater importance to instruments of collective party policy-making—the Democratic Conference and the Policy Committee.

The second study in this section focuses on two of the most important money committees in Congress: the Ways and Means Committee in the House and the Finance Committee in the Senate. Each illustrates the extent to which congressional decision-making on critical issues can be concentrated in the committees of Congress. Analysis of the two committees also indicates the wide range of behavior patterns exhibited by various committees, as well as the divergent leadership styles of committee chairmen. It should be remembered that these are not ordinary committees. Ways and Means and Finance are among the most sought after assignments in the Congress; their jurisdictions are more politically sensitive than those of most committees; the membership has more seniority and experience than most; and unlike other committees neither utilizes sub-committees.

The Ways and Means—Finance Committees study also provides insights into the differences between the House of Representatives and the Senate. Members of the House are more likely to become subject matter specialists than are Senators who have at least two committee assignments and normally more diverse and demanding constituencies. The success of House Ways and Means Committee in achieving its policy objectives over those of the Senate Finance Committee however, is indicative of the importance of the House of Representatives in spite of the fact that its activities and membership attract relatively slight press attention.

As both of the articles in this section illustrate, understanding American policy-making requires a good working knowledge of the complex congressional procedures. It is an institution whose leadership is fragmented among a series of strong standing committees (such as Ways and Means and Finance), which at the same time achieves a degree of policy coordination through the actions of its political party organizations and their leaders.

Mansfield reforms spark 'quiet revolution' in Senate
Andrew J. Glass

After a decade in office, Senate Majority Leader Mike Mansfield, D-Mont., is presiding over what he calls "a quiet revolution in the Senate."

The Mansfield initiative has two basic aims:

to respond to pressure from a new generation of Democrats seeking a larger voice in legislative affairs;

to provide Senate Democrats with forums to voice their collective views on important national issues.

Mansfield is trying to spearhead the reform drive without appearing to threaten the interests of the Senate establishment.

He is trying to get the Democrats to speak out on issues without sparking direct confrontations with President Nixon.

Leader's Role: While pursuing these objectives, Mansfield remains faithful to his long-held concept that the Majority Leader's office should serve as a unifying force for Senate Democrats.

"One reason I'm Leader is maybe I can keep the party together and prevent us from breaking up into argumentative fragments," Mansfield said in a recent interview with *National Journal*.

A prime goal of the multi-faceted reform drive is to allow Senate operations, which were bogged down by a series of filibusters in the 91st Congress, to function more smoothly.

But Mansfield recoils from any suggestion that new-found efficiency will swing the Senate back to the kind of tight-fisted control that marked the reign of Sen. Lyndon B. Johnson, D-Tex., as Majority Leader, which began in 1955 and lasted until 1961, when Johnson became Vice President.

One of Mansfield's closest associates, who asked not to be identified by name, in analyzing Mansfield's approach to the Senate, said:

"You don't organize chaos. You can't get it to operate in unison. The Senate is made up of strong individuals. If it is tearing itself apart on an issue, it is operating as it should be: 100 minds examining the issues of the day. To seek organizational solutions is to fail to recognize the Senate's basic function.

"It is in this context that Mansfield views his job. It is in this context that he tries to give them a hook; to structure the debate."

Mansfield's prime instruments for involving Senate Democrats in national issues are the Senate Democratic Policy Committee, an executive steering group, and the Senate Democratic Conference, to which all Democrats belong.

Indochina: At a policy committee luncheon Feb. 22, 1971, Mansfield presented a wide-ranging resolution that outlined party goals for the 92nd Congress.

It dealt in general terms with inflation, revenue sharing, government efficiency and law enforcement.

The sole detailed and controversial clause focused on the Indochina war, an involvement which Mansfield has opposed since the first U.S. troops were sent in.

In its final form, the resolution called for an "end to the involvement . . . and . . . the withdrawal of all U.S. forces and the release of all prisoners in a time certain."

The policy committee voted 6-1 in favor of the resolution, with Sen. Robert C. Byrd, D-W. Va., objecting to the words "a time certain." (Although the "time" is not specified, Mansfield noted that the resolution was for the life of the 92nd Congress, implying a deadline of January 1973, when the present Congress expires.)

One participant in the policy committee session, who asked not to be quoted by name, said:

"The issue before us was, shall we put in the language 'time certain', without which we could have gotten unanimity. And the policy committee decided, we're going to lead the group and take a few losses if we have to. Anyway, having a few losses on an issue like this gives greater impact to what we've done."

On Feb. 23, after a three-hour debate behind closed doors, the conference voted, 37-13, for the Indochina clause, with two more Senators announced in favor except for the words "time certain." (On this occasion, Byrd reversed himself and voted with the majority.)

It was the first time in conference history that a leadership initiative split party ranks. But the policy committee source said: "If something had come out of that caucus with John Stennis and 'Scoop' Jackson in favor of it, it wouldn't mean anything."

(Sen. John C. Stennis, D-Miss., is chairman and Sen. Henry M. Jackson, D-Wash., is a member of the Senate Armed Services Committee. After the conference ended, Jackson told reporters that the Indochina resolution amounted to yet another congressional attempt to impose a deadline for troop withdrawal.)

White House: But Mansfield contended that Stennis, Jackson and the other Senators who had spoken out against the resolution failed to recognize an essential element: that he intended it to be "helpful to the President." Mansfield said the resolution meant, in effect, "If you take moves to get out, you're not going to be hurt by partisan criticism."

Mansfield has never been known to attack a President directly, although he has differed sharply on such policy issues as Indochina and NATO troop commitments with both the Johnson and Nixon Administrations.

Over the years one of Mansfield's favorite phrases, in referring to any President, has been: "He's doing the best job he can."

Mansfield's attitude is one reason why the current relationship between the Nixon White House and the Senate Majority Leader is a good deal warmer than is generally known. (Mansfield was stung in April 1970 by the President's failure to inform him of his plans to invade Cambodia; the incident led the White House to reform its information policies before the U.S.-assisted invasion of Laos in February 1971.)

A White House source told *National Journal* that Mansfield is "a frequent visitor" to the White House. Most often, the source said, "the President and the Majority Leader meet over breakfast without anyone else being there." Mansfield also meets frequently with the Nixon congressional liaison staff.

The Nixon staff is well aware that Mansfield's leadership poses an unusual challenge for a Republican President. For his part, Mansfield continues to call on the Senate Democrats to function "as a responsible Senate majority."

As Mansfield put it in a meeting of the Democratic Conference Jan. 20, 1970: "It is our highest obligation; it must take precedence over political concerns."

REFORMS

The reforms adopted by the Senate Democrats at the start of the 92nd Congress elicited no open opposition—a fact one veteran Senator privately ascribed to "Mansfield's uncanny ability to take really precedent-smashing moves without appearing in the least to threaten entrenched interests."

Yet another observer, Sen. Philip A. Hart, Mich., told *National Journal:* "We've shifted our way of doing things in a bloodless coup, and outsiders have hardly noticed.

"If he (Mansfield) had tried something like this eight years ago—or even five years ago—he would have had a full-fledged revolt on his hands. Even at that, I wouldn't make book that it would have happened under other leadership."

Harris Initiative: Much of the impetus for the changes that have occurred this year came from Sen. Fred R. Harris, Okla., a past chairman (1969-70) of the Democratic National Committee.

In the waning days of the 91st Congress, Harris sent Mansfield a detailed memorandum spelling out his ideas for reform. He also circulated the memo to other Democrats and, on Dec. 3, 1970, he put it into the *Congressional Record.*

In the published version, Harris stressed that "this effort in no way intends to be critical of the Senate leadership—and certainly not of Sen. Mansfield—but of the system itself and of the outdated and archaic rules and procedures."

Among Harris' suggestions:

Senate Democrats should confer as a body once a week or, at the very least, once a month, and these meetings should be public.

The Democratic Conference should have the power to pass judgment upon individual committee assignments voted by the 17-member Democratic Steering Committee, whose sole function is to serve as a committee on committees.

The Democratic Conference should empanel a special committee on reforming the seniority system and on party loyalty, with the view of creating prospective guidelines on loyalty.

Harris later broadened his Senate reform campaign by staging informal hearings Jan. 18-19 (jointly with Sen. Charles McC. Mathias Jr., R-Md.), during which he termed the seniority system "an archaic and undemocratic method of running the Senate and Senate committees.

Mansfield Response: In his public statements and in a Feb. 10, 1971 speech to the conference, Mansfield took the view that such zeal was unwarranted.

Thus, Mansfield told reporters: "The whole issue of seniority is one which in my judgment has been greatly exaggerated . . . . With it, as with just about every rule, practice and procedure, the Senate has not been bound or restricted to any measurable extent. . . . Most of the machinery of the Senate is in good working order."

Against this backdrop, Mansfield:

agreed to convene the Democratic Conference whenever any of its 55 members requested a meeting;

established the precedent that the conference may nullify by majority secret ballot any committee assignment, in particular retaining the power to name committee chairmen;

formed a special three-man committee, headed by Harris, to study both seniority and party loyalty.

Conference Sessions —
In 1959, Sen. William Proxmire, Wis., publicly called for "regular caucuses (of all Democrats) with specific agendas (to consider) our legislative program."

When the Democrats convened for the second session of the 86th Congress, on Jan. 7, 1960, Proxmire moved to hold a meeting every two weeks or whenever 15 Democrats requested one. But the motion was withdrawn when the Senator at whom it had been directed, Lyndon Johnson, pledged to call a meeting at the request of

Fred R. Harris

any Democrat.

Prompted by Proxmire and other Senate reformers, Mansfield held more meetings in the early 1960s than had his predecessor, Johnson. But attendance was poor at these sessions. They became less frequent, until the Democrats, once having organized themselves for the new session, met only on rare occasions. It was at this point that Harris raised the issue anew.

Committee Chairmen —
Mansfield had a lesser precedent to work with when he conferred far-reaching powers on the conference to remove committee chairmen.

Senate Democrats have only twice denied a chairmanship to the member who had served longest on the committee: In 1859, they removed Sen. (1847-61) Stephen A. Douglas, Ill., from the now-extinct Territories Committee because of his anti-slavery views; in 1913, they denied one-eyed Sen. (1895-1918) Benjamin R. Tilman, S.C., chairmanship of the Appropriations Committee because of

his advanced age (66) and poor health.

It is Mansfield's position that the conference "is empowered to decide all questions of committee membership, including chairmen, ratios, distribution and the basis on which assignments are made."

According to one participant at the Jan. 26, 1971, conference, "Mansfield did not read the names of the committee chairmen as an announcement, which had always previously been the case. Instead, he read them as a proposal, subject to ratification, and leaving room for objection. Of course, there was none."

The Majority Leader also listed committee assignments, including the Senators (both newly elected and transferees) with fresh assignments from the Steering Committee. "If there had been a request for a roll call, it would have been granted," he later told *National Journal.*

However, in announcing the revised procedure to the press at the time, Mansfield chose to stress continuity rather than change.

"The conference procedures," he said, "accommodate adequately any individual challenge to a given recommendation for a chairman or a committee assignment. The fact that there was no challenge this year does not render these procedures any less effective."

Although Harris did not raise the point, the conference, at Mansfield's behest, approved a policy that Democrats will be allowed to serve as "ranking" members of only one committee in the event that the Democrats become the minority party.

This conforms with a change

106 enacted by the Republicans this year.

Floor Action—Mansfield also joined Harris in co-sponsoring a resolution (S Res 17) that revises Senate Rule XXIV to require the Senate to elect, one by one, the chairman and the ranking minority member of each committee.

Another section of the resolution formally recognizes for the first time the existence of the Democratic and Republican Conferences as executive bodies within the Senate structure. It charges them with the responsibility of nominating chairmen and ranking minority members.

The Harris-Mansfield resolution (Mathias is leading the fight on the Republican side) is currently before the Subcommittee on Standing Rules of the Senate, a unit of the Senate Rules and Administration Committee headed by Majority Whip Byrd.

After Byrd held an open hearing on the plan Feb. 12, 1971, the full committee voted Feb. 26 to report the resolution to the Senate "unfavorably." The report said that the "abolition of the seniority practice might promote unseemly struggles for the election of chairmen ... whereby lobbyists, pressure groups and even the White House could influence the election of their favorites."

Special Panel—Along with Harris, Mansfield named Sens. Herman E. Talmadge, D-Ga., and Hubert H. Humphrey, D-Minn., to the special study group.

In addition to reviewing the seniority issue, the panel will:

consider and make recommendations to the conference on the credentials of Senators who run on other than the Democratic ticket and then seek to join the conference;

study assignment procedures for conference committees with the House conferees to ensure fair representation.

In creating the study panel, Mansfield ensured that an attempt would not be made in the conference to take action against Sen. Harry F. Byrd, Ind.-Va., who ran in 1970 as an independent but voted with the Democrats to organize the Senate on opening day, or against Sen. John C. Stennis, D-Miss., who ran (with nominal opposition) on a party slate that had

---

SENATE MAJORITY LEADERSHIP

The Democratic leadership in the Senate for the 92nd Congress is composed of:

Mike Mansfield, Mont., Majority Leader, chairman of the conference, chairman of the policy committee, chairman of the steering committee.

Allen J. Ellender, La., President Pro Tempore of the Senate.

Robert C. Byrd, W. Va., Majority Whip.

Frank E. Moss, Utah, secretary of the Democratic Conference.

The Senate Democratic Policy Committee: This group formulates policy for the party, and is composed of the four Senators in the leadership, members of the Legislative Review Committee and, in order of seniority:

Warren G. Magnuson, Wash.	J. W. Fulbright, Ark.
John O. Pastore, R.I.	Philip A. Hart, Mich.
Stuart Symington, Mo.	Herman E. Talmadge, Ga.

The Democratic Legislative Review Committee: It participates fully in all of the policy committee's deliberations. Its members are:

Edmund S. Muskie, Maine (chairman)	Ernest F. Hollings, S.C.
	Harold E. Hughes, Iowa
Daniel K. Inouye, Hawaii	

The Senate Democratic Steering Committee: This panel serves as a committee on committee appointments and transfers. Its members are composed of Mansfield, Byrd and Moss, who sit ex officio, and, in order of seniority:

Allen Bible, Nev.	Vance Hartke, Ind.
Allen J. Ellender, La.	John Sparkman, Ala.
John L. McClellan, Ark.	Henry M. Jackson, Wash.
Harrison A. Williams Jr., N.J.	Quentin N. Burdick, N.D.
Clinton P. Anderson, N.M.	William B. Spong Jr., Va.
Stuart Symington, Mo.	Edward M. Kennedy, Mass.
William Proxmire, Wis.	Lawton Chiles, Fla.

MAJORITY LEADER MIKE MANSFIELD: 'THERE IS NO MEANNESS IN HIM'

In January 1966, Senate Majority Leader Mike Mansfield, D-Mont., was summoned to the White House for one of the bipartisan advice-seeking sessions favored by former President Lyndon B. Johnson on the eve of major policy decisions.

When it came Mansfield's turn to speak, he unfolded a three-page typewritten statement drafted in the dry style of a college professor—which he once was. He argued in the statement that air raids over North Vietnam, which had been suspended for a month-long "peace offensive," should not be resumed.

Some days after the White House meeting, Mansfield watched on television in his Capitol office, S-210, as Mr. Johnson announced that the bombing halt was over. "I feel so sorry for him," Mansfield said. "I can imagine what he's going through.

Character: The remark reflected a compassionate side of Mansfield's complex character. Sen. Hubert H. Humphrey, D-Minn., once alluded to this quality when he observed that "there is no meanness in him."

"Keep in mind," Humphrey added in an interview, "the things he says, no matter how critical, do not spring from personal ambition, but rather as a reflection of his own mind and conscience."

Mansfield now says of the Johnson period: "It's not easy to say 'no' to the President in that oval office, where he is surrounded by all of his advisers and chiefs of staff. I guess I had to do that half a dozen times."

Mansfield's forgiving approach to politics remains one of the chief reasons why a Senate in which personal ambition is no stranger manages to function with a minimum of rancor.

While the Mansfield and Johnson political styles are poles apart, Mansfield shares with Johnson, who was his predecessor as Majority Leader, a somewhat mystical sense of the Senate's dignity and integrity. In spite of his forgiving nature, Mansfield cannot abide behavior that tends to throw the Senate into disrepute.

Senate Minority Leader Hugh Scott, R-Pa., describes Mansfield as "the most decent man I've ever met in public life. He's fair. And his word rates in fineness above the gold at Fort Knox."

There is a certain bleakness to the Mansfield landscape: his smile, while warm, is not quick in coming. Mansfield's public life is increasingly governed by the credo once espoused by the 17th-century English poet John Dryden when he wrote:

"For all the happiness
Man can gain
Is not in pleasure,
But in rest from pain."

At 67, Mansfield is six feet tall and weighs 170 pounds. He speaks in short declarative sentences in a flat style that has been compared to that of a sheriff of the Old West. The Majority Leader has long been one of the most casual dressers in the Senate. Lately, the contrast with his colleagues has sharpened; he often appears in the Senate wearing a sport jacket and yellow socks.

Career: Michael J. Mansfield was born March 16, 1903 in Manhattan's Greenwich Village. He was reared in Great Falls, Mont., the first son of Irish immigrant parents who ran a grocery store below their apartment.

As a youth, Mansfield ran away from home three times, ending up twice in the Great Falls city jail, the second time overnight, before his third and successful attempt.

He entered the Navy on Feb. 23, 1918, at age 14, for the duration of World War I. In 1919, he enlisted in the Army for one year, and then enlisted in the Marine Corps for two years, serving mainly in China.

In 1922, he returned to Montana to work in the Butte copper mines, 3,000 feet below the surface, for the next eight years.

While working as a miner, he met Maureen Hayes, a Butte school teacher. Miss Hayes encouraged him to resume his studies (he had never finished grade school) while Mansfield encouraged her to marry him, which she did.

He attended the University of Montana at Missoula from 1930 to 1934, where he received his bachelor's and master's degrees. Mansfield then embarked upon a new career as an associate professor of Latin American and Far Eastern history at the university, where he taught for 10 years. He still retains permanent tenure there as a professor of history.

Mansfield ran for Congress in

1942 and served five terms in the House (1943-53). He was elected to the Senate in 1952 and reelected in 1958, 1964 and 1970. Johnson engineered his election as Majority Whip in 1957. When Johnson became Vice President in 1961, John F. Kennedy persuaded a reluctant Mansfield to serve as Majority Leader. He has held that position longer than any other Senator.

Montana: Mansfield wields the full power inherent in his position only to protect the interests of his 682,000 Montana constituents.

Mansfield has been known to keep Cabinet officers waiting in his outer office while he chatted amiably with a touring Montana family.

Over the years, copper mining legislation and other measures of direct interest to his state have been safely guided through the Senate.

Should Mansfield come to feel that Montana has been short-changed in its slice of federal funds, he is apt to summon the agency chief to his office for a head-to-head talk. This is a fearsome and parochial side of Mansfield which outsiders rarely see.

In non-election years, he returns to Montana only a few times a year, mainly to speak on college campuses.

Mansfield's campaign style is to come into a hotel lobby an hour or so before the scheduled start of a political dinner and to stand quietly in a corner with his wife, smoking a pipe. As soon as he is recognized, a reception line forms and everyone comes up to shake his hand.

Last year, in an Oct. 28 Great Falls campaign speech, Mansfield said: "Every candidate who runs for public office has the duty and obligation to lay his whole life before the people he seeks to represent."

In 1970, Mansfield ran against Harold E. (Bud) Wallace, a Missoula sporting-goods salesman. Wallace accused Mansfield during the campaign of "being soft on communism." The issue failed to take root when President Nixon sent an Air Force plane to Glasgow Air Force Base in Glasgow, Mont., to fly Mansfield to New York, where he accompanied the President on an Oct. 23 visit to the United Nations.

Mansfield ignored his opponent, never mentioned him in the campaign, and won 150,060 to 97,809.

Schedule: While in Washington, Mansfield usually arrives at the Capitol before 7 a.m. in a car chauffeured by Lorenzo M. Lee.

He has breakfast with his closest friend in the Senate, George D. Aiken, R-Vt., and Aiken's wife, Lola, who is her husband's administrative assistant. By 8:15, he is in his Capitol office, dictating letters, drafting speeches and conferring with his senior staff.

Mansfield leaves the office 10 minutes before the start of a Senate session for his daily press conference behind the Majority Leader's desk on the Senate floor. Normally, he skips lunch; when he does eat, it is alone in his office.

Depending on the nature of the business before the Senate, Mansfield will remain on the floor or ask his deputy, Sen. Robert C. Byrd, D-W.Va., to monitor the debate.

He will see visitors throughout the afternoon, coming off the Senate floor or from the cloakroom retreat to meet with them in his office.

In late afternoon, Mansfield usually returns to his "Montana office," a six-room suite in the old Senate Office Building, where he dictates and signs mail until he leaves for home.

The Mansfield's social schedule is comparatively light. He prefers to be home by 10 p.m. The Mansfields' only child, Anne, is an economics writer in London.

Senate Life: Humphrey once observed that Mansfield "is a political leader who refuses to be pressured. He resents outside contacts. He calls that 'lobbying.'"

Mansfield also abhors the idea of acquiring or exercising power for his own account. When he became majority leader, he halted the practice of conducting the kind of painstaking pre-ballot senatorial head counts that Robert G. (Bobby) Baker once handled for Lyndon Johnson in their years together. The White House filled the void until 1969; since then, the policy committee staff has quietly resumed headcounts—without the vote-by-vote fine tuning that marked the Johnson years.

Mansfield is unwilling to say whether the Johnson high-pressure power-broker system or his own far more gentle approach ("Senators will have to live up to their responsibilities; all Senators are equal") works best in the long run.

"We're different personalities, and we have faced different problems," Mansfield said in an interview. "It's just not a fair comparison. But Johnson was the greatest Majority Leader the Senate ever had."

In 1970, most rank-and-file Senators quite predictably favor the Mansfield technique. As former Sen. John J. Williams, R-Del. (1947-71) once observed:

"When Lyndon was the leader, he liked to play tricks on you. The game was always trying to outfox Lyndon. But I would never try to pull anything like that on Mike. Why, he'd just turn around and say, 'The Senator, of course, is perfectly within his rights. . . .'"

---

shunned the integrated group which had been recognized as the official Democratic Party of Mississippi at the 1968 Democratic National Convention.

Procedural Changes: On a parallel track, with Mansfield's eventual blessing, the Senate has altered its method of doing business by trying to run itself more efficiently.

The initiative for these changes came from Sens. Alan Cranston, D-Calif., and William B. Saxbe, R-Ohio, who are close friends. Afterwards, Sens. Harold E. Hughes, D-Iowa, and Richard S. Schweiker, R-Pa., were enlisted as co-sponsors.

Content—Some of the revised procedures must be adopted daily by unanimous consent, a chore that Majority Whip Byrd has assumed. Others have been implemented through the discretionary powers of Mansfield and Minority Leader Hugh Scott, Pa.

The changes require the Senate to adopt these procedures:

Organize the Senate day so that short speeches come first, routine business is transacted next, with long speeches and controversial bills held until the other work is done.

Organize the legislative year with pre-planned recesses so that Senators and staffs can schedule their time out of Washington without missing a vital vote (under this plan, the Senate does not meet on the last five days of the month; but votes will not be held off because key Senators cannot make it, as has sometimes previously been the case).

Organize major debates so that each side has 15 minutes to sum up its arguments before the vote. As a further step, a blinking light has been added to warn Senators that a roll call is in its final five minutes. Consequently, slowdowns in the roll call to accommodate tardy Senators have been banned.

Style—A Senate source who asked anonymity said: "It was terribly important in our method of handling it (the reform drive) not to appear to threaten the authority of the leadership."

Another Senate source observed, also privately: "Perhaps it was easier to effect because it clearly came from the grass roots. Mansfield isn't exactly known for his order and organization. Frankly, some of this stuff wouldn't have been necessary if the Senate were better run by the leadership."

While Mansfield was initially warm to the plan when Cranston approached him, he later expressed his doubts in a private memo to Scott. The GOP leader sought, with some success, to reassure Mansfield that the authority of the leadership was not at stake.

However, in the final compromise, the new plan must be readopted each day the Senate meets, rather than have a six-month or session-long trial, as its four sponsors had hoped.

Mansfield told *National Journal:* "I am delighted at the initiative taken by the younger members. In fact, I've asked them to continue serving as an ad hoc committee to monitor the procedures and to suggest additional reforms as they are needed."

POLICY COMMITTEE

Mansfield's low-keyed reform drive has also left its mark on the Democratic Policy Committee, which he heads.

The 14-member group, founded in 1947, entered a new phase in 1969, after the Nixon Administration came to power, when it began to examine and adopt positions on policy issues.

Changing Role: A participant in committee sessions said privately: "When the 91st Congress opened, Mansfield noted to us that we were in a whole new ball game. For one thing, there was a Republican President in the White House. For another, Speaker (John W.) McCormack (D-Mass., 1928-71) was over the hill, and we really couldn't expect too much from the House. Finally, the Democratic National Committee was very weak and in hock up to its eyeballs. So the initiative had to come from the Senate and, particularly, from the Democratic leadership."

In an interview, Mansfield said that during the Kennedy and Johnson Administrations, the policy committee refrained from issuing statements, on the theory that the Democratic position should be enunciated from the White House. "When the Democrats were in charge," he said, "we bowed to the President. Under Nixon, we function primarily as a policy-determining committee."

Since 1969, the group has passed a series of resolutions, some of which have not been publicized. Mansfield said that most were approved without active opposition. "Where an issue might divide us, we just don't touch it," Mansfield said before the Feb. 23, 1971, debate on Indochina.

The new policy role has left little time for the panel to pursue its more traditional task of regulating what legislation would be debated in the Senate. Currently, legislative scheduling is left almost entirely to the majority leader and his staff.

(The Democratic Policy Committee has been described as the Senate equivalent of the House Rules Committee, but the comparison is only partly valid. The Senate group has no minority members, no authority to issue rules, impose limits on debate or bottle up pressures for floor action.)

The recently broken string of unanimous resolutions has still spared Mansfield from invoking a Mansfield rule that a two-thirds majority is needed in committee in order for him to bring a resolution before the Democratic Conference for ratification. (None of these resolutions is binding on Senate De-

mocrats, on or off the committee.)

At a Feb. 20, 1971, meeting of the policy group, Mansfield distributed a list of prior accomplishments and asked the members what they thought the committee should stress in 1971.

Among the topics discussed were the domestic economy, the welfare program, health care, revenue sharing and the Indochina war.

The far-reaching nature of the resolutions, and the relative ease with which they were adopted, prompted Hart, a member since 1959, to observe to *National Journal:* "I am somewhat surprised that under his (Mansfield's) leadership we have moved as quickly and as far as we have. It's all to the good."

Procedure: The policy committee met only sporadically during the Kennedy-Johnson years, but now meets at least twice a month whenever the Senate is in session.

Timing—Normally, the committee meets for lunch every other Tuesday. Occasionally, the group will gather over coffee in Mansfield's private office. The regular meetings begin at 1 p.m. and last about two hours.

"Mansfield eats quickly and starts right in," a participant who asked not to be quoted by name reported. "There is a surprising freedom of expression because everyone knows that his political flanks are protected. We've never had a leak."

Agenda—A written agenda and, usually, an opening statement, are prepared under Mansfield's direction by Charles D. Ferris, the committee's general counsel and staff director. Ferris takes

notes throughout the meeting and keeps the minutes, which are not available to non-members.

"The meeting is always firmly under Sen. Mansfield's control," Ferris said. "He keeps a tight rein on the proceedings."

But Sen. Stuart Symington, Mo., a senior member, said in an interview that there was "no problem at all" in bringing up a new topic that had not been listed on the prepared agenda. "They are very constructive luncheons. ... Mike likes to hear all sides of a question. I view the committee as a way to meld sectional views on legislation. But it's also an excellent place to discuss the President's program."

One participant, who asked not to be quoted by name, reported that Sens. J. W. Fulbright, Ark., John O. Pastore, R.I., and Symington are at present the most active speakers at meetings. Another participant confirmed this report and said that Sen. Edmund S. Muskie, Maine, "is particularly good at getting people together when things become stalled."

Francis R. Valeo, secretary of the Senate and a longtime Mansfield associate who, at $36,000, is the highest-paid Senate employee, told *National Journal,* "One of the committee's key functions is to identify and then to exploit areas of commonality—where we can take a stand together effectively."

Announcements—Valeo added that "the Majority Leader does not seek to maximize publicity on some of the issues that come before the committee. In fact, some of their decisions are not announced. On those things, he feels it's preferable to work in the background with committee chairmen to bring about change."

Publicity is further diminished because policy committee sessions are never announced in advance to the press, as are virtually all other open and closed committee meetings on Capitol Hill. Consequently, reporters rarely have an opportunity to question the participants after a meeting ends.

Ferris said that "perhaps a dozen different methods" have been employed to disseminate the committee's decisions. They include Senate speeches by Mansfield; Mansfield statements issued to reporters; private letters to Senate Democrats; announcements to the Democratic Conference and personal chats between Mansfield and affected committee chairmen.

Outsiders: Mansfield has also instituted a policy of inviting experts to the luncheons where they brief the Senators on important issues.

Among those who have participated are: Stanley S. Surrey, a tax expert who formerly served as an assistant secretary of the Treasury (1961-69), now a Harvard Law School professor; David Rockefeller, chairman of the board of the Chase Manhattan Bank; and Charles L. Schultze, a former director of the budget (1965-67), now a senior fellow at the Brookings Institution.

Economics — Symington recalled that one of Schultze's briefings prompted him to ask Mansfield to invite Alfred Hays, president of the Federal Reserve Bank of New York and a close friend of Symington's, to a subsequent luncheon "so that the group could have a more balanced view of the economic picture."

Another economist who has lunched with the group is Arthur M. Okun, a former chairman (1968-69) of the President's Council of Economic Advisers in the Johnson Administration.

Okun, who is also a senior fellow at Brookings, recalled that last summer Sen. Edward M. Kennedy, D-Mass., "invited me over for a drink at his home. He seemed disturbed that Congress was doing so little to reverse the slide in the economy.

"Somewhat later, I got a call from Sen. Mansfield asking whether I would be willing to brief the Democratic Policy Committee on the economy. (At the time, Kennedy was Majority Whip and an ex-officio member of the policy committee.)

"I gave a little briefing, trying to calm their worst fears that the present situation was parallel to the Depression. It struck me at the time that some of those Senators were taking notes like college freshmen. It's really amazing how inadequate sources of information are for Senators."

Subsequently, Mansfield asked Okun, Walter W. Heller and Gardner Ackley—all of whom had served as chairmen of the Council of Economic Advisers under either Mr. Kennedy or Mr. Johnson—to prepare a report for the committee on the economy. (Heller served from 1961 to 1964; Ackley, from 1964 to 1968.) The report was released Sept. 23 without editing by the committee.

"It was no secret," Okun said, "that it was intended in part as a campaign document."

Television—On April 7, 1971, Mansfield invited the newly elected Democratic National Chairman, Lawrence F. O'Brien, to meet with the policy committee at a "get acquainted" session that was also intended to minimize friction between the two groups.

The O'Brien session led Mansfield to name a special panel, headed by Muskie, to seek means of increasing the amount of television exposure available to the Democrats.

In 1970, Mansfield also played a crucial role in getting the policy committee to approve a packaged televised response to President Nixon's State of the Union speech.

Kennedy, the moving force behind the planning for the program, asked Robert D. Squier, head of the Washington-based Communications Co., to serve as its executive producer.

(The program was spliced together from tapes of congressional leaders as they exchanged views on various issues with typical constituents. Kennedy, who was scheduled to appear in his capacity as Majority Whip, declined to go on at the last minute.)

According to a participant at a committee session, who asked not to be identified, "Squier pushed the program hard to the policy committee for half an hour and then was asked to step out.

"The deal was criticized by Pastore and Symington as too ambitious. Some others saw it as a rehab job for Teddy. But Mansfield managed to turn them all around, and the show was produced in less than 20 days."

Appointments: Whenever policy committee vacancies occur, the Majority Leader fills them.

Consultation—"I am under orders to take geography and philosophy into account when making appointments," he said in an interview. "I make the selections after discussing them with Byrd and Moss. (Frank E. Moss, D-Utah, is the conference secretary.) I also discuss them with Ellender although I am not bound to do so. (Allen J. Ellender, D-La., is the President Pro Tempore of the Senate.) In the last analysis, a certain amount of discretion is left to me."

When Mansfield feels sure of his ground, consultation on appointments with other members of the leadership is apt to be merely perfunctory.

Thus, shortly before announcing the new steering committee slate to the Democratic Conference, Mansfield was reminded by an aide that he hadn't shown the names to Moss, who was seated at his right. "This is all right with you, Frank, isn't it?" Mansfield said before reading the list.

Russell—After Sen. Richard B. Russell (D-Ga., 1933-71) died Jan. 21, Mansfield named Russell's fellow Georgian, Talmadge, to the vacancy on the policy committee.

Russell had been a major force on the policy committee, speaking far more freely on such issues as the Indochina war than he ever did in public. Until his final illness, he rarely missed a meeting, always taking a seat reserved for him at Mansfield's right.

Several members of the policy committee privately told *National Journal* that Russell was instrumental in thwarting Mansfield's desire to name Sen. William B. Spong Jr., D-Va., to the committee. They reported that Russell objected to Spong on the grounds that the Virginian declined to attend meetings of the Southern Caucus, an informal group of Senators from nine Southern states, which Russell had headed. (The seat went instead to Sen. Ernest F. Hollings, D-S.C.)

Asked for comment on Russell's part in the appointment, Mansfield said: "Russell never exercised veto power. He had no special influence."

STAFF ROLE

Legislation which created the Democratic and Republican Policy Committees (60 Stat 911) provided for separate staffs "to assist . . . in study, analysis and research on problems involved in policy determination."

The Republican Policy Committee, headed by Sen. Gordon Allott, R-Colo., has a 20-member staff that performs research on legislative and political issues.

By contrast, the Democratic policy staff—which, by Mansfield's choice, is one-fourth the size of its GOP counterpart—plays a central role in facilitating Senate operations.

Policy Staff: "It is a Democratic staff in a broad sense," Mansfield said. "They serve all the Democrats, but they are answerable to me."

While the Senate is in session, Charles Ferris is usually seated several paces in front of the Majority Leader's desk, facing the Senate, at a long mahogany table. Normally, Daniel E. Leach, the associate general counsel, is seated at his left.

The Ferris-Leach team briefs Senators on the day's legislative complexities. A principal task is to inform them when major bills and amendments are likely to come up, what position the leadership will take and what the likely outcome might be.

Even more important, they work with Mansfield in devising legislative tactics to cope with an immediate parliamentary problem, as well as in planning legislative strategy.

In the course of their work, Ferris and Leach remain in constant touch with most of the Democratic Senators and their staffs, as well as with important Senators and staff men on the GOP side of the aisle.

Operations—Ferris played a major role in the successful drive to deny G. Harrold Carswell of Florida a seat on the Supreme Court.

Published accounts of the Senate struggle failed to mention Ferris' role. Said Ferris: "I much prefer to work in the background."

(Several Senate reporters, who have known Ferris over the years, regularly tap him for "guidance" on Senate issues. But they never reveal him as a source of information.)

"We are an intelligence-gathering network," Ferris said in an interview. "As such, we must keep our heads down."

Ferris maintained a close relationship with the late Sen. Robert F. Kennedy (D-N.Y., 1965-68). Some years ago, both Robert Kennedy and his brother, Edward, made a special trip to Boston to attend the funeral of Ferris' father. Ferris is also close to Sen. Humphrey, with whom, at Mansfield's request, he drafted civil rights legislation during the years (1961-65) that Humphrey served as Senate Majority Whip.

Sen. Walter F. Mondale, D-Minn., told *National Journal:* "Increasingly, the conservatives recognize him (Ferris) as an agent of the liberals. That must make things tough for Charlie at times."

Ferris acknowledges that he works easily with the "liberal group" but adds: "I try to keep things in balance. When (Sen. James O.) Eastland (D-Miss.) calls, I give him a hand if I can, and liberals may not hear about it."

Ferris and Leach are circumscribed in their operations by Mansfield's firm policy against using the majority leadership as a political office.

As Mondale put it: "For as long as I can recall, Mike has taken the position that he wants the policy staff to work on Senate matters and not on political matters. It's up to the (Democratic Senatorial) Campaign Committee to do the other. To the extent they (the campaign committee) try, they've got to do so through privately collected funds."

Finances—The fiscal 1972 budget calls for an appropriation of $282,675 each for the Democratic and Republican Policy Committees. The GOP customarily disburses its entire allotment. Mansfield, however, regularly returns about $150,000 a year in unspent policy committee funds to the Treasury.

Some junior Senators have privately criticized Mansfield's decision not to use all available funds on the grounds that the Democrats could use the added research aid. (One Senator who feels this way is Adlai E. Stevenson III, D-Ill.)

Asked for comment, Mondale, who confers regularly with Harris, Cranston, Hughes and other members of the reform-minded group, said: "I would have assumed there is really no point in raising that. In all of our organizational meetings (on proposed reforms), I don't really remember that coming up."

Ferris conceded that there has been "some grumbling" over the spending policy, but he said: "Mansfield abhors bureaucracy. He much prefers to work with a tight staff."

Ferris also said that the Democrats are not doing without needed research, because "we can and do pick up the phone and get the most expert research help in the country anytime that we want to."

GOP—Ferris also maintains "special relationships" with perhaps a half-dozen Republican Senators "whose names I won't reveal." They rely on him to keep abreast of the legislative schedule and, at times, for legislative advice—despite the fact that the GOP maintains a parallel legislative apparatus through Minority Leader Scott and J. Mark Trice, secretary for the minority.

Ferris' contacts within the upper echelons of the Nixon Administration, and particularly with the White House, are nil. "They never call," he said.

Valeo—On an average of three times a week, Mansfield confers with his top legislative advisers: Ferris, Leach and Valeo, who, unlike the policy committee staff men, is an elected officer of the Senate.

(These sessions tend to be businesslike and lacking in the cynical humor and personal gossip that characterize many Senate staff meetings. Ferris, who is well-acquainted with Senate tempers and Senate egos, said in response to a question that "Sen. Mansfield is always a perfect gentleman in dealing with his staff.")

Under Valeo's predecessor, Felton M. (Skeeter) Johnson (1955-65), the office of the secretary of the Senate was largely a ceremonial one. His personal office, which adjoins the Democratic wing of the Senate, often served as a late-afternoon clubhouse with a well-stocked bar.

"All that has changed," Valeo said. "I must be responsive to the Mansfield leadership." (Mansfield serves his staff and his visitors coffee but no liquor; Valeo does the same.)

Valeo is also the chief administrative officer of the Senate. His office supervises a network of parliamentary experts, art curators, legislative clerks, record keepers, financial officers, librarians and messengers.

The secretary of the Senate is also responsible for some Senate functions, such as the payroll. He coordinates the Republican aspect of his work through Scott and his staff.

By training, however, Valeo is an expert in foreign affairs, particularly on Southeast Asia policy. He has accompanied Mansfield on several world tours. Mansfield's statements on the Indochina war are invariably written in consultation with Valeo.

During the recent push for reform, Valeo has advised Mansfield to take care not to weaken the authority of the leadership inad-

114 vertently.

On the issue of whether Byrd of Virginia should be allowed to take a seat in the Democratic Conference, Valeo said: "You are a Senator before you are anything else. That has to be recognized. It is easy, you know, to play these games of exclusivity; you can become a minority anytime you want to."

Kimmitt—Mansfield's chief assistant for non-legislative Senate business is J. S. (Stan) Kimmitt, secretary for the majority. "Stan is the man who is there with who wants what," Mansfield said.

Kimmitt's chief task is to keep track of the many senatorial requests for committee transfers, which often involve conflicts of geography, ideology and seniority. His advice was often solicited during the six closed meetings of the Democratic Steering Committee early in the session that formulated committee assignments for the majority.

In addition to the standing, select and joint committees, Kimmitt watches over various nonlegislative special committees, extracurricular commissions and international delegations, whose Democratic membership is under Mansfield's control.

The Montana-born Kimmitt is the direct successor to Robert G. (Bobby) Baker, who was convicted in 1967 of income tax evasion, theft and conspiracy, and who is currently serving a one-year federal prison term in Lewisburg, Pa.

Kimmitt's present official duties bear no parallel to Baker's previous official duties. A Senator close to Mansfield, who asked not to be quoted by name, said: "Stan was hired because of his impeccable record. Mike has chosen to deliberately play down the importance of the office (Kimmitt occupies) until, hopefully, the taint of scandal is lifted by time."

Ferris, Leach, Valeo and Kimmitt are the only Senate aides who regularly attend meetings of the Democratic Policy Committee and the Democratic Conference.

THE SYSTEM

Ralph K. Huitt, a political scientist who once worked for Johnson when he was Majority Leader, has observed that "leadership in the Senate is highly personal and exceedingly complex. People who know a great deal about it are the ones most reluctant to talk about it."

Mansfield View: In discussing the subject with *National Journal*, the Majority Leader said:

"I'm not a king and I have no princes. I have less power than any other Senator. . . .

"This is a job which is not in the Constitution. It (the power available) is whatever the Senate gives us in the way of cooperation. Basically, we have less power than all the other Senators. But the power of the Senate is tremendous. Yet my power is neither defined nor understood.

"Senators realize that they are treated as I'd like to be treated—as mature men. Their independence is not infringed upon. They know that everything is on the table. They know all about our moves ahead of time. There are no surprises.

"Lyndon Johnson once said—and he was quite right about this—that 'the only power available to a leader is the power of persuasion. There is no patronage; no power to discipline, no authority to fire Senators like the President can fire members of his Cabinet.'

"Johnson was an effective Majority Leader. But I look toward the long range. I'm not interested in immediate victories. We're trying to keep the party together despite all the pressures that might divide us."

One divisive pressure, Mansfield acknowledged, would be any contest to succeed him as Majority Leader. Mansfield, however, said he would never seek to designate a successor as had former Speaker McCormack in choosing to support Rep. Carl Albert, D-Okla., for the Speakership. "Senators are grown men and can make up their own minds," Mansfield said.

Analysis: A Senator who took his seat in 1953, as did Mansfield, agreed to comment on Mansfield's remarks if he would not be quoted by name. He said:

"I'm not at all surprised, al-

Hugh Scott

though of course it isn't true that he has less power than any other Senator.

"He doesn't believe that for a moment. But what he was trying to say—and what he *does* believe very strongly—is that other Senators are able to twist and to turn this way and that to suit their political needs—exploiting the rules or even abusing them—whereas Mike to remain effective must play fair. His attitude is sometimes interpreted as one of weakness, but that isn't it at all."

Another Senator who knows Mansfield well and who similarly declined to be quoted by name said:

"The only time I've seen Mike get up tight is when someone crowds his authority as leader. But he has no ego-trip hang-ups and so the others like to work with him. He is also scrupulously fair.

"I've heard him say, as I'm sure you have, that there is no difference between the oldest and the newest Member. While, strictly speaking, that isn't true, it is Mansfield's approach."

A Southern Democrat told *National Journal* privately: "Mansfield has an acute awareness that Senators must play different and conflicting roles and that the task of his leadership is to structure a situation so that a Senator can select a role that will allow him to stand by his party."

Asked to comment on the statement, Mansfield reflectively chewed on his pipe for several moments and then said: "I guess that's fair."

Power Base: In his book *The Congressional Party: A Case Study,* David Truman wrote: "The Ma-

jority Leader builds his influence upon a combination of fragments of power."

Roles—Mansfield is, at one and the same time:

majority floor leader of the Senate;

chairman of the Democratic Policy Committee;

chairman of the Democratic Conference;

chairman of the Democratic Steering Committee.

Each title adds to his influence and to the size of the professional staff that he controls, although Mansfield is anything but an empire builder.

Republicans divide these tasks among four Senators. Currently, Scott serves as minority floor leader; Allott as chairman of the policy committee; Sen. Margaret Chase Smith, Maine, as chairman of the Republican Conference, and Sen. Wallace F. Bennett, Utah, as chairman of the GOP committee on committees, which is the equivalent body to the Democratic Steering Committee.

Recognition—Mansfield also possesses what Lyndon B. Johnson once termed "the power of recognition." This is essentially the time-honored duty of the Vice President or whomever is presiding over the Senate in his stead, to recognize the Majority Leader above the claims of all others whenever he wants the floor. (Once a Senator is recognized, he may speak or control the debate, until he agrees to yield the floor.)

The "power of recognition" has evolved by tradition and is not stated in any Senate rule. (The first presiding officer who announced that he would abide by the policy

was Vice President (1933-41) John N. Garner.)

This year, the Senate for the first time adopted a unanimous consent agreement, requested by Mansfield and Scott, that the two party leaders be automatically recognized before any other Senators are permitted to speak at the start of each Senate day. The agreement, which will remain in effect for the duration of the Senate session, ensures that the leadership will retain day-to-day control.

Internal Pressures: Several political scientists have observed that the powers of the Majority Leader are limited by:

the direct relationship between Senators and their own constituencies, which the leader cannot usually penetrate;

the national constituencies of some Senators, including those who are running or weighing a race for the presidency; and

the system of standing Senate committees with virtually preemptive jurisdiction over wide areas of legislation.

Chairmen—A member of the policy committee, who is also a committee chairman, said privately: "Around here, committee chairmen are tribal chiefs to be bargained with, not lieutenants to be commanded.

"The persons who are least enthusiastic about a strong policy committee composed of committee chairmen, as has been suggested in some quarters, are the chairmen themselves, who have no desire to trade their sovereignty for a vote in council."

Mansfield is sensitive to the power of committee chairmen to bottle up legislation. In order to keep his lines open, he makes it a practice to confer with the chairmen of the Senate's 17 standing committees on a regular basis, usually over lunch in his office.

Pressure, when applied, is of the gentlest sort. For example, in early February, Mansfield informed Senate Finance Committee Chairman Russell B. Long, D-La., that the policy committee had approved a resolution arguing that social security, welfare reform and trade matters be considered separately and not as part of a package, as had occurred in the waning days of the 91st Congress.

Mansfield himself has little time for committee work. (He is a member of the two most prestigious Senate committees—Appropriations and Foreign Relations.)

Mansfield ranks behind Fulbright and Sen. John Sparkman, D-Ala., on the Foreign Relations Committee. But Sparkman is already chairman of the Banking and Currency Committee, so if Fulbright should die, resign or retire, Mansfield would be in line to succeed him.

But Mansfield told *National Journal* that "under no circumstances" would he serve in the Senate as a committee chairman.

Senators—Although Mansfield said he is willing at all times to confer in private with any of his fellow Senators, he sees his colleagues only rarely on that basis.

One Mansfield staff aide explained: "The older guys know better than to bother him, and the younger guys are in awe of him."

Another Mansfield aide who also requested anonymity said: "Mansfield is an arms-length guy. He'll play a straight and honest game with Senators and with Nixon. He won't have it any other way.

"The type of politican he can't stand is the guy who will go whisper in the corner. With him, it's all on the table, head-to-head."

Southerners—Mansfield devotes particular attention to "bringing along" relatively junior Democrats from Southern states by using his influence to ensure that they receive responsible committee posts early in their Senate careers.

In this vein, he has named South Carolina's Hollings to the policy committee, and Virginia's Spong and newly elected Sen. Lawton Chiles, Fla., to the steering committee.

In addition, with Mansfield's help, Hollings this year won a seat on the Appropriations Committee while Spong, again with a push from Mansfield, was named to the Foreign Relations Committee.

"We've got to look to our younger Members," Mansfield said. "They are a new generation, and they look at the problems of the South in a new way.

"It should be clearly recognized within their constituencies that the Senate in general and the Democratic Party in particular welcomes them and will provide for them. I have told all the new Senators—North and South—that I expect them to be seen and heard if they have something to say."

In commenting on Mansfield's "Southern Strategy," Minnesota's Mondale said: "Spong and Chiles represent a shift toward moderation. That probably explains the election of (Sen. Gaylord) Nelson (D-Wis.) to the Finance Committee and of (Sen. Daniel K.) Inouye (D-Hawaii) to the Appropriations Committee.

"It is not a revolution, but it's a change, in my opinion in the right direction. I think it's almost unprecedented to reach behind a whole army of Senators and pick a brand new freshman and put him on the steering committee—which is what he did with Chiles."

External Pressures: Mansfield blocks off a wide swath of potential pressure by refusing to see any Washington or out-of-town lobbyist, in or out of his office, no matter what his background or his cause.

Thus, when such major issues as tax reform, civil rights or the effort to repeal Section 14(b) of the Taft-Hartley Act (61 Stat 136) have reached the Senate floor, Mansfield has remained aloof from the large and diverse group of lobbyists who have sought to affect the course of the legislation on Capitol Hill.

But Mansfield will readily see any constituent from Montana who comes to Washington or will talk with any long-distance caller from the state with a legitimate reason for telephoning him. He does not regard any of his fellow Montanans as lobbyists, and he personally dictates replies to all his mail from the state.

(During the intensive lobbying effort by anti-war groups on Capitol Hill last May, which followed in the wake of the Nixon Administration's incursion into Cambodia, several college students told Mansfield that they were from Montana in order to win an audience with him. Although Mansfield's questions soon determined that they were not from Montana, he agreed with their views and good-naturedly consented to talk to them anyway.)

Press—In contrast with lobbyists, congressional reporters enjoy easy access to the Majority Leader. While Mansfield is held to be an extremely poor "leak" on Senate matters that have not been publicly announced, he is most willing to discuss his own views on issues with a candor that is rarely seen on Capitol Hill.

All of Mansfield's conversations with reporters and editors are "on the record," in contrast to other Washington politicians who often talk with correspondents on a "not-for-attribution" or "not-for-publication" basis.

SENATE LEADERSHIP: A 20TH CENTURY INNOVATION

In 1885, Woodrow Wilson wrote in his book, *Congressional Government,* that "No one is *the* Senator. No one may speak for his party as well as for himself. . . . "

The Conference: Well into the 20th century, the Democrats and Republicans elected a chairman for their respective conferences, but no Senator was elected to serve as the Majority or Minority Leader, as those offices are known today.

The party conference is in theory the supreme organ of the legislative party, as the national convention is of the national party.

But, until Senate Majority Leader Mansfield, D-Mont., recently revived the conference machinery, its principal function was to elect party leaders at the start of each session.

In the view of Lyndon B. Johnson, once a Senate Majority Leader (1955-61), not much can be accomplished in a conference. Johnson maintained that the issues that divide a party cannot be settled in a plenary forum, even when it is held in secret.

The Floor Leader: On Jan. 15, 1920, a Democratic conference was called for the first time for the purpose "of selecting a leader for the Democrats of the Senate."

They elected Sen. (1915-27) Oscar W. Underwood, Ala., as "Minority Leader." (The Republicans elected a leader of their own in 1925.)

But down into the 1930s, it was common practice for committee chairmen to take up a bill on the Senate floor without consulting the party leader.

The office of Majority Leader is not mentioned in any Senate rule. But the leader is recognized by law in that special funds are appropriated each year for the office.

(Mansfield currently earns $49,500, a $7,000 premium over the annual salary of other Senators. In addition, he is entitled to several special staffs and such additional perquisites of office as the use of a telephone-equipped Cadillac.)

Since 1927 and 1937, the Democratic leader and the Republican leader, respectively, have continuously occupied the front row seat on their party's side of the center aisle.

The Policy Committee: In 1946, the Joint Committee on the Organization of the Congress, then in GOP hands, reported that "strong recommendations" had been made to it concerning the need for a body to express formally the main policy lines of the

majority and minority parties.

Birth—The Senate had provided for the creation of Republican and Democratic policy committees for each chamber in the Legislative Reorganization Act of 1946 (60 Stat 812), but the House deleted the provision from the bill.

The Senate established the committees by attaching them as a rider to the fiscal 1947 legislative money bill (60 Stat 911). The law fixed membership at seven Senators each, with the party leader to serve as chairman.

The original policy committee concept called for a membership chosen to provide both ideological and geographic balance, a concept that has been followed ever since. Committee chairmen were to be omitted from the roster. While this precept was also followed, committee members in time gained in seniority and influence. Many of them eventually became committee chairmen, but retained their policy committee seats.

Early Life—Sen. (1927-49) Alben W. Barkley, D-Ky., was Minority Leader when the policy committee was born. Barkley's Senate leadership, which began in 1937 and lasted until he resigned to become Vice President, was personal, intuitive and highly informal. While he set out to hold weekly meetings of the policy committee, he seldom did.

Barkley's successor, Sen. (1939-51) Scott W. Lucas, D-Ill., utilized the policy committee to formulate the legislative schedule and help map floor strategy. But no votes were ever taken, and no decisions were ever held as binding. Barkley came to the meetings and added his weight as Vice President.

Lucas established the principle that the leader cannot be forced to take a man on the committee that he doesn't want. He left a seat vacant for two years rather than name the only logical replacement, a Senator with whom he didn't get along.

Sen. (1941-53) Ernest W. McFarland, D-Ariz., who served one term as Majority Leader, viewed the policy committee as a kind of legislative cabinet. He said: "These are the men that the leader would have to deal with anyway, even if there were no policy committee, if he wanted to do his job, although he would not have to deal with them as a group."

LBJ—The committee declined in influence after Johnson became Minority Leader in 1953. Few votes were taken and few decisions made. The minutes were brief and confidential. Public announcements of committee actions were a rarity.

The committee's decline reflected Johnson's personal ascendance. "Lyndon ran his own show," Sen. Stuart Symington, D-Mo., a veteran policy committee member, told *National Journal*.

One Johnson innovation, dating from 1959, was the addition of three freshman Senators to the policy committee. This group, which was geographically balanced and subsequently expanded to four Senators, is known as the Legislative Review Committee. Originally, its main function was to keep track of minor bills which fellow Democrats objected to and to block their passage on the Senate floor.

Sen. Philip A. Hart, Mich., one of the original trio named by Johnson, recently told *National Journal*: "I remember the days when we ate with the policy committee and participated in the discussion. But it was a gray area whether we were allowed to vote. Johnson kept the issue from ever coming to a head."

The Johnson method of running the Senate eventually incurred the wrath of former Sen. (1953-71) Albert Gore, D-Tenn.

At a Democratic Conference which Johnson convened Jan. 12, 1960, Gore moved to remake the policy committee into "an organization for evolving coherent party policy on legislation." He sought to have its membership increased to 15 and selected by the entire conference. The Gore motion lost 51-12.

Mansfield does not have a press secretary. He is usually available to reporters for about 10 minutes before the start of a Senate session. On Saturday mornings, he often meets with the "regulars" within the press corps over coffee in his Capitol office.

Because he refuses to discuss personal relationships and often glosses over Senate disputes in his remarks to reporters, Mansfield has acquired a reputation among some reporters for being politically naive.

But one Senate colleague, who is well versed in this aspect of Mansfield's personality, said, "You can be sure that he knows what's going on, including all the bad blood between Senators. But he doesn't want to let on that he does know what's going on because he doesn't want to say anything that would tend to bring the Senate into disrepute."

Democrats—Mansfield maintains a distant, but still friendly, relationship with O'Brien and the Democratic National Committee. He agreed to attend a Feb. 9 dinner that O'Brien sponsored for the seven leading Democratic Presidential contenders. (Albert also attended.)

The Senate Majority Leader also agreed, at O'Brien's behest, to serve as the Democratic spokesman who replied for the party to Mr. Nixon's State of the Union speech. The format finally agreed upon was an interview with Mansfield by four television network correspondents on Jan. 26.

At first, Mansfield pressed Albert to make the response. When Albert (who felt it was undignified for the Speaker to answer the President) declined, Mansfield sought to make a joint appearance with Albert.

Finally, when that arrangement fell through, Mansfield reluctantly agreed to appear, informing the television audience: "I'm not enjoying it, but I'm doing what I think is a duty."

A high-ranking official of the Democratic National Committee privately told *National Journal:*

"I must admit that sometimes we get very frustrated with his statements. And, to tell the truth, we didn't know until the last moment whether he would actually go on."

The official concluded: "Mansfield lives in the institution of the Senate and not in the institution of the Democratic Party. In short, he's a Senate man, not a political man, and in many ways an inscrutable figure."

OUTLOOK

Mansfield is eager that the reform bloc recognize the depth of the changes that have occurred, despite the fact that many of them have been accomplished in a low-key or even imperceptible fashion.

To this end, he is preparing a detailed analysis of the Harris suggestions which purports to show that all of the suggestions have, in one way or another, been satisfied.

Harris, pleased to have Mansfield in the reform camp, is likely to refrain from making further statements while the special committee that he heads pursues its study.

West Virginia's Byrd is likely to play a pivotal role in determining the course of the reform movement. It was Byrd's subcommittee that, along with the full committee, decided to issue an unfavorable report on S Res 17, which would allow the Senate to elect its committee chairmen and ranking mi-

nority members. (The committee did not announce a formal vote in making its report to the Senate.)

In his capacity as Majority Whip, Byrd has spent more time on the Senate floor this year than has any other Senator.

He turns back questions from reporters on leadership matters with the assertion: "I'm just here to listen and to observe."

But Byrd's unpublicized decision to switch his vote from the policy committee to the conference on the Indochina resolution reveals his desire to work well with Mansfield. If Byrd continues to follow the course, the Senate scales could swing strongly toward further reform.

Two money committees wield power differently

Frank V. Fowlkes and Harry Lenhart Jr.

Two of Capitol Hill's most powerful committees guard the legislative path which every federal revenue-raising proposal must take to become law.

They are the House Ways and Means Committee and the Senate Finance Committee, and they share responsibility for all trade, welfare and tax proposals that come before Congress.

That is virtually all they have in common.

The House committee, chaired by Rep. Wilbur D. Mills, D-Ark., moves toward its decisions slowly and with little public notice.

The Senate committee, chaired by Sen. Russell B. Long, D-La., often wages noisy races against the clock to get its bills to the floor.

The Mills committee is shielded from special interest groups; the Senate committee is fully exposed to the pressures of private interests when corporate funds are involved.

They share a staff of tax experts and lean on specialists from the executive branch for technical advice on welfare and trade; but the experts are invited to speak more freely in the House than in the Senate.

But the committees have come together on revenue sharing.

POWERS

These two panels offer some of the most sought-after standing committee assignments in Congress.

Ways and Means: No appointment in the House is more coveted than a seat on the Ways and Means Committee.

A position on that oldest of House committees confers instant status on the most junior Member. Other House Members respect the committee for its expertise and the importance of its work. Constituents appreciate the impact which the committee has on their daily lives. Members of Ways and Means can and do use their membership as a plank in campaigning for reelection.

The committee is the key to success for many legislative initiatives. New members, whose legislative contacts had previously run to lobbyists and Legionnaires, find themselves courted by Cabinet officers and the White House.

This year, the proposals that bring White House courting include social security amendments, welfare reform, medicaid and medicare, trade, and the President's general revenue-sharing plan.

Constitution—The foundation of the Ways and Means Committee's power is a provision in the Constitution that revenue-raising law must originate in the House.

In 1802, the House vested original responsibility for drafting this legislation in the Ways and Means Committee, which had just been created as the first standing committee of the House. Until 1865, the committee also was responsible for appropriations and for regulating the banking industry.

Custom — Inherent in the power to levy taxes is the power to determine the level of over-all federal revenues. But the authority of the Ways and Means Committee today extends well beyond determining gross revenue levels.

The large volume of health and welfare legislation passed under the statutory umbrella of the Social Security Act of 1935 (49 Stat 620) during the past 35 years has given the committee a major voice in how the federal dollar is spent as well as in how it is collected. Because it is funded by a payroll tax, the Act fell naturally within the jurisdiction of the committee.

It has since proved the opening wedge for the committee in the general area of health and welfare legislation, much of which has been enacted as amendments to the original Act.

On that technicality, the committee now has jurisdiction over programs such as medicaid and welfare, even though they are funded from the general treasury.

It has the power to determine both the amount and the manner in which money will be spent in the broad area of social security, health and welfare. In one step, it performs both the authorization and appropriation functions.

Expansion—Even so, both Chairman Mills and ranking Republican John W. Byrnes, Wis., would like to see Ways and Means more involved in determining over-all government spending levels.

There is too little coordination

between Ways and Means, which determines revenues, and the House Appropriations Committee, which determines expenditures, to plot a rational fiscal course, they told *National Journal*.

"That's one of the weaknesses around here," said Mills. "We don't have the close working relationship between the committees which the Reorganization Act of 1946 (84 Stat 1440) envisioned."

"I think it would help if the Appropriations Committees would follow the lead of Ways and Means and the Senate Finance Committee by setting up a joint staff through which our staff (the Joint Committee on Internal Revenue Taxation) could communicate with theirs," said Byrnes.

Mills, who agrees that the joint staff approach would be desirable, said that the Appropriations Committee had always resisted the idea, fearing that it would undermine the tradition that appropriations bills originate in the House—a tradition which, unlike the House prerogative on revenue matters, has no constitutional or other legal sanction.

At present, the committee's authority to fix the federal debt ceiling is the only means it has of affecting spending. At best, the ceiling is a blunt tool, and Mills discounts its usefulness as a check on appropriations. He is accustomed to pointing out that refusing to raise the debt ceiling amounts to giving the President an item veto on programs, giving him authority which rightfully belongs to the Congress.

Finance: The Senate Finance Committee spends more time in hot water than does Ways and Means, but it is no less a choice assignment.

"It is," said one White House aide, "the most powerful committee in the Senate."

There is, for example, no closed rule in the Senate—as there is in the House—to prevent bills from being amended on the floor. Because bills handled by Finance affect many people profoundly and thus can affect more votes more directly than, perhaps, any other legislation, the amendments to the committee's bills come in droves.

When the Tax Reform Act of 1969 (84 Stat 2059) was being considered on the floor, some 111 amendments were offered, 73 of which were accepted.

Last Resort—Finance deals with the hot spots in a revenue bill. It listens to complaints and demands of interest groups and does the fine tuning it thinks is needed to make the measure palatable.

It is the court of appeals where decisions of Ways and Means can be adjusted to reflect new facts, to prevent specific injustices and to forestall intended or unintended financial injury to specific groups.

In that role, it is often the nemesis of expensive social programs—as it was with the Administration's Family Assistance Plan (HR 16311) in 1970—and the broker benefiting business interests—as with the Trade Act of 1969 (HR 18970).

Finance is put in this position because few special interest groups see a final version of a revenue bill until it is out of Ways and Means and well on its way, unamended and virtually amendable, through the House.

Only after the hill reaches the Senate do interest groups have a clear shot at it.

On the House side, pressure is applied surgically by an exclusive group of sophisticated Washington tax lawyers who are intimately acquainted with the tax-writing process. In the Senate, people from across the nation get into the act and persuasion tends to be carried out in full public view with a club, swung at the grass-roots level.

No other committee in the Senate, said a Yale University doctoral candidate, David E. Price, in a 1969 dissertation dealing with Finance and two other Senate committees, is "the target of more wealthy, powerful, or politically active interest groups than Finance."

Critics and Campaigns—Few congressional committees have been as much vilified as Finance— partly because of its role as the visible point of access for pressure groups; partly because of the wheeler-dealer reputations of some of its most influential members, past and present; and partly because, as a committee, it has long been ideologically out of step with the Senate as a whole.

The critics say it is the champion on Capitol Hill of big business and the defender of special tax privileges for the rich and powerful.

They say that it is the chief protector of the oil and minerals depletion allowances and of other tax loopholes as well.

It is the place to go to get a tax favor, its critics say, in return for campaign contributions.

In his book, *The Great Treasury Raid* (Signet), Philip M. Stern tells of a high-ranking member of Finance who was asked by a newsman about his uncharacteristic sponsorship of several pro-insurance company amendments to a tax bill. The Senator candidly explained: "This is the way we finance our campaigns. Hell, I wish there was a tax bill up every year."

WAYS AND MEANS

The influence of Chairman Mills' committee arises in part from its hidden powers as well as its obvious ones, from its membership and from its expert tax advisory staff.

Hidden Powers: The influence of Ways and Means members is even greater in the House than their power to set tax rates implies.

Closed Rule—Bills which the committee reports to the House floor move under a so-called closed rule, which prevents their being amended.

This means that the committee version and the final House version are identical, except in rare instances when a Ways and Means bill has been recommitted for modification.

Only twice in the 13 years since Mills became chairman has the House recommitted a Ways and Means bill—once in 1958 and once last year.

The 25 members of Ways and Means, in effect, speak for all 435 Members of the House on tax, trade and welfare matters.

Members Bills—The intra-House influence of Ways and Means members is further enhanced by the peculiar institution of "members day."

On members days, which are generally held toward the end of a session, Ways and Means members are given the opportunity to offer small tax or tariff bills designed to amend laws that are burdensome to constituents.

"These are little exceptions for special interests in our districts," explained one Republican member.

The ability to introduce "members bills" also gives a committee member a chance to help colleagues who are not on the committee. In a session which sees no omnibus tax legislation come before the committee, a non-member can have a tax proposal considered only on members days.

Each committee member arranges his bills according to their priority and the bills are taken up in sequence around the committee conference table on members days. Generally, each committee member will get two bills considered.

Veto—The informal rules under which the committee operates hold that none of these special bills will be reported if a federal agency or any single member of the committee objects. Even if bills are reported, they are brought to the House floor under unanimous consent and are again vulnerable to defeat by a single vote.

These checks on the system are not 100 per cent reliable, however. Former Rep. (1951-68) Thomas B. Curtis, D-Mo., who was a member of Ways and Means, told *National Journal* that it was considered unsporting for one member to oppose another's bill; that logrolling and threats were common; and that, on a number of occasions, only his vote kept a bill from being reported out over the objection of a federal agency.

A Treasury official said the department's decision to oppose or not oppose a member's bill occasionally was colored by political considerations, such as whether Treasury's opposition might alienate a member whose vote might become important to the Administration on more significant matters.

Patchwork—Students of the committee have criticized the "members bill" system as an avenue of special interest legislation. One current member calls the bills "little patches on big problems which take off the pressure for tax reform."

In defense of the system, however, they point out that members bills are very susceptible to Presidential veto—something that cannot be said of Senate special interest amendments which arrive on the President's desk as riders to major bills.

Committee on Committees: For Democrats, there is a bonus in appointment to the Ways and Means Committee. Democratic members of the committee serve as the party's Committee on Committees, the body which, with rare exceptions, decides which Democrats will serve on which committees. (The committee does not appoint Ways and Means members.)

This privilege would make the committee highly desirable even if it had no legislative functions. Indeed, there are Democratic members of the Ways and Means Committee for whom work on legislation is secondary to their work as members of the Committee on Committees.

A place on the Committee on

Committees is a source of personal influence in the House. The power to parcel out seats on choice committees such as Appropriations gives a Member leverage with his fellow Representatives. The ability to stack a given committee with Members favorably disposed to Administration programs gives the Committee on Committees member influence with House party leaders, particularly when a Democrat is in the White House.

This personal influence is translatable into benefits for a Member's constituents. It gives him, if he is an artful horse trader, a leg up in bartering for pork barrel projects and other constituent benefits outside the committee's official jurisdiction.

COMMITTEE MAKEUP

New members of the Ways and Means Committee are carefully selected and measured against three yardsticks: party loyalty, geographic distribution, and disposition toward a number of issues within the committee's jurisdiction.

Democrats: Committee Democrats are appointed directly by the Democratic Caucus.

The views of the House Democratic leaders—and of the White House during a Democratic Administration—carry substantial weight in the selection process, as does the view of Chairman Mills.

Mills told *National Journal* that since 1958, when he became chairman, no Democrat had been appointed to the committee without his support.

Issues—For years, while the late Rep. (1913-61) Sam Rayburn,

D-Tex., was Speaker, it was widely accepted in the House that no Member need apply for a place on the committee unless he was committed to retention of a 27.5-per cent oil depletion allowance.

Under the Democratic Administrations of John F. Kennedy and Lyndon B. Johnson, support for medicare was a prerequisite.

In 1960, the committee rejected the medicare proposal, 17-8, with seven of 15 Democrats voting against it.

Between 1960 and 1965, the Democrats filled nine vacancies on the committee, and careful screening ensured that all but one of the new members was for medicare. By 1965, the committee's over-all disposition toward medicare had shifted to 13-12 in favor.

The only anti-medicare Democrat who was allowed to join the committee was former Rep. (1933-35; 1947-67) Clark Thompson of Texas; the leadership supported him only to head off the candidacy of another Texan, former Rep. (1951-67) Walter Rogers, who was unacceptable to the leaders on other counts.

Geography—The fact that an anti-medicare Texan was chosen for the committee illustrates the importance of geographic considerations in selection of Ways and Means members. Thompson replaced still another Texan—former Rep. (1951-61) Frank N. Ikard.

The geographic consideration is twofold. Because Democrats double as members of the Committee on Committees, an attempt is made to ensure that every major region of the country is represented by a Member who might be

expected to appreciate its constituent interests.

Thus, James A. Burke of Massachusetts represents New England and New Jersey on the Committee on Committees. Phil M. Landrum of Georgia has a zone which includes Georgia and the Carolinas. Charles A. Vanik is responsible for his home state of Ohio and for West Virginia.

The Committee on Committees zoning has anomalies. Sam Gibbons of Florida also has Hawaii and Alaska in his zone.

Big Districts—Where the geographic pattern fails to achieve balance, it is because the power of the Democratic Party is not distributed uniformly throughout the nation. It is easier for a Member with a large and important Democratic constituency to get on Ways and Means than it is for one from a small, marginal district.

"You can tell more about the Democratic power structure in the country by looking at the Ways and Means Committee than at any other institution," said one committee member. "It is no accident that all the big cities—Chicago (Dan Rostenkowski), Detroit (Martha W. Griffiths), Los Angeles (James C. Corman), New York (Hugh L. Carey), Cleveland (Vanik), Philadelphia (William J. Green)—are represented on the committee. The big cities are the seat of Democratic power."

The tendency of the Democrats to pick members from the party power centers means there are some states—such as New York, Illinois, California and Texas—that have what amount to permanent seats on the committee.

Selection of members from

In 12 years as chairman of the House Ways and Means Committee, Wilbur D. Mills has built a reputation as Congress' most skillful legislator.

Each year, it falls to Mills to shepherd some of the Administration's most controversial and important legislation through the House. Yet he rarely loses control of his committee, and he almost never suffers a defeat on the floor.

How does Mills do it? What are his tactical secrets? *National Journal* interviewed committee members, committee staff, departmental officials, White House staff, lobbyists and Mills himself for answers to these questions. Their responses support the following conclusions.

Options—Mills keeps his options open. He rarely commits himself to a position before he has a clear reading of sentiment among his members. In this manner, he avoids intra-committee tests of strength and skirts unnecessary defeats. "Mills plays his cards close to his belt, and so do I," said ranking Republican John W. Byrnes of Wisconsin. "We try to look for areas of agreement and try to get resolutions rather than make issues."

Committee members said they frequently do not know where Mills stands on a controversial provision until the committee has nearly completed action on a bill.

His technique for exploring issues has led to a reputation for inscrutability, said a committee staff member close to the chairman. "If Mills seems inscrutable," he said, "it is because he keeps a completely open mind. He literally works out his position right there in front of the committee."

Soundings—Mills takes careful note of sentiment in the House at large before reporting out a bill.

Before each day's session, Mills customarily arrives early. Pushing aside the large swinging doors behind the rostrum, he enters the Speaker's lobby, seats himself in the corner of a beige leather sofa, inserts a small Madison cigar in a holder and lights up. That is the signal that the chairman is ready to hear what is on the minds of the Members.

For as long as he remains on the sofa, a nearly steady stream of Members come by to sit with him and talk about their problems concerning issues before his committee.

By making himself accessible to the Members, Mills avoids quixotic attempts to push legislation which his contact with the House tells him is counter to majority wishes.

"If the chairman is at odds with a consensus of the House," said Byrnes, "he will see what he can do to accommodate that consensus, though his solution may not be the same as that proposed by the consensus."

The characteristic, which students of the committee have described as "followmanship," spares Mills the loss of influence suffered by other chairmen who tilt at legislative windmills.

Homework—A good measure of Mills' influence within the committee stems from the fact that he is far more expert in the intricacies of the committee's legislative jurisdiction than are most of the other members.

This is particularly true in the tax area. Except on provisions where members have clear constituent interests, therefore, they tend not to take issue with the chairman.

"Mills knows his stuff so well that he can afford to be a benevolent autocrat; he can swamp any member with his expertise," said one staff source.

"The complexity of the statute (the tax code) is one of the things that gives Mills and Byrnes so much power," said Thomas F. Field, a former Treasury lawyer now head of Taxation without Representation, a public interest tax lobby. "They are the only two who really understand it."

Hard Work—In addition to being more expert than other members, Mills is willing to work longer and harder than most.

He has focused his life on the work of the committee with Benedictine dedication.

Mills has few interests to divert him from Ways and Means. He plays no golf, attends no cocktail parties, goes home early at the end of the day and generally declines to take telephone calls at home.

Only his frequent trips to his Arkansas district to talk with constituents takes his attention from the committee. For a man of national stature, Mills takes his home-district relations very seriously. It is generally harder for the

EFFICIENT, ABLE, SKILLFUL, POWERFUL

press to get an appointment with Mills in Little Rock than it is in Washington.

"Mills' ability to put together consensus on the committee is often a product of the grinding pace he sets," said one Democratic member. "The executive sessions just go on and on. People get tired, worn out, willing to let Mills have his way. One problem is that the committee is always working as a whole. There is so much stuff to be covered that some members are smothered by it. There is no question that this gives Mills and Byrnes an advantage."

Dropouts—The physical and intellectual rigor of the committee's work has caused some members in effect to drop out of active participation.

"There are a number of people on the committee who couldn't care less about its legislative function," said one Republican member. "This means that Mills' de facto power is far greater than his de jure power.

"There is no question but that he comes to any issue with a working majority in his pocket of people who are willing to rely on him for the technical details."

This view was echoed by a veteran Democratic member. "Mills can pretty much control the votes of all but a handful of the Democrats on the committee," he told *National Journal.*

Mills defends his members on the question of individuality, denying that he carries proxies.

"These are myths," he told *National Journal.* "I don't know how

they get started. Some of them to embarrass me, I guess. Some of them by folks who think it will enlarge my stature and that I'd like that.

"I don't feel that way about it. I can talk to any member of the committee and if I can persuade him, that's one thing. But each member of the committee is an individual. All 25 of us make a contribution of some sort to every piece of legislation of any magnitude that comes out of the committee. You'll find something that each member advocated and got into any major bill. Maybe they won't get everything, but some of what they advocate will end up in the bill."

Low Key—The willingness of some members to defer to the chairman's judgment is reinforced by Mills' courtesy and consideration for their interests.

In four weeks of interviews with members of the committee, *National Journal* heard not one word of personal criticism of Mills. "I've worked with a lot of people in the past, but Wilbur has got them all beat," said one junior Democrat.

"He is the lowest key leader I ever saw. He will talk to you any time and give you all the time in the world. His greatest characteristic is that he is just a very, very nice person."

Respectful—Mills' consideration for the other members manifests itself in several ways, which tend to ensure his hold on the committee.

Every member is given all the time he wants to question wit-

nesses or express his views. No Ways and Means member is given reason to feel that he is being cut off. Mill has held to this policy under considerable duress. When former Rep. (1950-68) Thomas B. Curtis, R-Mo., was on the committee, he frequently drove other members to doodling with his lengthy inquisitions.

Mills also is respectful of the constituent interests of his members. He is careful not to abuse his leadership prerogatives by asking members to do themselves political damage with a vote.

"Take Danny Rostenkowski (D-Ill.)," said one member. "Danny knows that Wilbur knows the areas in which he has to be protected. It's a relationship of trust, not just a bald-faced transfer of power. People can give Mills their proxies with assurance that he won't misuse them and leave them exposed to their patrons."

Cool—Mills also suffers opposition graciously. On the few occasions where there is substantial opposition to his viewpoint within the committee, he avoids an overt display of resentment which could breed division on future issues. When seven members of the committee narrowly missed handing the chairman a major embarrassment in floor action on the trade bill last year, it did not alter their relations with Mills. Both Sam M. Gibbons, D-Fla., and James C. Corman, D-Calif., leaders of the attempt, told *National Journal* there had been no hint of retribution for their actions.

Challenge—Although Mills

averted defeat on the question of how the trade bill should be considered, he did lose last year on a motion offered by committee member Jackson E. Betts, R-Ohio, to recommit the social security bill with instructions to add a cost-of-living escalator.

Committee members interviewed by *National Journal* deny that Mills' grip on the committee is slipping—Gibbons calls it a "hug" rather than a grip—but at least one Administration official who has dealt with Ways and Means feels that Mills' control is exaggerated.

Though he would not speak for the record because of his dealings with the committee, the official criticized the White House for being too timorous in challenging Mills.

"Mills has expertly used his reputation for being unbeatable, just as a poker player uses his. People fold when they don't have to," he said.

"This is not right. It was only a couple of years ago people were saying you couldn't take on the Appropriations Committee on the floor. Hell, they've been beaten; they've been rolled.

"Ways and Means had its pants taken down twice last year on roll-call votes. Betts beat Mills, and Gibbons almost beat him. He can be had."

One group which is doing its part to ensure that Mills cannot be had is the Japanese textile industry.

The Japanese textile companies have elected to comply with an export agreement which they negotiated with Mills even though the agreement was conditioned on the United States signing similar agreements with other Asian countries, which have yet to be reached.

The reason, according to a Japanese trade official, is that the companies fear that failure to comply will make the Mills effort appear futile and undermine the chairman's influence to the advantage of those who advocate legislated quotas.

these states to fill seats varies somewhat from the rule in that the state delegation in the House exercises the controlling influence. Where the state delegation is closely-knit, local influence is important. The appointment of Rostenkowski to the Illinois seat was made largely at the urging of Chicago Mayor Richard J. Daley, who had polled the delegation and found Rostenkowski's support greater than that of another Chicago aspirant, Roman C. Pucinski.

Republicans: The selection of Republicans for the Ways and Means Committee is done by the Republican Committee on Committees.

"There is a tradition in the Republican Party that someone doesn't get on Ways and Means unless he is from a fairly safe district," said Barber B. Conable Jr., N.Y. "I wouldn't have gone on unless I had moved my plurality from 53 per cent to 68 per cent."

The safe-seat criterion ensures that Republican members are relatively invulnerable to constituent pressures and that the Republican side of the committee will stand united behind the party line, which it does with more regularity than the Democrats.

Another reason why unity is the rule for committee Republicans is the close screening their Committee on Committees gives to prospective members' stands on issues.

Byrnes, the committee's ranking Republican, told *National Journal* that an effort was made to pick members who represent the middle of the party.

"Since the party is generally conservative on fiscal matters, we tend to pick people who are conservative on fiscal matters, people who represent the middle of the party," he said.

In the 91st Congress, the average Republican member of the committee voted in accordance with the position of National Associated Businessmen Inc., on 85.8 per cent of selected votes. Democrats agreed with the association only 30.1 per cent of the time. No Republican voted with the NAB on fewer than 66.7 per cent of its votes.

The NAB, founded in 1946, each year presents "watchdog of the treasury" awards to Members of Congress who, according to the association's literature, "vote for economy and against inflation."

On the other hand, the average Republican committee member in the 91st Congress voted with the AFL-CIO's Committee on Political Education on only 20.5 per cent of selected votes, whereas Democrats averaged 66.6 per cent.

Like the Democrats, Republicans tend to assure representation on the committee from several big states. "We try for regional balance, but some states like California, New York and Pennsylvania have sort of permanent seats," Byrnes said.

Influential Members: The fact that volunteering for Ways and Means is not enough if a Member's politics and geography do not have the proper mix means that some committee members have less than consuming interest in the complex and often tedious work of the committee.

Because the committee generally considers omnibus legislation which pools numerous bills, almost every member is apt to have an interest in one or more provisions. But relatively few members consistently take an active interest in all aspects of every bill.

There are a handful of members, including Mills and Byrnes, who can be seen at almost all open meetings. The majority attends sporadically. With a few members, it requires the patience of a birdwatcher to record a sighting at an open session.

National Journal asked committee members, former members, Hill staff members, lobbyists and Administration officials who deal with Ways and Means which committee members were most active and influential in the committee's decisions. Their lists were very similar.

At the top of everyone's list were Mills and Byrnes, whose influence was rated far above that of other members.

"The mindless operation of the seniority system has somehow brought the two natural leaders to the top," said one Republican member. "Mills and Byrnes, under any rational system, would be the leaders."

Those interviewed rated the following in order, behind Mills and Byrnes: Conable; second-ranking Democrat Al Ullman of Oregon, who, at age 57, is a possible successor to Mills because ranking Democrat John C. Watts of Kentucky is already 68; Corman of California, intelligent and effective; and Gibbons of Florida, a dogged attender and the committee rank-and-file's most diligent worker.

While active members have the greatest over-all impact on the committee's work, officials who work on and with the committee told *National Journal* that, on any specific issue, the senior Democrats have the greatest influence.

"If you have some small bill that you want to get through," said one Republican member, "the most effective thing to do is go to Watts, Burke or Ullman, the ranking Democrats. They are close to Mills and he will listen to them."

Those questioned generally declined to rate the four new members of the committee—Carey of New York; Joe D. Waggonner Jr., D-La.; John J. Duncan, R-Tenn.; and Donald G. Brotzman, R-Colo.—who have been there less than a year.

Philosophy: On the surface, the balance of power in Ways and Means might seem to have shifted in the 92nd Congress.

In the 91st Congress, members who could be expected to support Democratic leadership positions held a 13-12 edge on the committee, although the actual party lineup in that Congress was 15 Democrats and 10 Republicans.

But the 10 Republicans—when they voted together—could normally expect two Democrats to join them—Landrum of Georgia and Omar Burleson, Tex.

When Rep. Hale Boggs, D-La., left the committee to become Majority Leader, he was replaced by Waggoner who often has voted with Republicans on issues which divide the House generally along party lines.

During the 91st Congress, he voted with the Democrats on only 35 per cent of the votes which pitted a majority of the two parties against each other. Boggs voted with the Democrats on 71 per cent of those votes.

But Waggonner's voting record is deceptive when it comes to predicting how he will vote on Ways and Means.

During debate on the Legislative Reorganization Act of 1970, for example, he lined up with the House reform group on the issue of recording teller votes. Furthermore, he gets along well with Chairman Mills.

Given Mills' approach to consensus, a one-vote shift in balance on the committee would not likely have meaning. Typically, Mills tinkers with whatever legislation is before the committee until no more than a half-dozen members still oppose it.

WOODWORTH: MAN IN THE MIDDLE

When the House and Senate considers a tax bill, the man in the middle is Laurence N. Woodworth.

As chief of staff of the Joint Committee on Internal Revenue Taxation, Woodworth, 53, is chief technical adviser to both the Ways and Means Committee and the Senate Finance Committee.

It is a dual role which requires strict professionalism. When the House and Senate go to conferences to reconcile their differences, there must be no reflection of inconsistencies in Woodworth's advice. He must serve two masters but wear one hat—that of the impartial expert.

By all accounts, Woodworth is a master. Under his predecessor, the late Colin F. Stam, the joint committee was occasionally accused of foisting its viewpoint on the other committees.

Woodworth, who took over from Stam in 1964, has carefully avoided this pitfall. His job, as he sees it, is to outline alternative courses of action and to offer the pros and cons of each. He offers his opinion as to which is the preferable course only when it is solicited.

Woodworth has won the praise of Stanley S. Surrey, former assistant treasury secretary for tax policy (1962-69) and a critic of Stam. Surrey described Woodworth's role for *National Journal*.

"You have to be an able and sensitive person to work successfully in that job. You must deal with both committees in such a way that they have confidence in you. Only a person who is sensitive to his responsibilities in that regard can accomplish it. Woodworth is.

"When he is dealing with the Ways and Means Committee, his job is to see to it that the members understand the issues, to sense where they want to go and to assist them in accomplishing their objective without making mistakes and without their obviously understanding all the contours of a given problem in all its sections.

"When he goes to the Senate, his job is partly to explain why the House did what it did, but also to make apparent to the Senators what the issues are in case they want a different result. If they do want a different result, he must work it out with them at that time.

"When it comes to conference, he has to be in the position of really explaining the issues and letting them decide how to resolve them. He must be as helpful as possible in offering ways of resolution, while recognizing the interests of both groups. It's a difficult job. I think he carries it off well."

For Woodworth, the joint committee, which he joined in 1944, has been almost his entire professional life. He has a master's degree from the University of Denver and a doctorate from New York University.

MAKING LAWS

Among House committees, Ways and Means is unique in a number of ways—in its ties with executive experts, in the way it works from notes and not draft bills, in its protection against amendments from the floor, and in the fact that it has no subcommittees.

Executive Activity: Consultation between the Administration and the committee begins well in advance of the time a formal proposal reaches the Hill.

On major legislation, the White House asks Mills and Byrnes for their views before it makes a final decision.

The White House—When Mr. Kennedy was President, Mills visited the White House almost daily. He visited President Johnson at least weekly.

Mills has had far less contact with President Nixon.

On two occasions in the first two months of this year, however, Mr. Nixon invited Mills and Byrnes for private conversations with him and his Cabinet officers about legislative proposals destined for Ways and Means.

"I've gone down there every time they have asked me to," Mills told *National Journal*, "except to dinners or something like that. I don't go to the White House dinners."

If it is inconvenient for Mills to come to the Administration, the Administration often goes to Mills. In 1969, while Congress was in Easter recess, the Treasury Department and the White House were putting the finishing touches on tax-reform proposals which

Ways and Means would consider that year.

Before announcing them, Charles E. Walker, Treasury undersecretary, and Edwin S. Cohen, assistant secretary (tax policy), held long talks with Byrnes and all the committee Republicans. Walker flew to Little Rock, Ark., to go over the proposals section by section with Mills.

Mills is so important to the Administration on tax policy that he is consulted even on matters not under direct control of his committee.

In January of this year, when the Administration was preparing to announce administrative revision of depreciation schedules, David M. Kennedy, who was then Treasury Secretary, and Assistant Secretary Cohen again went to Little Rock to talk with Mills, even though the action did not require Ways and Means approval.

While the Administration's eagerness to consult committee leadership allows for congressional influence on the executive branch, some committee members complain that it also means the Administration has too great a say in the final outcome of the committee's work.

"Mills is greatly influenced by conferences with the President," said one Democratic committee member, speaking before the recent rift between Mills and the White House over the textile question.

"He is substantially controlled by people in the executive branch—the White House, the Treasury, the social security people. The Administration people have more influence than the com-

WAYS AND MEANS STAFF
SMALL, DISCREET, NON-PARTISAN

For a committee which handles so much important legislation, Ways and Means has a small professional staff.

There are just nine professional members, two of them specialists in social security and welfare matters, two specialists in tax matters and one a specialist in trade.

As a result, the committee leans heavily on other sources for its legislative expertise. Most of the staff work in the tax area is done by professionals of the Joint Committee on Internal Revenue Taxation and the Treasury Department.

On welfare and social security, the committee gets most of its technical advice from the HEW Department and from the Congressional Research Service at the Library of Congress.

On trade legislation, the committee draws on the staff of the Tariff Commission and on a host of interested departments of the executive branch.

The small complement of in-house experts which the committee retains is not divided between the parties as is the case with most congressional committees. Committee experts serve both majority and minority members, and *National Journal* heard no complaints from members about staff partisanship.

The size and character of the Ways and Means staff are in part a reflection of chairman Wilbur Mills. Mills prefers a small staff, several committee members said. "It was like pulling teeth to get Mills to add one trade staffer," said former committee member (1951-68) Thomas B. Curtis, R-Mo. Curtis also said that Mills resisted his requests to build up the social security staff. He recalled that Mills responded: "Damn it, Tom, you can't trust them."

The staff's small size, plus Mills' willingness to deal personally with the most trivial legislative detail, has prevented the emergence of any staff Richelieu or Mazarin as the power behind the chairman.

The man who would hold that power, if it existed, is Chief Counsel John M. Martin Jr. But Martin, 53, is the personification of discretion in his role as liaison between the committee and the press and the lobbyists.

Some committee counsels freely air their views on the inner workings of their respective committees, but not Martin. Even in off-the-record comments, the courteous Tennessee lawyer declines to criticize members, assign motives or hazard predictions about what the committee will do.

Martin's principal duties are administrative. He organizes hearings, schedules witnesses and makes staff assignments. On non-tax bills which the committee considers, he is also the committee's chief staff expert, attending all markup sessions and occasionally participating in the drafting sessions as well.

Martin has been with Ways and Means since 1956 when he joined as a professional staff member. In 1957, he was made assistant chief counsel and served in that capacity until he became chief counsel in 1968.

Martin's counterpart for the minority side is Richard C. Wilbur, 35. As minority counsel and a taxation specialist, Wilbur's primary duties are to research tax issues for the Republican members. A 1962 graduate of Notre Dame Law School, Wilbur came to the committee in 1964 from the Office of Chief Counsel of the Internal Revenue Service.

---

mittee members. Many members don't come to meetings. I used to wonder why; then I realized you just sit there for hours and you really don't accomplish anything. Why sit there 30 hours a week if you are not going to make any difference?"

Staff Work—Although the executive branch's influence with the chairman on major policy questions is ebbing—it has ebbed on revenue sharing—the Administration's influence on technical details is not affected.

This is true because the most important point of contact between the committee and the Administration is at the staff level. In some areas of its jurisdiction, Ways and Means has virtually no staff aside from that which it borrows from the executive branch.

The one area in which the committee has a strong staff of its own is taxes. The staff of the Joint Committee on Internal Revenue Taxation, which serves both Ways and Means and the Senate Finance Committee, has a complement of nearly 20 tax attorneys, economists and statistical analysts. Even in the tax area, however, the committee makes extensive use of technical experts from the executive branch.

The joint committee staff, headed by Laurence N. Woodworth, is in almost constant communication with Treasury tax experts; the Treasury is represented at all executive sessions of the committee.

Committee members, by contrast, are not permitted to bring their personal staff to executive sessions.

On trade legislation, social security, and welfare legislation, the Ways and Means Committee has only a skeletal staff. As a result, it must rely almost exclusively on the executive branch for staff work.

When the trade bill was under consideration last year, the committee borrowed three men from the Tariff Commission on a full-time basis to provide technical assistance. Moreover, the committee had additional help from executive departments (the Tariff Commission is an independent agency).

Subcabinet Officials — In closed markup sessions on the trade bill, committee members were greatly outnumbered by Administration representatives. Attending meetings of the subcabinet convention which the committee had assembled were: Carl J. Gil-

bert, the President's special representative for trade negotiations; Paul A. Volcker, Treasury under secretary (monetary affairs); Herbert N. Blackman, deputy assistant secretary of Labor; Stanley Nehmer and Lawrence A. Fox, deputy assistant secretaries of Commerce; Raymond A. Ioanes, administrator of the Agriculture Department's Foreign Agricultural Service; and representatives of the State Department, the Interior Department, the Tariff Commission and the Customs Bureau. Accompanying staff was limited only by the size of the room.

"The Administration position was sought section by section," recalled one Administration man who attended. "We were asked for alternative language, and we offered it. It was as if we were the staff of the committee."

By contrast, when the Senate Finance Committee marked up the same bill later in the year, no Administration representatives were invited to participate.

For staff work in the welfare and social security areas, Ways and Means, which has only two staff experts of its own in the area, relies on the Library of Congress' Congressional Research Service and on technical experts at the Department of Health, Education and Welfare. Frederick B. Arner, chief of the Education and Public Welfare Division of the Congressional Research Service, has been assisting the committee in his area of specialization for 15 years.

Concern — The committee's close ties to the executive (the former HEW chief actuary, Robert J. Meyers, was listed formally as the committee actuary as well) worry some students of the committee, who say that its independence may be undermined.

Former member Tom Curtis says that Ways and Means is more independent of the Administration when legislating on tax matters, where it has in-house competence, than it is in the other areas, where it must lean on the expertise of the executive branch.

This is a minority view, however. Most committee members and staff members say that the help they get from the executive departments comes primarily from technicians who have no political axes to grind.

"We use the personnel downtown as sources of information," said John M. Martin, chief counsel. "It's the only place you can get certain types of information. If you need to know the number of social security beneficiaries in a given age group, you can get that only from the Social Security Administration."

Hearings: Unlike most committees, Ways and Means rarely has a specific bill before it when it begins hearings. This is partly by design and partly because the committee has so many bills referred to it each year that it must combine them into omnibus legislation.

Gerard M. Brannon, associate director of the Office of Tax Analysis at the Treasury Department, explained to *National Journal* that the Administration sends tax measures to the hill in the form of proposals rather than as draft bills.

"Tax legislation is different from other legislation because a bill pretty much spells out who is going to have to pay what. Each

taxpayer can look at a tax bill and see how it is going to affect him. Thus, if there is a draft bill before the committee when the hearings begin, a lot of special interests will show up to complain that this or that section says diddley-doo instead of diddley-dump."

Ways and Means, therefore, seldom has a draft bill until the markup session is completed. This explains, at least in part, why pressure for special interest amendments focuses on the Senate Finance Committee rather than on Ways and Means.

Nevertheless, Ways and Means hearings have been criticized by students of tax legislation for the fact that after Administration witnesses have said their piece, the rest of the hearings are taken up by a parade of special interest witnesses.

Chief Counsel Martin, who is responsible for putting the hearings together, conceded that special interests come forward to plead their cases, but he says the committee tries to ensure that all points of view are heard.

"On some issues, the variety of special interests ensures that all sides are heard," Martin said. "When that has not been the case, we have made efforts to see that the public interest and the unrepresented sides of the issues are heard. We have set up discussion panels and we have called in specialists."

To conserve time and to prevent the committee from being subjected to saturation bombing campaigns, Martin tries to get witnesses with similar points of view to consolidate their testimony.

In addition, veteran witnesses

are sophisiticated. They understand that it can be damaging to their interests to mislead Ways and Means. "That committee has an institutional memory because it deals in figures," said White House lobbyist Richard K. Cook.

"Ways and Means has a small staff, so it must rely on industry for information. But industry better not try to pull the wool over the committee's eyes, or it will get it in the neck the next time around."

Cook was a minority staff member of the House Banking and Currency Committee from 1965 to 1969.

Subcommittees: The Ways and Means Committee is unique among House legislative committees in that it has no subcommittees. It is within the authority of the chairman to create subcommittees if he sees fit, but Mills does not want standing subcommittees.

"Everything we do is of such importance and affects so many people that we would just be killing time to start off with a subcommittee," Mills said. "What good would it do to have a subcommittee of nine members to conduct hearings and report legislation when the full committee would have to hold a hearing on the subcommittee's report before it could ever know what to do?"

Byrnes stands firmly behind Mills in his opposition to subcommittees and for the same reasons. Other members say, however, that there are personal advantages to Mills in keeping all legislation in the full committee. Delegating jurisdictions to subcommittee chairmen could create specialized experts within the committee who could diminish Mills' influence as the reigning expert in all areas.

"Look at the Appropriations Committee," Curtis said. "There isn't any full committee any more. Mills knows that knowledge is power. He squirrels away information rather than elucidating issues."

Markup: A frequent complaint about the operation of Ways and Means is its secrecy.

Secret Sessions — All its markup sessions are behind closed doors, and the committee does not make its votes public.

"You don't want to let people know what's going on, or you can't control it," said Curtis. "If you make a mystery of it you can control it."

Other committees accustomed to closed markup sessions have opened them up only to find the result disruptive. Two years ago, Chairman Wright Patman, D-Tex., opened the House Banking and Currency Committee's markup of the one-bank holding company bill, and the session turned into a shouting match, with much of the noise generated for the ears of the lobbyists in the audience.

Curtis says Ways and Means members would not behave similarly. "To perform (for the lobbyists) you have to do your homework. Most members would run out of material pretty soon."

While Curtis was on the committee, he ignored the secrecy rule and made a point of telling anyone who asked whatever they wanted to know about what went on in the meetings. Even without Curtis, major Ways and Means votes are still regularly given to the press by members who do not respect the secrecy rule.

Procedure—In markup, members come down from the curved dais where they sit during hearings and gather around three sides of a square of large felt-topped tables in the area between the dais and the audience, which is generally packed with interested representatives of the executive branch.

Along the fourth side of the square, their backs to the audience, sit Administration advisers and committee staff.

If the committee is marking up a tax bill, Mills will invite the joint committee's Woodworth to get the discussion under way.

"Out comes the blackboard and Larry Woodworth begins to teach basic tax law," said a former Treasury Department participant. It can be a grueling process.

Generally beginning with the least controversial provisions, Woodworth describes alternatives and the pros and cons of each. If asked—and generally only then—Woodworth also will state a preference. The views of Administration representatives are solicited and heard. Each member is permitted to speak his piece and to question any witness.

At this point, members seldom know where Mills stands. Little has been predetermined. Mills and Byrnes may have had private discussions before markup, but both men said they make no effort to settle differences in advance.

MILLS' REPUBLICAN COUNTERPART

Since 1963, Rep. John W. Byrnes of Wisconsin has been the ranking Republican on the House Ways and Means Committee.

As leader of the minority, Byrnes does not draw the headlines or attract the attention that Chairman Wilbur D. Mills, D-Ark., does. But his influence among committee members is only slightly less than that of the chairman.

"Byrnes' role is probably understated on the committee," said a top committee staff member. A Democratic committee member agreed. "Mills is hesitant to ignore Byrnes," he said. "Byrnes is at least as influential with the Republicans as Mills is with the Democrats."

One reason Byrnes must be reckoned with is that he is almost totally independent. It was Byrnes who last year bucked Mills and forced through a social-security cost-of-living escalator. It was Byrnes who in 1970 refused to introduce the Administration's revenue-sharing proposal.

His refusal to support the bill involves a historical irony. Byrnes was a classmate of Walter W. Heller, who is considered the father of revenue sharing, at the University of Wisconsin, where he was graduated in 1936.

Before he was elected to Congress in 1944, Byrnes served three years (1938-41) as Wisconsin's special deputy commissioner on banking and four years (1941-44) in the Wisconsin state senate.

"Often I don't know where Mills or Byrnes stand before the session," said a top staff aide. "I can generally see the drift of the discussion, but I never feel a provision will stick until I sense agreement between Mills and Byrnes."

Substitute for Votes — The committee seldom votes during these sessions.

"You don't have to have votes," said Mills. "It just delays." Instead, Mills picks his way through the viewpoints, discarding points that involve irreconcilable differences, aggregating points on which there is agreement until he has a version which most members can support. At this point, Mills asks Woodworth to prepare a draft; the committee moves on to the next provision.

Frequently, committee members—particularly if they have arrived late—are not certain what agreement has been reached.

Drafting—Woodworth is one of three partners in the drafting process. Treasury and House Legislative Counsel staff members also are involved. All during a discussion, Woodworth's staff takes notes, as do the staff members from Treasury and the legislative counsel's office.

When markup is completed for a day, Woodworth and the Treasury representatives leave the committee room and go to the House Legislative Counsel's office where, with a member of that staff— usually Ward M. Hussey, deputy legislative counsel—they compare notes and draft the section. Often, these sessions run late into the evening.

The following morning, committee members are presented with the draft language which, barring objection, formally becomes a part of the bill.

Again, the committee usually avoids record votes.

"Any member can demand a vote, but it is considered something of an affront to do it," said a staff member.

"I used to demand votes," recalled Curtis. "Of course, you'd run into the boys who would try to frown you down to avoid pressure."

One committee member told *National Journal* that members were not given enough time to study the drafts to make sure they reflected their understanding of the previous day's agreement.

Floor Action: Bills reported by the Ways and Means Committee nearly always go to the floor under a closed rule; this restricts changes.

Complexity Argument—The argument in favor of closed rules, which the House Rules Committee has always imposed in response to Mills' requests, is that the committee's legislation is too complex and too vulnerable to perforation to permit normal amending procedures on the floor.

The handling of the revenue bills in the Senate, where there are no closed rules and where a host of amendments often are added to the House version, is often cited to support the argument.

"That's a lot of crap," said Curtis. "The way to hold power is to say to the House that this is too difficult to explain."

Curtis said former Rep. (1913-32; 1933-52; 1955-64) Carl Vinson, D-Ga., "used to do the same thing when he was chairman of Armed Services. He'd get unanimity in the committee, then if anyone from outside asked a question, he'd say, 'Oh well, military science is so complicated that you couldn't understand.'"

A Democrat now on the committee said he saw one serious disadvantage in the closed rule.

"Because of the closed rule, the House has never been forced to learn much about taxes, trade or welfare legislation," he said. "They don't have any say in the shape of the legislation, so they don't bother to study the details closely."

Challenge—Mills jealously guards the committee's closed rule. When seven members of the committee campaigned last year for a modified closed rule on the trade bill (HR 14870) and won the initial procedural vote on the floor, Mills threatened to take the bill back to committee rather than allow it to be considered section by section as the modified rule would have permitted.

He carried the day. The House defeated the modified rule, and Mills averted a precedent-setting action that could have weakened the exclusive grip of the committee on legislation within its jurisdiction.

Skill, Caution — Were Ways and Means in the hands of another chairman, its use of the closed rule might raise more opposition than it does. Though it circumscribes the franchise of the House at large by limiting members to an up or down vote, Mills is so well attuned and responsive to the will of the House that it rarely has the effect of thwarting the wishes of the majority.

His skill at reading House senti-

134 ment has prevented him in a dozen years as chairman from suffering a serious defeat on the floor.

Some students of the committee attribute this to simple caution and say that Mills would rather trim his sails than risk a close vote on the floor, where a defeat could weaken the committee's authority in the future.

Those who make that charge most often attribute Mills' caution to his experience with the first bill he ever reported out of the committee—a 1958 unemployment compensation bill which the Eisenhower Administration had requested. The bill was sent back to committee with instructions to delete one of its titles.

Mills says today that the deleted title was added to the bill as a lightning rod to draw opposition away from the rest of the legislation.

"I had set it up like a lame duck; I knew we'd never pass it," he said. "But they keep harking back to that and saying that the first bill I brought out of committee was defeated. Well, it wasn't defeated. It passed overwhelmingly" when it was reported again.

Mills contends that his cautiousness is largely mythical.

"They've written that I wouldn't bring a bill on the floor of the House until I'd counted the votes to be sure of passage," he said. "My God, I've brought bills out on the floor when I couldn't count 180 votes. . . . I've never had a controversial bill when I have had 218 people ahead of time for it."

Pragmatism — Nevertheless, Mills concedes that he can see no point in reporting legislation that is likely not to be passed.

"Hell, the whole process here is to legislate," he said. "Why would you vote out anything if you know it can't pass?"

Legislation coming out of another committee may represent only a few days of the full committee's time and only one of the matters before it, but legislation coming out of Ways and Means generally represents the sum of everything the full committee has done for months. It would be a waste of the committee's time to report legislation that had little chance of passing.

Fewer than half the members of Ways and Means have time to sit on second committees. Most of those second committees are involved with taxes or spending—the Joint Committee on Internal Revenue Taxation, or the Joint Committee on Reduction of Federal Expenditures.

During the 91st Congress, 3,432 bills were referred to Ways and Means. The committee held 96 days of hearings on 11 major subjects, heard 1,198 witnesses in person and received testimony that filled 47 volumes.

LOBBYISTS

Because of the committee's taxing powers, lobbyists for special interests could generate unbearable heat if the members did not have some insulation.

They are insulated in three ways:

by the fact that the committee works without a bill before it;

by the fact that the lobbyists traditionally concentrate on the Senate Finance Committee;

by Mills' skill at avoiding a commitment without appearing to do so.

By working without specific legislation, the committee makes it difficult for an interest group to tell whether or how its ox is likely to be gored by tax legislation until the measure is already on the House floor.

"The big conservative money is generally too slow getting started to be effective in the Ways and Means Committee," said one oil lobbyist. "Generally, they don't jump until they see a bill, and they don't have a bill until Ways and Means has already done its bit."

As a result of the first layer of insulation, lobbyists are more experienced in working with the Senate Finance Committee, which goes to work on tax legislation with the House bill before it. The Senate Finance Committee offers lobbyists a repechage, should they lose out in the House.

The third factor which helps shelter committee members is the difficulty of extracting a commitment of any sort out of Chairman Mills.

"In lobbying the committee, you really can't deal with Mills directly," said one Republican member. "He is too slippery. People have gone to see Wilbur and come away thinking they had a commitment. But that was only because they didn't listen carefully enough."

Because Mills rarely lets his position be known and because the committee tends to follow his lead, it is difficult for a lobbyist who concentrates his efforts on committee members to know whether or not he is making any headway.

Most members of the committee and lobbyists interviewed by *National Journal* agreed that the most effective way to lobby the Ways and Means Committee is to take the indirect approach. One veteran tax and oil practitioner said the first step is always to go to the Tax Legislative Counsel's Office at the Treasury Department on the theory that its technicians will have a major input into whatever the committee does.

After seeing the people at Treasury, he said, his next step is to go to the Joint Committee on Internal Revenue Taxation to talk to Woodworth or his staff. Woodworth confirmed that a number of lobbyists have decided that is the way to approach the committee.

"We see them, we see them," he told *National Journal.*

On a tax bill, assurance of support from Treasury and the joint committee is money in the bank. They represent almost all of the technical advice which the committee hears; both have considerable influence with Mills and Byrnes, and neither is likely to be gainsaid by other members of the committee less familiar with the arcana of the tax code.

Shotgun Approach: An even less direct approach to the committee, which has been successful, is to aim a lobbying effort at all 435 Members of the House and at the general public. The theory behind this type of lobbying is that Mills' penchant for reporting passable legislation means that the committee is more responsive to the mood of the House than are other committees.

"That's the way to go about it,"

said one Republican committee member.

"Sell your case to the people and to the House at large, and the general will position himself in relation to the troops."

Heavy emphasis was placed on this type of lobbying last year by opposing interests in the fight over whether the trade bill should include protectionist quotas on textiles and shoes.

Through newspaper ads, speeches and press releases, forces for and against the bill sought to create the kind of Main Street support for their positions which might turn the House in their favor.

David J. Steinberg, head of the Committee for a National Trade Policy, a free trade group, recalled his strategic thinking.

"I initially addressed my proposals to Mr. Mills with material sent to his attention," he said. "But, seeing that I wasn't going to get anywhere, I began to try to change the climate in the House, thinking that if Mills sensed the change, he would change his position."

Administration Lobbying: The White House puts great store in the effect of public opinion on Mills.

Revenue Sharing—The whole thrust of the Administration's lobbying campaign in favor of revenue sharing has been to build constituent support at the state and local level. Little has been done to try to persuade Mills and Byrnes, who the Administration knew in advance were opposed to the plan on principle.

"We made the decision last year that if we were going to get reve-

nue sharing through, over the opposition of Mills and Byrnes, we would have to sell it at the grassroots level," said Richard Cook, White House liaison man for the House.

The White House pushed the idea with mayors, Governors and state legislators and cooperated with the National League of Cities before the 1970 elections in sending letters to every congressional candidate. The letters outlined the proposal and asked each candidate for a commitment to the principle of revenue sharing.

Candidates who did not respond were approached in person by local politicians.

"The idea," recalled Cook, "was to get these people on record so we would have some leverage after the election when we went back to them. ... We are still relatively optimistic that the forces are there—out in the constituencies— to put together a majority in the House."

To hear Mills tell it, those who take their case to the House and to the public are on the wrong track. "I don't feel bound to go along with anything just because somebody else wants it," he said.

Medicare—"This story grew out of the fact that for a long time the Ways and Means Committee was against the Administration's proposal on medicare. I'm against it to this good day."

Mills explained that his support of medicare was not a capitulation to the will of the House, but the result of the committee's having rewritten the Administration proposal to conform to another approach which Mills had favored all along.

136

"Hell, if I had been against medicare, it never would have passed," he said. "How do I know? Because when John Byrnes offered his motion to recommit the committee bill to put all the costs under the general fund and do away with the payroll tax, we just beat him by 32 votes. If I have any strength in the House at all I could get more than 32 votes. I could have joined him (Byrnes) and made it into something entirely different from medicare."

Procedures—The Administration is the most active single lobbying force with which Ways and Means must contend. The high-level contact between the committee and the Administration, which begins in the pre-proposal stage, generally continues until the matter is settled.

The coordinating organ for the Administration is the White House. Under a system which has evolved over the past two years—and which is used for dealings with other committees as well—top White House aides meet on a when-necessary basis with relevant Cabinet officials to discuss where they stand with the committee.

The purpose of the meetings, explained one participant, is to make certain that the Administration is speaking to the committee with one voice, that whoever the spokesman is has all available information, and that the Administration is able to move quickly when necessary. Said the same source:

"The Administration man in the committee must be able to move just as fast as the committee or he will lose control. That committee has a certain pace, and you have to keep up with it or get lost."

Textile Quotas—Although the current split between Mills and the President is likely to reduce the effectiveness of Administration pressure this year, its lobbying efforts met with reasonable success in the 91st Congress.

The Administration was successful in getting Mills and the committee to add textile quotas to the trade bill despite Mills' historic opposition to protectionist measures. Inclusion of quotas was the result of an agreement between the chairman and the President designed to strengthen the U.S. hand in negotiations with Japan for voluntary export limitation. Mills feels that the President did not stand by his part of the agreement, which was to withhold White House support for legislated quotas.

Tax Legislation—The Administration was also successful in pushing through a proposal to speed up collection of estate and gift taxes to provide $1.5 billion in non-recurring revenue gains. An Administration participant recalled that, despite a "storm of protest" when the proposal was first announced, it was quietly pushed through after negotiations at the committee staff level.

"We worked with Larry Woodworth and with all the bar association people, and took the best of everything that was suggested," he said. "We took a lot of time, talked to many members of the committee, talked to everybody, let everybody get everything off his chest. In the end, despite the fact that the public testified unanimously against it, the thing went through the committee, and the Senate Fi-

nance Committee didn't even hold public hearings on it. I think it's an illustration of the kind of staff work you have to do."

The Administration failed, however, to win committee approval of another portion of the same revenue package, a proposed tax on lead additives in gasoline. Although Treasury Under Secretary Walker and James E. Smith, assistant secretary (congressional relations) visited all committee members, they could not sell the lead tax.

Legality—Technically speaking, the lobbying done by the Administration is illegal. Federal law (62 Stat 792) prohibits the use of appropriated funds to pay for lobbying Members of Congress either to favor or oppose legislation. The prohibition is largely ignored, however.

"You hear the complaint of illegal lobbying every once and a while when someone steps over that gray line and says something that is too crude or inappropriate," Cook told *National Journal.* "But Congress for the most part has come to live with executive lobbying, just as we at the White House have come to live with congressional lobbying."

CROSSING THE LINE

The most bitter arguments between House and Senate over taxes, trade and welfare come when the House believes the Senate has overreached its power in amending a House bill.

Clause One: The same clause in the Constitution—Article 1, Section 7, Clause 1—which requires the House to originate all revenue bills also declares that on these bills "the Senate may propose or concur with amendments as on other bills."

The Senate traditionally has construed those words to be an undiluted grant of authority to work its will on revenue legislation so long as the bill it shapes originated in the House.

Finance sometimes makes radical changes in House-passed revenue bills; it adds new and often wholly unrelated provisions that would be inadmissible under the strict rules of germaneness in the House. On rare occasions, it even discards the House language altogether and substitutes—as an amendment—a creation of its own, retaining only the House bill number and its enacting clause.

House Outrage: When a revenue bill has been radically altered by the Senate, some House Members protest that the Senate's authority to amend is proscribed by the subject matter of the House bill.

On those grounds, Rep. H. R. Gross, R-Iowa, challenged Senate amendments to the Revenue and Expenditure Control Act of 1968 (82 Stat 251) which came back to the House amended to include a 10-per cent income tax surcharge and a $6-billion reduction in spending.

"I do not claim that the Senate has no power whatsoever to amend a revenue bill of the House," Gross said on the House floor.

"But I do say it cannot, under the guise of an amendment, propose new revenue legislation. And that is exactly what has happened in this instance."

FINANCE COMMITTEE: A DISTINGUISHED HISTORY

In 1959, a special committee headed by John F. Kennedy selected five men as the most distinguished Senators in United States history.

All five were at some point in their careers members of the Senate Finance Committee—Henry Clay, John C. Calhoun, Daniel Webster, Robert M. LaFollette, and Robert A. Taft.

Three Presidents had been members of Finance while they were in the Senate—Martin Van Buren, John Tyler, and Lyndon B. Johnson.

The Senate did not organize standing committees as early as the House did, but in December 1815, a temporary (or select) committee was formed to consider a bill proposed by President Madison to raise tariffs and to charter the Second Bank of the United States.

That committee was made a standing committee a year later when the Senate decided to adopt the House committee pattern.

Initially, Finance had jusisdiction over tariff measures for revenue purposes only, such as the duty on salt.

Tariffs on manufactured goods designed to protect the nation's infant industries were the province of the Senate Committee on Commerce and Manufactures.

Finance succeeded in extending its jurisdiction over all tariffs in 1834, partly as a result of reaction to the ultra-protectionist "tariff of abominations" of 1828—a creature of the Commerce Committee.

By the eve of the Civil War, Finance—like Ways and Means—had extended its jurisdiction to appropriations, the national debt, and banking and currency.

The back-breaking workload this wide jurisdictional net produced during the Civil War led to formation in 1867 of the Senate Appropriations Committee to relieve Finance of part of its burden.

Not until 1913, however, did Finance lose its jurisdiction over banking and currency bills. Ways and Means lost its authority over appropriations, banking and currency in 1865.

Finance today still has a somewhat wider legislative jurisdiction than Ways and Means, despite its loss this year of responsibility for veterans' benefits.

In addition to responsibility for tax matters, social security and medicare, welfare assistance, unemployment compensation benefits, the public debt and tariff and trade legislation, which both committees hold, Finance also has responsibility for sugar quota legislation, which in the House is handled by the Agriculture Committee.

Domestic sugar producers have been protected from sugar imports since the first federal tariff law in 1789. But, since 1934 the protection has been afforded through a complex system of quotas—rather than a tariff—which involves an excise tax on domestic producers.

Finance had jurisdiction over sugar policy when it was implemented through tariffs and it has kept that authority since the introduction of the quota system (in the Jones-Costigan Act of 1934) because of utilization of the tax. Ways and Means had jurisdiction over sugar as well, until 1937 when, according to David Price, a Yale University scholar, "a personal deal was struck" between the chairmen of Agriculture and Ways and Means. The quota system periodically comes up for renewal in Congress and, because of the stakes, is the subject of intense lobbying by foreign and domestic sugar producers.

The stakes are high because, as Price explained in his doctoral dissertation on Finance, "by limiting the total amount of sugar that could be marketed, the quota system stabilized prices in the United States considerably above those prevailing in most other countries, and thus made the possession of a generous quota highly profitable. The result was constant jockeying among various classes of producers, domestic and foreign, for an increased share of the market."

There is little doubt where sugar stands in the list of priorities of Finance Chairman Russell B. Long, D-La. The chairman's interest in sugar is exceeded only by his concern for the oil industry, both being of prime importance in Louisiana.

Until this year—when the Senate Committee on Veterans' Affairs was organized—Finance also had jurisdiction over veterans' benefits, which, on the other side of the Capitol, has long been handled by the House Veterans' Affairs Committee, not Ways and Means.

Finance tried to head off formation of the new committee, which veterans groups had lobbied intensely for, by setting up a standing subcommittee of veterans legislation with Sen. Herman E. Talmadge, D-Ga., as chairman—this despite a long tradition weighing against permanent subcommittees.

Veterans' pensions and annuities were closely related to the committee's authority over other public income maintenance programs, Talmadge argued.

But the veterans lobby felt that its constituents were treated as stepchildren in the Senate, and it was awarded the separate Senate committee in the Legislative Reorganization Act (84 Stat 1140) of 1970.

In his book on Ways and Means, *The Politics of Finance* (Little, Brown 1970), John F. Manley concluded that "the House is unwilling to let constitutional niceties stand in the way of the resolution of pressing political demands."

In the 1968 debate, the heat was on to impose the surcharge to check inflation, and Article 1, Section 7, Clause 1 was not allowed to stand in the way.

Mills Leverage: It is clear that the Senate amends at the sufferance of the House.

"The Senate looks on its amending power as being unlimited on any House revenue bill," said Thomas L. C. Vail, chief counsel to the Finance Committee. "But we can't make that view stick anywhere but in the Senate.

"If the House takes the attitude, as they sometimes have, that they will be strict about our amending power, there is nothing we can do about it."

Mills has a variety of ways to persuade the Senate not to take too many liberties with House-passed revenue bills.

The most important is his dominance of the joint House-Senate conference committee where members of the two committees meet to reconcile differences over legislation.

Anticipation of what Mills will accept in conference frequently is a significant factor in Senate deliberations. Mills plays on that, even threatens not to call a conference at all when the Senate, in his view, is using its amending powers too freely.

He made the threat, although to little avail, when the Senate was

Gross offered a resolution to return the bill to the Senate as unconstitutional; it was tabled after heated debate.

Mills himself opposed the Gross resolution, arguing that the Supreme Court had repeatedly held that the Senate had wide latitude to amend revenue bills as long as they had originated in the House.

adding trinkets to the "Christmas tree bill" of 1966—the Foreign Investors Tax Act (80 Stat 1541), which came back to the House trimmed with pork barrel amendments.

He delivers on the threats just often enough to give them validity. He refused to go to conference on unemployment compensation amendments in 1966, telling the Senate to accept the House version or let it die.

Backed by the Johnson Administration and organized labor, Long had won in the Senate with an amendment to the House bill (HR 15119), calling for federal minimum unemployment benefit standards. When Long refused to accept the Mills version, the bill died.

Waiting on the House—The hegemony of Ways and Means extends even into the Finance Committee's hearings calendar.

There is a tradition in the Senate of "waiting on the House." It was followed assiduously by Long's predecessor, the late Sen. (1933-65) Harry F. Byrd, D-Va. Byrd never began hearings on a bill until Ways and Means had finished, even though as adjournment approached it left the Senate in a weak position to make changes.

Long is not the stickler about waiting on the House that Byrd was, but the rule is followed out of necessity.

"Generally, Finance doesn't know what to hold a hearing on until Ways and Means gets through," said a top Finance staff member.

House Rule: After prolonged debate, the House amended its rules on germaneness of Senate amendments as part of the Legislative Reorganization Act of 1970 (84 Stat 1140).

Under the rule proposed by Rep. James G. O'Hara, D-Mich., House conferees no longer can bring a non-germane Senate amendment back to the House floor as part of a conference report on a bill.

These amendments would have to be reported "in disagreement," giving House members an opportunity to vote yes or no by a simple majority on each amendment.

Significance—How significant the new rule will be is problematic. It caused no comment at all when the reorganization bill went before the Senate.

"If we had challenged everything, there wouldn't have been a bill," said Eli E. Nobleman of the Senate Government Operations Committee staff.

First Test—Although a top Finance Committee staff member said the new rule could cause trouble, it failed to do so on its first test.

The House bill calling for an increase in the debt limit (HR 4690) came back from the Senate on March 16 with a popular 10 per cent increase in social security benefits written into it.

The amendment was not germane to the House bill, but Mills asked for unanimous consent to suspend the new rule. John Byrnes, supporting Mills, pleaded with Members "not to impose hurdles at this time on this important legislation."

Political reality prevailed and the measure was adopted.

Jealousy: Manley ascribes some of the House antagonism toward Senate tampering with its bills to a feeling in the House that "Ways and Means does most of the work on the legislation and the Senators irresponsibly amend it in response to their own wishes or, more likely, the wishes of interest groups and executive department officials who are dissatisfied with the decisions reached by Ways and Means."

To Ways and Means members, Manley wrote, "the Senate is characterized by irresponsible logrolling and by capitulation to politically popular but unwarranted demands."

"There's tremendous jealousy of the Senate in the House," said former Sen. (1949-67) Paul H. Douglas, D-Ill., and a former Finance Committee member.

"We were snobbish toward them, they thought," Douglas recalled, "and that excited, naturally, their opposition. But the House always wanted to score points on us. It has an inferiority complex."

Media: Another factor in House antagonism is the superior power of Senators to command media attention.

"The guy who's 10th in seniority on Ways and Means is out of sight," said a former Johnson Administration official who has worked with both committees. "He's a hell of a lot lower than the guy who's 10th or even 16th on Finance."

Finance members can float an idea, get publicity for it, tack it to a House bill and hope that in three or four years it will have developed enough public support that Mills will accept it.

140

Sen. Abraham A. Ribicoff, D-Conn., a member of Finance, may ultimately get tax credits for college tuition written into the tax code that way. He succeeded in adding his proposal to the Tax Reform Act of 1969 (83 Stat 487), but it did not survive conference.

FINANCE

The pressures that shape amendments to House revenue measures start in the Senate Finance Committee, but, unlike the practice in the House, they follow the bill to the Senate floor.

Cauldron: Even when interests clash in Ways and Means, it is a quiet pond compared with the cauldron of Senate Finance.

"It's a far more mysterious body than Ways and Means," said Thomas F. Field, former Treasury tax lawyer now with Taxation With Representation, a public interest tax lobby.

What emerges from Finance, said Stanley S. Surrey, former assistant treasury secretary for tax policy (1961-69), is "a composite of personal results." What emerges from Ways and Means, he said, is a "committee result."

The Finance Committee traditionally is less receptive than the Senate to ambitious social legislation such as medicare and redistributive tax reform measures.

Medicare was defeated in Finance, 6-11, in 1964, but it was passed, 49-44, on the Senate floor after Sen. Clinton P. Anderson, D-N.M., decided to fight the committee.

It was dropped in conference that year. A year later, after Ways and Means had lined up for it,

Finance backed medicare, too.

Finance also rejected, 8-8, what ultimately became the centerpiece in the Tax Reform Act of 1969, the proposal by former Sen. (1952-71) Albert Gore, D-Tenn., to increase the personal exemption for individual taxpayers from $600 to $850.

Gore pared the figure to $800 and won on the floor, 58-37, then pared it again to $750 to save it in conference.

This kind of performance led one labor lobbyist, who asked not to be quoted by name, to label Finance "probably the most overruled committee in the Senate."

Long told *National Journal* the title was "100 per cent wrong" and undeserved.

All of those interviewed by *National Journal*—including Long and Sen. Wallace F. Bennett, R-Utah, ranking minority member—were unanimous in placing the committee several degrees to the right of the Senate as a whole with respect to issues that go before the committee.

Yet Long, a consummate horse-trader, has confounded those who would pigeonhole the committee by extracting from the cauldron a lopsided vote in favor of a revolutionary proposal giving taxpayers the option of designating on their tax returns that a dollar of their tax liability should be diverted into a fund for financing Presidential campaigns.

In 1970, Long won committee backing for a health insurance proposal for catastrophic illness, which would pay 80 per cent of all hospital costs after the 60th day of confinement and all medical costs above $2,000 for anyone under the

age of 65 who was insured under social security.

The plan was tied to the ill-fated social security-welfare reform-trade package (HR 17550) that died in the final hours of the 91st Congress.

THE MEMBERSHIP

Finance is one of the Senate's "big four" committees—ranking with Foreign Relations, Appropriations, and Armed Services as the places to be.

Attraction: A seat on Senate Finance does not confer the incidental powers over colleagues that go with Ways and Means membership.

The attractions are the importance of the legislation the committee handles and access to campaign funds.

"When you go on Finance, boy, do you make friends," said Wilbur J. Cohen, former HEW Secretary (1968-69), who has worked with the committee in various capacities since the early 1930s. Cohen is now dean of education at the University of Michigan.

Said a former aide to a Finance Committee member:

"It's easy to get your campaign war chest filled up when you go on Finance, if you're willing to work for the special interests. But all a liberal who fights for the public interest can do on that committee is make enemies."

A former committee member, who asked not to be quoted by name, said the basic split on Finance is between Senators with a public-interest bias and Senators who have a private-interest orientation.

Said Yale scholar Price after a study of the 89th Congress: "Only Douglas, Gore and Williams seemed to have serious misgivings about using their committee positions to promote home-state or other interests." Former Sens. Douglas, Gore and John J. Williams, R-Del. (1946-71), were then on Finance. These three fought a running battle with other committee members.

Campaigns—Yet, the lure of the committee for all three was overpowering, and they all waged long campaigns for appointment.

It took Douglas seven years. Gore made it in four, which Long said is "about par for the course."

Sen. William Proxmire, D-Wis., "tried like hell to get on," Douglas said, but he did not make it.

The main sticking point for all of them was their stand on the oil depletion allowance.

Gore—In his book, *The Eye of the Storm* (Herder and Herder, 1970), Gore, who had been a Member of the House for 14 years before joining the Senate, explained his determination to get appointed to Finance:

"I watched tax bills ... come out of Ways and Means, go through a pro forma House debate, and then be voted on as a package—usually by overwhelming majorities with few questions raised. ...

"For fourteen years as a Congressman, I was never able to offer an amendment to a tax bill, though I felt deeply that tax inequity was one of the blatant injustices of our society. One of the reasons I sought election to the Senate was that I might be able to act more effectively in this area. ... It

seemed to me, furthermore, that it would only be by assignment to the Senate Finance Committee that I could really be effective in implementing my views on tax inequities."

Democrats: The Finance Committee's attractiveness and its traditionally low rate of turnover has loaded its membership with senior Senators with relatively safe constituencies.

Four members, for example, are chairmen of other Senate committees—Anderson of Aeronautical and Space Sciences; Herman E. Talmadge, D-Ga., of Agriculture and Forestry; J. W. Fulbright, D-Ark., of Foreign Relations; and Vance Hartke, D-Ind., of Veterans Affairs. Only the Appropriations Committee has more members who are chairmen of other committees; it has five.

When Byrd was chairman of Finance, Senators with what he considered liberal leanings were deliberately blocked from membership. "He liked to have a membership that didn't get too far from his views," the late Sen. (1950-69) Everett M. Dirksen, R-Ill., once said.

Dirksen went on the committee at Byrd's urging to block another Republican—unpalatable to Byrd—with less seniority who was then trying for appointment. Byrd's gatekeeping power on Finance membership was a natural adjunct of his position in the Senate inner club, which kept a tight grip on all committee assignments.

The musical chairs game was constantly in use to keep the committee to Byrd's liking. Fulbright was persuaded in 1961 to give up the Banking and Currency Com-

mittee, which he liked, according to a veteran Senate aide, by a combination of oil and gas interests in his state who wanted his voice in Finance and the Senate grandees who wanted to block Proxmire from getting on the committee.

Douglas was turned back repeatedly when vacancies occurred because a more senior applicant suddenly materialized. In the case of the late Sen. (1926-49; 1955-56) Alben W. Barkley, D-Ky., Douglas was implored to step aside out of courtesy to the former (1949-51) Vice President.

Lyndon Johnson joined the committee in 1955 to block Douglas, according to a Senate staff member who would not be quoted by name.

Opening Up—Douglas succeeded in 1956, and there followed a flurry of appointments to the committee following a Johnson rule that efforts would be made to get each Democrat on the committee of his choice.

Former (1958-71) Sen. Eugene J. McCarthy, D-Minn., and Hartke were among them. The positions they later took on oil legislation in Finance led Douglas to write in a 1967 article in *American Scholar*: "I sometimes suspected that the major qualification for most aspirants for membership on the Finance Committee was a secret pledge or agreement to defend the depletion allowance against all attacks. I suspected, also, that campaign funds reinforced these pledges."

Long Influence—Long does not have nearly the grip on membership selection that Byrd had, largely because these matters are

142

handled in a far more democratic way in the Senate now than when Byrd was there.

In an interview with *National Journal*, Long said he had a "small amount of influence, not a great deal" over who gets named to Finance.

Long said that he had always favored a balanced committee. "I supported Senator Douglas to go on the committee," he said, "and used what little influence I had then to help get him on, and knowing what his position on oil was, and knowing his position on sugar—both of which were contrary to mine.

"But I felt the committee needed him because it needed that balance of a Northern liberal at that particular time. I supported Senator Gore and urged that he go on. He probably gave me more headaches than any Democrat on the committee but I felt that he should be on there."

Four Democrats have been named to Finance since Long became chairman: Sens. Lee Metcalf, Mont.; Fred R. Harris, Okla.; Harry F. Byrd Jr., Va. and Gaylord Nelson, Wis. Of these, only Byrd, the son of Long's predecessor as chairman, can be considered a fiscal conservative.

Metcalf resigned in 1969 after only two years on Finance when Senate Democrats decided that each Senator should be limited to two major committees. Metcalf was on three. He had gone to Finance, reluctantly in the first place at the insistence of Sen. Mike Mansfield, D-Mont., the Majority Leader.

Nelson—The manner of Nelson's appointment to the commit-

tee this year showed that the oil lobby still has a powerful hand in the selection of committee members.

Nelson, who has been in the Senate since 1963, nosed out freshman Sen. Lloyd M. Bentsen Jr., D-Tex., for the job by a single vote in the Senate Democratic Steering Committee.

Nelson has consistently voted to cut depletion allowances. Bentsen was expected to protect his home state's oil interests.

The vote reflected the fact, said one lobbyist, that "the oil and medical people both were looking for friends." The proposals for a national health insurance plan with the likeliest chance of success—those tied to the social security system—would go through Finance.

Long would not say, in an interview, whether he supported Nelson's candidacy, but, he said, "I was pleased to see him named. His name was being suggested along with two other men, any one of whom I'd have been happy to have on the committee."

Other Senators who sought the Finance assignment, according to one veteran lobbyist, were Thomas F. Eagleton, D-Mo; Walter F. Mondale, D-Minn.; James B. Allen, D-Ala.; and Mike Gravel, D-Alaska.

Although Long and Nelson disagree on oil they are good personal friends. When Long took over as chairman of Finance, he gave up to Nelson his Monopoly Subcommittee of the Select Committee on Small Business—which he could have retained. Nelson thereafter made headlines with his subcommittee hearings on drug costs.

Nelson voted for Long in 1968, when Long was challenged and defeated for the Democratic Whip's job by Sen. Edward M. Kennedy, D-Mass.

Republicans: In the 91st Congress and now in the 92nd, the senior Republican on Finance has had formal authority to screen Republican applicants for the committee. John Williams was chairman of the Republican Committee on Committees in the 91st Congress and Wallace F. Bennett, Utah, who became ranking Republican on Finance when Williams retired, holds that position now.

Seniority—Bennett said, in an interview, that the Republican committee assignments are made strictly on the basis of seniority. "The most senior man requesting a committee gets it."

Sen. Robert P. Griffin, Mich., the Senate Republican Whip, was named to fill the one Republican vacancy on Finance this year. Sen. Charles H. Percy, Ill., had sought the assignment, but Griffin is seven months senior to Percy.

"The Republicans," said Democrat Lee Metcalf, "have what amounts to a policy of putting their most conservative men on the Finance Committee. Just look who is there."

"Griffin is the first Republican to get on that committee in the memory of man who hasn't been an absolute troglodyte," said a labor lobbyist who follows the committee's work.

White House Role—There were press reports at the time of Griffin's appointment that the move was engineered by the White House to give it a strong committee spokesman for its welfare-re-

RUSSELL LONG: EXTENDING THE KINGFISH DYNASTY

Russell Billiu Long, scion of one of the nation's most colorful political dynasties, is emerging from a difficult time of his life.

Six years ago, Tom Wicker of *The New York Times* called Long "a hot betting choice" to succeed the late Sen. (1949-63) Robert S. Kerr, D-Okla., as "uncrowned king of the Senate.'"

That was just after he was elected Senate Democratic Whip, succeeding Hubert H. Humphrey who had become Vice President.

He was then considered a good bet to succeed Sen. Mike Mansfield, D-Mont., as Majority Leader when and if Mansfield decides to step down.

His senatorial powers increased even further in January 1966 when he succeeded the late Sen. (1933-69) Harry F. Byrd, D-Va., as chairman of the Finance Committee—although because of Byrd's failing health he had been de facto chairman since the death of Kerr in 1963.

Long had won high praise for his skill as floor manager of a landmark $18-billion income tax reduction bill in 1964, which was the keystone of the Kennedy-Johnson Administration fiscal policy. So effective was Long that an opponent of the hill, Sen. William Proxmire, D-Wis., paid him this tribute:

"If a man murdered a crippled, enfeebled orphan at high noon on the public square in the plain view of a thousand people, I am convinced after today's performance that, if the Senator from Louisiana represented the guilty murderer,

the jury would not only find the murderer innocent, they would award the defendant a million dollars on the ground the victim had provoked him."

But in 1967, his Senate power began to fade almost as quickly as it had grown.

He snapped the patience of the Senate with a runaway, single-minded filibuster in defense of what he considered one of his greatest achievements—an amendment authorizing taxpayers to apply $1 of their tax liability to Presidential campaign funds.

Long pushed the campaign contribution proposal to enactment in the 89th Congress, but former Sens. John J. Williams, (1947-71), R-Del., and Albert Gore (1953-71), D-Tenn., came into the 90th Congress determined to repeal the law because of its cost.

They ultimately succeeded, but Long postponed defeat with a series of parliamentary maneuvers which kept the Senate tied up for five solid weeks.

So exasperated were Senate leaders by the delay that columnists began writing think pieces that all but pronounced the last rites on Long's admitted ambition to become Majority Leader.

Shortly thereafter, the Louisiana Senator announced he would defend former Sen. (1959-71) Thomas J. Dodd, D-Conn., against charges of misusing political funds. In an often belligerent performance, which again stalled Senate business for weeks, Long ridiculed the Senate Ethics Committee for recommending censure of Dodd

and made the charge—for which he later apologized—that most of the men on the committee could not stand the scrutiny Dodd had undergone.

Despite the fact that Long's defense did Dodd more harm than good, it was a characteristic act of simple charity on Long's part; he helped a man other Senators were treating as a pariah.

When Sen. Edward M. Kennedy, D-Mass., challenged Long for his post as Whip and won, it came as no surprise. For one thing, Mansfield had found Long less than dependable as a lieutenant.

Long's personal fortunes declined further in 1969. He was divorced by his wife of 30 years. An embarrassing incident in a Washington restaurant in which Long was alleged to have "bumped or shoved" two Connecticut policewomen dining there was reported in Washington newspapers.

And in 1970 a federal grand jury in Baltimore named Long as well as Rep. Hale Boggs, D-La., in a report charging a Baltimore contractor, Victor J. Frenkil, with conspiring to defraud the federal government on a contract involving underground parking facilities for the House of Representatives. A subsequent Justice Department memorandum on the incident said that no elected official had committed any wrongdoing in the case.

The alleged conspiracy involved an attempt by Frenkil to get federal approval for $5 million in extra costs over and above the original $11.7-million contract figure. Long told *The Washington Post*

144

that at the request of former Sen. (1963-69) Daniel B. Brewster he had asked his administrative assistant, Robert Hunter, to inquire into the merits of Frenkil's claim.

One of Long's friends believes that in the Frenkil case, as in the Dodd defense, it was the Louisiana Senator's easy generosity that got him tangled in a web of problems.

Yet this same quality has earned him the great affection of a wide circle of friends inside and outside the Senate. "He's frank, warm-hearted and not a hypocrite and I personally like him very

much," said former Sen. (1949-67) Paul Douglas, D-Ill., in an interview.

Long's friends say that he has changed since his remarriage in December 1969 and that the change has meant renewed effectiveness in his Senate work.

Born 52 years ago in Shreveport, La., he was first named Huey Pierce Long after his father, the Louisiana Kingfish. But his father, who had just embarked on his political career, feared the name might be a burden and renamed him Russell Billiu.

Long is the only Senator in United States history who was preceded in that august body by both his father and mother. His father served in the Senate from 1932 to 1935. His mother, Rose McConnell Long, was appointed to her husband's seat in the Senate after he was assassinated, and served out his term, which ended in 1937.

Long's desk on the Senate floor is the same one his father occupied—and the same one used by John C. Calhoun, who was chairman in the 29th Congress of the Senate Finance Committee.

form and revenue-sharing plans.

A White House aide told *National Journal* that "those reports were entirely wrong."

"We work with Bennett," said the aide. "He's the ranking Republican. And he's a good leader. He's evolving into a Mansfield type of leader on the committee. He gets things done by tact and consideration of everyone's needs and feelings."

But, at the outset, according to a labor lobbyist who keeps a close watch on Finance, "the White House had to sweat blood to get any Republican support on that committee for their position on the family assistance plan."

Bennett at the time did not dismiss out of hand the speculation about Griffin's expected role in the committee.

"I went to Senator Griffin about those reports," Bennett told *National Journal*, "and asked him how much he was involved in them. He replied: 'I'm going on as the junior member of the committee and that's the way I plan to

conduct myself.' So I think the reports were perfectly ridiculous. The White House doesn't need anyone to bring messages to me."

Philosophy: The turnover on Finance in 1971 was unusually large. Three Senators left the committee: Gore by defeat, McCarthy and Williams by retirement. But there were only two vacancies in the 92nd Congress because the committee membership was reduced by the 1970 Legislative Reorganization Act. Finance was cut from 17 to 15 originally, but it was raised to 16 when the 92nd Congress convened (although the statutory limit remains at 15). The rationale behind the reduction was to bring committee strengths more nearly in blaance with each other. The reduction also means that the character of the committee will be harder to change with new appointments.

Packing the Finance Committee with younger, more progressive members in order to dilute its control by "the Senate Establishment" had been one of the prime objec-

tives of former Sen. (1956-69) Joseph S. Clark, D-Pa., a critic of congressional organization.

Clark wanted to increase the committee's membership to 21. Finance operated in a vacuum "removed from the disturbing fiscal theories of the modern world," Clark said in his 1964 book, *Congress, the Sapless Branch* (Harper Trade Books).

By contrast, said Clark, Ways and Means had "begun to adjust itself slowly but surely to the fiscal needs of the nation" and "can act when a majority of the body it represents is ready for action."

Byrd's Committee—When Clark wrote the book, Harry Byrd Sr. was chairman of Finance and—as one Senate staff member put it—"The atmosphere in Finance was six degrees below zero." Long, who said he considers himself "an old-time populist" on many issues, quickly removed the logistical system with which Byrd had frozen out junior members when he took over in 1966.

Byrd, for example, leaned exclusively on the staff of the Joint Committee on Internal Revenue Taxation for assistance on tax bills. Finance itself had only a clerical staff whose quarters, according to Price's dissertation, "resembled nothing so much as the tax assessor's office in a Southern county courthouse."

Membership on the joint committee is confined to the five senior members of Finance and of Ways and Means. The staff, then headed by Colin Stam, served only those ten men. As a result, junior members of Finance had no specialists to assist them in picking their ways through complex amendments to the tax code.

"And the damn code is very complicated," said Douglas, who never made it into the inner circle of the committee.

Long's Changes—Long asked and was granted Senate permission to hire a six-man professional staff. Finance, by then, already had one professional, Vail, who had come from the joint committee staff in 1964 at Long's request.

The staff buildup was opposed by Williams, Bennett, and Sen. Carl T. Curtis, R-Neb. Williams argued that the joint staff was sufficient. Long overruled the objection, and the staff was hired. Vail became chief counsel and Long stressed that the staff was available to all committee members.

Stability—Although Finance emerged from the Southern courthouse era and junior members were brought in out of the cold, the philosophical makeup of the committee did not change appreciably. As new members arrived, the more effective challengers to the committee's leadership—such

as Douglas and Gore—left.

In view of one congressional aide, who has kept in close touch with the committee for many years, "It has unquestionably veered to the right from where it was a few years ago."

It remains, in the judgment of a top aide to one of the committee's members, "one of the most autocratic committees in the Senate."

"Its ideological makeup is far more conservative than that of the Senate," said Sen. Harris in an interview. "It's just not reflective of the Senate. That's why I moved this year to try to keep the number of members up and have the vacancies filled by those who are more progressive."

One of the committee's top staff members said, however, that Finance better reflects the Senate of the 92nd Congress—in which President Nixon believes there is an ideological majority behind him— than the committee in 1970 reflected the Senate of the 91st Congress.

Ratings—If the members of Finance were grouped on a see-saw according to their ADA (Americans for Democratic Action) and ACA (Americans for Constitutional Action) vote ratings in the last session of Congress, the see-saw would drop like a ton of bricks on the conservative side under the weight of at least 10 of 16 members.

The ADA calculates a member's "liberal quotient" based on selected votes, and the ACA ratings reflect evaluations of selected votes from a conservative viewpoint.

Both organizations placed Sens. Bennett, Long, Griffin, Talmadge,

Byrd, Curtis, Clifford P. Hansen, R-Wyo., Paul J. Fannin, R-Ariz., Len B. Jordan, R-Idaho, and Jack R. Miller, R-Iowa, on the conservative side of the see-saw, with most of them clustered near the tip.

Both ADA and ACA placed Harris, Ribicoff, Nelson, Hartke and Fulbright on the liberal half, with only Harris, Nelson and Ribicoff at the tip.

New Mexico's Anderson produced the only disagreement between ADA and ACA, with ADA giving him a moderately conservative score and ACA giving him a moderately liberal rating. Indeed, he has played the swing man in Finance on occasion.

Those rated conservative by ADA and ACA have the best attendance records and are the most active participants in committee work, although Ribicoff and Harris did have significant roles last year during consideration of the family assistance plan.

Ideological Lines — Bennett told *National Journal* the committee divides in its votes more on ideological than on party lines.

"What you get," Bennett said, "are ideological-line votes with some Democrats joining Republicans, most of whom are on the conservative side."

"There's a kind of community of interest among members of the committee, both Democrat and Republican," said a White House aide, "which even tends to cut us out occasionally."

"They will have a point of view different from ours."

That Finance is more conservative than the Senate as a whole, Long told *National Journal,* is "a fact of life that you can't do much about." The reason for it, he said, is that "the fellows who have to pay for things become cost conscious."

"I've heard them—some of them very good men whom I regard highly—say that the way to stay in the Senate is to vote for every appropriation and against every tax. But if you're one of the fellows with the majority in the Finance Committee, it becomes your unhappy duty from time to time to go out there and ask that Senate to raise taxes to pay for what we've done and to oppose amendments where we don't have the money to pay for it."

Representation: Griffin of Michigan is the only committee member representing a state that is among the 10 most populous; he is also the only member whose state contains one of the 10 largest metropolitan areas (Detroit).

None of the five most populous states—New York, California, Pennsylvania, Texas and Illinois—is represented on Finance.

Seven members represent states that are among the 20 least populous; five are Republicans. Only Ribicoff comes from the heavily populated Northeast.

Urban-Rural—Some of this imbalance results from the constitutional compromise that brought about creation of a bicameral legislative branch, with one body representing people and the other states.

But the imbalance has been exaggerated by the screening of applicants for membership conducted by Byrd and his predecessors that for years prevented men from urban states, such as Douglas, from getting on Finance.

The screening practices resulted in a committee that over time has been highly responsive to specific industries and relatively insulated from labor and urban interests.

Geographic—The South, with its traditional fixation on tariff policy along with its stake in petroleum, sugar and other commodities, is heavily represented.

Five members—almost a third of the committee—represent Southern and border states.

The sparsely populated Rocky Mountain states, with big stakes in mining and the petroleum industry, have three members. The Southwest, also dependent on mining and oil, has two.

Although it is unusual for both Senators from a state to serve on the same major committee, mineral-rich Colorado for 11 years (1943-54) had double representation on Finance. For nine years (1951-60), both of Delaware's Sen-

---

BENNETT: THE RANKING REPUBLICAN

Wallace F. Bennett, Utah, 72, the new ranking Republican on the Finance Committee, is a self-effacing man but the weight of his views is always an important factor in setting a direction for conservative Republicans in the Senate on financial questions.

He works very closely with the White House staff and he has a good relationship with the President.

"When there's a problem in the committee, I have the kind of relationship with the President that makes it possible for me to initiate contacts quickly, but I really see the President very infrequently," Bennett told *National Journal*. "I'm not one of those who personally attempts to get time with the President on a regular basis."

Bennett was elected to the Senate in 1950 and took his place in the upper chamber at the same time as another freshman Republican, Richard M. Nixon, who had just been elected Senator from California.

He graduated from the University of Utah in 1918 and was an infantry lieutenant in World War I. He went to work for his father's firm, the Bennett Glass & Paint Co. in Salt Lake City. He later became its president. He founded the Bennett Motor Co. in 1939, served as vice president of the National Paint, Varnish and Lacquer Association, and, in 1949, was president of the National Association of Manufacturers.

He is also a member of the Senate Banking and Currency Committee and was its ranking Republican until 1971 when he stepped aside for Sen. John G. Tower, R-Tex., upon assuming the top Republican position on Finance. He is also vice chairman of the Senate Ethics Committee, and serves on the Joint Committees on Atomic Energy, Defense Production and Internal Revenue Taxation.

ators were members. Delaware's economy is dominated by E. I. du Pont de Nemours & Co. Inc., an aggressive advocate of protectionist tariff and trade policies, particularly when chemicals are involved.

With jurisdiction over legislation involving such crucial urban problems as welfare assistance, Finance remains less representative of centers of population than most standing committees. When the 17 Senate committees are ranked according to the total population represented by the "average member" of the committee, Finance ranks 12th. Appropriations, which ranks 15th, is the lowest among the "big four" committees, with Finance just above it.

FINANCE PROCEDURES

Treasury officials routinely touch base with "the people in Finance" when they are preparing to send a tax proposal to the Hill.

That means a call on Tom Vail, and sometimes courtesy visits to Long and Bennett.

Preliminaries: At that point in the tax legislative process, however, the calls are not in the same category of imperatives as the de rigueur call on Wilbur Mills.

For Treasury, getting into details with the Finance Committee does not come until the bill has passed the House. Officials in the HEW Department operate essentially the same way on social security and welfare proposals.

This modus operandi results partly from the constitutional requirement that revenue bills originate in the House. In the view of Wilbur Cohen, however, it is dictated partly by the desire of Finance Committee members to keep all options open.

"The Senators like to be a little bit more distant," Cohen said. "They want to reserve their rights. They don't want to be tied down by what the Administration says, whether it is Democratic or Republican."

When a bill arrives at Finance, the committee subjects it to a hard but frequently brisk going-over.

The difference, according to Surrey, is that when Ways and Means clears a bill, "they decide for the House, whereas, when the Senate Finance Committee decides, it doesn't necessarily decide for the Senate."

Time Bind—Finance also often has little time for study.

Ways and Means, for example, began hearings on the Tax Reform Act of 1969 in mid-February of that year, and did not report out a bill until Aug. 2. The House acted five days later.

Finance began hearings Sept. 4, with Chairman Long under intense pressure from the Senate Democratic leadership to report out a bill by Oct. 31—a deadline he met despite the fact that he was in a difficult period in his personal life, having just been divorced by his wife of 30 years.

His handling of the bill was described by one Treasury official as "masterful."

During that time, Finance took testimony from 298 witnesses and received close to 1,000 pieces of correspondence on the bill for entry in the record, which filled 6,777 pages and seven volumes.

Public Hearings: Finance "isolates the problems" in public hearings, said a Treasury official.

First Forum—The "conceptual work" has been done in Ways and Means, which produces what could be called an initial draft of the bill. "When it emerges from Ways and Means, that is the first time the experts on the outside have seen the legislation. And their first opportunity to zero in on the problems they see in the bill is before the Finance Committee," the Treasury official said.

"At that point," said Surrey, "many more people in the country are looking at the results." The Ways and Means bill, he said, tends to be shaped by "a more closed group of people who understand how the legislature works and are Washington-based."

"Once the bill comes out of Ways and Means, then lawyers all over the country begin to look at it, begin to see it in light of their clients' problems and tend to bring in some of those problems to the Finance Committee."

Witnesses—In preparing for hearings, other Senate committees frequently encounter problems in developing a list of witnesses who will reflect a broad cross-section of opinion on the problem under study, and thus witnesses frequently must be solicited to fill the blanks.

Finance almost never does this, said a committee aide. It does not have to. A press release is issued announcing the date hearings will start, and then comes a deluge of requests to testify.

There were some 400 requests to testify following announcement of the welfare reform hearings. Only 200 witnesses could be heard. In sorting out the requests, of course, an effort is made, said the aide, "to get as many different views voiced as possible."

Little Liaison—In the same way, no elaborate effort is made to keep in close touch with what Ways and Means is doing with a bill, in preparation for the day it arrives in Finance.

"There is surprisingly considerable separation between the two bodies," said one committee staff member. "I frankly don't think the Finance Committee members give a damn what happens in the House to a bill."

Another staff member said that he and his counterpart on the Ways and Means staff in the same area of specialization are good friends and there is a free flow of information between them.

"But one of the accepted protocols is that I won't call him to ask what the Ways and Means Committee did in closed session today," he said.

Markup: A door at the rear of the Finance Committee hearing room, which opens off the dais from which the committee hears testimony, leads into a room barely big enough to hold a long rectangular table.

It is to that room on the second floor of the New Senate Office Building that the committee retires to mark up the House bill after it has held hearings.

As in Ways and Means, it is in markup sessions that the tough work is done and the hard bargaining takes place.

Chalk-Talk—Laurence Woodworth of the joint committee staff starts the discussion on any tax bill with a point-by-point explanation of each section of the bill and of what it is expected to accomplish.

He resorts to the blackboard more often in these sessions than he does for Ways and Means members.

Tom Vail is an active participant, particularly in discussing Senate amendments. The Treasury Department officials are there to answer such questions as the potential revenue effects of a particular amendment, and to act, within limits, as advocates for the Treasury position.

Committee Print—The text which serves as the point of departure for Woodworth and the committee in markup is called the confidential committee print.

Typically, it contains a section-by-section exposition of what is in the House bill, an analysis of existing law and how the bill would change it, the likely effect of the change and the Ways and Means Committee's reasons for thinking the change is desirable.

It reports new facts that have come to light since House passage. It outlines the views of those who testified in public hearings and their alternative proposals, if any. It concludes with a staff recommendation.

The committee print is prepared by Woodworth and his staff and reviewed by Vail and his staff.

During markup on the 1969 tax reform bill, Finance dealt each day with sections of the bill in an agenda that had been published in advance, with a different confidential print covering each day's sections. Woodworth arrived each day with a stack of prints for the next day's agenda and distributed them to Senators at the end of each markup session.

Although they are supposed to be closely held documents, many tax lobbyists boast of having a complete set of them.

Fast Pace—The pace is much faster in Finance markups than in Ways and Means. Long becomes impatient with dawdling over minutiae. In his early days as chairman, Long often cut off particularly long-winded members in mid-sentence to hurry matters along. He does that less frequently now.

Delaware's Williams used to be the chief time-consumer. Jack Miller has inherited that role.

"You could have a great big bill involving $5 billion," recalled a former Administration official who sat through many markups "and Miller or Williams would insist on taking a close look at Section 302 involving $1.98.

"Miller would haggle about small things until the committee would finally say, 'Let him have what he wants; it's not important, anyway,'" the former official said.

Fair Treatment—The consensus of participants in Finance markups who were interviewed by *National Journal* is that Long is eminently fair and democratic in his conduct of the meetings, although he is preoccupied, according to one aide, with "moving matters along."

"If anything, he's too democratic," said one participant. "He will sit there and say: 'Gentlemen, what is your pleasure?' And he votes last. He doesn't try to influence them by letting them know how he is going to vote. He lets them put anything on a bill. And, although he may vote against it, it inevitably then is painted as

'Long's Folly' in the press."

Voting—In contrast to the Ways and Means practice, there are frequent votes during Finance markups.

"The chairman has a rule that any Senator can vote on anything he wants to in the committee," said Oklahoma's Harris. "You can often get into parliamentary snarls where, under Robert's rules or the Senate rules, you would have to vote on the substitute first and the amendment to the substitute, and all that. But Long always says that a Senator is entitled to have a clean vote on whatever he wants voted on—unencumbered—and then we'll vote on these other things. He's always been very open about things like that."

The liberal vote rule is essentially a device Long uses to cut off random debate, said one committee aide. Long will frequently say: "All right, let's stop talking and vote."

But the rule has been pushed, on occasion, to the point where a member has asked for a vote on whether a vote should be taken. And a vote, once taken, almost never precludes reopening the issue at a later time in the markup. Underlying all this, said the committee aide, is Long's frequently voiced objection to any set of rules that could work to frustrate the will of the majority.

Hot Spots—Finance does not aim at duplicating the section-by-section winnowing and sifting that Ways and Means does. What it does, said a frequent outside participant in markups, is "restructure some of the concepts in the House bill, deal with inequities that may have been identified, write excep-

tions to some of the rules set forth in the bill, and, sometimes, change the basic concept in the bill, where necessary."

Finance operates on a "hot spot" basis, Vail said, dealing mainly with problem areas. If Ways and Means has resolved most of the problems in the bill that it reports out, then the Finance Committee's consideration of it is likely to be much less thorough than it otherwise would be, he said.

Executive Staff—The Finance Committee is unique among Senate committees—as Ways and Means is among House committees—in the degree of executive branch participation that it countenances in markup sessions.

One participant in Finance markups described them as a kind of mannered "free-for-all" marked by a three-way exchange, if it is a tax bill, between Woodworth, Vail and either Edwin Cohen or Nolan. If it is a bill involving social security cash benefits, Michael Stern of the Finance staff is the committee's principal adviser; but Robert M. Ball, commissioner of the Social Security Administration, functions in much the same role as does Woodworth on a tax bill, according to Sen. Harris.

Robert A. Best, the Finance staff trade specialist, would be the important staff man in a trade bill markup, but there would also be someone in the session—usually the general counsel—representing the Tariff Commission.

But in Finance markups, in contrast to Ways and Means, the executive branch participants are never allowed to forget that they are invited guests. During consid-

eration of the 1969 tax reform bill, Edwin Cohen was politely but firmly threatened with ejection when he pressed Treasury's position vigorously.

"On the House side," recalled Wilbur Cohen, "you can get up and say: 'Look, I want to talk, too.' You're not supposed to let them do something that's stupid, that's not workable. Mills can shut you off. He can say 'No.' He's said it to me a hundred times. But, man, if you sit there and you let him do something that you come back later and say was a goof, his answer is: 'Well, why the hell didn't you speak up? What the hell we got you there for?'"

Cohen was no less outspoken in Finance than in Ways and Means when he was an HEW official, but the atmosphere was much less permissive. And, he recalled, "the Senate (committee) once or twice kept us out when we were advocating something they didn't like."

Because Finance markups are held in a much smaller room, Administration officials are not permitted to bring the same retinue of aides that would accompany them to a Ways and Means markup. Wilbur Cohen would have perhaps 10 aides with him in Ways and Means, but only one or two in Finance.

Senatorial Staff—The members of Finance themselves are not permitted to bring personal staff men to the markups, a bar almost unique among Senate committees. The result is that a Senator offering a proposal which represents a departure from the recommendation of the Joint Tax Committee and Finance staffs, and which is opposed by Treasury, is at a disadvantage in the markups.

When Albert Gore was battling in markup for an increase in the personal exemption rate during consideration of the 1969 tax reform bill, he stationed a legislative assistant, Paul R. McDaniel, right outside the committee's door and periodically left the room to consult with him.

McDaniel was ideally suited for the job. He had been a tax attorney at Treasury and, as one of Nolan's principal aides, had sat through the Ways and Means markups on the tax reform bill. He was forced to leave Treasury after Sen. Henry Bellmon, R-Okla., insisted that McDaniel, a Democrat and a former aide to Stanley Surrey in the Johnson Administration, should not hold a high post in the Nixon Administration..

On the day the personal exemption battle took place in the markup session, the Treasury and the joint committee staff produced a raft of charts to buttress their positions on the issue.

"It takes a considerable amount of expertise and experience to be able to look at one of those charts and find out what it means," said McDaniel, who now teaches at Boston College Law School.

"Gore is a very, very smart man and thoroughly knowledgeable in tax matters," said McDaniel in an interview, "but it was impossible for him to try to sustain the burden of his argument, on the one hand, and then try to analyze the technical details of a chart they'd just laid before him, on the other. So he asked permission for me to come in and they refused. They voted against it."

Neither the Finance staff nor the joint committee staff could give Gore the kind of detailed day-to-day assistance he required during the markup, because each night after the Senators had left, they were engaged—often until 2 a.m. or 3 a.m.—in drafting into legal language the decisions the committee had made in markup that day.

Drafting—The drafting sessions are crucial, especially when a tax bill is involved. "The real key to tax bills, very often, is not political but technical," said a Washington tax attorney in an interview. "Control of the words is vital."

The sessions are held in the Senate Legislative Counsel's library on the 6th floor of the New Senate Office Building.

Harry B. Littell, a senior counsel, is the chief tax draftsman and, in the words of Tom Vail, "an unsung hero of the tax wars." Woodworth, Vail, Cohen and Nolan are there when any but routine matters are being drafted. However, on the two occasions during work on the 1969 tax bill when Cohen and Nolan were not invited into the markup, they were also not invited into the drafting sessions afterward.

If a policy question arises in the course of a drafting session, Littell looks to Vail, or the Treasury staff, for its resolution. But often, the problems will have to be taken back to the committee, or to Long, for resolution.

Members' Influence: When a bill emerges from Finance and goes to the Senate floor, the committee members who, with Long, have had the most influence over its shape almost invariably are Bennett and Talmadge, according to the consensus of those interviewed by *National Journal.*

The Chairman—Long is unquestionably in control of the committee. He is, however, more erratic and less well organized than Mills. "He's got the quickest mind on the committee," said a one-time participant in Finance markups.

Price found in interviews during the 89th Congress that "impatience and a lack of tact compromised Long's effectiveness, though his intelligence and ability to comprehend issues received the opposite evaluation." He has worked to curb his impatience, according to those who frequently work with him. Indeed, Bennett described Long as "very patient" and said he "gives every point of view an ample hearing."

Ranking Republican—Bennett, once president of the National Association of Manufacturers, is regarded by the Republicans as "their most expert financial man," said a former member of the committee. He was virtually de facto leader of committee Republicans even before Williams retired. Williams was too much a maverick to be looked to for leadership, whereas Bennett has always been viewed as solid and sensible by his GOP colleagues.

The Others—Talmadge is influential because he is "a strong Southern conservative," according to one source familiar with the committee's work, and because he does his homework. He is the third-ranking Democrat.

Anderson, the second-ranking Democrat, once was a power but is in declining health and no longer makes a significant contribution. He still has a good attendance record.

Curtis, the second-ranking Republican, has less influence than his position might warrant. "He's really had very little influence in that committee since he's been on," said a source close to the committee. "He's always fighting some battle of 20 years past. He'll get some little tiny things once in a while, but he really is a drag on that committee." Similar impressions were voiced by other Capitol Hill sources.

Miller, a tax lawyer and former Internal Revenue Service official, could have much more influence than he does, but according to a former Finance member, he dissipates much of it because of a passion for minutiae.

Fulbright, chairman of the Foreign Relations Committee, takes little part in the work of Finance. He did, however, attend nearly all the executive sessions last year on the welfare reform bill.

Ribicoff is an effective voice on the committee, even though he often disagrees with the leadership. He is frequently looked to by other members for guidance on welfare and medicare legislation because he is a former HEW Secretary. He gets on well with Long, but his attendance is sporadic.

Harris is "too liberal" to have influence, according to a one-time participant in markups who has kept in touch with the committee's work. He plays too much of a lone role and is unwilling to moderate his position to win support, the source said.

"Hartke," according to the same source, "gets a lot out of the committee because he makes himself a nuisance on the floor with all of his amendments; yet he doesn't have any particular persuasive power in the committee about anything big. But he's a dogged, persevering fellow on what he wants."

Jordan, Fannin, Hansen and Byrd have made no significant mark on the committee, although Hansen has gained a reputation as the oil industry's staunchest defender in the committee, surpassing even Long.

It is still too early to evaluate Griffin and Nelson, according to committee sources.

PRESSURES

Outside pressures are exerted on the writing of a revenue bill at every point in the path it follows through Congress.

"We fought for taxation with representation," said Gerard M. Brannon, a Treasury tax economist, "and, by God, that's what we got."

The pressures are, by all accounts, most intense along the legislative path that leads through the Senate.

Administration: No one from the White House staff sits in on markups or in the conference. That would erase the already blurred line between the executive and legislative branches on tax, trade and welfare.

But the White House is a hovering presence. Its congressional liaison staff is responsible for contacts with Senate Finance and is in almost constant communication with Bennett.

Special Interests: Most of the outside pressure comes not from the White House or even from broad-gauged interest groups like the AFL-CIO or the National Association of Manufacturers, but from special-interest groups like the oil lobby, the coal lobby and the cement lobby.

"Seeing lobbyists is one of our functions," Vail told *National Journal*. "I would be doing the members of the committee a disservice if a lobbyist got a Senator to sponsor a proposal, and, when it was offered, I was not prepared to explain the logic, or lack of it, to the committee."

A special-interest taxpayer with problems is in good shape, according to an experienced Washington tax lawyer, if he is the constituent of a Senator with power whom he can interest in his case.

"The Podunk Beer Distributing Co. has more leverage than General Motors," he said. "Congress is inordinately responsive in national tax questions to people with parochial problems."

"The public interest is diffused and hard to marshal," said Paul Douglas. "But the special interests are highly concentrated and thus have more weight."

Access—The Finance staff observes a strict guideline against helping lobbyists who visit them in search of sponsors for proposals. "The last thing we want to do is give the impression we are screening them for a hearing by individual Senators," said a Finance staff man.

Yet, one of the primary duties of Joe H. Ward, one of the tax specialists on the Finance staff, is "special research projects" for members of the committee involving "constituent tax problems."

Lobbyists are sealed off from access to Harry Littell and his draftsmen when a revenue bill is being recast on the Senate side.

But when questions occur on a proposal specifically designed to assist one organization or group, if the sponsoring Senator cannot clear it up—which he usually cannot because he normally does not have the required intimate familiarity with the case—Littell or his aides are referred to the beneficiary organization.

On one occasion in 1959, when a tax bill affecting life insurance companies was being drafted, representatives of a company with a particularly thorny technical problem were invited into the drafting room.

Loopholes—A mix-up in signals on one special-interest amendment tacked to the Revenue Act of 1951 (65 Stat 452) still produces chuckles among veteran tax attorneys.

The amendment was drawn to give relief to the Bridgeport Brass Co. The company's Washington lawyers had written the amendment and gotten it into the bill, and it had become law.

But, because of a change in the company's accounting system that Bridgeport officials had failed to tell their lawyers about, the firm was disqualified from using its own loophole.

Timing—One reason that most loophole writing has occurred in the Senate is that the Senate is near the end of the tax-writing sequence. There is less opportunity at that point to focus on a special-interest amendment and mobilize opposition to it.

The more legitimate the de-mand, the more likely it is that a strong effort will be made to get it into the Ways and Means bill.

"You prefer that the Ways and Means bill comes out right rather than letting it come out wrong and hoping to cure it in the Senate," said a former Administration tax official.

If attracting attention to a proposal in Ways and Means would rock the boat for a special interest, then the best strategy is to wait until the bill reaches Finance, the official said. If even less attention is desirable, he said, then one waits until the bill is on the Senate floor, so that a successful attempt to amend it would give the proposal "a run for its money in conference."

The Foreign Investors Tax Act of 1966 (80 Stat 1541) attracted a parcel of late amendments because Long had given the signal that the bill would be a good "horse" for any riders the Senators had in mind.

Sen. Williams said on the Senate floor that one amendment, which Hartke got through, meant a $2-million windfall for Harvey Aluminum Co. of Los Angeles. The amendment survived the conference.

Long submitted an amendment raising the depletion allowance for clam and oyster shells used for their calcium carbonate content in making cement. Hartke also won a special cut in the excise tax on hearses, many of which are assembled in Indiana. Fulbright and Talmadge won higher depletion rates for alumina-bearing clay, which is processed in the making of aluminum and is an important resource in Arkansas and Georgia.

Former Sen. (1945-69) Bourke B. Hickenlooper, R-Iowa, said: "I think it is the most odoriferous bill I have seen in many years. It is utterly indefensible. I think it stinks to high heaven."

Cement—One of the most effective lobbying groups, according to Thomas Field, is the Portland Cement Association.

"The cement industry people really have become lobbying experts," Field said, "because over the years they have had to convince state legislatures that cement is better for road building than tar."

The officials of the Lone Star Cement Corp., of Greenwich, Conn., contribute to the Lone Star Voluntary Political Fund, for example.

John C. Mundt, senior vice president of the company, administers the fund.

Lone Star executives contribute between 1 and 1.5 per cent of their annual salaries. The money is distributed, Mundt said, among "key members of committees concerned with highways, construction, taxes, and public works," and to business-oriented Members who "understand the problems of the free enterprise system."

The Lone Star fund contributed $1,000 to Long's reelection campaign in 1968 and $700 to Harry Byrd's 1970 campaign.

Compromise—Treasury officials try to defend the public interest, Field said, and try to oppose special tax breaks in the Finance Committee.

Often in executive session, he said, the price they must pay to head off a special-interest amendment is a promise to provide administrative relief.

"A promise to dispose of the matter administratively is extracted in return for not doing something much worse legislatively," he said.

Tax Lawyers: Pressure on Finance comes also from a cadre of Washington tax attorneys representing individual corporate clients.

Parts of many tax bills often are written in Washington law offices.

One Finance staff member spent close to one-third of his time during consideration of the 1969 tax reform bill with Washington tax attorneys, going over their briefs on various sections of the bill.

"They would come to you," he recalled, "and say that 15 cases were decided in the courts this way and that the proposed provision would reverse those decisions and cause all kinds of inequities. They are actually a tremendous help."

THE COMMITTEE'S BILL

Because Finance Committee bills do not travel to the Senate floor with the protection of a closed rule, they invite ambush.

Whether the Finance chairman should try to resist amendments to his bill is a matter of debate among Senators and their staffs.

A veteran lobbyist who has worked with Finance for many years told *National Journal* that "to counter-balance the lack of a closed rule, what you need is an authoritative Finance Committee chairman."

On the Floor: He said the late Sen. (1922-57) Walter F. George, D-Ga., "had great authority. He'd kill all those extraneous amend-ments offered on the floor because he held enough respect in the Senate to quash them."

The late Sen. (1941-1957) Eugene D. Millikin, R-Colo., had "massive authority," according to the lobbyist. (George was chairman in 1943-46 and 1949-52; Millikin was chairman in 1947-48 and 1953-54).

"Long lacks that authority," the lobbyist said. "He lacks the respect of members of the Senate's Inner Club."

A former member of the committee took issue with that assessment.

"I would say that it's a virtue of Russell's—the free and easy sort of way he does things," he said. "Millikin and George were, I think, worse chairmen. They were more subject to the influences of big business and to venality in the tax structure and carried it off with such an air that their judgments seemed to be the voices of God himself. No one could ever think that Russell's ideas came from God."

Riders—"I don't think it's a chairman's duty or right to hold a bill clean on the floor," said Talmadge in an interview. "The committee is a creature of the Senate. The Senate is not a creature of the committee."

Long told *National Journal:* "I suppose, to my regret, I've educated Senators to the fact that if you want to put a rider on a bill, it'd be a good idea to put it on a horse, so to speak, that's strong enough to carry the rider.

"If you put a controversial measure on a minor bill, it's not likely to survive. Sometimes we've passed major bills without a single floor amendment that we didn't want added to them. We've lost some votes. But the amendments that we don't agree to are, for the most part, defeated."

Anticipation—Long, like any chairman, tries to anticipate the Senate in shaping a bill in committee. He said:

"The committee is somewhat more conservative than the Senate as a whole, and knowing that I, for one, try to keep in mind when I'm voting (in committee) what I think the Senate's going to do. I don't see much point in recommending something that the Senate won't agree to."

Long's openness to amendments may actually help in building support for a bill; when the bill clears the Senate, it is more likely to be in line with the demands of constituents and interest groups than it was when it passed the House or when it was reported out by Finance.

By the same token, Long's willingness to accept amendments in committee or on the floor has, in Price's view, intensified the focus of interest group activity on Finance, which was already intense because of the committee's position in the tax-writing sequence and its role as appeals court.

Conference: "I don't think Russell cares very much what the floor amendments are going to be," said Sen. Metcalf. "He knows that this is complex legislation and that it is going to be written in conference and that it is going to correspond pretty much to what the House conferees will accept."

The conference committee is "the $64,000 place," said Wilbur Cohen. "That's where the real decisions are made."

Mills Dominant—By nearly

any reckoning, Mills is both captain and navigator in conference. This is largely because of his technical expertise, his prestige in the House and the unanimity he is usually able to maintain among House conferees. The Senate conferees are a less cohesive group.

When Metcalf resigned from Finance in 1969, he told a reporter that the Senate committee was little more than a "rubber stamp" for Mills.

"No matter what amendments were put on in the committee, or later on the floor, involving things I was interested in such as welfare or tax reform," Metcalf recalled in an interview, "we always lost those things in the conference. So I didn't see any advantage in staying on a committee that was just a rubber stamp."

"Paul Douglas would complain to me," said Wilbur Cohen, "that the Finance Committee could do anything in the world but it wouldn't make a damned bit of difference because everything was really decided in H-208."

Room H-208 on the House side of the Capitol is the site of the Ways and Means-Finance conferences, which is expressive in itself of the power relationship. A virtual civil war broke out in 1962 between the House and Senate over the site of appropriations conferences—which traditionally had been held on the Senate side of the Capitol.

Mills and Long have an amicable relationship. Disputes between them in conference are always handled with politeness.

Mills does not dominate through force of personality; Long is the more flamboyant, pugnacious and volatile of the two.

BOBBY BAKER AND FINANCE

The 1957 trial of Robert G. (Bobby) Baker, former secretary to the Senate Democratic majority (1955-63), provided a rare detailed look at an effort by a special-interest group to get from the Senate Finance Committee a tax bill to its liking.

The trial focused on money given by California savings and loan association officials to Baker to be distributed for use as campaign funds by the late Sen. (1949-63) Robert S. Kerr, D-Okla., then ranking Democrat on Finance.

Baker was convicted of keeping $8,000 of the $99,600 which had been raised by the California group.

Tax proposal—The Administration was trying to end a special-treatment tax long enjoyed by savings and loan associations by reducing the amount of earnings they could declare as tax-free reserves against bad debts. The Treasury Department estimated the entire industry was then paying little more than $7 million a year in taxes. The change would have increased the industry's taxes by some $20 million a year.

The Administration backed a Ways and Means Committee proposal allowing all savings and loan associations—mutuals which are owned by depositors as well as stock companies owned by shareholders—to hold 60 per cent of earnings as tax-free reserves. The House approved the proposal.

When the bill reached Finance, Kerr won approval for an amendment that, while keeping tax-free reserves for mutuals at 60 per cent, cut stock companies' tax-free reserves to 40 per cent.

Finance approved that formula July 20, 1962. A week later—on July 27—the committee voted to raise the stock company reserve figure to 50 per cent. According to one estimate, the original Senate version would have cost the stock S&Ls $10 million more a year than the House version.

Washington Gossip—A former member of the Finance Committee told *National Journal* that it was common gossip in Washington that between July 20 and July 27, "a committee from California came in with money and gave it to Kerr."

That was not established during the trial. Baker testified that they came to Washington in September. The bill passed the Senate Aug. 7.

Baker's Role—Baker testified that he received a phone call Sept. 24 from Glen S. Troop, vice president and lobbyist for the U.S. Savings and Loan League, saying that Kenneth D. Childs, former president of the Home Savings and Loan Association of Los Angeles, wanted to meet Kerr. Baker said the meeting was scheduled and that Childs later told Baker that "as a result of his conversation with Senator Kerr," he planned to recommend to his California colleagues that "they make a substantial contribution to Senator Kerr to be used in the 1962 election."

Childs testified that Baker suggested to him that the industry raise $100,000 for senatorial candidates "so that there would be an open door when legislation came along affecting their interests."

Conference—The day after Kerr's meeting with Childs, Ways and Means and Finance members went into conference on the tax bill.

The Senate abandoned the Kerr amendment and agreed to the original House provision that both mutuals and stock companies could declare 60 per cent of their earnings as tax-free reserves.

In October and November of that year, Baker collected $99,600 from officials of the Great Western Financial Corp. of San Francisco, the First Charter Financial Corp. of Los Angeles, and from Childs of Home Savings and Loan.

Trial—Eight Senators and Chairman Wilbur D. Mills, D-Ark., of the House Ways and Means Committee, appeared in court to testify that they had received no part of the funds.

Although all were sworn in, only Mills, Sen. J. W. Fulbright, D-Ark., and former Sen. (1946-71) John J. Williams, R-Del., had actually testified before Baker's attorney conceded they had not received any of the money.

The central figure, Kerr, had died on New Year's Day 1963.

Mills dominates because he knows more than anyone at the table about the subject and about the bill.

"He knows more, is technically more equipped, is more politically adroit, is a better ballet dancer and, at the same time, has all the leverage," said a former Administration official who has participated in numerous conferences.

Long is clever, he is quick on his feet and he is facile," said a lobbyist who knows him well. "But Mills is both facile *and* profound."

Long's Power—If Mills dominates, said one Finance Committee aide, it is because Long is not interested in dominating. "On something Long feels strongly about, Mills always gives him what he wants. And when he has gotten that, he doesn't care what Mills does. He's not interested in being the country's number one tax authority. His interests are broader than that."

"I don't ever have the feeling that Mills dominates," said Bennett. "But they have the advantage because of the nature of House rules and because the discipline inside that committee is much tighter than in ours."

Long believes the Senate does well in conference. "I think we've been far more successful since I became chairman than we were in the past in making the Senate position prevail," he said. "My impression is that we've been successful in persuading the House to take about two-thirds of the things we initiate. And I wouldn't expect to do any better than that no matter who I was conferring with."

Stratagems—When the Senate recedes on an amendment, it often is because the amendment was unacceptable to Long and the committee majority in the first place but was added to the bill, over their objections, on the floor.

Often they are what Long described as "shoot-the-moon type amendments that'd cost us $20 billion without one line of financing in the bill to pay for it. We just have to take the amendment, see if we can bring back some part of it, but feel no apology whatever if the House won't take any of it. Come back and say: 'Well, I'm sorry, but those fellows said they sent us a bill to pay for itself, and they're not going to take some irresponsible amendment such as that one.'"

Often, too, a Senate amendment accepted by the House conferees is one that Mills inspired.

"Part of Mills' strategy," said Wilbur Cohen, "is to shift some of the burden to the Senate. If something is to be done that is distinctly controversial, what Mills will tell somebody is: 'Go over in the Senate and get it on and I'll take it in conference.' In other words, Mills doesn't try to pass the perfect bill. He knows that the Senate Finance Committee's role is to have something that's different from the House so there is room for a compromise."

Outsiders—Sitting with Mills and Long in H-208 are the ubiquitous representatives of the executive branch who, as in the Ways and Means and Finance markups, are an integral part of the decision-making process in those sessions.

The influence of the Administration is thus less an outside pressure than an inside constraint.

"If you're gonna hold these people responsible for the administration of it later on," said Wilbur Cohen, "then you gotta ask them when you do it: 'Is this workable?' There's no point in passing a law that says two times two is five."

4   THE PRESIDENT

The complex American political system depends heavily on the President for policy direction and coordination. His position at the head of the huge federal bureaucracy, the actions of which affect the lives of all citizens, his special role and powers in foreign and national security policy, and his special relationship to the public because of a communications revolution that focuses national attention on him give the President influence and power far beyond the scope of that conceived by the Founding Fathers. Indeed, the President's powers are such that virtually all who are involved in the governing of America in some way and at some time find themselves dependent upon the President to do their jobs.

The President's central position within the American political system mean that the decisions he makes about the kind of President he will be are extremely significant. There are many different ways of being President—different ways of viewing the extent of pres-

idential legal authority, different ways of organizing the Executive Office of the President; delegating and sharing authority, and selecting subordinates.

Some Presidents such as Dwight D. Eisenhower, create highly formalized organizational structures within the Executive Office of the President, make extensive grants of authority to subordinates, rely heavily on their personal popularity with the American people, and are relatively nonaggressive in seeking to initiate policy changes. Others such as Lyndon B. Johnson organize the White House in a loosely structured manner and make certain that they are involved in the control of all major decisions. They also take an expansive interpretation of presidential powers and aggressively use their powers to influence American domestic and foreign policy.

President Nixon, like his predecessors, has organized and staffed the White House to meet his particular vision of the office. The Nixon White House is a more for-

mally structured institution than was that of Lyndon B. Johnson. The White House staff is larger than at any time in history. Some activities previously performed within the regular departments of the Executive Branch are now being handled directly by the White House. This is particularly true in the field of foreign policy where the office of Henry Kissinger, Assistant to the President for National Security Affairs, overshadows the Department of State. A large White House staff also reflects a presidential need for personnel to help him supervise and maintain control over the growing number of federal agencies and programs.

The first two articles in this section provide insights into the White House of Richard M. Nixon through an analysis of work and roles of two key aides—Robert Haldeman and John Erlichman. These presidential intimates play quite distinct roles. Haldeman is charged with organizing the supervising of the management of the

158 White House and to a certain extent controls the President's time. He plays a critical role in determining who will see the Chief Executive and which matters will reach his attention. His actions therefore help shape presidential policy.

Erlichman's role is more directly concerned with shaping the domestic policies to be pursued by the Administration. In an effort to gain greater coherence and coordination in domestic policy, President Nixon reorganized the White House to create a Domestic Council to coordinate domestic policy-making in much the same way as does the National Security Council in foreign policy. Erlichman heads the staff of the Domestic Council. He is charged with helping formulate the President's domestic program and with bringing to the President various policy alternatives.

The impact of policy statements and the public's conception of the President are influenced by the manner in which the President's views are transmitted. Great care is therefore taken in the writing of each presidential pronouncement. The volume of required presidential statements is so great that all modern Presidents have required the assistance of speech writers. Even though President Nixon frequently drafts major statements personally, his White House, like that of his predecessors, has a stable of skilled "wordsmiths." The final selection of this chapter deals with the critical role played by presidential speech writers.

The three articles in this chapter by focusing on the roles and significance of key presidential staff aides provide insights into the leadership style of Richard M. Nixon. They also vividly point up the extent to which the President sits a top a large bureaucracy of his own within the Executive Office of the President. The Presidency, though influenced by the particular conception of the incumbent, is also a highly institutionalized organization. Certain jobs such as appointments secretary, press secretary, speech writer, domestic policy advisor and national security advisor have become an expected part of each administration. Formal advisory bodies such as the Council of Economic Advisors and the Domestic Council also exist. In a real sense then, the Presidency is more more than one man—it is an institutionalized organization.

Haldeman directs staff as President's alter ego   *Dom Bonafede*

At approximately 9 a.m. each day, President Nixon presses a small, black button on his desk. A buzzer sounds and a red light flashes on a communications console in the large, cool-green office of Harry Robins (Bob) Haldeman. No matter what he is doing, Haldeman unhesitatingly drops it and strides the few feet to the President's Oval Office. At that moment, the daily business of the Administration begins.

Together, the two men map the President's day. Thoroughly attuned to each other politically and personally, after 15 years as friends and associates, they speak in almost muted tones, Haldeman reporting to the President on Administration developments and the President conveying instructions to Haldeman.

Through Haldeman, the President administers the White House and hence, much of the government. Virtually every person (with notable exceptions) and every piece of paper which reach the President go through Haldeman, whose title is assistant to the President.

Specifically, Haldeman sees that the President deals with what historian Richard E. Neustadt calls "action-forcing deadlines": documents awaiting signature, vacant positions to be filled, officials seeking hearings, newsmen probing for answers, interest groups requesting audiences, intelligence reports requiring responses.

Just as Haldeman is the first to see the President officially in the morning, he is the last to see him officially at night.

All that, as Haldeman himself acknowledges, places him among the small elite group who stand at the peak of the Nixon Administration hierarchy.

Yet, because Haldeman deals directly and almost exclusively with the President and is responsible only to him, his influence is more passive than active, more custodial than creative, more private than public.

ROLE

Inasmuch as White House staff structure differs with each President, Haldeman's role, as he said, is hard to define. "There is no analogy with any predecessor, and it doesn't quite fit anybody in the modern Presidency," he said.

Haldeman acts as appointments secretary, staff manager, staff secretary, timekeeper and communications director. He is chief of Mr. Nixon's personal White House staff as opposed to the President's institutional staff, which includes, for example, the Office of Management and Budget.

Adams Comparison: Haldeman said that, in view of his broad mandate, "I come closer to Sherman Adams than anyone else." Adams, who was the assistant (1953-58) to President Eisenhower, was known as an autocratic staff director who became deeply involved in major policy decisions.

As for differences, Haldeman said, "Adams spent little time with the President but a lot of time acting for him. I spend a lot of time with the President. I act *at* the President's direction; I transmit and coordinate *with* the President's direction. I don't directly act in policy matters."

Commenting on the same theme, Bryce N. Harlow, who served as counselor (1969-70) to President Nixon and congressional relations assistant (1953-61) to President Eisenhower, said:

"Haldeman has eschewed policy-making in major domestic matters; Adams was heavily engaged in these matters. Adams handled Presidential (political) appointments; Haldeman does not.

"Also, the White House staff structure is different. Part of it is organized by law, as the Domestic Council and the OMB. It is a multi-legged creature which reports to the President rather than to his chief of staff."

Comparing the two men, Harlow said, "Haldeman is far less known than Adams, is younger, less experienced and has had no public service; Adams was a Governor (R-N.H., 1949-53) and a Member of Congress (R, 1945-47). Haldeman's relationship to the President is closer than Adams' was to Ike. Haldeman is in and out of the President's office constantly; he travels with him; he sees the President more than anyone else; he is used by Mr. Nixon as his action agent."

On their similarities, Harlow said, "Haldeman is a brusque man by instinct; Adams was, too. Both are highly efficient."

Harlow said Haldeman is "indispensable to the President; his loyalty quotient is measureless."

The Broker: Haldeman further described himself as a broker who is responsible for feeding into the President all available options on any given issue. "When a decision has been made, then I definitely become an advocate," he said.

However, another White House aide, who asked to remain anonymous, said that the option system has its limitations.

"It's a form of security and survival for senior White House aides who fear that if they advocate a proposal that runs counter to the President's views, they will be banished," he said. "About the only White House guy who is not afraid to push his own views and say no to the President is George Shultz," former OMB Director and current Secretary of the Treasury.

Policy: The extent of Haldeman's involvement in the policy-making process has been a question of considerable debate among Washington politicians, bureaucrats and newsmen since the beginning of the Nixon Administration.

His proximity to the President (one Washington scale of measurement to determine power) is considered prima facie evidence of his influence. Yet, because of the man's low visibility, his influence has been difficult to gauge.

Several incidents, however, indicate Haldeman's standing:

After the Senate, in April 1970, rejected G. Harrold Carswell, Mr. Nixon's choice for Associate Justice of the Supreme Court, the President sequestered himself aboard the Presidential yacht *Sequoia* to plan his strategy with only two close advisers—Attorney General John N. Mitchell and Haldeman.

When it became apparent that Secretary Robert H. Finch's position at HEW was becoming untenable, it was Haldeman who urged that he be brought into the White House.

During an internal White House debate over the Cambodia incursion in April 1970, Haldeman, according to a Presidential aide who asked anonymity, argued in favor of the action. "It's the right thing to do; it's well thought out," Haldeman is quoted as telling the President.

Daily Staff Meeting—Haldeman is in charge of the daily 8 a.m. meeting for senior White House aides. Held in Haldeman's office, it is the most select of the White House staff meetings and covers the total scope of the Presidency, including broad policy, scheduling, congressional relations and follow-up activities.

Regular participants in the meetings (other White House aides attend by invitation only) include Counselors Finch and Donald Rumsfeld; Domestic Council Executive Director John D. Ehrlichman; Clark MacGregor, counsel to the President for congressional relations; Henry A. Kissinger, assistant to the President for national security affairs. Prior to their appointments to Cabinet posts, Shultz and Commerce Secretary Peter G. Peterson (former executive director of the Council on International Economic Policy) attended.

At 8:30 a.m., Press Secretary Ronald L. Ziegler, Herbert G. Klein, director of communications for the executive branch, and William E. Timmons, assistant to the President for congressional relations, join the group. The meeting then becomes an operational planning session.

Meeting with Mr. Nixon—Almost immediately afterwards, Haldeman meets with the President. What was discussed at the earlier meetings may be relayed to the President, if Haldeman sees fit.

The discretion which Haldeman uses in transmitting information to the President, the priorities he gives to the President's time and his decisions on prospective visitors all have an impact on policy.

Devil's Advocate — Questioned about his policy role, Haldeman acknowledged, "It's hard for me not to be involved in policy; yet, I'm not directly involved in the creation of policy.

"I'm involved in the sense I'm involved in anything that goes to and from the President. My role is more that of a devil's advocate, to see whether all the input is there and whether it is put together to give the President the full picture, with all the pros and cons. . . . I'm the one point through which all these things flow. I can't avoid getting involved.

"But I do not get involved by expressing my personal opinion. I see that all the arguments are fully considered. If the President seems to favor Point A, I'll argue for B. It is our responsibility to see that the President makes a decision for the right reasons. We make sure the reasons are there."

Haldeman will often suggest during a meeting that the White

House assistant who has a special expertise on the topic under discussion be called in. This may be John C. Whitaker on environmental issues, for example, or Kenneth R. Cole Jr. on health matters, or Egil Krogh Jr. on government reorganization.

STAFF

Although Haldeman's area of responsibility covers most of the White House, with exceptions such as the National Security Council and the Domestic Council, he has only three aides in his personal office: Lawrence M. Higby, his administrative assistant, and Gordon Strachan and Bruce Kehrli, staff assistants. They are primarily concerned with following up Haldeman's directives to see that deadlines are met, assuring that background material on particular meetings goes to the President, arranging Haldeman's schedule and taking care of other "housekeeping" duties. Three secretaries are also assigned to the office.

Other White House aides work within Haldeman's purview, however.

Chapin—Dwight L. Chapin, special assistant to the President, is a Haldeman deputy. He is concerned with long-range schedule planning for Mr. Nixon. This involves scheduling the President sometimes more than a year in advance.

For instance, a calendar in Chapin's office shows that during December 1971 the President is due to hold National Security Council and Domestic Council meetings, leave on an out-of-town trip and receive a state visitor.

Chapin also is responsible for the President's travel schedule and is in charge of the advance teams which precede the trips and ensure that the arrangements are proper and in order. Ron Walker, the chief White House advance man, reports to Chapin.

Assisted by Mark Goode, Chapin also oversees special television projects involving the White House. For example, when producers of CBS-TV's "60 Minutes" program wanted to do a special on a state visit they dealt with Goode and Chapin.

Also working with Chapin is David Parker, who receives most of the bids for Mr. Nixon's time, such as requests for a Presidential speech or for a visit with him. Generally, the request is forwarded to the top official in the designated area. If it involves foreign affairs, for example, it would go to Kissinger for an advisory. This would be routed back to Chapin and to Haldeman for final approval.

Requests from Members of Congress are generally relayed through MacGregor or Timmons. Important members, such as Senate Majority Leader Mike Mansfield, D-Mont., have merely to telephone Haldeman for an appointment.

Butterfield—Alexander P. Butterfield is Haldeman's deputy for administration. Chapin's duties run up to the day of the scheduled event; Butterfield takes over from there. He sees that the schedule is executed and handles all the paper that goes in and out of the President's office. Butterfield also is involved in non-substantive matters concerning the Cabinet and ar-

ranges the Cabinet meetings.

Working with Butterfield is John Meade Huntsman, a recent appointee, who serves as staff secretary and helps route Presidential papers. Mr. Nixon frequently annotates documents and memorandums which must be forwarded to certain aides for implementation. Each of these is logged and given an "action-due" date.

Mr. Nixon's comments on the margin are transcribed and forwarded to the appropriate aide. The original papers, with the President's inscribed remarks, are stored in a vault in the White House basement.

More and more, Butterfield is taking over Haldeman's routine administrative duties. Haldeman, an aide said, "is preparing for the long pull and looking toward 1972."

Bull—Stephen Bull is Butterfield's counterpart with respect to Presidential visitors. He brings people into the President's office and makes the presentations ("Mr. President, I would like you to meet . . .").

Bull also arranges special White House ceremonies, such as the swearing in of new Presidential appointees.

It is his responsibility to see that the appointments schedule runs smoothly and on time.

Most meetings with the President are for 15 to 25 minutes; groups sometimes are allowed 45 minutes. However, Administration officials frequently are given only five minutes, which the staff maintains is just as useful as longer meetings since it requires the visitor to state his case concisely without embellishment.

MR. NIXON'S WASHINGTON WORKDAY

President Nixon operates on an orderly, tightly programmed schedule, in keeping with his habits and temperament. Subject to variations—for an out-of-town trip, the delivery of a major speech or the arrival of a state visitor—this is a normal Washington workday for the President.

7:30 a.m.—Shortly after arising, the President does three or four hundred jogs in place in his bedroom. After dressing, with the aid of his Cuban-born valet, Manolo Sanchez, Mr. Nixon has a light breakfast (which frequently, but not always, includes Wheaties) in the White House residence. Generally, he takes a quick look at the morning newspapers at breakfast, especially *The New York Times* and *The Washington Post.*

Unlike Presidents Kennedy and Johnson, Mr. Nixon does not confer with aides in his bedroom suite. In those Administrations, it was considered a mark of status for a White House aide to be admitted to the President's living quarters. In these relaxed, private surroundings, the aide had an opportunity to promote his special viewpoints. That special privilege, which often provoked infighting among White House staff members, is denied Mr. Nixon's assistants.

8:30 a.m.—Mr. Nixon walks from the residence to the Oval Office in the West Wing (until recently, he arrived at his office about half-an-hour earlier), where he turns first to a blue, looseleaf notebook embossed with gold lettering, "The President's Daily News Briefing." This contains a summary of news items and editorials compiled under the direction of Patrick J. Buchanan, a one-time editorial writer for the *St. Louis Globe-Democrat.* Mr. Nixon devotes 15-to-30 minutes to it.

9 a.m.—Mr. Nixon buzzes H. R. Haldeman, his chief administrative aide, to come into his office. This is the President's first daily contact with his official staff. Mr. Nixon and Haldeman review the President's schedule for that day and examine overnight developments. They also consider current policy and staff matters.

9:30 a.m.—Henry A. Kissinger, assistant to the President for national security affairs, enters the office, and Haldeman leaves.

Kissinger briefs the President on security and foreign affairs matters and goes over the latest developments in the Indochina war.

Between nine and 10 o'clock, Presidential Press Secretary Ronald L. Ziegler passes in and out of the Oval Office to discuss the latest news breaks with Mr. Nixon prior to the daily 11 a.m. White House press briefing.

10 a.m.—The morning appointments schedule begins. During this period, the President receives official and private visitors. He may also meet with the Cabinet, see Members of Congress and receive foreign diplomats.

1 p.m.—After the last visitor leaves, Haldeman returns to the Oval Office and brings the President up-to-date on developments and discusses the day's remaining agenda.

Alexander P. Butterfield, deputy assistant to the President, comes in with papers and memorandums requiring the President's perusal. Next, the President summons staff members, such as John D. Ehrlichman, executive director of the Domestic Council, to review particular matters.

2 p.m.—Typically, Mr. Nixon enters a sitting room off his office and, in solitary quiet, eats a light lunch, such as cottage cheese and pineapple, from a tray. Usually, he will read material from a pale blue "FYI folder" brought to him by Butterfield. It includes internal memorandums, representative letters sifted from the 2.5 million sent each year to the White House and magazine articles.

3 p.m.—The afternoon schedule begins. Ehrlichman and the director of the Office of Management and Budget, meet with the President to discuss domestic affairs issues.

3:30 p.m.—The afternoon appointments begin.

6:30 p.m. or thereabouts—After the final appointment, Haldeman reenters the President's office to brief Mr. Nixon on the latest events. Butterfield brings in the night "immediate-action folder."

7:30 p.m. or thereabouts—Mr. Nixon returns to the residence, where he will have a quiet dinner with his family unless there is a White House social function.

A white-tie formality prevails at social events. Mr. Nixon mingles with the guests, but, unlike Lyndon Johnson, he does not dance. Generally, he will leave before midnight and go upstairs to the family living quarters.

9 p.m.—Often, the President repairs to his "hideaway" office in the old Executive Office Building next door to the White House, where he works alone and reads and studies lengthy papers requiring his attention.

Sometimes, instead of going to the Executive Office Building, Mr. Nixon works nights in the Lincoln Room, to the accompaniment of stereo music by such composers and conductors as Mantovani, Rodgers and Hammerstein, Percy Faith and Andre Kostelanetz.

During these nocturnal working sessions, Mr. Nixon makes numerous telephone calls on official and private business. Haldeman estimates he receives two phone calls at home each night from the President.

12 to 1 a.m.—The President retires for the night.

Mr. Nixon's schedule is more flexible when he is away from Washington.

Nonetheless, even while on sojourns to Key Biscayne, Fla., and San Clemente, Calif., he takes along chores that have to be done—polishing the budget or drafting a major speech. It is up to

Haldeman to see that the people and the papers are there when the President needs them.

Other staff members who generally accompany the President when he is away from Washington include Kissinger, Ehrlichman, Ziegler, Dwight L. Chapin and a military aide.

Occasionally, when Mr. Nixon journeys to nearby Camp David, Md., for the weekend, he is accompanied only by a military aide and Secret Service agents, plus members of his family. An elaborate radio station keeps him in touch with the outside world.

(A few top officials—such as Ehrlichman, Kissinger and Shultz—have almost carte blanche access to the President if they believe the situation warrants it.)

Occasionally, senior White House aides will bring in people and introduce them to the President.

Before a visitor sees the President, both he and the President are briefed on the nature of the call. The caller is also informed how much time he is allotted. If necessary, Bull will terminate the meeting by a subtle gesture to the visitor. The President, of course, may allow the meeting to run beyond the allotted time, which he sometimes does.

"For the most part, people are conscientious about using the President's time and do not try to stay longer than they're supposed to," Chapin said.

A log of the President's activities is meticulously kept for each day, covering every hour of the President's time, the visitors he has seen, the times they entered and departed, the nature of their business and the agenda of official meetings. This goes into a daily packet, which also includes records pertaining to the President's actions for that day and is preserved for historians.

Others: A number of high-level White House aides report to the President through Haldeman in his role as Mr. Nixon's chief administrative assistant. They include Charles W. Colson, special counsel for liaison with organized groups; Harry S. Dent, special counsel for political affairs; John Wesley Dean III, counsel to the President, who acts as the White House legal officer; and Frederic V. Malek, special assistant for personnel.

Ziegler reports directly to the President, but he frequently consults with Haldeman.

Haldeman deals individually

with Cabinet Secretaries on upper-level personnel matters and on non-substantive policy issues.

Raymond K. Price also reports to Haldeman. Price, a former editorial writer for *The New York Herald Tribune* who heads the speech-writing team, also takes care of some of the White House mail.

The estimated five million pieces of mail received since Mr. Nixon entered the White House have been handled this way: Mail dealing with random subjects goes to a professional staff; personal mail goes to Rose Mary Woods, Mr. Nixon's personal secretary; mail dealing with substantive matters is forwarded to the appropriate department or agency; a cross-section of mail considered useful and thought-provoking, reflecting the mood and consensus of the public on certain issues, is handled by Price's staff and submitted to the President.

Haldeman is never far from the President, thanks to an elaborate communications setup.

One of the five buttons on a telephone console on the President's desk connects him directly with Haldeman on the only phone which rings in Haldeman's office. (Other calls reach Haldeman through his secretary.) The President may also summon him by a buzzer system or through the White House switchboard. A direct telephone line connects the White House and Haldeman's home in Chevy Chase, Md.

If Haldeman wants to reach the President, he telephones him through the White House switchboard and is put through directly to the Oval Office by the operators. This is a privilege accorded only to Haldeman, Kissinger, Butterfield and Ehrlichman.

Haldeman, like other top White House aides, can learn the President's whereabouts in the White House at any hour by means of a security device known as the "locator board." This consists of a display with seven electronic buttons, each corresponding to a White House location—such as the East Wing, the residence, or the Executive Office Building. White House police light up the appropriate button from a control board to mark the President's location.

Making of the President: Theodore H. White wrote in *The Making of The President—1968,* "Half a dozen names form the constellation of Richard Nixon's communications group—Leonard Garment, Frank Shakespeare, Wil-

HALDEMAN'S TOP STAFF ASSISTANTS

At the start of the Nixon Administration, more than 30 members of the White House staff were 30 years old or younger. Several of them had worked with H. R. Haldeman during the 1968 campaign. Background information follows on principal members of Haldeman's staff and others who work in his area of responsibility.

Dwight L. Chapin, 30, special assistant to the President, was Mr. Nixon's personal aide in the Presidential campaign. He was responsible for getting the candidate up in the morning, putting him to bed at night and looking after his wardrobe, meals and schedule. Born in Wichita, Kan., he migrated with his family to California, where he was graduated from the University of Southern California. He subsequently worked for the J. Walter Thompson advertising firm.

Alexander P. Butterfield, 44, deputy assistant to the President, was born in Pensacola, Fla. The son of a career naval aviator, he followed his father in a military flying career. He retired as a full colonel in the Air Force in 1969 to join the White House staff. His military credits include service as a parachutist, as wingman on the jet aerobatic team, The Skyblazers, and as commanding officer of a jet squadron in Vietnam, where he flew 98 combat missions. He also served as military assistant in the office of Defense Secretary (1961-68) Robert S. McNamara. He is a graduate of UCLA and of the National War College.

Stephen Bull, 29, staff assistant to the President, was born in New York City and graduated from St. Lawrence University. He served three years in the Marine Corps, including one year in Vietnam, rising to the rank of captain. On his return to civilian life, he became administrative assistant to the president of the Canada Dry Corp. In July 1968, he took a leave of absence to work in the Nixon campaign.

Lawrence M. Higby, 25, staff assistant to the President and administrative assistant to Haldeman, helped set up office assignments when the Nixon team moved into the White House. He majored in political science at UCLA and earned a master's degree in business administration at the same university. He and Haldeman met during Haldeman's tenure as president of the UCLA Alumni Association, when Higby was student body vice president. He later worked part-time under Haldeman at J. Walter Thompson and was Haldeman's aide in the 1968 campaign.

Jon Meade Huntsman, 33, special assistant to the President, was appointed Feb. 23, 1971, with the assignment of staff secretary. Formerly with HEW as associate administrator of social and rehabilitation services, he managed the Cuban refugee program in the United States. Previously, he was president of the Dolco

Packaging Corp. and board chairman of Continental Dynamics Inc., a Los Angeles tape and phonograph production company, which he founded in 1966. Born in Blackfoot, Idaho, he graduated from the Wharton School of Finance at the University of Pennsylvania and received a master's degree in business administration from the University of Southern California.

liam Safire, Herbert Klein, Harry Treleaven, H. R. Haldeman. These men, collectively, had greater importance and greater impact than any other communications group in any Presidential campaign; but the governing philosophy can perhaps best be traced to H. R. Haldeman."

In support of this thesis, White cited a late 1967 memorandum which Haldeman wrote for candidate Nixon.

In the memorandum, Haldeman maintained that the traditional marketing of political candidates had become obsolete; that the candidate can reach more people in a half-minute of television than in 10 months of barnstorming; that a favorable column in a nationally circulated news magazine is worth more than two dozen press releases or position papers, and that the physical strength of the candidate must not be wasted through excessive campaign stumping.

The Haldeman memorandum, wrote White, "framed the Nixon campaign."

The Public Pulse—Chapin says Haldeman's advertising background prepared him well for his White House position.

"Advertising men know public attitudes, what is acceptable and not acceptable. You can't deceive the people. You can use advertising techniques, but the end results are not always what you want," Chapin said.

"A good advertising man has a responsibility to his client and must have a good knowledge of the cross-section of the American

ACCESS TO THE PRESIDENT

According to one White House aide, "The name of the game is access to the President. Some guys know how to 'roll' the White House; others never learn, and, like (former Interior Secretary, 1969-70, Walter J.) Hickel, they're the soon forgotten ones."

However, White House spokesmen such as Press Secretary Ronald L. Ziegler and Presidential Deputy Assistant Dwight L. Chapin, say that any Cabinet member or top-level Administration official can get through to the President if his business is urgent enough.

"For example," Chapin said, "Gov. Volpe (Transportation Secretary John A. Volpe, a former Massachusetts governor, 1961-63; 1965-69) may call and say he would like to talk with the President about something, say hijacking, and that he will be in his office between 3:30 and five. We then put a note on the President's desk saying that Gov. Volpe will be in his office at that time and would like to speak with him about hijacking."

The access routes to the President's Oval Office vary.

Some enjoy a special relationship with the President: Attorney General John N. Mitchell, Secretary of State William P. Rogers and Presidential Counselor Robert H. Finch, because of their long association with Mr. Nixon; Defense Secretary Melvin R. Laird, because of his position as head of a vitally important federal department. These people usually reach Mr. Nixon by notifying Presidential Assistant H. R. Haldeman.

"The President's relationship with Finch is like father and son," said a White House aide. "He likes to talk with him on the phone."

Pass-through System—In most cases, however, access to the President follows a circuitous path, with Haldeman the final traffic light. HUD Secretary George Romney, for example, deals with the White House essentially through John D. Ehrlichman, executive director of the Domestic Council, or the Assistant OMB Director for Human Resources. But Haldeman is at the President's door and is consulted.

A spokesman for Labor Secretary James Hodgson told *National Journal:*

"There is no one channel; it all depends on the subject. If it's about reorganization and revenue sharing, we deal with Ed Morgan (on Ehrlichamn's staff); if it's high economic policy, we contact (former OMB Director) George Shultz; if it's a labor problem, we'll see (Charles W.) Colson, since he is the White House liaison with labor organizations.

"The Secretary has very little dealing with Haldeman unless he wants an audience with the President."

Structural Maze—The White House is not set up like a corporate structure: its organizational lines may cross each other or purposely remain fuzzy.

On the White House organization chart, Russell E. Train, chairman of the Environmental Quality Council, reports directly to the President. Usually, however, Train first confers with John C. Whitaker, a deputy to Ehrlichman.

Outside organizations conduct their White House affairs through individuals associated with a specific government area or function. Many will deal with Colson; others, such as George Meany, president of the powerful AFL-CIO, with Shultz. Black organizations and spokesmen contact Robert J. Brown, a special assistant to the President.

Personal friends of the President outside the government reach him through his private secretary, Rose Mary Woods.

Sen. Jacob K. Javits, R-N.Y., said in a December 1970 speech in Houston that Mr. Nixon "runs the risk of being too closely insulated from the country, with his reading material screened, with his personal meetings limited and with staff assessments of what are the moods and the needs of the people."

Haldeman's responsibilities include all three of the sources of isolation Sen. Javits listed: screening reading material, clearing visitors and helping assess the mood of the public.

The Real Target—Haldeman concedes that he is the real target of charges by the press and some Members of Congress that Mr. Nixon is isolated. He says, however, that the charges are without foundation.

public. I think that advertising helped him (Haldeman) develop his mind and accentuated qualities which are beneficial to him now.

"He has a good sense of organization, which comes from looking at a number of clients; he has a good public awareness. For example, during the Cambodia thrust, he had a good feel on how the public would react, not just at the moment but far in the future."

Haldeman is not involved directly in Presidential public relations. But he is brought into all White House activities related to it. For instance, he has a subordinate on an ad hoc White House panel which meets irregularly to discuss the President's public relations.

Included in the group are Ziegler, Klein, Dent, Chapin, and Patrick J. Buchanan, a speech writer.

Isolation of the President:

HALDEMAN ON NIXON

During a *National Journal* interview in his White House office, before a fireplace with crackling logs, H. R. Haldeman offered insights into Mr. Nixon as President and into the Presidential decision-making process.

"President Nixon is an enormously prodigious worker and a complete perfectionist. Before a meeting, he wants to know the background of the subject. He doesn't like someone to come in and present an original case with which he is unfamiliar. That's counterproductive. He wants to be given everything about an issue, including other views and the pros and cons, so he can get right to the point, rather than start from scratch. He prefers to get rid of the preliminaries.

"In 10 minutes he can go through a background summary and have a good idea of what it's all about instead of taking 45 minutes in discussion.

"Some visitors are overawed in a meeting with the President and don't ever get to the point."

Haldeman said that during a break in his schedule, the President may sit around with senior staff aides and chat informally on various topics. But even then, Haldeman said, Mr. Nixon likes to probe and ask questions.

"For example, today (Feb. 19, 1971) he is meeting with a group of *Fortune* magazine editors. This almost certainly will stimulate ideas. Afterwards, he will review their points, ask questions about them and note that they challenged the Administration on this or that. He may call in Peter Flanigan (assistant to the President) or Paul McCracken (former chairman of the Council of Economic Advisers) and talk to them about it.

"We try to allow him time to do that. It is a much more important use of Presidential time than most of what appears on the President's schedule, much of which is partly ceremonial. Also, he has a remarkable knack of turning social functions into the decision-making process by talking to people and getting their views and ideas."

Haldeman said he did not believe that the Presidency had changed Mr. Nixon very much.

"Everybody changes with time, of course. But Mr. Nixon came into the Presidency with a complete familiarity with the office. He had served as Vice President, and he sought the Presidency in 1960. I don't think that anything has surprised him. He has sort of phased into it.

"He has always worked hard and long, more than he should be doing now. That is one of my responsibilities—seeing that he has periods of relaxation—where I have been least successful.

"He doesn't take long, periodic vacations. President Kennedy would go to Palm Beach and Lyndon Johnson to his Texas ranch. But he won't do it. He will move the physical base of work to Key Biscayne or San Clemente, and he will change his work patterns.

"For instance, he likes to work in the Executive Office Building. It's a way of leaving behind the ceremonial part of his office. There he can work in depth at his own pace. And he can bring people in on an unstructured basis. Weekends at Camp David also are very useful. There, he uses the bowling alley and swims in the fresh-water pool—although he prefers ocean salt water—and he can work out on the sun terrace."

Another form of relaxation for the President is reading, mostly histories and political biographies.

"Kissinger provides him with reading suggestions, and he has asked Pat Moynihan (former Presidential Counselor, 1969-70, who returned to Harvard to teach) to recommend reading material," Haldeman said.

In a May 24, 1970, speech at UCLA, which had named him alumnus of the year, Haldeman said Mr. Nixon is "the most unisolated President in recent times."

The President, he said, carefully weighs each option and listens to arguments by people in and out of government, representing a wide range of thought, before he makes major decisions.

The charge of isolation, Haldeman said, is a fabrication by the press.

Another Critic — Walter N. Thayer, former president of *The New York Herald Tribune* and a special consultant to the President to direct the activities of the Advisory Council on Executive Organization, might take issue with Haldeman.

Thayer was denied access to Mr. Nixon when he attempted to present him with a report on the council's activities. Protesting vigorously, Thayer indicated that he would resign as consultant if he did not see the President personally. Eventually, he saw the President.

Never Say No—Ever since the flap in November 1970 over the dismissal of Interior Secretary Walter J. Hickel, who said he had been unable to obtain a private meeting with the President, the White House has adopted a policy of never saying no to a high Administration official seeking a Presidential interview.

"There are other ways of handling them if the President is unavailable," said a White House aide. "In such cases, we get other qualified people in the Administration to take care of them. We try not to antagonize them. We have all read George Reedy's book and are very much aware of this."

(Reedy, former press secretary, 1964-65, to President Johnson, suggested in his book, *The Twilight of the Presidency,* that U.S. Presidents have become isolated from the feelings and concerns of the people.)

Views from the Senate—Several Republican Senators' offices indicated to *National Journal* that communications with the White House have improved but are still inadequate.

An aide to Sen. Clifford P. Case, R-N.J., said privately, "The Senator feels that the best way to communicate with the White House is from the floor of the Senate."

Case once tried to reach the President by telephone, the aide said, and Haldeman returned the call. "The Senator told him he didn't want to speak with him, that he wanted to speak only to the President. Subsequently, he was put through to the President."

William Hoiles, administrative assistant to Sen. William B. Saxbe, R-Ohio, said: "Things have improved between the Senate and the White House, although it's not where we would like it to be. Top assistants there certainly don't lavish attention on top assistants here.

"Sometimes, communications are snafued, but not for lack of effort—more for lack of experience and coordination."

An aide to Sen. Richard S. Schweiker, R-Pa., said privately, "Relations with the White House have gotten better, particularly with recent efforts ... to explain the legislative package and the briefings on the State of the Union and the budget. ... It remains to be seen how well things go once the battles get under way."

An assistant to Sen. John Sherman Cooper, R-Ky., said that things are smoother now, and it's a more leisurely operation since the November (1970) elections."

Each of the Senators attributed the improved relations between the Hill and the White House to Mr. Nixon's appointment on Dec. 1, 1970, of Clark MacGregor as counsel to the President in charge of congressional relations. MacGregor was a Republican House Member from 1961 to 1970; he was defeated by former Vice President Hubert H. Humphrey in the 1970 Minnesota Senate race.

MacGregor outranks William E. Timmons, who, according to some Members of Congress, did not have sufficient influence at the White House.

Several Senators—including Case—also said that the November elections seem to have had a sobering effect on the Administration, prompting it to be more cooperative with the legislators.

In this connection, Mr. Nixon frequently has had breakfast with important Members of Congress, such as Majority Leader Mike Mansfield, D-Mont., and Rep. Wilbur D. Mills, D-Ark., chairman of the House Ways and Means Committee.

Impressions: Reflecting on his White House responsibilities, Haldeman said, "I've found it harder than I expected to get things done. The difficulty to get the bureaucratic structure of the government to move is a real one. You've always heard that, but you can't really believe it until you've been here. There's a basic problem there."

On his role as the President's man, he said, "My whole existence is pointed toward carrying out another man's directives and being of service to him. That automatically changes one."

Ehrlichman acts as policy broker in Nixon's formalized Domestic Council

Dom Bonafede

Once or twice a day, Presidential aide John D. Ehrlichman's special White House phone rings sharply, and, as often as not, the caller asks, "Are you busy? If you're doing something, tell me."

The voice belongs to President Nixon, inquiring as to the availability of his chief advisor on domestic affairs.

Normally, a Presidential summons, no matter how graciously couched, is an order of highest priority. All other business is immediately abandoned in response.

But, "with sufficient frequency," Ehrlichman may decorously inform the President that he is engaged in a pressing task or conferring with a Cabinet officer or two and ask if it would be convenient if he checked back.

"Some time ago," Ehrlichman explained, "I had some important visitors in my office, and the President called. When I got to his office, he asked if I had been free, and I mentioned the visitors. He then told me, 'I shouldn't have called you out. Let me know when that happens again.'"

This Presidential deference reflects both Ehrlichman's standing at the White House and his personal relationship with Mr. Nixon.

In power-conscious Washington, proximity to the President is the cachet of ultimate status. Ehrlichman's status is all the more remarkable in that less than three years ago he was little known beyond the city limits of Seattle, Wash., where he practiced law as a partner in the firm of Hullin, Ehr-lichman, Roberts and Hodge.

Equally remarkable is the fact that, except for a summer stint as a postal clerk in Santa Monica, Calif., in 1942, he had never worked for the government before going to the White House with Mr. Nixon.

His relationship with Mr. Nixon, which dates only from 1959, is far briefer in time than that of other close Presidential associates, such as H. R. Haldeman, assistant to the President and White House chief of staff; Robert H. Finch, counselor to the President; and Herbert G. Klein, director of communications for the executive branch.

Dual Role: In his dual role as assistant to the President for domestic affairs and executive director of the Domestic Council, Ehrlichmann, 47, serves both the personal Presidency of Mr. Nixon and the institution of the Presidency.

He is intimately involved in the creation of domestic policy proposals, in their refinement and remodeling, in their packaging and promotion. In some instances, he is responsible for aborting them. He screens, winnows, evaluates and, in general, passes on every domestic policy matter that comes before the President.

In the equation of national politics, that almost equals unparalleled clout.

Referring to Presidential aides of Ehrlichman's status, political scientist Richard E. Neustadt observed, "(They) outrank in all but protocol the heads of most executive departments."

Of his relationship with Mr. Nixon, Ehrlichman says, "There is almost nothing I wouldn't feel completely easy about taking up with him. . . . We have a sense of mutual confidence."

PERSONAL PORTRAIT

Ehrlichman's official power base is the Domestic Council, established in May 1970 when Congress cleared Reorganization Plan No. 2 of 1970.

As executive director—he was appointed on the following June 10—Ehrlichman is in charge of both the council's day-to-day operations and its long-range planning.

His conduct of the council's business over the past year has brought Ehrlichman into contact with a variety of public officials and private citizens. As a result of these contacts, Ehrlichman is beginning to come into focus as a force in government and as a personality.

Manner: How does he seem to shape up against the men who were his near-counterparts in recent Administrations?

He is neither as articulate as Theodore C. Sorensen, special counsel to the President in the Kennedy Administration, nor as authoritarian as Sherman Adams, the assistant to the President in the Eisenhower Administration, nor as passionately partisan as Joseph A. Califano, special assistant to the President in the Johnson Administration.

Ehrlichman fits neatly with the private Presidency of Mr. Nixon, which puts a premium on order, corporate-chart efficiency, competence and restraint.

He is low on flair, bright but not brash, keen-minded but more technician than theoretician. "Firm but affable" is a common description of Ehrlichman's nature.

Whereas his close friend "Bob" Haldeman gives an impression of earnest but studied informality, Ehrlichman is genuinely relaxed and casual. He slouches in a chair to talk with a visitor and sports moccasins at a Cabinet meeting.

"He's low-keyed and very cool," said Tod Hullin, aide de camp to Ehrlichman and son of his former Seattle law partner.

"I've never heard him raise his voice."

Edward L. Morgan, one of Ehrlichman's principal deputies, said, "He's easy to work for but definitely not lax or sloppy. ... I've worked for him the whole time in the White House, and we never seem to operate in a taskmaster atmosphere."

Ehrlichman is a Christian Scientist, and he neither drinks nor smokes. An advocate of old-fashioned virtues, he sent a box of candy to each of the White House telephone operators on Mother's Day. And when the head of the Army Signal Corps detachment at the White House was promoted to general, Ehrlichman forwarded a congratulatory note.

Press Image: This side of Ehrlichman does not conform to the press image he shares with Haldeman as "Prussian guards," overly zealous in their desire to protect the President.

"That image came out of the campaign," said Ehrlichman, "and there's been a certain amount of carry-over ever since. From the nature of our jobs, we didn't have an easy rapport with the press. Also, it's colorful; we've got Germanic names, and it makes for lively press copy. I can't say it bothers me."

Another deputy, Kenneth R. Cole Jr., said that much of the criticism directed at Ehrlichman and Haldeman arises from the fact that "they're not running around the embassy party circuit."

Bryce N. Harlow, who served as counselor to President Nixon (1967-70) and congressional relations assistant to President Eisenhower (1953-61), and now is an executive with Procter & Gamble Co., noted that press criticism of White House aides is endemic to the American political system.

"It is normal for people serving the President to be criticized because they are close to power. And they can't please everybody," he said.

"You'll remember Joe McCarthy (Sen. Joseph R. McCarthy, R-Wis., 1947-57) called President Eisenhower's staff 'that motley crew'; Kennedy aides were the 'Irish Mafia'; Johnson's were 'the Texas rangers' and now Nixon and the 'Prussian guards.'"

Ehrlichman has defended Vice President Agnew's attacks on the media as criticism that needed to be expressed. And, although he himself is hardly indifferent to the press, he has no bitter complaints about it. "As a general proposition, I don't have too much complaint about press treatment of the President. But the Administration has had poor results in getting its accomplishments across to the people through the media," he said.

"When I go out into the country and enumerate the things we've

Ehrlichman and President Nixon on White House grounds

done, people say, 'I didn't realize that.' Somehow or another, we're not getting through. I'm not sure where the blame lies, and I can't point out specific cases where we have been subject to unfair treatment. But I'm not prepared to say the world is against us."

No Headline Hunter: Although the era of White House aides with "a passion for anonymity" ended (if it ever existed at all) with the advent of electronic communications, Ehrlichman is not a headline hunter.

He is sometimes accessible to the press, but he does not court it. During recent speculation that he was in line to succeed Attorney General John N. Mitchell, he asked Robert Finch to spike the reports rather than make an announcement himself.

He has strong views about officials who assume the posture of Administration spokesmen.

"It is too likely we would be taken as alter egos of the President," he said. "The President should make statements of a policy nature and Cabinet officers on matters of a departmental nature.

"In order to be efficient, a person in a situation like mine has to enjoy the confidence of the President and the Cabinet.

"A lot of personal appearances and public statements do not tend to build that confidence but to erode it."

Briefings—Nevertheless, the White House often calls on Ehrlichman to brief the press, Members of Congress and special interest groups on substantive policy issues.

Less frequently, he makes public speeches and press statements.

Spokesman—In December

1970, as a stand-in for the President, he spoke on the Administration's revenue-sharing proposal to the National League of Cities convention in Atlanta. And, prior to the 1970 midterm elections, he told newsmen at the California White House in San Clemente that Congress was "fiscally irresponsible" and said he hoped that the new Congress would be more sympathetic to the Administration.

During the President's visit to Birmingham on May 25, 1971, Ehrlichman briefed Southern editors and publishers on the merits of the Administration's departmental reorganization plan.

As the 1972 election approaches, he likely will be doing more of the same. Yet, he said, "I'm very content *not* doing those things."

The Lawyer: Ehrlichman's background as a lawyer has equipped him ideally for his White House job, which essentially requires him to provide the President with deeply researched briefs containing all possible arguments and their potential ramifications.

Little is known publicly of John Ehrlichman, attorney at law. Invariably, biographical accounts state that he specialized in cases concerned with "urban affairs and conservation of natural resources." The statement is accurate to a point. Ehrlichman also handled litigation in corporate and business law and in insurance cases. He represented both individual clients and companies.

John A. Roberts, a former law partner, described Ehrlichman the lawyer: "A very strong advocate, an excellent lawyer, very hard working. He enjoyed a fine reputation with fellow lawyers, as well as

with the courts. He had a tremendous capacity for long hours. There is a lawyer's adage that for every hour in court, you spend five out of court working on the case. John did that."

In one case which received some notice in the Seattle newspapers, Ehrlichman represented the owner of a railroad car that had been damaged by the Northern Pacific Railway Co. The company was willing to settle out of court for about $2,000. But Ehrlichman and his client took the case to court and eventually were awarded a $60,000 verdict.

Religious Scruples: Roberts said that Ehrlichman is not "straitlaced" to the extent of not understanding the behavior of people with ethical standards different from his own. Yet his religious principles are basic to his way of life and his work.

"As an attorney, I tried personal injury cases—without noticeable harm to my clients," Ehrlichman said.

"But I have been scrupulous about not getting into the Administration's health-care program. I've asked Ken Cole to take it over exclusive of any help by me. Those people involved have a right to assume the decisions were not influenced by a Christian Scientist."

Ehrlichman's abstention from the White House's formulation of the health-care program came after discussion with President Nixon and with his approval.

DOMESTIC COUNCIL

What power does Ehrlichman exercise as executive director of the Domestic Council? How does the council operate in his charge?

The Domestic Council, as envisioned by Mr. Nixon, has a broad mandate. Its principal functions are to define policy issues and devise proposals for dealing with them; to assess national needs; to provide the President with prompt advice in times of domestic crisis; to help set national priorities for allocating resources; and to maintain a check on programs and recommend reforms as needed.

Chaired by the President, the Domestic Council includes the Vice President, the Secretaries of Cabinet departments (with the exception of the State and Defense Departments), the OMB director, the chairman of the Council of Economic Advisers, Presidential counselors and anyone else the President designates. It meets only once a month, normally.

Title VII of the 1970 Housing and Urban Development Act (84 Stat 1770), which provides the framework for a national urban growth policy, requires the President, through a standing Domestic Council committee, to file a biennial report on urban growth. This is the Domestic Council's only statutory requirement.

Supporting the Domestic Council is a permanent, institutional staff which operates under Ehrlichman's authority.

The Domestic Council's sister agency, the OMB, concentrates on budgetary and managerial activities, including program coordination, legislative clearance, executive manpower development and informational systems.

The basic difference between the two agencies—according to the White House—is that the Domestic Council is concerned with set-

JOHN D. EHRLICHMAN: A HIGH 'DEDICATION QUOTIENT'

John D. Ehrlichman, 47, is a bear of a man (a shade over six feet tall and about 200 pounds) who, one is constantly told, can be tender or rough. This ambivalence has been the hallmark of his White House career.

Leaders of the House black caucus insist that it was Ehrlichman who persuaded Mr. Nixon to delay meeting with them because they might make political propaganda out of the confrontation. Yet, he supported the Philadelphia Plan requiring minority hiring in federally funded construction projects, and he supported welfare reform and the war on hunger.

With easy dexterity, he has defended both Vice President Agnew and Daniel F. Moynihan—symbols of two opposing schools of American political thought.

Even his current bedside reading ranges widely: from *Ball Four,* by Jim Bouton, to *Khrushchev Remembers.*

Ehrlichman simply does not consider himself an ideologue but rather a Presidential aide imbued with what Mr. Nixon once described as a high "dedication quotient."

Self-assured, a believer in religious principles, with an expanding waistline and receding hairline and the air of a Westerner with a slight distaste of the Washington scene—Ehrlichman looks and acts the part of a Nixon aide. Ehrlichman's assistants say that the two "mesh well together."

Ehrlichman himself observed in a ceremony marking the second anniversary of Mr. Nixon's inauguration, "We appreciate the qualify of life here at the White House. The days here are long, but the years are short."

Though obviously possessed with an evangelical sense of duty to his chief, Ehrlichman has not been awed by the thrust from relative obscurity to national prominence.

"The immersion was so gradual—we went through the campaign, the election, the transition and now here—it probably saved me from the bends," he said in an interview in his second-floor White House office.

Like the man, the office is unadorned by the normal appurtenances of political status. There are no photos of himself with the great and near-great, no glowing tributes or appointments written in script. Instead, there is a hand-lettered scroll of a quotation which Ehrlichman jotted down during a private chat with Mr. Nixon:

"Let us not fall into the dreary rut of just managing chaos a little better. Let us use the great power of this place to do something for the nation."

Early Years—Ehrlichman was born March 20, 1925, in Tacoma, Wash., but grew up in Seattle and in Santa Monica, Calif. His father, who was in the investment business, retired and moved to Southern California while John was still a boy.

Early in World War II, the elder Ehrlichman, who was too old for the U.S. Army Air Corps, became an officer in the Royal Canadian Air Force. He was killed in a plane crash in Canada in 1942.

After serving as a navigator in the U.S. Army Air Corps, young Ehrlichman went to the University of California at Los Angeles. There, he met H. R. Haldeman, who was campaign manager for Ehrlichman's wife in her unsuccessful bid for vice president of the student body. That was the first of a series of joint political ventures which eventually led to the White House.

He got his law degree at Stanford in 1951.

In 1959, Haldeman introduced Ehrlichman to Mr. Nixon. At Haldeman's urging, Ehrlichman worked in Mr. Nixon's 1960 Presidential campaign and in his 1962 California gubernatorial campaign.

Ehrlichman was doing well in law practice in Seattle when the call came in 1968 to join the Nixon campaign. He was ready. His main responsibility was to see that the Nixon entourage traveled on schedule.

Staffing the White House: The day after the election, the President-elect met with his top lieutenants at Key Biscayne, Fla., to discuss his White House staff structure.

Included in the meeting were Haldeman, Ehrlichman, Robert H. Finch and John N. Mitchell.

Finch and Ehrlichman were prepared to propose the formation of a domestic affairs policy council. But Mr. Nixon opted for the "star system," which meant attracting such men as Arthur F. Burns, Bryce N. Harlow and Daniel P. Moynihan.

One of Mr. Nixon's first appointees, Ehrlichman was given the title of counsel to the President, with assignments bearing on a wide range of domestic problems. He also performed legal work involving the President's personal financial affairs. In the meantime, he had severed connections with his Seattle law office.

A former partner, John A. Roberts, said, "A law firm is like a marriage. But we never had a harsh word. ... You get the impression that John is a hard-nosed, unbending person. The amazing thing is that that is furthest from the truth. Numerous times he deferred to majority rule."

Political Experience—One of the criticisms leveled at Ehrlichman is that he lacks practical political experience. In response to this, he said, "My approach might have been different, but I'm not sure whether that is good or bad."

He conceded that more experience in dealing with Congress "might have been an advantage."

Harlow, an expert in the area of congressional relations, remarked, "It can be said that the more one knows about Congress

ting policy, and the OMB, with seeing that policy is carried out.

In practice, however, their activities frequently overlap.

Role Defined: Ehrlichman perceives his primary function on the Domestic Council as policy broker, responsible for developing and delivering to the President painstakingly thorough, factual compendiums on domestic issues, complete with options, alternatives, supportive material and potential effects.

Ehrlichman is accountable to the President for scheduling the material so that Mr. Nixon has adequate time to deliberate on the wide range of choices and to arrive at a decision before a prescribed deadline.

The President tries not to reveal his early attitudes on issues, according to White House aides, in order to preclude the possibility that he will get only recommendations that his advisers think he wants. Often, he will call in assistants and Domestic Council staff members and pepper them with questions about a particular problem without tipping his hand on how he feels about it.

Neither does the President want memorandums heavily weighted toward one position.

"The President has made it clear that he doesn't want slanted papers," said Cole.

Paper Route: Ehrlichman's deputies send policy papers to the President in the form of loose-leaf notebooks, which may be from 50 to 150 pages long.

Each includes a cover memorandum written by Ehrlichman which summarizes issues, important points and alternatives. This is the better it is. I'm not sure.

"It's entirely correct that neither John nor Haldeman had much federal experience. But they traveled on the campaign with Mr. Nixon, so neither are exactly political neophytes."

Bureaucratic Battle—Despite his White House rank, Ehrlichman has found it difficult to budge the bureaucracy—as did most of his predecessors.

Shortly after taking office, Mr. Nixon asked Ehrlichman to see that the row of temporary World War II Navy buildings was removed from the Capitol Mall. The President had worked briefly in the buildings during the war as a young Navy officer.

Despite Ehrlichman's insistence and the fact that he was acting on behalf of the President, a year passed before the buildings were dismantled.

Ehrlichman's Day— A normal working day begins for Ehrlichman when a White House limousine picks him up at 6:30 at his Great Falls, Va., colonial-style house. During the ride to the White House, he scans the morning newspapers and attends to some of the paperwork in his briefcase.

At 7 a.m., he has breakfast at the White House mess with Kenneth Cole, one of his deputies, and Tod Hullin, his administrative aide. Edward L. Morgan, another deputy, sometimes joins them.

During breakfast, Ehrlichman is briefed on news events and office developments. In turn, he issues instructions for the day and reviews his schedule. His meal usually consists of juice, three eggs (fried or scrambled) and coffee.

At 7:30 a.m., he attends the large White House staff conference in the Roosevelt Room.

At 8 a.m., he moves to Haldeman's office for the daily meeting of senior White House aides.

Between 9 and 9:30 a.m., he starts in on the day's work schedule. Normally, Hullin charts Ehrlichman's day hour by hour.

Lunch is almost always at the White House.

At 3 p.m., he and the OMB Director meet with Mr. Nixon in what is a standing appointment. Cole sits in for Ehrlichman when he is unable to attend.

At 6 p.m., he turns to his personal and official mail, takes care of "priority reading" and checks press releases from Press Secretary Ronald L. Ziegler's office.

At 8 to 8:30 p.m., he returns to Great Falls for dinner with his wife and the four children living at home. Their oldest son, Peter, attends Stanford University.

Ehrlichman prefers to keep his family out of the spotlight of publicity. He and Mrs. Ehrlichman attend "must" social events. They favor quiet evenings at home or with friends, such as the Haldemans, showing home movies.

presented in such a way that the President can use it as a checklist. In addition, Ehrlichman marks what he considers the most cogent material. The books are tabbed so that Mr. Nixon can readily turn to identified sections.

The purpose of all this is to conserve one of the President's most precious possessions—his time. Generally, Mr. Nixon will read the notebooks at night in the Lincoln Room or in his office in the Old Executive Office Building next door to the White House. The heftier reports are reserved for weekends and for longer sojourns at Camp David, Md., Key Biscayne, Fla., and San Clemente, Calif.

The President's habit is to write commentaries and instructions in the margins.

"Sometimes a paper will go down," Ehrlichman said, "and we'll get it right back. Other times, it will wait three or four days. He will want to sleep on it."

Picking Issues: The President determines what major issues the Domestic Council will take up after consultation with Ehrlichman, Shultz and other close advisers. Sometimes, Mr. Nixon will simply send a memorandum to the Domestic Council staff, instructing it to look into the a matter. Cabinet officers and Domestic Council staff members often make suggestions. The staff also keeps abreast of expiring legislation, which may lead to new fields of policy exploration.

The President often calls on Ehrlichman to perform service apart from his organizational duties.

For example, he arranged ceremonies for the departure of William McChesney Martin Jr. (1951-70) as chairman of the board of governors of the Federal Reserve System.

Operational Structure: Although the Domestic Council has been called a White House minibureaucracy, the President and Ehrlichman have attempted to make it a heterogeneous body, cutting across departmental lines.

Cabinet Input — Ehrlichman has asked Cabinet officers and their staffs to participate in the policy-making process much more than they had anticipated.

And, at least theoretically, the Domestic Council is neutral in interdepartmental rivalries.

"We deliberately arrange to bring people in from the departments," Ehrlichman said. "They participate in policy proposals; they have a stake in them; they understand them. When there is a decision from the President, they are more likely to be aboard."

Interagency Mix—Under the present working setup, once a policy issue has been determined, a Cabinet-level committee is recruited from the departments to form an over-all group.

Then, a project group or task force is assembled at the assistant-secretary level. It is generally composed of Domestic Council staff members, representatives of the affected departments and agencies and OMB officials. Sometimes, outsiders with special interests or expertise are included.

Five to eight people—occasionally more—are in each unit.

The committee on health, for example, included representatives from HEW, OMB, the Veterans Administration, the Defense Department, OEO, the Treasury Department, Council of Economic Advisers, the Labor Department and the Office of Science and Technology.

The purpose of the mix is multifold: Most governmental problems are interagency in scope; by their very nature, the departments and agencies have built-in biases, plus alliances with special constituencies; and, acting alone, they are unlikely to be objective. As Ehrlichman has noted, it is easier to get departments and agencies to endorse programs and policies which they have helped develop.

The Tasks — The project groups, under the supervision of Ehrlichman's deputies, make the studies, conduct the research and draft the working papers. Invariably, they call on specialists in other areas of the government.

Most of the papers are channeled to Cole, who is Ehrlichman's deputy administrator. He sees that the papers are in proper order and forwards them to Ehrlichman—and, by that route, to the President.

Occasionally, Ehrlichman or Cole will kick back papers which are "loaded" toward one position, leave questions unanswered or are otherwise inadequate.

Infrequently, some policy proposals—such as the Administration's general revenue-sharing plan—are designed almost exclusively within the Domestic Council staff framework.

Policy issues the Domestic Council has studied include national energy, health care, environmental problems, drugs, government reorganization, military retirement benefits, revenue sharing, welfare reform and model cities.

The Domestic Council's two-tiered committees and subcommittees are fashioned as ad hoc, temporary groups. Once the President has accepted their reports, the panels are disbanded. They may be reestablished, however, to help develop legislation.

Objectivity: Under previous Administrations, the custom was for policy papers to originate at the White House or in departments and then to circulate to other departments for advisory comments.

"We are more concerned with objectivity than with advocacy," Cole said.

But, because Ehrlichman acts as impresario over the whole operation, the question arises as to his objectivity in policy matters.

"There is no sure thing as a completely sanitized presentation," Ehrlichman said. "You have to ask yourself all the time if it is sufficiently unweighted to give him (the President) a fair shot at it.

"Of course, if he asks me for an opinion, I'll give it to him."

Skepticism—Despite Ehrlichman's contention regarding staff objectivity and Cabinet-level participation, one long-time opponent of the Domestic Council concept remains unconvinced.

Rep. Chet Holifield, D-Calif., chairman of the Government Operations Committee, told *National Journal*:

"I think the same about the Domestic Council as I did before. I have not made any evaluation of its work, but the principles of my objections are still valid. It sets up a 90-member council of political

EHRLICHMAN AND THE LEVERS OF POWER

John D. Ehrlichman has demonstrated staying power and buoyancy in the face of White House shakedowns and organizational changes. Appointed a Presidential aide following the 1968 campaign, in which he had served as "tour director" in charge of logistics, he has risen to positions of the highest influence and authority within the White House hierarchy.

The frustration of some of the President's staffing plans and the mutual antagonism of two of his close advisers helped to bring Ehrlichman to prominence.

During the transition period between election and inauguration, Mr. Nixon indicated that he would select generalists as his aides; that personality cults within the White House staff would be discouraged; that the staff would be smaller than under previous Presidents; and that powers held in the White House would be decentralized.

President-elect Nixon intended to appoint Cabinet Secretaries endowed with "extra dimension," through whom the federal departments would regain some of the prestige and power that had been increasingly concentrated in the Office of the President.

But, according to a White House aide, once the Administration got under way, it became evident that the implementation of some of these intentions was ineffective.

"Coordination was lacking within the White House and between the various executive offices," he said.

Cults sprang up, particularly around Arthur F. Burns, counselor to the President and his chief economic adviser, and around Daniel P. Moynihan, assistant to the President for urban affairs—two White House intellectuals-in-residence with conflicting political ideologies.

Shifts of Power—Robert F. Ellsworth, national political director for the Nixon-Agnew campaign who had been appointed a top White House aide with responsibility in both domestic and foreign fields, was shunted to NATO as the U.S. Ambassador when it became clear that he did not see eye-to-eye with other Presidential advisers, including Ehrlichman and H. R. Haldeman, assistant to the President.

John P. Sears, a former member of Mr. Nixon's New York law firm who had been named deputy counsel in charge of political liaison, also drifted from the center of power.

From the start, Mr. Nixon leaned heavily on the National Security Council for advice, enlarging the scope of its functions under Henry A. Kissinger, assistant to the President for national security affairs.

But the lines of communication within the domestic affairs area remained disorganized.

In the summer of 1969, Burns and Moynihan were locked in an internecine battle over the design of the Administration's welfare-reform plan. The President turned to Ehrlichman to reconcile the differences. The result was a thick memorandum titled *Welfare Proposals and Commentary*.

This document served as the basis for the President's welfare plan. Ehrlichman's star was on the rise.

Ash Council—In an effort to put his house in better order, the President on April 4, 1969, announced the formation of the Advisory Council on Executive Organization, headed by Roy L. Ash, president of Litton Industries Inc., a California-based conglomerate.

The council was told to study the executive branch thoroughly, including the Office of the President, and to recommend ways to make it a more efficient instrument for public policy.

A White House-drafted scenario of the study later disclosed: "The President hoped to develop reorganization plans prior to taking office; but this proved impossible, due to time and legal restraints. Therefore, both Cabinet and sub-Cabinet officials were warned to expect substantial reorganization early in the Administration's tenure."

Acting on one of the first Ash Council reports, the White House announced a major realignment on Nov. 4, 1969, one year after the election. Burns became chairman of the Federal Reserve Board. Moynihan and Bryce N. Harlow, a veteran of the Eisenhower Administration who supervised congressional relations for Mr. Nixon, were elevated to the position of counselor.

At the same time, Ehrlichman, then counsel to the President, became assistant for domestic affairs with jurisdiction over "all substantive matters concerning domestic affairs."

The shakeup meant that Moynihan's urban affairs council and Burns' economic policy-making cluster would be shifted to Ehrlichman's domain.

Ehrlichman had emerged as the domestic counterpart to Kissinger.

Revamped Structures — Shortly afterwards, in May 1970, Congress cleared Reorganization Plan No. 2 of 1970. The plan established the Domestic Council and restructured the Budget Bureau, which became the Office of Management and Budget.

On June 10, President Nixon named Labor Secretary George P. Shultz as director of OMB, and Ehrlichman as executive director of the Domestic Council.

The reorganization plan went into effect July 1. It was then certain that the levers of power at the White House were shared by a quartet composed of Kissinger, Haldeman, Shultz and Ehrlichman.

With the reorganization, the Nixon White House assumed its characteristic style, which contrasts with the organization and style of recent Administrations.

President Eisenhower preferred a chain-of-command system; John F. Kennedy's White House was staffed with colorful and precocious friends; the Johnson White House operation was personalized and free-wheeling.

The Nixon White House operates somewhat as an appeals court, with the President acting as the supreme magistrate who, in the solitude of his chambers, weighs all the arguments before making his decisions.

In another legal image, President Nixon once referred to himself as "counsel for all the people."

If that is the case, Ehrlichman is the President's junior partner in charge of domestic affairs.

appointees, which, in effect, is doing the work, making the policy determinations and setting the priorities which heretofore had been made by the various Cabinet departments and the Bureau of the Budget.

"It constitutes a method by which the Domestic Council deliberations have the respectability of Cabinet participation. But it doesn't replace Cabinet-level decision-making."

Insulation for Nixon—Holifield further faulted the Domestic Council for the fact that Ehrlichman and his staff enjoy executive privilege, which, he said, means they are "not answerable to Congress" for their actions.

In a Jefferson-Jackson Day speech at San Jose, Calif., May 15, 1971, Sen. Ernest F. Hollings, D-S.C., revived the contention that the Domestic Council serves as a barrier between Congress and the Presidency. Said Hollings:

"It used to be that if I had a problem with food stamps, I went to see the Secretary of Agriculture, whose department had jurisdiction over that program. Not any more. Now, if I want to learn the policy, I must go to the White House and consult John Price.

"If I want the latest on textiles, I won't get it from the Secretary of Commerce, who has the authority and responsibility. No, I am forced to go to the White House staff and see Mr. Peter Flanigan. I shouldn't feel too badly. Secretary Stans has to do the same thing."

Price, a special assistant to the President, and a member of Ehrlichman's staff, specializes in urban-rural affairs. Flanigan, an assistant to the President, deals primarily with business and trade matters.

Staff: The Domestic Council has a staff of 49—28 professional and 21 secretarial people. This is considerably fewer than the 80 allowed under its statutory ceiling (and the 90 mentioned by Holifield).

The holddown is attributable to several factors: a desire to maintain a low profile to allay fears in Congress and the federal bureaucracy that the Domestic Council is running the domestic side of the government; the inclusion of OMB and departmental specialists in the operation; uncertainty over qualifications and talents required for Domestic Council professionals.

"Our needs are not for great visionaries," said Cole, "but for generalists who are bright and have a good grasp of problems; people who have demonstrable talents and can work with people."

The council will take on additional staff members next year, he said.

Ehrlichman said that the Domestic Council was deliberately being built "very slowly." He said he was wary of setting up a big organization, because it might appear to justify criticism that the council is another wall between the Presidency and other branches of government. He said there could be "a measure of truth" in the criticism.

"That's one of the reasons why I conceive of our role as more catalytic than monopolistic," he said. "I don't want to see us develop an organization that would sterilize the input the President gets by having it developed by a closed corporation."

The Deputies: Below Ehrlichman on the Domestic Council organizational chart are five deputy directors, each with a personal staff. For the most part, the deputy directors have assigned areas of jurisdiction:

Edward L. Morgan—welfare reform, school desegregation and labor. (Morgan also serves as Ehrlichman's operational director and is charged with coordinating President Nixon's "six great goals.")

Egil Krogh Jr.—drugs, crime and law enforcement, housing, government reorganization and transportation.

Edwin L. Harper—revenue sharing and budgetary procedures.

John C. Whitaker—environment, agriculture and national growth policy.

Kenneth Cole—Ehrlichman's administrative director and staff manager. (With Ehrlichman, he makes staff assignments and determines who sits on the committees and working groups. He acts as Ehrlichman's alter ego in administrative matters.)

In keeping with the Domestic Council's flexibility, none of the deputies is confined solely to his

specialty. They often cross over into other fields of study.

Four project managers involved in promotional and legislative coordination in connection with major programs are also on the staff.

Backgrounds—Ehrlichman's staff aides are mostly young (average age 33) and have little previous experience in government. They come mostly from business and professional fields, rather than from political backgrounds. Many of them served in secondary positions during the 1968 Nixon campaign.

A White House aide, who is not a member of the Domestic Council staff, had this private comment about them:

"It is often said disparagingly that Ehrlichman's crew is composed mainly of advance men, which is partly true. But these are guys the President is comfortable with, the ones he has been living with and trusts—the Morgans, the Coles, the Whitakers and so forth. They've been tested by time.

"I can't imagine anyone usurping that influence. You can't start making friendships after you've become President."

Partly because of their relative youth, some of Ehrlichman's staff have antagonized high-level department executives, including Cabinet Secretaries, who say that they sometimes act in such a way as to isolate the President.

Former Interior Secretary Walter J. Hickel and his successor, Rogers C. B. Morton, have made this complaint. And a HUD official said that Morgan once insisted that everyone below the rank of assistant secretary leave a meeting.

"I'm certainly not unaware of these complaints," Morgan said. "But I'm not a career government official; I'm here for one reason—the interests of the President. On the other hand, I don't presume to be the President's Secretary of Labor or HEW. . . .

"Somebody has to keep it all happening, make sure we're all tracking together. We're not trying to usurp the authority of the Secretaries or crack the heads of the guys in the departments. We're trying to help, not grind an ax with the departments."

Many of the departmental gripes about the White House domestic policy staff predate the Domestic Council. Before the council was established, domestic staff members served as "desk men" assigned to liaison work with the various departments and agencies. That function has now shifted to the OMB, and that agency now gets a share of the complaints.

Department Dealings: As a case in point, HUD's dealings with the White House went through Richard P. Nathan, former assistant OMB director.

Analyzing HUD's relationship with the Office of the President, particularly with the Domestic Council and the OMB, a top aide to Secretary George W. Romney described it as "a curious arrangement and certainly not a clear division of responsibility."

Romney's aide said, "I guess you could say in political science terminology that the Domestic Council serves essentially as the institutional interface between politics and policy. On purely legislative and programmatic issues, we relate to OMB. That covers the nitty-gritty, as well as our major legislative initiatives—special revenue sharing and departmental reorganization."

Politics—"But when things get into the political, as well as the programmatic area, then Ehrlichman gets heavily involved. For example, we worked with OMB on drafting the special revenue-sharing plan. But the moment that the policy initiative began to raise political problems—in this case, it was the possible termination of the model cities program—then Ehrlichman and the Domestic Council stepped in. It was Ehrlichman's decision to extend model cities into the next fiscal year," the aide said.

An assistant to HUD Under Secretary Richard C. Van Dusen said that Ehrlichman and the Domestic Council—not OMB—were now handling the politically sensitive issue of dispersing federally assisted low-income housing into the suburbs.

"Fair housing doesn't really get into program or legislation, but into general policy—and therefore politics—so on that issue we and the Justice Department have been relating to the Domestic Council. It is their staff—along with ours and the Attorney General's—that has been drafting the Administration's policy on this issue.

Transportation Under Secretary James M. Beggs said that his department generally gets along "amicably" with Ehrlichman and the Domestic Council staff.

"We've had various and sundry arguments; most have been family-type policy arguments that have finally been resolved," he said.

Money—He reported that the most serious disagreements involved budgetary considerations.

"We have argued for higher levels in mass transit and highway funds from time to time. But somebody has got to decide how much total money will be spent and who gets what, and these are the things that are decided on John's level," Beggs said.

Variations on a Theme: The Domestic Council operation is not a new concept.

In a speech at Los Angeles in July 1968, Hubert H. Humphrey, then the Vice President, said:

"A National Domestic Policy Council should be established to provide the same comprehensive, systematic and reliable analyses of domestic problems which the National Security Council and its staff produce on foreign policy and national defense issues."

Earlier Models—During the Johnson Administration, Califano created a de facto domestic policy staff, which was a model for Mr. Nixon's formalized version.

A domestic council, said Califano, is "absolutely essential" to the modern Presidency. "There are lots of decisions that involve more than one department and agency, and someone has to pull it all together."

Califano, now a Washington lawyer who serves as counsel for the Democratic National Committee, said he was a personal admirer of Ehrlichman. He described his counterpart in the Nixon White House as "a fine person doing a tough job."

The big difference between his operation and Ehrlichman's, he said, was that he had fewer people.

Harlow recalled that in the Eisenhower Administration the Cabinet functioned as the Domestic Council. Follow-up action was handled by a Cabinet Secretary, he said, and programs were developed in ad hoc committee meetings chaired by Sherman Adams.

"That system, which was fashioned out of the British War Council, was the one most comfortable for President Eisenhower, for the times in which we lived, for the problems then and the size of the staff he had," Harlow said.

"But President Kennedy didn't like Cabinet meetings. He had no domestic council at all. For President Nixon, this is better than anything else. He knew how it was in the Eisenhower Administration; he sat through it.

"Adams was a mix of Haldeman, Ehrlichman and Shultz. The only area he had to be delicate about was national security; otherwise, he was the substance of the programs, he handled personnel and he was the President's chief aide. There is no Adams now."

Evaluation—Harlow said there is no way of deciding whether one system is better than another; that it depends on the man in office.

Answering charges that the Domestic Council staff is not accountable to Congress, Harlow said:

"The staffs of congressional committees and those serving Members of Congress are not held accountable, and many of them have immense influence. The same charge has been made about the National Security Council staff. But you've got to remember that a confidential relationship exists between the President and his assistants."

Furthermore, Harlow said, "The President is held accountable for his Administration."

NSC Comparison: Inevitably, the Domestic Council is said to be similar to the National Security Council. One is the President's advisory arm for foreign affairs, and the other, its equivalent for domestic matters.

But there are institutional and operational differences. The size of the NSC has been estimated at 110 to 140, perhaps three times larger than the Domestic Council. There is less give-and-take and greater rivalry between the NSC and the departments concerned with national security—notably, State and Defense.

Also, it is not rare for Domestic Council members to be called in to confer with the President; NSC staff members almost never meet with Mr. Nixon; indeed, several have complained that they seldom see Kissinger.

Over-all, the Domestic Council's operation is considerably more informal than the NSC's, partly because of the confidential nature of NSC work, but more because of the personal relationship between Ehrlichman and his staff.

Power Struggle?: In the beginning, the big question mark over the Domestic Council and OMB was how well Shultz and Ehrlichman would get along.

The success of the two agencies hinged on the compatibility of their directors.

No sooner had they been appointed to their present positions than speculation arose over a probable power struggle of titanic proportions.

DOMESTIC COUNCIL STAFF CHIEFS

Domestic Council staff members have a variety of backgrounds—in law, advertising, science and higher education. Many came to the White House from the 1968 campaign. Following is background information on top-level members of the staff.

Kenneth R. Cole Jr., 33, is deputy assistant to the President for domestic affairs and assistant director of the Domestic Council. He was born in New York City and grew up in Scarsdale, N.Y., and Westfield, N.J. He was graduated from Bucknell University with a degree in business administration. From 1961 to 1965, he was on active duty in the Navy, rising to the rank of lieutenant. He was later an account executive with the J. Walter Thompson advertising agency in New York. He served as coordinator of advance men during Mr. Nixon's campaign. He and his wife live in Bethesda, Md., with their two daughters.

Edwin L. Harper, 30, is special assistant to the President. He worked formerly for the Arthur D. Little Co., specializing in urban affairs consultation, and for the Bureau of the Budget. He taught political science at Rutgers University and was a guest scholar at Brookings Institution. He attended Principia College and the University of Virginia, where he received a doctoral degree in political science. Harper is a native of St. Louis, Mo. He is married and has one daughter.

Edward L. Morgan, 34, is deputy assistant to the President for domestic affairs and assistant director of the Domestic Council. He was born in Lorain, Ohio, and grew up in Tucson, Ariz., where he attended the University of Arizona, majoring in political science. In 1963, he received a law degree from the university. After service as an officer in the Army Adjutant General's Corps, he practiced law in Phoenix, Ariz. During the 1968 Nixon campaign, Morgan served as an advance man. He is married and has one daughter.

John C. Whitaker, 46, is deputy assistant to the President for natural resources and environmental areas. He was born in Victoria, Canada, of American parents, graduated from Georgetown University in 1949 and received a doctoral degree in geology from Johns Hopkins University in 1953. From 1958 to 1966, he worked for Litton Industries. He later became vice president of the International Aero Service Corp. of Philadelphia. Whitaker, his wife and their five children, live in Bethesda, Md.

Egil Krogh Jr., 32, is deputy assistant to the President and assistant director of the Domestic Council. He was graduated from Principia College after which he served in the U.S. Navy as a lieutenant from 1962-65. Following graduation from the University of Washington Law School in 1968, he joined the Seattle law firm of Hullin, Ehrlichman, Roberts and Hodge. He and his wife have two children.

Events—It was regarded as significant that Shultz moved into the White House in an office comparable to Ehrlichman's, even though the OMB's base of operations was in the adjoining Old Executive Office Building.

Next, Shultz took over the daily 7:30 a.m. White House staff meetings, which Ehrlichman had chaired. Then, during the budget process, Shultz' presence was pervasive in Washington.

In addition, all the ingredients of a feud were there: The jurisdictional line between the two agencies was exceedingly fine; OMB was wary of Ehrlichman, because he was viewed as a threat to its traditional policy-making role and because he was believed to have been influential in the abrupt departure of Budget Director Robert P. Mayo from the agency; and, finally, there were the disparate backgrounds of Shultz, the reserved academician, and Ehrlichman, the politically oriented lawyer.

No Evidence—Nonetheless, one year later, there was no overt evidence of a collision. The two ranked as co-equals. They fixed the lines of authority between them on a mutually agreed basis; they met together with the President at a 3 p.m. daily conference, and, in addition to frequent face-to-face consultations, they conferred two or three times a day over the "hot line" which connects their second-floor White House offices.

As for the 7:30 a.m. White House meetings, Shultz chaired them because his was the operational agency. According to witnesses, Ehrlichman sat at the other end of the table and participated equally with Shultz.

"At first, John seemed to be rather quiet, but that's not so any longer," commented a White House aide. "Actually, the meetings were livelier and wittier when John chaired them."

Teamwork—After working in tandem for a year, OMB has proved a match for the Domestic Council in political infighting and is now less fearful of losing its blue-chip status.

Commenting on his dealings with Shultz, Ehrlichman said:

"We seem to hit it off very well. His wife and mine have become very good friends. We spent a weekend at their farm in Massachusetts.

"We've never had very serious differences of opinion. He's very low key, reasonable and fair in personal relationships. It's possible to talk out problems with him."

The jurisdictional overlap between the two agencies is reflected in the fact that Ehrlichman in June 1971 met with OMB section chiefs to talk about fiscal 1973 domestic policy questions.

EHRLICHMAN SPEAKS

During an interview with *National Journal*, John D. Ehrlichman made observations on several random subjects:

Political polls—"I don't think the polls at this time are very significant. It's like the guy who says, 'How's your wife?' And the other guy says, 'Compared to what;' We're not in a position to compare alternatives."

Young People—"Part of my job is to be thinking about things, to be aware of what people are thinking. I've had many fruitful contacts with young people. I find it different than meeting with special interest groups and trade associations. It's important that I know what young people think, too. We're very much concerned about young people. They're an important element of our society. So much of what we do will be important four or five years from now."

Presidential Chats—"Sometimes, late on a Saturday night or at San Clemente or someplace, we'll have an unstructured, rambling conversation about people, things, a book he is reading."

Life Style—"My life style has changed. I have always worked for myself. We have less time for family activities now. Before, we could go camping, skiing, and boating and spend a lot of time together. Those things create a close-knit family. Now we can't do those things often. It's been an adjustment for my family."

Economic Issue in 1972—"I happen to De one who believes trends are more important than fixed levels. In a given situation, if the trend is towards improving the situation, it is politically as important as the percentage level."

Later he and Shultz jointly led lengthy policy discussions among White House aides at Camp David.

In anticipation of the session, Ehrlichman sent a memorandum to the departments and agencies, inquiring as to "action-forcing events," expiring legislation and intrinsic matters that should come to the attention of the White House.

These preparations enabled Ehrlichman and Schultz to go into the President's June review to discuss domestic policy and national economic issues.

OUTLOOK

The Domestic Council so far has neither lived up to the potential its advocates foresaw nor achieved the power its critics feared.

The reasons for this are Ehrlichman's middle-way approach and Shultz' personal standing—plus the recognition that policy (the Domestic Council) and performance (OMB) are interdependent.

However, the Domestic Council has shown it can deal with the totality of public issues, within the demands of President Nixon, and that it is less vulnerable than the departments to pressure from Capitol Hill and special-interest sources.

One of the hazards of the concept is that White House aides who are too closely in harmony with the President may fail to provide fresh insight and tend to emphasize rather than offset his weaknesses.

Ultimately, the success—or failure—of the Domestic Council in this Administration rests on the fragile human relationship of two men.

Speechwriters play strategic role in conveying, shaping Nixon's policies   *Dom Bonafede*

In this McLuhanian era of instant communications and mass-selling techniques, a white blizzard of paper spews forth each day from the White House.

The cascade includes proclamations, messages, reports, pronouncements, policy statements, declarations, executive orders, fact sheets, presidential remarks, transcripts of briefings and press conferences, official correspondence and toasts made by the President at ceremonial events.

The papers may range from a proclamation declaring Safe Boating Week to a 15,000-word State of the Union text.

Each word written for the President by his large corps of speechwriters is carefully selected, weighed and polished in the knowledge that it may well endure as part of the history of the Administration. Even discarded drafts of speeches almost incomprehensible with Mr. Nixon's editing marks are stored in the National Archives.

While still fresh, presidential utterances are sent around the world on the wings of communications technology. In foreign capitals, corporate board rooms, offices of Congress, political party headquarters, editorial offices and scholarly retreats, they are studied and scrutinized for possible nuances and shifts in position and policy.

Few statements by the President in the performance of his office are considered so inconsequential that they are not printed, cataloged and distributed to the press and public.

The Uses of Words: More than a half million words annually flow out of the White House in a torrent of paper and ink. About 180,000 words are devoted to major policy actions. The 1970 volume of the public papers of President Nixon covers 1,168 pages, as well as another 42 pages which index material not included in the text.

The purpose of this Niagara of words is to communicate and convince, to impart information which will arouse support and enlist the energies of the audience, whether it be a partisan group or the vast American public.

Accordingly, in his Jan. 25 statement on hitherto secret peace negotiations with Hanoi, President Nixon reported he was making the disclosure to attract widespread support and perhaps "break a secret deadlock."

Although not acknowledged by the President, the address before a nationwide television audience also carried a political thrust in that it served to portray him as a statesman for peace during this election year.

Signs of the Times: The President's speeches act as signposts, pointing up the problems, proposals and issues with which he copes.

Mr. Nixon accepts congratulations after a speech

Thus, Mr. Nixon's talks on drugs, crime, welfare, hunger, environmental quality and urban decay can be read as a social commentary of the time.

His speeches are also an extension of his philosophy and personality. For the most part, they are well-organized and well-researched, somewhat in the style of a legal brief. They are meant to be more expository than literary; they contain few inspirational flashes of passion. This, however, is in keeping with the public demeanor of the President, who, in his Inaugrual Address, proposed that Americans "lower our voices."

In the light of such an appeal, it is ironic that President Nixon has set up the largest speechwriting section in White House history.

On this point, Theodore C. Sorensen, President Kennedy's top aide and speechwriter, said in an interview, "We had a very small staff involved in writing speeches. LBJ more than doubled it and President Nixon, I suspect, has tripled it."

Contributing Factors: At least partly responsible for this are the increasing demands on the President as the symbolic leader of the nation and innovator of federal legislation, the blanket media coverage given the Presidency and the artful use of television as a political device. The office of Herbert G. Klein, director of communications for the executive branch, reported that Mr. Nixon has made at least 60 major television appearances since taking office.

Consequently, television has changed the technique of presidential speechmaking. Speeches often must be measured to fit a time slot. Also, the manner of delivery is tailored to television's specifications if the President is to be persuasive.

This puts TV speechmaking close to the realm of show business, complete with makeup, special background settings and professional lighting arrangements. For in the theater of politics, visualized rhetoric serves as music to soothe a troubled constituency.

Staff Lineup—However, it is the projection of the written word which most concerns Mr. Nixon's speechwriters. Headed by Raymond K. Price, Jr., 42, who was chief editorial writer for the old *New York Herald Tribune,* the staff includes three other front-line writers: Patrick J. Buchanan, 34, a one-time editorial writer for the *St. Louis Globe-Democrat;* William L. Safire, 42, another former newspaperman who later established his own public relations firm and the Rev. John J. McLaughlin, 45 former associate editor of the Jesuit magazine *America* and the first Catholic priest to serve officially in the White House. All hold the title of special assistant to the President and are unabashed admirers of Mr. Nixon.

On the next level are eight backup writers: Lyndon K. Allin, Eliska A. Hasek, Lee W. Huebner, John K. Andrews Jr., John McDonald, Harold Lezar, Noel Koch and David R. Gergen, who also acts as an aide to Price.

Assisting the writers are four researchers led by Cecilia B. Bellinger, a former *Time* magazine researcher. Under her are Ann M. Morgan, Pamela A. Giles and Maureen W. Brown.

Another four aides help Allin put together the "President's Daily News Summary" under the overall supervision of Buchanan.

Organized   Group—Price's unit, the first formally structured White House speechwriting office, officially is known as the Writing and Research Department in line with the President's penchant for neat organizational groupings.

Mr. Nixon's immediate predecessors preferred a loosely structured speechwriting operation.

President Johnson had a stable of a half-dozen aides who doubled as writers, including Horace Busby Jr., Bill D. Moyers, Jack Valenti, McGeorge Bundy, S. Douglass Cater Jr. and Richard N. Goodwin.

President Kennedy relied almost solely on Sorensen for major speechwriting chores. He, in turn, occasionally got help from White House aides Myer Feldman, Arthur M. Schlesinger Jr., Lee C. White and Goodwin.

In effect, Mr. Nixon has institutionalized White House speechwriting. But as Sorensen observed, each President must organize his staff in a manner most compatible to his personal and professional needs.

The   Beginning — James Keogh, a former *Time Inc.* executive who was in charge of the White House writing group until his resignation in December 1970, said its formation was "more or less a conscious thing."

He said: "It evolved from the campaign days before the nomination and as the need grew more people were added. Buchanan, Price and Safire were already with Mr. Nixon in those early days. I

---

didn't join the group until after the nominating convention in 1968.

"At that time, it was the sort of structure that Mr. Nixon dealt with himself, with Bob Haldeman (H. R. Haldeman, now assistant to the President) sort of running it. I came aboard to be manager and editor. No one had been coordinating it. The candidate didn't have time and Haldeman was busy doing other things. I operated with the writers as would senior partners in a law firm.

"After the election, the structure was transferred to the White House and enlarged. I brought in Huebner and others. Mrs. Bellinger had worked in the Johnson and Kennedy Administrations in another writing capacity when I discovered her and added to her role somewhat.

Ideological Spread—Within narrow limits, the staff by its own description covers an ideological span with Price on the left, Safire in the middle and Buchanan on the right. Huebner is a former president of the Ripon Society, a progressive Republican youth organization.

"Philosophically, a White House writer should be aligned with the President," Price said. "He has to believe in what he's doing and have a sense of mission. But that doesn't mean he has to agree with everything."

PRESIDENTS AND 'GHOSTS'

Presidential ghostwriting has been an accepted, conventional metier since the birth of the Republic when Alexander Hamilton penned George Washington's Inaugural Address.

Obviously, no President has the time—even if he possesses the talent—to perform such a prodigious task. Abraham Lincoln and Woodrow Wilson, however, did compose many of their own speeches.

Nixon's Involvement: Price and his associates contend that Mr. Nixon is more involved in the creation and composition of his speeches than any other President since Wilson.

"He prefers to write his own when he has the time," Price said. "At other times, he will supply the ideas, the emphasis and the organization. He taught me everything I know about speechwriting. Writing for the printed word and the spoken word is entirely different. He's like a tutor; he'll tell you how to reorganize a draft, what to put in and leave out and how to use highlights."

The announcement of his China trip was completely written by Mr. Nixon without consultation with any of his speechwriters, Price said.

"He knows what he wants and how he wants to say it," Buchanan said. "With each draft, it becomes more his own material. He fights each word, paragraph after paragraph, page after page. Afterwards, it's wholly his own."

Buchanan recalled that Mr. Nixon once edited out every line of a six-page draft submitted by a colleague.

Safire said the President "sweats over every line. When he gets to a crucial thought, he may devote 20 minutes to it."

He recalled that while drafting a 1966 speech on academic freedom at Rochester, N.Y., Mr. Nixon rewrote a line several times until it accurately reflected what he was trying to say. The reconstructed line read: "The man of thought who will not act is ineffective; the man of action who will not think is dangerous."

According to Safire, the President's practice of outlining and drafting his own important policy statements has several inherent advantages.

"It's a form of discipline; it can be used as a deadline for policy implementation; it is a signal to the rest of the government or a way of giving orders; and it is a way of exhorting and leading people."

Organization: McLaughlin said of the President as a speechwriter:

"He's a self-starter and self-originator. He knows what its content, form and organization should be. He knows how to use a distribution of emphasis, moving toward some sort of climax, saying it to meet the demands of a mass audience and keeping it reasonably absorbable. He does not want it to be or try to be anything but Nixonian, meaning putting a sharp limitation on the range of allusions and quotations. If he is not familiar with a person, he's not comfortable in quoting him, as, for instance, a behavioral scientist who may be nouveau. . . .

"He organizes material by the systematic heightening and subordination of ideas. Logic is a part of rhetoric and the whole structure must stand up. He believes in persuasion by citing facts; assemble the facts and the facts will speak for themselves. He likes going back to familiar material and ideas that he has gone over in his own mind."

McLaughlin perceives the function of Mr. Nixon's speechwriters as being analogous to music arrangers who work with someone else's composition.

"After receiving the President's outline and contributions from other sources, we strip it down, reassemble and rewrite it, reemphasize parts of it, get rid of some of the fat and go with some new stuff," he said.

The End Product—The President's writers, however, are not always pleased with the end product. One complained, "After he goes through eight or 10 drafts, he's drained the life out of it; it's bloodless."

Another White House aide said, "The legal approach has to be balanced by a more flourishing type of verbal construction. The President has a tendency to ramble, to take five paragraphs for what he should say in one. That's why you hear White House staff members say, 'If the public could only hear him in private.'"

But the President has the final say and the speech that the public hears invariably bears the mark of Mr. Nixon's own hand.

SPEECHWRITERS' ROLE

The role of a White House speechwriter is probably the most ambiguous of all presidential assistants. Questions historically revolve around him: Is he a technician or a policymaker? Is it possible for him to sublimate his personal and political ideologies while writing prose in the service of another man? Should he remain an anonymous figure?

Speechwriters disagree among themselves on these questions. But on one point there is unanimous agreement; a presidential speech, regardless who conceived and nurtured it through its various stages of growth, is solely the President's, including every line, every indelible phrase.

Identity: An unwritten code within the brotherhood of the craft prohibits White House writers from openly assuming credit for any portion of it.

In this regard, Samuel I. Rosenman, a speechwriter for Franklin D. Roosevelt, said in his book, *Working with Roosevelt* (Harper & Bros., 1952), "The speeches were always Roosevelt's. They all expressed the personality, the convictions, the spirit, the mood of Roosevelt. No matter who worked with him in the preparation, the finished product was always the same—it was Roosevelt himself. And nothing I write here should obscure that fundamental fact."

Indeed, Price prefers that it not be known what writer worked with the President on any particular speech.

However, the age of faceless speechwriters ended with the Roosevelt Administration. Among the colorful crew of writers and thinkers assembled by Mr. Roosevelt, besides Rosenman, were playwright Robert E. Sherwood, Thomas G. ("Tommy the Cork") Corcoran, poet Archibald MacLeish, Raymond Moley and Rexford G.

THE PRESIDENT'S TOP WORDSMITHS

President Nixon's three veteran speechwriters are all loyalists tested in the fire of the 1968 campaign. One of the trio recently observed that the respect they have for the President must be mutual "Or why would he keep three rather temperamental guys as his speechwriters?"

Raymond K. Price Jr., the lead man in the group, is the son of a Wall Street broker. Reared on Long Island, he was graduated from Yale and later wrote editorials for *The New York Herald Tribune.* Earnest, studious and youthful-looking, he lends an air of quiet solidity to the rather mercurial speechwriting operations. Upon the recommendation of Walter Thayer, former *Herald Tribune* president, Mr. Nixon in February 1967 invited him to join his staff at a three-hour lunch at Mr. Nixon's New York apartment. "I spent the next weekend extensively thinking about 1968," Price recalled. "I reviewed history and decided he was my candidate. A week later, I phoned him and said I'd be delighted to come to work for him." A bachelor, Price is known as a workhorse who frequently does not leave his office until 8 or 10 p.m.

Patrick J. Buchanan, a utility man with diverse responsibilities, possesses the political convictions and looks of a young John Wayne. A graduate of Georgetown University and the Columbia Graduate School of Journalism, he went from being an auditor and accountant in a firm owned by his father to editorial writer for the *St. Louis Globe-Democrat*. In 1965, he met Mr. Nixon at an event in Belleville, Ill., and said he would like to join his staff. The following year, Buchanan went to work at Mr. Nixon's New York law firm, handling correspondence and helping with speeches and a syndicated news column. In addition to speechwriting, which takes only a small portion of his time, Buchanan also oversees the President's Daily News Summary, draws up briefing materials for the President's press conferences and takes on special assignments from H. R. Haldeman, assistant to the President.

William L. Safire, newsman, public relations specialist and author, is the most facile of the White House writers. A New Yorker with a casual manner (he sometimes works in his office with his shoes off), he almost disguises an alert intellect and an expertise in the modern use of the American language. Safire already occupies a footnote in history. As a public relations consultant, he was in charge of promoting the model U.S. kitchen where Mr. Nixon and Soviet Premier Khrushchev engaged in a now-famous debate at the Moscow Trade Fair. "I yelled, 'This way to the typical American home!' and they followed," Safire recalled. "That night Nixon told me, 'We shall put your kitchen on the map.'" Safire also took the photograph of the pair which was flashed around the world. He is the author of *Relations Explosion, The New Language of Politics* and coauthor of *Plunging into Politics* and has written for publications ranging from *Harvard Business Review* to *Playboy*.

working with Mr. Nixon on the State of the Union message at Camp David, Md., early in January.

Also, the White House acknowledged that Safire was among the chosen presidential aides present at Camp David the weekend of Aug. 13 to help formulate Mr. Nixon's new economic policy. He was the only speechwriter present and assuredly was involved in releases emanating from the meeting.

Technician and/or Policymaker: The range of the White House writer's role is determined by the President.

As President Kennedy's alter ego, Sorensen was intimately involved with policy decisions. None of Mr. Nixon's writers occupies a position at a comparable level of power.

Rosenman's view was that aides having a hand in drafting White House policy statements "are in a peculiarly strategic position to help shape that policy."

He said, "So much depends on the choice of words and phrases, on shadings of meaning and emphasis. Language enunciating a policy may be bold and forthright; or words may be used that obscure, understate or circumscribe the policy."

Mr. Nixon's stand on the issue of policy involvement by speechwriters was reflected in an interview published in *Redbook* magazine in June 1962. Mr. Nixon criticized Sorensen's role in the 1960 campaign, claiming that Mr. Kennedy had been "a puppet who echoed his speechmaker."

Mr. Nixon added it was essential that the President "communicate directly . . . even if it's pedes-

Tugwell.

Subsequent Presidents added literary figures and intellectuals to their speechwriting staffs.

Washington lawyer Clark M. Clifford wrote for President Truman, as did academician Malcolm C. Moos for President Eisenhower. Besides Schlesinger, a Pulitzer Prize-winning historian, President Kennedy recruited economist John Kenneth Galbraith. For a time, novelist John Steinbeck helped President Johnson with his speeches.

Phrasemakers—Despite the alleged altruistic nature of Presidential speechwriters, many are identified with memorable lines spoken by their bosses.

Rosenman is credited with popularizing the term, "New Deal."

Galbraith reportedly authored, "Let us never negotiate out of fear, but let us never fear to negotiate."

Emmet John Hughes, journalist and writer, is associated with the pledge made by Gen. Eisenhower: "I shall go to Korea."

Sometimes the father of a phrase is lost among conflicting parental claims. Credit for the term Alliance for Progress has been given variously to Goodwin, writer Karl E. Meyer and economist Ernesto Betancourt.

Ban Broken — Occasionally, Price's edict against identifying the writer with the speech is broken. Price himself was photographed

trian and dull."

Duality—Price said that Mr. Nixon's speechwriters "are a little of both (technician and policymaker). But mostly we have to be technicians. We touch a lot of bases and put together a lot of ideas and divergent views. The Administration may be monolithic on the outside but not always on the inside."

Frequently, he said, Mr. Nixon's writers "urge him to take something out or put something in; essentially we serve in an advisory and assistance role."

In the event of a difference of opinion between the President and his speechwriters, he said, "We'll discuss it and ask why. If he has a reason for wanting something in, he'll explain why. Maybe it's a word or a paragraph or an idea. Sometimes, he'll spin out his ideas to test them on us. He's very good about knowing the biases of people and likes to bounce ideas off them."

Sorensen System—Sorensen's influence ran considerably deeper.

"I wrote speeches in addition to my involvement in the decision-making process," he said. "There is a great advantage in this. You know the President's arguments, comments and ideas; how he wants to say it and why. . . . I had direct access to the President. There were no sharp differences between us. After all, we had been working together for several years. I could write a draft of the very words he wanted to say. It wasn't that I was putting words in his mouth that he didn't believe. He could depend on me to come up with material he could rely on.

"Writing speeches for John F. Kennedy gave me an opportunity to have a voice in what was being said and heard far more than I could accomplish on my own. It increased my role in the decision-making process. The man who helps the President decide he is going to say it also helps in the decision.

"In many ways, the answer in the Cuban missile crisis was not resolved until it was decided whether the answer was consistent with our objectives and effectively worded."

Sorensen reported the Kennedy White House received few complaints from departments and agencies which felt their views were not being adequately presented in Presidential speeches.

"Because of my responsibilities in the White House and my relationship with the President," he said, "I didn't have much trouble with the agencies telling me what to put in speeches."

Buchanan and Policy: There is evidence that in some instances Mr. Nixon's writers have been closely involved in policy matters.

Day-care Veto — Buchanan was one of the President's assistants consulted during White House discussions on the $2-billion child care bill (S 2007). The bill would have provided health, nutritional and educational serv-

WORDS OF THE NIXON ERA

White House speechwriter William L. Safire, a lexicographer of some renown and author of *The New Language of Politics* (Random House, 1968), has updated a section of the book to include words and phrases coined during the Nixon Administration.

As Safire noted, "The memories of an era can be evoked by a look at its inventory of political phrases. Some are coined by a President, some by his Cabinet, others coined for use against him."

In the new list of phrases and popularizations identified with the Nixon years, some of which he minted himself for Vice President Spiro T. Agnew, are:

Coinages
black capitalism
bring us together
effete snobs
game plan
hack it
instant analysis
lift of a driving dream
nattering nabobs of negativism
New Federalism
old wine in new bottles
radic-lib
silent majority
strict constructionist
Vietnamization
workfare

Phrases Used in Attacks on the Administration
benign neglect
Nixonomics
Southern strategy

Phrases That Came from Outside the Administration
heartland
household word
Middle America
new politics
Nixon doctrine
psephology (study of elections)
quality of life
reordering priorities
social issue
winding down

SORENSEN: MEMORIES OF THE NEW FRONTIER

More than eight years after Dallas, Theodore C. Sorensen, President Kennedy's intimate adviser, friend and speechwriter, works as a lawyer for the New York firm of Paul, Weiss, Rifkind, Wharton & Garrison. Yet, the Kennedy legend is never far away. Sorensen's office in a Manhattan skyscraper on Park Avenue contains paintings, original cartoons and photographs of the Kennedys and other prominent members of the New Frontier.

For almost 11 years, Sorensen walked in the shadow of John F. Kennedy. Now when he talks about the assassinated President a distant look comes into his eyes and he says, "Things would have been different."

If he thinks about how it might have been, he also thinks about the way it was.

"We were so close, I knew his style and thinking and could draft a speech almost with the words he would have used," Sorensen said during an interview. "We had a standing joke: the material he took out of one draft always showed up in another speech."

The Kennedy Style—Sorensen acknowledged that the quality of the speeches was enhanced by President Kennedy's delivery.

"He wasn't that good in the beginning; he later developed a natural, sincere manner. On a major address for which there was a text, President Kennedy almost never made any changes. But when making a political speech or a dinner talk, he almost always made changes.

"I remember the television address on civil rights he made in June 1963. My first draft was finished four minutes before he went on the air. He had been concerned and was making notes. During the speech he used the notes extemporaneously."

Shaping a Speech—Sorensen said a good presidential speechwriter must have access to the President and the ability to formulate what the President wants to say philosophically and stylistically. "To just say a lot of eloquent things in a speech does not make it a great speech," he said.

"First, you must identify the date, audience and subject. Sometimes one commands the others, such as the State of the Union message. Or the subject may be shaped by the event, like the Cuban missile crisis. Also, the audience may be fixed, the United Nations or Congress. . . .

"Then you round up material from the departments and agencies involved and set a deadline. On the basis of the material, plus my own involvement in the decision-making process and the material in my own files, I would put together the first draft."

Next, President Kennedy and Sorensen usually would sit down together and go over the draft. A painting of the two reviewing a speech in the White House Cabinet Room hangs in Sorensen's office.

"He'd make comments, suggestions and recommendations," Sorensen said. "I'd draft it again and it might be circulated to interested

officials with the request that their comments be sent to me by a certain time. On the basis of their comments, I'd put together a third draft. When the President had another look at it, I'd put together the final draft."

Sorensen said that pattern was not always followed.

"Sometimes, speeches were created in the back of an automobile on the way to the platform," he said.

The President, he said, "never believed in long speeches. Normally they were 20 or 30 minutes."

Mutual Convictions—Sorensen said that the President and his speechwriter should share the same political convictions.

"If they don't, they won't feel comfortable working together. The President may sense this. It adds to the strain and impairs the effectiveness of both.

"Secondly, the writer is going to feel somewhat cheapened, as though he was prostituting his skills."

Sorensen said it was paramount that the speechwriter be constantly aware that a presidential address is directed at a multiple audience.

"He may make a speech in the Deep South, yet it is heard in Harlem," Sorensen said.

He said he did not think that speechwriters ought to have much trouble keeping their individual biases and ideologies out of their bosses' speeches.

"A priest can defend Rome or be the devil's advocate and a lawyer can defend or prosecute a client."

Nixon and Agnew—Asked about his opinion of President Nixon's speeches, Sorensen said:

"It's difficult for me to separate the speech from the content. I so often disagree with him. Great speeches have great content.

"Secondly, it's hard for me to separate the literary style from the delivery. President Nixon lacks a lot there. He is not solid or inspirational; he's patronizing and unctuous.

"He frequently has good phrases in his speeches but his manner of delivery handicaps him. I thought his Inaugural Address had some good phrases—but none of them are memorable."

Mr. Nixon, he said, "is a pro in politics and in the use of the media. The President can't be overexposed if the events justify" a special television address.

Of Vice President Spiro T. Agnew, Sorensen said, "He has a good sense of humor. I think that is important. And he has attention-getting phrases."

Hits and Misses—He acknowledged that he had made a blooper in a speech for Mr. Kennedy.

"We once took a figure and said 17 million Americans go to bed hungry every night. The Republicans got hold of it and replied, 'Yes, and most of them are on Metrecal.'

"We hadn't made the differentiation between hunger and malnutrition. But when you look at things today, maybe we weren't wrong."

He said that President Kennedy felt that an address he made June 10, 1963, at American University was one of his best speeches. On that occasion, the President proposed an arms de-escalation between the United States and the Soviet Union.

"He felt it was an important speech; he was very satisfied with it," Sorensen said.

"We discussed whether it should be vetoed, how to veto it," Buchanan said. "We argued and debated. Involved were John Ehrlichman's Domestic Council staff and the departments."

Buchanan recommended that the bill be vetoed, a point of view which prevailed. On Dec. 10, President Nixon rejected the proposed legislation.

In the veto message, written by Buchanan, Mr. Nixon said, "The child development (program) envisioned in this legislation would be truly a long leap in the dark for the United States government and the American people. I must share the view of those of its supporters who proclaim this to be the most radical piece of legislation to emerge from the 92nd Congress."

The President further said "neither the immediate need nor the desirability" of such legislation had been demonstrated and that, if adopted, it would "lead toward altering the family relationship. ... . For the federal government to plunge headlong financially into supporting child development would commit the vast moral authority of the national government to the side of communal approaches to child rearing over against the family-centered approach."

On Feb. 5, Sen. Fred R. Harris, D-Okla., charged that the language in the veto message represented "the most demagogic rhetoric of the right" and "blatantly misrepresented" the intent of the legislation.

Military Affairs—Buchanan also was involved in the writing of Mr. Nixon's Air Force Academy address on June 4, 1969, in which the President vigorously defended the defense establishment against "skeptics" and "neo-isolationists." And he helped draft the President's speech on the Cambodia incursion on April 30, 1970.

"The President is aware of my ideology," Buchanan said. "He's intelligent; he knows I'm conservative. That's why he asked me to work on the Cambodia speech. He knew I'd support it."

Special Activities: Occasionally, Mr. Nixon's speechwriters engage in activities beyond their normal responsibilities.

Last September, Safire called several reporters and suggested they check into a report that Senate Majority Leader Mike Mansfield, D-Mont., had threatened to withhold campaign funds from Democrats who failed to support him on an end-the-war amendment. Mansfield denied the report on the Senate floor. Sen. Lloyd M. Bentsen Jr., D-Tex., suggested that Mr. Nixon "publicly reprimand his speechwriter."

There is no indication that Mr. Nixon did as Bentsen advised.

PROCEDURE AND STYLE

No two major policy statements are drawn up quite the same way. The process of their construction varies, if only slightly, with each speech.

Presidential Draft: Normally, the creation starts with the President himself. Explaining the procedure, Price said:

"The President will provide a lot of draft material; he'll dictate his thoughts and ideas into an IBM machine and the tapes will be transcribed. Or he will write them down on a yellow legal pad. He's thinking out what he wants to say, the points he wants to emphasize, the basic theme and the tone. He's not thinking about the language. . . .

"He likes to read history while working. He may wake up in the middle of the night when deeply in a speech as ideas come to him and he may dictate as many as 16 pages of text, memos and ideas. They will be on my desk in the morning. He might also communicate by phone or memo or through Haldeman and Ehrlichman."

Agency Contributions: Meanwhile, memoranda are coming into the White House from the departments and agencies concerned with the issue. A speech on foreign affairs, for example, will produce substantive material from the National Security Council, the State Department, policy people at the White House and perhaps the Treasury Department.

Traditionally, the involvement of the agencies in the speech making process is a delicate affair since they primarily are concerned with promoting their special areas of interest.

"The departments get upset when their stuff is not used," Price said. "To them, their world is the most important."

Invariably, their submissions are cut considerably. As Keogh put it, "Department drafts don't survive."

Safire said, "We must be completely scrupulous in reflecting the views of the departments. But we also have a hell of a responsibility in keeping out biases."

The departmental impact is mostly evident in messages to Congress on proposed legislation relating to their fields. At such times, they work through the Office of Management and Budget and the Domestic Council.

One-to-one System: Usually, the President works with one writer during the preparation of a speech.

The committee system, popular in the Roosevelt Administration wherein several writers worked together to produce a major speech, seldom is used. Nor does the President, as did some of his predecessors, assign more than one writer to the same speech without informing each of the other's participation.

Mr. Nixon's writers are considered generalists but over the years some have acquired a facility for writing in certain areas. Safire, for instance, does a lot of writing on economics, Price on foreign affairs.

Polishing the Draft: Once the writing begins, the drafts are sent to the interested agencies and officials and to Mr. Nixon, who almost always returns them heavily marked up with suggestions and notations in the margins.

Seldom does a speech go through fewer than four or five drafts. An important speech has about a two-week gestation period, sometimes longer. The State of the Union message, begun in early December, took more than six weeks to produce and was delivered by the President on Jan. 20.

"About six or seven people pass on a draft," Price said. "At the end, it is the President himself."

Often, the President will make changes right up to the moment of delivery.

Consultation: Sometime during the process, the President and the writer may consult one another directly.

"He is very considerate of his writers," Safire said. "He will usually call the writer after a speech and explain the changes. This is to teach you for the next time."

One writer recalled that after Haldeman had made a change in a speech, the President said, "This doesn't scan any more. Give it to the writer to change."

When Mr. Nixon is unhappy about a speech, Price is likely to hear about it "in a gracious way."

The writers also appreciate the fact that they each get a turn at accompanying the President on foreign trips. Buchanan was picked to go to China. According to some White House aides, he was a political choice who was chosen because of his ideological views "to assuage the right."

Price is scheduled to go to Moscow with Mr. Nixon later this year.

Style: As a speechmaker, Mr. Nixon is more concerned with substance than language.

Keogh, who recently completed a book called *President Nixon and the Press*, said: "He wants his speeches to be as interesting as possible so they will carry the message well. He wants clarity and always brevity. One thing he doesn't want them to be is dull. Above all, he wants to get over the point."

Price said, "The President likes to quote certain types, although he doesn't quote as much as Kennedy did. He prefers political figures—Jefferson, Wilson, Disraeli, Lincoln and Teddy Roosevelt. The Bible, also. He doesn't like to quote precious types and he's not much on quoting poetry."

Evolution—A perusal of Mr. Nixon's speeches shows a slight evolution in his style. He now tends to shy away from the grand promises similar to those he made in his 1971 State of the Union Message when he offered his "six great goals." What formerly was called Communist China is now the People's Republic of China. And he no longer quotes econo-mist Peter Drucker, author of *The Age of Discontinuity* (Harper & Row, 1969).

He still favors the use of the contrapuntal device, such as in his Feb. 9 State of the World radio address: "By facing the realities of the world . . . we can make peace a reality."

And he likes to hammer home a point by employing a repetitious phrase. In his Vietnam peace plan speech of Jan. 25, he stated three times in one paragraph, "Nothing is served by silence."

Political Tool—Politics is injected in his speeches with greater frequency as the election draws near. Deviating from the major thrust of his State of the World speech, he struck out in the speech against critics of his "policies to bring peace."

Also, one White House aide maintained that the "excessive language" of the child care bill veto was used for political purposes.

He said: "It was not much of a public issue but it was an emotional issue on the Hill. It (the veto message) was meant to cut off the legs of John Ashbrook (Rep. John M. Ashbrook, R-Ohio) and other conservatives. It showed the adrenalin of the President. What else has he been able to serve up to the conservatives? From that point of view, it served a purpose and Buchanan did a good job."

ices to low-income families through Head Start and other day-care programs.

Presidential Editing: A presidential speech is never completed until the President delivers it.

State of the World—In the case of the State of the World address, Mr. Nixon changed about 20 per cent of it the last hour before he spoke to the nation.

Among the changes was the cutting of an introduction with a quotation from Winston Churchill. He also eliminated a section on the Soviet military buildup and interjected his reply to his critics.

In one sentence, he exchanged the word harmonize with negotiate. And he added the word naive in the line which read: "I will go to that meeting (in Moscow) in May with no naive illusions but with some reasonable expectations."

In all, the speech, which was

A PRIMER ON WRITING FOR PRESIDENTS

Two premier presidential speechwriters—Samuel J. Rosenman and Theodore C. Sorensen—are mainly responsible for elevating the technique into a near art form. In books written by them they tell of their White House experiences.

Rosenman and Roosevelt—In *Working With Roosevelt* (Harper & Bros., 1952), Rosenman wrote:

"Those who helped with his speeches would have been useless to him if they had been mere yes men . . . As soon as he (the speechwriter) is ready to accept as sacrosanct or immune from criticism anything that the President has written, he might as well go home—he is going to be of no use to the President. If he is to be helpful to him at all, he has to feel free to criticize, and even to urge a complete discard of the material that the President has dictated. . . .

"The preparation of some of the speeches or messages took as many as 10 days, and very few took less than three. That does not mean actual writing time. But there were long memoranda and proposed drafts to be read, and information and statistics to be gathered. Irrelevant data had to be separated from relevant data. Many people had to be interviewed, sometimes a dozen or more for a single message. Some were consulted during the preparatory period before the speech began to take shape, others during the actual writing of the speech—either to check data or to canvass views on questions of policy. The President often asked that a full draft of a speech or certain paragraphs in it he checked by several departments and agencies. Sometimes a speech went through as many as 12 or 13 drafts before the President was finally satisfied. Obviously, for him to undertake so exhausting and time-consuming a task from beginning to end was impossible if he wanted to continue to carry on his other duties."

Sorensen and Kennedy—Sorensen, in *Kennedy* (Harper & Row, 1965), said:

"The Kennedy style of speech-writing—our style, I am not reluctant to say, for he never pretended that he had time to prepare first drafts for all his speeches—evolved gradually over the years. ... Our chief criterion was always audience comprehension and comfort, and this meant: (1) short speeches, short clauses and short words, wherever possible; (2) a series of points or propositions in numbered or logical sequence, wherever appropriate; and (3) the construction of sentences, phrases and paragraphs in such a manner as to simplify, clarify and emphasize.

"The test of a text was not how it appeared to the eye but how it sounded to the ear. His best paragraphs, when read aloud, often had a cadence not unlike blank verse—indeed at times key words would rhyme. . . .

"Words were regarded as tools of precision, to be chosen and applied with a craftsman's care. . . . For he disliked verbosity and pomposity in his own remarks as much as he disliked them in others. He wanted . . . his language to be plain and unpretentious, but never patronizing. . . .

"He used little or no slang, dialect, legalistic terms, contractions, cliches, elaborate metaphors or ornate figures of speech. He refused . . . to include any phrase or image he considered corny, tasteless or trite. . . .

"Except for joking about the political liabilities of his own religion, he avoided all ethnic references as well as all off-color remarks in public (although not in private). . . .

"We kept a collection of appropriate speech endings—usually quotations from famous figures or incidents from history which, coupled with a brief peroration of his own, could conclude almost any speech on any subject with a dramatic flourish. On many of the hectic precampaign trips of 1957-59, he would leave one community for the next with a paraphrase from a favorite Robert Frost poem:

Iowa City is lovely, dark and deep
But I have promises to keep
And miles to go before I sleep."

condensed from a 236-page report compiled by the National Security Council and the State Department, went through six drafts.

Economic Policy—Much of Mr. Nixon's famous Aug. 15, 1971, speech on his new economic policy was written by the President himself in the early morning hours of Aug. 14 at Camp David.

Because there were only three sheets of White House stationery in his quarters, the President wrote the draft on both sides of the paper. A notation shows that it was written at 3:17 a.m.

Safire, who was drafting a text at the same time in his room, was unaware of the President's activity. When he took his draft to Rose Mary Woods, the President's private secretary, at 6:30 a.m. he found her busily typing.

"Is there another speechwriter here?" Safire asked. She said yes and pointed to the President's lodge.

Later, Safire took Mr. Nixon's draft and prepared a text. About seven or eight drafts were made before one was approved.

"The President said he did not want it written by a committee," Safire said. "I was to show officials only those parts which concerned them. Since Rogers (Secretary of State William P. Rogers) was not there, I read his part over the phone."

News Summary: The "President's Daily News Summary," a compilation of news items to keep Mr. Nixon informed, has been revised over the last several months. Previously, it had been divided into sections according to the me-

194

THE PRESIDENT'S DAILY NEWS SUMMARY

The following is a page from the news summary prepared for President Nixon on Feb. 4. A similar summary is compiled each day.

NEWS SUMMARY

February 4, 1972
(Thursday nets, wires, mags)

The major stories of a day on which each net chose a different lead:

Secy. Rogers makes an unscheduled appearance to sharply criticize Muskie's attack on RN's peace plan (ABC lead and film on all nets with Muskie's rebuttal on one.)

The VC apparently reject RN's plan but issue a new proposal calling for negotiations with a Thieu-less GVN and all POWs back when all US forces are out. Seen to be more flexible. 2 nets noted this in comparison to Muskie's statement that RN's plan wouldn't lead to progress. NBC however tended to agree that RN's program had been rejected despite Rogers' statement to the contrary.

W. Coast dock strike seen close to settlement but NBC lead said House Labor's subpoena of the two sides slows things down.

Tension building in N. Ireland as Catholics refuse to call off another big—and illegal—protest march for Sunday. Sevareid raps EMK's call for US involvement and takes on Jackson and Muskie at same time for proposing that US pay for resettlement in Israel of Soviet Jews.

Ways and Means will allow debt to increase by only $20 B, thus forcing Admin to return in June for more—could be embarrassing in an election year.

Admin is willing to go along with FAP pilot project and anticipates whole program will eventually pass. (Note by 1 net.)

A woman with whom author Irving spent time in Mexico says there's virtually no way he could have met Hughes there as she was with the author almost all the time. (CBS lead.)

Hartke, HHH and Chisholm were subject of network film reports.

dium: newspapers, magazines and television. Now it includes all in each news summary.

"Before it was too big: this way, it eliminates redundancy," Buchanan said.

The average digest is about 21 single-spaced pages of about 6,000 words. It is one of the first things the President reads each morning. It once went only to Mr. Nixon and a few top aides, but currently it is delivered to several dozen.

Surprisingly, the text includes informal condensations, such as RN for Richard Nixon and Veep for Vice President Agnew. Many reporters are identified by their last names only. Sometimes, a rather frivolous news development is included, such as the Howard R. Hughes-Clifford Irving caper.

"In 25 minutes the President can get a comprehensive view of what's going on in the world," Buchanan said. "Talk about his being isolated is ridiculous. We try to keep out puff pieces and slanted news. He's an intelligent man, he knows such things when he sees them.

"We try to give him an accurate reflection of the intensity of feelings on issues and use it as a barometer of national thought."

Sometimes Buchanan will take a single news item and make a separate report on it.

SUMMING UP

Presidential speeches add—or detract—from the totality of his performance.

"There is always so much more that needs to be done," Price said. "We're always thinking how the President's ideas and philosophy can be gotten across to the country.

"We have not been as successful as I had hoped. His basic philosophy has been explained well but it's hard to get people to listen to it. . . .

"It's a burden-of-proof type of thing. We're assumed to be lying until proven otherwise. I thought we'd be able to change things sooner."

5   THE ADMINISTRATIVE PROCESS

The Executive Branch, as viewed by most citizens, appears to be a monolithic structure headed by the President, and managed as a standard hierarchical organization. It would appear from organization charts and statutory requirements that power and authority flow from the White House to the Cabinet secretaries and agency directors and down to their subordinates of the career civil service.

In fact, however, government agencies are only partially dependent upon the President. Each agency was created by a separate set of statutes and was thereby given specialized programs to administer. Each agency must deal with a different group of congressional committees. An agency's functions and programs give it a particular set of clients, enemies and supporters both within and without the formal governmental structure. Finally, each agency is manned by a different collection of career service specialists. These personnel have their own policy preferences, traditions, and ways of thinking and acting. To survive and achieve any of his policy objectives, the agency administrator must therefore come to terms not just with his superior in the White House, but also with committees of the Congress, agency personnel, and agency clientele groups. In short, government administrators serve many masters.

These multiple dependencies of agency administrators, not to mention the sheer size of the executive establishment, impose severe limits on a President's control of the agencies he is constitutionally charged to direct. One of the President's principal means of gaining control over the far-flung federal bureaucracy is the budget. The agency responsible for developing and implementing the federal budget is the Office of Management and Budget (OMB) in the Executive Office of the President. How the OMB, reorganized under President Nixon, seeks to achieve Administration policy objectives is portrayed in the first article in this section. This analysis also provides insights into the interplay of OMB, Congress, and interest groups in shaping budgetary policy.

Just as the federal bureaucracy is non-monolithic and difficult for the President to control, so too are the individual departments. This is particularly true of an agency as large and as varied in functions as the Department of Health, Education, and Welfare which now surpasses the Pentagon in expenditures of public funds. Here, too, the budget is a powerful weapon in the hands of the Secretary in shaping departmental policy. But as the second article of this section illustrates, the Secretary wields his budgetary authority under the careful scrutiny of interested congressmen, senators and interest group-clientele leaders.

The interrelationships and patterns of influence that grow up among the White House, departments and agencies, congressional committees, and interest groups are vividly presented in the final selection in this chapter. President Nixon, by proposing significant realignments of existing federal departments and agencies into what he considered more functional and efficient units, created a storm of controversy because his reorganization plan threatened to disrupt some of the existing patterns of influence.

Budgets, departmental reorganizations, and the admistrative process are not normally what most Americans think of as national politics and policy-making. But as these three studies dramatize, the administrative process is critical in shaping the policies which affect our lives.

The making of the President's budget: politics and influence in a new manner   *Dom Bonafede*

Editor's Note: The following article was prepared prior to George P. Shultz's appointment in May, 1972 to the post of Secretary of the Treasury. Shultz was replaced as Director of the Office of Management and Budget by his former Deputy, Casper W. Weinberger.

President Nixon's 1972 budget went to Congress Jan. 29, 1971, closing out the shakedown run of controversial new White House budget procedures.

In most respects, the new budget was like its predecessors— a 2,000-page blur of statistics bearing no visible signs of the six months of infighting, conniving and pleading that went into their production.

But the document is unique in that it is the first product of the President's new Office of Management and Budget, which:

set out in July 1970 deliberately to break up carefully-nurtured relationships between career budget professionals in the federal agencies and professionals in the budget bureau;

tried, and failed, to write a budget without giving Cabinet officers the right to appeal budget bureau decisions;

had to scramble to meet its deadline, partly because of the unprecedented effort to put total control of the budget process in the hands of presidential appointees.

As with all budgets, the fiscal 1972 version will be larger than the one before it—more than $225 billion as compared with $200 billion in fiscal 1971.

It will be the product of a family argument almost entirely confined to the executive branch; Congress and pressure groups stand aside during this first step in setting national priorities.

Drafting a budget, according to Commerce Secretary Maurice Stans, himself a former budget director (1958-61), involves "the uniform distribution of dissatisfaction."

"One of our most delicate areas is our relationships with the departments," said Arnold R. Weber, associate director of the OMB.

"George Romney is sensitive about it. We get excellent cooperation from Transportation. Defense is an institutional problem; there is Defense and 11 other departments."

What emerged from the process was a document setting the philosophic tone of the Nixon Administration for two more years.

It reflected Mr. Nixon's view of the needs of the nation in the most meaningful way they can be expressed—backed up by commitments to invest money to meet them.

The budget called for revenue sharing, welfare reform, start-up costs for a volunteer army and increased social security benefits. Larger amounts were requested for social programs and for defense.

Reflecting the Administration's move toward an "expansionary economy," the deficit budget was designed to slow down the rate of inflation and reduce unemployment, both of which could be crucial to Mr. Nixon's reelection plans for 1972.

NEW SYSTEM

For five decades, the Bureau of the Budget was an elite group of career civil servants functioning more in the British tradition of government than any other agency in Washington.

Only the director was appointed by the President. The director's top deputies and the 350 professionals—many with two or more college degrees—stitched together the federal budget no matter who was in the White House.

That pattern was substantially altered on July 1, 1970, when the Office of Management and Budget was set in motion.

Shultz—George P. Shultz left his position as Labor Secretary and took a $17,500-a-year cut in pay to move into the White House as the first director of the OMB.

Since then, he has established himself as Mr. Nixon's principal adviser in domestic affairs. Working with handpicked aides, he has modified the original concept of the office as a purely policy-implementing agency by assuming some policy-making functions as well.

Triumvirate: The budget director was absolute ruler of his operation under the old system, reporting directly to the President with 21 top-level career professionals reporting to him.

While Shultz was Director, OMB was managed by a triumvi-

Budget planners aboard Presidential jet: (from left) John D. Ehrlichman, Caspar W. Weinberger, Robert H. Finch and George P. Shultz

rate—Shultz, Deputy Director (for budget) Caspar W. Weinberger and Associate Director (for management) Weber.

"Weinberger is the 'B' in OMB and Weber is the 'M,' Shultz said.

Because Shultz' time was at the call of the President, Weinberger, a former California legislator and state finance director, and Weber, an economist and educator, shared general supervision of the office.

"We keep him (Shultz) informed, and all major decisions are brought to him," Weber said.

Budget Assistants: Reporting directly to Weinberger were three assistant directors—James R. Schlesinger, Donald B. Rice and Richard P. Nathan.

The jobs are filled by appointment rather than career advancement, a break with budget bureau tradition.

Nathan told *National Journal* he believes the change has helped make the "legislative, budgetary and management review processes more reflective of the President and the Presidency."

Rank and Status—The appointments also were designed to break another old tradition—in which Cabinet officers would create traffic jams in the director's office because they refused to deal on important issues with anyone of lower rank.

The three budget assistants are presidential appointees with the rank of Executive Level V and salaries of $34,500 a year. The jobs were upgraded to put the three men on more nearly equal footing with Cabinet officials.

Chain of Command—The budget assistants have line responsibility in the budget process for the departments, agencies and offices, which are assigned to six different program divisions, two each to an assistant director.

Schlesinger was in charge of national security and international programs; Rice handled economics, science and technology and natural resources; and Nathan supervised human resources and general government.

Each program division is headed by a division chief who supervises a corps of budget examiners responsible for program analysis and evaluation, and budget formulation and execution.

Division chiefs report to assistant directors, who report to the deputy director, who deals with Shultz.

Influence—According to one veteran budget official, who declined to be quoted by name, the three assistant directors are "among the most influential guys in town." He said, for example, that when HEW Secretary Elliot L. Richardson had a budget problem in his early days at HEW, he dealt with Edward L. Morgan, a White House staff member assigned to John D. Ehrlichman, assistant to the President for domestic affairs. Now Richardson deals directly with Nathan.

Morale: At the time of the transition, morale in the budget bureau was low, because employees felt that Director Robert F. Mayo (1969-70) lacked influence at the White House.

There was no visible improvement in morale immediately after the reorganization.

"Many people resented the changes per se," Weber said. "Others believed we were not doing what we should. Some were unhappy because they didn't see the director; this is very much a collegium, you know."

Morale has picked up in recent months, but one veteran agency official, who asked not to he identified, said: "Morale is still not as good as it should he."

Politics—The change in the method of appointing the top budget deputies has drawn some criticism on grounds that it makes the budget process too political.

"This makes the agency a direct political extension of the White House," said an OMB career executive, who declined to be quoted by name.

The three budget assistants and three other top officials who serve at Executive Level V may be reassigned, but they retain bumping— or seniority—privileges over career executives below them, some of whom have 25 years in government.

Weinberger—One official of the OMB, who asked not to be quoted, said Weinberger's work style had also created some ill will.

"He holds a daily meeting at 8:15 a.m. with his senior people," the official said, "but he has almost no communication with the staff below that level. He communicates with them by telephone and memo; this they resent."

Impact: "Fortunately," Shultz told *National Journal*, "we inherited a crackerjack outfit. Our problem was to build on it and to bring a new consciousness of management practices."

William L. Gifford, Shultz' aide for congressional relations, said he believes the director's close association with President Nixon has given the office "a new vitality and excitement."

Nathan, a carryover from the old budget bureau, said, "Significant differences are already discernible. We are deepening the professsional staff capacity of the President and tying it into the White House decision-making process."

One major difference in operation, according to a veteran budget officer, is that "we bureaucrats no longer talk to the other bureaucrats about the budget—that's all handled by the policy people."

Under the old system, he said, requests for hudget increases often were originated by department budget officers with their counterparts in the budget bureau.

"Now these discussions are carried on by Rice, Nathan or Schlesinger with ranking policy people in the departments, under secretaries or deputy under secretaries."

DRAFTING THE BUDGET

The views of the budget process from the top, or White House, level and from the lower levels of the federal government differ sharply. Discussions at OMB of how the budget was put together are calm and self-assured. Recollections of the process within the agencies and departments often are tinged with desperation.

From the Top: The outline of the fiscal 1972 budget began to take shape in July 1970 only a few days after OMB began operation.

For three days, Mr. Nixon met with Shultz and other aides, including Weinberger, Treasury Secretary David M. Kennedy, Paul W. McCracken, chairman of the Council of Economic Advisers, Arthur F. Burns, chairman of the Federal Reserve Board, and Ehrlichman.

"The President became deeply involved early in the process," Shultz said. "He made the major decisions back in July on the broad framework on which we were going to work."

Cabinet officers were briefed on the President's budget strategy in a series of meetings the week of July 27 at the western White House in San Clemente, Calif., during which they were given what Shultz called "reasonable targets" for their departments' budgets. The departments and agencies then were given their preliminary budget ceilings and told to respond by Sept. 30. As instructed, they came back within the deadline period with estimates of the funds they would need during fiscal 1972.

"It added up to being outside the boundaries of the President's strategy," Shultz said. As a result, a second round of estimates was proposed at a Cabinet session in October.

Hearings—A round of meetings began between department and OMB officials on budget proposals. Sitting in on the hearings was Edwin L. Harper, a representative of Ehrlichman's Domestic Council.

From time to time, agencies received new directives on the budget from Shultz, Weinberger and assistant budget directors.

"The budget is a responsive process," Shultz said. "It's a back-and-forth process in which you look at all the parts over and over until it jells."

Following the November elec-

THE CHANGING BUDGET PROCESS

The establishment July 1, 1970, of the Office of Management and Budget—referred to by President Nixon as "something entirely new in the history of reorganizing the executive department"—was received with apprehension by its critics and caution by its advocates.

Acknowledging this concern, Mr. Nixon said: "The question that many will ask is, is this another layer of government on top of too much government already? . . . If it is, it will have been a great mistake."

The OMB, with its companion agency, the Domestic Council, was conceived during a 1969 study by the President's Advisory Council on Executive Organization, headed by Roy L. Ash, president of Litton Industries Inc.

As envisioned by the Ash group, the Domestic Council would be a White House-based, institutionally staffed, "mission-oriented" body, charged with advising the President on all domestic policy. The OMB would use as its base the Bureau of the Budget. In addition to budgetary and legislative review activities, the council said the OMB should concentrate on program evaluation, management, interagency coordination, executive manpower development and improved information systems to facilitate the decision-making process for the President.

In submitting Reorganization Plan No. 2 of 1970 to Congress on March 12, 1970, Mr. Nixon said that creation of the OMB represented a new concept. While the new agency would continue to prepare the federal budget and oversee its execution, the President said, that would "no longer be its dominant, overriding concern."

He said, "The Domestic Council will be primarily concerned with what we do; the OMB will be primarily concerned with how we do it; and how well we do it."

History: The forerunner of the budget bureau was established in 1921 by Congress, which assigned the mission to the Treasury Department.

Until 1921, the financial needs of departments and agencies were communicated informally to Congress with no coordination by the executive branch.

Roosevelt—With the New Deal social programs and the threat of World War II, President Franklin D. Roosevelt felt he needed a personal budget staff, responsive to his office. He said it was "humanly impossible" for the President to function properly "because he is overwhelmed with minor details and needless contacts arising directly from bad organization and equipment of the government."

In 1936, Roosevelt named Louis Brownlow, government scholar, to head a three-man President's Committee on Administrative Management. The committee recommended creation of an Executive Office of the President, which Congress approved in 1939; the budget bureau became an arm of the Presidency.

Problems—With the tremendous growth in government agencies, personnel, programs and expenditures, the budget bureau had trouble fulfilling its mandate. There was no system for evaluating programs, coordinating activities or following up on policy.

Nor was there any systematic method for converting national goals into workable programs, for mobilizing executive talent and assigning it prudently. The President was inundated with raw data, but there was no organized information system in the bureau to translate the statistics.

President's Men—Because the executive office is the President's personal staff, existing to serve his needs, accommodate his habits and bend to his political philosophy, he is free to modify it as he sees fit.

The reorganization sought by Mr. Nixon has led to the dismantling of the budget bureau, one of the most sacrosanct of government offices. Lean (seldom more than 550 employees, of whom some two-thirds were professionals) and powerful (because of its budgetary power), the bureau was a fiscal Swiss Guard, with a constituency of one. The budget director was the only presidential appointee of Cabinet rank who did not require Senate confirmation. He was "the President's man."

Reorganizing: Under federal law, a reorganization plan submitted by the President becomes effective in 60 days unless either the House or Senate rejects it by a simple majority vote. Opposition to the Nixon plan soon surfaced.

Rep. Chet Holifield, D-Calif.,

then the ranking majority member of the Committee on Government Operations and now its chairman, attacked the proposal on grounds that it would create a privileged "faceless bureaucracy," deeply involved in policies and programs but protected from congressional review by executive privilege.

Officials of the American Federation of Government Employees (AFL-CIO) and the National Federation of Federal Employees said the OMB would infringe on the jurisdiction of the Civil Service Commission and duplicate commission functions.

Other opponents, including Rep. John E. Moss, D-Calif., said the plan would endanger the apolitical nature of civil service by providing for the appointment of six new Level V supergrade positions on the OMB under the umbrella of civil service tenure.

Plan Adopted: On May 13, 1970, after a vigorous White House lobbying campaign, a resolution (HRes 960) to disapprove the reorganization plan was defeated, 193-164, and the plan was adopted.

On June 10, the White House announced that Budget Director Robert P. Mayo was being appointed counselor to the President and that Labor Secretary George P. Shultz would become OMB director.

Caspar W. Weinberger, Federal Trade Commission chairman, was named deputy director.

Despite Mayo's reservations about the plan, both John D. Ehrlichman, assistant to the President for domestic affairs, and H. R. Haldeman, assistant to the President, urged Mr. Nixon to appoint Mayo to the OMB job. The President rejected their recommendation.

"Shultz was the President's personal choice," a staff member of the Ash Council said.

201

tions, a budget meeting was held with subcabinet members. By this time, the departments were trying to work out something within range of the new ceilings which had been set for them.

Director's Review—The most dramatic moment of the budget process is the director's review. This takes place in October and November and involves a series of confrontations between the budget director and various examiners responsible for recommending agency budget levels.

The reviews are conducted in the director's high-ceilinged room at the Executive Office Building. In the center of the room is a large oval table, cluttered with paper. Each participant is backed up by a number of technicians.

In the past, the budget director conducted the reviews. This year, they were chaired by Weinberger. Shultz attended some meetings, moving in and out as his schedule dictated.

In this atmosphere, the director challenges the examiner's recommendations and the examiner defends them.

"Weinberger doesn't know economics," complained one veteran budget official, who declined to be quoted by name, "All he wants to do is cut, cut, cut. He has a tendency to talk when he should be listening."

"The operating agencies are always sure the budget people don't understand their problems," said Weinberger.

Andrew M. Rouse, executive director of the Advisory Council on Executive Organization, says the director's reviews should be abolished.

"The budget decisions could be made between the assistant directors and the agencies," Rouse said. "As it is now, they spend three minutes on an item costing $2.5 billion and three hours on something involving $150,000."

Rouse said Weinberger spent almost a month on the director's reviews "when it could have been done in five days" through assistant directors.

A former budget bureau official, who asked not to be identified, disagreed with Rouse.

"The director's review is the way the director gets to know his staff. Whose judgment can he trust? Which ones really do their homework?"

The Mark—Sometime in December, agencies were notified of their "mark" by the OMB assistant directors. (The "mark" is the dollar figure at which the director draws the line for each agency after his review. To seek to go beyond the mark, an agency or department must file an appeal.)

The View Below: Several agencies went into budget negotiations persuaded that the punch cards were stacked against them.

NASA—Just when serious negotiations were getting underway, National Aeronautics and Space

Administration Thomas O. Paine resigned and was replaced by his deputy, George M. Low, who was appointed acting administrator.

Several officials close to the space program, who asked not to be named, said they were concerned at the time about Low's appointment at this critical time.

Said one: "George Low is an extremely able guy, but he's just not a political animal. He's ill at ease among politicians and is not knowledgeable about the tactics agencies have to use to defend their interests."

An OMB official, however, said Low's political naivete worked in some ways to his and NASA's advantage. "He's probably not a good politician," said the official, "but possibly for that reason—and for the fact of his undoubted integrity—everybody trusts him. We knew that he was never trying to pull a fast one on us, that he always played it straight. You never knew what Paine was up to, but Low you could depend on."

There was also a difference of opinion about the effect of President Nixon's failure to appoint another administrator in the four months after Paine's resignation.

Russell D. Drew, technical assistant with primary responsibility for space programs in the Office of Science and Technology, doubted it made any difference.

But James E. Webb, former NASA administrator (1961-68), said "the lag in appointing a new man becomes significant as people begin to take it as an indication of the President's interest in the space program. Had he appointed some well-known and able man and told him, 'You are my man. You and

OMB's BROAD CHARTER: EXECUTING POLICY AND 'COPING'

On the day that George P. Shultz was named director of the Office of Management and Budget, John D. Ehrlichman, assistant to the President for domestic affairs, was named executive director of the Domestic Council.

The council's role was to set domestic policy. The OMB's role was to carry out that policy.

The media immediately began speculating about a coming struggle for power between the two.

"I get along just fine with Ehrlichman," Shultz said, dismissing the notion of any infighting. "He's very bright, sensible and, personally, a fine person to deal with."

Equal Access: The fact remains that both men are engaged in the same policy area and both sit at Mr. Nixon's side.

At 3 p.m. each day, Shultz and Ehrlichman meet with the President. "There is no agenda," Shultz said. "We have things we want to get a reading on. Sometimes, the President has things on his mind that he wants us to get cracking on."

"Some days I'll see the President all day long," Shultz said. "Some days hardly at all."

Ehrlichman has said that he sees his White House role as expediter, not advocate, as one who presents the President with all available options.

Shultz perceives his role in about the same light, but he considers himself more an advocate.

"I have views on things," he said. "In this kind of a role, you have a responsibility to present all sides to get a presidential choice. And you lean over backwards when you have a strong view to see that the President is exposed to other points of view. If you don't, people don't trust you. You want people to feel that the President's decision was made on its merits and he was exposed to the total picture."

Management: The OMB's management section, under Associate Director Arnold R. Weber, consists of five divisions:

Organization and Management Systems—This division concentrates on improving management and organization of the executive branch and promotes uniform financial management systems and the simplification of contract and grant requirements; it provides technical assistance to departments and agencies.

Program Coordination—This division provides on-site aid in the coordination of federal programs in the field, responds to requests for special assistance in crisis situations, follows up on presidential initiatives, and deals with special departmental problems.

Statistical Policy and Management Information Systems—Created by the consolidation of the Office of Statistical Policy and the Management Information Systems staff, this division is concerned with an integrated statistical collection and reporting system for government managers.

Legislative Reference—The responsibilities of this division, which existed in the old Bureau of the Budget, were not changed by the reorganization. It prepares and clears legislation and coordinates department and agency views on legislation.

Executive Development and Labor Relations—This division is responsible for executive recruitment and training programs; it helps evaluate and formulate union-management policies in the federal government.

Coping—Shultz said that "one of the OMB's responsibilities is not on the organization chart; it's only in my head. That is 'coping'. We spend a lot of time coping with things whether we generate them or somebody else does. When you cope, you cope with immediate operating matters and you resolve them in terms of immediate pressures."

Mine Disaster—As an example, he cited the OMB's role following a recent mine disaster in Hyden, Ky., in which 38 miners were killed. After a New Year's Eve White House meeting with Sen. Marlow W. Cook, R-Ky., and other members of the Kentucky delegation, Mr. Nixon directed Shultz to coordinate an emergency program to help survivors.

Within hours, Weber and his staff began contacting federal and regional government offices, such as HEW, Social Security Administration, Labor Department, Agriculture Department and the Veterans Administration.

The next day, William A. Boleyn, a senior OMB official, was sent to the disaster area to expedite relief for widows and children, including workmen's compensation, social security payments, veterans death benefits and, for those in dire need, food stamps and public assistance.

Reaction—A subsequent critical report by an investigating group guided by Ralph Nader, the consumer advocate, said that the federal officials "did not fully protect all of the widows' rights."

Sen. Cook, however, praised the OMB's efforts. "We have received no complaints from the families; they seem to be very pleased," said A. Mitchell McConnell, the Senator's legislative assistant.

Programs: The OMB has helped create several national programs, particularly in cases where the President had to respond quickly. Most of the programs were the responsibility of William H. Kolberg's Program Coordination Division, a section of Weber's management team. Now comprising 10 members, the division is to be increased to more than 30.

Among the programs:

Sky marshal plan—The OMB assisted the Treasury and Transportation Departments in putting together an interagency anti-hijacking program. OMB officials met with Lt. Gen. Benjamin O.

Dave Packard get together and work out a compatible and defensible program, and I'll back you,' it would certainly have made a difference. In the absence of this indication, NASA is bound to be in a weaker position."

HUD—Since the bulk of the HUD Department's spending for urban development is at administrative discretion and not mandated by statute, the HUD budget is easier than most to slice. HUD's two big money programs—urban renewal and model cities—had been in particular difficulty since the start of the Nixon Administration. And just when the budget process was beginning, the department's biggest programs were publicly attacked by presidential aide Ehrlichman. Later in the year, Vice President Agnew joined the attack.

In an interview with *The Seattle Times* on July 10, 1970, Ehrlichman said, "Urban renewal is a good example of a program without a purpose. It hasn't helped the poor and hasn't beautified the cities.

"And take model cities. The waste and frustration of that program is terrible. In Seattle, only one of the five model cities projects is delivering."

In November, Mr. Agnew told the editors of *The Daily News* (New York) that HUD's budget would be deeply cut to free money for more important domestic initiatives. He predicted that the savings would be transferred to a revenue-sharing program which had a high priority in the Nixon Administration.

Environment—The new Environmental Protection Agency had

Davis (USAF-ret.) when he was appointed Sept. 21 as head of the security force. They worked out plans for putting government resources at his disposal and arranged for the recruitment and training of 2,500 air marshals.

"We considered and rejected a suggestion we use deputy marshals from the Justice Department," Kolberg said. "We believe this is a relatively temporary thing and we didn't want to institutionalize it."

OMB management experts also set up an interagency committee to deal with the hijacking problem. Gen. Davis is chairman and Boleyn sits on the committee as the OMB representative.

"Our role in the program has been that of coordinator, expediter and enforcer," Kolberg said.

Railroad strike plan—During a threatened rail strike in December 1970, Shultz convened a meeting of federal departments and agencies to draft an emergency transportation plan under a priority system.

The OMB is now working with the Labor Department in an effort to reach agreement with railroad unions before the March 1 strike deadline.

Railpax—Working in conjunction with the Transportation Department, the OMB helped develop a national grid for rail passenger service operated by a quasi-public corporation.

its hands full just getting organized during the crucial early days of the budgeting process.

The agency—first new line agency to be established by the Nixon Administration—assumed control of the principal federal antipollution programs Dec. 2.

To ensure that the new agency could commence operations on schedule, a special OMB task force supervised by Dwight A. Ink, assistant director for the Organization and Management Systems Division, started work last summer, soon after the July 9 announcement of the plan.

The task force shaped the superstructure of the new agency and arranged the transfer of its component parts—whose fiscal 1971 budget had totaled some $1.4 bil-

lion—from the Interior, Agriculture and Health, Education and Welfare Departments and other offices.

EPA was without a top command during this stage. Not until Nov. 6 did the White House announce the nomination of William D. Ruckelshaus as administrator. Ruckelshaus had been assistant attorney general (civil division) in the Justice Department.

Meanwhile, the 15 offices being drawn into EPA still were under the jurisdiction of their departments as fiscal 1972 budget preparations got underway.

Budget justification and review sessions, normally held in late summer and early fall, were thus conducted in a bureaucratic limbo. Budget cuts inflicted on depart-

ments were shifted, at least temporarily, to agencies the departments knew they were giving up.

OEO—The fiscal 1972 budget process was particularly painful for the Office of Economic Opportunity.

Not only was the poverty agency forced to work with a fiscal 1972 target that was 23 per cent below its fiscal 1971 appropriation; but the fact was leaked to the press, which increased tensions between the agency and the President's budget staff.

The press reports were based on OEO documents leaked by employees and former employees who were seeking to generate public pressure for raising the mark.

POVERTY NEGOTIATIONS

OEO's strict budget limits produced strong feelings within the agency. A mid-December memorandum to acting Director Frank C. Carlucci, written by John O. Wilson, assistant OEO director for planning, research and evaluation said:

"I sincerely doubt whether the agency could survive cuts such as these."

One OEO official with previous budget bureau experience warned not to consider the budget figures contained in the leaked memoranda as final. "The budget process is a bargaining process," he said, "and the OEO is in no way, shape or form different than any other agency in that regard. OEO became the symbol simply because of the leaks."

The budget office established what it considered the target for OEO's fiscal 1972 budget in an

Aug. 5 letter to Donald Rumsfeld, then OEO director and now counselor to the President. The target was $960 million. OEO's fiscal 1971 budget is $1.3 billion.

Nathan: OEO's budget was under the jurisdiction of Nathan, who was not enthusiastic about the agency's approach to fighting poverty.

One OEO official, who asked not to be quoted by name, said Nathan "has certain deeply committed philosophical approaches; one is income transfer as opposed to rendering services to the poor, such as OEO does."

"By emphasizing the income strategy—give the poor money and not services—he de-emphasizes other things," the OEO official said. "He comes down too hard on the programmatic approach that OEO takes." (The Administration also favors an income strategy over the service-rendering approach taken by OEO.)

Examiners: Thomas Ubois is OMB's budget examiner for OEO. Fiscal 1972 was Ubois's first poverty budget. OEO had a steady turnover of examiners in the old budget bureau.

"We've always had a problem in that regard," an OEO official said. "They get a little committed to our program and lose their usefulness to OMB. I've watched that happen two or three times in both (the Johnson and Nixon) Administrations."

Analysts: OEO's Program Analysis Division, headed by William Plissner, is the antipoverty agency's budget shop. It examines the requests of the various OEO programs at the first level in the development of the agency's budget.

One OEO official, who declined to speak for attribution, said the program analysis office "wears two hats."

"They are the nasty bastards in the agency who ask the hard questions of the program people," he said. "And once a figure is established, program analysis must develop a justification for its expenditure to present to OMB."

Four people who now work in OEO's Program Analysis Division or oversee it formerly held positions in the old budget bureau. They are James E. Connor, director of OEO's Office of Planning and Program Analysis; Clifford Parker, deputy director of the Program Analysis Division; Richard D. Redenius, chief of community betterment in program analysis; and J. Susanne Meyer, a program analyst.

One OEO official said privately: "The standard governmental pattern is to recruit your (OMB) examiner. If he knows how to find it he knows how to hide it." However, none of the four former budget bureau officials now at OEO was responsible in his previous position for the OEO budget.

OEO's stringent budget limitation forced the Program Analysis Division to take a hard look at every operating program and activity, regardless of its station in the agency.

Rumsfeld—With Rumsfeld serving as OEO director and as an assistant to the President, many OEO employees had at first assumed that he would protect the agency's budget interests at the White House. One OEO official said privately:

BUDGET TERMINOLOGY

Many of the terms used by federal budget professionals can be found in official government glossaries. As often happens, some of the most common expressions have no official status. Among them are:

Mark: A mark is the budget level for an agency which is approved by the Office of Management and Budget for inclusion in the President's budget. It can also mean the level at which anyone involved in the budget process believes his budget should be, as in the Secretary of Defense's mark.

Ceiling: The agency budget limit set by the OMB before the budget process begins.

Planning Target: Nearly the same as a ceiling, but more flexible.

Priority Bands: Agency programs, grouped by level of priority in an agency director's judgment, with the most expendable programs at the bottom and the most important at the top.

Director's Review: Meetings between the budget director and his examiners as a last step before setting the OMB mark.

Examiner: The OMB staff member responsible for examining an agency's budget.

Desk Man: An OMB official with responsibility for the budget of a particular area of government. The term usually applies to one of the three assistant budget directors, but it could be applied to an examiner, as in the Transportation Department's desk man.

"The general feeling in the agency when Rumsfeld was director was, 'Forget the budget bureau, we have our own man in the White House, our own ties to the President.' This attitude prevailed, particularly when Mayo was director. Perhaps it was inaccurate, but it prevailed."

Rumsfeld made his presence felt on behalf of OEO in top-level, morning staff meetings at the White House, according to one poverty official.

Using Channels—A White House aide to Rumsfeld said, "Without question his having an office in the west wing had an impact on OEO's budget, but he consistently followed the normal budget process. He would not make use of his position in the White House to undercut OMB. He got his appeals in through the normal route."

Rumsfeld told *National Journal* he emphasized the importance of using the proper channels for budget appeal. Asked whether he ever circumvented the process, Rumsfeld said, "I never worked that way. We were always very proper."

FUNDING THE ENVIRONMENT

To coordinate budget planning for the Environmental Protection Agency, a special unit was established last summer in OMB's Natural Resources Programs Division.

Examiners Wesley Sasaki and Glenn Schleede were assigned to the unit; they report to Donald E. Crabill, chief of the division, who in turn reports to assistant director Rice.

Staff: Meanwhile, the management task force at EPA tapped Eldon Taylor, a veteran budget expert with NASA, to chair the group's program and budget group.

Taylor sat in on many budget sessions at OMB, serving as adviser to OMB and at the same time preparing options for the then-unannounced new EPA administrator.

Taylor, who is now EPA's acting deputy assistant administrator for resources management, was assisted by Matthew Pilzys, former budget aide at the Federal Water Quality Administration and now EFA's acting director of budget operations. The water agency has handled EPA's biggest budget items—grants for sewage treatment plants, which totaled $1 billion in fiscal 1971.

Also involved in budget sessions were Alvin L. Alm and J. Clarence Davies III from the staff of the Council on Environmental Quality (CEQ), the President's advisory board on environmental policy. Both Alm and Davies are former budget bureau officials.

Council member Robert Cahn said of the CEQ effort in behalf of the new environmental agency: "We wanted to make sure that they didn't come in like a new baby with no clothes and no crib."

Ruckelshaus—Several days before his nomination was announced, Ruckelshaus plunged into his new duties as EPA administrator.

One of the first moves was to meet with Taylor and plug himself into the fiscal 1972 preparations.

This required a line-by-line review of the original budget submissions, briefings with program managers and a crash course in environmental policy and programming.

OMB gave the new administrator special treatment because of the unusual circumstances surrounding the EPA budget and allowed Ruckelshaus to make late requests for funds without instituting a formal appeal.

Ruckelshaus conferred with Assistant Director Rice at OMB on several occasions. He also talked with John C. Whitaker, chief aide to the President on environmental matters.

New Legislation: Complicating matters further, Congress late in 1970 was acting on several bills with a direct bearing on EPA operations. One agency official said new bills were "coming in over the transom."

The 1970 Clean Air Act amendments (84 Stat 1676), for example, authorizing massive increases in air pollution control and a new Noise Abatement and Control Office in EPA, cleared a conference committee one week before Christmas.

While officials of the National Air Pollution Control Administration had previously estimated their extra requirements under the new bill, the final version nevertheless caused last-minute budget changes.

HUD BARGAINING

The impact of the White House attacks on HUD was made clear on Dec. 24, 1970, when the department received its initial spending marks for fiscal 1972. Urban renewal was to be cut from $1.2 billion to $800 million; model cities was to be cut from $575 million to zero in one mark, and to $250 million in a later mark; water and sewer funding was to be cut from $350 million to $200 million.

Process: Secretary George W. Romney's budget problems were complicated by the new process at OMB.

In preparing the fiscal 1971 budget, the budget bureau gave departments "planning targets" along with instructions to justify, in order of priority, areas where they felt they could not work within the planning targets. The bureau provided detailed steps for Cabinet officials to take to appeal spending levels to the budget director and the President.

The process for fiscal 1972 was different.

Targets were replaced by ceilings, and, as one ranking HUD official said: "This year, we were given ceilings and we were told they were the President's ceilings, not OMB's."

Nevertheless, he said, "every major agency came in over its ceiling."

Attack: Budget ceilings were sent to the department on September 15. On Sept. 30, HUD sent written justifications for higher spending levels; it followed up during several weeks of hearings with a verbal case for more money.

Under Secretary Richard C. Van Dusen led off hearings in mid-October with a presentation of HUD's over-all case to Weinberger, Nathan and members of their staff.

After Van Dusen's presentation, HUD's assistant secretaries argued for their own programs to their respective examiners. Both Rom-

ney and Van Dusen then concluded the series of hearings with a final general plea to the same OMB officials who were present at the first meeting. OMB then asked the department for additional written materials answering questions raised during the Shultz-Ehrlichman conference.

Representing OMB on the HUD budget were Weinberger, Nathan, Paul H. O'Neill, division chief for human resources programs; Harry S. Havens, assistant division chief for housing and urban development programs; and Ubois, who examines model cities as well as poverty programs.

Budget specialists for HUD are Nathaniel J. Eiseman, director of the office of the budget; John R. McDowell, deputy director; and Albert J. Kliman, director of program budget development. All three are career men; they have a total of 63 years on the job.

HUD's budget office consolidates and revamps the budgets prepared by the budget officers attached to each of the seven assistant secretaries.

The Marks—After HUD made its October arguments for more money, Weinberger and Nathan filtered out the major differences between the OMB and HUD positions and took them to Shultz and Ehrlichman.

After those answers were in, Weinberger, Shultz, Nathan and Ehrlichman took the President what they regarded as the crucial remaining differences. Mr. Nixon personally resolved them.

The end product represented HUD's spending marks, and they were transmitted to the department the day before Christmas.

The National Aeronautics and Space Administration had no way to go but up after the drubbing it took during negotiations on the fiscal 1971 budget. The agency had gone to the budget bureau in October 1969 with a $4.1-billion request and left in January 1970 with about $3.3 billion—several hundred million dollars of which it had managed to gouge out in the last few weeks before the President's budget was released.

While the agency may well have stemmed the panic in the aerospace industry, events during 1970 did not foreshadow a comeback.

Though NASA remained optimistic about fiscal 1972, said one NASA official, "we found as the year went on that the over-all temper of the country and the Congress, as well as the continuing problems on inflation and Vietnam funding, meant we couldn't expect any great change in the coming budget."

Science Office: The reemergence of the President's Office of Science and Technology as an important voice in setting priorities for federal science programs strongly influenced the formulation of the fiscal 1972 NASA budget.

David—As he did with Shultz and Weinberger in OMB, President Nixon has made it clear his new science adviser, Edward E. David, has his complete confidence and is listened to. In a reversal of last year's decision to bar OST officials, for example, men from the science office were present at the final OMB director's review sessions in November.

David's appointment came on Aug. 19, after the budget process was well along.

During the autumn, David received a forced-draft education, leaning on the office staff for advice. In the case of NASA, this meant turning to space specialist Russell Drew. Drew told *National Journal* that soon after his appointment, David began discussions with Low and then with some of NASA's associate administrators. As he had in years past, Drew said he kept in close touch with the NASA examiners at the budget office.

Influence—During the final rounds of negotiations in the fall, OST staff members independently questioned NASA officials on matters of particular concern to the scientific community.

Said Drew: "Our interests and approach are somewhat different from OMB's. Our goal is always to see that the scientific and technological values of programs are kept to the fore. We also try to look for alternatives, or other possible options, for issues that initially seem to be questions of black and white."

An OMB official said of OST's impact this year: "David and Weinberger established a close working relationship, and on a number of important final decisions OST did exercise a sizeable influence."

According to Drew and to David Z. Beckler, assistant to the director of OST, when NASA appealed certain OMB decisions this year, OST entered to make direct recommendations both to top OMB officials and to the President himself.

Beckler and Drew also stressed that the fiscal 1971 and 1972 budgets are based on the recommendations of the President's own Space Task Group report of Sept. 1, 1969.

The report was entitled, *The Post-Apollo Space Program: Directions for the Future*. OST provided much of the staff work required to formulate policy options.

Negotiators: Participants in NASA's negotiations with OMB included Low; William E. Lilly, assistant administrator for administration; Joseph F. Malaga, director of NASA's Resources Analysis Division; Willis H. Shapley, associate deputy administrator and a one-time NASA examiner in the budget bureau, and the agency's associate administrators.

THE FINAL TOUCH

When the Office of Management and Budget was created, nobody could foretell how it would get along with the departments.

"Having been a Cabinet officer, I understand their problems," Shultz told *National Journal*. "Our job is to see that we use the available resources to further the objectives of the President and the Cabinet. But there is always the possibility you can't do everything."

Then, with a wry smile, he said: "You'd think that if you were in charge of $200 billion, you'd have friends everywhere. But it doesn't work out that way."

Appeal Process: In previous years, an agency's mark was considered the director's mark. If an agency chief disagreed with his mark, he could appeal over the director's head to the President.

That system has been modified by Shultz in one of the more significant changes in the budget process.

"We told the agencies," Shultz said, "that we were giving them the President's mark; if they had new information and facts and figures to support their appeals, they had to put it in writing.

"They were told not to put it in a 100-page document but to keep it in a form that the President can look at. Beyond that, if there is a need for discussion with him, we will arrange it."

Nixon Meetings—Early in January, responding to complaints from departments, Mr. Nixon met first with his Secretaries and then with his under secretaries.

He admonished them that 1971 was a tough year all through the federal government and that belts had to be tightened. At that time, he told them appeals could be made.

Any Secretary who felt he could not live with his ration was permitted to send a two-page memorandum to the President. That in turn would be accompanied by a report from Shultz. If Mr. Nixon decided against a Cabinet officer on the basis of his memorandum, the officer could ask for a meeting in person.

No Takers—As of mid-January, Shultz said, "There has not been an occasion when a Cabinet member said, 'I've just got to see the President.'"

Weinberger said that "lots" of requests for reconsiderations had been made by the departments and agencies; they were taken up with the President.

Shultz said Cabinet members

who have gripes about their budgets often get a chance to talk to the President about them at Cabinet sessions.

Under the current format, he said, when an agency head requests a budget reevaluation he is in effect asking the President to reconsider his own judgment.

Romney—HUD Secretary Romney was one who was restive under the earlier ground rules for bargaining with OMB. He felt the new process was keeping him not only from the President but from Shultz, said one HUD official who asked not to be identified.

"The OMB people were always between us and the President," he said. "They were getting there firstest with the mostest when it came to adjudicating our appeals."

In the early stages of budget negotiations, said one HUD budget officer, who asked not to be quoted by name, there was no formal appeals procedure. "During our preliminary hearings, we kept asking our examiners how to appeal and they kept communicating the feeling that there would be no appeals mechanism."

Bargaining—One aide to the Secretary said Romney's success during negotiations on the fiscal 1972 budget reflects his close involvement with the department's work in putting together its requests.

"He really prides himself on that," the aide said; "because of his business achievements, he believes he really shines on using the budget as a management tool; it's a real plus for him."

Results—Romney has been able to restore his prized housing subsidy programs—one for home ownership assistance and one for rental assistance (Sections 235 and 236 of the National Housing Act, 12 USC 1715z, 1715z-1)—to their existing levels of $140 million and $145 million respectively.

NASA: Although no formal appeals procedure had been announced at the time, NASA officials also decided in mid-December to appeal their final judgments from OMB.

"We appealed because we felt that there were some factors that had not been taken into account," Lilly told *National Journal.*

"We felt the President should be made aware of the implications of certain decisions. For these reasons, we asked for a reconsideration on certain items."

The deliberations, according to Lilly, went on for some time, during which the agency continued to feed information into the White House.

OST also entered the debate directly, according to Beckler and Drew, with communications to Shultz, Weinberger and the President.

Regarding NASA's arguments in the appeal, an OMB official said: "The documents were much more intellectually defensible this year. They did present a rational case, and there was a good deal less of the adversary content to them."

Lilly said the appeal resulted in a compromise in which NASA got essentially what it asked but gave up other things in partial compensation.

BUDGET CRITIQUE

Department officials who dealt with OMB agreed that old-line professionals at the budget office had less to say about policy during preparation of the fiscal 1972 budget than in years past. Beyond that, they agreed on virtually nothing about the new system.

In one case, officials from the same agency could not agree on whether the new approach was a step forward or a setback.

OMB—Weinberger said he thought the work on the budget "went well, considering that it was an enormously difficult job."

"We got off to a slow start, he said. "The budget is a great downhill-rolling ball, and it's hard to control it even if you catch it at the top of the hill."

Catching Up—Joseph Laitin, assistant to the director for public affairs, said the job of putting together the budget did run behind for a long time; but he said that in the end OMB was able to beat their deadline for delivery of the final package.

Laitin said the fact that Congress failed to take action on many fiscal 1971 appropriations bills until the closing days of the 91st session hampered the OMB effort.

"We had to see what Congress was going to do before we could go ahead with 1972," he said.

Another OMB official said the transition made necessary by reorganization of the budget bureau "cost us about six months."

"Don't forget," he said, "the budget process really should begin the day after the President submits his last budget."

President's Time—Weinberger said he thought the new process led to more efficient use of the President's time on budget matters than was possible in past years.

"It was not wasted," he said. "There was substantial presidential involvement, but there was no wasted motion. I'm told that has not always been the case.

OEO: One poverty official said he found the budget process "more confused than last year, simply because they had gone through a major reorganization."

"The people at the OMB were not as sure of their signals as before," he said.

Another OEO official, who asked not to be quoted by name, said it was clear during the process that "control of the old budget pros had been loosened."

"I think we paid a certain price for that," he said, "but how it balances out, I think it's too soon to judge."

The same official said the new approach led to "some fairly productive, high-level conceptual conversations early in the game" that helped educate budget office officials.

In one conversation, he said, "the OMB got a better view of how OEO's neighborhood health centers and its family planning program linked up and how they related to other government programs. There is a tendency at OMB not to relate, not to sweep across the government.

HUD: One HUD official said his department had the opposite experience when it came to relating programs.

"In two of our programs, where activity in one supports activity in another, they eliminated the basic program and left the supporting program at the requested level," he said.

"I attribute this to the new structure," the HUD officer said. "Their examiners seemed as much

CRITICISM OF OMB-DOMESTIC COUNCIL

For the most part, early opponents of the formation of OMB and the Domestic Council remain critical of the operation.

Holifield: Rep. Chet Holifield, D-Calif., chairman of the House Committee on Government Operations, says the Domestic Council has inherited policy-making functions formerly vested in the budget bureau.

"The Domestic Council makes policy and hands it over to the OMB," Holifield said. "It (the Domestic Council) takes a look at the programs and says cut this 5 per cent, this 10 per cent and this 20 per cent. The OMB no longer considers policy along with dollars. The budgeteers have become skilled bookkeepers and accountants; they're a mathematical, computer bunch, rather than instruments in setting policy."

Holifield said further that the Domestic Council "is taking the place of the Cabinet. You are going to see the deterioration of the prestige that goes with the Cabinet. Prominent people will refuse to become a Cabinet member. They'll realize they are just a front."

Employees: Employee organizations, which fought the plan from the start, still oppose it, although the chairman of the Civil Service Commission so far sees no threat to government employees.

Wolkomir—Nathan Wolkomir, president of the National Federation of Federal Employees, said:

"Nothing has been done to change our opposition to it. In fact, our original stand has been confirmed. The OMB concept increases the Administration's responsibility over the lower levels of government employees and promotes more political appointments.

"When you inject policy-making types of appointees down to lower levels, it is the spoils system. This is reflected when people who are career employees are told to clear out their desk in five days."

In reference to OMB's executive development program, Wolkomir said, "For almost four years, the Civil Service Commission has been making studies and conceived an executive assignment system. Then Nixon comes up with his reorganization plan and says the hell with it. For 53 years we have been fighting for the merit system; now this contaminates the whole idea."

Griner—John Griner, president of the American Federation of Government Employees, AFL-CIO, told *National Journal:*

"We haven't changed our opposition to it one bit. The OMB will take over the prerogatives of the Civil Service Commission and affect the merit system, which God knows is weak enough already. And because it is close to the President—not just in this Administration but in all Administrations—there is bound to be politics involved."

Hampton—Despite the apprehension voiced by the union leaders, Chairman Robert E. Hampton of the Civil Service Commission said, "I've seen no evidence the OMB is going to encroach in our business so far . . . , and I have no fear they will. I have 10 times the number of people they have."

However, Hampton said, "We haven't worked out what they'll be doing and how it will relate to us. Or what we'll be doing and how it will relate to them."

Involved in the personnel management issue are 2,857,849 government employees (as of October 1970) and a $28-billion personnel budget.

Moynihan: Before he left the White House early in January 1971, Daniel P. Moynihan, counselor to the President, said: "Whether it's a better budget bureau or not is unknown at this time, but institutionally it's better."

in the dark as we were. Of course, it was not wholly unsatisfactory. A lot did go smoothly; but not in the problem areas, and of course that is where you have to spend most of your time.

NASA: Officials at the space agency gave the new budget team high marks.

"It was a much better situation than last year because we had clear indications all the way through that our requests were being considered in a more responsible and efficient way," said NASA's Lilly. "This meant, finally, that the White House got a more accurate picture of the rationale behind the requests we were making."

Lilly said the negotiations were "more formal and structured but at the same time more straightforward."

Professionals: Lilly said he and other NASA officials felt during the process that OMB's professionals were uncertain about their positions in the new structure and were trying to prove themselves to the new management.

A career OMB official, who asked not to be quoted by name, said Lilly's impression was correct.

"What we've got over here now is an old professional bureaucracy and a new management group," he said. "The old bureaucracy did try very hard during the recent negotiations to prove their loyalty to the new ways of doing things."

One of the reasons for changes at OMB, he said, "was to end the rounds of sub-negotiations between budget bureau staff people and agencies. There had been a lot of scurrying back and forth during the past, and this sometimes led to crossed signals. This year, after the director's review, there was no more talking. Weinberger held the review and then held his counsel. This made the whole process more efficient and less cluttered with internal sub-negotiations."

The official said the end result was that "we weren't almost driven mad as we were last year—particularly at the end—by the White House people fiddling around with figures."

HEW Department, largest federal spender, seeks to funnel more money to the poor

John K. Iglehart

The HEW Department, biggest spender among the federal agencies, carved up the controllable segments of its mammoth budget in a new way this year, seeking to better target resources on the poor and other dependent segments of the population.

In a major shift from past practice, Secretary Elliot L. Richardson attempted to apply department-wide goals in weighing funding requests, and his techniques have caught the interest of other big domestic departments.

Richardson imported as his chief planning aide a former systems analyst for the Pentagon and the National Security Council, Laurence E. Lynn Jr., and Lynn played a leading role in the effort to develop over-all strategies and priorities in the department's budget process.

In memoranda and in top-level meetings, Lynn pressed, with Richardson's support, the view that individual education programs should not be viewed merely in the context of other federal educational activities, and that welfare and health programs likewise should be considered in light of less parochial objectives than in the past.

The department, largely as a result of the policy, requested additional funds for compensatory education, education of the handicapped and vocational rehabilitation, all programs that serve the dependent.

Indian health programs, family planning, alcoholism and drug

HEW's main building: heart of a vast complex

abuse prevention and community mental health centers also fared well under the policy, although these programs also had political forces working for them in the budget process.

In seeking to advance the thrust, Richardson ran headlong into fiscal constraints, a lack of discretionary dollars and, in seeking to shift funds from lower to higher priority programs, a sacred tenet of federal budget-making: programs are generally granted annual budget increases, regardless of their priority, either at the request of the President or the insistence of Congress.

After the President's budget had been finally approved and printed, Richardson said that he generally was pleased with the new review system. "In terms of the gross department budget, the definable impact of the strategies is

relatively small," he said. "But the strategies are significant in imparting a direction. They reflect a cutting edge of the department's future direction."

By Richardson's estimate, HEW shifted, retargeted, or increased funds totaling $1.3 billion to advance his department-wide goals.

The figure represents less than 2 per cent of the department's total fiscal 1973 budget estimate.

Fast Growth: HEW's fiscal 1973 budget request is a landmark for the department. For the first time, if spending projections are correct, HEW will surpass the Defense Department as the biggest spender among federal agencies. The budget projects that HEW outlays will total $78,953,000,000, or 32.1 per cent of the projected budget total of $246,157,000,000, while the Pentagon will spend

$77,722,000,000, or 31.6 per cent.

HEW's budget is growing faster than the total federal budget. Its projected outlays for fiscal 1973 represent a 10-per cent increase over the spending level estimated for fiscal 1972. In contrast, total federal outlays are projected to increase 4 per cent.

Noncontrollables—The rate of growth is in part a result of the increased attention that the Administration and Congress are giving to social programs, but it also is a reflection of the rapid escalation in the "noncontrollable" category of departmental expenditures.

Noncontrollables are outlays in programs such as social security, medicare, medicaid and public welfare, where the government is responsible, by statute, for paying out benefits to eligible individuals, regardless of their number.

The level of spending in these programs is controllable only through a change in the authorizing legislation, not through the congressional appropriations or regular budget process.

As operator of the largest federal income maintenance programs, HEW has a disproportionate share of federal noncontrollable outlays—$68 billion out of an estimated total of $169 billion in fiscal 1973.

Domination of the HEW budget by noncontrollables is likely to continue. The department's planning office, in a five-year projection of HEW spending, estimated that in fiscal 1977 the department would spend $117 billion, including $104 billion in noncontrollables.

Controllables—Richardson found, as have other recent HEW Secretaries, that his influence over the department's budget is sharply limited by the size of the noncontrollables, but he was determined in the fiscal 1973 budget cycle to exert as much influence as he could by bearing down on program requests over which he had some discretion.

Richardson discovered obstacles of varying natures standing in his way as he sought to retarget portions of the $13 billion in controllable funds at his disposal.

Richardson said in an interview that he was struck "with renewed force" at the countless pressures at work to automatically grant budget increases and to continue business as usual at HEW.

"The awareness of the hardships that can be brought about by any sharp discontinuity in support of ongoing activities" was one of two principal sources of pressure, he said, and the other was "the inescapable awareness of the political repercussions that would attach to disappointing the well-organized constituencies that look to us."

The department also found that the Office of Management and Budget constituted an impediment to the total advancement of Richardson's plans.

OMB considered HEW's budget only partly in the light of the goal that Richardson had embraced as his department developed the document for fiscal 1973.

Much of OMB's examination of the HEW budget was in the traditional fashion—line-by-line—and not in terms of an overriding goals, thus hindering its advancement. OMB also imposed tight ceilings on HEW early in the budget process.

But by the end of a long and intense bargaining process, and after imposition of the President's wage-price freeze which eased HEW's fiscal problems a bit, the department was generally pleased with its fiscal 1973 budget.

One ranking HEW budget official said: "(Caspar W.) Weinberger (OMB's deputy director) must have given up trying to hold the line. We're not kicking about the outcome of our budget."

Richardson appealed only one item to the President and that was done in a letter. The Secretary urged Mr. Nixon to reject OMB's proposal to transfer hospitalization costs totaling an estimated $350 million from the federal government to medicare patients through an earlier copayment requirement.

Richardson argued that Mr. Nixon's political credibility with the over-65 population would be hurt if the Administration adopted OMB's proposal. In a reversal from previous policy, the President accepted HEW's position. The Administration had advanced and lost on a similar proposal in fiscal 1972.

Developing a Strategy: The settling on a new department thrust evolved in September from an intense exercise that engaged Richardson's budget and planning staffs. For the first time, the two staffs entered the budget development process as equals.

At Richardson's request, the staffs developed a number of strategies from which the Secretary could elect an area of concentration for future department funding.

From the alternatives raised,

Richardson selected two department strategies that will seek to focus many of HEW's 270 programs in the future on the reduction of human dependency and the promotion of institutional reform.

In the main, the strategies translate into a greater commitment on the part of HEW to target its dollars more closely on segments of the population that suffer from handicapping conditions of any kind.

Richardson views the strategies as particularly relevant to relieving problems in the nation's inner cities caused by the increasing concentration of poor and black people there.

"I certainly regard our programs and budget decisions as having a greater relative impact in coping with that problem than any other given area of urgent national concern," the Secretary said.

Philosophical Shift: With the adoption of these strategies, Richardson rejected a total emphasis in the future on the income-transfer approach to alleviating poverty in favor of extending more and better services to the poor.

The Administration has touted the income approach—give the poor money instead of services—since President Nixon delivered his message on welfare reform in August 1969.

Richardson is not opposed to the income approach, but believes that in the future the federal government must strike a balance between providing income and services to the most dependent segments of society.

The Johnson Administration, in its "war on poverty," advocated expanding services to the poor,

Laurence E. Lynn, Jr.

and it pushed creation of the Office of Economic Opportunity (OEO) for this purpose. The OEO has fallen on hard times during the Nixon Administration, partly because of its service-rendering orientation.

Congress: In a number of major pieces of legislation already put forward, the Administration has sought to target the bulk of the resources on the neediest people.

HEW's success in pushing this line on Capitol Hill has been strictly limited, and for this reason Richardson blasted congressional Democrats Nov. 2 in his sharpest public criticism of Members of Congress since he took over HEW.

In a statement that he penned in longhand moments before a news conference, Richardson said: "I am sick of hearing this Administration attacked for lack of sufficient concern for the poor and disadvantaged. Right at this moment we are engaged on three fronts in fighting to keep resources targeted on the needs of the disadvantaged."

Richardson identified these fronts as the Administration's emergency school aid bill (HR 2266, S 195), its higher education bill (HR 5191, S 1123) and the day-care provision of its welfare-reform bill.

He said: "Our liberal opponents, self-styled in each case, are advocating alternatives that could only have the effect of diluting scarce resources."

Congressional Democrats are intent on exacting legislation that provides higher education aid and child-care opportunities tó the middle class. Rep. John Brademas, D-Ind., stated their position during public hearings on higher education legislation.

Brademas said: "In all candor, I resent being told I have to trade off middle-income bodies against low-income bodies. What I don't understand is why we can't help both."

Despite Richardson's harsh words, he recognizes that his goal of better targeting HEW's resources cannot go forward without congressional support.

"In the end, the usefulness of trying to identify and be guided by specific strategies depends upon our success in communicating persuasively to Congress why we did what we did," he said.

THE PROCESS

HEW's conduct of its budget exercise this year was different from past years. New actors with new powers were on stage, front-and-center.

The offices of the assistant secretary-comptroller and assistant secretary for planning and evaluation shared, at Richardson's behest, the responsibility for drawing the budget document.

In years past, the comptroller's office dominated the process and made most of the substantive decisions on the budget under the guidance of the Secretary.

The process previously culminated at HEW when the Secretary, in torturously long meetings, went through the budget line-by-line and made what one ranking department official described as largely "seat-of-the-pants decisions."

In this process, the program operators held the upper hand. The Secretary was not equipped with the information necessary to probe lofty claims of program chiefs and hence he was a reactive force in weighing requests.

Richardson's fiscal 1972 budget was in large part of this character because he became HEW Secretary late in the cycle and had little time to closely study funding requests.

This year, Richardson went into the budget process equipped with information designed to relate the programs in a fashion that would give him a better idea of what he was buying.

Budget Office: Over the years, HEW's comptroller has enjoyed immense power over the department purse-strings.

An overriding reason was James F. Kelly, a forceful personality and respected budgeteer, who held the post for 16 years until he resigned in August 1970.

In addition, HEW's budget office deals directly with other centers of power in Washington, working closely with the congressional appropriations committees

HEW's PLANNER, LAURENCE E. LYNN: DEFENSE, WELFARE AND BLUEGRASS

The influential involvement of HEW's planning staff in the making of the department budget this year is testimony to the strong will of its chief, Assistant Secretary Laurence E. Lynn Jr.

Lynn, 34, made his forceful entry into the department in June 1971 with a mandate from HEW Secretary Elliot L. Richardson to upgrade the planning capability of that far-flung bureaucracy.

Lynn and his planning staff used this mandate to produce for Richardson in the later stages of the budget development process an overview of the department from a vantage point which differs from the perspective offered by HEW's agency chiefs.

The overview and subsequent memoranda identified department-wide goals which Richardson could adopt in drawing HEW's fiscal 1973 budget and the actual funding decisions that would be required to implement them. Richardson's receptiveness to this approach identified Lynn as a force the department's program operators must reckon with in the future.

The degree of Lynn's impact was enhanced by the relationship that developed between him and James B. Cardwell, HEW's comptroller and the key day-to-day actor in the development of the department's budget.

Of Cardwell, Lynn said: "He was a strong and consistent supporter of our approach to planning. A man with a narrower view of the comptroller's role could have made it difficult or impossible to do what we did."

Lynn had made a reputation as an incisive analyst of policy issues in the defense and national security sectors before he came to HEW.

He served as deputy assistant secretary of Defense (systems analysis) in the Johnson Administration and was regarded as one of former Defense Secretary (1961-68) Robert S. McNamara's most effective "whiz kids."

Lynn moved from the Defense Department to the National Security Council in 1969, where he served as director of program analysis under Henry A. Kissinger.

Facelifting: Since coming to HEW, Lynn, an economist (Yale, Ph.D., 1966), has transformed the office he heads into an operation that more nearly matches its description—the Secretary's arm for planning and evaluation.

Under the previous assistant secretary for planning and evaluation, Lewis H. Butler, the office was a far different place. As a confidant of former HEW Secretary (1969-70) Robert H. Finch, Butler enjoyed tremendous influence on questions of policy, but he never professed to be a planner.

He was not a manager either. Butler, a lawyer, liked best to immerse himself personally in individual policy issues and resolve them. Thus, he let his staff go its own way. Without precise direction, the planning and evaluation office was a more free-wheeling operation than it now is under Lynn.

Lynn was lured to HEW by the prospect of returning to the Washington world of public policy making, particularly in Richardson's department. Lynn has made a number of staff changes that reflect his interest in well-directed planning and analysis.

"Lynn wanted to build a well-coordinated team; the team does the work under his direction," said his executive assistant, Glenn D. Frederick. At HEW, Lynn is viewed as a task-master who demands first-rate work from his staff.

Philosophy: During the development of HEW's fiscal 1973 budget Lynn strongly urged emphasizing an income strategy as the best means of alleviating poverty.

Under this approach—one the Administration has promoted since introducing its welfare-reform legislation (HR 1) two years ago—the poor are given cash, instead of more government services, to improve their lot.

Lynn consistently pointed out that HEW faced a choice between a department strategy that would further emphasizing improving the poor's position in society by increasing direct payments to them and a strategy that would further expand HEW-supported services.

Richardson decided that the Administration's welfare-reform bill would move HEW far enough in the direction of an income approach for the present. As a result, he elected to emphasize in HEW's fiscal 1973 budget an improvement in services to the poor and other dependent segments of society.

Program Meetings: HEW's agency chiefs first did substantive business with Lynn in meetings Richardson held in early September to air issues surrounding the budget.

The Secretary, flanked by Cardwell and Lynn, examined their funding requests and asked the agency chiefs to defend them in the light of competing demands on HEW resources. The atmosphere grew tense at times.

Education—For example, the session with the Office of Education surfaced a sharp conflict between the Secretary's office and the Office of Education commissioner, Sidney P. Marland Jr., over how to spend new education dollars. In one instance, Lynn and Cardwell criticized Marland's proposal to expand OE's career-education program as not well-enough developed to justify expenditure of substantial new funds.

John R. Ottina, OE's deputy commissioner for development, conceded in an interview that the analysis of education programs turned out by Lynn's office "had a great deal of influence" in developing the budget.

Noncontrollables—The influence of Lynn's office in the and with OMB.

By and large, HEW's planning operation remains out of the mainstream of political life.

Kelly, who left HEW to become vice president for administrative affairs at Georgetown University, never worked particularly closely with department planners although he says now he never opposed their work.

Kelly was succeeded by his deputy, James B. Cardwell, a career bureaucrat with a personal style far less domineering than that of his predecessor and fewer qualms about working with HEW's planning office.

LYNN'S ARRIVAL

Cardwell was not publicly taken aback last June when Richardson brought on Lynn as assistant secretary for planning and evaluation. From the outset, Lynn argued forcefully for the integration of the budget and planning processes.

"My belief in the need to integrate these processes is based upon a number of assumptions," Lynn said in a memorandum to Richardson less than a month after his arrival.

"The Secretary of this department is a unique actor. His position gives him a different perspective from anyone else in HEW—he must look at all of the department, not just the pieces.

"Thus he ought to have a complete picture of HEW programs, policies, resource allocations, their relationships and alternatives. In other words, he ought to see this information displayed by agency, by substantive area so that the trade-offs he must consider are explicit."

Richardson bought the idea of

budget process as it related to the department's noncontrollable expenditures was more limited, partly because the dollars are not as easily shifted from program to program. One ranking planning official said: "We did not make huge inroads but we did have an impact."

Among noncontrollable proposals that were aired, Lynn, along with other HEW officials including Under Secretary John G. Veneman, successfully opposed the inclusion of funds for another across-the-board social security benefit increase as suggested by the Social Security Administration.

Lynn and his staff instead favored using any new funds to provide, at an earlier date, increased aid to the adult welfare categories as authorized in HR 1 and inclusion of prescription-drug coverage under medicare. No decision has been made on these suggestions.

Background: Lynn was born and grew up in California. Tall and thin, he is an unassuming dresser and wears his hair very long.

Divorced and the father of four children, Lynn resides alone in a home he bought in Northwest Washington. He relaxes with a banjo, often arising early and practicing for an hour before heading to work.

A bumper sticker on his green hard-top reflects his preference in music. It reads: "Blue Grass Music Will Make You Free." His favorite weekend haunt is Ruby's Restaurant, a truck stop 30 miles south of Washington which features Cliff Waldron's music group and the Cameron Street Grass Band.

While at the Defense Department, Lynn was largely responsible for building the conceptual framework used by the Pentagon to persuade Congress of the need to upgrade the nation's strategic mobility through construction of the C5-A aircraft.

One of Lynn's former Defense colleagues said: "There probably would never have been a C5-A without the conceptual ground that Larry laid for the need for such a craft. But the later screw-ups, the cost overruns, were not of Lynn's making. They were a procurement problem."

At the National Security Council, Lynn directed studies on policy was a key force in developing the U.S. approach to the Strategic Arms Limitation Talks (SALT) with the Soviet Union.

Lynn left Washington for Stanford University in 1970 to teach for one semester a course he suggested and developed on decision making in the public sector.

He returned last June after Richardson, at the suggestion of Butler, personally recruited him to be assistant secretary for planning and evaluation. As under secretary of State, Richardson had come to respect Lynn's work at the National Security Council, particularly as it related to the SALT talks.

Lynn's office is at work developing HEW's program and budget integrating the two processes for the development of the fiscal 1973 budget in mid-July.

At that point, Lynn said in an interview, his office faced a tough choice because budget deadlines already were close by.

Recalling the time, he said, "We could have undertaken to provide the Secretary with a complete picture of HEW or just a view of one agency.

"I finally decided that we should undertake a complete look at the department, but because of the time constraints, compress it. I thought the time would never be better."

Program Memos: Starting in mid-July and working through August, Lynn's staff developed an overview memorandum for Richardson and four program memos which dealt with health, education, social services and income maintenance.

The first overview memo, dated Aug. 25, set out for Richardson a breakdown of how HEW spends its money, the key issues before the department and a number of strategy alternatives.

The memo noted among other things the HEW planners' estimate projecting a department budget of $117 billion by fiscal 1977 with health and income maintenance costs accounting for $105.7 billion, education, $6.1 billion and social services, $5.3 billion.

The four later memos dealt in greater detail with the issues facing HEW's programs. The education memo, written by P. Michael Timpane, director of education planning, surfaced conflicting views between the planning office and options for fiscal 1974. He hopes his office will have a greater impact on next year's budget. Lynn and the Secretary also expect that HEW's agencies will become more intensely involved in the planning process in the future, to avoid the notion that it is being imposed from above.

the Office of Education on which programs should be expanded in fiscal 1973.

Meetings: Richardson used the program memos as discussion papers in a series of four meetings with HEW agency heads in early September. In the sessions, Richardson, flanked by Cardwell and Lynn, asked the agency heads to justify their budget requests.

One top-ranking HEW official who attended the sessions said the agency heads were "confronted by analysts and planners who were thinking of trade-offs. Trade-off became a byword around here."

Lynn said the meetings were part of a plan to apply Richardson's leadership more directly on the discretionary budget decisions that the department must make every fiscal year.

The program meetings underlined what the Secretary's office felt was the lack of concrete goals on the part of HEW's program managers. The agencies "have done little or no strategic thinking, choosing instead to advocate 'good things,'" Lynn said in a memo following the meetings.

Nevertheless, most participants in the sessions considered them as a productive first step in providing Richardson a framework in which he can discuss trade-offs between HEW's programs.

Beyond that, the meetings provided Richardson an opportunity to focus on questions of HEW's future and to select program strategies with which to face it.

Strategies: "Three fundamental department goals have survived our recent series of memoranda and meetings," Lynn told Richardson Sept. 16 in an "action memorandum."

"These are equalization, nondependency and institutional reform," Lynn said.

Richardson decided to embrace two of the three strategies—reducing human dependency and reforming institutions although the flavor of the third is not lost in HEW's fiscal 1973 budget.

Lynn's action memo detailed future program directions that seemed the most appropriate.

Reducing Dependency—Emphasizing the reduction of dependency, the memo suggested that funds be increased or retargeted in the right-to-read, dropout prevention, bilingual education and education-for-the-handicapped programs.

In health, based on the nondependency strategy, HEW would expand or retarget maternal and child health, family planning, community mental health centers, drug abuse and migrant health programs.

In social services, the reduction of dependency translated in Lynn's eyes to mean an expansion of its aging, vocational-rehabilitation and child-development programs.

Institutional Reform—The adoption of a strategy to reform HEW and the institutions with which it deals has implications beyond the department's programs.

To a significant degree, the strategy represents a further manifestation of the Administration's interest in consolidating federal grant programs and revenue sharing.

HEW's institutional reform strategy will attempt to reform the department through grant consolidation and integration of its service programs. HEW will also work with state and local government agencies in an effort to improve their capacities to deal with HEW's clientele.

Richardson points to the new approach to social services delivery that President Nixon outlined in his State of the Union address as one element in an institutional reform strategy.

Mr. Nixon said the proposal "would strengthen state and local planning and administrative capacities, allow for the transfer of funds among various HEW programs and permit the waiver of certain cumbersome federal requirements."

In terms of programs, the strategy would mean a targeting of interest subsidy construction funds on community colleges; increased funding to strengthen state education department capabilities, an expansion of education renewal and career education programs and a levelling of the budgets of small categorical aid programs.

The changes in HEW's health sphere would include a strengthening of grants management in research; improvement in the management of medicaid and medicare and a closure of gaps in coverage;

better control of the quality and prices of hospital care and possibly pursuit of a special revenue-sharing proposal for health.

Less Impact: HEW's decision makers, reflecting the political difficulties inherent in cutting budgets, were less precise in coming down hard on programs that do not relate to the strategies.

Richardson said: "It was a matter of selecting things for increases and leaving others with smaller increases or leaving them substantially level. . . . Had we followed a different course the result presumably would have been an emphasis on programs other than those we did choose."

In general, HEW programs that suffered in the fiscal 1973 budget process were programs already unpopular with the Administration and susceptible to cuts.

Examples of such programs would include federal impact aid to school districts—a favorite on Capitol Hill that Members have made impervious to cuts—higher-education institutional aid and school and hospital construction funding.

Impact of Freeze: As the year progressed, Richardson found that he had more discretionary funds than he had anticipated, primarily because of the wage and price controls imposed by the President Aug. 15, 1971, and the cutbacks some states have made in the level of their welfare payments.

HEW's budget office is projecting that as a result of the controls imposed on physicians' fees and hospital bills, the department will realize a savings of $393 million in the operation of medicare in fiscal 1973.

With the state cutbacks in welfare expenditures—principally in the aid to families with dependent children category—and medicaid savings through price controls, HEW estimates it will save $1.3 billion compared with its earlier projections.

The Office of Management and Budget based its Aug. 9, 1971, ceiling on HEW's fiscal 1973 budget on estimates that were calculated before the wage-price freeze was imposed and before the extent of state welfare cutbacks was known.

As a result, HEW was able to take the projected savings realized from noncontrollable expenditures and use them to expand programs over which Richardson maintained a greater degree of discretion.

Wilford J. Forbush, the director of HEW's budget division, said: "The thing that saved us this year was the economic stabilization program."

Forbush is credited by his colleagues with devising the plan that provided HEW with a financial cushion.

From the onset, one department official said, OMB approved shifting of HEW's funds under its overall budget ceiling.

STRATEGIES' IMPACT

From year to year, HEW's 270 programs fare well or poorly in the budget process depending on vagaries that are only partially under the department's control.

This year, for example, a number of programs profited from their relevancy to Richardson's newly articulated strategies, but that was only the first of several tests.

The OMB, second hurdle in the budget process, more often than not shaves even what HEW considers austere requests. This year was no exception.

Title I: The compensatory education program, authorized under Title I of the Elementary and Secondary Education Act (79 Stat 27), is a prime example of a program that fared well at HEW but lost out at the White House.

Title I is the principal federal thrust to upgrade the education of disadvantaged children. Of the estimated 50 million children enrolled in public and private schools, 7.9 million participate in Title I programs.

The Administration never has been convinced that the program effectively serves the poor. This skepticism has been reflected in the fact that the Administration's requests have remained at $1.5 billion for the past two years.

For fiscal 1973, however, HEW requested a $100-million increase over the current Title I appropriation. The proposal was based largely on Richardson's belief that Title I is a vital link to the advancement of his strategies of nondependency and institutional reform.

Timpane, HEW's director of education planning, strongly advocated an expansion of Title I. He argued in a memorandum, addressed to Richardson and endorsed by Lynn, that "Title I should expand in fiscal 1973 and thereafter, even if other priority concerns must advance more slowly and risks must be taken in cutting popular but low-priority programs."

Timpane said that experience under Title I programming is "just beginning to show the way to successful remediation for poor children'"

In California, for example, where Title I programs are run on a basis of $300 per child—a much higher funding level than in most states—a Rand Corp. evaluation has revealed pupil improvements that one HEW official described as "tantalizing."

OE Position—The Office of Education asked for no increase in the Title I budget and, in fact, Commissioner Sidney P. Marland Jr. later argued against one in a rejoinder to Timpane.

Marland said in a memo to Richardson: "Title I is already, by an overwhelming margin, our largest, single program. Any significant percentage increase in this $1.6-billion program virtually eliminates the possibility of any other new initiatives at the low budget level."

Marland stressed that he was in total agreement with Richardson's contention that the first order of HEW's business in education is redressing the impact of poverty on children. But he urged that any new funds be put in other programs that also serve the impoverished.

Marland also said that OE still has reservations about the effectiveness of Title I and, beyond that, the Administration's emergency school-aid bill (HR 2266, S 195), if enacted, would funnel the bulk of $1.5 billion in new funds into an estimated 60 per cent of the 17,000 Title I school districts.

The President's new budget, largely following OMB advice, requested no new funds for Title I. One OMB official said that "Title I is not a stand-alone program. The President's emergency school aid program has a high incidence of overlap" with Title I districts.

Marland's Thrust—One major reason for OE's standpat attitude on Title I was Marland's intent to put a portion of any new funding into what he calls an "educational renewal strategy."

Marland delivered an "interim accounting" of the strategy Nov. 16, 1971, in a speech to the Chief State School Officers' annual meeting in Louisville.

His label "interim" was based on a feeling of uncertainty about just how the strategy would fare in the assembling of HEW's fiscal 1973 budget.

Marland said the strategy called for "redirecting a good share of our discretionary funds" and concentrating them, in a "critical mass," on some 2,000 schools in an effort to use the latest techniques to upgrade the educationally disadvantaged.

Funding for the project would be drawn from discretionary funds OE has available in a number of its programs, including teacher training, dropout prevention, experimental schools, the right to read, bilingual education, and the Teacher Corps.

Lynn and Cardwell applauded the renewal concept but argued that HEW's financial commitment to it should remain small until the idea was better developed.

The renewal theme fared worse at the OMB during the first round of fiscal 1973 budgeting—one department official said it was "emasculated"—but, after an appeal by Richardson, OE recovered enough money to launch the plan.

Marland also became personally involved in turning the budget agency around on his renewal strategy. He exerted "tremendous pressure" on OMB's education examiner, James L. Blum, to allow more funds to finance the idea, one HEW official said.

Education for Handicapped: In the mind of Edwin W. Martin Jr., associate OE commissioner for education of the handicapped, his program is an outstanding example of a beneficiary of Richardson's strategy to reduce human dependency.

Based largely on an early and strong commitment from Marland, OE requested an increase of 63 per cent in fiscal 1973 funds for educating the handicapped.

Martin said in an interview: "When we hit the Secretary's office initially with our request ($184.9 million) there were a lot of questions, such as 'Is this a priority? Is a dollar spent on the handicapped better than a dollar spent on the disadvantaged?'"

"The first response was less supportive, particularly our intent to use federal assistance to states as a catalyst," Martin said. "But in the final analysis, as the non-dependency strategy came forward, it was clear that our priority increased. Our request jumped from a modest increase to more support."

HEW's planning office advocated a smaller budget increase for education for the handicapped, arguing in a memorandum that "OE has not demonstrated the need for federal support of the excess costs of education of all handicapped children, irrespective of family income or severity of handicap."

Richardson sided with OE and

HEW requested $148 million for education for the handicapped in fiscal 1973, compared with a fiscal 1972 appropriation of $115.7 million. The President's budget requests $131.1 million for the program.

Martin described HEW's fiscal 1973 budget request for his program as "a symbolic breakthrough" and he credited Marland's strong support and the nondependency strategy. "If the funds loosen up in the future we'll be in a good position to cash in based on these factors," he said.

Health: Other factors—largely political—were at least as important as the new strategies in the proposed expansion of selected health programs operated by the department.

Health programs have entered a period of great expansion at HEW, largely because of the widespread assumption that federal intervention into health affairs will greatly increase in the 1970s.

Anticipating this trend and counting on the enactment of national health-insurance legislation, HEW's planners project that the department's health expenditures will grow from $17.6 billion in fiscal 1972 to $35.6 billion by 1977.

Interim Plan—A tentative Administration plan to withhold health program funds appropriated by Congress for fiscal 1972 well illustrates the appealing politics of health.

Congress appropriated $689 billion more than the Administration requested for HEW health programs in fiscal 1972. Anticipating that OMB would not want to spend all of these funds, HEW developed and submitted to OMB an "interim funding plan" that listed programs from which appropriated monies could be withheld.

Programs affected by the proposed plan included community mental-health centers—construction funds ($9.8 million), regional medical facilities ($35 million) and biomedical research funded by the National Institute of Health ($38.7 million).

The Administration never publicly revealed the interim funding plan, but program operators disclosed its contents to their constituencies and Members of Congress, who, in turn, went to work lobbying.

Under pressure from Members of Congress, and the psychiatric and biomedical research lobbies, the OMB dropped consideration of the plan to withhold health funds in fiscal 1972.

Without mentioning the interim funding plan, HEW announced in a news release Dec. 27, 1971 that all fiscal 1972 health funds would be spent.

Abandonment of the plan was important to the affected programs, not only because it made available additional fiscal 1972 dollars, but because it forced the OMB to accept higher funding levels for fiscal 1973.

Health programs that fit most naturally under a thrust to reduce human dependency—alcoholism and drug-abuse prevention, community mental-health centers and family planning—all fared well in the budget process.

But to a large degree, these programs already had been marked for expansion by the President or Congress and for HEW to treat them differently would have been to fly in the face of political reality.

Alcoholism—Forces beyond the nondependency strategy proved profitable to the rapidly expanding alcoholism program operated by the new National Institute of Alcohol Abuse and Alcoholism.

One official in the office of Dr. Merlin K. DuVal Jr., assistant HEW secretary (health and scientific affairs), said: "When we discussed alcoholism with the OMB, nobody ever mentioned the strategies. They mentioned Sen. (Harold E.) Hughes (D-Iowa)." Hughes is chairman of the Senate Labor and Public Welfare Subcommittee on Alcoholism and Narcotics. A recovered alcoholic himself, Hughes is a powerful advocate for a massive expansion of federal efforts to combat alcoholism.

Hughes' forceful advocacy contributed to the Administration's decision to allow the expenditure of all fiscal 1972 funds—$84.6 million—appropriated for alcoholism treatment and prevention. The Administration had requested $34.6 million.

NIH—Political pressures also played a part in the shape of the budget of the National Institutes of Health (NIH).

Renewed interest in cancer research earlier had prompted talk of giving the cancer program independent status. Proposals to step up heart research provoked similar proposals to move the program outside of NIH.

"We're all influenced by outside stimuli," said Cardwell. "The cancer effort caused us to take a closer look at heart. We want to preserve the integrity of the NIH."

Cardwell was making reference

222

ASCENSION OF THE ADMINISTRATION ON AGING: POLITICAL POWER OVERCOMES ORDERLY PLANNING

When representatives of the nation's elderly citizens gathered in Washington late last year for the decennial White House Conference on Aging, they were determined to impress further upon political leaders the electoral benefits which could be reaped by appealing to their interests. They succeeded, and the strength of "senior power"—a slogan of groups representing the elderly—is reflected in the HEW Department's fiscal 1973 budget. It already has been reflected in action on Capitol Hill.

Reaction to the growing political consciousness and activism of the elderly is transforming HEW's Administration on Aging into a major social agency. AOA never has been popular within the department, but nonetheless it has suddenly found that it has big new responsibilities and a lot more money than it ever had before.

The growing importance of AOA illustrates the fact that pure politics can have as great an impact on the department's budget development as the planning exercise which HEW took its budget process through this year.

Competing for Votes: The conference on aging lasted from Nov. 28 to Dec. 3, and during that week Mr. Nixon told conference delegates that he wanted to increase the AOA's budget of $21.1 million "nearly fivefold" in fiscal 1973. Congress, by way of upping the ante, granted the increase but made it effective in fiscal 1972.

While Mr. Nixon and Sen. Edward M. Kennedy, D-Mass., were the key voices on behalf of the AOA, members of the congressional appropriations committees, in their acquiescence to the agency's financial windfall, made up the supporting cast. And virtually every Member of Congress played a part by not opposing the budget increase.

The federal decision makers were competing for the political favor of 3,400 White House conference delegates and a national constituency of 20 million Americans aged 65 and over.

The aged population increased 15.5 percent between 1960 and 1968, compared with an 11.4 percent boost for the entire population, and by 1980 there will be more than 27 million elderly persons, the Census Bureau estimates.

The over-50 population votes Republican more often than the under-50 group. In 1968, the Gallup polls showed, 47 percent of voters over 50 years old cast their ballots for Mr. Nixon; 41 percent favored Hubert H. Humphrey.

AOA's Role: The political currents sparked by the 1961 White House Conference on Aging resulted in creation of the AOA, but it has never been an overly popular agency on Capitol Hill or at HEW.

Congress traditionally has responded to pressure from lobbies representing the elderly by granting social security benefit increases. Until this year, providing services to the elderly beyond income benefits has never been very appealing politically.

From the outset at HEW, the AOA operated from a position of weakness.

Two former HEW Secretaries were critical of AOA's creation. Anthony J. Celebrezze (1962-65) testified against its creation. Another former Secretary, Wilbur J. Cohen (1968-69), criticized Congress for placing the AOA, by statute, in the Office of the Secretary.

Two years after its creation in 1965, the AOA was downgraded from an independent agency reporting to the Secretary to one of six operating programs in what is now called HEW's Social and Rehabilitation Service.

Haphazard planning accompanied the AOA's lowly status in its first years. The AOA's mandate was to serve as a federal advocate of the elderly and also as the operator of service programs. With the small budgets the agency had to work with, the functions often came in conflict.

The AOA has always been a target of the White House budget office. In fiscal 1971 and 1972, the Office of Management and Budget sliced $27 million from HEW's request for it.

In 1971, HEW's planners recognized that with the White House conference coming the politics of the aging would be running at full speed. The task of deciding how this would affect the AOA was left largely to a Cabinet-level committee on aging chaired by HEW Secretary Elliot L. Richardson.

Richardson favored a more visible advocacy role for the AOA, but he questioned the need to greatly expand the agency.

Richard G. Darman, HEW's director of interagency policy analysis, noted in a memorandum that discussed issues concerning the AOA's fiscal 1973 budget: "The political benefit of more than doubling the AOA budget will be great and at a very low cost in terms of the over-all HEW or SRS (Social and Rehabilitation Service) budget. But there is merit in preserving flexibility with regard to program content."

In essence, Darman recognized the political need to increase AOA's budget in light of the White House conference without planning precisely how the funds would be spent.

HEW measured the need to respond to the White House conference by calling for a doubling of the AOA's fiscal 1972 budget of $21.2 million. On Nov. 15, 1971 the department requested $43.2 million for AOA in fiscal 1973 in its budget submission to the OMB. OMB shaved the request but this decision was reversed after the President voiced the Administration's final position in his White House conference speech.

Congressional Action: In this politically charged environment, Kennedy opened the congressional bidding on behalf of the elderly on Nov. 30, two days after the conference was convened.

Working in close concert with Sens. Thomas F. Eagleton, D-Mo., and Charles H. Percy, R-Ill., Kennedy urged Senate approval of a bill (S 1163) authorizing creation of a nutrition program for older people.

The bill authorizes the expenditure of $100 million in fiscal 1973 and $150 million in fiscal 1974 for HEW grants to states to finance the operation of feeding and nutrition programs. If approved, it would be the largest federal service program operated exclusively for the elderly.

Although the Administration opposed the measure in earlier congressional hearings on grounds that it planned to introduce a more comprehensive proposal, no Republican Senator opposed the bill and it passed 89-0.

The timing of the Senate's consideration of the bill and the White House conference was no accident. James J. Murphy, counsel to Eagleton's Senate Labor and Public Welfare Subcommittee on Aging who is respected by Democrat and Republican Members alike, said: "We wanted to neutralize the Administration's opposition."

"We looked to the White House conference as an opportune time to move legislation on the elderly that the Administration opposed. We had several other bills we wanted to push through, but congressional committee jurisdiction questions cropped up and we ran out of time," Murphy said.

After Senate passage, the measure was forwarded to the House, and Kennedy, in a telephone call to Rep. John Brademas, D-Ind., chairman of the House subcommittee handling the legislation, urged that the measure be expedited.

Brademas and the chairman of the full Education and Labor Committee, Rep. Carl D. Perkins, D-Ky., sought immediate House consideration but Minority Leader Gerald R. Ford, R-Mich., objected on grounds that no House panel had aired the measure.

President's Speech: Two days after Kennedy's triumph on the Senate floor, Mr. Nixon addressed the White House Conference on Aging. In the space of 36 minutes, he articulated a number of significant proposals that would greatly benefit the elderly.

The AOA was a principal beneficiary of the President's efforts to capture from congressional Democrats, and particularly Kennedy, the major credit for helping the elderly.

Mr. Nixon said he would increase "the present budget of the Administration on Aging nearly five-fold—to $100 million." The President speculated that the delegates might wonder why this figure had been chosen, and he provided them with a glimpse into the emotions of the fast-moving decision-making process.

"I must say, I heard from a number of you and I heard from Arthur Flemming (conference chairman). He didn't know about the number until this morning because it was $80 million last night, and I decided, why not $100 million."

Supplemental Vote: The Senate responded the following day by approving a Kennedy amendment to a supplemental appropriations bill (HR 11955) calling for an additional $55.2 million for AOA in fiscal 1972.

The budget amendment, subsequently approved by the House, brought the funding of programs authorized under the Older Americans Act of 1969 (83 Stat 108) up to $100 million.

Although the President proposed to infuse the AOA with $100

million in fiscal 1973, rather than the current fiscal year, the White House had no real choice politically but to support the supplemental appropriation. Percy conveyed this position on the Senate floor.

HEW's position on the AOA's supplemental appropriation was "passive concurrence," said one official in the department's office of legislation.

Politics vs. Planning: The speedy action on behalf of the elderly and the AOA has catapulted the agency into big-time social programming but with no definitive plan for spending the money.

One HEW official spoke critically of the dearth of planning that accompanied the anticipated expansion of the AOA's service programs to the elderly. He said:

"Planning has to anticipate the environment in which developments are going to take place. The fact is that what has happened was very predictable. HEW should have developed long-range plans for this occurrence.

"When these things get into a political environment, the programs, not the budget cutters, win out. Presidents are politicians, not planners."

Future Directions: The bidding for the elderly's favor is by no means over. President Nixon urged Congress in his State of the Union speech to eliminate the $5.80 monthly fee now charged the elderly under Part B of medicare— a $1.5-billion item.

He also promised aggressive pursuit of a 1971 initiative, a crackdown on substandard nursing homes.

The Administration also is con-

sidering a number of other major proposals, including the expansion of medicare coverage to include prescription drugs—the largest single out-of-pocket health outlay for the elderly.

Congressional Democrats are prepared to up the ante at every turn for the over-65 population. Sens. Eagleton and Frank Church, D-Idaho, chairman of the Senate Special Committee on Aging, have summoned Flemming to appear before their committees Feb. 3 to relate how the Administration plans to implement the White House conference recommendations.

The debate that will ensue when Congress considers extending the Older Americans Act, which expires June 30, will provide another opportunity for upping the federal commitment to the elderly.

to a bill (S 1828) that President Nixon signed into law Dec. 23 to establish a greatly expanded attack against cancer.

The new law provides that the budget of the National Cancer Institute must go directly to the President. Anticipating passage of the bill, HEW sent the fiscal 1973 request of the cancer institute— $550.8 million—directly to the OMB without altering it.

The President's budget requests $430 million for the cancer institute in fiscal 1973. The institute is currently operating with an appropriation of $337.5 million.

Heart—HEW's response to the perceived need to elevate the place of the National Heart and Lung

Institute at NIH resulted in a department budget request for fiscal 1973 of $243.8 million.

The President requested $254.4 million for fiscal 1973, compared with a current appropriation of $232.1 million.

One of the pressures at work for expanding the federal attack against heart disease is the report of a government-sponsored task force formed by the director of the heart institute, Dr. Theodore Cooper.

The task force recommended Dec. 9, 1971 a massive research program on heart disease, the nation's No. 1 killer. Cooper maintained at that time that the task force's report "is not a counter

balance or a gimmick to compete with the cancer attack program."

Beyond the report of the task force, there are firm indications that the federal fight against heart disease is going to become a far more expensive proposition than the Administration's fiscal 1973 budget allows.

Congressional consideration of the heart research program is likely to dominate Capitol Hill's attention to biomedicine during election year 1972, and Rep. Paul G. Rogers, D-Fla., is prepared to lead the fight.

Rogers, chairman of the House Interstate and Foreign Commerce Subcommittee on Public Health and Environment, is preparing a bill that would likely lead to significantly increased expenditures for research on heart and lung diseases.

Rogers' subcommittee has jurisdiction over NIH and it was largely through his influence that the cancer institute was kept within NIH rather than being made an independent agency.

Rogers said in an interview that his heart initiative is a "rather direct ruboff" from the congressional consideration of the cancer issue.

Rogers said he expects his heart-research legislation to lead to funding that is substantially higher than what the Administration is requesting for the heart and lung institute in fiscal 1973.

Relevancy: Throughout the budget process a continuing debate occupied the department's health officials over the relevancy of their programs to Richardson's strategies.

Assistant Secretary DeVal took the position, for example, that all health programs relate to the reduction of human dependency.

But Lynn's planning and evaluation staff viewed health programs in a more specific and limited context. In essence, his staff maintained that nontargeted biomedical research should not be expanded when measured against an emphasis on reducing human dependency.

In fact, all of the strategy alternatives that Richardson considered during the course of developing the budget called either for a reduction or a leveling off of biomedical research expenditures.

NIH, naturally, responded to the selected strategies with misgivings. But one health budget officer in the Secretary's office said that the agency was not hurt in fiscal 1973 by the strategies.

Like many of the agencies, the framework of NIH's fiscal 1973 budget was largely in place before the Secretary's planning exercise got moving.

In one meeting at which Lynn and his staff explained the strategies, Dr. T. J. Kennedy Jr., associate NIH director (program, planning and evaluation), questioned whether the strategies could be applied to the budget decisions NIH would have to make.

Kennedy's attitude toward the planning initiative is not shared by all officials at NIH.

Others are less skeptical, but they still are uncertain about how the agency will fare in the long run under the Richardson approach.

NIH Director Robert Q. Marston and Stuart H. Altman, deputy assistant HEW secretary (health planning and analysis), argued at a management meeting Jan. 13 over the extent to which NIH is cooperating with the planners. Richardson sat in on the debate but remained silent.

One NIH official, who declined to speak for attribution, said the attitude of HEW's planners is "away from biomedical research and toward 'let's take care of the patient.' NIH has always fared poorly in the executive branch. It fares poorly in this department because it has a very large share of the controllable dollars."

He said that for the most part "outside forces are controlling NIH's budget through their representation to the Congress. I don't see how Flood and Magnuson will understand these nondependency and institutional reform strategies, particularly if they work to the detriment of NIH."

(Rep. Daniel J. Flood, D-Pa., is chairman of the House Appropriations Subcommittee on Labor-HEW and Sen. Warren G. Magnuson, D-Wash., is chairman of the counterpart Senate subcommittee.)

FDA: The Food and Drug Administration was a big winner in the fiscal 1973 budget sweepstakes as played at HEW and at the OMB, but Richardson's strategies had little to do with that. The agency profited largely from the Administration's intention to respond—particularly in an election year—to the consumer movement.

HEW estimates that 38 cents of every $1 spent by consumers goes for products regulated in some way by the FDA. Yet, the agency long has lacked the manpower to cope with its mandate. FDA's fiscal 1972 budget—$110.8 million—is less than one-tenth of one percent of the sales of FDA-regulated industries.

Richardson's executive assistant, G. Marshall Moriarty, sent a short note to HEW's budget office last spring saying that the Secretary was concerned about the level of the FDA budget and wanted to increase it.

Richardson's concern with FDA was stimulated by the continuing controversies that swirl about the agency when products whose manufacture it regulates must be recalled because they are found contaminated.

In the latest incident, which generated a great deal of publicity, soups and other canned products packed by Bon Vivant Soups Inc.

of Newark, N. J., were removed from the market in August 1971 after botulism, a deadly poison, was detected in vichyssoise which the company had processed.

Shortly after the seizure of the soup, FDA Commissioner Charles C. Edwards told the House Government Operations' Intergovernmental Relations Subcommittee that his inspectors visit food plants an average of only once every six years.

The FDA has 210 full-time food inspectors to police the products of 60,000 food companies. Edwards told Congress that his agency needs five to six times its present manpower and budget in order to do its inspection job properly.

Responding to this need, the Administration is asking for a fiscal 1973 budget of $188 million, a 70 percent increase over the agency's appropriation of $110.8 million for fiscal 1972. The bulk of the new money will be used to add 2,600 new positions in FDA's work force, which now totals 5,500.

Increasing its capacity to inspect food products is only one of the uses to which FDA plans to put its new money, and more frequent inspection is not really the agency's most pressing need at that.

FDA's consumer product-safety bureau will reap the greatest number of new dollars in fiscal 1973— $29.4 million—if Congress goes along with the Administration's request.

The rationale for the increased funding is two-fold: to expand FDA's capacity to inspect products and enforce safety standards and to attempt to thwart congressional efforts to create a new independent consumer product-safety commission.

One ranking HEW budget official said the more generous level of funding was an attempt on the part of the Administration to "head off at the pass" advocates of a new product-safety agency by beefing up FDA.

The Administration also has earmarked funds to implement proposed legislation that would expand federal inspection of fish and fishery products (HR 3666, S 700) and regulate medical devices (HR 12316, S 3028).

Social Services: HEW also is planning to use its new budget approach to make states account more strictly for the federal funds they spend for administrative, social services and personnel training costs in welfare programs.

In effect, the initiative is HEW's latest attempt to get a handle on an open-ended appropriation that Congress has refused to close.

In the last two years, the Administration has sought legislation to limit matching grants to 110 percent of the previous year's outlay. At present, appropriations are open-ended to the extent that the federal government is committed to match whatever level of funds the states are willing to commit from their own resources.

Under pressure from Governors and state welfare directors—particularly from the big industrial states where increased welfare expenditures have had the most severe political consequences— Congress has rejected the request each time.

Since HEW's initial effort to close the open-ended appropriation for social services and admin-istrative expenses, federal outlays have increased from $842 million in fiscal 1971 to an estimated $1,363 million in fiscal 1972.

By requiring states to document the way they spend federal funds under what is now loosely described as social services, HEW expects to save $184 million in fiscal 1973.

A more favorable matching rate (75-25) is available to states for social services expenditures as opposed to welfare administrative costs (50-50).

HEW officials believe that the states hardest hit by increased welfare costs have lumped administrative expenses in with social services to take advantage of the more favorable matching rate.

To date, HEW has been lax in monitoring the way states spend the money, largely because of a lack of manpower. To more effectively police the problem, the Administration is asking for 427 new positions at HEW. The tougher accounting method was largely developed by Tom Joe, an assistant to HEW Under Secretary John G. Veneman.

Rehabilitation—Richardson's nondependency strategy hit the department's vocational rehabilitation program in two ways. One resulted in an HEW request for substantially more dollars and a second communicated the Secretary's intent that the program concentrate on rehabilitating welfare recipients.

The President's budget requests $675.8 million for vocational rehabilitation in fiscal 1973, an increase of $58 million over 1972 levels. HEW had asked for $710 million in fiscal 1973.

The program, a favorite on Capitol Hill, has grown ten-fold over the last decade, but it has largely served a population that, while needy, is not impoverished. Welfare recipients represented 14 percent of the program's 291,272 rehabilitants in fiscal 1971.

One HEW official said: "There were pressures from state vocational rehabilitation agencies to maintain the current kind of program. The nondependency strategy and its emphasis on rehabilitating welfare recipients tips the scales toward a new kind of vocational rehabilitation program."

Edward Newman, commissioner of the Rehabilitation Services Administration, maintains that his program for the welfare population is constantly improving, and Richardson's thrust provides impetus to that movement.

But, unlike some of HEW's program operators, Newman did not argue that Richardson's nondependency strategy lacked impact on the level of fiscal 1973 budget requests. "If you're a loser under the strategies, it's rhetoric, if you're a winner, it's great," he said.

PLANNING'S UTILITY

In the course of their work on HEW's fiscal 1973 budget, Lynn and his planning staff learned anew the hazards of planning for the future in a department whose goals and policies are constantly changing.

Due largely to the size and complexity of HEW, the need to make limited resources does not end with the completion of the budget cycle.

John M. Seidl, deputy assistant

HEW secretary (program systems), observed in a paper entitled, Planning in HEW: A Month of Order and a Year of Chaos:

"Since the conclusion of the planning meetings and the Secretary's decisions, a number of events have taken place which call into question the necessity, utility and structure of our planning process. In fact, the problems ... raise again the question: Is planning possible in HEW?"

Seidl's treatise was used Dec. 1-2, 1971 as a discussion paper for a meeting Richardson held at Camp David, Md., with the department's agency chiefs and other top officials.

Among problems Seidl said frustrate efforts to plan rationally was the introduction of $9 billion worth of fiscal 1973 congressional and departmental initiatives into the picture after the September planning meetings Richardson held.

Of the $9 billion, about half involved Social Security Administration proposals that were considered before the White House Conference on Aging.

The Social Security Administration had advanced none of these proposals during the course of HEW's regular planning exercise. A number of social security proposals were aired within a Domestic Council committee on aging.

HEW's planners attribute the lack of Social Security's involvement to a streak of independence that runs through the agency and its own capability to plan.

Lynn said: "SSA has easily the most competent research and analysis staff of HEW's agencies. It's fair to say that, because of the

quality of the operation, the Secretary's office has not been able to lay a hand on SSA."

Master Calendar: To better cope with the chaos Seidl identified, HEW's planners have developed a master calendar that identifies key dates in the process which leads ultimately to the submission of the department's budget to the OMB.

The calendar would be a key tool in carrying out Richardson's intent to institutionalize the role of his planning office in the budget process.

The first deadline on the calendar, Feb. 15, is the target date for completion of a memo which will provide strategic and fiscal guidance to the agencies for fiscal 1974-78.

The document, which HEW calls its "planning guidance memorandum," is largely a product of Lynn's operation, but the offices of legislation and budget also contribute to it.

In essence, the memo seeks to guide HEW's agencies in the directions Richardson wants to see them move before they get down to the business of developing their individual budgets.

This early imposition of secretarial guidance should give Richardson a firmer grip on the future directions of HEW and perhaps make possible more explicit trade-offs between the department's programs.

"I hope this will be possible," Richardson said, "but of course the question of whether the program has a high enough priority to be increased significantly is a question on a rather different footing than whether another program is such a low priority that it ought to be decreased.

"It's difficult in the range of most of the things that we do to identify things that we not only feel should be cut back but which offer any realistic opportunity for actually cutting back."

Lynn, meanwhile, hopes to see a resurgence in the influence of planning as it relates to tough policy judgments that federal departments must make every day.

He said his counterparts at the Labor and Interior Departments are "intensely curious about what we're doing."

"They are eager to upgrade their own planning processes," he said. "What may be happening is a revival of planning in a more realistic framework" than the Johnson Administration efforts to apply to government generally the Planning, Programming, Budgeting System (PPBS) developed in the early 1960s by the Defense Department.

Nevertheless, Richardson and Lynn clearly recognize that in the end the analysis to which their staffs subject budget requests is only a part of the process, and that politics is perhaps a more important element.

Richardson said: "It's important to have fully and clearly in view the limitations of a purely rational process for allocating resources. What we need to do in substance is to make the decision process—the difficult choices among competing claims—as conscious and articulate as possible attitudes, values must have ultimate and controlling weight.

"It is legitimate, therefore, that political process in the broad sense should make itself felt in our own budget process as it inevitably will in the congressional appropriations processes."

Community development proposal pits President's influence against established lobbies   *William Lilley III*

One of four Nixon Administration proposals designed to reshape radically the executive branch has a chance of enactment before the President's first term ends.

It would merge significant elements of the Transportation and Agriculture Departments, along with other agencies and programs, into the HUD Department—to create a giant Department of Community Development.

Strong rhetoric has surrounded the reorganization proposals. The New American Revolution encompassed two of the "six great goals" set by Mr. Nixon in his January 1971 State of the Union address, and was designed, he said then, to return "power to the people."

Rhetoric vs. Action: The approaching action on the community development proposal is in many ways a dramatic test of the Nixon Administration—its commitment to its programs, its credibility with Congress, its ability to get things done in Washington.

On Capitol Hill, influential Republicans and Democrats, too, are viewing Mr. Nixon's performance on the issue as a measure of how much belief to place in his Administration's famous dictum to "watch what we do and not what we say."

Rhetoric has exceeded action to date.

The Administration has won two important allies in the Democratic chairmen of the House and Senate Government Operations subcommittees which have jurisdiction over the reorganization proposals.

But that is not enough to assure passage, by any means. Other powerful committee chairmen in Congress, as well as two of Washington's most powerful lobbies—the farm lobby and the highway lobby—are firmly opposed to the change.

It is with these interests that the Administration must deal if it is to succeed. But negotiations have not even begun.

Still Committed: Nonetheless, the President reaffirmed his commitment to reorganization in his Sept. 9, 1971 address to a joint session of Congress.

His closest advisers insist he means it.

"Executive reorganization is very top priority," said George P. Shultz, former director of the Office of Management and Budget.

"The President wants this done. He is always asking about how it is moving ahead. It is just very important to him."

Former Treasury Secretary John B. Connally said: "To me, reorganization of the executive branch holds as much promise of being responsive to the needs of this country as anything that could be done.

"The Administration just feels terribly strong about it."

Connally said that he was "very anxious to get back to reorganization," and that he intends "to put a lot more time in on it."

Connally and Shultz were the Administration's lead-off witnesses when House Government

Operations Committee Chairman Chet Holifield, D-Calif., held hearings on the plan.

Reorganization Test: Holifield and Sen. Abraham A. Ribicoff, D-Conn., chairman of the Senate Government Operations Subcommittee on Executive Reorganization, have decided to tackle the community development bill (HR 6962) before the other three reorganizations because they believe that it has the best chance of approval. If it should fail, they say, reorganization is dead for the 92nd Congress.

But should it succeed, then the prospects would be excellent for action on the bills to create a Natural Resources Department (HR 6959) and a Human Resources Department (HR 6961). At present, there is no inclination in Congress to move on the controversial Economic Affairs Department (HR 6960); that proposal, for all purposes, is dead.

History attests to the difficulty of creating new Cabinet-level departments. Only two—Transportation and HUD—have been established in the past 18 years, and those by President Johnson at a time when he was enjoying large Democratic majorities in Congress. And those two were not created without months of persuasion and compromise.

Community Development Challenge: Creating a Department of Community Development will require the most adroit and persistent politicking.

The President has proposed to

230 consolidate into HUD the Federal Highway Administration and the Urban Mass Transportation Administration from the Transportation Department, the Farmers Home Agriculture, and the Rural Electrification Administration from Agriculture, the Economic Development Administration and five regional commissions from Commerce, the community action program from the Office of Economic Opportunity and the Appalachian Regional· Commission. Other minor programs also would be included.

The most important transfers are Transportation's highway program and Agriculture's rural development programs. Together, they have fiscal 1971 budget authority totaling about $8 billion, more than twice the total of all of HUD's programs.

Along with the money go powerful constituencies—the farm and highway lobbies—which believe the transfers would give their political enemies control over their economic interests.

As the highway lobby sees it, residents of the inner city, HUD's principal clients, have been the major opponents of highway development. The farm lobby has watched the big cities, with their growing political power, take an increasingly large bite of the federal budget, at the expense, in its view, of rural development.

Taking the Heat: It is a stroke of luck for Mr. Nixon that Ribicoff and Holifield are handling the bill in Congress.

Both men are outspoken supporters of the reorganization, and each is prepared to deal with the lobbies which oppose it. Of the

highway transfer, Ribicoff said: "I don't mind the heat from the lobbies when something is right." And Holifield said: "I've handled every reorganization bill since 1949. I'm used to the heat; it doesn't bother me."

Although both Ribicoff and Holifield are ready to go to bat for the Administration's plan, both say they will need help in negotiating with the highway and farm interests and with the congressional committees which service them.

Help has not yet come, and Ribicoff says, "It is often the case with things the Administration promulgates. They throw them on the table with lots of fanfare and then walk away from them.

"Already their performance is par for the course. They are not systematically working with Congress and the interest groups. Down the line with their proposals, it has been the same story."

Working the Lobbies: Although the Administration fielded a top-flight array of witnesses for Holifield, the White House has not yet begun the business of behind-the-scenes persuasion that will be necessary if the plan is to succeed.

White House lobbyist Richard K. Cook said Administration officials have not yet been given their lobbying assignments for the plan, although many of the affected interest groups and congressional committee chairmen are openly hostile to the new department.

Thus, little has been done to dispel the impression, prevalent among some in Washington, that the reorganization proposals were made essentially as a political publicity stunt.

"We have seen these proposals as fraught with so many fights that they can go only one way—down," said Ralph L. Tabor, top lobbyist for the National Association of Counties. "We haven't considered taking positions on the proposals because we've seen them as a political thing for 1972—too far out and not politically realistic. They were never meant to be passed."

NACO's position should be cause for concern at the White House. Helping local governments is one major reason for establishing a new Department of Community Development. But NACO, usually a supporter of the Administration, is indifferent if not openly hostile; the White House now can look for strong support only to the nation's mayors.

PROPOSAL

Experts in the theory and practice of government have hailed the community development proposal as bold and progressive.

Witnesses from the National Academy of Public Administration and from major universities praised the idea during overview hearings Holifield held in June and July of 1971 to review the scope of all the reorganization proposals.

The academic community—not often a supporter of Mr. Nixon—was joined in its praise by prominent Democrats who had served in President Johnson's Administration.

But the community development plan, like most other reorganizations, has little political appeal, and no amount of presidential rhetoric is likely to generate much grass-roots support. Thus, despite the support of public-administration theorists, the key to success lies in dealing with what author S. Douglass Cater Jr., special assistant to President Johnson from 1965 to 1968, calls the "subgovernments" of Washington—the parochial but powerful economic-interest groups.

Democrats: Praise came during the Holifield hearings from the two leading reorganization specialists of the Johnson Administration: Joseph A. Califano Jr. and Ben W. Heineman.

Califano, a special assistant to Mr. Johnson from 1965 to 1969, managed the negotiations that led to creation of the Transportation Department in 1966. Heineman, president of Northwest Industries Inc., chaired three major reorganization task forces for Mr. Johnson.

Heineman told the Holifield committee that "there is great similarity" between Mr. Nixon's community development plan and one he had recommended to Mr. Johnson. Califano said the reorganization made "abundant good sense" and was "not a partisan issue."

Holifield asked Califano about the impact the transfers would have on transportation programs, and Califano replied: "I agree with the move the President has proposed in this area."

Helping Locals—Califano repeatedly stressed his view that reorganization was desperately needed to aid local governments now "at a loss to find the federal programs they need to help them serve their citizens." Consolidating development programs, he said, would greatly assist "city governments attempting to put together a coherent plan of action."

Federal Czar—City development programs had become so scattered throughout the federal government, Califano told the committee, that President Johnson toyed with the drastic idea of appointing "expediters in the cities, a man who would be in charge of all the federal programs going into a certain city." The President eventually abandoned the idea, fearing that the expediter would end up with more money at his disposal and more power than the mayor.

Horton: The desire to strengthen local government, cardinal to Republican ideology, was a strong motivating factor behind the community development proposal. The idea has helped win the support of many Republicans in Congress.

Among the principal proponents is Rep. Frank Horton, R-N.Y., ranking minority member of Holifield's Subcommittee on Legislation and Military Operations, which will consider the plan.

Horton says the worst aspect of fragmentation in government programs is its effect on local officials and in turn on the men and women who represent them in Congress.

"The time has come to regroup and put like functions together," Horton said. "It's absolutely essential for local officials and for Congressmen."

Horton's district, which is rapidly growing in population and industry, includes parts of the city of Rochester along with suburban and rural areas north and east of the city.

In an interview, Horton talked of the problem local officials in his district experience in dealing with the federal bureaucracy—and of the impact of their troubles on his own time and on that of his staff.

Shilling for Mayors—"What we have got to do," Horton said, "is help the mayor of Rochester, who has innumerable agencies to deal with, and in all those agencies the problems are all decided at the very top levels.

"A mayor comes to me now, from Rochester or a smaller city, and he doesn't have the expert staff like New York City does to go the proper bureaucratic route—to hustle the right kind of application and eventually get a grant.

"So the problem ends up in my office and we in turn end up shilling for the mayors. That's why we have to get one-stop service."

Preoccupation of Staff—Horton continued: "Our number-two man in the office does nothing but ramrod local applications for community development projects. Seven other staffers in the office work part-time on community development projects. And I spend more than a third of my time on this local community development business. Yet, we are supposed to be legislating.

"I don't know if my situation is any worse or better than other Members', because we are a fast-growing area and I have to do all three kinds of community development—urban, suburban and rural. I range all the way from urban renewal and model cities—city development programs—to EDA for rural development. My district just missed coming under the Appalachian Regional Commission or else I would have had them all."

Percy: Horton's views were

echoed by Sen. Charles H. Percy, R-Ill., ranking minority member of the Senate Government Operations Committee and the Senate's leading advocate of executive reorganization.

"We have got to simplify the job of the mayor," Percy said in an interview.

"The mayors' main complaint is the federal government's complexity; one mayor has to go so many places. What's a mayor's average tenure—four or five years—and he has to spend two of those just figuring out how things get done.

"The cities just have to be run better; that's the highest priority, I think. And the Department of Community Development would help a lot."

Biting the Bullet: "The President really bit the bullet on this one," Percy said in reference to the difficulties associated with transferring the highway and rural programs.

The proposed transfers already have aroused stiff opposition and resentment from affected pressure groups. And unfortunately for Mr. Nixon, he will have great difficulty rallying public opinion as a countervailing force.

The public at large just does not care much about executive organization, Califano said in an interview. "It is basically a Washington problem between the interest groups and the Hill, not a grassroots problem."

In the view of Rep. Clarence J. Brown, R-Ohio, the Administration could actually suffer, at least in terms of its relations with farm and highway interests, if the reorganization is approved.

Brown, an active member of the Government Operations Committee, said: "Chet Holifield sees this, and properly so, as *not* an issue on which you can make partisan hay. Indeed, the way the Democrats could hurt the President with the parochial interests is to pass it. The reorganization has very limited sex appeal at the nationwide level, but it has big sex appeal to the parochial interests like the highway and farm lobbies."

"Must Transfers": But White House officials say the fight must be waged—that the highway and farm rural programs are what will enable the new department to deal with *community* development, not just urban development as now is the case with HUD.

The White House reorganization coordinator, Alan L. Dean of the Office of Management and Budget, called them "must transfers." And Shultz said they would "establish the concept of goal-oriented departments which group together like functions."

Leverage—The success of the community development proposal—and probably that of the other reorganization plans as well—hinges on the highway and rural program transfers.

If the programs are moved, then the other elements of the proposed new department will follow. The narrow constituencies of the other elements also oppose the community development idea, but they are not powerful enough to resist without the farm and highway interests at their side.

Further, Holifield and Ribicoff view the community development bill as a test run for Mr. Nixon's entire reorganization agenda. The passage of this bill, they say, is the key to the adoption of the other proposals.

Case Prepared—The White House has prepared a broad-ranging defense of its transfer proposals.

In part, it will seek to demonstrate that the transfers are in the interest of local governments and the general public. In part, it will argue that the transfers will benefit the programs and their lobbies.

The latter case will be by far the harder to make, at least to the satisfaction of the interest groups.

CASE FOR RURAL TRANSFERS

The proposal to transfer the rural development programs has generated the most vocal opposition so far.

At present, the programs are scattered among several agencies, although most have duplicate functions. The transfers include:

From the Agriculture Department, two agencies with budget authority totaling about $2 billion: the Farmers Home Administration, which provides low-cost loans for rural and small-town housing and grants for water and sewer development; and the Rural Electrification Administration, which provides low-cost loans for construction of rural electric generating, transmission and distribution facilities.

From the Commerce Department, the Economic Development Administration ($253 million), which provides grants and loans for public works development in depressed rural areas; and the Regional Action Planning Commissions ($54 million), which provide staffing money for regional economic planning.

From the Executive Offices of the President, the Appalachian Regional Commission ($302 million), which provides grants for highways and public facilities in 13 states stretching from New York to Mississippi.

The National Grange, which speaks for the small farmer, and the National Rural Electric Cooperative Association are united in loud opposition to the transfers. Rural needs, they say, would get short shrift in any department which also counted the big cities among its clients.

The farm groups also argue that stripping any programs out of Agriculture would start a "ripple effect" which could lead to the department's demise.

But the White House says it wants to make the transfers so that more attention, not less, will be given to developing rural America.

Shultz: By far the most persuasive Administration spokesman is Shultz.

"We want to have the rural development programs in a community development department so that we can build up rural communities," he said.

"We think that rural development is so important that it should be approached in a coherent way. The present administrative response forces a dispersed governmental response to rural development problems. What we want is a focused effort, not a dispersed effort."

Aggregated Impact—Shultz said that "the farm groups fear their interest will be submerged in a community development department. But it won't happen that way. We plan for rural development to get major attention. The current way of doing things has actually worked to submerge the rural interests, not promote them. The various program components are so dispersed throughout the government that they cannot be effectively aggregated. Therefore, they have no real impact on the problem. What the farm groups are deploring—the whole submerging of interest thesis—is precisely why their programs should be integrated. Their own argument is actually the most powerful one for putting those programs into the new department."

No "Ripple Effect"—Shultz also discounted the "ripple effect" argument against the transfers. "Taking those programs from Agriculture has no impact on the viability of that department," he said. "Agriculture is gigantic, a really big enterprise, and losing those programs does not affect it.

"In fact, I'll make a deal right now with the farm groups. They will never hear me using the argument that because the rural development components have gone to Community Development, then Agriculture cannot stand on its own feet."

Rouse: The community development plan, like the Administration's other reorganization proposals, was based on recommendations by the President's Advisory Council on Executive Reorganization (the Ash Council), which completed its work late last year.

Andrew W. Rouse, who served as executive director of the Ash Council, said that "the farm lobbies have a good political case against Farmers Home and REA going to DCD, but a lousy substantive case."

Rouse, who now works at Arthur D. Little Inc. as a consultant specializing in government structure, said the lobbies are in the tough political position of not being able to question any part of Agriculture, no matter how peripheral it is to farming, because that seems to threaten the department itself.

Farmers Home—"But Farmers Home is not farm housing. It's really a rural development program, with most of its mortgages in towns and not farms," said Rouse.

"Given that situation, the question is where should you have the expertise: in a department which is agriculture oriented or one that is community development oriented?"

Small Farms Dying—"Rural towns are in trouble to the degree that small farms, and in particular the historic family farm, are dying. The towns, in turn, are looking for substitutes to the agricultural economy, not for more agricultural development. So Farmers Home should be lodged where the community development expertise is.

"Ever since Orville Freeman was Secretary, the department has made political efforts to change its mission from agriculture to rural development. But that would be redundancy of skills. No point basing that expertise in a department—Agriculture—where the economic and demographic trends are running irreversibly against small-time agriculture. We cannot recreate the family farm as a viable economic unit. Let's get away from that fiction and face up to reality.

"When you do that, you have to ask yourself if the small farmer is going to be adequately represented in a department which has to care most about food production. Thus, it worries about the 20 percent of the farmers who produce 80 percent of the food."

Democratic Applause: The proposal to transfer the rural development components to a Community Development Department is seen as a bold administrative reform and a still political challenge.

Sundquist—James L. Sundquist, who served as deputy under secretary of Agriculture from 1963 to 1965 and before that as a staff member on the Senate Banking and Currency Subcommittee on Housing and Urban Affairs, said that "the rural areas will get short shrift in a big HUD department. But they are getting short shrift now. It's a sideline in Agriculture and it's split among three other departments. Granted it would be a sideline in Community Development, which would favor big city and metropolitan area clients. But at least it would have unified leadership."

While favoring the concept, Sundquist said "it will have pretty hard sledding. The rural groups have a lot of political moxie and can make real trouble. If they are opposing, why would congressional Democrats want to alienate the groups tied in with the Farmers Home and the REA, programs with strong popular support, in order to make a Republican President look good?"

Semer—Milton P. Semer, a counsel to the President specializing in housing (1966-67), said the Johnson Administration always had favored consolidating all housing programs into one agency. But in the end Farmers Home was left in Agriculture.

"We talked a lot about it—how it would be good for government, good for housing, good for the farmers and good for the environment," Semer said. "But we were afraid to go for it. We just made the political decision that it was a waste of time to try to give to HUD part of Agriculture."

The political realities have not changed, in Semer's opinion. "With this Administration, I think you have to ask yourself: Does Nixon have any more strength than LBJ to add to HUD? By asking the question that bluntly, you answer it. Obviously not," he said.

"Of course, they have made their political compromises too. For example, and this seems a glaring one if you are appraising functional compatibility, why aren't the Veterans Administration housing programs put into the new department? There is certainly nothing functionally special about them. They would fit right in with current Federal Housing Administration programs. Well, it is a political decision. They think that the veterans lobby is just too tough for them to tangle with."

CASE FOR HIGHWAYS TRANSFER

In terms of money, by far the biggest proposed transfer involves the Federal Highway Administration, which had budget authority totaling about $5.8 billion in fiscal 1971.

White House officials make no bones about why the change was proposed. They see highway development as involving more social than economic issues, and they want the federal bureaucracy to manage it with that in mind.

The pitch to the highway interests is equally blunt. Administration spokesmen claim that the highway lobbies had better come around to the Nixon position, or be prepared to suffer the worst economic consequences. They say that unless the social consequences of highways are reduced, growing community opposition will eventually stop all development. That, they argue, is an increasingly obvious fact of life.

Shultz: "Moving the highways into a Community Development Department is advantageous to the highway lobby," said Shultz. "It gives them an opportunity for more effective work on highway development. They have got to realize that 'effective' no longer means buying the cheapest cement, but how you relate highway development to the other human systems in a community.

No Choice—"It's just a very simple situation to my way of thinking: either the highway people come around and realize this or else highway building in this country is going to come to a stop," Shultz said.

HUD-Transportation: "You can hardly talk about community development without talking about a community's transportation system. It's totally artificial, for example, to separate housing development from transportation development. That's why there have to be so many working relations between HUD and DOT now."

Dean—Reorganization coordinator Alan Dean said that "the big issues in highways now are relocation, land-use planning, viability of communities, environmental and aesthetic impact.

"We as a nation have reached that point in our development that highway development should be administered in conjunction with those concerns.

"Moving the highways to keep pace with changing conditions is nothing new. In fact the Federal Highway Administration is the most peripatetic federal bureaucracy. It's traveled from Agriculture to the Federal Works Agency to the General Services Administration to Commerce and to Transportation.

"Each one of those shifts has reflected the evolving character of transportation. Now transportation is essentially a community development question."

Urban Members: The White House hopes to win the support of urban-oriented Members of Congress on the highway transfer. It is looking for most help from those who have had to field numerous complaints about highways disrupting local communities.

Percy considers himself a good example. "It is becoming essential for a politician to look at transportation in light of how it will affect communities," he said.

"Right now the people of Chicago are furious because there is so much highway repair in and out of the city. For example, the only way that I can get from the airport to downtown is by helicopter.

"It is going to get worse and worse all over the country. And automobiles are not going to provide the pleasure and the efficiency they once did.

"I just don't see how the highway people can say that their program should not be administered in conjunction with the city and community development programs. The interstate part of their program is virtually finished.

"The real problem ahead is finishing and improving the highways in the cities, and that's where the people get so furious."

INTEGRATION CONFLICT

The highway and farm lobbies are particularly irritated by an unpublicized feature of the Administration's plan for the new department—complete integration of programs in a regional and state office structure.

The White House hopes that decentralized decision-making on all community development programs—by federal officials responsible for jurisdictions as small as states—can provide to the hard-pressed mayors a one-stop shopping service closely attuned to their individual needs.

But clients of the Farmers Home Administration and the Federal Highway Administration have long enjoyed the benefits of highly autonomous local administrative operations, managing only programs of interest to them. The farm and highway interests are overwrought at the idea that these local operations might be merged into field offices which would deal with a whole range of other problems.

Power to the People: The decentralization strategy is in line with actions already taken by the

Reps. Chet Holifield (left) and Frank Horton with chart showing proposed reorganization, including Department of Community Development

236 Administration to establish 10 common regional offices for major domestic agencies.

On its own, HUD has gone further, and has established 42 state-level offices, thus becoming the most decentralized of federal agencies.

The Nixon plan would integrate the autonomous farm and highway structures into Community Development state and regional structures to be built around the nucleus of HUD state and regional offices.

Thus, highway, housing, rural and urban development programs could be meshed at administrative levels below those in Washington.

A planning document now being quietly circulated among federal departments makes a few concessions to farm and high interests on field structure, but pursues the objective of total integration of programs.

Highway Opposition: The highway lobby is very much opposed to the field integration plan. Especially adamant is its leading spokesman, A. E. Johnson—the longtime and influential director of the American Association of State Highway Officials. He said flatly that nothing more detrimental to the highway program could happen than to have its field operations meshed in with other community development programs, especially the HUD programs.

"Our state highway officials are expediters," said Johnson. "But the clock turns very slowly at HUD, if at all. They aren't expediters; all you have to do is look at how they manage urban renewal.

"Under the proposed structure, Frank Turner would have to deal with a regional Community Development director, rather than directly with his own regional highway administrator as he does now. Thus Turner would have to go through one of Romney's regional guys in order to get to his own people."

(Francis C. Turner is administrator of the Federal Highway Administration. Ever since Turner and Johnson worked together in the Bureau of Public Roads in the 1930s, they have been close friends. Both men plan to retire at the end of 1972.)

Johnson also said that "because the state highway operation would be integrated with the HUD or Community Development state operation, the highway program would be further downgraded."

White House Rebuttal: Shultz strongly refuted Johnson's arguments. "I don't see how the new setup will complicate Frank Turner's relation with his state operations," Shultz said. "We've deliberately integrated the field and regional administrative structures in order to facilitate highway construction, not hinder it."

HUD Rebuttal: Emil Frankel, a high-ranking HUD official, said that the "highway transfer means symbolically and structurally that highway construction has to be coordinated with the other community development programs. Thus the key thing is to get the highway guys coordinated *in the field* with the housing and community development guys."

He said, "The highway program cannot be transferred but continue as a self-contained bureaucracy. If so, it really doesn't matter where it is. If all the highway construction-

community interest conflicts have to be resolved here in Washington under the new structure, just as they are under the existing multi-department structure, then the whole thing really makes little difference. Look out my window, we're across the street from them right now, and we communicate all the time, but Washington-level coordination really doesn't help local development.

"What we have really got to do for better community development

Charles H. Percy

Abraham A. Ribicoff

is to make highway planning part of the total community planning process. And what we are worrying about is Congress writing into the DCD law the autonomy of the Federal Highway Administration. I don't think it would be worth all the trouble if we were to end up in a straitjacket."

Van Dusen Group—Frankel, formerly the principal legislative assistant to Sen. Jacob K. Javits, R-N.Y., now is the top aide to HUD Under Secretary Richard C. Van Dusen. Van Dusen is chairman of a task force—including the under secretaries of Agriculture, Commerce and Transportation, and the deputy director of OEO—charged with drafting the administrative structure and procedures of the new department. Frankel, in turn, chairs a working group composed of top aides to the various under secretaries. To date, the Van Dusen and Frankel groups have met secretly, and without consultation with the interest groups.

The Van Dusen group has drafted a field structure which modestly compromises the objective of full integration

One compromise lets the top highway bureaucrat in each state, the division engineer, report directly to the Community Development regional administrator. That way the highway man does not have to go through the department's state office director, and so functionally is his equal. Another administrative compromise allowed the Farmers Home Administration to retain its 1,700 county offices.

The White House has not officially approved the final proposal of the Van Dusen group, nor has the proposal been shown to the Government Operations Committees or the interest groups. But Administration sources told *National Journal* that it would not be changed.

LOCAL GOVERNMENT LOBBIES

On grounds that creation of the Community Development Department is designed to strengthen the hand of local politicians, the Administration is expecting a strong show of support from local government lobbies.

Most influential is the city lobby, represented in Washington by the National League of Cities-U.S. Conference of Mayors. Less potent but gaining in influence is the county lobby, the National Association of Counties.

In pressing Congress for reorganization, White House officials had planned to exploit a tactic that worked well when they were seeking to dramatize their case for revenue sharing—parading a solid phalanx of local politicians—both city and county—before House and Senate committees.

City Lobby: The mayors plan to lend all the support they can to the new department.

Allen E. Pritchard, the deputy executive vice president of the National League of Cities said: "We have absolutely no problem with it. We think it's a sound proposal. We've already supported it publicly when Lugar was on the Hill testifying."

(Richard G. Lugar, the Republican mayor of Indianapolis, is president of the National League of Cities.)

"We support all the transfers," said Pritchard, "even those where we are the major clients, as in the case with the Urban Mass Transportation Administration. We want that transferred. We are very unhappy with the way that UMTA has been run by the Transportation Department. We'd like it in the new department. We've already begun pressing the private transit lobbies to go along."

County Lobby: Unhappily for the Administration, the county lobby will not join the phalanx this time.

NACO once was a rural-oriented interest group, but recently it has taken on a suburban and even metropolitan cast.

The counties now want to share fully in the government's subsidy programs for community development, especially the ones which HUD has historically administered.

But HUD, with its strong city bias, has always looked coolly at county government. As a result, the county lobby views dimly the prospect of a new department to be organized around a HUD nucleus.

Hillenbrand—Bernard F. Hillenbrand, the executive director of NACO, said, "Our general reaction is that HUD has been a dud. They cannot get on top of anything—that's the general consensus around town. It takes them forever to get anything done.

"Then they always want to grab off pieces from other departments when they cannot administer what they already have. For example, they have been critical of the Farmers Home Administration, apparently—if I understand it

238 right—for being too efficient.

"Besides all that, HUD is just not sympathetic to counties. They have no county orientation. I am leery of getting involved with the HUD people any more than necessary."

Tabor—NACO's chief lobbyist, Ralph Tabor, said the county lobby has no official position on the new department and would not testify before the Holifield committee.

"We would have to put an awful lot of work into it," said Tabor. "Because it affects so many federal programs, virtually all of our legislative committees would have to review it. Our feeling all along has been that only the proposed Natural Resources Department had a real chance in the real world, not the public relations world."

Image Problem: The Nixon Administration has close ties to the county lobby, and although it has not yet tried, it should be capable of persuading NACO not to take a hostile position.

But it seems very doubtful that NACO, at this late hour, could be converted to active support.

The city lobby is better at rounding up votes and getting the attention of Congress and the media, but still the county lobby will be missed when the Administration gets around to pressuring Congress.

County politicians are supposed to be major beneficiaries of the community development reorganization, and their silence will not go unnoticed on Capitol Hill.

In fact, it may increase the Administration's difficulties in convincing Congress that its program is meritorious and fully supported by the President.

6 LAW AND JUSTICE

The recent emergence of "law and order" as a political issue and the increase in crime have drawn public attention to the role of law enforcement and the key part played by lawyers in the American system of justice. Courts certainly occupy a key place in the judicial arena, but it is one that is heavily dependent upon effective enforcement of the law and capable advocacy by qualified lawyers. In this section, therefore, we have concentrated on selections that explore these two components of the judicial system.

The death of J. Edgar Hoover in mid-1972 brought to an end a forty-seven-year era that spanned the entire history of the Federal Bureau of Investigation. The appointment of L. Patrick Gray III as his temporary successor will almost certainly usher in a new era of substantial long-range change in the operations of the Bureau. Public popularity has in the past made the FBI virtually impervious to presidential and congressional pressures. A new assessment of its role in the Department of Justice, its relationship with the Attorney General, and its accountability is almost certain to be undertaken. Even so, the controversial nature of the activities of the FBI will probably guarantee continued and vocal interest by those who see themselves as defenders and detractors of the agency.

One of the innovative concepts effectively implemented by the Nixon administration was the "strike force" idea. Strike forces, as noted in the second article in this chapter, have emerged as a major arm of the Federal government's efforts to curb organized crime. The strike forces have tested the ability of federal agencies to cooperate to overcome bureaucratic entanglements and jealousies. In the process they have compiled an impressive statistical record during their first three years. An interesting corollary to the strike forces has been increased anticrime efforts by existing agencies.

The American Bar Association, one of the best known organized interest groups in the nation, has a much broader mission than lobbying and other pressure-type activities. It has served as a screening agent for judicial nominations for every president since Harry S. Truman and also for the Senate Judiciary Committee. It has attempted to reach internal agreement on matters such as consumer protection, environmental quality standards, and legal services to the poor, but with mixed success. It has compiled a strong legislative record with regard to constitutional amendments and in the realm of criminal and tax law. It has long recognized a special role for itself as an advisor to government in the fields of reform and public service. Its impact upon government, law making and administrative decision-making makes it a part of any discussion of American law and justice.

FBI at end of Hoover era lacking blueprint for transition   *Richard S. Frank*

Editor's Note: *On May 2, 1972, J. Edgar Hoover died at age 77 after almost 48 years as director of the Federal Bureau of Investigation. President Nixon has appointed Patrick Gray, III, assistant attorney general in charge of the Justice Department's Civil Division, to serve as acting director, but will not submit the name of a permanent successor to Mr. Hoover to the Senate for confirmation until after the November election. This article was written in December 1971 prior to Mr. Hoover's death.*

J. Edgar Hoover, who is not known to take criticism lightly, was in a jovial mood recently when he took note of the increasingly frequent demands for his retirement after more than 47 years as director of the Federal Bureau of Investigation.

Speaking Oct. 22 at a dinner of the Washington chapter of the Society of Former Special Agents of the FBI, Hoover spoke of the delays which have pushed back the scheduled completion of the new FBI building to late 1974 or early 1975. (Completion was originally scheduled for 1968.)

"There are some who maintain that the only reason I am staying on as director of the FBI is to be present at the dedication," Hoover said.

"This is absolute nonsense. At the rate the building is going up, none of us will be around by the time it is completed."

Hoover may have been joking, but the general expectation in Administration and congressional circles is that someone else will be moving into the executive suite when the mammoth FBI structure on Pennsylvania Avenue—the most expensive government building ever erected in the capital—is finally occupied.

No Transition Plans: Hoover is 76 years old. He will be 77 on New Year's Day. It would therefore come as no great surprise if he were to step down inside of a few months. Many in and out of government who admire him or fear him are already looking ahead to the time when there will be an FBI without a J. Edgar Hoover.

Some see his prospective departure as an opportunity to institute the changes—in structure, in duties, in operating methods—that they believe are desirable but cannot be accomplished while Hoover sits in the director's chair.

Others look to his retirement with concern, fearing that the man who replaces Hoover will almost inevitably find it more difficult to insulate the bureau from political interference.

"When he goes," a congressional aide said, "the wolves will come in."

Despite this mixture of anticipation and apprehension, however, there is no evidence that any hard plans are being developed in the Justice Department, in the White House, or in Congress to prepare for that day.

There is, on the contrary, every indication that nothing will be done until Hoover's retirement is actually announced and the search for his successor has begun. Despite the rumors and reports of Hoover's imminent retirement, the wait could stretch well beyond a few months.

Old Rumors: Hoover retirement rumors are nothing new. As far back as the beginning of the Eisenhower Administration in 1953, there was talk of the FBI director stepping down.

The rumors recurred when John F. Kennedy was elected President in November 1960, but the announcement that Hoover would remain at his post was almost the first act of the President-elect (as it was of President-elect Richard Nixon in 1968).

Hoover's 70th birthday and the age of compulsory retirement came on Jan. 1, 1965, and Kennedy, so the reports had it, was prepared to choose a new director, once his own reelection was a fact.

But Kennedy had been dead six months when President Lyndon B. Johnson, on May 8, 1964, signed an order (ExecOrder 11154) exempting Hoover from the automatic retirement rule, telling Hoover that "the nation cannot afford to lose you."

YEAR OF OUTCRY

The talk of imminent departure was renewed vigorously in the past year as Hoover was subjected to a steady barrage of criticism and complaint.

Ironically, the criticism may have served to prolong the director's stay in office. President Nixon made this point before the American Society of Newspaper Editors last April 16, when he suggested that the criticism of Hoover would not lead to his retirement but "would tend to have exactly the opposite effect: not to hasten his retirement but to have him dig in."

Critical Barrage: The extent and the intensity of the criticism are unparalleled in the 47-year career of Hoover as head of the FBI.

Since the beginning of 1971:

Hoover's resignation has been demanded by two potential Democratic presidential candidates, Sens. Edmund S. Muskie of Maine and George S. McGovern of South Dakota.

The FBI director was accused by McGovern of trying to destroy the career of an airline pilot who had criticized the bureau for its handling of the hijacking of a plane he was piloting.

The bureau was reported to have cut its direct liaison with the Central Intelligence Agency because the CIA refused to tell Hoover who in the FBI had leaked information to the CIA.

The American Civil Liberties Union went to court to demand an end to FBI surveillance of "lawful political and social activity" on the part of American citizens.

The FBI was accused of engaging in widespread surveillance of anti-pollution rallies on Earth Day in 1970, including one in Washington attended by Muskie.

House Majority Leader Hale Boggs, D-La., said the FBI had tapped the telephones of Members of Congress.

More than 1,000 documents were stolen from an FBI office in Media, Pa., and some of them were selectively released over the next few months, embarrassing the bureau and revealing some details—perhaps distorted—of the FBI's domestic intelligence activities.

Critics continued to blame Hoover for announcing, in advance of an indictment, that the FBI had uncovered a plot to blow up underground electrical and steam systems in the capital and kidnap a high government official.

The government agreed to an out-of-court settlement with an FBI agent, John F. Shaw, who said he was forced out of the bureau by Hoover after writing an academic paper critical of Hoover's administration of the FBI.

A flurry of high-level retirements and resignations in the bureau, including one by an official considered by some to be a leading candidate to succeed Hoover as director, gave rise to speculation that Hoover was attempting to eliminate internal dissent.

Ambivalent Support: Hoover could draw comfort from a Gallup Poll conducted for *Newsweek* during the height of the criticism last spring.

The poll showed that 70 percent of the sample believed Hoover had done a good or excellent job as head of the FBI and rated his agency favorably.

But the 76-year-old director may have been less pleased by the same poll's revelation that 51 per-

cent of the cross section felt that the time had come for him to retire.

Attorney General John N. Mitchell, as recently as this month, repeated the official Administration position: that Hoover could remain as director as long as he wanted to and as long as he continued in good health. Hoover himself has said his health is excellent.

Whether this represents Mitchell's own view is another question.

Richard W. Kurrus, who served as the first chief counsel to the House Select Committee on Crime, recalled recently that he and Rep. Claude Pepper, D-Fla., the committee chairman, called on Mitchell at the Justice Department shortly after the committee was established in the early summer of 1969.

In talking about the Justice Department, Kurrus said, "Mitchell told us the real problem he had in the department was J. Edgar Hoover, and that Hoover was more of a detriment than a help."

Kurrus, now in private law practice, said, "Mitchell indicated that Hoover would shortly be phased out. He told us the department had no control over Hoover and that Hoover had been sanctified and that he couldn't direct him and couldn't gain his cooperation."

The Attorney General turned down a request for an interview on the subject, his press spokesman telling *National Journal* that "the Attorney General doesn't consider it very productive to sit there and defend the FBI."

FBI Studies: At a conference

242 Oct. 29 and 30 on the campus of Princeton University, most of the same complaints about the FBI were sounded again, along with some proposals to alter the legal responsibilities of the bureau, change its structure or institute new controls over its operations.

A few weeks later, a group called Friends of the FBI, calling the Princeton conference biased against the FBI, commissioned a study of the bureau by the Chicago-based Americans for Effective Law Enforcement in an effort to redress the balance.

Whatever their differences over the merits of the FBI, the sponsors of the conference and of the new study share this goal: to have an impact on whatever studies Congress may undertake on the present and future activities of the bureau.

On the Hill: Of the various committees and subcommittees with the appropriate jurisdiction, however, not one has any plans to take on such a study.

Nor do committee aides expect that any comprehensive studies will be undertaken while Hoover continues to serve as director.

In 1968, as part of the Omnibus Crime Control and Safe Streets Act, Congress adopted a provision (82 Stat 236) which shifted the power to appoint an FBI director from the Attorney General to the President and required that the Senate give its advice and consent to such appointments.

"That's the best toehold Congress has to look at bureau policy," said a committee aide.

In the meantime, however, proposals for meaningful congressional studies of the FBI—its procedures, its relations with the At-

torney General, with the President and with the Congress—have been put on the shelf.

STATUS AT JUSTICE

The FBI has prepared a 26-page booklet, *99 Facts,* which sets out the bureau's official positions in the form of questions and answers. The booklet asks: "What safeguards are there against abuses of authority by the FBI and its director?"

The official answer: "The FBI's activities and operations are under constant scrutiny and review by the Attorney General, committees of Congress, the Bureau of the Budget (now the Office of Management and Budget), the courts and the nation's press."

Just how extensive this oversight is has long been a matter of considerable dispute.

On the official organizational charts, the FBI has a clearly subordinate status within the Justice Department, ranking below the legal and administrative divisions, each of which is headed by an assistant attorney general.

The bureau is no more important—on the charts—than the Bureau of Prisons or the Immigration and Naturalization Service, for example.

It is, in short, part of the department (the largest single part in terms of employees) and not an independent nor even a quasi-independent agency.

That this is sometimes forgotten, even by Justice Department officials, was made evident by the testimony of Assistant Attorney General Robert C. Mardian, head of the Internal Security Division,

before the Senate Judiciary Subcommittee on Constitutional Rights last March 17.

Sen. Edward M. Kennedy, D-Mass., was pressing Mardian about the department's role in conducting surveillance of private individuals, and wanted to know if the department had formal guidelines to limit its activities in this field.

"We do not engage in . . . surveillance ourselves," Mardian responded. "The only information we have available to us comes in the form of FBI reports of actions, civil disorders."

William H. Rehnquist, the assistant attorney general who has since been appointed to the Supreme Court, was sitting next to Mardian, and leaned over and whispered to him.

"Well, Mardian continued, "Mr. Rehnquist reminds me that the FBI is a part of the Justice Department."

When Kennedy asked him for an explanation of the FBI's guidelines for surveillance, Mardian replied: "I think it would be more appropriate to direct that inquiry to the bureau."

Uncharted Status: As the Mardian testimony demonstrated, the FBI's true status cannot be determined by its place on the organizational chart. Its status is a function of the unique influence in Washington of its director. And the exact source of Hoover's influence—although a frequent subject of speculation—is elusive. An important ingredient is that he is a recognized master of bureaucratic infighting. Another, perhaps, is simply that he has survived so long. Mr. Nixon is the eighth President Hoover has served and Mitchell the 16th Attorney General since Harlan F. Stone (1924-25) appointed him director in 1924.

In any event, Hoover has managed to defy the wishes of Attorneys General and to thwart their programs from time to time with impunity, or at least without any visible scars.

Former Attorney General (1967-69) Ramsey Clark thinks that part of the reason is that "the bureau, after all, tends to run itself, and the Attorney General is busy, typically is inexperienced in this area and very much impressed with Mr. Hoover's status."

Clark, in a recent interview, said that "in most parts of the department, when the signal is finally called, everyone will do his job." This is not necessarily so with the FBI, Clark said.

Inhibiting Force: Even when the bureau offers no resistance to an Attorney General's initiatives, the possibility of resistance can be inhibiting, the former Justice Department chief said.

During his term as Attorney General, said Clark, "ideas were questioned before they really got started, in anticipation of FBI resistance.

"I think there's a psychological analogy to self-censorship there. You don't want to take on fights that would be difficult and harmful unless they're quite important."

Even when change was achieved, it came slowly because of FBI reluctance, said Clark. "You never felt you had a firm hand on the wheel."

Ideology Gap: Almost two years after Clark left office, he was described by Hoover as "like a

jellyfish . . . a softie," and called the worst Attorney General Hoover had ever served under, "worse than Bobby Kennedy."

In part, this was Hoover's reaction to Clark's book, *Crime in America* (Simon and Schuster, 1970), which had just been published, and contained some equally harsh words about Hoover.

But it was also a reflection of the wide ideological gap between Hoover and Clark, a gap which may also have accounted for at least some of the problems the former Attorney General had with the FBI director.

Biddle—One of Clark's predecessors as Attorney General, Francis Biddle (1941-45) tells of his own efforts to win the cooperation of Hoover, who by that time—1941—had already held his office for 17 years.

In his second volume of reminiscences, *In Brief Authority* (Doubleday, 1962), Biddle says that Harlan Stone, who had appointed Hoover FBI chief, "gave me a key to Hoover's complex character: if Hoover trusted you he would be absolutely loyal; if he did not, you had better look out; and he had to get used to his new chief each time."

Biddle writes that he came into the Attorney General's office "with the stamp of a 'liberal,' and Hoover must have suspected that I would be too soft, particularly now that a war was on. . . . "

"Temperamentally Hoover was a conservative," writes Biddle, "although such an easy classification hardly describes a temperament which was clearly not reflective or philosophic. Edgar Hoover was primarily a man of immediate ac-

tion."

Biddle relates that "I sought to invite his confidence, and before long, lunching alone with me in a room adjoining my office, he began to reciprocate by sharing some of his extraordinarily broad knowledge of the intimate details of what my associates in the Cabinet did and said, of their likes and dislikes, their weaknesses and their associations."

Kennedy—Hoover's relations with Attorney General Robert F. Kennedy (1961-64) were often stormy, and the loyalty which Biddle believed was so important for a smooth relationship was never, apparently, established.

An official in the Criminal Division of the Justice Department in those years said recently that "you had to negotiate with the FBI. You couldn't order them to do something. Well, you could, but you usually didn't."

Hoover himself has confirmed one report that he had resisted Kennedy's pleas to recruit more black agents for the FBI.

"He wanted me to lower our qualifications and to hire more Negro agents," Hoover told *Time* last December.

"I said 'Bobby, that's not going to be done as long as I'm director of this bureau.' He said, 'I don't think you're being cooperative.' And I said, 'why don't you get a new director?'

"I went over to see President Johnson," Hoover continued, "and he told me to 'stick to your guns.'"

Mitchell—For his present Attorney General, Hoover has nothing but kind words.

"There has never heen an Attorney General for whom I've had

higher regard," Hoover said last year of Mitchell, whom he also described as "an honest, sincere and very human man."

But there has been some minor friction between the Attorney General and the director, such as the time last spring when Hoover turned down Mitchell's request for him to speak at a meeting in Washington on crime control, presumably because Hoover objected to some of the participants at the meeting.

More recently, the department's Office of Public Information, which is responsible directly to Mitchell, began editing FBI crime reports and news releases prepared by the bureau's crime records division, which handles FBI public relations.

As one result, the reports on national crime trends, as interpreted by Mitchell's press staff, have been more encouraging than those released directly by the FBI.

News Policy: During the Clark regime at Justice, FBI releases were routinely cleared through the office of the department's information director, according to Clifton F. Sessions, who held that post.

Sessions said in an interview that he never turned down an FBI release, although he sometimes suggested changes with which the bureau went along.

"But I've always had the feeling that if I turned one down, they'd get their story out anyway."

Ray Arrest—Sessions recalled one instance when the FBI issued a news release without clearance from his office and aroused Clark's ire.

It was on June 8, 1968, the day of Robert Kennedy's funeral, and James Earl Ray had been arrested in London, several hours before the funeral, on a charge of shooting the Rev. Martin Luther King Jr.

While the funeral service was in progress in New York City, the FBI in Washington issued a release announcing Ray's capture.

Before the release was handed out, Sessions learned it was coming; he informed Clark's deputy, Warren Christopher, who called the FBI about it.

"They wouldn't tell him anything," Sessions said, "and that's what got Clark mad. He rarely gets mad. I've seen him that way two or three times—and that was one of them."

HOOVER AND THE WHITE HOUSE

In an interview last year, Hoover said that he had not spoken to Attorney General Kennedy for the last six months of Kennedy's tenure at the Justice Department.

That this period began shortly after the death of Kennedy's brother, the President, is no coincidence, but rather a demonstration that Hoover knows where the power lies—in the White House.

Robert Kennedy was still Attorney General after Nov. 22, 1963, but his brother was no longer President, and his power and influence over the FBI was no longer what it had been.

Direct Lines: During Ramsey Clark's term as Attorney General, according to Sessions, "the FBI maintained direct relations with the White House."

Sessions recalled that he once asked Clark, at a time when Clark was particularly disturbed over an incident with Hoover, why he didn't fire the director.

"Clark said he could do that if he wanted, and he was sure he would be fired by the President in five minutes and Hoover would be rehired."

Nixon — Under President Nixon, the personal relationship between the FBI director and the chief executive continues to exist.

But Attorney General Mitchell has much the same kind of relationship with the President as Robert Kennedy had with John Kennedy; he is the President's chief political adviser and is intimately involved in domestic and foreign policy decisions which go far beyond the scope of his Justice Department office.

Thus, Mr. Nixon has reportedly let it be known that he expects the FBI to subordinate itself to the Attorney General and to take his problems and complaints to Mitchell, not to the White House.

Appointees — The White House does deal directly with the FBI on the investigations it requires before it appoints someone to a federal office.

One recent FBI check, run on CBS News correspondent Daniel Schorr, caused a minor furor when it was revealed that Schorr knew nothing about the investigation or about the job he was ostensibly being considered for.

What concerned some people was the fact that Schorr was considered an Administration critic, and the fear that the FBI might have been used to intimidate him.

"The use of the FBI for political purposes is reminiscent of the use of arbitrary police power to intimidate and throttle the free press in Nazi Germany and the Soviet Union," Rep. James H. Scheuer, D-N.Y., said after the Schorr investigation became public.

Scheuer was critical of the White House, not the FBI. Ramsey Clark, however, questioned whether the bureau did not have "an obligation to stand up and question this—to ask, is it a real job check or not."

Independence: What troubles some of the FBI's critics is the thought that another director, lacking Hoover's independence and prestige, might find it hard to stand up to an improper request from the President.

On the other hand, the Schorr investigation may be a sign that Hoover himself—his once broad reservoir of public and political support diminishing—is less able to withstand such a request. Hoover clearly is more dependent on keeping the favor of the President and the Attorney General now than he has been at any time in his long career.

Victor S. Navasky, in his recent book on the Robert Kennedy years in the Justice Department, *Kennedy Justice* (Atheneum, 1971), writes that with all the difficulties of an independent FBI, "the virtue of an independent intelligence operation is that it cannot be used for "political" purposes—a Gestapo to carry out night raids on behalf of the Administration in power."

PRIORITIES AND PERFORMANCE

"It doesn't do much good to order the FBI to do something, to shout and push and bang your head on the table," Ramsey Clark said. "You've got to make them want to do it."

Clark described his frustrated effort, during his term of office, to reduce what he considered the bureau's undue emphasis on investigating interstate car thefts.

"I felt very strongly that this was a waste, a deception and a harm, and that a good deal of case time for agents was wasted on this kind of thing."

Dyer Act: The Dyer Act of 1919 (18 USC 2311) makes it a federal crime to transport stolen vehicles across state lines, and each year the FBI points proudly to its record of recoveries of stolen cars, noting in its budget presentations to Congress that the number of recoveries has again risen to an all-time high.

In fiscal 1970, for example, 30,599 stolen vehicles which had been moved interstate were recovered in FBI-investigated cases, Hoover told the House appropriations subcommittee which handles his budget.

These recoveries figure prominently in a chart labeled "FBI Accomplishments and Appropriations," which the director presents to Congress each year and which compares the bureau's spending to the money it brings to the federal treasury as a result of fines, savings and recoveries.

Each year, the latter is greater than the former. Thus, last March, Hoover could tell the subcommittee that the bureau brought in $410,974,099 as compared with an appropriation of $256,857,292, or "an average return of $1.60 for each $1 of direct funds appropriated to the FBI in the 1970 fiscal year."

Clark, however, insists that the statistics on recovered cars are "a deception because it is represented that the bureau is making the arrests when actually the local police have."

Convinced that Congress, in passing the Dyer Act, was concerned about interstate car-theft rings, not joyriding youngsters who steal cars and drive them into another state, Clark attempted to get the FBI to devote less of its time and energies to car thefts and more to areas which he believed deserved higher priorities.

"But it's a part of their budget-justifying process," Clark said. "It's important with them on the Hill, and it has the appearance of high productivity."

The FBI resisted and, as a result, Clark said, he was unable to accomplish the shift in priorities which he, as the nominal Justice Department policy maker, felt was desirable.

FBI Position: The bureau's answer, supplied by a spokesman for Hoover, is that "if the American public doesn't want the FBI to enforce that law (the Dyer Act), all it has to do is repeal the statute. But as long as the Act is on the books we will enforce it."

The FBI spokesman (Hoover turned down a request for an interview) asked rhetorically, "Wouldn't we be subject to criticism if we turned down a case referred by a local police department, if we decided which cases we will and will not accept for investigation?" The FBI, he said, "made its reputation as an impartial investigator of federal offenses. But now we're being criticized for enforcing a law."

Clark, however, insists that "priorities must be set," and that the FBI could properly spend less of its time on stolen vehicle cases and more, for example, on civil rights violations.

Civil Rights: In defending itself against charges that it has been less than energetic in the field of civil rights enforcement, the FBI takes the opposite tack, contending that it cannot investigate civil rights cases unless instructed to do so by the Justice Department.

"If there's any failure to act in civil rights cases," the FBI spokesman said in an interview, "they'll have to take it up with the Department of Justice, not the FBI. We can't drag our feet. If they (Civil Rights Division officials) ask us, we do it. The division sets policy, not us."

Doar—But John Doar, a key Civil Rights Division aide during the early days of the civil rights struggle in the South, recalls that the FBI did, in fact, resist the initiatives of the Civil Rights Division in the first few years of the last decade.

Doar, who served in the division from 1960 through 1967, most of that time as the No. 2 man in the division, summed up the bureau's performance in that early period at the recent Princeton conference on the FBI:

"The bureau didn't know the first thing about its job and didn't do anything to learn it. The division had to teach the bureau."

"Why didn't we get tough with the FBI," Doar asked, "just give them the job and make them do it?"

"We knew," he said in answer to his own question, "that if the

FBI's FAR-FLUNG DOMAIN

With 21 percent of the budget and 45 percent of the personnel, the Federal Bureau of Investigation is the single largest unit within the Justice Department.

Its current appropriation of $334.5 million is surpassed only by the $698.9-million aid program administered by the Law Enforcement Assistance Administration, and its staff of some 8,900 agents and almost 12,000 clerks dwarfs LEAA's roster of barely 500 employees.

About one third of the FBI's staff works at what bureau Director J. Edgar Hoover refers to as the seat of government: FBI headquarters in the Justice Department building in Washington and scattered offices in the capital.

The bulk of its employees work out of 59 field offices across the country, at the FBI Academy in Quantico, Va.; at liaison posts in 17 foreign countries, and in several hundred resident agencies in smaller towns.

Centralized Control: Direction and control of the bureau are centralized in Washington, with Hoover sitting at the top of the pyramid.

Under Hoover is his long-time associate director, Clyde A. Tolson. Directly below Tolson is the recently created post of assistant director-deputy associate director (all one title), held by W. Mark Felt.

Two assistants to the director, John P. Mohr, who supervises the administrative branches of the bureau, and Alex Rosen, who heads the investigative divisions, rank next in the chain of command.

Ten divisions and an office of legal counsel are each headed by an assistant director, the next step down the ladder. The 59 field offices are each under the command of a special agent in charge.

Jurisdiction: The FBI has investigative jurisdiction over all federal criminal statutes except those specifically assigned to other federal agencies. Among these the most significant are narcotics matters, which are handled by the Justice Department's Bureau of Narcotics and Dangerous Drugs, and tax violations, which are handled by the Treasury Department.

In testimony before a congressional committee earlier this year, Hoover submitted a list of some of the 185 investigative classifications under which the bureau operates, including in the criminal and civil fields:

Admiralty Matters	Atomic Energy Act—Applicants for Sensitive Positions
Antiracketeering	
Antiriot Laws	Bank Robbery
Antitrust	Bribery and Conflict of Interest
Assaulting or Killing a Federal Officer	Civil Rights
	Crime Aboard Aircraft—Including

Hijackings
Crimes on the High Seas
Departmental Applicants
Deserters, Harboring Deserters
Destrucion of Aircraft
Election Laws
Escaped Federal Prisoners; Parole, Probation and Conditional Release Violators
Explosives and Incendiary Devices
Extortion
Federal Train Wreck Statute
Fraud Against the Government
Illegal Gambling Business
Interstate Transmission of Wagering Information
Interstate Transportation of Obscene Matter
Interstate Transportation of Motor Vehicles
Interstate Transportation of Stolen Property
Irregularities in Penal Institutions

Kidnapping
Labor-Management Reporting and Disclosure Act
National Bankruptcy Act
Obstruction of Justice
Selective Service Act
Theft from Interstate Shipment
Theft of Government Property
Unlawful Flight to Avoid Prosecution, Confinement or Giving Testimony
White Slave Traffic Act

In the security field:

Espionage
Internal Security
Black Panther Party
Sabotage
Security of Government Employees
Sedition
Treason

bureau didn't want to do the work, it wouldn't do a good job."

Beginning in 1964, however, the FBI's performance began to pick up significantly, and "from that time on," Doar says now, "the FBI really performed."

In the spring and summer of 1961, the Civil Rights Division called on the FBI to investigate allegations of voting discrimination in 34 Southern counties.

The bureau did the work, but Doar pointed out at Princeton that in each of the reports, "we got exactly the information we asked for—no more, no less."

If the division failed to anticipate particular kinds of discriminatory practices, then "the bureau's investigation would fail to bring out those practices." Fur-

ther, while the bureau had no problem getting whites to talk to its agents, the division's own attorneys had to conduct most of the interviewing of black witnesses.

The Treaty—In fact, in what Doar has described as a "treaty" between the division and the FBI, division lawyers had to act as investigators as well as attorneys in voting cases in the South.

It was also necessary for division attorneys to draft their requests for FBI interviews "in the most minute detail," according to Doar, who cites one request in 1962 which ran 174 pages, "explaining, anticipating, cautioning and coaching the bureau agents."

In another group of cases, Doar said, "the FBI produced voluminous reports . . . and numerous

agents conducted interviews. But the investigation was superficial. There is no other way to describe it."

From 1961 to 1963, the FBI investigated many cases of voter intimidation, and the fact that it had conducted an investigation "did some good but it made few, if any cases," said Doar, "and its performance—for the bureau—was far from adequate."

This was partly because the bureau was understaffed in the South, especially in Mississippi, said Doar, partly because its resident agents in that state shared the attitudes of their fellow Southerners and partly because the FBI in Washington did not understand the problems in the field.

FBI Shift—The big change came in the spring and summer of 1964, beginning with a memo from Attorney General Kennedy to President Johnson describing the problem in Mississippi, proposing that the FBI expand its role in that state and telling the President he was dispatching a crack team of organized-crime investigators to Mississippi to investigate terrorist activities.

Two weeks later, the President sent the late Allen W. Dulles, retired director (1953-61) of the Central Intelligence Agency, to Mississippi to survey the scene.

Dulles returned with a recommendation that the FBI force in that state be substantially expanded. On that same day, Hoover decided to open an FBI field office in Jackson, and Doar is convinced "that Mr. Dulles' recommendation was the proximate cause in changing the bureau's operation in the South."

Doar also suggests that the competitive threat from the special investigating team which Kennedy sent to Mississippi helped to bring about the accelerated FBI role in that state.

It was, said Doar, one of the factors which "combined to produce a magnificent change in the bureau's performance in Mississippi."

In 1964, Doar added, "when a deep-seated change came upon America, ... the bureau changed as well."

From then on, he said the FBI showed "exactly how and why it had earned its reputation for thoroughness, persistence and tough-mindedness in responsible law enforcement."

In a lengthy paper on the FBI's civil right performance prepared for the conference at Princeton, Doar concluded:

"Perhaps in retrospect there were ways to have made the bureau do better. But in evaluating the FBI's performance in protecting the right to vote, let us be sure we do not transfer our impatience with America itself onto the FBI simply because of its visibility—or our prejudices—or because we feel more comfortable criticizing a bureaucracy than criticizing ourselves."

Organized Crime: FBI critics point to the field of organized-crime investigations as another area where the FBI followed the lead of the Attorney General only with great reluctance.

Hoover, interviewed by *Time* last year, said flatly of his relations with Robert Kennedy: "There was no disagreement about organized crime."

THE BUREAU BEFORE HOOVER

J. Edgar Hoover and the FBI have been synonymous for so many decades that it is a little hard to remember there was a Bureau of Investigation (the "F" for Federal wasn't added until 1935) long before Hoover came along.

The Department of Justice had no organized investigative unit until the bureau was created in 1908. Until then, the department hired private detectives for specific investigations or borrowed Secret Service agents from the Treasury Department for general investigative work.

Small Start: In 1908, at the request of Attorney General (1906-09) Charles J. Bonaparte, Congress appropriated funds for a small but permanent detective force for the department.

With the money, Bonaparte hired nine Secret Service agents away from Treasury, combined them with 14 examiners and agents already on the Justice payroll, and set up a permanent unit under Chief Examiner Stanley W. Finch.

J. Edgar Hoover: In 1917, Hoover, a recent graduate in law from George Washington University, joined the Department of Justice. He was 22 at the time.

Starting as a clerk, Hoover by 1921 had been appointed an assistant director of the Bureau of Investigation.

In 1924, with the Justice Department reeling in the aftermath of the Harding-era scandals, a new President, Calvin Coolidge (1923-29), and a new Attorney General, Harlan Fiske Stone (1924-25), looked about for someone to revitalize the bureau. Their choice was the 29-year-old Hoover.

That was more than 47 years ago, and Hoover has held the post ever since. During the same period, the bureau's budget has climbed from $2,245,000 in 1924 to $334,486,000 in the current fiscal year.

Navasky—In his book on the Kennedy years in the Justice Department, Victor Navasky says that the FBI came late to the fight against organized crime, denying even the existence of organized criminal groups long after the leadership of the department made the breakup of organized crime one of its major goals.

In the end, the FBI bowed to Kennedy's demands and increased its activities in this field, although Navasky says that "Mr. Hoover had won by losing," that the FBI had increased its independence and power by taking on the added assignments.

Navasky speculates that the FBI was reluctant to get involved in the organized-crime fight for fear that its statistical batting average of convictions would drop if it took on the necessarily lengthy organized-crime investigations.

Hundley—William G. Hundley, who headed the organized crime section of the Criminal Division under Kennedy, recalled recently that "it was like pulling teeth" to gain the cooperation of the FBI.

Hundley had previously worked in the Internal Security Division, where the relationship with the FBI was "close and intimate and cooperative."

Apparently, he said, Hoover felt that the organized-crime program was not as popular as "communist hunting."

Eventually, he said, the FBI began to perform effectively in this field, except where interagency cooperation was required. There, he said, "the bureau just would not play that game."

Clark—Ramsey Clark, who was an assistant attorney general under Kennedy, said recently that the FBI's hesitancy to enter the organized-crime field was, in part, the result of a "personality clash" between Hoover and Kennedy, "the director not being willing to play second fiddle to Bob Kennedy."

By the time Clark himself became Attorney General in 1967, "the FBI seemed to be ready to make a record" in the organized-crime field.

Strike Forces—Clark's principal contribution to the federal government's war on organized crime was the institution of the strike-force program, which brings to each section of the country with an organized-crime problem a team of specialists from the major federal agencies with jurisdiction in the subject.

The FBI, of course, is one of these agencies, but from the beginning it refused to join the interagency teams.

Clark said the FBI's reason for declining to participate—that it did not want to lose control and direction of its own agents—made some sense.

But he suggested that the main reason the bureau did not join in was that "they wanted the credit to be the FBI's and not someone else's."

Under Mitchell, the picture was improved, and the FBI is now cooperating in, although still not participating in, the work of the strike forces.

Jurisdiction—The bureau's response to the criticism is that it had no effective jurisdiction against organized crime at the time Kennedy became Attorney General and decided to move extensively into that field.

"We couldn't go out and investigate people when there's no federal law," an FBI spokesman said.

The first of the organized-crime laws which gave the bureau the required authority, he said, were not enacted until 1961.

"Look at the statistics beginning in 1963, after these laws had been on the books long enough to produce some convictions," he said.

The statistics, as presented to congressional committees this year, show that FBI investigations resulted in the convictions of 64 "organized crime and gambling figures" in fiscal 1964, 281 by fiscal 1968 and 461 in fiscal 1970, the last year for which data were published.

Intelligence: In no area has the FBI been more roundly denounced nor more strongly defended than in that of intelligence gathering, a function which was not among the bureau's original responsibilities when it was established more than 60 years ago.

Since World War II, however, it has become an important—some say the most important—part of the FBI's assignment.

Shortly before the outbreak of the war, the bureau was handed the job of coordinating and gathering of information on the activities of alleged or potential subversives and spies.

It is an assignment which has never been revoked, and it involves such sensitive and controversial techniques as the surveillance of individuals and groups, the compiling of dossiers and files and the use of telephone taps and other forms of electronic bugging.

Complaints—Critics have complained that the bureau has been too free in disseminating information from its files, that it has been indiscriminate in its tapping and bugging and that, in general, its intelligence-gathering role is a threat to free expression.

There have been charges that Hoover has shared information from its files with Members of Congress, and, in fact, those who sit on the House Appropriations Subcommittee on State, Justice, Commerce, and the Judiciary, which processes the FBI budget, acknowledge that the director tells them things in confidence about pending cases and individuals and groups under surveillance that could not be told in public.

Expressions of concern about the extent of FBI bugging and

tapping are widespread, and Hoover himself, testifying before a Senate Appropriations subcommittee last June, used the term "tap-mania" to describe the state of those who believe their phones are tapped.

President Nixon, at a news conference in May, called it "hysteria," and pointed out that the taps "are always approved by the Attorney General."

Wiretapping—In á long letter declining an invitation to have an FBI representative at the Princeton conference last October, Hoover defended the bureau from criticism that it was acting without proper authority.

"Some critics would have the public believe that the FBI has acted totally outside the law," Hoover wrote, "when the fact is that we simply followed the legal advice given to us by the Attorney General."

A former Justice Department attorney familiar with organized-crime taps, however, said recently that the approval of a tap by the Attorney General doesn't necessarily assure its desirability. And, because of the historically unequal relationship between Hoover and his nominal superiors at Justice, it doesn't assure that the real initiative has rested with the Attorney General.

CONGRESS

Congress, say critics of the FBI, has failed in its responsibility to oversee the activities of the bureau.

Its legislative committees are reluctant to look at the bureau's practices, its appropriations committees are distracted by the FBI's dazzling display of facts and statistics and fail to ask the proper questions, its critics charge.

An aide to a House committee which shares jurisdiction over the Justice Department, and therefore over the FBI, said recently that "no one in Congress was questioning the FBI about some things it should be asked about."

But his committee, he said, had no hold over the bureau, no real way of getting at the policy issues involving the FBI.

Leverage: "The place where leverage can be applied," he said, "is in the appropriations process."

Here is where Hoover could be made to account for his bureau's actions and inactions, the committee aide suggested.

As for his own committee, he said, the members feel obliged to deal on policy issues with Hoover's superior, the Attorney General.

"If it's a policy matter, it's an insult to the head man if you don't go to him. It's the boss Congress should be aiming at."

This is an argument which Hoover readily endorses. It is the bureau's position that it is an investigative agency, which neither makes nor comments on policy. This, however, is a position which is not always strictly adhered to.

Testimony—As a general rule, Hoover will testify only before an appropriations committee. When asked by a legislative committee, he will usually respond that the request for testimony should properly be addressed to the Attorney General.

In 1969, for example, the newly established House Select Committee on Crime invited the FBI director to appear before it to answer questions about how much of its annual budget was used to fight crime and how much to maintain internal security.

The word came back by telephone from one of Hoover's assistants that Hoover testified only before the appropriations panels, and then only in closed sessions.

Try the Criminal Division of the Justice Department for the information, the committee was told.

Rep. Pepper, the committee chairman, angered by the refusal, warned he could subpoena Hoover, but said he would not because he didn't want to embarrass the director.

Exceptions—Hoover's rule has been bent from time to time, however. The most famous instance was the director's testimony, on Nov. 17, 1953, before the Senate Judiciary Internal Security Subcommittee at his own request.

Hoover told the committee that former President (1945-53) Harry S. Truman's promotion of Harry Dexter White, a Treasury official accused of being a member of a Soviet spy ring, had hampered the work of the FBI.

Hoover testified, an FBI spokesman said recently, because "his integrity had been questioned and he was setting the record straight."

Whatever the reason, Hoover's testimony on what was then such a sensitive subject caused a storm of controversy.

Policy: Hoover has also not hesitated to discuss policy during his sessions with the House and Senate subcommittees which process his budget. These hearings are invariably closed to press and public, but a transcript is later published, excluding the off-the-record exchanges of Hoover and the committee members.

The FBI director tries to avoid commenting on specific legislation—at least during the on-the-record portions of the hearings—but even in this there are exceptions.

Consular Offices—In March 1965, in testimony before a House appropriations subcommittee, Hoover responded to a request to comment on a treaty then pending in the Senate which would authorize the exchange of consulates between the Soviet Union and the United States.

Hoover stated that this would "make our work more difficult." So influential is Hoover with Congress on the subject of subversive activities that this remark was sufficient to put the treaty into serious trouble in the Senate, despite the fact that the President and the Attorney General were on record as favoring it.

The treaty was finally approved after Secretary of State (1961-69) Dean Rusk wrote to Hoover, saying that he did not agree with the general interpretation of Hoover's statement as one of opposition to the treaty.

Rusk said he thought Hoover only meant that such a treaty would complicate the problem of internal security "without, of course, implying that the problem could not be handled by the FBI."

Hoover could not easily disavow Rusk's flattering interpretation, and wrote back to the Secretary that his interpretation was indeed correct.

Repeaters—Even in the routine course of budget hearings, Hoover's views on crime and the law are solicited and given.

Last June, for example, during his appearance before the Senate Appropriations Subcommittee on State, Justice, Commerce, and the Judiciary, which processes his budget, Hoover was asked for his recommendation on what to do with criminal repeaters.

"The difficulty," said the director, "is with district attorneys who make deals and judges who are too soft.

"Some are bleeding hearts. In some big cities, it is like a revolving door. They go in and come right out again.

"Then last, but not by any means least, you have the abuse of parole and probation."

Drug Addicts—In the same hearing, Hoover was asked how he would cope with hard-drug addicts. His reply:

"Enforce the laws that are on the books at the present time, particularly those aimed at the pushers, who sell the drugs. I am not particularly in favor of reducing the penalties in regard to the possession of marijuana and hard drugs."

It is the congressional legislative committees, incidentally, not the appropriations panels, which process bills on drug pushing or on criminal recidivism.

Privacy—As a general rule, however, the appropriations committees do not—on the record, at least—spend much time quizzing Hoover on policy questions.

The director, for example, appeared before the House appropriations subcommittee on the morning of March 17 this year to testify on his budget request, while assigning one of his assistants to go to a nearby hearing room and read a Hoover statement to the Senate Judiciary Subcommittee on Constitutional Rights, which was holding hearings on the invasion of privacy by government.

Hoover presented the House subcommittee with what amounted to a briefer version of that statement.

Not a single question was asked of him on record nor, so far as the printed transcript indicates, off the record.

Off the record: The parenthetical phrase "discussion held off the record" dots the published versions of Hoover's closed-door committee testimony.

What is said off the record is, of course, intended only for the ears of the committee members, who are proud of their ability to keep what they hear to themselves.

Hints—Nevertheless, the general nature of the off-the-record discussions are hinted at and even described by members of the two panels.

Rep. John J. Rooney, D-N.Y., who has chaired the House Appropriations Subcommittee on State, Justice, Commerce, and the Judiciary for 21 of the last 23 years, said in an interview that the committee finds out what it needs to know to process the FBI budget during the off-the-record phase of the hearings.

"You must imagine this is a very interesting part of the day," Rooney said. "We get information no other committee of Congress gets . . . and it's never divulged."

Rooney's Republican counterpart, Rep. Frank T. Bow of Ohio, who is also the ranking Republican in the full House Appropriations Committee, said "you do find some sharp questioning" in the closed sessions.

Other committee members have similar reports.

"Anything we want to hear," said Rep. Neal Smith, D-Iowa, "he'll tell us about," including cases pending in court. "It gives us an idea of what they're up against in the coming year."

Hoover, said Rep. Mark N. Andrews, D-N.D., "has to be frank with us so we know how much money he needs to run his shop and to anticipate problems."

"Most of the probing questions we ask come up when we are off the record."

Berrigans—Hoover got himself into hot water and simultaneously gave the public a rare glimpse of the kind of information given out during off-the-record committee sessions when he appeared before a Senate appropriations subcommittee Nov. 27, 1970 to request supplemental budget money.

An FBI spokesman said Hoover did not realize the committee intended to release copies of his statement; others say the FBI itself made copies available in advance of the testimony.

In any case, Hoover made headlines that day by telling the subcommittee of "an incipient plot" by the East Coast Conspiracy to Save Lives to blow up underground conduits and steam pipes in Washington "to disrupt federal government operations" and to kidnap a high government official and hold him for political ransom.

The leaders of the east coast conspiracy group, said Hoover, were the Revs. Philip and Daniel Berrigan; the high official was later identified as Henry A. Kissinger, President Nixon's assistant for national security affairs.

For publicly revealing details of an FBI investigation in advance of grand jury action, Hoover was sharply criticized.

Participants in appropriations committee hearings say Hoover privately gives out this kind of information on a regular basis during off-the-record sessions. In November 1970, he did it on the record.

Fears: There is a widespread feeling on Capitol Hill that the FBI's vast files contain folders on each Member of Congress, and that the potential for abuse of the files exists.

Dossiers—At the Princeton conference in October, Bernard Fensterwald Jr., former counsel to the Senate Judiciary Subcommittee on Administrative Practice and Procedure, explained why he believed Congress would never investigate the FBI:

"Hoover's got a dossier on everyone on the Hill, and they know it."

While many share Fensterwald's suspicions, others are convinced that even if there are dossiers, the FBI would never use them for fear of arousing the enmity of the entire Congress.

Taps—The recently voiced suspicions on the part of some Members of Congress that their office phones were being tapped has put Hoover on the defensive.

When questioned last March by a House subcommittee member about fingerprint records of Members of Congress, Hoover volunteered: "I would like to add, also, we have never tapped a telephone of any Congressman or any Senator since I have been director of the bureau."

In June, before the Senate subcommittee, Hoover said, "I want to take this opportunity to reiterate what I told the members of the House subcommittee on appropriations last March, that the FBI has not tapped the telephone of any Congressman or any Senator since I became director in 1924."

The suspicions remain, however, and they were not dispelled by recent court testimony that the FBI had bugged the office (though not tapped the phone) of Robert T. Carson, administrative assistant to Sen. Hiram L. Fong, R-Hawaii, in the course of investigating a bribery charge against Carson and that the telephone of a man calling Rep. John Dowdy, D-Tex., at his Capitol office had been tapped during a probe of a similar charge against Dowdy.

Accountability: Despite his relative freedom from close congressional supervision, "Hoover is accountable up here," a Senate aide, who did not wish to be identified, said; "not day to day, year by year, line-item by line-item, but he knows what Congress wants and doesn't want."

The aide said there are a series of "informal checks and balances, and these are what keep the bureau in line." When Hoover is finally replaced, he said, "the new man will have to learn this."

BUDGET

The FBI asked for $334,486,000 for the current fiscal year, and as is usually the case, got every penny of it.

In the past 23 years at least, the FBI has gotten all it asked—and in two of those years, more than it asked.

This is true not only of what the bureau gets from Congress but of what it is authorized by request by its superiors in the Justice Department and in the Executive Office of the President.

Justice: Leo M. Pellerzi, the assistant attorney general in charge of Justice's Administrative Division, said in a recent interview that historically the FBI's budgeting procedures have been "much better than the rest of the department" and that for this reason the bureau has been treated differently from all other units of the department in the preparation and processing of its spending requests.

The FBI, for example, does not participate in the internal review process within the department which precedes the formal submission of budget requests by the department's subdivisions.

But it is involved in "the daily give and take" with departmental budget analysts, and at this stage of the process, its budget requests are treated much as those from other units of the department.

Budget Cuts—The Administrative Division has, on occasion, recommended cutbacks in FBI spending. But Pellerzi said that since he joined the department in 1968—and for at least several years before that—no bureau cuts have been sustained.

"Hoover can be very persuasive with the Attorney General," who has the final word on the size of the department's budget, said Pellerzi.

"If he says he needs it to do the job, his personal stature is such that there is very little you can do to knock that down."

After Hoover—Hoover gets what he asks for, in the department and on Capitol Hill, said Pellerzi, because his budget is carefully prepared and well justified.

When finally a new director takes over at the FBI, "it would be almost a natural consequence that the budgets would be looked at a lot more closely, and it would be essential from the point of view of the Attorney General and the OMB (Office of Management and Budget) to do this," Pellerzi said.

OMB: At OMB, the FBI budget is usually reviewed during a half-day session attended by Clyde A. Tolson, Hoover's long-time associate director; by John P. Mohr, the veteran assistant to the director, and by Nicholas P. Callahan, assistant director in charge of the administrative division of the bureau.

The FBI budget has survived the OMB review without change for at least the last few years, according to Pellerzi, who added that "from this you shouldn't conclude that the review is cursory—you can have a very thorough review of the budget and still not cut it."

The FBI budget fares well at OMB, explained Mark W. Alger, chief of the general government programs division of OMB, because "the FBI has not been an agency that has continually asked for increases in personnel except in response to specific legislation or presidential direction."

Congress: Hoover personally leads the FBI budget team before
the annual sessions of the House appropriations subcommittee and the occasional hearings held by its Senate counterpart.

"Mr. Hoover spends months preparing for his budget testimony," an FBI aide said, "because he knows the budget is the key to operating the bureau."

Hoover often takes the budget documents home with him during this period, and the results show in his testimony on the Hill.

Rooney—House subcommittee Chairman Rooney has a reputation as an impatient questioner of witnesses before his panel. He is quick to spot and to land upon a witness who is unsure of his facts.

Of Hoover, Tolson and Mohr, the trio which usually presents the FBI budget to the subcommittee members arrayed on one side of the long, narrow, felt-covered table in the center of the committee room, Rooney said:

"You can ask them any question, anywhere in their budget, and you get an answer right then and there."

Rooney complained that other witnesses are inclined to dodge hard questions by promising to supply the answer later for the committee record. "Hoover never does this," he said.

Why has the FBI fared so well at the hands of the committee, Rooney was asked.

"Because it's the best-run agency in town, administratively," he said.

The bureau's budget rises each year, said Rooney, "because of additional duties given to it gratuitously—and not sought by the FBI—by the Congress itself."

When he first became subcommittee chairman, Rooney recalled, "I started out trying to trip up Mr. Hoover, and I really got frustrated.

"I never could lay a glove on him. I might be able to get his goat—he has a low boiling point, you know—but I never could get anything that would justify reducing the budget."

Rooney's predecessor, Rep. (1935-51) Karl Stefan, R-Neb., gave him some advice when he took over the subcommittee:

"He said to me, 'Consider carefully before you cut the FBI budget, because it means so much to our country.' I've taken that advice."

Bow—The senior Republican on the subcommittee, Rep. Bow, shares Rooney's attitude toward the FBI.

"The FBI always lays its cards on the table for us," he said. "They never try to put anything under the table that we can't see."

Bow, like Rooney, insisted that

McCLELLAN AND ROONEY: FRIENDS OF THE FBI

If any one man can be said to dominate the relationship between Congress and the FBI, it is Sen. John L. McClellan, D-Ark., a 33-year veteran of Capitol Hill.

McClellan wears three hats while acting out this role.

He is chairman of the Senate Government Operations Committee, which is empowered to investigate and monitor the activities of the entire executive establishment. He is also chairman of the committee's Permanent Subcommittee on Investigations, the forum in which McClellan built his reputation as a stern prober of organized crime, labor corruption and government waste.

He is chairman, as well, of the Judiciary Subcommittee on Criminal Laws and Procedures, which processes most of the legislation in the field of organized crime, gambling and racketeering, with major jurisdiction over the laws which the FBI enforces.

Key Post: Most important, McClellan heads the Senate Appropriations Subcommittee on State, Justice, Commerce and the Judiciary, which passes on all budget requests from the FBI.

McClellan's most significant role in the future, however, may derive from his Judiciary subcommittee chairmanship if he is still in the Senate when the nomination of a new FBI director is sent up for confirmation.

That nomination will be handled by the Judiciary Committee, and McClellan, because of his subcommittee position, may be influential both in the choice of a new director and in the nominee's approval by the Senate.

McClellan, at 75, is a year younger than the FBI director. He served two terms in the House, from 1935 to 1939, and then returned to Arkansas to private law practice until 1942, when he successfully ran for election to the Senate.

He will complete his fifth term in the Senate on Jan. 3, 1973.

An aide to the Arkansas Senator, asked if McClellan's relations with Hoover and the FBI were satisfactory from McClellan's point of view, said in an interview that the question answered itself: "McClellan can't have a bad relationship with the FBI. He has too much power over it—when he chooses to use it."

McClellan is considered ideologically to be in the same camp as Hoover, and therefore the need to use his legitimate and purse-strings power over the bureau rarely arises.

Three in House: McClellan's three hats are worn by as many men in the House.

The House government operations Subcommittee on Legal and Monetary Affairs, which oversees the work of the FBI, among other agencies, is headed by Rep. John S. Monagan, D-Conn., a member of the House for 13 years.

The dean of the House, 83-year-old Rep. Emanuel Celler, D-N.Y., who has heen in the House since 1923, is chairman of the Judiciary Committee, which has general legislative jurisdiction over the FBI.

The House Member who has the most influence over the FBI, however, is Rep. John J. Rooney, like Celler a Democrat from Brooklyn, who has been in the House since 1944 and has been chairman of the House Appropriations Subcommittee on State, Justice, Commerce and the Judiciary since 1949 (except during the two Republican years of 1953 and 1954).

Rooney's subcommittee processes the FBI's budget and is one of the very few panels to take testimony regularly from Hoover.

Approval: The Full House Appropriations Committee rarely overrides the spending recommendations of its subcommittees, and the full House does not often tamper with what its Appropriations Committee proposes.

In the case of the FBI budget, the subcommittee has always approved at least as much as the bureau has asked for, and this approval has always been sustained by the full committee and by the House.

Rooney's views on the FBI are perhaps best exemplified by a statement he made on the House floor last June 14 in reaction to a television documentary critical of Hoover and the bureau.

"As a citizen of the United States," Rooney said, "I am deeply disturbed at this continuing attempt to discredit a devoted and exemplary public servant, FBI Director J. Edgar Hoover. He has selflessly molded the FBI into perhaps the finest investigative agency in the world.

"To my mind, the FBI represents one of the best-managed and most efficient government agencies it has been my privilege to observe in more than a quarter of a century on the Hill.

"This evaluation of the FBI is not made from any infatuation with or, as some critics would maintain, a fear of Mr. Hoover. It is made from the cold, hard analysis and comparison of government operations from a vantage point few others have had."

the committee examined the FBI budget "as closely as we do the others. It's the manner in which the FBI has handled its budget which makes it look easier."

GAO: The General Accounting Office, an arm of Congress, has general auditing authority over all agencies of the federal government.

There are some exceptions, however, for funds relating to intelligence activities, and the FBI—like the CIA—is free from GAO auditing.

"We've never set a foot inside the door of the FBI," said a GAO official who declined to be identified.

"As a practical matter, we doubt if the FBI would give us access to their records."

REFORM PROPOSALS

There is no shortage of proposals to reform the FBI, to restructure it, to increase its responsiveness and accountability, to protect it from the grasp of political manipulators.

Princeton: A sheaf of suggestions emerged from the October conference at Princeton, including several calls for legislation to limit the FBI to the enforcement of criminal laws, stripping it of its intelligence-gathering function.

Emerson—Professor Thomas I. Emerson of the Yale Law School made that proposal, and also recommended that a board of overseers be established to watch over the FBI, and an ombudsman appointed to process citizens' complaints against the bureau.

Elliff—John T. Elliff, an assistant professor of politics at Brandeis University, said the FBI suffers from the fact that it has gone a half-century without a public accounting.

He proposed that a permanent domestic intelligence advisory board, a counterpart to the board which advises the President on foreign intelligence, be created to give the chief executive advice in this field.

Chairman—A statement issued in the name of the three conference chairmen—Burke Marshall, Norman Dorsen and W. Duane Lockard—urged Congress to convene a "national commission of inquiry" that would explore some of the questions raised at the conference.

AELE: Americans for Effective Law Enforcement, a Chicago organization created originally as a counterweight to the American Civil Liberties Union, has been given a $70,000 grant by Friends of the FBI to make its own study of the bureau.

The Princeton conference was biased and its studies were prejudiced, Frank Carrington, executive director of AELE, told a news conference in Washington recently.

"Our study is necessary, therefore, if this nation is to have a full discussion of the FBI's role in our society," he said.

Carrington said the new study "will be prejudiced in only one respect. We will recognize the conflict between the need for a governmental institution that contends with radical and revolutionary groups, and the constitutional rights of those groups.

"We will not resolve that conflict entirely in favor of the radicals, as has been done by the ACLU and the CPJ (Committee for Public Justice, a cosponsor of the Princeton conference).

In Congress: Sen. Muskie, the front-running candidate for the Democratic presidential nomination, has called for a domestic intelligence review board, responsible to the President and Congress, that would oversee all government surveillance activities.

Sen. Gaylord Nelson, D-Wis., has sponsored a bill to establish a legislative commission to study all domestic surveillance by government agencies, including the FBI.

In the congressional hopper but, like Nelson's bill, without any signs of hearings, are two bills which would set conditions on the selection of a successor to Hoover.

Rep. Charles H. Wilson, D-Calif., has sponsored a bill which would set a 10-year term for the director of the FBI and prevent reappointment at the end of the term. It would also let the President remove the director from office before the term is up.

Rep. Walter S. Baring, D-Nev., is the author of a bill that would require the President to appoint the next FBI director from among those who have served in the bureau for at least 10 years.

OUTLOOK

There is little sign of any real desire—in the Justice Department, the White House or Congress—to get involved now in a full-scale study of the organization and activities of the FBI.

Administration: Wallace H. Johnson, an associate deputy attorney general who is the Justice Department's chief legislative representative, said in a recent interview that the Administration had no plans for any legislation in this direction.

"As far as I know, there has been no legislation proposed, considered, submitted or encouraged to restrict the FBI or circumscribe the director's term," Johnson said.

Congress: A Senate committee aide who follows the legislative fortunes of the FBI closely predicted recently that "nothing will be done until Hoover actually steps down."

Staff members of other committees with jurisdiction that could permit them to embark on an investigation of the FBI were equally confident that any study of that kind would await Hoover's retirement.

Last April, the Justice Department briefly proposed and quickly rescinded an invitation for a full-scale congressional investigation of the bureau.

Nothing more has been heard of the suggestion.

There may be some committee studies and investigations which peripherally will involve the FBI.

Ervin—Sen. Sam J. Ervin Jr.'s Subcommittee on Constitutional Rights has invited two White House aides, Frederic V. Malek and Charles W. Colson to testify on the abortive FBI check of CBS newsman Schorr early next year as part of Ervin's hearings on press freedom.

The subcommittee is currently working on a report and legislation based on this year's hearings into government surveillance which may affect the FBI, at least incidentally.

Rights Panel—The Organized Crime Control Act of 1970 (84 Stat 960) established a National Commission on Individual Rights, composed of 15 members, seven named by the President and eight by Congress, to study federal laws and practices relating to wiretapping and bugging, among other things.

The commission was given authority to demand data from any federal agency as part of its determination as to whether such laws and practices "infringe upon the individual rights" of Americans.

The role of the FBI would be a logical part of such a study—if it ever comes about.

To date, the commission has not been named and money to run it has not been appropriated, even though the commission was to have begun its work on Jan. 1, 1972.

Advice and Consent: There is much optimism on the part of FBI critics, about the provision of the 1968 Safe Streets Act which requires the President to submit the nomination of Hoover's successor to the Senate for confirmation.

They are hopeful that the Senate will exercise its review privilege as vigorously as it has on Supreme Court nominations during the past few years.

"I was very pleased to see the directorship put under Senate confirmation," Ramsey Clark said, "because I thought it possible the wrong man could get in."

A congressional aide who differs with Clark on many issues, shares with him his feeling that the confirmation requirement is desirable and "is likely to produce a moderate, able nominee."

Stephen Gillers, director of the Committee for Public Justice, which sponsored the Princeton conference, said a book which includes the papers prepared for the conference and much of the two-day proceedings, will be ready next fall and if the timing is right, he hopes the volume will have an impact on congressional consideration of a new director.

"We're also prepared very quickly to put together a panel of people to testify at a confirmation hearing," Gillers said.

"At the least," he added, the Princeton papers "can serve as a vehicle for a public airing and a way to put the new director on the record."

New Man: That there will be a new director before too long is widely accepted.

When the new man is in office, predicted Clifton Sessions, "a lot of people will be testing to see what they can do and get away with—whether the old power still exists."

Francis Biddle, writing in 1962, drew upon his experience as Hoover's boss during the war years and asked:

"When Hoover resigns or retires or dies, what will happen—can the same freedom be given to another man, the virtual freedom from control?

"I do not believe it can. But the tradition of good work over these long years will carry it along and perhaps hold it above the corruption and misdirection which has infested so many police forces.

"A successor to Hoover must be found who is outstandingly competent, but who is also humane."

Federal strike forces dominate government's war on organized crime   *Richard S. Frank*

Federal strike forces—teams of investigators and prosecutors combining their efforts in a single geographic area—have become, in less than three years, the government's principal weapon in its war on organized crime.

This has happened in spite of bureaucratic jealousies that could have destroyed the teams and in the face of an almost constant struggle for dominance between strike-force teams and the U.S. Attorneys in whose districts the forces are assigned.

Today there are 18 strike forces, more than twice the number there were on Jan. 20, 1969, when the Nixon Administration took office. They now account for the major share of the more than $77 million the federal government plans to spend this year to combat organized crime.

The strike-force concept dates from 1967. In practice, it brings to each part of the country with a significant organized-crime problem a team of specialists from the principal federal agencies which have responsibilities and expertise in the subject.

Each team is expected to pool the intelligence-gathering, investigative and prosecutorial efforts of the agencies and bring them to bear on organized crime and racketeering in its geographical area.

The strong acceptance of the strike-force concept by the Nixon Administration has come about despite an influential study group's recommendation to President Nixon that the program should, in effect, be scrapped as a centrally directed instrument of the federal government and be made subordinate to the U.S. Attorneys.

That recommendation, made two years ago by the Advisory Council on Executive Organization (Ash Council), was rejected by Mr. Nixon, one of the very few times a proposal by the panel had been turned down.

In making that decision, the President leaned heavily on the advice of Attorney General John N. Mitchell, who inherited the strike-force program from his predecessor, Ramsey Clark, and promptly made it his own.

Many of the problems have survived the change of Administrations.

Some U.S. Attorneys still feel threatened by the strike forces and see them as challenges to their authority as chief federal prosecutors in their districts.

Some federal agencies still are only reluctant participants, and the FBI, the most important of all these agencies, remains relatively aloof from the strike forces.

Nevertheless the Administration considers the program a success, and the evidence seems to bear out this conclusion.

ACTIVITIES

There have been strike forces for nearly five years, and while the precise composition and function of each differ from city to city, there is a fixed basic outline.

Each team is headed by a law-yer-member of the Justice Department's organized crime and racketeering section, and includes several other attorneys from the section as well as representatives of agencies with an active general interest in organized crime or with a specialized interest in a particular strike-force city.

Teams: Typically, a strike force will include agents from the Justice Department's Bureau of Narcotics and Dangerous Drugs and its Immigration and Naturalization Service; Treasury's Internal Revenue Service, Bureau of Customs and Secret Service; Labor's Office of Labor-Management and Welfare Pension Reports; and the U.S. Postal Service's inspection service.

Conspicuous by its absence is the Federal Bureau of Investigation, which has never assigned its agents as members of the strike force but which, in recent years at least, has cooperated—often at arm's length—with the strike-force teams.

The strike force in New York City (the Southern District of New York) is a joint federal-state force, with representatives of police and prosecuting agencies in New York State and New York City holding membership on the force.

Similar federal-state-local cooperation exists in Detroit, on an informal basis, according to William S. Lynch, chief of the Justice Department's organized crime section, and a formal joint force is in a formative stage in Newark.

Intelligence — Thomas J. McKeon, who headed the Detroit

strike force in 1968 and 1969, has written of the "jurisdictional blinders" which federal investigative agents so often wear and which must be removed if the strike-force concept is to work.

And Fred M. Vinson Jr., former assistant attorney general (1965-69) in charge of the Criminal Division, said in an interview recently:

"Most investigators tend to get tunnel vision."

The Ash Council, in its study of strike forces in 1969, found this example of the breakdown of interagency cooperation which the strike-force concept was intended to correct:

The Treasury Department's Bureau of Customs and Justice's Bureau of Narcotics and Dangerous Drugs each independently assigned agents to tail a narcotics smuggler from the Mexican border to a large Midwestern city, where a pickup was expected to be made.

Neither agent was aware that the other was on the same case. When they spotted each other at the pickup spot, each thought the other was the pickup man, and each opened fire on the other. Fortunately, neither was killed.

Clearly, the Ash Council study concluded, had the two agencies coordinated their operations by exchanging their information, the incident could have been avoided.

Investigative agencies are also chary about sharing their informants, or stool pigeons, with personnel of another agency. The strike force is intended to break down this barrier to cooperation.

Relations—Thus, the relationships among the agencies in the organized-crime field are critical to the success of the strike-force program, and this includes not only the agents who sit on the strike forces but their agency colleagues back in Washington and in the field.

Equally critical is the relationship between the strike forces and the U.S. Attorney, who represents the federal government within his district and who is chief prosecutor on behalf of Washington.

It is in the area of organizational and personal relationships that most of the early troubles with the strike forces arose.

Growth: The strike-force concept was initially sold to federal law enforcement agencies as a pilot project, and Buffalo was chosen as the demonstration city.

Robert D. Peloquin, who headed that first strike force, said in a recent interview that "originally the strike force was to be a hit-and-run group." A team of outside investigators, he explained, was to move into a city, do its work and then withdraw.

But the Buffalo experience convinced the Justice Department that the concept was sound and that strike forces should be assigned to other cities on a permanent basis.

Many of the problems which strike forces face today result from that early decision to institutionalize the team concept and to make the strike forces a permanent—and now the most important—part of the federal effort against organized crime.

Under Clark—The decision to give permanent status to the strike-force program was made by Clark. Thus, by the end of his term as Attorney General, on Jan. 20, 1969, there were six new strike forces in Brooklyn, Chicago, Detroit, Miami, Newark and Philadelphia.

The original Buffalo strike force disbanded a few months later, but a new team was sent to Buffalo the following September.

By the spring of 1968, the first Buffalo strike force had sufficiently impressed the Justice Department with its results that Vinson was describing the concept to a congressional committee as "the most fruitful technique available for major impact on organized crime."

The department intended, he said, to locate strike forces "in all areas of major concentration of racketeers."

As a result of the increased emphasis on strike forces, the staff requirements of the organized crime section, which supervises the teams and supplies the Justice Department team members, grew rapidly during the Clark-Vinson regime.

Where there were only 48 lawyers in the entire section in fiscal 1966, Vinson told the committee, by the spring of 1968 there were already 67, and the department was hoping the number would be up to 85 by the following year, with most of these lawyers assigned to strike-force duties.

Under Mitchell—Even before he took office as President, Richard Nixon was advised that the strike-force program was one he should hold on to.

In December 1968, the House Republican Task Force on Crime, headed by Rep. Richard H. Poff, R-Va., told Mr. Nixon that the strike forces "ought not only be retained but also expanded."

The advice was taken. In one of his first messages to Congress (on April 13, 1969), the President said he was instructing his new Attorney General to establish 20 "racketeering field offices" in as many cities "to instutionalize and utilize the valuable experience that has been gained by the 'strike forces' under the direction of the Department of Justice."

The attempt to substitute a new name for the Clark-initiated program has long since been abandoned, and the concept has been implemented virtually without change.

Under Attorney General Mitchell, strike forces have been assigned to Baltimore, Boston, Cleveland, Kansas City, Los Angeles, New Orleans, New York City, Pittsburgh, St. Louis and San Francisco and have been reassigned to Buffalo.

There is also a Washington-based strike force, with nationwide jurisdiction, appointed last July to investigate the infiltration of legitimate business by organized crime.

Today the organized crime section has grown to 125 attorneys, of whom all but 25 are assigned to the strike forces.

Numbers—The precise number of strike-force personnel from all federal agencies is classified, but according to Lynch, of the organized crime section, there are between 100 and 200 federal agents outside his section assigned to strike-force teams.

There are also, according to Lynch, "several thousand supporting personnel, in the field and in Washington."

FIGHTING ORGANIZED CRIME: 10 AGENCIES

Ask someone to name a federal law enforcement agency in the field of organized crime, and the chances are he will answer: "the FBI."

But the Federal Bureau of Investigation is only one of 10 agencies with major responsibilities in this field and one of several dozen government offices with some role to perform in fighting organized crime.

The 10 major agencies, including the FBI, have a combined budget of more than $77 million to spend on organized crime.

Following is a list of those agencies, a description of their duties in the organized-crime field and an estimate (provided by the Office of Management and Budget) of their budgets in this area for the current fiscal year.

Justice Department:

FBI—Investigates illegal gambling, violations of labor laws and general criminal activities of organized-crime figures. $21,386,000.

Bureau of Narcotics and Dangerous Drugs—Investigates illegal importation and domestic sale of narcotics, marijuana and dangerous drugs. $382,000.

Immigration and Naturalization Service—Acts to keep criminals and racketeers out of the country and to deport undesirable aliens. $344,000.

General Legal Activities—Includes U.S. Attorneys, U.S. Marshals, the Tax Division and the Criminal Division's organized crime and racketeering section. $13,908,000.

Treasury Department:

Internal Revenue Service—Through its Intelligence Division, keeps close tabs on the tax affairs of known or suspected organized-crime figures; through its Alcohol and Tobacco Tax Division, investigates illicit liquor and firearms traffic involving organized-crime groups. $34,201,000.

Secret Service—Investigates forgery and counterfeiting of government currency, checks and bonds. $1,555,000.

Bureau of Customs—Investigates smuggling of narcotics and marijuana. $1,375,000.

Labor Department: Its Office of Labor-Management and Welfare Pension Reports investigates attempted infiltration of or influence over labor unions by organized crime. $3,125,000.

Securities and Exchange Commission: Watches for involvement of organized crime in the nation's securities markets. $300,000.

U.S. Postal Service: Its inspection service investigates mail frauds involving organized-crime figures and the theft and counterfeiting of credit cards. $571,000.

ASH COUNCIL

In his April 1969 message to Congress on organized crime, the President announced that he had directed the Ash Council "to examine the effectiveness of the executive branch in combating crime—in particular organized crime."

The council, whose chairman was Roy L. Ash, president of Litton Industries, eventually focused its study on the strike-force program, by that time in operation in nine cities.

Study: The council staff worked on the strike-force study in the summer and early autumn of 1969, interviewing more than 100 law enforcement experts in Washington and in each of the nine strike-force cities and in several other cities where strike forces were planned.

Interviews—Among those interviewed were Attorney General Mitchell and other key Justice Department officials, the director and other officers of the Bureau of Narcotics and Dangerous Drugs, the assistant treasury secretary for enforcement, the commissioner of customs, 13 of the 93 U.S. attorneys, FBI Director J. Edgar Hoover and eight other FBI officials, 15 strike-force members, judges, local police, Members of Congress and private individuals.

The interviews ranged from half an hour to 1½ hours and were given on the understanding that the statements would not be attributed, in the hope that this would lead to frankness.

The resulting report was approved by the council and forwarded to the White House. It has never been made public; neither have its conclusions and recommendations ever been announced by the White House or the Justice Department.

Findings—The Ash Council, in its interviews, uncovered substantial evidence of friction among the agencies represented on the strike forces and between the forces and the U.S. Attorneys in the field.

The council found that while the individual members of a team worked well together, the agencies for whom they worked were reluctant partners at best and jealous rivals at worst.

It found that the strike force leaders were frequently suspicious of the dedication of U.S. Attorneys to the war on organized crime, and that the U.S. Attorneys commonly viewed the strike force as a threat to the independence and authority of their office.

Proposals—The council recommended a number of changes in the strike-force program, including one change so sweeping that it would have altered the program almost beyond recognition, had it been accepted by the Nixon Administration.

This was the proposal that the strike force in each city should be made responsible to the U.S. Attorney instead of to the Justice Department in Washington.

Thus, each U.S. Attorney's office in the cities with organized crime problems would, in effect, have had an organized-crime section staffed and paid by federal law enforcement agencies but under the direction of the federal prosecutor.

The Ash Council also recommended that communications between the Justice Department in Washington and the U.S. Attorneys in the field be improved; that liaison between Justice and other enforcement agencies, and among the various agencies, he increased; that a high-level coordinating council be created; and that additional investigators be hired by each agency engaged in organized-crime activities.

Response: The council report, along with a lengthy appendix containing the interviews (many of them unattributed), was sent to the White House and to the Justice Department.

Although the Administration's reaction, like the report itself, was never made public, a participant in Justice Department discussions of the study recalled recently that Mitchell, by now a staunch strike-force advocate, was "incensed" by the council's criticisms and its recommendations.

Justice—Andrew M. Rouse, who was the council's executive director until it disbanded last spring and is now with Arthur D. Little Inc., a management consulting firm, was involved in the next step.

"After the report was approved by the council," Rouse said in an interview, "there was a kind of formal discussion with Attorney General Mitchell and Will Wilson (then assistant attorney general in charge of the Criminal Division, who resigned Oct. 15, 1971).

"Wilson made a presentation to the council about all they were doing in the organized-crime field. It amounted to a plea in confession and avoidance, which is a lawyer's way of saying we admit everything you say is true, but we've already begun to correct our faults."

For one thing, Wilson told the council, the Justice Department was already working on improved liaison with the other agencies in the strike-force program. For another, he said, the Administration was already moving to provide more personnel for the organized-crime units of federal law enforcement agencies.

As for the proposal that a coordinating council be established, Wilson said that President Nixon had already decided to set up a National Council on Organized Crime for that purpose.

The principal recommendation, that strike forces be subordinated to the U.S. Attorneys, was summarily rejected, Rouse said, with the Attorney General leading the opposition.

"The Attorney General was pretty convincing," Rouse said, "and I imagine he was convincing with the President as well."

White House—In his subsequent establishment of the National Council on Organized Crime (ExecOrder 11534) the following June 4, the President made no reference to the Ash Council's proposal to this effect.

Instead, the chief executive said that "creation of such a council is the inevitable result of the success of the federal strike forces. . . . "

SORE POINTS

The problems spotted by the Ash Council have not been eliminated by the Nixon Administration, and they have not disappeared with the passage of time.

The strike-force program has been plagued since it began by interagency rivalries and jurisdictional disputes.

U.S. Attorneys: The point of friction which most concerned the Ash Council and which led to its principal recommendation was between the strike force and the U.S. Attorney—or perhaps more accurately, between the Justice Department's central office in the nation's capital and its prosecutorial field offices, in the person of the individual U.S. Attorneys.

"You have to take a look at this in terms of the historic struggle between the U.S. Attorneys and the office of the Attorney General," a member of the Ash Council study team said recently.

While there has been an Attorney General since the birth of the Republic in 1789, there has been a Justice Department only since 1870.

Before that time, the U.S. District Attorneys (now simply U.S. Attorneys) were completely independent of the Attorney General. Since 1870, these federal prosecutors have come under the supervision of the Attorney General and are part of the Justice Department.

The relationship has always been touchy; the U.S. Attorney is a presidential political appointee, while the Justice Department attorneys, with whom he principally deals, are career employees, or, at the least, nonpolitical jobholders.

The typical U.S. Attorney is also politically ambitious, and therefore is particularly resentful of nonpolitical types, who represent a challenge to his authority.

Complaints—The Ash Council concluded that the smooth relationship in Buffalo between Peloquin as strike-force leader and John T. Curtin as U.S. Attorney was the exception, not the rule.

In the spring of 1969, for example, a new U.S. Attorney, H. Kenneth Schroeder Jr., took office; four months later, a new strike-force team arrived in Buffalo.

The new prosecutor and the head of the new strike force immediately disagreed over questions of jurisdiction and authority. The council study quotes Schroeder's complaint:

"It is the U.S. Attorney's job to coordinate information to the various agencies in the area. It is *his* job to direct the government effort *and* emphasis.

"I am responsible to the people here for both the good and the bad of the federal effort. If the people from Washington come out here to work with me as my assistants, that's fine."

The strike-force leader, of course, disagreed.

In Chicago, according to the Ash Council study, the U.S. Attorney fought the strike-force arrival "tooth and nail." A participant in the strike-force program there told the council it was greeted with a "stone wall."

In Detroit, where McKeon was put in charge of the second strike force, "he and the U.S. Attorney were at each other's throats," according to Peloquin, who, with McKeon, now runs International Intelligence Inc.

In another city, according to the Ash Council study, a U.S. Attorney learned that a new strike-force chief had been assigned by reading the local newspapers.

"I had heard nothing from Washington about this prior to the announcement—and still haven't," the prosecutor told a council interviewer at the time.

The complaints of U.S. Attorneys crossed party lines. A new Republican prosecutor told the council:

"Bobby Kennedy would have abolished the office of U.S. Attorney, if he could have, because he wanted more complete control in Washington. I am sorry to see that this seems to be the same line of thought under the new Administration."

Another fear expressed to the council by federal prosecutors was that the assignment of a strike force to their district implied that they were lax in their duties.

One attorney told an interviewer for the council that the Justice Department should stay out "unless they don't think the U.S. Attorney is doing his job. Indeed, if that is the case, he should be relieved of his duties."

Another prosecutor summed up his opposition to the strike-force concept in these words:

"I feel Justice has made a mistake in structuring the strike force the way they have, i.e., as a satellite of the U.S. Attorney's office rather than as a part of it.

"I don't want the strike force's work—my men have 400 cases as it is. All I want is to be able to do my job, which is to coordinate the Justice Department setup here.

"To do that, I have to know what is going on. The Justice functions should not be fragmented, as it just creates ill feelings and resentment."

The heart of this argument, persuasive enough to be endorsed by the Ash Council, is that the U.S.

Roy L. Ash

Attorney is central to effective federal law enforcement in his district, and that what irritates and upsets him diminishes that effectiveness.

The Other Side—This argument is not universally accepted, especially by Justice Department officials, who question whether the U.S. Attorneys were ever effective against organized crime.

"They think that the presidential plaque on the wall gives them expertise in all subjects," one official said of the federal prosecutors.

The official is a career employee of the department, who has served under Democratic as well as Republican Attorneys General, and his remark reflects the gap between the professional, Washington-based organized-crime fighter and the temporary politically appointed prosecutor in the field.

A former high-ranking Justice Department official who served during the formative days of the strike-force program, said in a recent interview:

"U.S. Attorneys come in all

ranges of competence—from terrifically dedicated to incompetent—just a few of those. The large bulk range from mediocre to good.

"But even the best just don't have the time to head a strike force. You've got to have an experienced, full-time guy. No U.S. Attorney can be full time at it. Without the help of the investigative agencies, you've got nothing, literally nothing."

The Ash Council's proposal to eliminate the friction between Justice and the U.S. Attorney by subordinating the strike-force teams to the prosecutor is totally rejected by the department.

William Lynch, the organized crime section chief, said in an interview that "if you do that, then you might as well abolish this section."

He added that "it also means taking a giant leap of faith forward that the U.S. Attorneys' office will work as they haven't before."

Meeting—What Lynch has described as "the natural tension" between the department and the U.S. Attorneys has continued into the Mitchell regime at the Justice Department.

But some of the earlier rough spots have been smoothed over, and earnest efforts have apparently been made to open up better lines of communication between Washington and the district prosecutors.

The problem may have come to a head early last year, when a majority of the U.S. Attorneys with strike forces in their districts ("10 or 11," Schroeder, the Buffalo prosecutor, recalls) met with Wilson.

Schroeder said in a recent interview that the situation in late 1969 and early 1970 "was like the tail (the strike force) trying to wag the dog (the U.S. Attorney). There was no real recognition of the position and the role of the U.S. Attorney, who is the lawyer for the U.S. government within his district."

The meeting with Wilson was held at the request of the prosecutors to air their grievances, Schroeder said.

Out of the meeting, he said, emerged "the concept of mutuality, and a recognition that the U.S. Attorney is not going to play a subservient role or no role at all."

His particular problem in Buffalo, Schroeder said, was settled by the replacement of the strike-force chief.

One result of the meeting between the attorneys and Wilson was the issuance of formal guidelines governing the relations between strike forces and U.S. Attorneys in April 1970.

Guidelines—The guidelines represent a compromise between the rival claims for ascendancy.

They stipulate, for example, that the strike-force chief shall be chosen by the head of the Criminal Division "with the advice of the United States Attorney of the district where the strike force is located."

They spell out that the chain of command in all litigation shall be from the Criminal Division to the U.S. Attorney to the strike-force chief.

And they provide that press releases issued within the district "shall generally be issued in the name of the United States Attorney."

But the guidelines also provide

NATIONAL COUNCIL ON ORGANIZED CRIME

In its 1969 study of strike forces, the Advisory Council on Executive Organization (Ash Council) recommended that a high-level coordinating body be created to supervise the work of the strike forces and of other federal efforts against organized crime.

In June 1970, either in response to the recommendation or independently, President Nixon issued Executive Order 11534 establishing the National Council on Organized Crime.

It was, as it turned out, the only major recommendation of the Ash Council strike-force report ever put into effect.

The council, charged by the President "to formulate a national strategy for the elimination of organized crime," is headed by the Attorney General and includes the heads of all the principal agencies with some responsibilities in the organized-crime field.

The council has created six permanent staff committees, each headed by the assistant attorney general who heads the Criminal Division. Their subject areas—narcotics; gambling rackets; infiltration of business; state and local effort against organized crime; labor; and counterfeit, stolen funds, securities and credit cards—indicate the extent of the government's efforts against organized crime.

There are also two special committees serving the council. The Project Plan Committee is working, along with the Office of Management and Budget, on ways to evaluate the effectiveness of the various federal organized-crime programs.

The Trial Committee has been given the task of analyzing trials in organized-crime cases, comparing them with other criminal cases and proposing ways to minimize trial delays.

The national council itself has tactical and policy-making functions.

Last December, for example, it directed a coordinated raid, involving agents of the FBI and Internal Revenue Service, against illegal sports-betting operations in 26 cities.

The council recommended earlier this year the establishment of a strike force in Washington with nationwide jurisdiction to investigate the infiltration of legitimate business by organized crime. On July 27, Attorney General John N. Mitchell created the force.

If a decision is made to create more strike forces, the council will be asked to choose the new cities.

that disputes between the strike force and the prosecutor—over investigative assignments, whether or not to indict, and like matters—shall be settled by the Criminal Division, which has the final word.

THE FEDERAL GOVERNMENT AND ORGANIZED CRIME: THE BUFFALO STRIKE FORCE

The federal government has been involved in the fight against organized crime since the 1920s and early 1930s, the heyday of the G-man and the T-man.

But interest apparently waned with the close of the Prohibition era and was not revived again until the Kefauver hearings in 1951 (the Senate Select Committee to Investigate Organized Crime in Interstate Commerce, headed by the late Sen. Estes Kefauver, D-Tenn., 1949-63).

One of the committee's recommendations was that the federal government play a greater role in combating organized crime, and, in partial response, the Justice Department in 1954 created the organized crime and racketeering section within the Criminal Division to coordinate federal enforcement activities in the organized crime field.

Three years later, the section had a total of 10 attorneys. A decade later, Assistant Attorney General Fred M. Vinson Jr. was to describe the section's achievements during that early phase as "marginal: the problem was too great and the section was too small."

Turning Point: The real turning point in the federal concern with organized crime came in the autumn of 1957 with the revelation that more than 60 men, most with long criminal records and all with ties to criminal groups in various parts of the country, had met at the home of an organized-crime leader in Apalachin, N.Y.

On the list, the government concluded, were many of the principal leaders of organized crime in the nation, meeting there to settle jurisdictional and other problems.

Crime Group—In partial response to the Apalachin meeting, Attorney General (1957-61) William P. Rogers appointed a Special Group on Organized Crime the following April.

The group set up regional offices, gathered information on all those at the meeting and conducted grand jury investigations, which culminated in the indictment and conviction of 20 men who attended the Apalachin conference for conspiracy to obstruct justice.

Convictions Reversed—The convictions were subsequently reversed on procedural grounds by the 2nd Circuit Court of Appeals. By that time, the special group had disbanded.

The Syndicate: The object of this and subsequent government attention is the group known variously as the Syndicate, the Mafia or, in more recent years, La Cosa Nostra.

There are strong differences of opinion over whether there is such an organized, ethnically homogeneous grouping of criminals in the country.

But whether there is or not, federal law enforcement officials have for some years believed there is, and have acted upon this belief.

Commission Report—The President's Commission on Law Enforcement and Administration of Justice, headed by former Attorney General (1964-66) Nicholas deB. Katzenbach, concluded in 1967 that "the core of organized crime in the United States consists of 24 groups operating as criminal cartels in large cities across the nation."

Altogether, there are some 5,000 members of these groups, or "families," with a commission representing the major families responsible for settling organizational and jurisdictional arguments, according to the Katzenbach study.

"Organized crime in its totality thus consists of these 24 groups allied with other racket enterprises to form a loose confederation operating in large and small cities," the presidential commission said.

"In the core groups, because of their permanency of form, strength of organization and ability to control other racketeer operations, resides the power that organized crime has in America today."

Reaction—When the late Robert F. Kennedy became Attorney General in 1961, he drew upon his experience as counsel to a Senate committee investigating the penetration of labor and business by organized crime and pushed successfully for an increase in the organized-crime section staff.

By 1963, the staff had 60 lawyers, compared with 37 when Kennedy took office. The number of convictions resulting from the section's activities rose in the same period from 73 to 288.

After Kennedy left office in late 1964, the momentum slowed again, picking up during Ramsey Clark's tenure (1966-69) as Attorney General.

Trend—Significantly, during Kennedy's term as head of the Justice Department, a trend began toward the centralization of federal organized-crime efforts in the department in Washington and the diminishing of the influence of the U.S. Attorneys in the field.

In its 1967 report to President Johnson, the Katzenbach commission recognized and applauded this trend, calling for "a national strategy against organized crime" and urging the rapid enlargment of the organized-crime section staff.

While insisting that the organized-crime program "should not be the exclusive province of either the OCR section or the U.S. Attorneys," the commission nevertheless said that "the section should have final authority for decision-making in its relationship with U.S. Attorneys on organized crime cases."

A Step Further—Clark accepted the recommendation and went a significant step further, adopting an idea developed within the organized-crime section for a unified attack on organized crime—the strike force.

In his book *Crime in America,* (Simon and Schuster, 1970) Clark explained why the strike-force concept had appealed to him:

"The demands of the marketplace and the desire for success in its ventures and security from police have compelled crime to organize. We might ask, then, if crime can organize, why can't law enforcement?

"To be effective against organized crime, law enforcement must organize itself. The concept of the federal strike force was developed in 1967 to attack organized crime in city after city on a highly coordinated basis."

Clark thus made the decision to try out the new concept in one city, and Buffalo was the choice.

Buffalo: In choosing Buffalo for the pilot strike-force programs, the Justice Department was guided in part by the evident enthusiasm of the U.S. Attorney there and by the virtual absence of recent prosecutions of organized-crime figures in the upstate New York district.

Robert D. Peloquin, who took leave from his job as an assistant chief in the organized crime section to head the strike force, said in a recent interview:

"The U.S. Attorney is a very important figure in the success of any strike force. In Buffalo, Curtin liked the idea and he grabbed right on to it." (John T. Curtin was U.S. Attorney for the Western District of New York, 1961-67.)

In addition, Peloquin recalled, "nobody had given Buffalo a good shaking, and that was one of the reasons it was selected for the experiment."

The lack of any significant government attack on organized crime in Buffalo, he said, meant that it would be easier to measure the success or failure of the strike-force experiment.

Thus, in November 1966, the first strike-force team, with Peloquin at its head, moved into New York's second largest city.

Veterans—The team included representatives of the Bureau of Customs, IRS intelligence and Alcohol and Tobacco Tax Divisions, the old Bureau of Narcotics, the Immigration and Naturalization Service, the Labor Department's racketeering unit, five attorneys (including Peloquin) from the organized crime section of the Justice Department, and agents of the Royal Canadian Mounted Police.

They were "the cream of the crop" in terms of experience and seniority within their own agencies, Peloquin said, averaging 16 years in experience.

The Treasury Department's Bureau of Customs, for example, assigned the head of its law enforcement office; the Narcotics Bureau detailed the chief of its organized crime office and the RCMP named its chief of intelligence to work with the strike force.

Before the team moved into Buffalo, its members took three weeks of training at Justice to familiarize themselves with the jurisdictional authority of each of the agencies.

They then returned briefly to their own agencies to gather information on the Mafia family headed by Stefano Magaddino; armed with this data, the strike force went to work.

Methods—Every member of the Magaddino group who was in jail was sought out and interviewed to determine if he was ready to talk; some were.

Strike-force members also interviewed or "debriefed" their own agencies' informants and pooled the results.

The Advisory Council on Government Organization (Ash Council), in a 1969 study, noted that Peloquin and Curtin immediately developed a strong personal relationship which, in the council's view, was a crucial element in determining the success of the pilot strike-force project.

Curtin made available to Peloquin an office which was adjacent to his own. The two men conferred daily, and the U.S. Attorney sat in on strike force meetings when he had the time.

Curtin was also given assurances in advance that the strike force did not intend to seek out publicity for itself, and that he would be able to reap the publicity—and political—benefits of strike-force successes.

When strike-force members found a case with good prospects for success, the entire team concentrated on developing evidence for the case, brushing aside jurisdictional boundaries in the effort to make the case.

Results—The Buffalo strike force won 36 indictments from the grand jury, including those of a number of key men in the Magaddino "family."

Three "lieutenants" were convicted and sentenced to 15 years in prison, and the family's underboss received a term of 25 years.

In addition, information developed by the strike force led to the firing of several managers of a union pension fund, according to the Ash Council study.

Peloquin who now heads (Intertel), a consulting firm in the field of crime control, believes that the Buffalo strike force was a success in that "it made a major impact on the Mafia family up there."

In any event, the Justice Department was convinced that the concept was a success, despite the refusal of the FBI to assign any of its agents directly to the strike force and despite an open skepticism on the part of local agents of other federal law enforcement units toward the Buffalo strike force.

They also call for strike-force attorneys to handle grand jury presentations, either by themselves or along with one or more assistant U.S. Attorneys.

In practice, the guidelines are flexibly applied. This, in fact, is the principal reason there were no formal guidelines before last year: a fear that they would work against the flexibility which was seen as desirable.

U.S. Attorney Schroeder said the guidelines "are treated as suggestions, rather than hard, fast, dogmatic rules. When grown men sit down, they don't need guidelines to get the job done."

His colleagues agree. Herbert J. Stern, U.S. Attorney for New Jersey (Newark), said of the guidelines: "These are for all over, and you may have different needs in different places.

"I don't think there's any doubt in anybody's mind about who's in charge in Newark. Under the guidelines, the U.S. Attorney is very clearly the chief law enforcement officer in the district."

In Philadelphia, Louis C. Bechtle, U.S. Attorney for the Eastern District of Pennsylvania, said that "whatever they say in writing, there's no question here about where the federal prosecutor's office is."

Agencies: The Ash Council found the same fear of implied criticism among representatives of the federal law enforcement agencies as it did among U.S. Attorneys.

"By and large," a council interviewer said recently, "the investigative agencies were reluctant partners, primarily because of traditional operational prejudices but also because the very existence of the strike force was an implicit criticism of their work."

The passage of time and the institutionalization of the strike-force program seems to have reduced this fear, but the bureaucratic rivalries and jealousies experienced at the outset have lingered on.

"Bureaucratic inertia is a problem," said Lynch. "Any agency is reluctant to change its ways."

Rivalry—Even in the successful Buffalo pilot project, the strike force was plagued by agency-to-agency hostility, despite personal cooperation among the individual members of the strike-force team.

"Cooperation among the strike-force members was not a problem," an Ash Council participant said of the Buffalo program.

The council study quotes one strike-force member there: "There is a large overlap of people each agency is interested in. Customs may want a man for one thing, the Secret Service for another and the Bureau of Narcotics and Dangerous Drugs for something else. Cooperation is only natural, if we are working in the same office."

In Buffalo, as in the other strike-force cities, the problem was in coordinating the investigative efforts of the agencies, not of the strike-force members.

Another Buffalo strike-force

member told the Ash Council that "Customs and others are hostile to the strike force. Orders have gone out to some of these people that they must send memos to Washington every time they get a telephone call from a strike-force member."

This agent found himself being "frozen out" by his own agency, he told the council interviewer, because of his membership on the strike force.

Peloquin, the head of that first strike force, suggested that money may have a lot to do with this interagency hostility:

"The lifeblood of any agency is its statistics—its arrest records and so forth. It needs them to get its money from congressional appropriating committees.

"If we take away their statistics, by absorbing them into the statistics of the strike forces, that hurts them."

Peloquin added that "hopefully the congressional committees have learned this by now."

Staffing—When the original plans for the Buffalo strike force were being prepared in 1966, a decision was made that the force must be made up of supervisory representatives of the investigative agencies if the idea were to succeed.

Participation of supervisory personnel would not only raise the level of the investigations but would also help to break down the walls between the agencies and the strike force.

Thus, the strike-force members in Buffalo were senior agents who, as a former Justice Department official put it, "have some clout with their supervisors."

As the strike-force program has expanded, however, the rank and the influence of team members has been diluted.

U.S. Attorney Stern has observed this with the strike force assigned to his district in Newark.

"Every time another strike-force office opens up, personnel are robbed or borrowed from the existing strike forces. That is a problem."

FBI: The major problem by far of interagency relations involves the FBI, the federal government's predominant law enforcement agency.

Hoover and Clark—FBI Director J. Edgar Hoover said in a letter to the House Government Operations Subcommittee on Legal and Monetary Affairs on Nov. 20, 1967:

"The FBI has clearly indicated to the (Justice) Department that we will handle any investigation which it desires us to conduct and which falls within our investigative jurisdictions.

"Our position is that the supervision of these investigations should remain within the FBI and that we continue to direct the activities and the assignment of our personnel so that the maximum utilization of available agents can be achieved at all time."

Vinson told the same subcommittee that while the FBI was not a member of the strike force, "we rely heavily upon that agency for the intelligence information critical to the operation of the strike force."

Vinson added that the FBI had agreed to "investigate promptly any matter within its jurisdiction which is referred to it by the strike force."

Thus, the FBI, alone among the federal agencies, remained outside the strike-force program. How closely it did actually cooperate with the strike forces remains a matter of dispute.

Hoover, in his letter to the subcommittee in 1967, said the FBI had "maintained daily contact" with the Buffalo strike force since it began a year earlier.

"It is therefore certainly not true that we have failed to cooperate with this task force, even though we do not at the present time have any agency personnel assigned exclusively to work with it."

The Ash Council came to a different conclusion.

It characterized the FBI special agent-in-charge in Buffalo as "hostile from the start," in the words of a council investigator.

Relations between FBI agents and strike-force members were poor, the council found, quoting one participant as saying of an FBI agent: "He was trying to stick me, and I was trying to stick him. It was as simple as that."

There was also a rather heated exchange of letters between Hoover and his nominal superior, Clark, each protesting the other's position.

In one of them, according to a former Justice Department official, Hoover characterized the strike force as a group of "amateurs and bunglers."

"It was a sniping war, sort of bureaucratic in nature," another ex-official of the department said of the exchange of letters and memos.

The bureau did turn over extensive files on organized crime in the Buffalo area to the strike force, but some strike-force members complained later to Ash Council interviewers that the FBI was only inundating them with a flood of largely useless data.

A top Justice Department official at the time recently described FBI cooperation during the Clark regime as "a sometime thing."

The strike force, he said, "was, after all, a real bureaucratic threat" to the FBI and the other agencies, especially as it became evident that the concept would spread to other cities.

Clark's judgment of the FBI's motives is harsher than this. In *Crime in America,* he wrote:

"The FBI has so coveted personal credit that it will sacrifice even effective crime control before it will share the glory of its exploits.

"This has been a petty and costly characteristic caused by the excessive domination of a single person, J. Edgar Hoover, and his self-centered concern for his reputation and that of the FBI."

Hoover and Mitchell—The FBI will still not participate in the strike-force program to the extent of assigning its agents to the team.

But there is some evidence that the bureau cooperation has increased since Mitchell became Attorney General almost three years ago.

Whatever improvement there has been is in large measure the result of a political bargain struck between Hoover and Mitchell soon after Mitchell took office.

As a former official of the department explained it, Hoover agreed to cooperate more than he had in the past and Mitchell

Ramsey Clark

agreed not to press the FBI about actual strike-force membership.

Lynch, of the organized-crime section, while declining to discuss details, said recently that what problems formerly existed in his office's relations with the FBI "have been resolved."

U.S. Attorney Stern, in Newark, said of the FBI: "I do think the bureau has recognized the usefulness of the strike-force concept."

Hoover, in a recent letter to the editors of *The Washington Post* in response to a critical column by Jack Anderson, described his bureau's present role this way:

"The FBI, with the approval of the Attorney General, has assigned liaison agents to the strike forces in the field and at headquarters and uses many hundreds of agents to combat organized crime and develop cases which are prosecuted by the strike forces."

Hoover said that "this workable, effective, cooperative relationship has contributed to a growing record of accomplishments against organized crime across the country."

In his contribution to the most recent (for fiscal year 1970) annual report of the Justice Department, Hoover wrote of "significant gains against organized crime" on the FBI's part, and added:

"Numerous underworld leaders throughout the country were brought to justice during fiscal year 1970 as a result of the bureau's intensive investigative activity in this area and dissemination of criminal intelligence data to other law enforcement agencies."

This is the closest the FBI director came, in his report, to mentioning the strike forces. Neither here nor in his testimony on the FBI budget before a congressional committee last March did Hoover use the words "strike force."

EVALUATION

Not surprisingly, Justice Department officials say the strike-force program works; the statistics they offer as proof appear to bear them out.

Box Score: The simplest way to judge the effectiveness of the program is to look at the indictment and conviction rates.

In terms of what the department calls "high echelon" members of organized crime syndicates, the number of individuals indicted climbed from 38 in fiscal 1968 to 106 in fiscal 1971, and the number of convictions rose from 23 to 61 in the same time span.

For all kinds of organized-crime defendants, the pattern is similar: 1,166 indicted in 1968 and 2,122 in 1971; 520 convicted in 1968 and 679 in 1971 (by comparison, a decade ago 49 were indicted, the same number convicted).

The department attributes 82

percent of the fiscal 1971 indictments (406) and 60 percent of the convictions (1,738) to the activities of the strike forces.

Attorney General Mitchell, in his annual report to the President for fiscal 1970, pointed to other results: the heads of six of the 24 Mafia families, he said, "were brought under federal prosecutive action" that year.

Wiretaps: Another factor, however, complicates the task of evaluating strike-force performance in such statistical terms.

In 1968, the use of court-authorized wiretapping in organized crime cases was made possible by the Omnibus Crime Control and Safe Streets Act of 1968 (82 Stat 197). The Johnson Administration declined to use this tool but it was sanctioned by President Nixon almost as soon as he took office.

Mitchell, in a speech last month at a conference on crime reduction, said the court-ordered tapping "has proved to be an extremely effective method of obtaining evidence in organized-crime cases where other methods are ineffective or too dangerous."

His deputy, Richard G. Kleindienst, recently said that 253 court orders of that kind were obtained in 1969 and 1970 and that all but 12 proved productive.

More than 800 arrests, he said, resulted from these taps, but only 72 convictions through last February (his latest available figures), with other cases pending in court.

Mitchell, in his annual report, claimed "substantive inroads against organized crime," and said the results came about "largely through the restrained use of wiretapping and the operation of strike forces."

His statement points up the difficulty of separating the results of wiretapping from those of strike-force operations.

Measuring: The problem of measuring results is recognized by the Justice Department.

Lynch, for one, said that the number of indictments and convictions would probably have been lower if wiretapping were not employed.

But he insisted, nevertheless, that the number of indictments and convictions remained "the only objective measurement."

The National Council on Organized Crime has established a project plan committee to work with the Office of Management and Budget in developing a performance-measurement system to evaluate the effectiveness of the strike force and other organized-crime programs.

An indirect but important way of measuring the success of the strike forces is in terms of the spur they may have provided to the activities of the FBI and other federal enforcement agencies.

The Ash Council found, in its 1969 study, that the FBI agents in Buffalo the previous two years were, in the words of a strike-force investigator, "breaking their necks to get information; but this wasn't to cooperate with us. They were in competition, which was a byproduct of the strike force—a good one."

The council also found evidence of a swift expansion of FBI organized-crime activities in other cities.

Whether this was to help the strike forces or to compete with them is hard to discover. What is clear, in any case, is that the overall federal effort increased, at least in part because of the strike-force program.

Thus, even a former Ash Council staffer who participated in the 1969 study and remains critical of the program conceded recently that the program had at least one positive result:

"The FBI has broken its back to succeed in the fight against organized crime in the face of this bureaucratic threat."

Future: Mitchell's announced goal soon after he took office was to establish strike forces in 20 cities; to date there are forces in 18.

According to Lynch, no final decision has been made about whether to continue to pursue this goal or to put the money and men into an expansion of the existing strike forces.

There is another kind of goal: the "breaking up of organized crime within six years."

This was set earlier this year by the National Council on Organized Crime and published as part of the Administration's budget documents for the current fiscal year.

Thus, the Administration would be well into its second term before its goal could be realized.

Ramsey Clark agrees that the goal is not unrealistic. In his 1970 book he said, "There is no reason why La Cosa Nostra should not be relegated to history within a few years. It is on the ropes now."

But he added this warning:

"We must not deceive ourselves—organized crime is a very small part of America's crime. . . . The greatest harm we could suffer from organized crime would be to permit it to distract us from the major problems we face if we are to control crime in America."

Ponderous, public-oriented American Bar Association has an image crisis   *Richard S. Frank*

The legal profession, as represented by the 155,000-member American Bar Association, is having image problems in Washington.

Its opposition to no-fault auto insurance has exposed the ABA to charges that its concern for the lawyer's wallet is greater than for the public's purse.

Its disapproval of a trio of prospective Supreme Court nominations last autumn enraged President Nixon, the first lawyer to occupy the White House in a quarter century, and may have embittered relations in general between the Nixon Administration and the ABA.

Its unwillingness—some say inability—to move swiftly and precisely to formulate positions on major legislative issues has tended to diminish its influence with Congress.

Jealous of its reputation, the association is moving away—though not as rapidly as some of its members would have it—from all-out opposition to no-fault insurance toward a compromise between no-fault and the present lawyer-oriented tort-liability system.

It has made overtures to the Administration in an effort to resume its consultative role on high court nominations which has injected it into so many political controversies in the past three years.

But with lawyer-like circumspection, it is not willing to take shortcuts through its internal policy-making process in the mere pursuit of greater legislative clout.

"We sometimes are too slow," ABA President Leon Jaworski conceded in an interview. "But that's better than rushing in without knowing what we are doing or by ignoring the view of others."

LOBBYING

As an organization of men— and some women—who share a common profession, the ABA is in some ways a typical trade association.

Its membership is open to any lawyer in good standing in his state, and about 50 percent of the entire legal profession does belong.

Like any trade association, it seeks to support policies and legislative proposals which benefit its members and to oppose those which harm them.

Yet the ABA, as both its critics and its friends observe, is a different breed of trade association. Its interests are far broader than those of other associations, and many of its lobbying activities can only be classified, in lawyers' terms, as *pro bono publico:* for the public good.

The ABA's leadership in the successful campaign for a constitutional amendment on presidential disability and its major role in the unsuccessful effort to reform the presidential electoral system, for example, cannot be explained away as special-interest lobbying.

Its study of the Federal Trade Commission in 1969, culminating in recommendations for major changes in the structure and policies of that agency, falls into a similar category.

Influence: The ABA differs from some other trade groups and from labor organizations in another important particular: it has no money to contribute to anyone's campaign chest, and it has no significant number of votes it can marshal for or against a candidate or an issue. What it has, says Donald E. Channell, director of the bar association's Washington office since 1957, is "disinterested expertise."

Congress and the Administration, say Channell and other ABA officials, know they can look to the association for expert technical advice and rely on it for objective comments on matters of policy.

In Washington, where so much political influence is based on campaign money and potential votes, the ABA can only fall back on its prestige and on the credibility it has built up over the years.

This accounts for its concern over the attacks on the legal profession for its opposition to no-fault insurance, its unhappiness over the President's anger and its distress about congressional criticism.

Techniques: Channell heads one of the smaller lobbying staffs in Washington. He, one assistant director who works with him in the lobbying field, and a second assistant director for public information, constitute the total professional roster.

(A third assistant director devotes all of his time to his work as staff director of the ABA's Criminal Law Section, which operates out of, but is not part of, the Washington office.)

This is only the smallest part of the ABA's lobbying effort, however, because the Washington office can call on hundreds of volunteers, each of them expert in his field, from the ranks of the association.

"Other associations have to have specialists on their Washington staffs," Channell explained in a recent interview. "We call on volunteers. Our role in one sense is to coordinate and get our experts together with the experts in the executive branch and on the Hill."

The Washington office can also call on a network of influential ABA members, and on leaders of the state bar associations, to bring their personal relationships with key Congressmen to bear on legislative matters the ABA is interested in.

In letters last November to all Members of Congress, asking them to support a controversial legal services corporation, for example, Jaworski made certain copies also went to the presidents of each of the 50 state bar associations—and that each Congressman knew about it.

"If they agree with us on an issue," said Channell, "we can call on the state bars for help."

Lowell R. Beck, who was Channell's deputy from 1960 to 1967, and is now the ABA's associate executive director, related another example of the indirect influence the association can call upon from time to time.

On an issue important to the ABA about a decade ago, said Beck, the key stumbling block appeared to be Rep. William N. McCulloch of Ohio, the respected ranking GOP member of the House Judiciary Committee.

Attempts to persuade McCulloch to support the bill backed by the association failed until Sylvester C. Smith Jr., then ABA president and general counsel to the Prudential Insurance Co. of America, joined the effort.

"Smith spoke to an old friend in Ohio who had done a lot of Prudential legal business there, a man who happened to be a friend of McCulloch," said Beck.

"The man came to the ABA office in Washington, familiarized himself with the bill, then went and talked to McCulloch and finally persuaded his old friend to support the bill. He did, and the bill passed."

As Beck tells the story, the point, he said, is that "the ABA has in it men and women of enormous power and influence in their own right."

Responsiveness: The ABA is anxious to work closely with Congress and the executive branch, and usually responds when invited to offer advice or information.

It made a study of electoral college reform in 1966-67 at the request of the Justice Department.

In 1969, it accepted President Nixon's invitation to form a commission to review the activities of the FTC.

At the request of congressional committees, it reviews bills within its areas of expertise—criminal law, constitutional changes, legal services, for example.

"If the ABA has any lobbying clout," says its executive director, Bert H. Early, "it's because we are increasingly responsive, helpful and public service-oriented."

From the viewpoint of Congress, ABA endorsement of legislation can have some real impact.

"When they come out for something, you get a terrific amount of prestige," said one congressional aide. "They can't get you votes, perhaps, but they can keep you from losing some votes. And they lend the respectability of the organized bar."

Complaints: For this reason, the same aide is disappointed that the ABA has so far been unwilling to take a position on the school busing issue, and particularly on the merits of a constitutional amendment to prohibit busing for the purpose of racial desegregation.

But the ponderous decision-making machinery of the ABA, together with its general reluctance to get caught up in bitter and divisive political battles, has kept it from speaking out while the issue is boiling in Congress.

The ABA has also found itself unable to speak out on the increasingly important subject of environmental law, and specifically on the question of citizens suits against polluters, because the issue has not yet been resolved within the association itself.

"But you can't effectively respond overnight to all issues," says executive director Early, "not if you wish to remain responsible." And responsibility, respectability and credibility are what the ABA is selling when it lobbies in the halls of Congress and the corridors of the executive branch.

ORGANIZATION

As with so many organizations, the real power within the ABA is not necessarily revealed by the organizational chart or the association's literature.

Board: The ABA's central organ, according to these guides, is its 307-member legislative body, the House of Delegates. But effective control is vested in the Board of Governors, a 21-member executive committee which can act for the House when that body is out of session and which has the dominant voice in deciding what shall be on the House's agenda.

Sitting on the board are the current president, the past president and the president-elect of the association; the secretary and treasurer of the ABA; the editor-in-chief of the ABA's *Journal,* and one member from each of 14 geographic districts, elected by the House of Delegates.

House: Legislative authority in the ABA is lodged with the House of Delegates, and it must normally approve policy positions before they can become the official policy of the association.

The ABA has no authority to bind state and local bar associations by its actions; nevertheless, there is a relationship between the ABA and the bar groups in each of the states and in most big cities and large counties.

Each state bar association has at least one delegate sitting in the House of Delegates, and larger associations can have up to five.

Local bar groups can also have delegates, depending on their size and on the number or percentage of ABA members in their associations.

In addition, each of the sections into which the ABA is divided is entitled to one member of the House, as are affiliated legal groups like the American Law Institute and the National Conference of Bar Examiners.

There are also 15 delegates chosen by the members who attend the annual association meetings; other seats are reserved for the Board of Governors and for former ABA presidents and House chairmen.

At the heart of the House system, however, are the 50 state delegates, elected by ABA members living in each state.

The state delegates nominate the ABA officers, the district members of the Board of Governors and the chairman of the House.

The actual election of officers is conducted by the full House, but as in most organizations of this kind, the decisions are almost always made during the nominating stage.

Sections: The ABA acts in large measure through sections and standing and special committees.

The sections, with membership ranging from a few hundred to several thousand, are composed of lawyers who have special interests in particular areas of law.

There are, for example, sections on criminal law, on taxation, on natural resources and on antitrust law.

The 21 sections, each of them governed by a policy-making council, are divided in turn into committees. The bulk of the ABA's $11 million in income is spent on staffing the work of these sections.

There are more than 60 standing and special committees, appointed by the association president, in such areas as legal aid, environmental law and federal court nominations.

With few exceptions, proposals for new legislation or for federal policy positions originate in the sections and committees, are reviewed by the Board of Governors and must be acted upon by the House of Delegates before it can be said that this is the ABA's position.

Staff: The ABA is serviced by a staff of about 250, headed by Early, executive director of the association since 1964, a lawyer and member of the ABA who serves at the pleasure of the Board of Governors.

The staff is centered in Chicago in a complex of office buildings which also houses the American Bar Foundation and eight other national legal organizations.

The Washington office, with a staff of only six, operates on a budget of about $190,000 a year, as compared with the $11.5-million budget for the entire association.

AUTO INSURANCE

Few things are as likely to touch a sensitive nerve in the ABA hierarchy as the charge that it is no more than a trade association dedicated to protecting and improving the economic status of its members.

Thus the ABA's movement—timid and slow as it may be—in the direction of no-fault automobile accident insurance must be seen and understood in terms of the association's susceptibilities.

In an editorial in last May's issue of its own publication, the *American Bar Association Journal*, the ABA acknowledged that "since fees from automobile accident cases represent a substantial segment of lawyers' income, the public might draw the inference that lawyers are fighting for their own economic advantage rather than for the best possible system."

The editorial goes on to reject the inference and affirm its conviction that "our profession would not put its own economic welfare above the public good."

Nevertheless, the suspicion that the legal profession is acting in a self-serving manner on the no-fault issue clearly exists.

No-fault: Under the existing tort-liability system, a motorist is legally responsible for any injury or damage caused by his own negligence, and buys auto-accident insurance to protect himself against the claims of his victims.

Under no-fault, the accident victim would collect from his own insurance company, not from the other party, without regard to who is at fault.

It would thus work like the workman's compensation system, and is advocated in protecting accident victims from economic loss.

No-fault insurance would reduce litigation and thus cut into legal fees (a pure no-fault system would eliminate suits and lawyers' fees entirely), particularly suits for pain and suffering, where the big money lies.

In 1970, the last year for which records are currently available, lawyers collected about $1.3 billion in legal fees arising out of auto-accident suits, and this is a measure of the importance of the no-fault debate—and its sensitivity.

Powers Report: In August 1969, the ABA's House of Delegates approved the report of the ABA Special Committee on Automobile Accident Reparations, which, under the chairmanship of George B. Powers, had conducted an 18-month study of the auto insurance system.

The committee opposed plans for no-fault insurance while putting forward more than 50 recommendations for improving the existing tort system.

Its report, as accepted by the House of Delegates, remains to this day the official position of the ABA.

Nevertheless, it is clear that the association's policy is changing, even though no formal revision of its official position can be made until its annual meeting in San Francisco next August.

Reardon Panel: Since that 1969 decision in opposition to no-fault insurance, two things have happened to persuade the ABA to adjust its stance:

No-fault, in one form or another, is obviously an idea whose time is fast arriving; in Congress and in an increasing number of state legislatures, the only real question now is what form no-fault should take.

The American Trial Lawyers Association, which represents lawyers in negligence practice, has taken an adamant stand against no-fault to the point where many think it has become counterproductive. The ABA, it is evident, is anxious to establish a clear distinction between its position and the ATLA's on no-fault.

ATLA, founded in 1946 and with a roster of more than 20,000 lawyers, has actively lobbied in Congress and in the state legislatures against no-fault insurance legislation.

By contrast, the ABA has been virtually inactive on the lobbying front, while awaiting the report of a new Special Committee on Automobile Insurance Legislation, created last May and headed by John T. Reardon, of Quincy, Ill.

Report—Reardon's committee submitted its report at the winter meeting of the ABA in New Orleans in February.

The committee concluded that many of the recommendations of the earlier study were sound, but said that others should be revised in the light of recent legislative and insurance industry developments.

What the Reardon panel recommended is a modified form of no-fault insurance which would provide a minimum of $2,000 to cover medical and economic losses resulting from an auto accident without regard to who was at fault in the accident.

The committee said this would cover the total losses of almost 95 percent of all traffic accident victims.

But the committee proposal would leave standing the individual's right to sue under the existing tort-liability system, thus giving the innocent victim the option of suing the other party or collecting from his own insurance company.

Further, the committee would preserve the right to sue for intangible damages, the pain and suffering suits "where the gravy is," as one lawyer familiar with the no-fault debate commented.

But such suits could not be filed for an amount greater than the victim's medical expenses, unless those expenses exceed $500 or the injury results in death or serious disability or disfigurement.

While this would eliminate many pain and suffering suits, it would leave most of the big-money suits intact.

Action—The Reardon committee, in turning its report in to the ABA House of Delegates, asked the House not to take formal action until the annual ABA meeting next August.

Officially, this will give ABA members a chance to review the complex proposals; unofficially, it gets the ABA off the hook of all-out opposition to no-fault insurance without precipitating an immediate battle within the association.

Reardon, in presenting the recommendations to the House, observed that "there is practically no subject as challenging to lawyers as no-fault insurance."

"The credibility of the bar," he warned, "is being challenged in the entire country" on the no-fault issue.

Early, the ABA's executive director, said in an interview during the House of Delegates meeting:

"The ABA is in the process of taking a second look (at no-fault). It would be absurd, in the face of what's going on in the states, to ignore this."

Jaworski, the ABA president, put it more bluntly in a separate interview: "We wouldn't have had a committee studying it," he said, "if our official policy against no-

fault hadn't really changed. No-fault may not be a panacea, but it's not something we can sweep under the rug."

Bill: The principal bill now pending in Congress is S 945, sponsored by Sens. Philip A. Hart, D-Mich., and Warren G. Magnuson, D-Wash. It is before the Judiciary Subcommittee on Antitrust and Monopoly Legislation, which Hart heads.

Dean E. Sharp, assistant subcommittee counsel who has been handling no-fault legislation, is critical of the ABA's role.

"They are burying their heads in the sand," Sharp said of the ABA's decision not to take up the Reardon report until its August meeting.

He would like to have the ABA's backing for S 945, but admitted in an interview that "the ABA's silence is better than its opposition."

JUDGES

The ABA speaks loudest in the area of judicial nominations, and especially those made by the President to the U.S. Supreme Court.

Through its standing Committee on the Federal Judiciary, the association passes judgment on the qualifications of presidential nominees to the high court as well as to federal district and appeals benches.

Totally devoid of any legal authority to approve or disapprove of judicial candidates, the ABA, through its committee, has nevertheless been able to wield an effective, if wholly informal, veto over presidential choices.

The Committee: In an excep-

tion to the ABA's general policy, the Committee on the Federal Judiciary is authorized to speak and act on behalf of the entire association, even though its judgments on judicial nominees are not submitted to the House of Delegates for ratification.

Thus the committee, composed of only 12 men, speaks with the full authority and prestige of the ABA.

It is headed by Lawrence E. Walsh, a former federal judge who, during his tenure (1957-60) as deputy attorney general, was responsible for the executive branch side of the judicial nominating and review process.

The eleven other members, each of them a prominent attorney, are selected on a geographical basis.

It is this panel which, through a combination of personal interviews and solicitation of opinions from lawyers across the country, rates judicial nominees on the basis of their qualifications for the bench.

Background: Since the Presidency of Harry S. Truman (1945-53), the ABA has been screening potential appointees to the federal judiciary.

Under Truman, however, the bar association made its evaluations for the Senate Judiciary Committee, and the President ignored its recommendations if they disagreed with his.

Under President Dwight D. Eisenhower (1953-61), the ABA was invited to comment on prospective nominees for the lower federal courts, but not on candidates for the Supreme Court.

Beginning with the 1956 nomination of William J. Brennan Jr. to the high court, and down to the present Administration, Presidents have asked the ABA for its views on Supreme Court nominees as well.

The key point, since that time, has been not whether the ABA's comments were sought but whether they were invited before or after the President formally announced his nominations.

When President Nixon took office in January 1969, he announced that while he would continue to seek the views of the ABA committee on appointments to the lower federal courts, he would not consult it on Supreme Court nominations.

The President kept that promise in choosing and nominating Warren E. Burger for Chief Justice in 1969.

Nevertheless, because its views were still sought by the Senate Judiciary Committee, the ABA panel made an after-the-fact investigation of Burger, and pronounced him "highly acceptable."

In his nominations of Clement F. Haynsworth Jr. and G. Harrold Carswell to the Supreme Court, Mr. Nixon followed the same procedure; in each case, the ABA committee reviewed the qualifications of the nominee at the request of the Senate committee.

Haynsworth was found "highly acceptable," and Carswell, under revised review standards, was deemed "qualified." Each nominee was rejected by the Senate.

In April 1970, Mr. Nixon nominated Harry A. Blackmun to the same Supreme Court vacancy, once again without consulting the bar committee first or asking its views afterward.

Once again the bar group, at the request of the Senate Judiciary Committee, reviewed the nominee's qualifications—this time with exceptional care—and, once again changing its qualifying standards, found Blackmun to have met "high standards of integrity, judicial temperament and professional competence."

Blackmun was confirmed easily by the Senate, but the bar committee, stung by the controversy over its ratings of Haynsworth and Carswell, said publicly it was thinking of dropping its review role entirely.

New Policy: Instead, the committee decided that it was performing a valuable function and would continue its review of Supreme Court nominations.

At the same time, it urged the Attorney General, on behalf of the chief executive, to consult with the ABA committee before nominations to the Supreme Court were announced.

A candidate's professional qualifications can only be properly considered before an announcement has been made, the committee said.

"Once he's nominated you get a bandwagon effect going," Walsh said in a recent interview.

Further, "it protects the reputations and feelings of those who are turned down," Walsh added, by allowing the Administration to drop the candidate quietly and without formal announcement.

That request was made in May of 1970. In July, Attorney General John N. Mitchell formally agreed to give the ABA panel "the names of persons I may consider recommending to the President for nom-

ination to the Supreme Court."

That agreement was short-lived, coming apart in 1971 during the process of selecting successors to Supreme Court Justices Hugo L. Black and John M. Harlan.

Poff—The President's first choice for one of the seats was Rep. Richard H. Poff, R-Va., a veteran member of the House Judiciary Committee.

In fulfillment of his pledge, Mitchell asked the ABA committee to review Poff's qualifications before any announcement was made.

Ultimately, the committee never formally reviewed the Congressman's qualifications. It had become obvious that Poff could not obtain the committee's highest rating—and might even be found unqualified—for lack of sufficient courtroom experience.

Walsh told this to Mitchell. The word was passed on to Poff, and the Virginian withdrew his name from consideration.

"It worked well with Poff," said an ABA official afterward, "except, unfortunately, that the President had so strongly hinted he would name Poff that Poff wasn't spared whatever embarrassment he did suffer."

Friday and Lillie—The committee was next presented with a list of six potential nominees, with instructions to give closest attention to two of them, Herschel H. Friday and Mildred L. Lillie.

The committee found the latter unqualified, and split evenly over whether Friday should be rejected or given the minimal rating of "not opposed."

Officially, all of this was done privately and confidentially. In fact, all six names had already appeared in the press, and the votes on Friday and Mrs. Lillie were reported almost immediately after they were cast.

Rehnquist and Powell—Even before the formal votes, when it was already clear the two candidates would not be endorsed, the President had invited Lewis F. Powell Jr., a former ABA president, to accept one of the nominations.

The day after the adverse votes, the President offered the other nomination to Assistant Attorney General William H. Rehnquist. That night, Mr. Nixon went on television to announce his choices of Rehnquist and Powell.

Walsh had been sounded out on Powell two days earlier, and had informally advised Mitchell that Powell would probably have no problem with the committee.

As to Rehnquist, "I didn't learn about him until eight minutes before Nixon went on the air," Walsh said.

Following its usual procedure, the Walsh committee then reviewed the qualifications of the two nominees at the request of the Senate Judiciary Committee, finding each of them well qualified.

Evaluation: Mitchell and President Nixon were furious over the premature disclosure of the earlier prospective nominees and over the bar panel's rejection of Friday and Mrs. Lillie and its adverse reaction to Poff.

Mitchell, in an angry letter, informed the ABA he was dissolving his agreement of the previous year, and would not henceforward give the committee a crack at Supreme Court nominees until after their formal nominations by the President.

The abortive agreement, he said, was "a well-intentioned experiment which proved impractical for reasons beyond our control."

Walsh, on the other hand, believes the experiment worked, to the extent that it kept from the high court several potential nominees which his committee felt did not belong on that bench.

There have been no Supreme Court nominations since those of Rehnquist and Powell, and there is no set procedure now to review the qualifications of the next nominee.

But Walsh has some hope that a new system can be established before the next nomination is made.

At his initiative, Walsh met in January with Mitchell and Richard G. Kleindienst, then Mitchell's deputy and now his successor as Attorney General, to discuss new arrangements.

No decision has been made, but Mitchell and Kleindienst agreed that after the next vacancy on the high court occurs, ad hoc procedures might then be formulated to allow for ABA review.

This is vague, but is about all the ABA can get from the Justice Department at this time.

Until that next nomination, it may not be possible to tell just how angry the Administration is with the ABA.

Scott: One who is still angry is Sen. Hugh Scott, R-Pa., the Senate Minority Leader.

In an interview, Scott said the committee review "performs a useful function by giving the bar's opinion about a judicial candidate."

But he sees no justification for the exercise of a de facto veto over candidates whom the bar committee does not like.

He is upset about Poff's failure to receive committee approval, saying, "I think he would have made one of the greatest Supreme Court judges. The President thought so too. The President's judgment should be worth as much as a bunch of lawyers, but it isn't, because of this absolute veto."

In its review of judicial candidates for the Supreme Court and the other federal courts, "the bar has done a good civic duty in many cases, but their judgment shouldn't be final," Scott said.

Scott has some personal reasons to be upset about the bar committee's review. Two of his proposed nominees to lower federal courts in Pennsylvania were vetoed by the Walsh committee on grounds of inadequate trial experience.

One was former Pennsylvania Governor Raymond P. Shafer, whom Scott and Sen. Richard S. Schweiker, R-Pa., had recommended for a vacancy on the 3d Circuit Court of Appeals.

The other was Lee A. Donaldson Jr., a former Republican leader of the Pennsylvania House of Representatives, proposed for the U.S. Court for the Western District of Pennsylvania.

"This question of prior legal experience weighs too heavily," Scott said. Prior administrative or legislative experience should also count, he said.

Lower Courts: Interestingly, in terminating the ABA review process for Supreme Court nominees, Mitchell left intact the three-year-old arrangement for review of lower-court choices.

Soon after he took office, Mr.

Nixon agreed not to nominate anyone to the lower federal bench who is not acceptable to the ABA committee. He has kept that pledge.

Of 160 persons nominated to the district and appeals courts by the President, all but one had been rated in advance as qualified, and that one exception was nominated inadvertently before the committee could complete its favorable report.

About 50 prospective nominees were eliminated from consideration by adverse informal action by his committee, Walsh said.

ABA President Jaworski is proud of this record, as well as the association's role on Supreme Court nominations.

"I think we're performing a tremendous service for the American people, and at our own cost," Jaworski said. "Who else can judge the qualifications of judges?"

CONSUMER PROTECTION

The ABA's urge to speak with a single voice has split the association into opposing camps in the field of consumer legislation.

At its midwinter meeting in New Orleans, the ABA's House of Delegates heard contradictory recommendations from two of the association's sections on a key provision in pending legislation to increase the power of the Federal Trade Commission to protect consumers against unfair or deceptive selling practices.

Dispute: At issue is Section 206 of the proposed Consumer Product Warranties and Federal Trade Commission Improvements Act (S 986, sponsored by Sens. Warren G.

Magnuson, D-Wash., and Frank E. Moss, D-Utah).

The FTC is now authorized (15 USC 46) "to make rules and regulations for the purpose of carrying out the provisions" of its basic act.

Section 206 of the Magnuson-Moss bill, which passed the Senate last November and is now pending before the House Interstate and Foreign Commerce Committee, would spell out the FTC's rule-making powers and give it the authority to issue legally binding rules, subject only to congressional veto.

The ABA's Administrative Law Section, composed principally of lawyers who practice before government regulatory bodies, endorsed this provision in principle, describing it in a report to the House of Delegates as "often the fairest, most expeditious and most effective way in which an administrative agency can meet its statutory responsibilities to protect the public interest."

The bar association's Antitrust Law Section, whose members usually represent or work for clients on antitrust litigation, submitted its own recommendation at New Orleans which would effectively negate the extension of rule-making powers to the FTC.

Two Voices—The conflicting recommendations were an echo of a similar split between units of the ABA over another consumer issue almost two years ago.

In the spring of 1970, the antitrust section had informed congressional committees of its opposition to class-action suits brought against sellers of faulty merchandise.

At almost the same time, the

ABA's standing Committee on Legal Aid and Indigent Defendants filed statements with the same committees in support of broad class-action legislation.

Both the committee and the section stressed, in their statements, that they were not speaking for the full ABA, but Congressmen confessed their confusion over who, if anyone, was speaking for the association on this issue.

To avoid a similar episode over the FTC rule-making legislation, the ABA's Board of Governors transmitted the conflicting recommendations of the two sections to the House of Delegates with the request that the dispute be resolved in that body.

Above all, the board urged, the House should "not adopt a position permitting the sections to present conflicting points of view to the Congress."

Resolution—The House of Delegates resolved the dispute by accepting the contention of the antitrust section that Section 206 "gives too much power" to the FTC and would allow the commission to act "by caprice."

This is now, by virtue of the action of the House of Delegates, the official position of the ABA and the view that will be presented to Congress on behalf of the association.

Not unexpectedly, the Administrative Law Section is unhappy with the outcome.

Ben C. Fisher, its representative on the House of Delegates, said in a recent interview that the House of Delegates, when it chooses not to take a position, should then allow each section to express its views before Congress.

Fisher, a Washington attorney, said "If the bar association wants to be of service to Congress, it ought to be able to present both of these views (on the FTC bill).

"Congress needs all the good, sound advice it can get. The legislative process would be improved if both sections go up to the Hill and give their views."

Fisher acknowledged that "the ABA has been burned" in the past when a section or committee leader has testified on behalf of his unit and left the impression he was speaking for the entire bar association.

"But in a highly technical matter, such as this one, Congress is really groping and looking for help," Fisher said, and the ABA can contribute by allowing each section to explain its position.

ENVIRONMENT

Sharp differences of opinion within the association can, however, blunt whatever effectiveness the ABA might otherwise have in influencing legislative decisions.

For that reason, association leaders are willing to push hard for compromise even at the expense of a strong and relevant legislative position.

Robert W. Meserve, who takes over as ABA president in August, cautioned that, "Congress isn't waiting with bated breath for us to take a stand. We have to sell them—and it's best, therefore, to speak overwhelmingly."

Citizens Suits: Meserve, in an interview, said this particularly applies to an issue such as the right of citizens to bring suit to enforce environmental quality standards.

"This is a matter on which lawyers can and do disagree," said Meserve.

ABA lawyers did disagree on this subject at the February meeting in New Orleans, and the result—in contrast to the resolution of the FTC dispute—was a decision not to take a stand.

At issue is the question of standing: who has the right to bring a civil suit to stop a company from polluting the water or to force the government to enforce antipollution laws.

The pending water-quality bill (S 2770), which passed the Senate last November and is now before the House Public Works Committee, authorizes suits by any individuals or groups.

Endorsement: The ABA's Special Committee on Environmental Law, established in the summer of 1970 in an effort to reconcile the split within the ABA over environmental issues, recommended at New Orleans that the association endorse the citizens-suit provision of the water bill.

With proper safeguards, the committee said, "the possibility of citizen-initiated enforcement actions can be expected to have a salutary effect on the diligence and vigor with which environmental protection agencies pursue their duties."

The Section of Natural Resources Law, whose members generally represent or are employed by the extractive industries—oil, gas, lumbering, for example—has a different point of view.

In its report to the ABA's House of Delegates in February, the section recommended that citizens suits be permitted only if

there is "demonstrated need" for the suits as a supplement to governmental action, and only when the plaintiffs can show that they will directly suffer economic loss.

These limitations, it is generally agreed, would drastically limit the number of suits which citizens and civic groups could bring.

Deferment—Confronted with what it acknowledged as "substantial disagreement" between the two units, the ABA's Board of Governors did what it often does in such situations: it urged the House of Delegates to defer action on the conflicting recommendations and to invite the special committee to continue in its efforts to reconcile the differences over citizen suits.

The house agreed, and the subject is off its agenda at least until its August meeting, by which time the water-quality bill may very well have been enacted or so entwined in political controversy that it will never become law.

Whether an ABA statement of position now could have made any difference is another question.

The House Public Works Committee has come up with a section on citizens suits which is close to that proposed by the bar's Natural Resources Section, and there is some doubt about which version will ultimately prevail.

Influence—Thomas C. Jorling, Republican counsel to the Senate Public Works Committee, said in an interview that an ABA endorsement of the Senate version would not have much impact. "It wouldn't cause the opponents of citizens suits in the House to back away," Jorling said.

An ABA statement opposing

the Senate position, however, "could have been troublesome," he continued, by reinforcing the arguments of the opposition.

In any event, he said, the ABA "has not done anything on the water bill, even though they were invited to."

Jorling recalled that he had testified at ABA hearings on the subject in Chicago more than a year ago, and had called the association "ineffectual." Nothing has happened, he said recently, to cause him to change his mind.

In the environmental field, Jorling said of the ABA, "it's not active and therefore not influential. It makes no effort to be involved and is reticent about becoming involved when invited."

Louis B. Potter, an assistant director of the ABA who worked with both the section and the special committee in New Orleans, said after the decision there to defer action on the citizens suit question that "quite obviously the ABA can't have an influence on the pending bill. The point will be moot by August."

It was clear, Potter said, that "there was no ABA consensus on this issue, and when consensus is lacking, the ABA generally does what it did in this case—defer action."

What the dispute shows, he said, "is that the ABA is not monolithic, and the decision to put the subject off is really an effort to represent the entire membership, not just that of a particular section on a particular subject."

Meserve, in defense of the decision not to act, said the subject of citizens suits "is an issue that's going to be around for a long time," and the ABA will have a chance to be recorded on it.

"ABA adoption of an uninformed opinion isn't going to help Congress," said the association leader. "If we are to have any influence, we should let Congress know this is really how the lawyers of this country feel. Going in half-cocked wouldn't be very useful."

LEGAL SERVICES

In terms of effectiveness and consistency, the ABA lobbying effort shows off to best advantage in its support in recent years of legal services to the poor.

Through its Washington office, the association has campaigned within the Administration and before Congress for larger budgets for legal services, and has fought against the frequent attempts to weaken or kill the program.

It successfully lobbied against efforts to give Governors an absolute veto over legal services programs in their states.

It attacked, with some success, the attempt by the Nixon Administration to take control of the program out of the hands of legal services lawyers.

More recently, it campaigned to create an independent legal services corporation, divorced from political influence.

Independence: The ABA's support for a separate corporation is illustrative of the association's willingness to work energetically on behalf of something it believes in; it also reflects the ABA's reluctance to take sides in a political fight.

Since 1965, the federal legal services program has been lodged in the Office of Economic Opportunity as part of the government's antipoverty program.

A series of incidents, culminating in the firing in November 1970 of the two top legal services officials by the head of OEO, convinced ABA leaders that the program should be separated from the federal agency and given some kind of independent status.

John D. Robb, of Albuquerque, N.M., then as now chairman of the ABA standing Committee on Legal Aid and Indigent Defendants, said in a recent interview:

"The concept of an independent program originated within our committee early in the Nixon Administration, in part because we found that conflicting OEO policies were not always in the best interest of the legal services program."

Studies: In the summer of 1970, Robb's committee, together with the ABA's Individual Rights and Responsibilities Section, began a joint study of the problem, and by early last year came up with the recommendation that an independent, quasi-governmental corporation be created.

Meanwhile, the Advisory Council on Executive Organization (Ash Council) had made its own study, and, in November 1970, recommended creation of an independent corporation for legal services.

Both studies left open what has since become the most contentious part of the corporation plan: the composition of its governing board.

The ABA Board of Governors, meeting last April, decided the association should actively support the concept of an independent corporation but, as Meserve put it recently, "refrain from entering the developing political contest over specifics."

John P. Tracey, who has been assigned to the legal services battleground since he went to work in 1967 as assistant director of the ABA's Washington office, recalled that the prevailing attitude of the board last year was that, "Look, there's going to be a helluva political fight over this, and it just isn't an ABA fight."

In addition, while several legal services corporation bills had been introduced in Congress at that point, the President's plan had not yet been formulated.

The ABA board, said Tracey, felt it would be a mistake to take a position on specific details before the President's proposal was made public.

Bills: Mr. Nixon's bill was presented to Congress in May, "and nobody saw any reason to change our position" of general support but noninvolvement in the dispute over the corporation's board, Tracey said.

ABA President Edward L. Wright, along with Robb, appeared before congressional committees to testify in support of the legislation, carefully refraining from taking sides while urging Congress to resolve the differences.

Essentially, the Administration proposal differs from the one finally adopted by Congress in the manner in which the corporation board would be appointed.

Mr. Nixon proposed an 11-member board, to be nominated by the chief executive and confirmed by the Senate.

S 2007, passed by Congress last December, provided for a board of 17 members, of whom only six would be freely chosen by the President.

The others would be selected by him from lists submitted by the ABA and other bar associations, by law schools, the federal court system and advisory panels of legal services clients and attorneys.

Mr. Nixon vetoed the bill, principally because of his objections to unrelated provisions in the measure's child-care title. But in his veto message he hinted that he would have vetoed the bill because of its unacceptable provisions on the legal services corporation board.

Despite this presidential warning, the House has again passed a bill with the identical legal services provisions, and it is now pending in the Senate.

ABA Acts: The ABA maintained its position of official neutrality throughout the long days of debate within the Senate and House committees.

"Congressmen, congressional staff members, legal services lawyers, they all beat us on the head to take a position," Tracey said. But the association would not budge until the bill had passed both houses of Congress and a conference committee had reconciled the difference over the composition of the board.

That was last November, and on Nov. 24, the ABA broke its silence and endorsed the corporation legislation in the form approved by the conferees.

A letter signed by ABA President Jaworski and sent to each Member of Congress urged support of the conference version.

The ABA continues to support that version as the only viable one before Congress. It has endorsed HR 12350, which, as passed by the House on Feb. 17, includes that version and will support it in the Senate.

If, however, a substitute is advanced which incorporates the President's recommendations, "we would have no position on it," Tracey said. "We would have to return to a position of neutrality."

Tracey, Robb and other ABA officials believe the association's unwillingness to take sides in the dispute between the President and Congress was sound, and that it was more important to battle hard for the independent corporation than to get caught up in the political fighting.

Rep. Lloyd Meeds, D-Wash., a member of the House Education and Labor Committee which processed the legal services bill, said recently he was not upset over the ABA's silence on the issue of the board's composition.

"They supported very strongly the concept of a private corporation," Meeds said, "and their support meant a lot."

The ABA, he said, "really carried the ball" on the legal services corporation, and helped to round up some important votes, particularly on the Republican side.

AMENDMENTS

Of all its legislative activities, the ABA is perhaps proudest of its advocacy and support of amendments to the Constitution, and especially the 25th Amendment on

282 presidential disability.

The association believes its expertise is particularly relevant in the constitutional field, and is eager to point out that it can have no vested interest in pressing for amendments such as those which provide for the orderly transfer of presidential power or call for reform of the Electoral College.

25th Amendment: In 1967, the states concluded the process of ratifying the 25th Amendment to the Constitution, establishing the procedures by which the Vice President succeeds to the Presidency and a new Vice President is elected.

From its inception through its congressional approval and down to its final ratification by the states, the amendment was shepherded along by the ABA.

Even before the assassination of President (1961-63) John F. Kennedy in Dallas Nov. 22, 1963, the ABA had been advocating a constitutional amendment to clarify the ambiguous language of Article 2, Section 1 of the Constitution, which provides for replacement of a disabled President.

"But there wasn't a great deal of interest in it," said Channell, the ABA's chief Washington lobbyist who played a leading role in winning approval of the 25th Amendment.

After Dallas, with the nation without a Vice President and no way of getting one until Jan. 20, 1965, the subject of presidential succession began to catch fire.

In January 1964, the ABA convened a conference of members and non-members in Washington which heard witnesses and then announced it had reached a consensus in favor of a constitutional amendment to settle the problem of presidential inability and succession.

Bayh—Meanwhile, Sen. Birch Bayh, D-Ind., as chairman of the Judiciary Subcommittee on Constitutional Amendments, began pushing his own proposal for continued change.

At a February meeting of the ABA that year, the House of Delegates unanimously endorsed Bayh's legislation and, from that point on, the ABA and the Senator worked together on the amendment, Bayh relates in his book on the subject, *One Heartbeat Away* (Bobbs-Merrill, 1968).

Channell and Beck, who was then Channell's deputy in the Washington office, cooperated with Bayh in mobilizing the support of the legal profession and helping to arrange testimony before Congress.

On July 6, 1965, Congress approved the proposed amendment, sending it to the states for the required ratification by three-fourths of them—38 of the 50 states.

States—Once again the ABA, through its 50 affiliated state bar associations, lobbied on behalf of the amendment in each of the states, and Bayh, in his book, gives the bar groups much of the credit for achieving ratification in 19 months, the 38th state acting on Feb. 10, 1967.

Electoral Reform: The team of Bayh and the ABA was far less successful in its campaign for a constitutional amendment to change the way Americans elect their Presidents.

"After the 25th Amendment was adopted," Channell recalled, "some people suggested we take a look at the Electoral College. Since we succeeded on the earlier amendment, they thought we might succeed on this one."

The ABA, in early 1966, established a Commission on Electoral Reform, composed of ABA members and non-members. ABA's Washington office served as commission staff.

In January 1967, the commission made its report, recommending that the Electoral College system be replaced by direct, nationwide popular vote, with a runoff election if no candidate received 40 percent of the total vote.

The ABA House of Delegates adopted the recommendation, making it official policy of the association.

"Then," Channell said, "we went to Celler and McCulloch and to Bayh to sell them on the merits of the proposal." (Rep. Emanuel Celler, D-N.Y., and McCulloch are the chairman and ranking minority member of the House Judiciary Committee, respectively.)

Forming a loose coalition with the AFL-CIO and the Chamber of Commerce of the U.S., the ABA lobbied for the amendment, first in the House where it passed in September 1969, and then in the Senate where it died one year later.

In helping to win in the House and to obtain a majority (but not the required two-thirds) in the Senate, the ABA's role, says Beck, "was to take the wind out of the sails of the conservatives."

A member of the House Judiciary Committee's staff agrees. "ABA endorsement establishes the respectable position on constitu-

THE MEMBERSHIP: BIG CITY, BIG FIRM LAWYERS DOMINATE

Richard Nixon used to be a dues-paying member of the American Bar Association, and 155,000 other lawyers still are.

Half the lawyers in the country are ABA members, contributing, in dues payments, 48 percent of the association's current annual budget of $11.5 million. (The rest of the ABA's income comes from foundation and government grants.)

Mr. Nixon, admitted to the bar in 1937, joined the ABA in 1951 and kept up his membership until shortly after he became President and resigned from many outside organizations.

Members: Most of the ABA's members are in private practice although many government lawyers—federal, state and local—belong.

Some 11,000 judges of all kinds, half the men and women on the bench, hold ABA membership. In addition, more than half the Congress (about 300 of 535 members) are lawyers, and while the ABA records do not show how many belong, many probably do.

More than a third of the ABA membership is officially classified as young—the 55,000 members of the association's Young Lawyers Section, which has an age limit of 36. There are also another 17,000 law school students, enrolled in the ABA's Law Student Division.

The median age of ABA members has dropped to 42; it will inevitably drop even further, judging by the rapid burgeoning of law school enrollments which could easily, if the pace continues, double the size of the legal profession by 1985.

Leaders: No matter how large the ABA grows, however, it will almost certainly continue to be dominated by the same small percentage of its membership.

The directory of the ABA lists some 3,700 members, those who hold office in the association or one of its sections or who serve on one of its committees.

The real power of the ABA is lodged with the handful who head the sections and committees, and the 307 members (including some of the above) who sit in the House of Delegates, among them the 21 members of the Board of Governors.

While about half the lawyers in private practice are in individual practice—no partners, no employees—the ABA tends to be dominated by members of large law firms.

ABA President Leon Jaworski, for example, is a partner in a Houston firm with more than 140 partners, associates and lawyer-employees.

William B. Spann, Jr., chairman of the House of Delegates, belongs to a firm in Atlanta with 49 lawyers among its partners and employees.

The Boston firm to which Robert W. Meserve, the ABA president-elect, belongs, has 57 partners and associates, and the Philadelphia firm which includes past president Bernard G. Segal has 99 lawyer-members.

There are smaller firms, of course, whose members are high up in the ABA hierarchy, but as a general rule, it is easier for a member of a big firm to find the time—and the money—to serve the ABA and to campaign for one of its offices.

Typical Member: A recent reader survey conducted by the ABA *Journal* gives a general picture of the "typical" member, though not necessarily the typical leader, of the ABA.

He is either a partner or an associate in a law firm (52.9 percent of those who responded), he has a total income of $21,260 (the median figure for those who answered the survey) and he lives in a metropolitan area rather than a small town.

The income figures show that 15.5 percent are in the $30,000-$40,000 category, while 13.6 percent earn $50,000 or more.

ABA members pay dues ranging from $7 to $40 a year, depending on the length of time they have been admitted to the bar.

Most of them, those who have been members of the bar for at least 10 years, pay the maximum amount.

ABA members are also eligible for membership in one or more of the association's 21 sections, paying additional dues to the section of about $10 a year.

Ideology: The ABA has long been considered conservative ideologically, as might be expected in an organization dominated by financially comfortable lawyers.

Only a little more than a decade ago, the ABA was on record in opposition to several Supreme Court rulings in the civil liberties field.

It was dominated by Southern lawyers and many of its views derived from its geographic slant.

This has changed to a considerable extent in recent years; several of its presidents have been considered liberals, and the association has become more hospitable to views that its leaders would once have considered radical.

Part of this is attributable to the increasing number of young members, and particularly to the stronger voice the young have been given through a more active Young Lawyers Section and by way of a recent decision to allot one of the 21 seats on the Board of Governors to a young lawyer.

Sections: The ABA's 21 sections, however, which initiate many of the ultimate policy positions of the ABA, remain dominated, in many cases, by lawyers with a built-in interest in the status quo.

The chairman of the Natural Resources Law Section, for example, J. P. Hammond of Tulsa, is assistant general counsel for Standard Oil Co. of Indiana. And the Insurance, Negligence and Compensation Law Section is headed by Don M. Jackson, of Kansas City, Mo., whose law firm lists a number of large insurance companies among its clients.

Theoretically, attorneys are expected to leave their special-interest concerns behind when they engage in ABA business. In practice, this is not always the case.

---

tional amendments."

Busing: The House committee aide expressed disappointment that the ABA, given this ability to grant or withhold respectability in the constitutional field, has not taken a position on proposed amendments to limit the busing of schoolchildren for the purpose of racial desegregation.

The aide made it clear, in an interview, that he would like to see the ABA oppose such constitutional limitations.

Beck agreed that the ABA's role could be influential, if it takes a position while the issue is before Congress.

The subject was discussed privately at the ABA's midwinter meeting in New Orleans in February, and Beck said it was likely that "between now and May (when the Board of Governors meets in Washington), the board will be taking some kind of position on busing."

He defended the ABA's failure to act at the February meeting, saying "we just can't—and shouldn't—act that fast on such an issue."

CRIMINAL LAW

In no area of federal policy is the ABA potentially more influential than in the field of criminal law.

That it wants to be is evidenced by its decision three years ago to move the offices of its Criminal Law Section from Chicago to Washington and to pick a former FBI inspector as the section's staff director.

The section is large (some 5,000 dues-paying members) and it is active. It maintaines systematic liaison with the Justice Department and the appropriate congressional committees; it reviews proposed legislation and initiates ideas of its own.

The results of this activity, however, as confirmed in interviews with congressional and Administration aides, are far less than the ABA would like them to be.

Said one congressional staff member of the Criminal Law Section: "Its influence is zilch, it's out of touch and its endorsement of a bill doesn't do much good."

Another congressional aide, equally active in the criminal law field, gave a somewhat higher rating to ABA endorsements, but said they were not influential enough to make or break a major piece of legislation.

Its power, said a high-ranking administration aide of the ABA in the criminal law field, "is not a consistent one. It is sometimes influential, sometimes not."

Crime Act: Oddly, on a bill which actively engaged the energies of the ABA, and on which its endorsement was eagerly solicited by the White House, Justice Department and Congress, the association's influence was not particularly great, according to those who followed the course of the legislation.

The bill is the Organized Crime

Control Act of 1970 (84 Stat 960), introduced on Jan. 15, 1969, five days before President Nixon's inauguration, and quickly endorsed by the President as partial redemption of his campaign pledge on law and order.

As enacted, it provides for such law-enforcement tools as special grand juries, immunity for witnesses, the use of antitrust laws against criminal infiltration of business and longer prison terms for dangerous offenders.

Nixon Letter—The Senate passed the bill (S 30) on Jan. 23, 1970. Four months later, when the measure bogged down in an unreceptive House Judiciary Committee, the President wrote a letter to ABA President Bernard G. Segal.

Congress has done virtually nothing to enact anticrime legislation, Mr. Nixon complained in his "Dear Bernie" letter, and asked the ABA to urge speedy action upon Congress.

The association responded with uncharacteristic speed. Two weeks after the receipt of the letter, the council of the Criminal Law Section convened in Chicago for a two-day review of S 30 and other pending criminal-law bills.

The results were disappointing to the Administration and its congressional allies, for the section council, in its majority report, found that "some of the provisions of S 30 are unacceptable in their present form" and recommended 22 amendments, some minor but some of major significance.

The minority report, however, said the ABA should make it clear that it "approves of the legislation and is simply suggesting minor modifications that it feels will improve it."

ABA Action—On July 15, the ABA Board of Governors, exercising its authority to act for the association between sessions of the House of Delegates, met in Chicago and, in effect, accepted the minority report, recommending seven amendments but approving the bill "in principle" and urging "its enactment by the Congress as soon as possible."

At its regular meeting in mid-August, the House of Delegates ratified the board's interim action.

In the meantime, ABA President-elect Edward L. Wright testified on July 23 before the House committee in support of the bill, and to dispel whatever doubts might have remained about the ABA's position, said the association would like to see its amendments accepted but supported the bill with or without the changes.

Lobbying—At the critical Chicago meeting of the Criminal Law Section, representatives of the Administration and Congress were on hand to present the case on behalf of the bill.

There for the Senate Judiciary Subcommittee on Criminal Laws and Procedures—whose chairman, John L. McClellan, sponsored S 30—was its chief counsel, G. Robert Blakey.

"We went out to Chicago to try to convince the section of what the score was," Blakey said in a recent interview.

Although the section's majority report was unsatisfactory from his point of view, Blakey said, the day was saved by the minority report which the Board of Governors ultimately accepted.

Sentencing—Some critics of the ABA are still upset, more than a year later, about the bar's role on behalf of the bill's controversial provisions for longer prison terms for "dangerous special offenders," those who have previously been convicted of two or more federal felonies or who in other ways give evidence of danger to society.

The Criminal Law Section had recommended, in general terms, that the provision as it had passed the Senate be changed to conform with the ABA's standards on sentencing.

On Sept. 11, more than six weeks after his testimony, Wright (by then president of the ABA), sent a letter to the House committee, suggesting specific language for an amendment to the disputed provision.

In his letter, Wright confessed that it was unusual for the ABA to urge particular language upon Congress, and said he had consulted the staff of McClellan's subcommittee, which actually drafted the suggested amendment.

Rep. Poff, a member of the House committee, took Wright's version and put it into a proposed substitute bill which he presented to the committee four days later.

As enacted into law, the act contains the ABA-Poff language, a fact which still galls House opponents of the crime bill.

Impact—These same critics, however, insist, as one of them put it recently, that "the ABA didn't make the difference on the bill—not for a moment."

Supporters of the measure agree. "The truth is," said one, "the bar association endorsement didn't make a lot of difference. The realities were being settled on a political basis."

Said an Administration official involved in preparing and supporting the bill: "The ABA was not influential over-all. The bill would have passed in any event. On some sections, but not the most significant ones, they played a role, but their influence was not crucial."

Why, then, did supporters of the bill seek out the ABA's endorsement in the spring and summer of 1970?

"It was defensive," one of them explained recently. "The ABA's support doesn't mean very much, but its opposition can be used by congressional opponents to reinforce their own positions."

"I think," he continued, "that they would like to have the same kind of veto on criminal legislation that they have on Supreme Court appointments. But they don't have the guns."

Justice: H. Lynn Edwards, the Criminal Law Section's staff director, said in an interview that the section works closely with the Justice Department on matters within its purview.

"The ABA represents expertise in the criminal-justice field," he said. Section members include prosecutors, defense attorneys and judges.

The official he works with most closely is Associate Deputy Attorney General Donald E. Santarelli, the Justice Department liaison with the ABA.

"While the Criminal Law Section is not consulted on a regular basis," Santarelli said, "it is, from time to time, on specific issues."

One problem, he said, is that the ABA procedure which leads to a formal stand is too slow sometimes to fit the timetable of the Justice Department.

All legislative proposals in the criminal-law field are reviewed automatically by the section, Santarelli said.

When an issue arises that is important to the department, he said, "I try to persuade them to endorse our position. But I don't consider that lobbying."

TAXATION

As a general proposition, the narrower and more technical the issue, the more effective and influential the ABA can be.

This is particularly true in the field of tax law, where the expertise of association members—especially those who are active in the Washington-based Taxation Section—can be brought into play.

On the major issues of tax policy, however—the Tax Reform Act of 1969 (83 Stat 487), for example, or the Revenue Act of 1971 (85 Stat 497), enacted during the economic emergency last December—the ABA plays little or no part.

ABA's Role: In fact, according to those who participated in the long legislative battle over tax reform in 1969 and in the much briefer process of cutting taxes to stimulate the economy last autumn, the association by and large stayed out of the debate.

In part, this is a consequence of the cumbersome machinery of the ABA, which ordinarily militates against quick policy decisions. "The 1969 act took about eleven months from introduction to final passage, and the ABA couldn't even get off the ground on that one," said a congressional aide who worked on the tax reform legislation.

The 1971 tax-cutting bill moved even more swiftly through Congress, and the same aide said he saw no sign of ABA activity on the measure.

Another factor is the prevalent feeling in government—shared by many in the ABA—that while the legal profession has special competence on narrow questions of tax law, it has none on issues of tax policy.

Thus the association's views will be considered, and even solicited, on questions such as what a provision of the Internal Revenue Code may mean or what the consequences will be if it is amended.

But the ABA's opinion on whether tax reductions are economically advantageous or socially desirable is considered no more relevant than that of any other professional or trade group.

Stanley S. Surrey, who served as assistant Treasury secretary for tax policy from 1961 to 1969, said whatever weight the ABA has had in the tax field comes from "the good technical comments" on legislation offered by the association's Taxation Section.

Surrey, now a professor at Harvard Law School, said, "On policy matters I don't think they play any role."

Lobbying: Surrey and congressional staff assistants are in agreement that the ABA does not lobby, in the usual meaning of that word, for or against legislation in the tax field.

"The ABA doesn't lobby as other groups lobby," said one aide who asked that he not be identified.

"They attempt to present an honest research effort," he said. "We're made aware of what their recommendations are, but they don't press for them."

The same congressional assistant said that "we respect their point of view and make use of it" in formulating tax policy.

The ABA, Surrey said in an interview, normally involves itself only in what he described as "the operative mechanics" of tax law, reviewing proposed regulations and making technical comments upon them, or proposing technical changes in the Internal Revenue Code.

At the recent midwinter meeting of the ABA, for example, the Taxation Section recommended (and the House of Delegates approved) nine amendments to the code to accomplish such things as limiting the civil fraud penalty or changing the requirements on sales of property by real estate investment trusts.

Special Interests—The ABA, says Surrey, "will rarely recommend a provision that will tighten up on anybody."

But while the legislative suggestions may often originate from the experience of individual lawyers and their clients, neither Surrey nor congressional aides would classify them as special-interest legislation.

"By the time they are mulled over within the Taxation Section, the proposals represent the broad interests of the entire bar," said one legislative assistant.

Views Sought—While the ABA, through its Taxation Section, generally volunteers its opinions to Congress and the executive

branch, its views are sometimes sought out, especially on technically intricate subjects.

A congressional aide said the ABA was asked to comment, for example, on a 1970 bill intended to relieve an innocent spouse of tax liability arising from the fraudulent omission of income from a joint return by the other spouse.

The association gave its professional advice and the bill was enacted (84 Stat 2063).

Surrey, during his years at the Treasury Department, consulted with the Taxation Section and its committees "at the early and late stages" of policy formulation on those issues in which he felt the section had special competence.

"Particularly if you felt they might have a different view about a technical issue," said Surrey, "you'd try to talk it out with the section. Any opposition, after all, can be a bother."

Taxation Section: The Washington office of the ABA has virtually no contacts with Congress or the executive on tax matters, leaving the field to the Taxation Section, which is one of two ABA sections (along with that of Criminal Law) staffed in Washington instead of Chicago.

The section's office is physically part of the Washington office, but that is as far as the relationship goes.

Its staff is primarily administrative and clerical, and the section's relations with Congress and the Administration are handled through its officers, particularly those who live in Washington or in close proximity.

The present section chairman, Mac Asbill Jr., practices law in

Washington, only a few blocks from the Treasury Building and a few dozen blocks from the Capitol; he handles much of the representational work of the section himself and assigns the rest on a voluntary basis.

There is an intimate relationship between the section and the government agencies with which it has most of its contacts.

"So many of the people now in government," says Surrey, "were at one time active members of the Taxation Section, and for this among other reasons, relations are cordial between the ABA and Treasury."

This is not a Republican phenomenon: Surrey himself was a member of the section's council (its governing body) before joining the Kennedy Administration in 1961.

Rule-making Powers: Another section of the ABA, that of Administrative Law, successfully intervened to challenge one aspect of a bill in a related field, the Economic Stabilization Act Amendments of 1971 (85 Stat 743).

This is the law under which wage and price controls are currently being administered.

The ABA section was upset that the Administration was seeking to exempt the Price Commission and the Pay Board from some of the routine provisions of the Administrative Procedure Act (5 USC 500 *et seq.*) in the interest of maximum flexibility, including such requirements as public notice before a rule could be issued.

Milton M. Carrow, the New York City lawyer who heads the section, said the group's council quickly held a meeting and decided to oppose the Administration efforts.

At Carrow's initiative, he was invited to testify before the House Banking and Currency and the Senate Banking, Housing and Urban Affairs Committees.

At the same time, he approached Administration officials in an attempt to persuade them to change their position.

He was told, Carrow said, that the Administration did not want to be hamstrung in administering the new wage-price program, but that it intended to institute proper safeguards of its own. ("Administrations always say, 'leave it to us,'" Carrow said.)

As enacted, the bill incorporates the principal rule-making provisions of the Administrative Procedure Act.

SELF-INTEREST

As sensitive as the ABA is to any suggestion that it is motivated by the self-interest of the legal profession, it is nevertheless not hesitant to advocate legislation or push for administrative changes that benefit lawyers as lawyers.

It was successful a half-dozen years ago in eliminating the requirement that lawyers would have to meet special tests to practice before federal administrative agencies.

And it has actively pursued legislation through the years to improve pension benefits for self-employed attorneys.

In a speech several years ago describing the lobbying role of the ABA, Channell, the director of its Washington office, pointed out that the association was "support-ing numerous measures that are directed at the legitimate but somewhat special interests of lawyers as professional men."

Agency Practice: One such measure was the Federal Agency Practice Act of 1965 (77 Stat 1281), enacted at the behest of the ABA.

Until passage of that law, an attorney who wished to represent his client before the Internal Revenue Service or a number of other federal agencies had to pass a special examination or meet other admissions requirements, even though he was a member of the bar in good standing.

To practice before IRS, for example, a lawyer needed what was known as a Treasury card. Without it, he could not appear before the agency, and Lowell Beck, then the assistant director of the Washington office, said IRS officials sometimes arbitrarily took the cards away from lawyers.

As enacted, the legislation eliminated admissions requirements for all federal agencies except the Patent Office.

"We lobbied hard for the bill and got it through," Beck said recently. "The membership of the ABA was mobilized to write letters and make phone calls to local Representatives and Senators," a technique not usually employed by the ABA Washington office, Beck said.

"It's clearly easier to mobilize the bar on a bread-and-butter issue like this than on public-interest issues," Beck admitted, adding that success on legislation helpful to lawyers makes it easier to get bar support for public service projects.

Pensions: Such a bread-and-butter issue is the campaign to expand retirement benefits for the self-employed, in whose ranks lawyers are numerous.

"I know some people will see this as a purely self-interest thing we shouldn't be involved in," said Beck.

Nevertheless, it ranks high on the ABA's legislative priority list.

In 1942, according to Channell, who personally handles this subject for the ABA, Congress made employer contributions to pension funds non-taxable to employees until they actually draw out the benefits upon retirement.

In effect, it amounts to a tax deferment to the advantage of the employee. Self-employed persons, however, had no equivalent tax break.

In 1962, in response to lobbying by the ABA, among others, Congress enacted the Self-Employed Individuals Retirement Act (76 Stat 809).

This bill was considered only a partial answer to the problem, since it placed an annual ceiling on contributions to a self-employed person's pension plan and permitted a tax deduction for only half the amount so contributed.

Legislation (S 3012 and HR 12272) sponsored by the Nixon Administration to raise the ceiling and increase the deductions was introduced late last year. Hearings have not been scheduled.

The ABA has already endorsed the proposals, which association president Jaworski has described as "a significant step forward toward equality in tax treatment for individuals in all walks of life . . . ."

Concern: That was in Jaworski's report to the ABA's House of Delegates at the February meeting.

In an interview with *National Journal,* he expressed the concern he shares with every other leader of the ABA that it not be stamped with the label of special-interest lobby.

About 90 per cent of what the ABA does, he said, is in the public interest.

"That bill," he said of the pension measure, "falls within the 10-per cent category. Yes, it affects lawyers as lawyers, but there's nothing sinister about it.

"There's no need of our leaning over backward to avoid criticism. We rightly should interest ourselves in this, and, in fact, the ABA has taken the lead among the professions in pushing this."

"We think," Jaworski said, "we're really correcting an inequality.

"But any time the American Bar Association gets to be an organization profession, I wouldn't want this job."

7 PUBLIC POLICY ISSUES

The shaping of public policy involves a complex and shifting (almost kaleidoscopic) pattern of interactions among legislators, executive officials, judges, pressure group and political party leaders, and private citizens. In the American political system, the participants and their relative power positions tend to vary dramatically from issue to issue. The articles in this chapter analyze a series of major foreign and domestic policy issues. The essays provide insights into the substance of these current issues and the stakes which various participants have in how these controversies are resolved. Further insights are presented into how governmental and nongovernmental forces interact to shape public policy.

DEFENSE AND FOREIGN POLICY

The interest of the Congress and the American people in foreign policy is sporadic and dependent upon the severity of the crisis at hand. Generally, however, the Congress has been content to let the President assume responsibility for foreign policy. Until recently most academic observers of the international scene have approved of this state of affairs since they have viewed the Congress as being parochial, isolationist, and too prone toward military solutions to foreign problems.

The frustrations caused by America's continuing involvement in the Vietnam war have created intense interest within Congress and academic and lay circles in the question of whether or not Presidents should be allowed to commit United States forces to combat without congressional approval.

The focal point of the present debate over the President's war powers is a bill that would limit the President's power to commit American forces in the absence of affirmative action by Congress. Though provocated by the disenchantment with the process by which the United States became involved in Vietnam, the bill has significance beyond the current controversy because it goes to the heart of the question concerning the respective roles of the President and Congress in national security matters.

This is not a new issue as the following article on the debate over the bill to limit the President's war powers indicates. A similar legislative battle took place in the 1950s over the so-called Bricker Amendment. This proposal would

have limited the President's power to make executive agreements with other nations. Such agreements have the effect of law, but do not require Senate ratification. In the 1950s, the forces favoring presidential latitude led by President Dwight D. Eisenhower carried the day and defeated the Bricker Amendment. Today after years of military conflict in Vietnam the political climate is different than it was in the 1950s and the alignment of forces is also different than it was then. It is impossible to predict the outcome of the present struggle over the respective powers of the President and Congress in foreign policy. As the article on the controversy makes clear, however, a major constitutional and foreign policy issue is in the process of decision.

Senate attempts to limit President's power to make war   *John Maffre*

Vietnam: Biggest undeclared war in American history

For the first time in two centuries, the Senate in 1972 moved vigorously to impose limits on a President's power to involve the nation in armed conflict.

By a vote of 68-16 on April 18, the Senate approved a bill (S 2956) to restrict presidential power to use force—except in emergencies—without the express permission and the constant monitoring of Congress.

One element of major significance influenced this Senate action. This was the widespread feeling that Congress had lost its influential voice in matters of defense and foreign policy, either by default or by presidential usurpation, and that it must reassert that voice.

A large number of Republicans voted for the bill, despite the objections of President Nixon, as well as key Democrats who are normally associated with a strong U.S. military posture.

Regardless of the outcome of the bill, which was not as highly favored in the House, the White House was served notice that its leeway in undertaking military adventures could no longer be taken for granted.

The Bill: The legislation reported by the Foreign Relations Committee on Feb. 9 (SRept 92-606) was largely based on proposals made by Sen. Jacob K. Javits, R-N.Y.

Its chief purpose is to ensure that a President will not undertake a lengthy war without affirmative action by Congress.

Thus, although the President would be given authority to commit troops to combat without prior congressional approval in emergency situations, he could only do so for 30 days. If Congress did not support continuation of the conflict within that period, it would have to be terminated.

Another key section of the legislation provides that U.S. troops could not be committed to combat under the terms of any treaty with another nation, unless the treaty was backed up by legislation specifically authorizing a combat role for U.S. armed forces.

Debate—The Nixon Administration argues that Congress already has enough authority to regulate U.S. involvement in war—primarily through its power to appropriate funds. Its spokesmen say that the Senate bill would dangerously restrict the President's ability to act. Further, they question the bill's constitutionality, and say that there is a better-than-even chance that President Nixon would veto it should it reach his desk in a form similar to the Foreign Relations Committee's version.

The driving force behind the bill, Javits says, has been the traumatic experience of Vietnam, where war never was declared by the United States. He and other supporters of the legislation maintain that it does not infringe on the President's powers—that it simply reasserts the voice of Congress in war-making decisions, a voice they believe has been dangerously muted in recent years.

ORIGINS OF BILL

On the floor of the Senate, in public speeches, in articles written for *The New York Times* and other major publications, Javits hammered at the theme that events—notably Vietnam—and assertive Presidents have diluted the authority of Congress in foreign policy and war-making issues.

Javits' Case: The United States' emergence after World War II in the previously "quite alien role" of dominant world power has led to a practice running "counter to the genius of our Constitution," Javits has said.

"Congress has learned from experience that it must devise practical new means for exercising, in relation to 'limited' and 'undeclared' wars, the war powers reserved to it in Article 1, Section 8 of the Constitution," he told a committee of the American Bar Association in New Orleans on Feb. 5.

"We have learned that the power of the purse, alone, is not an effective instrumentality for asserting congressional authority for undeclared wars."

Javits warned that recent moves by the Senate to reassert its powers had brought about a "hardening and intensification of unilateral and unfettered Presidential prerogative.

"Our action has stimulated a reaction. The situation is now one of dynamic tension."

Over the course of 25 years, Javits says, Congress has given up, on a piecemeal basis, much of its power to control war-making by enacting a series of so-called area resolutions, giving the President authority to use armed force in a specific area and for a specific purpose. The most famous of these is the Tonkin Gulf Resolution, enacted in 1964 and cited by President Johnson in justifying his actions in Vietnam. The resolution was repealed, with the support of the Nixon Administration, in 1970. Other area resolutions now in effect cover the Taiwan Straits, Cuba and Latin America, and the Middle East.

Some academics and officials of earlier Administrations—former Under Secretary of State (1961-66) George W. Ball and White House aide (1961-64) Arthur M. Schlesinger Jr., for example—have argued that the bill is dangerously restrictive of executive power. But Javits dismisses these criticisms as coming "from the perspective of the 'President's men.'"

Senate Dissent: Senate action on S 2956 followed in the wake of a number of actions the Senate has taken over recent years in an attempt to restrict presidential authority in the fields of defense and foreign policy.

The most dramatic instance came on Aug. 8, 1969, when the Senate came within one vote of rejecting continuation of the Safeguard antiballistic missile system; an amendment to defeat the program failed on a 50-50 tie.

In 1970, Sens. John Sherman Cooper, R-Ky., and Frank Church, D-Idaho, led a successful move to bar the use of U.S. ground troops outside of South Vietnam. Their proposal, made in the wake of a combined U.S. and South Vietnamese incursion into Cambo-

dia, was approved by the Senate, 58-37, on June 30. The provision was accepted by the House and it represented the first limitation ever voted on a President's powers as commander-in-chief in a combat situation.

In June of 1971 there was another bipartisan—but unsuccessful—bid to end the war in Vietnam.

Sens. George S. McGovern, D-S.D., and Mark Hatfield, R-Ore., proposed an amendment that would oblige the President to remove all troops from Indochina by Dec. 31, 1971. The amendment was defeated, 42-55, on June 16 in a roll-call vote.

A month earlier, the Administration mobilized dozens of leading public figures to oppose a proposal by Senate Majority Leader Mike Mansfield, D-Mont., to cut U.S. forces in NATO from 300,000 to 150,000 by the end of 1971. Mansfield's amendment was defeated by May 19, 36-61.

Mansfield's attempt to set a time limit on the Vietnam war also failed in 1971. The Senate approved, 57-42, his proposal requiring an end to combat in six months, providing all prisoners were freed. But a Senate-House conference changed the provision to read "at the earliest practicable date."

Congress, particularly the Senate, also has shown its concern about U.S. commitments abroad in action on foreign-aid requests in the past several years.

The Administration's request for foreign aid in fiscal 1970 was reduced from $3.6 billion to $2.5 billion. The same amount was voted in fiscal 1971, representing a cut of $300 million. Even the most vocal critics of foreign aid were stunned when the Senate, on Oct. 29 of 1971, voted, 41-27, to kill the fiscal 1972 foreign-aid bill entirely. A compromise on the measure was developed early in 1972, providing $3.2 billion, or $1.1 billion less than President Nixon had asked for.

ADMINISTRATION CONCERN

The White House was resigned to the success of the Javits bill in the Senate weeks before the April 13 vote.

"We just have to think of it in terms of being passed in the Senate, with such a broad spectrum of support from people like Stennis and Fulbright," Clark MacGregor said in an interview in February.

MacGregor, a former Republican member of the House from Minnesota (1961-71) became Counsel to the President for congressional relations in 1971.

"After that, the prognosis is uncertain, and probably not favorable for the bill. There's a different attitude in the House. I've talked with some thoug"tful people in the House, who are also constitutional lawyers, and they have their doubts."

The President had talked with him about it "in a preliminary way," he said. "And I've talked with Kissinger, and he has an acute interest in it—so does Haig."

Henry A. Kissinger is the President's assistant for national security affairs, and Brig. Gen. Alexander M. Haig Jr. is his deputy.

President Nixon gave a brief account of his views on war-powers legislation in response to a question at an April 29, 1971, press conference. "I believe that limiting the President's war powers, whoever is the President of the United States, would be a very great mistake. We live in times when situations can change so fast internationally that to wait until the Senate acts before a President can act might be that we acted too late."

Consultation — One White House aide, while opposing the strictures in Javits' bill, acknowledged that consultation between the executive and Congress on foreign policy matters was "deficient."

At an earlier time, he recalled, the Senate "was willing to delegate to a handful of its own Members the consultative role," citing in particular the late Sen. Arthur H. Vandenberg (R-Mich., 1928-51). "There were a few widely recognized Members who would breakfast with the President, and then come back and assure everybody. . . . Today's Senate won't buy that. You can't even consult with the full Foreign Relations Committee because Appropriations and Armed Services have to be told."

Strategy—Because of sympathy for the Javits' bill among such leading Republicans as Sen. Hugh Scott of Pennsylvania, the Minority Leader, Sen. Barry Goldwater, R-Ariz., led the fight against it on the Senate floor.

The Administration is anxious not to repeat what one aide characterized as "overkill" in its efforts to defeat the 1971 amendment offered by Sen. Mansfield to trim the U.S. troop commitment to NATO from 310,000 to 150,000 men. In that case, the White House rounded up so many elder statesmen, legislators and military leaders to denounce the amendment that it alienated many influential people on Capitol Hill.

"The best thing on our side is time," said a White House official. "We have a short year, what with the conventions and the campaign." In addition, he said, "it's a highly vetoable bill."

Rogers' Testimony — The most extensive presentation of the Administration's position on the war-powers legislation came last May, when Secretary of State William P. Rogers testified before the Senate Foreign Relations Committee.

His thesis was that Congress already had the powers it needed to regulate conflicts and that the President's ability to act quickly should not be fettered. Rogers conceded that closer consultation between Congress and the executive branch was imperative.

"Rogers went over that presentation word by word," a State Department aide said, "and he took more than the usual pains with it. That's not only the Secretary of State talking. That's also the voice of a guy who first learned his way around here as Attorney General in President Eisenhower's time."

Rogers said that too often a polemic approach was made to conflict between presidential and congressional power, "the implication being that these powers are somehow incompatible.

"I believe the contrary is true. The framers of the Constitution intended that there be a proper balance between the roles of the President and Congress, in decisions to use force in the conduct of foreign policy."

Precedent—Rogers then cited a number of cases when Presidents had acted without sanction of Congress, starting when President Jefferson sent warships to protect American merchantmen from the Barbary pirates. And he speculated on the reasons why there was "remarkably little complaint" from Capitol Hill.

"In the first place, I suppose that Presidents were acting in the context of a generally popular consensus in the country that the United States should assume a posture consistent with its emerging power, particularly in the western hemisphere.

"Second, a majority of the 19th and early 20th century presidential actions occurred in the Caribbean, where this country's power was so predominant that there was little or no chance of forcible response . . . In short, there being no risk of a major war, one could argue that there was no violation of Congress' power to declare war."

Rogers dwelt on the number of times since World War II that Presidents had acted, sometimes on their own and at other times relying on congressional actions short of declarations of war—for example, the Tonkin Gulf Resolution.

"The question is not whether these resolutions are useful to the President," he said, "but instead whether such open-ended delegations are an effective means for Congress to exercise its constitutional authority."

NIXON DOCTRINE

Then Rogers argued that changing perceptions in the executive

U.S. WARS: MOSTLY UNDECLARED

Sen. Barry Goldwater, R-Ariz., a staunch opponent of the war-powers legislation, argues on the basis of extensive historical research that congressional restrictions on the President's authority to commit U.S. forces to combat would invite disaster.

Goldwater and his staff have assembled a long list, which is continually being revised, of the number of instances in which the United States has used its military forces in combat, with or without a congressional declaration of water. Goldwar's count of the times Congress has declared war remains constant—at five—but the list of other military confrontations has grown from 153 last April to 197 this February.

Most of Goldwater's research has been performed by his legislative assistant, J. Terry Emerson, 36, a 1959 graduate of Duke University Law School. The information has formed the basis for articles published this year under Goldwater's name in the *Arizona Law Review* and under Emerson's name in the *West Virginia Law Review.*

It also has bolstered the Senator's case, at hearings and in speeches on the Senate floor, as he argues against the war-powers legislation now pending before the Senate.

Declarations of War: Goldwater's research has found congressional declarations of war in five instances:

The War of 1812. On June 18, 1812, Congress declared war on England. It was an indecisive fight that formally ended on Dec. 14, 1814, with the Treaty of Ghent.

War between the United States and Mexico, 1846-1848. The declaration came on May 11, 1846, and the Treaty of Guadalupe Hidalgo ended the war on Feb. 2, 1848.

Spanish-American War, 1898. This was the shortest declared war in American history. The formal declaration was made in April of 1898 and a peace treaty was signed in Paris in December.

World War I, 1917-1918. Congress declared war on Germany on April 6, 1917, and on Austria on Dec. 7. The Treaty of Versailles was signed June 28, 1919, but never was ratified by the United States.

World War II, 1941-1945. Congress declared war on Japan on Dec. 8, 1941, and on Germany and Italy three days later. War in Europe ended May 8, 1945, and Japan surrendered Sept. 2, 1945.

Other Instances: According to Goldwater's research, the United States has undertaken 45 major military actions for broad strategic purposes without a congressional declaration of war.

These include the sea war with France lasting from 1798 to 1800; the wars with the Barbary pirates in 1801-05; Commodore Matthew C. Perry's mission to open up Japan in 1853; the deployment of 126,000 troops—half of all U.S. armed forces at the time—to quell the rebellion in the Philippines in 1899-1901; the deployment of about 6,000 troops and 44 naval vessels to China in 1927 to protect American interests against Chinese attacks; the Korean war that began in 1950, and the Vietnam war, in which more than 2.5 million U.S. military men have served over the years.

Eighty-two of the 192 undeclared wars involved actual fighting, and 96 actions lasted more than 30 days. Under the Senate Foreign Relations Committee bill (S 2956), presidential authority to conduct an emergency military action would expire after 30 days in the absence of legislative action approving extension of the conflict.

One hundred and two, or slightly more than half, of the undeclared actions occurred outside the western hemisphere, starting with the wars against the pirates of Tripoli in 1801. With notable exceptions in the current century, most of the troop deployments were small, and the U.S. Marine Corps played a dominant role.

Goldwater's list includes 13 fights with Mexico and 10 incidents involving Cuba. It also shows that since 1789 the United States has had more incidents with China than with any other single nation. At the time U.S. and Chinese forces last collided in a shooting war—Korea—the two nations already had clashed 25 times.

---

branch of the proper use of military power had all but rendered moot the debate over the war-powers legislation.

"The very concept of that which best serves the national interest in the United States has undergone a significant change since the uses of force in the 1950s and 1960s," he said.

"The Nixon Doctrine represents a recognition that protection of our national interest does not require an automatic U.S. military response to every threat. The aim of the Nixon Doctrine is to increase the participation of other nations in individual and collective defense efforts. While reaffirming our treaty commitments and offering a shield against threats from nuclear powers aimed at our allies or other nations vital to our security, we now look to the nation directly threatened to assume the primary responsibility for providing the manpower necessary for its defense.

"I am sure this new approach will be of great help in achieving balanced executive-legislative participation in decisions regarding the use of balanced military force."

Quick Action—Rogers listed three reasons why the United States should be able to take quick, effective military action:

1. The nation has emerged as a world power committed to many treaties.

2. It has a commanding position in the field of nuclear weaponry, and the obligation to defend itself and its allies against nuclear attack.

3. "Third, the institutional capacities of the Presidency have facilitated the broad use of presidential powers. The nation must be able to act flexibly and, in certain cases, without prior publicity."

The White House has the capacity to act quickly, Rogers said, but Congress does not.

"Unlike the Presidency, the institutional characteristics of Congress have not lent themselves as well to the requirements of spped and accuracy in times of recurrent crises and rapid change. The composition of the Congress with its numerous Members and their diverse constituencies, the resultant complexity of the decision-making process, and Congress' constitutional tasks of debate, discussion and authorization inevitably make it a more deliberative, public and diffuse body."

Rogers said he opposed war-powers bills like Javits' because they would freeze something the framers of the Constitution had left unfrozen, the allocation of war powers.

Conclusions—To ensure that the responsibility for war-making would be shared, as provided by the Constitution, Rogers suggested:

"First, we are prepared to explore with you ways of helping Congress reinforce its own informational capability on issues involving war and peace. . . .

"Second, there needs to be effective consultation between Congress and the President, and we have tried to follow this policy. . . .

"Third, the Congress must effectively exercise the powers which it has under the Constitution in the war-powers area. . . .

"Fourth, there is the need to act speedily, and sometimes without prior publicity, in crisis situations. . . .

"Fifth, there is, in my view, the clear need to preserve the President's ability to act in emergencies in accordance with his constitutional responsibilities."

SENATE

Leading figures in the Senate have been associated with moves to enact a war-powers bill—including—Mansfield, Minority Leader Hugh Scott, R-Pa.; J. W. Fulbright, D-Ark.; John Sherman Cooper, the chairman and ranking minority member of the Foreign Relations Committee; John Stennis, D-Miss., chairman of the Armed Services Committee, and Robert Dole, R-Kan., chairman of the Republican National Committee.

Fulbright: Fulbright, whose committee reported S 2956 on Feb. 9, told Secretary Rogers why he thought legislation was needed during the hearings last May.

"You know," he said, "the more I observe this Administration the more closely I find it follows its predecessors' policies in nearly all respects with regard to foreign policy. You have gone about as far as Mr. Nicholas Katzenbach did when he came before this committee."

Rogers immediately protested that this was not "accurate at all," and said heatedly—three times—that he had publicly disagreed with a response that former Under Secretary of State Nicholas deB. Katzenbach gave on Aug. 17, 1967, to Fulbright, when the chairman

PROVISIONS OF THE BILL

The Senate Foreign Relations Committee's war powers bill (S 2956) is based on legislation first introduced in 1970 by Sen. Jacob K. Javits, R-N.Y.

Javits' bill saw no action in the 91st Congress. In February 1971 he introduced a revised version and throughout the year numerous competing war-powers bills were introduced by other Senators, including Thomas F. Eagleton, D-Mo.; John C. Stennis, D-Miss.; Robert Taft Jr., R-Ohio, and Lloyd M. Bentsen Jr., D-Tex.

The Foreign Relations Committee held prolonged hearings on the bills in March, April, May, July and October of last year.

By December a compromise approach had been developed, still largely along the lines of Javits' proposal, and on Feb. 9, 1972, the committee reported its bill to the full Senate (SRept 92-606).

The bill is intended, its preamble says, "to make rules governing the use of the armed forces of the United States in the absence of a declaration of war by the Congress."

Section 2 of the measure says that its purpose is to "insure that the collective judgment of both the Congress and the President will apply" when U.S. troops have been sent to war or are about to be sent. The section says the bill does not mean to interfere with the President's power to act in emergencies.

The next section spells out the emergency situations in which U.S. forces may be deployed in the absence of a congressional declaration of war:

to repel an attack on the United States or its possessions, to retaliate where necessary, or to forestall such an attack;

to repel an attack on U.S. forces abroad, or to forestall such an attack;

to protect and assist in the evacuation of Americans abroad in the event of combat.

A fourth paragraph of Section 3 says that U.S. forces may be deployed with other forces engaged in combat, or likely to be engaged, only by specific authority granted by Congress in advance. Troops may not be committed under any treaty, unless that treaty is backed up by legislation specifically authorizing introduction of U.S. armed forces.

Section 4 provides that whenever U.S. forces are deployed in emergencies, the President must "promptly" inform Congress and that he must continue to provide reports on the status of the hostilities—at least once every six months.

Section 6 provides that presidential authority to use U.S. forces in combat in an emergency situation shall only last 30 days, unless Congress specifically authorizes continuation of the conflict.

Section 7 says that Congress may enact legislation ordering

termination of the hostilities before the end of the 30-day period.

Other sections of the bill spell out procedures for fast action by Congress to "eliminate the risk of dilatory tactics"; provide that if one section of the bill was ruled unconstitutional, the rest of the bill would not be voided; and stipulate that the legislation would not apply retroactively—to include the Vietnam war. None of these provisions was changed during the Senate debate, and only three "perfecting" amendments were approved April 5 by a unanimous 59-0 vote.

Submitted by Javits, these authorized the President to: Protect and evacuate U.S. citizens and nationals endangered on the high seas, as well as on foreign soil; allow continued U.S. military cooperation in multinational headquarters operations such as NATO in Europe, the United Nations command in South Korea and the Canadian-U.S. North American Air Defense Command; continue using U.S. forces in combat after the 30-day limit if (a) "unavoidable military necessity" obliged those forces to be protected or (b) an armed attack prevented Congress from convening.

asked him if he thought it outmoded to declare war: "In this kind of context (Vietnam), I think the expression of declaring war is one that is outmoded in the international arena."

Fulbright was unimpressed, and insisted that he could not see "where the net result, the thrust of your remarks, comes out at a different place."

Amendments—In separate comments inserted in his committee's report on the legislation, Fulbright indicated that he was not satisfied with all aspects of the measure and that he would attempt to amend it on the Senate floor.

Fulbright objected primarily to a section of the legislation detailing the emergency situations under which a President could commit military forces to combat without congressional assent.

A provision allowing such action "to forestall the direct and imminent threat" of an armed attack on the United States could be construed as allowing "a preemptive, or first strike, attack solely on the President's own judgment," Fulbright wrote, and could be used "to justify the Cambodia intervention of 1970 and the Laos intervention of 1971, both of which were explained as being necessary to forestall attacks on American forces."

Fulbright also expressed concern that the bill did not address the question of a President's power, in a continuing limited conflict, to escalate by using nuclear arms.

He suggested an amendment that would allow the use of forces that would give the President general authority to act in emergency situations without defining those situations, explaining that this would make the President "accountable to Congress for his action to a greater extent than he would (be) if he had specific authorizing language to fall back on." A second clause of the amendment would absolutely prohibit initiating the use of nuclear weapons without explicit authorization from Congress.

Two months after his separate comments appeared in the committee report, Fulbright offered two amendments embodying his criticisms of the Javits bill. But they were defeated, 68-10 and 56-28.

Cooper: Cooper, in individual views filed in the committee report, said he believed it unrealistic to impose a 30-day limitation on undeclared hostilities, and that he felt it was beyond the power of Congress to end hostilities within 30 days by legislative expression.

Cooper also wanted to write in a procedure for calling Congress into session when U.S. forces were committed to a hostile zone.

However, Cooper did not submit amendments when the bill came up for debate.

Cooper, who had announced months earlier that he would not run for re-election in 1972, was critical in the report of the Foreign Relations Committee.

He said that on many occasions—in Taiwan, the Middle East, Berlin, Cuba, the Tonkin Gulf—attempts to require approval by Congress before armed forces could be used "were consistently opposed and rejected in the Foreign Relations Committee and in the Senate.

"I present these facts because I do not concur in one underlying theme of the committee report—which was never discussed in committee and never voted on—that the executive has taken from the Congress its powers.

"The record, if studied, discloses that the Congress, particularly since World War II, has not only acceded to but has supported executive resolutions requesting congressional authority to use the armed forces of the United States, if necessary, in hostilities.

"These are the settled facts of history. We can change our course, but we cannot revise and rewrite history."

Stennis: Stennis was a cosponsor of the Foreign Relations Committee's bill, and he last testified for it on Oct. 6, 1971. He said that various checks and balances were intentionally written into the Constitution "to insure that some actions would be taken by the federal government only after careful deliberation followed by a clear-cut decision. The decision to go to war is one of these actions."

Stennis added: "I want to make it clear, though, that I think the President has some power to act alone. I don't want him to sit there like a dummy, of course.

"Send carriers to the Mediterranean, yes; yes, there has to be some kind of influence. The Gulf of Tonkin—resist a display of force there, yes, resist it but not commit fully, not commit fully the nation to war on an incident like that. . . . "

Javits: In an interview, Javits described his war-powers bill as the most significant piece of legislation he had introduced during his service in Congress.

"This involves a historic confrontation involving the Congress and the Presidency," he said. "The President must use the power granted to him by the Constitution, when it comes to making war.

"Now, his power has come to be taken for granted. The tradition has grown up that we—the Congress, that is—would follow the tradition of simply relying on executive power. That's wrong, and Congress must assert itself."

Javits acknowledged that there has been no wide public discussion of the issue, but says "the steam will build up behind it when the President sticks to his idea of a residual force in Vietnam."

He predicted that the bill would be enacted in the 1972 Congress.

Goldwater: When Goldwater appeared before the Senate Foreign Relations Committee last April, he apologized for being "a layman and a non-lawyer." But he cited the extensive historical research he had performed with the assistance of his staff in support of his argument that giving Congress broad authority to restrict presidential war-making power would invite disaster.

"The war-powers bill prohibits any action for strategic purposes unless there is in effect a legislative instrument specifically covering the interest at stake," he noted.

"Of course, by the time Congress assembles and gathers a quorum for acting in the crisis, it then may be too late for anything but resolutions of condolence."

HOUSE

The House already has passed a mild war-powers resolution, and, according to its author, it was not likely that it would accept the Senate's version in its current form.

House Resolution: The bill was written by Rep. Clement J. Zablocki, D-Wis., chairman of the National Security Policy and Scientific Developments Subcommittee of the House Foreign Affairs Committee. It was first approved by the committee and passed by the House in 1970, but it died at the end of the 91st Congress when the Senate took no action.

The resolution (HRes 1) was approved again, by voice vote of the House, on Aug. 2 of last year.

The resolution states the sense of Congress that the President should consult with Congress before committing U.S. troops to combat. It says that in the event that the President, without prior authorization from Congress, sends troops to combat or substantially enlarges military forces already located in a foreign nation, he should "promptly" submit a written report to the House and Senate.

Zablocki, Fraser: Zablocki does not conceal his annoyance that the Senate had not acted upon his resolution.

"I know that Fulbright thought my resolution was wishy-washy," he observed in June, 1971 at the same time defending his proposal as a measure that had a fair chance of passing the House.

In an interview before the Senate approved Javits' bill, Zablocki said, "Fulbright just wants to see some strong language, a sort of sense of the Senate thing. He knows full well that would be ignored" in the House.

"The big problem around here has always been that there is no meaningful conference between the Senate committee and ours," he said.

"They take the adamant position that the House is not an equal body. The Senate would not think of any compromise, and it's always been that way. If they take a similar attitude on the war-powers bill, well. . . ."

He said there has been a good deal of change in House sentiment lately toward imposing limits on the President, "but certainly not to the extent that it would pass the Javits bill as it is now."

He said the chairman of the full Foreign Relations Committee, Rep. Thomas E. Morgan, D-Pa., "is of the same mind as I am."

"We've passed our bill. It's up to them to pass their own bill and then to ask for a conference."

Another member of the Foreign Affairs Committee, Rep. Donald M. Fraser, D-Minn., spoke in a similar vein. "Congress has all the controls that it could ever need," he said, "All it lacks is the guts to use them. We could end the war in Vietnam in 24 hours if we wanted to."

Bingham: Rep. Jonathan B. Bingham, D-N.Y., tried to find a middle ground between the Zablocki resolution and the Javits bill, but he had scant hope of success.

The Senate Foreign Relations Committee was receptive to Javits' bill, said Bingham, a member of the Foreign Affairs Committee, but "in the House, it's quite a different story. I don't seriously expect mine to be acted upon . . . ."

Bingham's bill (HR 12645) reflected his belief that the President should be able to "carry" on hostilities in the absence of a declaration of war so long as he has at

BRICKER: A HISTORICAL PERSPECTIVE

A former Republican Senator who came within a single vote in 1954 of winning Senate approval of a constitutional amendment to strictly limit presidential treaty-making power does not favor the pending war-powers bill of Sen. Jacob K. Javits, R-N.Y.

To John W. Bricker, 78, of Columbus, Ohio, it is one thing to try to protect American citizens at home from the reach of international agreements made by Presidents.

It is something else again, he said this month, to tie a President's hands in the conduct of foreign affairs or in the defense of the nation.

Bricker Amendment: On Feb. 26, 1954, there were 60 Senators present to vote "aye" for a somewhat diluted version of what is known to history as the Bricker amendment. Bricker's proposal would have provided that treaties could be effective as internal law in the United States "only through legislation which would be valid in the absence of a treaty." In that regard, the amendment was similar to Javits' bill, which would specify that no treaty could commit the United States to using armed force unless it was backed up by an act of Congress. Bricker also wanted to make executive agreements, which do not require Senate ratification, subject to congressional approval.

At the heart of the case for Bricker's proposed amendment was concern over agreements prepared by agencies of the United Nations, covering political, social and economic issues, which might be at variance with state or federal law.

Frank E. Holman, former president of the American Bar Association, claimed that these UN-sponsored accords posed a future threat when "a sufficiently internationally and socialistically minded President will be ready to sponsor and ratify them."

The Administration of President Eisenhower fought Bricker vigorously in the Senate, although the President himself was inclined to make concessions. Eisenhower, in a letter drafted for him by his Secretary of State, John Foster Dulles, told the Senate Majority Leader, Sen. William F. Knowland, R-Calif., that the proposed amendment would "shackle the federal government so that it is no longer sovereign in foreign affairs."

There were 91 Senators present on the day the Bricker amendment reached the Senate floor in 1954, and under the two-thirds rule for a constitutional amendment, 61 would have had to vote "aye." Four men switched their vote on the final tally to vote "nay," and two are still in the Senate: Henry M. Jackson and Warren G. Magnuson, both Democrats from Washington.

Views on Bill: In a telephone interview from his home in Columbus, Bricker said his amendment sought only to limit the impact of treaties on the internal affairs of the nation, while Javits'

proposal would limit the President's ability to make war.

"I don't think this bill is necessary, desirable or helpful in any way to the American people," he said. "In international affairs, in war, the President acts for me, for all Americans."

Today, Bricker still practices law in Columbus, as he has done since 1920. Gaps in the practice have come during extended periods of public service, including as assistant attorney general of Ohio (1923-27), state attorney general (1933-37), Governor of Ohio (1939-45), and U.S. Senator from 1947 to 1959.

---

least tacit approval of both houses of Congress."

The bill would ask the President to inform Congress promptly of commencement of hostilities, and would provide that Congress should be called immediately into session if it were in recess. Under Bingham's approach, the hostilities then could be ended by a resolution of either chamber.

In testimony before the Foreign Relations Committee in August 1971, Bingham said that the Zablocki bill did not go far enough, but that he took exception to several provisions of the Javits bill. He said that "it is quite futile and unwise to attempt specifically to prescribe the circumstance under which the President may engage in hostilities in the absence of a declaration of war" and that "any deadline on presidential or congressional action is ill-advised and probably unworkable."

"Third, I believe Congress should not be placed in a position where it must act for Presidential action to continue. . . .

"Rather, the responsibility and authority which the Congress now has—through the 'power of the purse'—to restrict or terminate presidential action should be spelled out clearly.

"What is now a blunt and awkward tool should be sharpened so that it can be used with more precision."

OUTSIDE VIEWS

There was no discernible organized pressure from private groups either for or against the war-powers bill, although the American Bar Association began in 1972 an extensive study of the issues involved.

Academics and officials of former Administrations—many of whom testified before the Senate Foreign Relations Committee—take widely divergent views of the need for the bill.

Against the Bill: Among those who testified against the bill was former Under Secretary of State Ball, who, along with others, had counseled President Johnson to wind down the Vietnam war.

Said Ball: "How does one draft a statute that would make it possible for the Congress to contribute its wisdom, and play at least a coequal role with the executive, in shaping fundamental decisions that may lead to war, without inhibiting the President in doing whatever is necessary in circumstances

of crisis and emergency to protect the vital interests of our country? . . . Let us be quite certain that Congress does not let itself be influenced in the design of that legislation by the transient mood of disillusion and disenchantment with our Vietnamese embroilment."

John Norton Moore, a constitutional law expert who teaches at the University of Virginia Law School, argued that the war-powers proposals "are similar in that they all delimit in advance the independent authority of the President to commit the armed forces to hostilities . . . . But to the extent that they restrict presidential authority beyond the area of exclusive congressional competence, they are of doubtful constitutionality."

Arthur Schlesinger Jr. argues that the problem of war powers "will not yield to neat structural solutions" such as those in the Javits bill.

Writing in *The New Republic* on Feb. 5, 1972, Schlesinger said: "It is more fundamental than that. It requires different states of mind—a new will to seek participation on the part of the executive, a new will to accept responsibility on the part of Congress. It requires much more systematic congressional skepticism about information and forecasts handed them by the executive. It requires an end to the idea that foreign policy is too sacred for secular debate."

Schlesinger wrote that the Javits bill "probably would have prevented President Roosevelt from protecting the British lifeline against Nazi submarines—and that it probably would not have prevented President Johnson from escalating the war in Vietnam."

For the Bill: Alexander M. Bickel, a professor of constitutional law at Yale Law School, attacked Schlesinger's position as "a counsel of despair" in a Jan. 22 article in *The New Republic*.

Bickel wrote that: "Singly, either the President or Congress can fall into bad errors, of commission or omission.

"So they can together, too, but that is somewhat less likely, and in any event, together they are all we've got. In emergencies requiring instant action, or for purposes of command decisions, the President alone is all we've got, as the war-powers bill fully recognizes, but that is true only in emergencies."

Testifying before the Foreign Relations Committee, McGeorge Bundy, who served as national security adviser to Presidents Kennedy and Johnson from 1961 to 1966, said that "Congress can and should put appropriate conditions on any authorization of limited hostilities. The constitutional power to declare war clearly includes the power to put limits on any hostilities that are authorized. This is what we have not properly understood in the past."

Similarly, George E. Reedy, who served as President Johnson's

press secretary in 1964 and 1965, told the committee: "One of the principal problems of the past 20, 30, 40 years has been the rise of that body of thought which ascribes a sanctity, almost a holiness to the presidential decision-making process and assumes that anyone questioning it, even in times when disillusionment has set in, is being rather presumptuous and is intruding in the fields of foreign policy where he has no business."

Bar Association—In July, 1972 the American Bar Association at its annual convention voted to conduct a study of war-powers issues, after turning down a resolution calling for unilateral withdrawal of U.S. forces from Southeast Asia and another resolution calling for a study of whether war crimes had been committed there.

The ABA study was contracted with Columbia University under an 18-month, $75,000 contract, directed by Abraham D. Sofaer, an authority on constitutional law at Columbia.

"It will be an objective, legal and historical analysis of the responsible powers of the Congress and the President to make and to conduct war," said George M. Wade, a New York lawyer and ABA member who was involved in negotiating the contract.

"The real danger to our security today," says Javits, "is not that the Congress might hamstring the President. The real danger is that Presidents can—and do—shoot from the hip.

"If the collective judgment of the President and Congress is required to go to war, it will call for responsible action by the Congress for which each Member must answer individually and for restraint by both the Congress and the President."

Earlier in 1972 the Senate had taken one action demonstrating its attitude towards executive authority to commit the nation to ventures abroad. On Feb. 16 it passed, 81-0, a bill (S 596) sponsored by Sen. Clifford P. Case, R-N.J., requiring the Administration to inform the Senate of any executive agreement reached with another nation within 60 days.

Agreements of that kind, unlike treaties, are beyond the reach of Senate ratification.

The Senate's action in passing the Javits bill by such a wide margin put the executive branch on notice: take Congress into consultation hereafter on matters involving defense and foreign policy, or face the prospect of legislative harassment and obstruction.

THE ECONOMY

Prices, wages, and jobs are real "gut" issues of American politics and accordingly leaders of both parties are highly sensitive to these economic concerns. Indeed one of the President's principal responsibilities is developing an economic policy that will achieve price stability and at the same time maintain a high level of employment. The economic dislocations caused by Vietnam war-inspired inflationary pressures and now the transition from a wartime to a peacetime economy has plagued President Nixon since he assumed office.

As the article on the President's Cost of Living Council illustrates, the task of managing the economy to achieve the twin goals of price stability and high employment is a delicate, often frustrating, and a politically controversial assignment. Once President Nixon had made his surprise announcement in the summer of 1971 that he was imposing wage and price controls, the job of implementing his policy rested with the Cost of Living Council. With a small staff—reflecting the President's opposition to a large World War II type wage-price control bureaucracy—the Council has sought to influence significantly the course of a diversified and growing economy with a GNP of approximately one trillion dollars. The extent to which the Council succeeds in its mission of price stability without unduly alienating significant segments of the economy is important because of the impact the status of the economy will have on the Republican chances in the coming elections. But beyond that, President Nixon's experiment in wage and price controls should provide additional information on what is required in the way of government policy if price stability is to become a reality.

Beleaguered Cost of Living Council set to focus efforts on major market forces   *Andrew J. Glass*

With its anti-inflation policies under attack, the Nixon Administration is giving serious thoughts to concentrating all of its efforts to control prices and wages on big corporations and big labor.

This policy initiative is being discussed quietly within the Cost of Living Council, which shepherds the economic-stabilization program for President Nixon.

If adopted, the Administration plan would decontrol large sectors of the economy on the theory that the larger units set wage and price trends.

The Administration also would be responding to a growing Democratic-led challenge in Congress. A Democratic majority on the Joint Economic Committee, following the advice of former (1964-68) Council of Economic Advisers Chairman Gardner Ackley, favors imposing controls selectively—only on those economic segments that hold "definite market power."

On the other hand, the plan is a rebuff to AFL-CIO President George Meany, who resigned in anger as a member of the Pay Board. The Meany alternative is to put the entire economy under controls, with an expanded bureaucracy to police the system.

Meany's abrupt resignation put the stabilization program under severe stress because it coincided with the announcement of an 0.5-per cent increase in the consumer price index for February, led by soaring meat prices.

The President responded to the challenge by persuading Pay Board Chairman George H. Boldt to continue operations with a reconstituted seven-member body.

At the same time, Mr. Nixon asked then Treasury Secretary John B. Connally, the Cost of Living Council's chairman, to confer with a dozen supermarket executives.

The meeting came at a time when meat prices were about to soften under natural market forces. But according to sources present, Connally persuaded the chain store executives to pass the lower prices on to consumers more quickly than they might otherwise have done.

"The Administration was in trouble," a spokesman for the council said, "so it trotted out its big guns."

Pace: Cost of Living Council Director Donald Rumsfeld privately said he believed that the post-freeze bulge in prices will extend through April but not through May.

Rumsfeld recently told an associate: "Unfortunately, you still have people who look at the wholesale price index and say, 'Ah ha, the controls aren't working.' That's an incorrect assumption. But some people are pretty loose about bridging the difference between the freeze and Phase 2."

In an interview, Treasury Under Secretary Charls E. Walker said: "Basically, we're pragmatists. We're dedicated to results."

Walker agrees with Rumsfeld that the economy is still moving through what Walker calls "the bubble." Yet Walker contends that the price and wage increases which followed in the wake of the freeze were actually at a lower level than the Administration had originally anticipated.

"What we're trying to do," Walker said, "is to speed up the transition to a peacetime economy—to produce, as it were, a 'hothouse' effect. In this new situation, demand-pull inflation is no longer a problem. So what we're trying to do is to navigate ourselves through cost-push."

Style: While the scope of the program may become more narrowly focused in the months to come, its character is unlikely to change before the national elections in November.

Questions still remain, however, over how large an administrative complex will be required to run the program in its evolving form—and where the bulk of that machinery should be deployed.

OPERATIONS

In part by accident and in part by design, White House control over the economic-stabilization program remains circumscribed.

The President initially ruled out creating a large agency to administer the program—a decision founded in his own experiences as a young lawyer in the Office of Price Administration during World War II. That decision dictated that wage and price controls would have to be self-administered, to a large extent, within the private sector.

At the same time, Mr. Nixon was eager to secure the active co-operation of the AFL-CIO for the stabilization program. Therefore, he bowed to demands from Meany and other labor leaders that the Pay Board be a tripartite body—with equal labor, business and public representation—and that its individual wage decisions be immune from a White House veto.

Having agreed to this demand last October—in what proved to be an abortive attempt to retain Meany's cooperation—the President was obliged to fashion an equally independent structure for the companion Price Commission.

Background: Mr. Nixon created the Cost of Living Council on Aug. 15, 1971, under Executive Order 11615 and charged it with developing policies needed to implement a virtually total 90-day freeze on prices, wages and rents.

Phase One—During this period, the council, under its chairman, Treasury Secretary Connally, and its first executive director, Arnold R. Weber, made all major policy decisions affecting the anti-inflation program.

The council issued policy statements, often in the form of questions and answers, which then were drafted as regulations by the Office of Emergency Preparedness, the agency charged with monitoring compliance during the freeze.

From the start, the council's skeleton staff was responsible for laying the groundwork for policy issues, coordinating compliance and enforcement procedures and providing information to the public.

The council also was authorized to request the Justice Department to seek injunctive relief, as required to maintain the freeze. More important, the council and its small staff were charged with developing and then recommending to the President procedures to be adopted during the post-freeze period, which was expected to last indefinitely.

For the most part, this work consisted of implementing broad policy options developed by a working group headed by Herbert Stein, chairman of the Council of Economic Advisers. Thus, the present council staff machinery reflects in large measure the original blueprints of the men who came to operate it.

Phase 2—With the lifting of the wage-price freeze, the role of the council and its staff was restricted to offering broad policy guidance.

Under Executive Order 11627, which Mr. Nixon signed Oct. 15, 1971, the council is responsible for setting the limits of the program, for adopting central budgeting procedures, for classifying units in the economy, for advising the President of developments that propel the economy toward or away from set program goals, for making recommendations to the President for modifications that would increase the program's effectiveness and, in general, for coordinating the program's various interrelated parts.

But, with the inception of Phase 2, responsibility for wage and price standards, as well as consideration of individual cases, was vested in the Pay Board and the Price Commission, where it remains. The

council and its staff review these standards but—neither in practice nor in theory—does the council hear appeals on specific cases.

The council still retains final authority for ensuring compliance with the program. (On April 3, in the first such action, Rumsfeld announced an IRS probe of 11 food chains that have exceeded allowable profit levels during Phase 2.)

Resources: These basic policy decisions have led to the formation of a small and select unit, closely tied to the White House, which monitors the over-all program and, in general, acts as an umbrella agency. This is the council staff.

Concepts—These decisions also have led to a subtle and complex relationship between the staff on the one hand, and the Pay Board, the Price Commission, the IRS, and its various staffs, on the other.

"Pay and price were set up autonomously and we respect their autonomy," said James W. McLane, the council's deputy director and a former Domestic Council aide.

"We try to look at it from the standpoint of the economic-stabilization program as a whole," McLane said. "One of the President's explicit goals was not to establish a huge bureaucracy of the kind that was set up during World War II or Korea. We're trying to do without that because we feel it would have been an overkill in terms of our companion goal: to get the economy moving again."

In the opinion of Richard B. Cheney, a veteran Rumsfeld aide and the council's assistant director for operations, "it would be fair to

President Nixon meeting with Cost of Living Council members in the White House Cabinet Room

say that we have been very true to the concept as originally outlined by the President. The Cost of Living Council is not an independent entity. It is an arm of the President. There is obviously no way the President can back off from what happens to the economy. The council is responsible for keeping tabs on the program and, to date, we have adhered very closely to the original concept.

Staff—To perform its assigned task, the council employs a staff of 97, compared with 140 at the Pay Board and 425 at the Price Commission (549 if 30 to 90 day detailees from other agencies are counted).

"There are really two types of people here," said Richard J. Alfultis, deputy director for administration. "There are career civil servants, some of whom are on leave from other agencies and who plan to return, sooner or later. And there are Rumsfeld people. However, they mesh very well. It's a

very happy wedding.

The entire council staff was nonetheless deeply shaken in mid-February by the violent death of Earl D. Rhode, 28, the council's executive secretary. Police reported that Rhode's wife, Delores, shot her husband and then killed herself in their Silver Spring, Md., home.

"Rhode was much more than an executive secretary," Alfultis recalled. "He grew up with the staff and stayed on top as it grew. He acted more as a deputy director than as a secretary. Since his death, the job has disintegrated."

McLane, who joined the council staff shortly after the murder-suicide in the Rhode family, concurred with this assessment. "Earl had pulled it all together and his job, in practice, has been eliminated," he said.

McLane belongs to the fresh layer of personnel assembled to staff the council needs after essential planning functions were com-

pleted. "It's a mixed bag now," McLane said. There are some OEO (Office of Economic Opportunity) people; some Weber people and some 'Rumsfeld's Raiders.' But I think it's getting more and more of a Rumsfeld quality every day."

"Yet, there's really no friction and that's one of the greatest things about this place. No one is worried about his turf and no one's worried about somebody's doing something in his area. We've got a job to do and we're doing it."

Coverage: A vital council task is to determine what sectors of the economy are to be covered by the program. (During the 90-day freeze, only 10 per cent of the economy was exempted; currently about 22 per cent is free from control.)

On average, five exemption requests come before the Cost of Living Council each week. These may originate from individual firms or from industry-wide groups.

"The requests are staffed out here and issue papers prepared," Cheney said. "A recommendation is made by the staff and, subsequently, by the working group of (Cabinet) under secretaries who meet before each (council) session."

Staff recommendations on coverage and classification are kept confidential. Usually, these also are reviewed in advance of their presentation to the council by the Pay Board and Price Commission staffs. Drafts sometimes are changed on the basis of these negotiations.

Yet the process remains exceedingly informal, at least by federal standards. Cheney said: "We say, 'We've looked at it. This is what we think. What do you think?'"

McLane put it this way: "I guess we could call (Price Commission Chairman C. Jackson) Grayson (Jr.) in and say, 'I'm a presidential appointee of higher rank.' This is the way it should be in theory, but that's not the way it works. And I'm not sure it would be a good way to work.

"It's really a very free-flowing type of thing. There isn't any time to stand on ceremony and invoke rigid procedures and make big studies and this is the way it ought to be.

"In a sense, they (the board and the commission) are in the pit more than we are. And we're not going to make it harder for them than necessary."

Informal checking procedures in regard to coverage standards—as well as toward other aspects of the stabilization program—do not, however, automatically ensure harmony.

McLane said: "This is a very sensitive matter. We're the umbrella agency. Yet they are supposed to be independent, although we control their budgets. So there's a built-in tension. It's designed to be that way."

Compliance: The chief remaining operational task delegated to the council staff is to develop a broad compliance and enforcement strategy and, in effect, to oversee the IRS' enforcement role.

In this respect, Cheney said, the council staff performs in the capacity of an inspector general, without, however, resorting to adversary proceedings.

More than any other aspect of the program, the compliance work requires the staff to keep close checks on pay and price trends. For this task, it uses the existing and elaborate economic monitoring machinery of the Labor Department and Commerce Department, as well as maintaining its

---

COST OF LIVING COUNCIL MEMBERS

The Cost of Living Council is made up of the 10 Cabinet and White House officials holding the specific offices designated in the presidential order establishing the council (ExecOrder 11615) as amended by the order setting up the machinery for Phase 2 (ExecOrder 11627). The membership is not fixed, however, and may include "such others as the President may, from time to time, designate," in the words of Executive Order 11627.

All of the powers conferred upon the President by the 1970 Economic Stabilization Act as amended (85 Stat 743) have been delegated to the council.

The chairman of the board of governors of the Federal Reserve System, Arthur F. Burns, is an official adviser to the council.

The present members of the council are:

George P. Shultz, Secretary of the Treasury *(council chairman);*

Herbert Stein, chairman, Council of Economic Advisers *(council vice chairman);*

Donald Rumsfeld, counselor to the President *(council director);*

Earl L. Butz, Secretary of Agriculture;

Peter G. Peterson, Secretary of Commerce;

George W. Romney, Secretary of Housing and Urban Development;

James D. Hodgson, Secretary of Labor;

Casper W. Weinberger, director, Office of Management and Budget;

George A. Lincoln, director, Office of Emergency Preparedness;

Virginia H. Knauer, special assistant to the President for consumer affairs.

own economic analysis unit under assistant director Marvin H. Kosters.

Cheney, who directs the compliance-monitoring strategy, also has contracted with the Bureau of Domestic Commerce in the Commerce Department to utilize their econometric model, which was developed after the freeze went into effect.

In addition, Cheney normally confers twice a week with representatives of a consulting firm which is developing basic monitoring guidelines.

(The firm, American Management Systems Inc. of Arlington, Va., has a contract to supply four man-years of support to the council. The contract, which expires at the end of the fiscal year, calls for a $182,000 payment for the six-month period ending June 30, 1972.)

Relationships: The council's staff work sets the stage for weekly meetings of the principals, who confer in the White House Cabinet Room each Thursday at 4 p.m.

The meeting, usually chaired by Rumsfeld, normally lasts two hours and is divided in two parts: an executive session, in which only the council principals take part, and a regular session, with broader attendance.

The executive meeting disposes of sensitive business, such as pending requests for exemptions, while the regular meeting usually is devoted to a broad review of the economic outlook.

Council meetings are preceded by meetings of the Senior Review Group, composed in the main of Cabinet under secretaries. This group initially takes up staff rec-

ommendations and passes them along to the full council.

McLane said: "Generally, we'll make a recommendation prior to a council meeting and a consensus will develop. The task of the Senior Review Group is to pre-decide a lot of stuff."

The council rarely rejects a recommendation from below, although sometimes members ask Rumsfeld to provide additional data and this, in turn, may lead to modifications. Most proposals are adopted intact, however.

Rumsfeld is also one of the few Administration officials who has easy access to the President—a personal relationship that facilitates council decision-making. Other members of the Nixon staff, not directly assigned to the economic sector, rarely interfere in council staff work.

In an interview, Rumsfeld characterized his relations with Grayson and Boldt as "cordial, direct and continuous." But Rumsfeld also observed that these relations are "to a degree specific and to a degree undefined."

No authority exists for the Pay Board and the Price Commission other than the President's executive order and the delegation of authority by the council.

Yet, in responding to the March 22 Meany-led walkout of labor members from the Pay Board, Boldt denied that any Administration official ever has attempted to influence votes of public members on the board.

As Cheney observed: "Obviously you could have argued for a system that is much neater and more efficient administratively. It probably would have led to a big-

ger system, more in the mold of a traditional government agency.

"But it also would have created a much more permanent sort of bureaucracy without the participatory quality which you get when you have part-time commission people. We decided that to have participatory processes was more significant than having a neat administrative structure. It does, however, make things a bit more difficult for us."

Internally, however, the council staff functions smoothly, despite intense outside pressures. For a government bureaucracy, the council staff is relatively new, relatively small and imbued with a clear sense of mission.

As Alfultis, the council's administrative officer, put it: "This is a swinging outfit."

POLICY

Rumsfeld and his top staff aides believe that the underlying goals of the Administration's economic-stabilization program are subtle ones and therefore not easy to project to the public.

In a Feb. 29 speech to the National Rural Electric Cooperative Association in Las Vegas, Rumsfeld said:

"A freeze psychology seems to exist whereby many people feel that no price can legally go up. Not only is that not the case, but if it were it would pinch the job situation so badly as to retard the economic recovery that is in process."

In a *National Journal* interview, Rumsfeld made the same point more succinctly. "The public liked the freeze," he said. "But you cannot play to a misconception."

Game Plan: Rumsfeld contends that the program must be aimed at both economic and psychological factors. In keeping with this view, the council has adopted a multi-faceted policy that would:

cut inflation to no more than 3 per cent a year by the end of 1972;

swing the jobless rate toward the 5-per cent mark, lower if possible, during the same period;

break the national inflation psychology—a state of mind in which most people expect prices and wages will continue to spiral upwards, despite official controls;

exempt from control those economic units that have no real impact on inflation or that are by their nature inherently uncontrollable.

Beyond the Freeze—Whether these goals are attainable under present policies in the time allotted remains an open question. In any event, Rumsfeld and his deputies are convinced that they are.

As Cheney explained: "Nearly everybody we talk to prefaces their remarks with the statement, 'We support the effort to control prices and wages, but we've got this problem or that problem.'

"That's why from the standpoint of perceived equity, the freeze was certainly a lot more attractive. But you can't continue the freeze for a prolonged period without incurring very, very serious economic problems."

Deputy Director McLane concurred with this assessment and added: "Politically, at least in the short term, we would have been better off by keeping the freeze on."

McLane acknowledged that "people are confused" because "they see prices going up and they have difficulty seeing that the controls are working. Yet there's a difference between a price rise and inflation. Prices are going to go up. It's a matter of priorities: *Where* are they going to go up?"

Small Units—At the staff level, the council is currently focusing on plans to hinge the anti-inflation program almost entirely on control of major economic units—the large corporations and major unions which, according to preliminary council data, set price and wage trends in the United States.

Under this policy, small businessmen and independent wage-earners, would be exempted from all controls.

James E. Connor, acting assistant director for program development, is completing a study of market forces for Rumsfeld that Connor hopes will better identify which economic sectors should be held under tight supervision and which could be safely excluded.

"You've got an incredibly complex situation because the American economy is a most complex creature," Connor said.

"We need to know how many people we need to cover to make the program work. You can have a grandstand show and perform an economic 'body count.' But the key question is how to maintain credibility."

"It's the finest damn line you can ever walk. And one of the real ironies of the situation is that there are very few things that have to be controlled in order to get results."

In discussing the same issue, Alfultis said: "The basic idea is that the big boys will tend to keep the price in line."

On Jan. 19, acting upon a recommendation from the Price Commission, the Cost of Living Council exempted from the program retail firms with annual sales of $100,000 or less—so-called "ma-and-pa" outlets.

Connor as well as other senior council staff aides feel that the exemption could have been pegged at $200,000 or $300,000 without materially affecting inflation rates. Asked why the council failed to do so, Connor said: "I guess they just chickened out."

Exemptions: In setting the stage for the post-freeze program, Rumsfeld announced Nov. 10 that a host of products and services would be exempt from coverage during Phase 2.

They include farm goods; seafood; custom-made goods and services; exports, imports and shipping rates; damaged and used products; government property; real estate; rents on commercial, industrial and farm property, as well as rents on new or rehabilitated dwellings; securities and other financial instruments; royalties; dues to noprofit organizations; life insurance; antiques and federal salaries.

Since that time, the council has been sparing in granting exemptions from coverage. But it has also left previously exempted areas intact.

Food—A major reason why prices have continued to climb since the freeze was lifted is a surge in food costs. As measured by the Department of Labor's consumer price index, food prices have risen 2.3 per cent since Phase 2 began and have accounted for

DIRECTOR RUMSFELD: ACHIEVING PRESIDENTIAL CLOUT

Donald Rumsfeld surveyed a roomful of assistants, fixed his gaze on a young man seated across the conference table, flipped his pencil towards him and softly said: "Go."

The young man responded by quickly summarizing his activities on the Cost of Living Council staff—a body that Rumsfeld has directed since last October, when the main outlines of the post-freeze economic program became known.

Rumsfeld's style in monitoring that program is crisp, precise, cool and direct. But his ability to get things done rests largely on his high personal standing with President Nixon.

While directing council activities, Rumsfeld, 39, remains counselor to the President, a $42,500-a-year position with Cabinet rank. Rumsfeld also has retained his White House quarters, which he uses interchangeably with his suite in the New Executive Office Building, where the council staff is headquartered.

Rumsfeld rarely discusses his role as a Presidential adviser, even with his associates. As he put it in a 1971 interview with *The Christian Science Monitor:* "The best policy as a counselor to the President, unlike a Congressman, is to counsel the President and not to counsel about how he counsels the President."

For Rumsfeld, recognizing the difference comes naturally: he was elected to Congress four times before being recruited by the President in 1969 at age 36 to head the Office of Economic Opportunity.

Background: After attending New Trier High School in Winnetka, Ill., a suburb of Chicago, Rumsfeld graduated in 1954 from Princeton University, where he majored in politics and won a varsity letter as captain of the wrestling team. He then spent 41 months in the Navy as a flier and flight instructor, becoming the all-Navy wrestling champion in 1956.

After the Navy, he worked on Capitol Hill, first for former Rep. (1957-59) David S. Dennison Jr., R-Ohio, and then for Rep. Robert P. Griffin, R-Mich., now a Senator. He left to work for a Chicago investment banking house, A. G. Becker & Co. Inc., but within two years, at age 30, he was back in politics, seeking a congressional seat.

Rumsfeld campaigned for the House in what was then the Illinois 13th congressional district (since split in two) and won easily, defeating three primary opponents, and going on to win the general election by a landslide.

Upon taking his House seat in 1963, Rumsfeld came to be regarded as a future party leader by many of his senior colleagues. But he feuded with Rep. Leslie C. Arends, R-Ill., the House GOP whip, over prospective reforms in House Republican procedures, which Rumsfeld and his allies were seeking.

As an activist "Young Turk," Rumsfeld was denied important committee assignments. Moreover, with Arends aligned against him, he lost the chairmanship of the Republican Research Committee to Rep. Robert Taft Jr., R-Ohio, now a Senator.

A longtime Rumsfeld acquaintance said privately: "You just don't discuss these things with Don. But he was bored silly in the House and he knew that he had nowhere to go."

Administration: Rumsfeld accepted Mr. Nixon's offer to join the Administration in May 1969 as assistant to the President and director of OEO.

Rumsfeld had voted against OEO when it was proposed by President Johnson in 1964. Nonetheless, he became an advocate of the anti-poverty agency. Although he trimmed its functional roles, he also protected it against attacks from the Republican right. Thus, he refinanced the controversial California Rural Legal Assistance program despite strong opposition from Gov. Ronald Reagan, R.

In December 1970, Rumsfeld left OEO to work full time at the White House. As a member of the Domestic Council, he has served on Cabinet-level committees on health and education policy and, more recently, on civil rights. He also has reported to the President on the international flow of illicit narcotics.

Despite his time-consuming duties as director of the Cost of Living Council, Rumsfeld maintains his wide-ranging role as a Presidential adviser. To stay on top of events, he arrives at the White House each weekday morning at 7 and attends both the 7:15 and 8:15 staff meetings before crossing Pennsylvania Avenue to preside over the council staff meeting.

Rumsfeld does not like press conferences; he has held only five since becoming council director. Consequently, Herbert Stein, chairman of the Council of Economic Advisers, and vice chairman of the Cost of Living Council, has emerged as the chief spokesman for the program, although Rumsfeld usually reviews Stein's prepared remarks beforehand.

Assessment: A former associate said: "There are two very different views of Don Rumsfeld in this town. One is that he's a hard-working guy who tries to get things done—that he's bright, able and honest. The other view is that he's very political and will do anything to advance himself."

Yet nearly everyone who comes into contact with Rumsfeld agrees that the strongest side of his character is his inherent private nature. As another former associate put it: "He's really not the kind of person that people get very close to."

58.3 per cent of the over-all increase in that period.

Rumsfeld initially exempted all raw agricultural products on the theory that they are subject to frequent changes in price, up and down, because of the large numbers of sellers in the market, the abrupt shifts in supply and continuing hazards of perishability.

Some Democratic leaders in Congress say they believe that the exemption was also politically motivated, although, so far, they have not made this charge publicly. (The President is known to be wooing the farm vote, which could hold the balance of power in the 1972 national elections.)

After consulting with the council, Price Commission Chairman Grayson announced March 23 that the commission would hold fact-finding hearings on food costs "because of the level of concern across the nation."

Other Exclusions — Since Phase 2 began, the council has approved general exemptions for the entire Commonwealth of Puerto Rico; U.S. workers employed overseas and in U.S. territories; several types of commercial insurance, including marine insurance; apartments renting for $500 a month or more, owner-occupied dwellings with four or fewer units and single-family dwellings rented on a monthly basis by a small landlord; fees charged in the trading of securities; residential land leases; tuition fees and other charges by private nonprofit schools, and dehydrated fruit.

In addition, on Jan. 8, the council approved a 23.9-per cent increase in third-class postal rates.

On the other hand, the council has denied about 30 exemption requests since the freeze was lifted.

Those who have been turned down include the National Association of Printing Ink Manufacturers, which unsuccessfully contended that printing inks are customized products; the American Orthotics and Prosthetics Association, which made the same argument for devices that correct spine and limb disabilities; The National Association for the Specialty Food Trade Inc., which cited low profit margins as its rationale for exception; the National Zinc Co. Inc., which cited cost burden on its zinc smelter operations; the New England Wholesale Meat Dealers Association Inc., which said processed meat should be excluded because of price fluctuations, and the Wine Institute, which asked for an industry exemption. (The council noted that any grape price increase was already an allowable pass-through cost.)

In addition, the council has denied exemptions for refined sugar, private educational institutions that are run for profit, newspapers and magazines, specialized business publications, yearbooks, legal advertisement rates, U.S.-flag oil tankers, goods shipped to Puerto Rico, floral arrangements and salaries of persons employed by the District of Columbia government.

Hearings: The Cost of Living Council has not held any hearings in reaching each of these determinations, a policy decision that has subjected its procedures to sharp judicial criticism.

In a March 8 ruling, Judge Gerhard H. Gesell of the U.S. District Court for the District of Columbia noted that such formal hearings are required "to the maximum extent possible" under the Economic Stabilization Act Amendments signed into law by the President last Dec. 22 (85 Stat 743; Section 207(c)).

Gesell asserted that the council's failure to adopt clear procedures and its record of making "imprecise rulings" make judicial review of its actions, as also provided by law, "difficult if not impossible" to achieve. Gesell said the council's contention that such hearings would be administratively infeasible was an "entirely inadequate" and indefensible position.

Although Gesell found "substantial confusion and informality" in the record, he upheld the council in full in denying a request for a preliminary injunction against a third-class postal increase filed by the Mass Retailing Institute and the Mail Advertising Service Association International.

In an interview, Rumsfeld said the council has no plans to hold hearings despite Gesell's findings. "For an agency such as the Cost of Living Council to hold hearings would be a very unusual thing," Rumsfeld said.

Moreover the President is known to feel that the council should not become under any circumstances an operational agency. In the process of holding hearings, this White House policy could be thwarted.

Congress: But in the legislative arena, Rumsfeld is looking forward to public hearings on the entire economic-stabilization program, which are planned by the Joint Economic Committee. The hearings were scheduled to begin April 14 and run for six days.

Rumsfeld has informed his senior staff that he views these hearings as a major opportunity to educate the public on the reason why some prices andd wages will continue to advance under a system of flexible controls.

Proxmire—In an interview, Sen. William Proxmire, D-Wis., chairman of the Joint Economic Committee, criticized the policies of the Cost of Living Council and said they would be subjected to close scrutiny during the projected hearings, which he will chair.

The Senator was especially critical of what he termed the council's "dim and indefinite relationship" with the Pay Board and the Price Commission.

He added: "As I see it, the Cost of Living Council is an impotent agency. It's really a public relations outfit. Rumsfeld is articulate and handsome and comes over well on television. But they have a real credibility problem."

Proxmire maintained that the stabilization effort should be revamped so that it concentrates on major economic units.

(When informed of Proxmire's view, Albert E. Abrahams, assistant director for congressional and public affairs, said he welcomed the Senator's suggestion and expressed pleasure at the fact that Proxmire's thinking in this respect so closely approximated the policy moves now being generated with the Cost of Living Council's staff.)

Patman—On March 12, Rep. Wright Patman, D-Tex., chairman of the House Banking and Currency Committee and vice chairman of the Joint Economic Committee, released a text of a letter to the President in which he assailed the stabilization policy and contended that the program is not being administered as Congress intended.

"Instead of strong enforcement," Patman said, "the stabiliza-

tion authorities seem to be resorting to Madison Avenue techniques." (Abrahams has contracted with the Advertising Council Inc. to prepare an anti-inflation media campaign, including television commercials. But Patman, who did not know of this arrangement, was making a more general charge.)

Unless prompt steps are taken to comply with congressional intent, Patman said his House committee "will be compelled to conduct oversight hearings."

The Cost of Living Council has no plans to mollify Patman, who is regarded within White House circles as an inconsolable critic. For his part, Patman has yet to announce whether the House committee will also hold hearings on the program.

Freedom of Action—Despite such attacks, the Cost of Living Council has remained relatively immune from broad congressional criticism—in part because the council is operating under legislation conceived and advanced by Democratic majorities in the House and Senate.

Requests from Capitol Hill for special help on behalf of industry or union constituents have also been relatively sparse and, for the most part, routine.

Nonetheless, Abrahams predicted that "we are going to have a continuing debate with Congress. We anticipate future criticism of the program.

"After all," he said, "it's 1972. And we're still in a bulge period so far as the economy is concerned, which gives the critics a target. But I think we can get there."

OUTLOOK

From the President on down, Administration policymakers remain convinced that the economic-stabilization program will take hold.

Yet they are bedeviled by what they regard as an unrealistic set of assumptions about the economy—assumptions that have languished in the minds of many Americans as a kind of post-freeze hangover.

Moreover, Administration planners recognize that in this year's intensely political setting, the Cost of Living Council is certain to come under pressure to achieve results quickly.

The chief apprehension in policy-making councils is that political pressure may yet force the White House to accelerate the anti-inflation drive in a way that could, as an unwanted side effect, endanger the current economic expansion.

Goals: Despite some discouraging economic indicators in February and March, there is no propensity within the Administration to alter the program's basic focus. The goal remains fixed: to break the back of inflationary psychol-ogy without creating a large government agency to enforce controls and without chilling economic expansion.

Abrahams said that there are no plans to unveil a "Phase 3" policy before the November national elections. "All the attention is on making Phase 2 work," he said.

In formulating council procedures, Abrahams said:

"We have never reached the point where we've decided that (procedures) won't be changed.

"But neither are we at the point where we've determined that they are failing.

"There is no thought of making a recommendation to the President to radically change the present organizational policy."

Nevertheless, the rising drum-fire of criticism from the ranks of organized labor—in which all of the Democratic Presidential aspirants have now joined—tends to put the council on the defensive.

Thus, Cheney remarked: "These are enormously important issues. Sure, there are some things that you might want to change in a minor way: the manner in which they (the Price Commission) han-dled this firm or that firm, or the way the Pay Board handled this contract or that contract. But that's not the ball game.

Future: Among the council's top staffers there is little concern over personal careers.

Kosters, the chief economic prognosticator, said: "We don't concern ourselves at all with how long our jobs will last. We regard that as irrelevant. We're willing to live with the question because we recognize that we do not have the basis on which to decide (how long the council will exist)."

"Moreover, I don't think there will ever be a day of decision. Instead, there will be a gradual accumulation of evidence on that score."

Whether or not this proves correct, it is already clear that the President has staked much of his political future on the proposition that the Phase 2 stabilization team can come up with a successful economic formula.

"There's a strong feeling in the White House that this just has got to go," Abrahams said. "The President has cast his lines. Now he wants results."

TRANSPORTATION AND COMMUNICATION

When the Constitution was being drafted by the "founding fathers" it was agreed that interstate controls over transportation and communications were to be a prerogative of the Federal government. As the two industries have developed it has become increasingly difficult for the independent regulatory commissions to arrive at the proper blend between the requirements of public service and those of private business.

In 1972 the question of transportation regulation has come down to a continuing controversy over the kind of railroad system that the nation shall have in the future. In the following article the positions of the industry, the regulators and the public are explored in depth as Congress wrestles with the question of whether to resolve the problems by tax benefits and subsidies, or nationalization.

In the field of communications recent attention has been focused largely upon the role of fairness in the dissemination of information by the radio and television media.

Charges and countercharges from officials of the Nixon Administration, interested congressmen, members of the Federal Communications Commission, and media representatives have beclouded the issue, and hanging over the entire controversy is the problem of Court interpretation of the First Amendment. The article included here considers all of the pressures that have developed as Congress attempts to formulate legislation to resolve the problem.

Congress plods through complex arguments over transport regulation *Vera Hirschberg*

Congress is reacting to conflicting advice about which way it must move to avoid nationalization of U.S. railroads by not moving much at all.

The Nixon Administration argues that relaxation of regulation is essential to keep the nation's common carriers prosperous and privately owned. The transportation industry argues it needs more, not less, regulation.

But industry and the Administration agree that the alternative to some action by Congress is federal railroads.

"Time is rapidly running out and the situation is critical," said John P. Fishwick, president and chief executive officer of the Norfolk & Western Railway Co. "Congres is not taking this problem seriously enough."

Lack of public interest, complexity of the issues and uncertainty about the impact of relaxed regulation on the transportation industry make it unlikely that any measure will be enacted in its entirety this year.

The industry proposal is the Surface Transportation Act of 1971, an omnibus program sponsored by the rail, truck and barge common carriers who are in unprecedented agreement on the program, which calls for subsidies, tax reforms and expanded regulation.

The industry approach is embodied in five House bills—HRs 11207, 11310, 11347, 11674, and 11694—and in one Senate bill, S 2362.

The Administration approach is being promoted by the Transportation Department. While it, too, includes financial aid and tax reform, it would relax many of the Interstate Commerce Commission's regulatory restraints on all three modes in an effort to spur competition among them and produce better service for shippers.

The program is incorporated into HR 11826 and S 2842, regulatory reform measures; and HR 11824 and S 2841, financial-aid bills.

The carrier plan first was introduced in the Senate in late July. The Administration plan did not surface until mid-November.

Several signs point to a slim chance for legislation this year.

A White House staff member said that White House lobbying for the Administration proposals has been minimal.

He said "it is very significant" that regulatory-reform legislation went to Congress as a Transportation Department bill rather than as "a Nixon bill," adding: "There isn't much action on the DOT bill from here because I don't think it's going to get anywhere. If the President says otherwise, I'll act otherwise. But he hasn't."

Transportation Under Secretary James M. Beggs said that although the Administration is "flexible" on the three most controversial regulatory provisions of its plan, his department and the carriers "are very far apart" on them. He said he doubts that agreement in principle can be reached.

A former high Transportation Department official who had a hand in drafting the regulatory legislation said he thinks the likelihood of anything's being approved in this election year "is very slender indeed." The congressional hearings, which began last November, "are not going anywhere this year" but will enable Congress to get a needed perspective on the problems involved, he said.

A lawyer representing a farmers' national trade association, which generally supports the Administration's proposals, said, "I'm just not very optimistic. I don't think we are going to get any kind of a bill; not in this session, anyway."

Alan S. Boyd, former Transportation Secretary (1967-69), said carrier unity, which has been a strong selling point for the industry plan, is endangered by "a gradual movement" within the railroad industry toward the Administration plan, which some railroads "believe has more good in it than bad."

PROBLEMS

Advocates of both proposals argue heatedly over their relative merits, but they agree that inaction increases the danger of nationalized railroads. Despite that, Congress is moving slowly and there has been little public discussion of the dilemma.

Stakes: "Unless there are some major changes in public policy, in time the railroad industry will be brought to nationalization through the back door," said Boyd.

Railroads—Former Sen. (1950-68) George A. Smathers, D-Fla., now one of the railroad industry's chief lobbyists, said: "If no legislation passes this year or next year then the situation could go one of two ways—either the government will have to nationalize the railroad industry, probably the worst and most expensive solution, or we'll have a great number of railroads in bankruptcy.

"The ICC says we already have 18 railroads that are marginal. Five are in bankruptcy. If more go into bankruptcy, railroads serving vast areas will have to stop or curtail service. The cost of transportation will go up and will help feed inflation.

"That alternative, which is just one step short of nationalization, is unrealistic and I can't believe Congress will allow it to happen."

Smathers is general counsel of ASTRO (America's Sound Transportation Review Organization), an industry-supported group that is publicizing the railroads' financial plight and the industry's solutions to its problems.

Administration—Beggs said he sees the stakes as "a slow deterioration" of railroads, "which neither I nor Secretary (John A.) Volpe want."

"We've got a lot of railroads that are doing rather poorly," he said. "It's a question of time. If we don't change the system there will be further deterioration until these roads go entirely bankrupt. Then there will be greater pressure to nationalize.

"And if we nationalize one railroad we would have to nationalize the whole system."

Beggs said nationalization cannot be dismissed as an alternative "if the situation gets that bad. And over the next decade one could expect that the situation could be that bad."

Truckers—Many transportation industry officials argue that once the railroads are nationalized their industries would not be far behind. Nationalization of truck and barge lines would be inevitable, they say, because the industries would be hard-pressed to compete with a government-subsidized system.

William A. Bresnahan, president of the American Trucking Associations Inc., the trade group of the regulated trucking industry, said he believes the nation already has witnessed "an ominous erosion of private enterprise in transportation," citing the takeover by many municipalities of their transit services and creation in 1970 of the National Railroad Passenger Corp. (Amtrak), a semipublic corporation that operates intercity trains.

"The possibility that freight transportation service—or at least substantial parts of it—might be nationalized no longer can be viewed by anyone as a remote or idle threat," Bresnahan says in many of his recent speeches.

Bresnahan told a group of leading shippers who make up the Transportation Association of America's User Panel on Sept. 21, 1971:

"In the trucking industry, we view this possibility not only as a threat to our own best interest, not only as a threat to the best interest of the total transportation system, but also as a threat to the national interest and the basic capitalistic system which sustains it."

Barge Industry—John A. Creedy, president of the Water Transport Association, which represents regulated barge companies, goes even further.

"The current talk is not of nationalization of the railroads," he told the House Interstate and Foreign Commerce Subcommittee on Transportation and Aeronautics March 28. "But it is clearly recognized that nationalizing the railroads would only be a preliminary to nationalizing the competitors of the railroads.

"And if all transportation is nationalized, why not rely on that solution when problems arise in utilities, in coal or in steel? . . .

"A fundamental start will have been made on large-scale nationalization of the entire economy," said Creedy.

Slow Pace: Although Congress has heard the nationalization warning often during the course of hearings on both proposals, it has shown little inclination to move quickly.

In opening hearings on the bills March 27, House Transportation and Aeronautics Subcommittee Chairman John Jarman, D-Okla., said that it would take time to deal with the proposals.

Jarman told a group of Administration witnesses, including Transportation Secretary Volpe, Agriculture Secretary Earl L. Butz, and Harold C. Fasser, assistant Commerce secretary (economic affairs), that enactment of their total legislative package "can't be achieved" before the 92nd Congress adjourns.

Nor is the Senate Commerce Subcommittee on Surface Trans-

320 portation, headed by Sen. Vance Hartke, D-Ind., about to move quickly on either proposal.

The subcommittee began hearings on the industry bill last November and they are still going on.

Although Hartke's subcommittee recently reported three non-controversial provisions to the full Commerce Committee with recommendations for approval, there has been no action.

"Unfortunately, it is difficult to get Congress to act unless there is a real crisis," said the N&W's Fishwick. "The fact that Penn Central appears to be moving along without a crisis now takes the heat off Congress in this regard."

Coverage: By and large, the national news media have ignored the hearings. *Traffic World*, a transportation industry trade weekly, and *The Journal of Commerce* (New York), a daily business newspaper, have given the hearings regular coverage. But little has been written for *The New York Times, The Washington Post,* and *The Wall Street Journal.*

Robert C. Fellmuth, a Ralph Nader aide who directed a Nader-sponsored critical study of the Interstate Commerce Commission in 1970, said of the lack of coverage: "I'm amazed that (they) haven't picked this thing up. It seems when you say ICC their eyelids close."

In Fellmuth's view, the media should be devoting more attention both to the Administration plan—which he generally supports—and to the carrier bill, which he calls the "worst bill ever written."

Both bills, he said, would affect the consumer and the price he pays for the hidden costs of transportation.

PROPOSALS

Although all carriers would be affected by both the industry and the Administration proposal, railroads are the big beneficiaries.

In recent years, railroad profits have lagged far behind those of the other modes and their financial situation is generally more precarious than that of the barge lines and trucking firms.

In 1970, for example, the rate of return (the ratio of net operating income to investment) for Class I railroads was 1.75 percent; it was 13.9 percent for regulated truckers and 11.5 percent for regulated water carriers.

In some respects, the proposals are similar. Both offer the railroads financial help, both would make it easier for railroads to abandon money-losing lines and both would give the railroads a break on property taxes in some states.

Industry Plan: The Surface Transportation Act was introduced by Hartke on July 28, 1971, and by Rep. Brock Adams, D-Wash., and nine co-sponsors, on Oct. 13.

Money—The industry bill would create a new Revenue Financing Division of the Treasury Department with authority to make or guarantee up to $5 billion in loans to help carriers buy equipment and otherwise improve services. Division operations would be patterned after the New Deal-era Reconstruction Finance Corp.

The division would not loan more than $750 million—or 15 percent of its total funds—to any one carrier. The loans would be repayable within 15 years, although on long-term projects, payments could be stretched beyond 15 years to the date of completion.

Abandonment—Railroads could drop lines that failed to make enough money to recover variable costs within seven and a half months after they had applied for permission to the ICC.

Property Taxes—Under the industry bill, no state could tax the property of a carrier at a higher rate than that paid by other businesses. The railroads would be the major beneficiaries of this provision.

Regulation—The bill would expand regulation in two ways. It would require water carriers to file rates for dry-bulk commodities with the ICC. Such rates now are exempt from any regulations, including the need to make them public.

It also would extend regulation to the for-hire trucking of livestock and some processed agricultural products, neither of which now is regulated.

Rate Making—The bill would require the ICC to develop criteria for determining the revenue needs of carriers by taking into account operating and capital costs and future replacement costs of equipment and facilities. The ICC also would be required to develop criteria for making interim rate adjustments.

Other—The bill would require states to spend at least 5 percent of their share of the Highway Trust Fund to improve railroad grade crossings and would permit the ICC to submit its budget directly to Congress, bypassing the

Office of Management and Budget. The Senate bill would extend to truck and barge companies the five-year amortization of equipment rules now enjoyed only by the railroads.

Hartke—In an interview, Hartke said he introduced the bill to provide a forum for debate.

"I am not committed or opposed to subsidies or to any change in the regulatory system," he said. "The mere fact that the Department of Transportation has come forward with deregulation is no reason for me to oppose it."

Administration Plan: The Regulatory Modernization Act was introduced on Nov. 11, 1971, by Sens. Warren G. Magnuson, D-Wash., chairman of the Senate Commerce Committee, and Norris Cotton, R-N.H. It was introduced a week later by Reps. Harley O. Staggers, D-W.Va., chairman of the House Interstate and Foreign Commerce Committee, and William L. Springer, R-Ill.

Money—The Administration bill would encourage railroads to buy more rolling stock by creating a Federal Railroad Equipment Obligation Insurance Fund which could contain up to $3 billion.

Unlike the industry bill, the Administration version would insure loans only to railroads, not to all carriers.

The legislation also calls for up to $35 million for research on a nationwide computerized car-control system.

Abandonment—The Administration proposal on abandoning rail lines assumes an end to service on 21,000 lightly traveled miles of track at an annual industry saving of $60 million. There are 205,000 miles of track in the U.S. railroad network.

The measure provides the ICC with standards for judging abandonment cases based on variable costs and would permit abandonment of any line that failed to generate one million gross ton-miles of traffic a year.

Property Taxes—As in the industry bill, the Administration would prohibit discriminatory taxation of railroads.

Regulation—The bill would relax ICC controls over entry into the regulated motor and water carriage by freeing carriers from certain routing and equipment restrictions and limitations on the types of commodities they can carry.

The bill also would eliminate the ICC's right to judge whether a prospective new entrant would have an adverse effect on competing carriers.

Rate Making—The Administration would create a so-called "zone of reasonableness" within which carriers could adjust freight rates up or down without ICC permission.

The zone would vary from a floor at variable cost to a ceiling of 150 percent above fully allocated costs in areas where there is no intermodal competition.

The system would be phased in gradually within a two-year period, with freedom to adjust rates 20 percent during the first year and 20 percent more the second year.

The Administration estimates that railroads would save $480 million a year if below-cost rates are eliminated and shippers would save $2 billion under the zone-of-reasonableness system. Shippers would save, the Administration says, because carriers no longer

would have to subsidize below-cost rates by charging higher-than-required fares on other shipments.

The bill also would limit the function of rate bureaus by limiting their antitrust immunity to the setting of joint rates—rates for cargo that moves on two or more different lines during the same trip. It also would prohibit the bureaus from protesting a rate filed by one of their members.

Rate bureaus are industry associations which set rates that must be charged by all carriers in a region, subject to ICC approval.

The bill also would shift the responsibility for setting per diem rates from the ICC to the Transportation Department. Per diem rates are those a railroad pays for the use of another railroad's freight cars.

Under the Administration bill, the ICC also would have exclusive jurisdiction over intrastate railroad rates if a state regulatory body failed to act on new interstate rates within four months after they were approved.

Other—The bill also would provide that no carrier could be forced to set a joint rate or division of rates below variable costs; would transfer from the ICC to Transportation the authority to establish certain cost-accounting procedures; and would restrict the right of the federal government to obtain free or reduced-rate shipping service.

AGREEMENT AND CONTENTION

While there are some areas of general agreement in both proposals, there are more areas of contention.

322

Agreement Areas: Stephen Ailes, president of the Association of American Railroads, told Jarman's subcommittee on March 28 that there are five general areas where the industry and the Administration agree in principle.

"Certainly, there seems to be almost universal agreement that some program of loans and guarantees is required for transportation," he said.

"Most people agree that discriminatory taxes exist, and that they ought not to exist because they constitute an intolerable burden on interstate commerce.

"Everyone agrees that greater efforts must be expended to improve safety at highway grade crossings.

"Most would agree that there is much redundant rail trackage which can never be economically justified and ought to be abandoned.

"And there is even general agreement that rate provisions ought to be adjusted so as to facilitate more adequate earnings."

Beyond that, however, the two advocates dispute virtually every word in each other's proposals.

Financial Assistance: Although both agree on the need for federal aid, they cannot agree on the form it should take.

Administration—Beggs said that in discussions with the carriers the financial-aid provision "is one of the most controversial points."

"They favor an RFC-type approach," he said, "but the bankers don't like it because they view it as competition. And the RFC concept is subject to some abuse if it were to provide direct loans to industry. Other industries would

soon be looking for similar privileges."

Beggs said that the RFC concept also might put government "pretty deeply into the operations of the railroads."

Claude G. Embrey, special assistant to the ICC's Bureau of Accounts, who served in the old RFC from 1941 until his retirement as its general counsel in 1957, supported the Beggs view.

Embrey said that while the RFC approach "would be a tremendous lift for the railroads, the bankers did feel that it was competition, although their view was completely unfounded. The RFC made loans only where they were denied in other quarters."

Embrey, too, felt government would be deeply involved in operations under the RFC approach. "Anytime you have collateral to watch, you almost always have to run the business," he said.

Carriers—Smathers said the Administration's opposition to the railroad financing plan did not make sense to him.

"If the bill were drawn tightly so that the Revenue Financing Division's loan provisions were limited to surface transportation carriers in trouble where there was a reasonable expectation that they would pay the money back, the concept is sound and ought to be adopted," he said.

Based on the old RFC experience, Smathers said, there were a few defaults on railroad loans.

But the RFC's railroad division loaned almost $1.1 billion to the railroads during its lifetime," he said. "When it folded (1957), after paying interest on the money and administrative expenses, it earned

a $100-million profit."

Smathers said he believes that rather than putting government into the railroad business, an RFD "is one way to keep it out."

"The RFD could lay down certain criteria to the railroads to get them to improve their services and management policies before granting the loans," he said. "It would relieve Congress of that responsibility.

"Members generally don't have time to go over railroad balance and loss sheets."

Easing Regulation: The bitterest arguments are reserved for the proposals that would relax transportation regulation.

Carriers—Industry leaders warn that the Administration plan would promote the very kinds of predatory competition and secret-rate discrimination that brought about regulation in the first place.

"The public would be the real losers in the case of deregulation," said Smathers, "because the really efficient, large carriers would get the cream of the business, the less efficient would get what's left and the marginal carriers would get the scraps.

"There would be chaos, with no one to service the small towns."

Asked how the carriers know this would happen, Smathers said: "We don't know. It has not been empirically proven. But our belief is that is what will happen. When everybody seeks the most profitable business, the public loses."

Bresnahan predicted to shippers last September that the end result of the deregulatory proposals would be "a great wave of new truck operation to compete not only with the more than 15,000 trucking companies already in existence, but also to harass the other modes of transportation."

With the new carriers going after only the most desirable traffic, Bresnahan said he foresees small towns and less-accessible areas being left without any transportation service.

Weakening of the rate bureaus' antitrust immunity and institution of the zone of reasonableness would be "equally destructive," he said, because it would lead to "predatory competition" within and between the modes.

Administration—Those advocating partial deregulation as envisioned by the Administration argue that the transportation situation today is vastly different from the time when regulation was imposed.

They say that railroads are no longer monopolistic and that truckers have established their industry as economically viable.

More rate flexibility and greater competition in the marketplace, they argue, would result in more efficiency, lower freight rates and better service.

But in many cases, deregulation advocates have presented no more proof of their claims than have the carriers.

For example, when asked how the Administration knew that the tests of the market would save shippers $2 billion a year under the Administration's plan, Beggs said: "We don't know. But we are not risking very much to allow this to happen."

Beggs said there is a small precedent for deregulation in Canada and "it appears to work well" in Australia.

"We are really not risking very much because if it doesn't work we can very quickly modify the rules again. We are proposing a very modest step. And if it were to work, we would propose a more radical change to total deregulation."

Philosophy: Charles D. Baker, one of the chief architects of the Administration plan, resigned last year as assistant Transportation secretary for policy and international affairs.

When Baker left office, Smathers said, he called Baker aside and "I told him that he could leave with a clear conscience and that philosophically and theoretically he had written a very fine paper. But it is just not practical. The only value I can see for it is that it gives impetus to the idea that something ought to be done."

Baker, who is now president of Harbridge House, a Boston-based management consultant firm, said: "George Smathers has forgotten more about the political arena than I'll ever know. But his argument has frequently been used by a variety of groups who both oppose and support our proposal."

Baker said that even though the track record on deregulation has not been good, "the issue deserves some thoughtful deliberation. The question is whether this kind of deliberation has a better chance than before. The answer is yes." Asked why, Baker said that 20 percent of railroad mileage in the nation is in receivership, other railroads are failing, and shippers are concerned over regulation, leading "to absolutely bellowing outrage" over poor service.

"The Interstate Commerce Act has many purposes but in the final crunch, transportation must be in behalf of the people who use it— the shippers," Baker said.

Baker claims, as do many Transportation Department officials, that the Administration bill is not a deregulation bill.

"It is a revised regulation bill," he said, "in which the ground rules of control are revised and in some instances relaxed. To suggest that the Administration bill is supportive of open entry is not supportive of the facts."

Adams, House sponsor of the industry bill, argues that the Administration bill is indeed "a deregulation bill." It is also "a jury-rigged bill," Adams said in an interview. "It is a highly theoretical bill that has picked up the deregulation concept from the Kennedy bill and it just won't work."

Adams said that transportation is closer to "a monopolistic public utility than it is to Adam Smith economics. The government must be involved in regulation and the antitrust laws must be used as an enforcer."

System's Defenders: In generally defending the present regulatory system, the carriers make it clear that they also defend the present regulatory posture of the ICC. They regard that oldest and largest of the regulatory agencies as their mutual protector both within each mode and in intermodal competition.

ICC—The ICC position in the legislative battle is that there is no need for change in the basic regulatory structure. The agency argues that it already has the power to initiate the changes the Administration would like to see

324

under its enabling legislation, the Interstate Commerce Act (54 Stat 899).

The ICC regulates 39 percent of truck traffic, all rail traffic and 10 percent of inland waterways traffic.

Though Adams supports the commission's claim that it does have the necessary powers he said "they haven't done anything in those areas because nobody has made them."

ICC Chairman George M. Stafford told the Jarman subcommittee March 28 that the "myth . . . to be dispelled is that provisions of the Interstate Commerce Act significantly impede the managerial discretion of regulated carriers."

Under the act and the ICC administration of it, Stafford said, "the initiative rests with the carriers . . . whether it be a quest for new or extended operating authority, a change in rates, or a merger or other financial restructuring, the carriers make the underlying decisions and determine the day-to-day and long-term course of their operations . . . The commission does not manage or control carriers; it regulates them."

In recent months, Stafford and other ICC commissioners have voiced their fears and doubts about the Administration proposal with increasing frequency in public speeches.

Stafford says often that the plan would create "rigidity and inflexibility."

Laurence K. Walrath, a senior commission member, has spoken of a return to the "law of the jungle" if the Administration proposal were adopted.

Carriers—The carriers back up

Stafford in his claim that the ICC already has the power to make changes proposed by the Administration.

Edward V. Kiley, the trucking associations' vice president for research and technical services, said in an interview that the present rate structure already is "cost based."

"Generally speaking, the floor is variable costs and the ceiling is fully allocated costs," he said. "In between this, we are not bound by any statutory restrictions as to the reasonableness of a rate."

System Criticism: Beggs said he disagrees with both Stafford and Kiley.

"If George (Stafford) thinks he can do these things why didn't he do them?" Beggs asked. "George is a good man. They're all good men at the ICC and have something between the ears—brains I mean.

"If there is a zone of reasonableness already, as they claim, how come it hasn't worked? If they have that authority already and are able to do it why haven't they done it? Clearly, the shippers are not getting good service.

"I think the Interstate Commerce Act is not sufficient to do the job. They are defending an outmoded system."

Beggs said the reason the carriers are not backing the Administration bill is twofold: lack of analysis and the fact that they have become too comfortable under the present system.

"The carriers are not very bright. I don't think they have thought this thing through. They think they have preferential rates now and are doing quite well. If they think they are being taken

care of now and can hold their own under any system, they are deluding themselves."

The carriers, Beggs said, have become used to a "well-worn system" of regulation and "are willing to take any inconvenience with it. Look at the state of the industry. Their problems have been going on for 20 years. The situation is chronic. It is clearly chronic."

Beggs said that relaxing regulatory restraints, particularly those in the rate-making area, "is the best thing that the government can do for the carriers.

"It will start them thinking about the cost of doing business as opposed to maximizing the tonnage they move. In the past and now they haven't paid enough attention to moving the stuff. I think it will force a rethinking of how they do business."

"Our proposal is based on the cost of doing business and as those costs change, clearly the zone of reasonableness changes. There is a great deal of flexibility there for carriers to move without ICC interference."

Beggs tackles the Walrath "law-of-the-jungle" argument this way:

"Like the Democrats, who are always raising the specter of the depression of the 1930s, the carriers and the ICC have a way of raising the specter of the 1890s.

"Walrath's statement assumes that the railroads, by virtue of the zone of reasonableness would lower a lot of rates below costs. The bill would prohibit them from doing this. I think that over a period of time the railroads are going to raise rates and offer better service."

Beggs noted that 80 years ago,

"the railroads drove the water carriers out of business. But today they don't have enough muscle to do this. And even if they did, the bill would not permit them do this because it doesn't permit predatory pricing. It forbids them to go below costs."

Beggs conceded that if the Administration's bill is enacted, some truckers and water carriers "would have life made so difficult that they would have to go out of business."

But as a general rule, he said, the bill would not make much difference in the relationships between the modes.

WHITE HOUSE

Although President Nixon initiated the push for regulatory reform and his top economic advisers favor it, the White House has not lobbied hard for the program.

Conciliation: Beginning in August, Peter M. Flanigan, assistant to the President for regulatory matters, held a series of meetings with shippers, carriers and Transportation Department officials to identify areas of controversy and measure potential support.

An official of one of the nation's major farm groups who attended a meeting of shippers in Flanigan's office in October, recalled that he asked Flanigan what the Administration's priorities were. Said the official: "He said their position was that the Administration wasn't going to be a Don Quixote—that they would only introduce the legislation if they thought it would be a political plus; and that they would not push it if they thought it wasn't."

Seeking Support: The official, who did not want to be identified by name, said that he felt the Administration came forth with the bill "after leaking its provisions to the press for months before, only when they got the reading from shippers that they were going to get our support."

Attending that same meeting were James V. Springrose, vice president of Cargill Inc., a big midwestern grain shipper; William K. Smith, vice president, General Mills Inc., and representatives of farm groups, paper manufacturers and the pharmaceutical industry.

Flanigan, said the farm group official, was most concerned at the meeting "with what the hell the carriers were going to say, rather than with the shippers' reactions."

COMET—To support and work for the Administration legislation, a group of large shippers formed the Committee On Modern Efficient Transportation (COMET) to lobby for the measure.

Formed in February, the group is supported by large shippers such as Cargill, Sears Roebuck and Co., General Mills and the Drug and Toilet Preparations Traffic Conference.

Jack Pearce, former deputy general counsel of the White House Office of Consumer Affairs (1970-71), is a registered lobbyist for COMET. Pearce worked with Flanigan as a member of the Transportation Subcommittee of the Cabinet Committee on Economic Policy, which drafted the regulatory reform legislation.

Caution—Pearce confirmed that Administration officials felt they needed shipper support before they could send their proposals to Congress.

"Flanigan always wanted the bill, but it is correct to say that he didn't want to commit the Administration publicly until he was assured of full shipper support," Pearce said.

Pearce said he believes Flanigan and Volpe still are committed to the bill, "feel strongly that it is needed and want to push it through."

He said the reason the measure went to Congress as a Transportation Department rather thatn a White House bill was that "some congressional aides around the President weren't sure that he should become involved in something that controversial at this time."

Kennedy Effort: While working in the Justice Department's Antitrust Division in 1962, Pearce also was involved in drafting a Kennedy Administration proposal for deregulation.

The plan never was enacted by Congress because of industry opposition.

Pearce said that as he watched the Kennedy proposal through hearings he was convinced that the Administration had not done its homework on the bill's economic impact.

By contrast, he said, the present deregulatory plan has a better chance of passage because "it does not try to pressure off the carrier modes against each other and it has the support of shippers and consumers."

Pearce said that the only way to get substantive changes in transportation legislation "is to look at the situation from the user point of view.

"I think this Administration has made an effort to do so to a considerable degree."

President: Mr. Nixon first hinted at his Administration's hope for "more reliance on the market mechanism" as "a step forward" for transportation in his February 1970 Economic Report of the President to Congress.

In his 1971 report, he spoke out more strongly on the theme, saying, "We must constantly review our economic institutions to see where the competitive market mechanism that has served us so well can replace the restrictive arrangements originally introduced in response to conditions that no longer exist."

Regulation was not mentioned in the 1972 economic message, but Mr. Nixon did plug the concept in his 1972 State of the Union address on Jan. 20.

He said he hoped that by adjournment the 92nd Congress would have accepted the Administration's recommendations "for revitalizing surface freight transportation."

"By encouraging competition, flexibility and efficiency among freight carriers, these steps could save the American people billions of dollars in freight costs every year," he said, "helping to curb inflation, expand employment and improve our balance of trade."

CEA—Although Mr. Nixon's 1972 message did not mention regulation, the report of his Council of Economic Advisers carried passages on it for the third straight year.

The council said that much of the problem in transportation "can be traced to regulation itself."

"Selective deregulation offers opportunities to improve efficiency of the industry and increase its ability to meet growing demand," the council said.

Saying that the Administration's proposal would save shippers $2 billion a year, the council warned that "failures to move forward, or even excessive delay could mean continued unsatisfactory performance of this vital service in the economy and may lead to increasing direct involvement by the federal government accompanied by large subsidies."

Houthakker—As a CEA member (1969-71), Hendrik S. Houthakker helped draft the Administration bill.

Houthakker, now a professor of economics at Harvard University, is currently circulating a statement to a group of 25 prominent transportation economists asking their support for the bill. He plans to submit the statement to both the House and Senate commerce committees.

In an interview, Houthakker said that several economic studies support the view that greater competition will reduce freight rates. But he is less sure about whether it will improve service.

"What we·do know is that an unregulated or a deregulated system will improve service. It has worked that way in Australia and Canada."

Houthakker said that if the Administration proposal is not enacted "there will be a further increase in freight rates and a further deterioration of service."

Nationalization of the railroad industry, he said "is a distinct possibility" if there are any more railroad bankruptcies.

Houthakker, noting that both Administration officials and the carriers speak of nationalization if their respective programs are not enacted, said: "They (the carriers) are saying it will happen if you keep the present system of regulation and don't make additional government money available to them. What we are saying is if you deregulate and avoid a massive infusion of government funds, you will avoid nationalization."

Lobbying: A White House aide confirmed that despite the statements by Mr. Nixon and the CEA, the Administration has kept its lobbying efforts for the legislation at a minimum.

Noting the failure of the Kennedy proposals to be enacted, the aide said: "Even the Democrats with a congressional majority couldn't get their proposals through. I'm not doing much because I don't want to give my time to something that's not going to go anywhere."

Asked how committed the Administration is to its bill, he said: "That's an embarrassing question."

"I'm not pessimistic," said the aide. "But I think that the beginning of a new term is the best time to promote this sort of thing. I think if we come back we will. These are just the kinds of issues our guys like to grapple with. It just bothers the hell out of them to see such a mess and they want to straighten it out."

THE PUBLIC

Although shippers are divided on the merits of some parts of the

Administration bill, they endorse the concept and reject the carrier proposal.

The concept also has substantial consumer support.

Shippers: Cargill's Springrose said: "The Surface Transportation Act does nothing but provide government subsidy to continue the wasteful practices in transportation today.

Two influential shipper groups, the User Panel of the Transportation Association of America and the National Grain and Feed Association, have adopted positions basically in support of the deregulatory package.

And at a February meeting in Chicago, the only nationwide shippers' group representing diverse interests—the National Industrial Traffic League—endorsed provisions of the Administration's legislation that would ease entry, curtail the powers of rate bureaus and hasten rail-line abandonments.

The league, however, rejected the zone-of-reasonableness approach.

Many members feared the shippers' traditional right to negotiate and challenge rates would disappear within the zone. A sizable faction within the league argued that a cost-priced rate structure, which would determine the limits of the zone, would preclude other factors involved in rate making.

Several members who favored the zone concept argued that without more rate freedom for the carriers and railroads in particular, the only alternatives would be enactment of the Surface Transportation Act, which one member described as "a more-regulation, more-subsidy bill conceived in a smoke-filled room," or nationalization of part or all of the railroads.

Donald E. Graham, general counsel of the National Council of Farmer Cooperatives, said in an interview that the carrier plan "is the most cynical piece of legislation I've ever seen."

Said Graham: "It's the biggest 'gimme, gimme' bill of them all. There's no obligation in it for carriers to give better service. The carriers took the approach of getting what was best for them and ignoring the needs of their customers, the shippers."

The industry bill, he said, has no shipper support. "There's nobody behind it. It is opposed by the NIT League and all the farm organizations."

Graham said that farm groups are united in favoring the deregulation concept. Generally, he said, they favor the zone of reasonableness, but are not sure that the Transportation Department has adequately studied what its limits should be.

"The idea of deregulation would save us money," Graham said. "There's no question about that. It would allow trucks to come back full instead of empty.

"Farmers just want to call a truck to move their stuff. They don't want to be bothered by certificates and prescribed routes. And they want to be able to let competition determine the price."

However, Graham said that many farmers fear abandonments because they mean "curtailment of service in rural areas."

Consumers: According to Shelby E. Southard, transportation chairman of the Consumer Federation of America, consumers would benefit greatly from deregulation.

In March, Southard wrote Sen. Magnuson and Rep. Staggers, chairmen of the congressional commerce committees, that "the scheme of regulation devised for the railroad monopoly of the 1880s and the Depression decade of the 1930s seems likely to need overhaul in the 1970s."

Southard said that although current regulation is not the cause of all the difficulties in the nation's transportation system, it contributes to these difficulties "and causes the over-all transport bill to be larger than it need be."

In the letter, Southard said that the public is not generally aware that the "less visible costs" of freight transportation have added about $136 to the cost of a $2,000 new car; 6 percent to the cost of utility services; about $1,800 to the cost of a $15,000 home and $4,800 to the cost of a $40,000 home.

Southard also is spokesman for the Cooperative League of the U.S.A., a CFA member. The league is a national federation of customer-owned cooperative businesses with urban and rural members. It claims membership of 20 million families.

In an interview, Southard said that although the league has not endorsed the Administration bill, "where competition is increased we are for it."

Southard said that league members take the position that where competition is increased there would be better service and more reasonable prices.

"What the consumer is concerned about in the transportation

quotient is how prices are affected by competition. To the extent that competition can be made more competitive and prices reduced, we think this will benefit consumers," he said.

Southard said he believes that the Transportation Department should work more fervently for its bill. "We think they are having second thoughts on the matter. There has to be more competition in rate fixing. Too much of it now is made in the board room."

Fellmuth—Robert Fellmuth headed the Nader research group that investigated the ICC in 1970. One of its conclusions was that the agency be abolished.

Fellmuth said in an interview that he has written an analysis of the industry plan's five titles for Nader, urging that Nader speak out against it.

"It is the worst bill ever written," said Fellmuth. "The end result would be a $5-million boondoggle for the carriers that would make the $250-million Lockheed loan guarantee bill look tame."

In Fellmuth's view the proposal would:

increase inefficiency;

raise prices;

be "unjust" for stockholders, and

"provide a new weapon for the Administration to use to elicit campaign contributions from the carriers."

"It would provide government welfare to corporations with monopoly power who have no claim of need; it would mean industrial socialism," he said.

The RFC provision, he said, would loan or guarantee $5 billion to carriers without adequately de-

PRICE GROUP AND DEREGULATION

The Price Commission has considered and rejected a plan to use its price-stabilization powers to bring deregulation to the surface transportation industry.

In mid-March, shortly after the commission delegated its price-stabilization powers over public utilities to state and federal regulatory agencies, the commission considered accomplishing by order what the Nixon Administration so far has failed to accomplish in Congress.

According to Norman Beebe, a Price Commission spokesman, deregulatory changes were among a series of options that the commission's general counsel compiled as a basis for dealing with transportation utilities in a different manner from other utilities.

The suggestion was rejected by the commission, said Beebe, "because there was an acute awareness that this would be legislation by fiat and not within the Price Commission's purview."

"It was weeded out very quickly," he said.

Among the measures the commission considered in an effort to hold down rate increases were:

forbidding the Interstate Commerce Commission to grant a railroad rate-increase request if it were determined that the railroad was subsidizing money-losing operations such as little-used routes or agricultural shipments which are hauled at rates below fully-allocated cost;

requiring the ICC to deny a rate increase if protestants could prove that the agency had denied an entry certificate to any firm willing and able to perform the service at lower cost;

using its persuasive powers to encourage the ICC to deny rate increases filed by rate bureaus on single-line rates. (If this were to be accomplished, it would—in effect—repeal the antitrust exemption for single-line rate-fixing by the bureaus.)

On April 24, the ICC suspended a proposed $489-million railroad rate boost. The average 4.1-percent increase was scheduled to take effect May 1 but it will be delayed for up to seven months while the ICC investigates the case.

The increase had been scheduled to replace a 2.5-percent emergency surcharge for the industry which the commission approved in February. The emergency surcharge will expire June 5.

The suspension is evidence that the ICC is reacting to pressures from the Price Commission.

In a letter to ICC Chairman George M. Stafford, which was made public April 18, C. Jackson Grayson Jr., chairman of the Price Commission, said that he was "not convinced" that the increase which was needed by the hard-pressed eastern railroads should be shared by the wealthier carriers.

Grayson said also that he had doubts about whether the ICC had given sufficient consideration to productivity as it affected the proposed rate boost.

He asked that the increase be suspended for the maximum period or until the ICC and the commission staff could study "its relevance to the needs of the carriers and its impact on the national economy." Grayson said the suspension request would ensure full study of the question.

fining minimum-interest requirements, and without adequate restrictions on use of the money or adequate criteria for repayment.

"If I were sitting in Congress," said Fellmuth, who currently is heading a Nader group investigating Congress, "I would vote for the Administration bill. Although I think it does not go far enough to remove entry bars, it moves in the right direction."

Advertising—Fellmuth helped to draft a March 28 letter to the National Broadcasting Co. Inc. and its Washington affiliate requesting equal free time to counter railroad industry-sponsored television advertisements for the carrier bill.

The advertisements feature former astronaut Walter M. Schirra Jr. urging public support for the act.

The letter was signed by representatives of five national farm groups—the National Council of Farmer Cooperatives, the National Farmers Union, the National Federation of Grain Cooperatives, the National Association of Wheat Growers and the National Farmers Organization. They were joined by Sen. Fred R. Harris, D-Okla.

The letter threatened a formal complaint to the Federal Communications Commission unless free time were granted to counter "propagandistic advertisements ... vastly overpresenting the case" for the industry proposal.

The groups requested that NBC and WRC-TV, the Washington station, "make known the ways in which they have fulfilled their fairness-doctrine obligation to provide balanced programming on the STA."

On April 21, Harris announced that a settlement had been reached through negotiation with the network and the station. He called it "a victory for the small farmers, average taxpayers and the American consumers."

The settlement included an agreement for three one-minute spots on network television during a weekend baseball game, a nightly news show and a Friday night movie.

The local station will air nine minutes of free time during news and variety shows, daytime programs, prime time and the "Tonight" show.

In commending NBC for the agreement, Harris said that the public "will now have a chance to argue against the increased prices, reduced service and outrageous government handouts that result from passage of this bill."

Transportation's Beggs and Rep. Adams, who is leading the fight in the House for the industry bill, said they would welcome a compromise. But the odds seem to be against such a settlement in the near future.

"I don't care whose title is on it," said Adams. "We'll give the Administration credit for passing a bill, just so long as we get a bill."

Said Beggs: "We'll be happy if the committee can come up with a better package to do the job. But it is no use tinkering with the mechanism. We've done this and it doesn't work. Clearly, the present regulatory situation is a national problem and a national disgrace."

The carriers, too, believe a compromise is necessary to get legislation enacted.

"We know we've got to get something done," said Richard E. Briggs, executive director of AS-TRO. "It's not a question of which provision is more expendable for us. The idea is not to see tradeoffs. The idea is to see how many common points of agreement there are."

Beggs' Priorities: Beggs hedged on the question of which provisions of its plan the Administration feels must be retained in any compromise.

"Our priorities are to get a meaningful change in regulation," he said.

Beggs and other Transportation Department officials negotiating for a compromise said that all of the provisions in their legislation are interrelated.

While they said they are flexible, Beggs said, for example, that dropping any single provision in its entirety "would kill the bill."

Beggs did say, however, that elements of the Administration program which it feels are "essential" are:

some freedom of rate making with a floor to prevent predatory pricing and a ceiling to permit freedom to respond to the marketplace;

some mechanism to ease abandonments;

some arrangement to loosen entry restrictions;

a watering down of rate bureaus' powers to protest rates proposed by one of their members.

Beggs said that the Administration is "flexible on the three most controversial elements of the proposal—entry, zone of reasonableness and rate-bureau provisions.

Carriers: But those are the very provisions on which the carriers say they cannot compromise.

"I see no possible compromise on those provisions so far as we are concerned," said Smathers.

In a like vein, Bresnahan said: "We are unqualifiedly, unequivocally and adamantly opposed to those three provisions and there is no room for compromise. We are opposed to them completely."

Briggs explained some of the thinking behind the carriers' opposition to the three provisions.

Entry—"If the idea is to create rate wars, it can't help us or transportation," he said.

"The proposal would expand the rights of everyone else and could hurt the railroad industry. If you expand the number of truckers and water carriers you cut down on the railroads' ability to handle marginal traffic."

Rate Bureaus—On what he calls the proposed "dismantling" of the rate bureaus, Briggs was just as emphatic.

"Allowing antitrust immunity only for interline rates means we couldn't operate in terms of setting stable routes when there are 70 or 80 different routes available. It would be impossible for the shipper to keep up with the rates and he could never know if he is getting best rates."

Zone of reasonableness—Briggs said that the railroads have no problem with the floor of the zone, but that the ceiling is troublesome because all railroads do not use the same method of calculating fully allocated costs.

He said: "The zone would hurt us at the upper end because unless there was effective intermodal competition we couldn't have any rate over 150 percent of fully allocated costs."

Adams: Adams said the three controversial provisions of the Administration bill "will never sell."

"Nobody on the political burner ever says they won't accept compromise or else they are going to be beaten. If I were to say that people would think I was a fool."

Adams praised the Administration proposal "as a very balanced, thoroughly worked-out system."

However, he said, compromise is necessary because "we're dealing with a very large, partially regulated, non-homogeneous private enterprise system.

"You cannot apply a nicely balanced, theoretical system to this hodge-podge of transportation all at one time.

"But you can take this system and begin to move it towards a privately managed, government-regulated plan where all shippers get fair treatment and carriers are prevented from committing suicide by carrying goods below cost."

Adams-Beggs: In separate interviews, Adams and Beggs outlined their views of possible compromises. There was little consensus.

Entry—Beggs said he believes that wherever there is a railroad abandonment, there ought to be a parallel opportunity for easier entry so that other carriers would be able to service an area.

"There has to be some liberalization of the ICC procedures that work to prevent entry," Beggs said. "Liberalizing or restating the rules by which the ICC judges entry might be an acceptable compromise.

"Private-contract carriage in trucking is growing very rapidly because there is unsatisfactory service and an inefficient system. The truckers are closing their eyes to the situation. I think they ought to take off their single-lens glasses and look at the future."

Though Adams favors strict regulation of entry, he said that, in talking with shippers, he got the impression that "what bothers them is not so much restrictions on entry as restrictions on commodity carriage."

As a final compromise, he said, he would favor a study of the whole question.

Zone—Beggs said that a possible compromise on the zone-of-reasonableness provision would be to make the zone narrower "and leave everything else to ICC rules."

If this were done, however, he

said, "it would be pretty bad news."

"The truckers and the water carriers like the floor but they don't like the ceiling because they don't want to give any more flexibility to the railroads to make them more competitive than they are. The railroads would like complete flexibility."

Adams is trying to write a formula by which the carriers themselves would set their own zone of reasonableness.

"The bottom would be pegged at variable costs. The top would be rates in effect now. Action would be allowed by exception," Adams explained.

Rate Bureaus—Beggs said "the carriers would be a hell of a lot better off if they did away with the antitrust immunity of the rate bureaus; they have used them as a crutch."

He said he wouldn't favor a study of the problem as a possible compromise because "it is clearly an industry practice to permit rate bureaus to protest a rate made by one of their members."

Also, he said, "We clearly have to address the problem of rate bureaus rescinding lower rates their members post."

Adams agrees with Beggs that the bureaus should not restrict their members from filing lower rates. He would free individual carrier actions on rates subject only to shippers' protests. Under such a system rate bureaus would be prohibited from protesting individual members' rate filings.

OUTLOOK

A high railroad industry official, noting that the railroads announced their coalition with the truckers and water carriers more than a month before the Transportation Department's proposal went to Congress, said:

"Frankly, I don't think there would have been an industry plan if the Administration hadn't delayed in sending up its legislation. They delayed so much that the bill became a legend in its own time."

He said that the present carrier coalition could easily fall apart "at the first crack in the wall."

Only the realization that the unanimity of the three modes will help their case in Congress keeps some wealthy railroads from speaking out publicly for the Administration legislation, the official said.

Although there is a slim chance for some noncontroversial segments of both competing proposals to come to the floor for a vote, indications point to no meaningful change in transportation legislation this year.

This opinion, shared by many on both sides of the debate, is reinforced by the complexity of both proposals, the claims and counterclaims of both sides and the fact that in an election year Congress prefers to steer clear of controversy.

Many observers in Congress also believe that it will not easily swallow the argument that nationalization of the railroads is inevitable if nothing is done.

A Senate staff official used a farmyard expletive to describe the argument that some legislation is needed to avert nationalization.

"There is only one candidate for nationalization and that's the Penn Central," he said.

"And even they are talking like they can make it. I don't think most Members of the Senate are convinced by that argument."

Smathers, who has talked to every member of the Senate Commerce Committee about the industry bill, is optimistic that "a bill beneficial to the railroad industry will come out in this session."

But the Senate official said Smathers' optimism may be unfounded.

"This is not the kind of an issue where the concern of the public is well known. And the subject is too esoteric for the press.

"With such a lack of public interest I don't think most Senators will be inclined to stick their necks out in an election year."

Broadcasters charge FCC and courts erode media freedom
Bruce E. Thorp

In the past year, partisan groups and individuals who feel they have been denied an opportunity to air their views on radio and television have moved significantly closer to gaining legally sanctioned access to the media. The gains have come through the Federal Communications Commission's rulings on its fairness doctrine and through court decisions on contested FCC rulings.

The fairness doctrine is an FCC requirement that radio and television stations—which are licensed by the commission—must treat all sides of controversial issues fairly.

For many years the commission has ruled on complaints from persons who have said that their viewpoints had been given inadequate coverage in on-the-air discussions. Often the commission has agreed, but then, except in isolated circumstances, has required only that broadcasters allow additional time for the neglected viewpoints, and not necessarily for the persons who had complained. The commission repeatedly has refused to establish an individual right of access.

In August, however, the U.S. Court of Appeals for the District of Columbia, skirting around the fairness doctrine and drawing on the 1st Amendment's guarantee of free speech, sent back an FCC ruling and said that broadcasters could not flatly deny access to persons wanting to buy air time to discuss controversial issues. As established by the court, this limited right of access does not depend on a determination that coverage of

an issue has been unfair; a person, in theory, can buy time to discuss any viewpoint on any issue.

Also in the past year, the FCC and this same court, ruling in separate cases, broke new ground by finding that gasoline and automobile commercials had raised controversial issues and needed balancing through other programming. This principle had been applied in 1967 to cigarette commercials, but with the promise from the FCC that it would not be extended to other types of advertisements.

So the year has been a good one for persons seeking access to the airwaves. "The most important new concept is that a broadcast licensee simply cannot monopolize the views that are broadcast over his station," said Tracy A. Westen, a lawyer with the Stern Community Law Firm, a public interest group in Washington. The public has gained some right to speak on licensed stations, he said. "There is a point at which a broadcaster can no longer censor things off the air."

The year has not been a good one for broadcasters, who never have liked the fairness doctrine because it necessitates government supervision of programming, and who see their control of their own stations continuing to erode as a result of the new FCC and court rulings.

Things really have not changed much in the last year, said John B. Summers, general counsel for the National Association of Broadcas-

ters. "We're just into it a little deeper," he said. "And we haven't yet gotten to the end."

Looking Ahead: Complaints about unfair coverage of issues are sure to continue, especially if partisans achieve continued success in their dealings with the FCC and the courts.

Also, next year is a national election year, and candidates and their supporters undoubtedly all will have complaints about coverage of the issues by the influential broadcast media. The Democratic National Committee already has been actively seeking redress for what it sees as excessive and unbalanced exposure of President Nixon on the air.

General Inquiry—In response to the continued turmoil over broadcast fairness and broadcast control, the FCC last June 9 began a general inquiry on the fairness doctrine. The commission asked for comments on how the doctrine has worked and how it could be improved.

It asked specifically for comments on whether groups and individuals have a right to use the media to respond to product commercials, whether access should be granted generally for discussion of controversial issues and whether present policies regarding political programming should be changed.

Court Decisions—Meanwhile, court decisions continue to define the fairness doctrine and access rights in ways that tend to restrict the commission's alternatives in modifying its own policies.

John Summers said that the FCC no longer could control the direction the fairness doctrine is taking, because the appellate courts have not backed up the commission decisions. Help for broadcasters, if it comes at all, "has to come from either the Supreme Court or Congress," he said.

Congress and Supreme Court—Congress, however, has shown little interest in amending the laws to clarify its intent in promoting fair discussion of issues on the airwaves. The Senate Judiciary Subcommittee on Constitutional Rights, chaired by Sen. Sam J. Ervin Jr., D-N.C., held hearings from Sept. 28 to Oct. 20 on the question of newsmen's rights and government interference with journalism, including broadcast journalism.

The Supreme Court has no fairness doctrine cases before it now, but the FCC has asked permission from the U.S. Solicitor General to appeal the lower court ruling that established the limited right of access for editorial advertising. Even if a Supreme Court ruling does result, no one can be sure if it will clarify broadcasters' and the FCC's responsibilities for fairness and access, or merely make administration of these policies more confusing and difficult.

ISSUES

The arguments being made about the fairness doctrine are much the same as they were a year ago.

Minority interest groups say that broadcasters, in order to get maximum audiences for their advertisers, produce bland program-

THE COURTS ON FAIRNESS AND ACCESS

Two recent decisions in which the U.S. Court of Appeals for the District of Columbia turned back rulings by the Federal Communications Commission could have profound effects on commercial broadcasting.

Both decisions tend to reduce broadcasters' control of programming by requiring them to accept at least some announcements on controversial subjects during time reserved for commercials, and to entertain responses, under the fairness doctrine, to product commercials.

Controversial Ads: The court, by a 2-1 vote, decided Aug. 3 that a flat ban on paid public-issue announcements violates the 1st Amendment.

The case involved two combined rulings of the FCC. One stemmed from a complaint from the Business Executives Move for Vietnam Peace (BEM), an antiwar group that had tried in 1969 to buy time on radio station WTOP, in Washington, D.C., for several antiwar announcemnts.

WTOP refused, following what it said was "its long established policy of refusing to sell spot announcement time to individuals or groups to set forth views on controversial issues." The FCC sided with the station.

The other ruling came after the Democratic National Committee requested the FCC to declare that a broadcaster "may not, as a general policy, refuse to sell time to responsible entities, such as DNC, for the solicitation of funds and for comment on public issues."

The FCC agreed that it "would appear arbitrary" if broadcasters did not sell time for soliciting funds, but it refused to declare that broadcasters must sell time for editorial comments.

In overturning the commission, the court did not mince words:

"We are convinced," it said, "that the time has come for the commission to cease abdicating responsibility over the uses of advertising time. Indeed, we are convinced that broadcast advertising has great potential for enlivening and enriching debate on public issues, rather than drugging it with an overdose of non-ideas and non-issues as is now the case. . . .

"Vigorous, free expression is promoted when members of the public have *some* opportunity to take the initiative and editorial control into their own hands on the broadcast media. . . .

"In the end, it may unsettle some of us to see an antiwar message or a political party message in the accustomed place of a soap or beer commercial. But we must not equate what is habitual with what is right—or what is constitutional.

"A society already so saturated with commercialism can well

334

afford another outlet for speech on public issues. All that we may lose is some of our apathy."

The court remanded the cases to the commission and said it should develop regulatory guidelines to deal with editorial advertisements and ensure that if a station or network sells time at all for advertising, some of it be for editorial spots.

Response to Ads: The other decision, also by a 2-1 vote, was made Aug. 16 in a case brought by Friends of the Earth (FOE), a national conservation organization.

FOE had complained to the commission that station WNBC-TV in New York City had denied the organization's request that it carry antipollution messages to balance automobile and gasoline commercials. FOE said the same fairness doctrine principle was involved as in 1967 when the commission ruled that antismoking messages must be broadcast by stations carrying cigarette commercials.

The FCC refused to honor the FOE complaint, on the grounds that cigarettes and the hazard they produced were unique, and that the fairness doctrine did not apply to other product commercials.

The court disagreed with the commission. It said: "When there is undisputed evidence, as there is here, that the hazards to health implicit in air pollution are enlarged and aggravated by such products, then the parallel with cigarette advertising is exact. . . . "

It remanded the case to the commission and ordered it to determine if in fact, the television station had given adequate coverage to the antipollution side of the issue.

ming that will not offend the majority of viewers. The fairness doctrine must be extended to ensure that minority views appear on the air, they say.

Broadcasters argue that the fairness doctrine infringes on their rights to control programming and puts the federal government into the business of media censorship. If more access were granted to minority interests, they say, audiences would dwindle and so would advertising profits. That could bring an end to today's system of broadcasting, and everyone would be the loser, they say.

Minority Complaints: Tracy Westen of the Stern Community Law Firm said that majority opinions dominate the present broadcasting system. Often, he said, the fairness doctrine does not even apply to programming considered controversial by some persons, because the viewpoints expressed in the program are considered to be noncontroversial. He listed military recruitment advertisements as an example, and noted that peace groups have not been allowed by the FCC to respond to these appeals.

J. Skelly Wright, circuit judge for the Court of Appeals for the District of Columbia, referred to this same point in writing the court's Aug. 3 decision that at least some time must be sold on the air for editorial advertising.

"All too often in our society," Wright wrote, "one particular ideology—that of passivity, acceptance of things as they are, and exaltation of commercial values—is simply taken for granted, assumed to be a nonideology, and allowed to choke out all the rest." Thus, he said, a flat ban against all editorial advertising cuts off the expression of viewpoints not eligible for fairness doctrine treatment and "establishes an unmistakable infringing of 1st Amendment liberties."

Westen said he thinks there has to be a provision in addition to the fairness doctrine to ensure that minority viewpoints are heard. "I think the problems of the fairness doctrine can be overcome to some extent by development of an access doctrine," he said.

Political Access: Joseph A. Califano Jr., general counsel to the Democratic National Committee, said in an interview that another serious weakness in the fairness doctrine is its failure to guarantee media access to the political party out of power after the President speaks on the air.

President Nixon can get on radio and television whenever he wishes to, and his appearances are "almost without exception partisan and controversial," Califano said. Yet, he explained, Democrats cannot get on the air to answer, and the FCC has dismissed their complaints by accepting broadcasters' explanations that the issues discussed by the President have been handled fairly through other programming.

Califano said the party should have an automatic right to respond to Nixon whenever he goes on the air. He filed a brief to that effect Oct. 20 with the Court of Appeals, in which the DNC asks the court to overturn an FCC ruling of Aug. 20. At the very least, the committee wants the commission to hold evidentiary hearings on these complaints to determine formally whether broadcasters have given fair treatment to issues raised by the President.

Califano said he expects the court ruling to be further appealed no matter who wins.

"And when we get to the Supreme Court, they're either going to have to give us a right of access or tell the FCC to hold evidentiary hearings," he said.

Broadcasters' Response: Roy Elson, National Association of Broadcasters vice president for government relations, said that a major problem with the fairness doctrine, even as it stands now, is that the federal government must step in after a complaint and determine whether additional programming is necessary to balance coverage of an issue.

"I'm very suspicious of the government deciding what people should see or hear," he said.

Richard W. Jencks, vice president of CBS Inc., in Washington, D.C., called the fairness doctrine "a bad idea whose time has come."

He characterized the new wave of fairness complaints as an attack on broadcast journalists and a display of distrust for their abilities to handle issues fairly.

Jencks said that broadcasters are reporting issues better today than ever, in interesting ways that hold large audiences. This provides more service to the public than if partisans were given time to

THE FAIRNESS DOCTINE: THREAT OR SAFEGUARD

Has government regulation of broadcasting jeopardized radio and television news coverage? Has the Federal Communications Commission's fairness doctrine curtailed broadcast journalists' rights under the 1st Amendment? Is there a government conspiracy against the electronic media?

These were among the questions addressed in the first series of hearings on freedom of the press held from Sept. 28 to Oct. 20 by the Senate Judiciary Subcommittee on Constitutional Rights, chaired by Sen. Sam J. Ervin Jr., D-N.C.

Newsmen Jeopardized: Two representatives of the CBS network were among those contending that government regulation is an increasing threat to broadcast newsmen.

Stanton—CBS President Frank Stanton testified Sept. 29 that "today, more than at any time in the history of radio and television, broadcast journalism is jeopardized by attempts to regulate its contents or its methods, including unreasonable application of the FCC's fairness doctrine."

Stanton is particularly sensitive to the government surveillance issue. Last spring he was subpoenaed to appear before the House Interstate and Foreign Commerce Subcommittee on Investigations in connection with the CBS documentary, "The Selling of the Pentagon."

Stanton appeared June 24, but he refused to supply the subcommittee with unused film from the program. Subcommittee members wanted the film to examine editing techniques used by the network. When Stanton refused to comply with the subpoena, the full committee, chaired by Rep. Harley O. Staggers, D-W.Va., sought unsuccessfully to have him cited by the House for contempt.

The FCC itself chose not to pursue the matter, but Stanton noted that in considering other fairness complaints, "the commission has engaged in microscopic examination of a licensee's coverage of an issue, going to such extremes as counting of lines in a broadcast script."

Cronkite—The day after Stanton testified, Walter Cronkite, CBS news correspondent, told the subcommittee: "Broadcast news today is not free. Because it is operated by an industry that is beholden to the government for its right to exist, its freedom has been curtailed by fiat, by assumption, and by intimidation and harassment."

Quoting from a speech in which Vice President Agnew criticized the networks, Cronkite said that even though censorship is disclaimed, "when the speaker is a high official of the Administration that appoints the commission that holds life-or-death power over the broadcast industry, a broadcast journalist and his employer might be excused for thinking that it sounds like a threat."

Others Disagree: Two experienced broadcast journalists played down the threat of government regulation.

Friendly—Fred W. Friendly, a former president of CBS news and now a Columbia University professor of broadcast journalism, said Oct. 12 that the larger threat of censorship comes from broadcasters themselves.

"The chilling hand that concerns me far more (than the FCC) is the corporate concern for maximizing profits," he said.

Responding to some broadcasters' arguments that the burden of the fairness doctrine has kept stations away from controversial programs, Friendly said, "It is the dollar sign, not the government's censorship stamp, that has drastically reduced the amount of air time devoted to documentaries and public affairs programming."

Brinkley—David Brinkley, NBC news correspondent, Oct. 19 acknowledged that politicians often had capitalized on public hostility toward broadcast journalism by attacking it, but he said: "As for intimidation by our critics, there is none that I know of. Anyone who can't stand criticism should not go into journalism."

Answering a question from Sen. Roman L. Hruska, R-Neb., Brinkley said it was all right to have constant surveillance of broadcast journalism from Congress as well as from everyone else.

Commissioners' Views: Two FCC commissioners who seldom agree with each other, Chairman Dean Burch and Nicholas Johnson, gave the subcommittee similar views on broadcast regulation Oct. 20.

Burch—The FCC chairman stressed that the commission is not "the national arbiter of truth." Citing "The Selling of the Pentagon" case as an example, Burch said that "in this democracy, no government agency can, or should try, to authenticate the news. Therefore, in a series of recent cases we have consistently and repeatedly stated that we will shun the censor's role and will not try to establish news distortion in situations where government intervention would constitute a worse danger than the possible rigging itself."

During questioning, Burch rebuked CBS President Stanton for having "promulgated the so-called conspiracy theory." The theory, Burch explained, is that Vice President Agnew "says something and the FCC will move in and do the dirty work by taking away licenses. . . .

"The only thing wrong with the theory is that it's false. And Dr. Stanton knows it's false. . . . I really am a bit disgusted that Dr. Stanton keeps bringing up this conspiracy theory, because it simply will not wash."

Johnson—Johnson is an outspoken critic of broadcasting, yet he told the subcommittee he was proud of the commission's "steadfast refusal to discipline the networks in any way in response to charges of distortion in news and documentaries. . . . I believe it

present their views directly, he said, because past experience shows that direct access programs tend to be dull, and audiences are small.

Solutions: "I would like ultimately to see the fairness doctrine disappear," said Westen, but only after a right of access is guaranteed to minorities and ownership of station licenses becomes more diversified. "That's a long way away," he said.

In the short run, even if some right of access is established, the fairness doctrine must be retained to keep broadcasters' own programming fair and to assure fair apportionment of access time, he said.

Westen expressed confidence that the courts would continue to hand down decisions favorable to groups seeking access. Without this prodding from the courts, he said, "I really don't have great faith that the FCC is going to do much in this area."

Califano said the only solution to the fairness problem would be to give the public more direct control over the electronic media.

"Like war is too important to leave to the generals," he said, "television is too important to leave to the broadcasters and the FCC."

Broadcasters, of course, want more control of their programming, not less. John Summers of the NAB said that the fairness complaints will not go away until the Supreme Court issues a strong decision making it very clear that groups and individuals do not have a right of access to the media.

Jencks of CBS said he thought it quite possible that fairness complaints will increase "and we will be crippled by the need to adhere to them."

He said that eventually the courts will become so overburdened by these cases that they will have to admit they cannot handle them. Then the responsibility for fairness will be given back to the broadcasters, where it belongs, he said.

The broadcasters who were interviewed said that nothing they could do would stop fairness complaints. "Some of those complaints are systematically organized," said Elson. "I don't think you're going to stop some of those complaints."

Jencks said he did not think that granting groups more access would reduce the complaints; it could encourage even more. For example, if groups from the far left got on the air to express their views, groups from the far right—who have not yet complained about a lack of access—would demand time for themselves, he said.

POSSIBLE LEGISLATION

Another way out of the fairness dilemma is through legislation that more clearly defines the intention of Congress in assuring fair discussion of issues on radio and television.

There is no legislation of this type proposed at the moment, but two men with experience in government regulation of broadcasting dealt with the question in recent speeches.

Whitehead's Idea: Clay T. Whitehead, director of the Administration's Office of Telecommunications Policy, told the International Radio and Television So-

would be unconstitutional for the FCC to engage in the task of validating the news performance of licensees."

Johnson did, however, offer a strong defense of the fairness doctrine. "The limited intervention of the FCC through the fairness doctrine is to insure that, after broadcasters have wielded the censor's knife, the public at least gets the right to hear diverse and antagonistic viewpoints with regard to what is on the air. . . . "

Members' Opinions: The hearings were rounded out by statements made by Members of Congress.

Springer—Rep. William L. Springer, R-Ill., ranking minority member of the House Commerce Committee, defended the role of Congress in keeping watch over broadcast journalism, as his committee did with "The Selling of the Pentagon."

He said the constant surveillance of Congress had helped make television coverage of public issues more fair now than it was four or five years ago. "Congress has had a constructive influence upon television," he said.

Ervin—Sen. Ervin expressed strong concern about the FCC's supervision of broadcast programming. "Whatever one's view of the fairness doctrine," he said in opening the hearings Sept. 28, "it must be clear to everyone that such a doctrine has placed in the hands of a federal agency a not very subtle form of censorship."

ciety in New York City Oct. 6 that the fairness doctrine should be eliminated.

But, he said, it should be replaced with a statutory right of access. Individuals should be allowed to buy radio and television time "on a first-come, first-served basis, at nondiscriminatory rates," he said.

Complaints of denied access should be handled through the courts, and not through the FCC, he said. Furthermore, broadcasters should not be held responsible for the content of the paid statements, except to guard against illegal material, he said.

In the same speech, Whitehead called for longer license periods and more assurance of renewal for broadcasters doing a good job.

In an interview, Whitehead explained his reasoning.

There are two ways to arrive at individual access rights, he said. The first is through the present fairness doctrine and the 1st Amendment, as the courts are now trying to do.

"The trouble with that theory is that it does not really lead you to an individual right of access, but to an idea's right of access," he said.

Because the broadcaster or the FCC must decide who gets the access to express the idea, it is not really a right to appear, he said.

The second method would be to admit that "access is not really a God-given, 1st Amendment right," Whitehead continued. But Congress could legislate a right of equal opportunity to purchase air time, he said, as he had suggested in his speech.

The danger of the first method

THE FCC's FAIRNESS DOCTRINE: AN INQUIRY TOWARD EVALUATION

The fairness doctrine has evolved over the years as the Federal Communications Commission has made rulings on complaints that broadcasters have been unfair to one side or another in presenting issues of public importance.

Each individual ruling has added substance, and often new meaning, to the doctrine, and the rulings, therefore, gradually have added to broadcasters' responsibilities in presenting controversial issues.

Critics have charged that these rulings too often have been made without enough thought to new principles they might be raising. Review courts have questioned the commission's apparent inconsistency from one case to another.

So now the commission has opened the doctrine to a full-scale inquiry, with a promise to take a broad new look at how the fairness doctrine has evolved and what the consequences of that evolvement have been.

"It is important to stress that we are not hereby disparaging any of the ad hoc rulings that we have made in these areas," the commission said in its June 9 notice of inquiry. "Rather, we feel the time has come for an overview to determine whether the policies derived largely from these rulings should be retained intact or, in lesser or greater degree, modified."

The commission emphasized that it would not consider extreme changes in the doctrine that would go beyond present statutory law. " ... this commission cannot abandon the fairness doctrine or treat broadcasters as common carriers who must accept all material offered by any and all comers," it said. It also asked that comments be aimed toward new policies that would be "consistent with the maintenance and growth" of the present commercial broadcast system.

Inquiry Divided: The commission divided the inquiry into four subject areas, which it set out in Parts II, III, IV and V of its notice of inquiry.

General Comments—Part II asked for general comments on the fairness doctrine, its strengths and shortcomings, and asked how it should be changed. The deadline for submitting comments under Part II has been extended to Dec. 10; reply comments are due Jan. 24.

Rights to Time—Part III asked for comments on whether groups or individuals have a right to free or paid time on the air to respond to product commercials that they feel represent one side of a controversial issue.

In 1967, the FCC ruled that broadcasters had to present opposing views to cigarette commercials. In only one case since then, which involved ESSO petroleum commercials that discussed Alaskan oil development, has the commission extended that ruling to any other product commercials. That ruling came June 30.

Six weeks later, on Aug. 16, the U.S. Court of Appeals ruled that commercials for leaded gasoline and high-powered cars raise environmental issues that require answering under the Fairness Doctrine. It remanded to the commission a case brought in 1970 by Friends of the Earth, a conservation group that complained that WNBC-TV in New York City had refused to carry antipollution messages. The court said the commission, to be consistent with its 1970 cigarette ruling, must determine whether the station had in fact presented the antipollution viewpoint adequately. This matter is now awaiting the outcome of the general inquiry because of the possibility that the commission could change the 1967 policy decision on which this court decision is based.

Comments in response to Part III of the inquiry were due Oct. 11; reply comments were due Nov. 11.

Access and Issues—Part IV concerned general access to the broadcast media for the discussion of issues. The commission asked for comments on whether there is a feasible way to allow people on the air to discuss issues "quite aside from the fairness obligation" or, in other words, even if their appearances are not in response to the presentation of opposing viewpoints.

The commission repeatedly has denied that any group or individual has a constitutional or statutory right to access. However, the Court of Appeals for the District of Columbia ruled Aug. 3 that once a broadcaster has decided to sell time on his station for commercials or other paid announcements, he violates the 1st Amendment if he does not sell at least some of the time to persons who want to present viewpoints on public issues.

This decision, which came on complaints filed by the antiwar group, Business Executives' Move for Vietnam Peace (BEM), and by the Democratic National Committee, is being appealed by the FCC to the Supreme Court. But unless it is reversed, it means that hereafter the commission must consider that groups and individuals have limited rights of access to the broadcast media to discuss issues.

Comments on Part IV are due Dec. 10; reply comments are due Jan. 24.

Political Broadcasts—Part V asked whether there should be any changes made in how the commission applies the fairness doctrine to political broadcasts. During formal campaigns, declared candidates must be given equal opportunities to appear.

In all other political broadcasts, with one exception, the fairness doctrine applies to issues discussed on the programs. The exception is that if a broadcaster sells or gives time to one political party, he must sell or give time to the rival party.

Two pending court cases challenge this commission policy. One was brought by CBS, which had been told by the commission Aug. 14, 1970, to give the Republican National Committee time to reply to the network's July 7, 1970, "Loyal Opposition" program. In that program, CBS had given time to Lawrence F. O'Brien, chairman of the Democratic National Committee (DNC), to offset previous television appearances by President Nixon. CBS contends that giving the extra time to the Republicans would again tip the balance in that party's favor.

The second case was brought by DNC after the commission on Aug. 20 refused to compel the three television networks to give the Democrats time to respond to three appearances by Mr. Nixon earlier this year. The commission ruled that the networks already had balanced the President's appearances with other programming, but DNC now is seeking a court ruling that whenever the President appears on television, opposition spokesmen must be given an opportunity to respond.

The commission has called for comments on Part V by Dec. 10, with reply comments due Jan. 24.

First Replies: The first replies to the inquiry—those dealing with access to respond to product commercials—have been predictable. Groups wanting access have argued that commercials should be subject to the fairness doctrine just like any other programming, and that free time should be granted to answer them. Broadcasters and advertisers have argued that the FCC should go back to its policy before the 1967 cigarette ruling and declare again that product commercials are not comments on public issues, and therefore are not subject to the fairness doctrine.

For Access—The National Citizens Committee for Broadcasting, a public interest group, suggested that in selling commercial time broadcasters should give preference to editorial comments on consumer products and services, and that up to 20 percent of the time should be held open for free access.

The committee argued that consumer-oriented groups would not have enough money to buy time for and prepare very much "counter-commercial advertising," so the present system of sponsored programming would change very little.

The Friends of the Earth, making this same point, assumed that there would be just one "counterad" to each five product commercials subject to fairness complaints, the ratio that was adopted in the case of cigarettes. "Thus, it is, to say the least, highly unlikely that 'free time' spot announcements would seriously affect the continued extraordinary profitability of the broadcasting industry," it said.

Against Access—CBS came to just the opposite conclusion. It told the commission that if television networks had been required to provide free time, at a 5 to 1 ratio, for groups to respond to cereal, automobile, gasoline and oil, drug and detergent commercials in 1970, the networks' $50 million profit would have turned into an $18 million loss.

CBS concluded that the commission could avoid disaster only by rescinding the cigarette ruling that gave birth to the principle that product commercials could raise issues that required answering under the fairness doctrine.

The same plea was made in joint comments filed for Time-Life Broadcast, Inc., the Radio Television News Directors Association and other broadcasters.

"Having broken with all precedent to order the carriage by broadcasters of anti-smoking messages to balance cigarette commercials, the commission is now finding it impossible to satisfy the courts with its explanation of why other matters of important national policy are not handled similarly," this group said in its comments.

The American Advertising Federation warned that advertisers would shy away from radio and television if their commercials were subject to response under the doctrine.

The National Association of Broadcasters said it assumed that in the future the FCC will hold some commercials subject to the fairness doctrine.

But, it said, little weight should be given to *implicit* messages in commercials, and "product commercials should give rise to licensee obligations only where it can be shown that the commercials have been placed for the purpose of influencing opinion."

---

of granting access, the method now being followed by the courts, is that it is "making the broadcaster a government agent," he told the society.

"'Big Brother' himself could not have conceived a more disarming 'newspeak' name for a system of government program control than the fairness doctrine," Whitehead said.

Loevinger Speech: The other reference to fairness/access legislation came Oct. 13 from Lee Loevinger, a member of the Hogan and Hartson law firm in Washington and a former member of the FCC (1963-68).

Loevinger told the Illinois Broadcasters Association in Chicago that "the troubles of this period for commercial broadcasting may be terminal," and listed the problems of license renewal and attacks on commercials as the two most serious. He suggested legislation to embody eight basic principles of broadcasting that stressed more freedom and independence from government.

One of the principles called for "either a fairness doctrine strictly defined by statute or, as a complete substitute, the statutory right of access suggested and described by Mr. Whitehead."

Both Whitehead and Loevinger said they could not specify precise legislative proposals, and it appears that no actual bills will be introduced in Congress in the near future. But the speeches have stirred interest among broadcasters, interest groups and others concerned with government regulation of the media.

Response: *Broadcasting* and *Television Digest,* the leading trade journals for the broadcast media, both hailed the Whitehead speech. They quoted an NBC spokesman as saying the proposals were "bold, innovative and like a breath of fresh air."

Statements made by broadcasters to *National Journal,* however, were more reserved.

John Summers of NAB said there had not yet been enough time to think through the implications of Whitehead's speech. He said he did not know in detail what Whitehead meant by access—how much time would be involved and, for example, during what period of the day.

Jencks of CBS welcomed Whitehead's acknowledgement that the fairness doctrine was not working well, but he said he was not sure that establishing a right to paid time—and eliminating the free access that is now sometimes available under the fairness doctrine—would be politically feasible.

Tracy Westen, speaking from the standpoint of minority groups wanting more access, said that this particular change would in one sense be "a step backward."

Whitehead's plan would "set up a system where only the wealthy could speak," he said. "The poor would be disenfranchised."

He also criticized a suggestion by Whitehead that a licensee's fair treatment of issues be considered only at renewal time.

Whitehead had said that broadcasters who handle issues unfairly should not be disciplined for each infraction, as they are now in response to individual complaints, but should lose their licenses if their over-all treatment of issues has been unfair.

"Whitehead is going toward capital punishment as the sole sanction," Westen said. Violators of fairness would either lose their licenses or suffer nothing, he said. (So far in the history of the FCC, no radio or television license has ever been revoked because of violations of the fairness doctrine.)

Not only would punishment become rare, if not nonexistent, under Whitehead's proposal, but there would be no real remedy left for those whose views had been kept off the air unfairly, he said.

Westen said he at least considered the proposal for a right of paid access an improvement over the present situation—"you can speak if you have the money"—but on the whole he said he was "not too thrilled" by Whitehead's speech.

Whitehead himself said that broadcasters responding to him about the speech "have been very happy." He said that some do not like the idea of a right of access, but "the more thoughtful ones have accepted that."

He said he also thinks most public interest groups liked the speech. He indicated that the FCC also had reacted favorably, although he said the FCC is not really able to do anything about the fairness and access problems. "The only way the thing can be resolved is from the outside," he said.

HEALTH EDUCATION AND WELFARE

Though education remains primarily a state or private responsibility, the realities of educational finance have caused educators at all levels—elementary, secondary, and college—to look to the federal government for assistance. During the 1960s the Congress responded to Administration and education lobby forces with vastly increased levels of federal funding to support all levels of education within the states.

In the 1950s and 1960s the major issue was whether or not there would be federal aid to education. That issue now seems resolved and there appears to be a consensus in Congress about the need for such programs. But controversy regarding the federal government's role in funding education is far from over as the article on higher education policy demonstrates. The nature of federal aid programs have a direct bearing on how educational institutions will function. At present Administration spokesmen in the Department of Health, Education and Welfare favor greater reliance on direct aid to students; while major components of the educational establishment prefer institutional aid programs under which the colleges and universities have control over the funds. The higher education aid controversy of 1972 thus illustrates how contending forces seek to achieve their objectives by influencing the nature of federal grant programs.

The 1972 bill also illustrates how quite different issues can become enmeshed. The higher education bill reached the House and Senate floor just as the public outcry against school busing to achieve racial balance was reaching a peak. The higher education bill therefore became the vehicle to which antibusing amendments were attached. The new controversy tended to overshadow the already significant issues surrounding the higher education bill and even threatened the life of the bill itself.

Legislation could revolutionize federal programs for higher education

Joel Havemann

After a marathon bargaining session of fifteen hours, House and Senate conferees came to a compromise agreement on a far-reaching higher education bill. Differing versions of this legislation had earlier been passed by the House and Senate and the Conference Committee's job was to resolve this difference.

Senate and House versions of the higher education bill (S 659) called for large expenditures—the Senate bill authorized $7 billion in 1973 and $24 billion over three years—and they differed on an estimated 250 particulars of substance. The differences were profound on almost every issue.

Controversial Riders: The higher education provisions are costly and controversial, but they have been overshadowed in recent weeks by debate surrounding the addition of antibusing amendments to the bill. The House attached strong provisions that sharply limit the use of busing to overcome school segregation, and the Senate approved much milder language after lengthy debate.

"This is a landmark bill for higher education, and it would be tragic if higher education were overshadowed in conference by busing," said Sen. Jacob K. Javits of New York, the ranking Republican on the Labor and Public Welfare Committee, which handled the bill.

Busing is not the only rider on the higher education bill. Both houses also attached controversial

Busing amendments threatened education bill

amendments to provide school districts with $1.5 billion to overcome segregation, and the Senate added provisions for Indian education, youth camp safety and ethnic studies.

Broad Reforms: Nevertheless, higher education was the original purpose of the bill, and many of the higher education provisions are far-reaching.

For the first time, both bills would authorize direct federal aid to colleges and universities for their operating budgets with no strings attached.

The Senate provision, which would cost $674 million in the first year if fully funded, directs federal aid to institutions according to the number of students receiving federal grants—and these students are

mostly from poor families.

The House provision, which would cost an estimated $1.14 billion, channels federal aid to institutions according to the total number of students earning credits, as well as the number with federal assistance.

Institutional aid is not intended to replace the traditional forms of federal aid to higher education—assistance for students and grants for particular campus projects. In fact, many of these programs are expanded and modified by both versions of the higher education bill.

On student aid, as on institutional aid, the Senate bill tends to favor the poor while the House bill tends to favor the middle class.

The Senate's goal of guaranteeing every student $1,400 toward his education would help the lowest-income students the most. The House keeps the student aid program substantially as it has been, with some new language designed to benefit middle-income students.

The institutional and student aid provisions of the Senate bill, according to one House Democrat, reflect the Senate's "obsession with the disadvantaged." The House bill, according to many Senators, shows that the House Democrats are abandoning one of their traditional constituencies—the poor.

Curious Coalition: One consequence has been a curious coalition in the House, with Republicans, the Black Caucus and a handful of other Democrats opposing the key features of the House bill and claiming to be on the side of the poor.

The Nixon Administration is supporting the coalition. HEW Secretary Elliot L. Richardson has been warning that the country cannot afford massive social programs for both the poor and the middle class, and has urged Congress to concentrate money on the poor.

"Our liberal opponents, self-styled in each case, are advocating alternatives that could only have the effect of diluting scarce resources," Richardson told a press conference last November.

In response, House Democrats have charged that money is scarce only because the Administration is spending it in the wrong places. During hearings on the higher education bill, Rep. Edith Green, D-Ore., wondered how the federal government could afford to save the Lockheed Aircraft Corp., and added, "We are not dealing with

our institutions of higher education very fairly in comparison with many institutions in our society."

House Divided: The chief sponsor of the Senate's higher education bill is Sen. Claiborne Pell, D-R.I., chairman of the Education Subcommittee. But the subcommittee's Republicans played a considerable role in shaping the bill.

"Everyone on the subcommittee co-sponsored the bill," said an aide, "and usually that happens only on something like a resolution congratulating Salk for his polio vaccine."

The House bill, on the other hand, is to a great extent the work of one woman—Mrs. Green, who is chairman of the Special Education Subcommittee. It reflects Mrs. Green's deep mistrust of HEW, and her conviction that many of the opportunities of middle-income America are being sacrificed to an inflationary economy.

Therefore the conference on the higher education bill will pit a unanimous Senate delegation against a divided House.

A majority of all conferees support the Senate approach on the key higher education issues of institutional aid and student aid. But this means nothing in a conference, where the Senate and the House delegations each have one vote.

The Senate position will prevail with little compromise only if Senators can persuade at least two House Democrats to abandon the other 10 and join the eight House Republicans. Otherwise, the outcome of the conference will be determined by trades and compromises.

It happens that exactly two

House Democratic conferees, John Brademas of Indiana and Frank Thompson Jr. of New Jersey, generally supported the Senate approach as the bill was being prepared.

"It's a lousy bill that the House approved," Thompson said. "I might join the Senate on some issues in conference, but I won't know until the conference begins.

Brademas also said he does not feel bound to vote with the other House Democrats in Conference. If he and Thompson switch, the House conferees will be split 10-10, and the Senators will find themselves in a strong bargaining position.

The already announced opposition of so many House conferees to key provisions of the House bill has aroused the ire of Mrs. Green.

"I am aware that the rules of the House require every House conferee to support the position of the House whether or not he agrees with the position of the House," she said on the House floor on March 8. "I am also keenly aware this rule does not always prevail."

INSTITUTIONAL AID

The most far-reaching of all the new higher education proposals is the one to give as much as $1.14 billion annually in no-strings-attached aid to colleges and universities.

For months, the higher education community has been telling Congress that it must get this kind of help in a time of financial crisis.

Six major national associations representing colleges and universities, public and private, got together to ask for federal aid for all institutions according to their enrollment. They said that most institutions were running deficits, and warned that many might have to close if they did not get help soon.

Different Formulas: In the Senate Education Subcommittee, there was heated reaction against the pleas of the educators for aid according to enrollment.

"You can't give federal aid to something just because it exists," said a subcommittee staff member who aided in preparing the Senate's bill. "There has to be a federal purpose."

Carnegie Commission—Pell found the federal purpose in the recommendations of the Carnegie Commission on Higher Education, a research and policy organization financed by the Carnegie Corp. of New York. In a report issued in December 1968, the commission rejected the enrollment formula sought by the institutions, because it felt that the routine operation of colleges and universities was a state and local, not a federal, responsibility.

However, the Carnegie commission found that ensuring equal educational opportunity was a federal responsibility. So it recommended federal aid to institutions according to the number of students receiving federal help.

This kind of formula would encourage institutions to recruit poor students, the Carnegie commission reasoned, and it would help cover the additional cost of their education beyond tuition, which rarely meets all the expenses of education.

Pell adopted the idea of aid according to the number of stu-

dents with basic federal grants, and he weighted the formula so that small colleges—those most likely to be in danger of closing—get the most help.

The smallest colleges would get $500 for every student recipient of a federal grant under the Senate bill, while the largest universities would get $100 for every recipient.

House Compromise—The House Special Education Subcommittee deadlocked on institutional aid. Mrs. Green and most of the Democrats favored aid according to total enrollment, while the Republicans and a few Democrats insisted on a formula similar to the Senate's.

Finally a compromise was worked out in the full Education and Labor Committee. Two-thirds of the money for institutional aid would be distributed according to total enrollment—$100 for each freshman and sophomore, $150 for each junior and senior and $200 for each graduate student.

The other third would be handed out according to the total dollar volume of federal student grants received on campus.

The House formula, like the Senate's, gives a bonus to small colleges by allotting $300 for each institution's first 200 students and $200 for the next 100. The Office of Education figures that some small colleges would get as much as 40 percent of their operating budget from the House formula if it were fully funded.

Mrs. Green—Mrs. Green said she favored the total enrollment formula because the financial crisis in higher education extends to almost every campus. She rejected the argument that the federal gov-

Edith Green

ernment has no general responsibility in higher education.

"I think it's in the national interest to help all colleges and universities," she said in an interview. "Is it not in the national interest to train future civilian leaders, just as the federal service academies train future military leaders?"

Her mistrust of HEW was a factor. She contended that if institutional aid were related to student aid, HEW could manipulate institutional aid by manipulating student aid. Under the total enrollment formula, she said, HEW could not arrange to increase or decrease aid to any school.

Mrs. Green also pointed out that the House formula, unlike the Senate's, distributes aid not according to current enrollment but according to academic credits earned by the previous year's enrollment. This provision, she explained, would guard against excessively rewarding institutions with open enrollment policies where many students enroll at the beginning of a year but drop out quickly.

Republicans—The House Republican conferees lined up solidly against the House compromise and in favor of a formula similar to the Senate's.

Among them was Rep. John Dellenback of Oregon, the ranking Republican on the Special Education Subcommittee. In an interview, Dellenback complained that the higher education lobbies had failed to justify their request for across-the-board aid. "I expected a heavy concentration of long-range thinking to come from the educators," Dellenback said. "But instead, they just held out their hands and said 'please.'"

Three Democrats—Thompson said he did not like either formula, but if he were forced to choose, he would take the Senate's.

"I have deep reservations about blanket aid to all institutions, particularly church-related institutions," Thompson said. "I'm not convinced that all institutions need federal money."

Brademas said he favored the Senate formula, but this did not necessarily mean he would reject the House formula in conference.

A third House Democrat who leaned toward the Senate formula was Augustus F. Hawkins of California, the only black conferee. The Senate formula would channel about twice as much money to black colleges as the House formula if the two were funded equally.

Senate Condition—The Senate bill as it now stands includes an important hooker. No institutional aid is to be distributed, it says, until all student aid provisions are fully funded.

"We wanted to make sure students came first," said Sen. Peter H. Dominick of Colorado, the ranking Republican on the Education Subcommittee and an original supporter of this provision.

House Democrats complain that the provision means there would be no institutional aid at all, because the newly expanded student aid programs could not be fully funded for years, and they believe this is one point where the Senate will yield.

Constitutionality: There is a possibility that the courts would find either formula unconstitutional. Both give federal aid to church-related schools with the requirement that the aid not be used for religious purposes.

Pell said the Senate formula is more likely to be found constitutional because it addresses a specific federal purpose—promoting equal educational opportunity.

Mrs. Green said that if one formula is unconstitutional, so is the other. It is the way the aid is used, not the underlying philosophy, that determines constitutionality, she said.

This issue was addressed during House hearings; and Thomas E. Kauper, a deputy assistant attorney general in the Office of Legal Counsel, said there is no way to be sure how the courts would act. But he added:

"Grants of financial aid to church-related institutions of higher education must probably be viewed as unconstitutional."

The Supreme Court ruled last June in *Tilton v. Richardson* that federal construction grants to church-related colleges and universities are constitutional only if the buildings are not used for religious education.

Administration: The Nixon Administration originally was opposed to institutional aid, but now it has rallied behind the Senate formula.

In House testimony a year ago, Richardson said more study was needed to find a formula that would put the money where it would do the most good.

"We do not believe that the proposals that have heretofore been presented represent anything more than very shallow common denominators of proposed support for institutions of higher education," Richardson told Mrs. Green's subcommittee.

Three months later, before the Senate Education Subcommittee, Richardson continued to condemn Mrs. Green's enrollment formula.

"It is hard to imagine a mode of financing less suited to alleviating an immediate, short-term crisis," he said. "It is much too blunt an instrument for dealing with acute problems of particular institutions, for it would provide support to all institutions regardless of their needs without substantially affecting those which are in the greatest difficulty."

But this time he proposed a formula of institutional grants equal to 10 percent of the total of federal student grants, work-study payments, and loans which are federally subsidized at each school.

When the Senate adopted its somewhat different formula, based on the number of students receiving federal-grant assistance rather than the amount of dollars they receive, Richardson supported it.

Pressure Groups: During House and Senate hearings, most of the higher education community lobbied for Mrs. Green's formula of institutional aid based on enrollment.

Education Lobby — Before congressional hearings began, an agreement to support this formula was made by the American Association of Junior Colleges, the American Association of State Colleges and Universities, the American Council on Education, the Association of American Colleges, the Association of American Universities and the National Association for State Universities and Land Grant Colleges.

These associations quoted at length from two reports documenting the financial crisis in higher education.

"The Red and the Black," published by William W. Jellema of the Association of American Colleges in January 1971, found that 261 of the nation's 362 accredited four-year private colleges and universities had deficits in 1970-71. The average figure at the bottom of the ledger that year was minus $115,000.

"Most colleges in the red are staying in the red and many are getting redder, while colleges in the black are generally getting grayer," the report concluded. "Taken collectively, they will not long be able to serve higher education and the nation with strength unless significant aid is soon forthcoming."

"The New Depression in Higher Education," written by Earl F. Cheit for the Carnegie commission and published in December 1970, studied 41 institutions and found 29 of them in financial trouble or headed for trouble.

The schools already in trouble ranged from black schools such as Fisk University and Tougaloo College to large, prestigious universities such as Stanford and the University of California at Berkeley.

In House testimony, John F. Morse of the American Council on Education argued that the pervasiveness of the crisis and the diversity of the troubled institutions meant that institutional aid must be distributed broadly among all kinds of schools.

"We don't really see the logic of seeking to assist institutions on the basis of some selected number of students," Morse said.

He added that schools have to spend just as much to educate a student who does not receive federal aid as they have to spend on one who does.

Governors—The educational establishment was joined late in February by the National Governors' Conference. A committee of Governors met during their convention in Washington with Pell, Mrs. Green and other Members of Congress of both parties who will be on the conference committee.

The Governors told the conferees that state support of higher education has grown dramatically in the last decade but is reaching the limit of state resources, and contended that all colleges and universities could put federal aid to good use.

Several of the Governors, including Richard B. Ogilvie, R-Ill., are under pressure from local educational officials because they have tried to hold the line on state aid to campuses.

Opposition: Despite the vehemence of the higher-education lobby, there still is opposition to both the House and the Senate institutional aid formulas in some highly respected places.

"The current House and Senate versions, or their likely compromises, bear little relationship to any coherent set of goals underlying institutional aid," said D. Bruce Johnstone of the Ford Foundation.

The Carnegie commission, whose recommendation is the basis for the Senate formula, opposes the small-college bonus that appears in both the Senate and House formulas. It contends that the small colleges may be too inefficient at a time when money for higher education is scarce.

Another skeptic is Frank Newman, associate director of university relations at Stanford University, and chairman of a higher education task force set up by Robert H. Finch when he was HEW Secretary.

He suggested that federal grants for particular projects, which now go largely to research universities, be expanded at the level of the small college, the black college and the community college.

It is too late now to substitute a new institutional-aid formula; all that can come from the conference committee is one based on the two existing ones. But because of the confusion and the closeness of the conference to the new fiscal year, many experts believe that little or no money is likely to be appropriated for institutional aid in fiscal 1973.

Emergency Aid: In addition to general institutional aid, the Senate bill also authorizes $150 million for colleges and universities threatened by financial extinction, as determined by OE. To get emergency aid, institutions must submit cost analyses and agree to financial and operational reforms requested by OE.

A similar measure made it through the House Education and Labor Committee but was defeated on the floor by a vote of 122 to 17.

Much of the support for emergency aid comes from Republicans, some of whom had hoped it could replace general institutional aid.

Dominick said he preferred emergency aid because no general aid formula could concentrate the money on schools that needed it most. Rep. William A. Steiger, R-Wis., said he would work in conference to have emergency aid restored.

Opposition to emergency aid comes mostly from conferees of both parties, notably Mrs. Green, who do not trust OE to distribute the money.

She contended that OE would have no way of identifying the schools in the most serious danger of closing. One institution might be in the black, she said, simply because state law prohibited a deficit and programs had to be cut. At the same time, a school that was in trouble because of bad management might be rewarded with federal aid.

Even HEW itself is not so sure it wants the $150 million. Christopher T. Cross, HEW's deputy assistant secretary for education leg-islation said the Administration is "uneasy" with this provision because it does not spell out what kinds of institutions should get help.

STUDENT AID

The student-aid provisions of the higher education bill are likely to be as controversial as its sections on institutional aid.

Again, distribution of federal resources is the key issue, and again, the Senate bill favors low-income persons to a greater degree than the House bill.

Each bill would extend and expand authority for direct and federally subsidized loans to students, for federal payments to students who work while studying, and for direct grants to pay part of the costs of students' education.

Grants: The grant program is by far the most controversial, and it is here that the greatest change in current federal practice may occur.

The Senate bill envisions a vast increase in direct federal grant assistance to needy students. Its goal is to assure that each student has a minimum of $1,400 a year at his disposal to spend on his higher education. The money would be distributed according to need, with the $1,400 maximum reduced to account for the family's ability to contribute to the students' education. The House bill is less ambitious.

Current Program—The Educational Opportunity Grant (EOG) program now is running at an authorization level of $170 million a year; in fiscal 1972, appropriations for the program were $165.3 million.

The money is distributed under a formula to the states, which in turn pass it along to their higher education institutions. Then, it is at the discretion of financial-aid officers in the colleges to select students "of exceptional financial need" to benefit from the federal program. Because student bodies vary widely in their ability to pay for education, the program does not operate on a nationwide basis according to need.

House Provisions—The House bill would continue the program with relatively minor changes. It would raise the maximum EOG from $1,000 to $1,500 a year, and would drop the current restriction against grants of less than $200, thus enabling students of only slight need to get aid.

No authorization figure is specified in the House legislation.

Senate Bill—But the Senate bill would completely overhaul the grant program. It would eliminate the state distribution formula and the role of the campus financial-aid officers.

Each student whose family contribution was less than $1,200 would get a grant (no grant could be made for less than $200) regardless of the school he attended, except that the grant could not be more than half the cost of attendance.

The Labor and Public Welfare Committee's report on the legislation estimated that the first-year cost of the provision would amount to $939 million, or more than five times as much as the government now is spending on education grants. The Office of Education's estimate is $1.14 billion.

In an interview, Pell conceded that Congress would not vote enough appropriations in the next few years to fully fund the program. But the bill provides, in that event, for so-called ratable reductions—under which each student's grant would be lowered by the same percentage.

The Senate bill also includes a new supplemental grant program that would provide additional money to students who could not afford the college of their choice even after the basic grants were handed out. As in the current EOG program, campus financial-aid officers would have control over distribution of the funds, and could make basic grants of $1,000 a year, or $1,200 a year for students in the top half of their class. The bill would authorize $200 million for the program in fiscal 1973.

Finally the Senate bill provides $50 in matching funds to aid states that establish new grant programs of their own for needy students. The program is aimed at encouraging establishment of such programs in the many states that have lagged in providing scholarship aid for the poor.

Despite these critical differences, the House and Senate bills have some important similarities, for example, each would make part-time students eligible for federal grants for the first time.

Congressional Views—Senate conferees, Republicans and Democrats alike, support the Senate's student-aid provisions. But the House delegation to the conference committee will not show a like unanimity in support of its own version, for the House Republicans are more inclined to accept the Senate's provisions.

Mrs. Green, with support from other House Democrats, is intent on giving middle-class students a chance at the action.

Although Pell and other Senate sponsors of the higher education bill insist that their grant program is intended only to equalize educational opportunity, Mrs. Green said she does not believe them.

Mrs. Green's mood about the Senate bill was reflected in this statement: "Why is it then in a national interest to make it possible for the financially neediest student to go to the most expensive school? The middle-income student does not have this option."

In fact, the Senate bill would not give poor students any special entree to high-cost schools, Pell said. "Low-income students would not be any better off than middle-income students. We're just trying to lift everyone to the $1,400 floor."

Under the current EOG program, college financial-aid officers can give grants to students even if their families are able to contribute $1,400, but that would end under the Senate bill, to Mrs. Green's chagrin. "I do not see that a young man or woman from a middle-income family would have any real assistance other than a loan which he must pay back," she said.

Mrs. Green sees little need for overhauling the current program, for she believes it has worked well. It already is helping low-income students, she says, claiming that 88 percent of the EOG recipients in 1970-71 came from families with incomes under $7,500. She also says campus financial-aid officers should retain discretion over the power to select grant recipients because they "are in a unique position to know how limited funds can best be used."

Mrs. Green and other House Democrats also point out that the Senate's ratable-deduction formula would reduce grants to each eligible student to almost nothing, unless funding of the grants program is vastly increased, a prospect they view as unlikely. The current EOG program is serving 297,300 students, but under the Senate's eligibility formula, some two million students could qualify for grants.

Aides to Pell's Senate Education Subcommittee say the bill was intentionally drafted so as to pose this problem. "The idea was to pressure the Administration and the appropriations committees into providing a lot more money," one said.

The Senate Committee, in its report on the bill, said: "A simple continuation of the present student-assistance programs would not fill the need for student aid."

Figures compiled by the College Entrance Examination Board showed that because federal funding was insufficient EOGs had to be denied to 300,000 students recommended by campus financial-aid officers in the 1971-72 academic year.

House Republicans who will serve on the conference committee unanimously support a formula similar to the Senate's. "It is only fair to give grants to the poorest students first, if money is scarce," said Rep. Albert H. Quie, R-Minn., ranking minority member of the Education and Labor Committee.

Quie likes the Senate bill for two additional reasons. Under both the current EOG program and the House bill, he said, money is distributed inequitably among the states; Hawaii, for example, would be able to meet 42 percent of the demand for grants under the House formula while the District of Columbia could meet less than 12 percent.

Further, eliminating the role of the campus financial-aid officers would mean that "the student doesn't have to shop around and find the college that gives him the best financial deal," he said.

Quie does object to the ratable-reduction formula in the Senate bill, and will seek to eliminate it in the conference and to specify that the $1,400 ceiling on the basic grant would be reduced to a figure that would fit the appropriation. This would have the effect of cutting only a little from the poorest students and everything from the least poor. An appropriation of $437 million, for example, would support a maximum grant of $800.

Administration—Originally the Administration proposed a basic grant of $1,000 minus family contribution, and now it supports the Senate formula, just as it does on institutional aid. It admits, however, that the Senate student-aid provisions could not be fully funded.

Richardson, in House testimony, complained that the House formula provides no federal uniformity for the distribution of grants. The kind of formula in the Senate bill, he said, makes sure that the neediest students get grants before the less needy.

"The primary thrust of our proposed student-aid reforms can be stated quite simply—to give every qualified low-income student the same financial access to a postsecondary education as a student from a middle-class family," Richardson said.

He denied a charge by Mrs. Green that low-income students would have even greater opportunities than middle-income students.

Interest Groups—Campus financial-aid officers, who would lose much of their authority to distribute grants under the Senate bill, generally support the House version.

Allan W. Purdy, of the National Association of Student Financial Aid Administrators, warned in an interview that the Senate bill implicitly promises more federal aid than can be delivered.

"We cannot object to assuring every student that if he's capable of higher education, economics should not stand in his way. But the economy at this time will not carry such a heavy load," said Purdy, the financial-aid chief at the University of Missouri.

Purdy claimed that financial-aid officers, given authority over student-aid money, have used it to attract low-income students.

"But we have not confined our help to the very low-income group," he added. "We have not disqualified the children of the working class."

The same independent associations that prefer the Senate's institutional-aid formula also tend to favor the Senate formula for student aid.

Clark Kerr, chairman of the Carnegie commission, warned in a letter to Mrs. Green that the House formula "Lacks any provision designed to ensure fairness and equal treatment of students."

"Each student with financial need should be able to count on a basic grant which would be available to him regardless of what institution he decided to attend," Kerr wrote.

Researchers at the Brookings Institution took a similar position. Alice M. Rivlin, a senior fellow and former (1968-69) assistant HEW secretary for planning and evaluation, warned in House testimony of possible "paternalism, arbitrariness and potential for abuse" in the House bill.

Lois Rice, director of the Washington office of the College Entrance Examination Board, said that youths in the bottom quarter of the nation economically are still three times less likely to be in college than those in the top quarter.

Even among youths of equal ability, she said, rich youths are more likely to be in school than poor ones. She concluded that more college opportunities must be opened for the poor—as the Senate bill would.

Work-Study: Both the Senate and the House versions of the higher-education bill extend the work-study program, under which the government pays up to 80 percent of the salary of students working on campus or for nonprofit organizations. The program is budgeted at $244.6 million this year, and it will aid some 545,000 students.

The Senate bill continues the work-study authorization at its current level of $285 million a

Distribution of Aid by Income Level

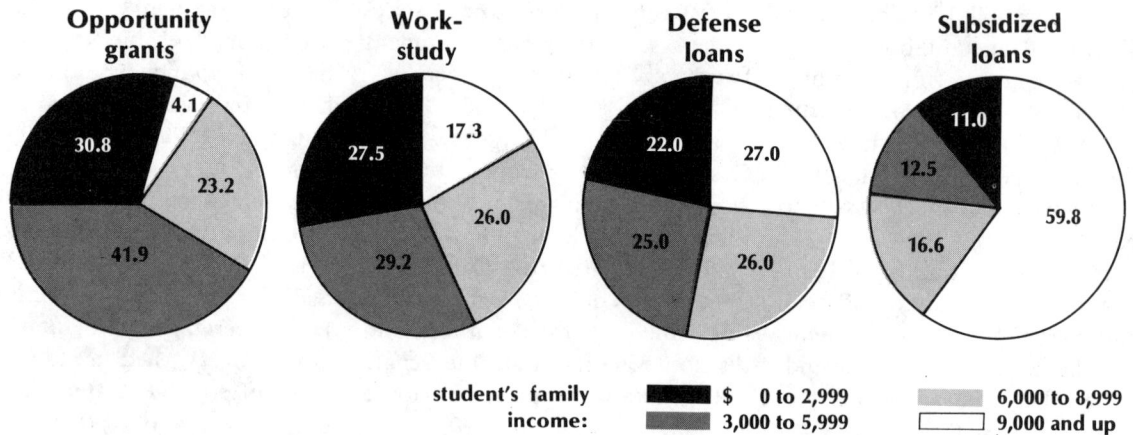

Opportunity grants	Work-study	Defense loans	Subsidized loans

Opportunity grants: 4.1, 30.8, 23.2, 41.9

Work-study: 17.3, 27.5, 26.0, 29.2

Defense loans: 22.0, 27.0, 25.0, 26.0

Subsidized loans: 11.0, 12.5, 16.6, 59.8

student's family income:
- $ 0 to 2,999
- 3,000 to 5,999
- 6,000 to 8,999
- 9,000 and up

The charts above show how money is distributed among students from families at various income levels under the four major federal programs to aid persons enrolled in higher education institutions.

Direct federal grants under the educational opportunity grant program and the work-study program have been made to 842,300 students in the current academic year—mostly from low-income families.*

Direct federal 3-per cent loans under the national defense student loan program went to 648,900 students, about evenly divided among income brackets

Finally, 1.25 million students, most of them in the relatively high income brackets, received private loans with federal subsidies on interest in excess of 7 per cent.

SOURCE: Office of Education

year, for students "from low-income families."

The House bill changes the preference in work-study to students "with the greatest financial need"—another reflection of Mrs. Green's concern for the middle-income student. The authorization would rise from $410 million in 1973 to $500 million in 1976.

Loan Programs: Both bills extend the National Defense Student Loan program, which benefits low-income students, and the federally subsidized loan program, which is used primarily by the middle class.

The defense loan program provides direct, 3-percent loans to needy students. It is budgeted at $293 million this year, and will aid an estimated 648,000 students. Under the Senate bill, the authorization for the program in fiscal 1973 would be $375 million; the House provides an open-ended authorization, and the Administration has budgeted $293 million.

In the subsidized program, students receive loans from private lenders and pay them back at 7-percent interest when they finish school. The government pays all the interest while they are in school and the excess over 7 percent when they finish.

Subsidized loans are specifically geared to middle-income students, and 60 percent of the students who received them in 1970-71 came from families with incomes in excess of $9,000.

The volume of subsidized loans has been greater than the volume of grants, work-study and defense loans combined, although the federal costs have been relatively low. In the current fiscal year, a federal budget level of $196 million has generated $1.16 billion in loans to 1,247,000 students, against an authorized ceiling of $1.4 billion.

The subsidized loan program most likely will expand in future years, because both versions of the bill would establish a Student Loan Marketing Association (SLMA, or Sallie Mae), designed to make loan money available to students even during times of tight money.

Sallie Mae is to be a semi-public corporation that raises money by selling obligations and uses it to buy student-loan paper from institutions that lend money to students.

The goal is to let lending institutions turn over considerable amounts of money to students without tying up their cash, and this would make it much easier to reach the authorized loan ceilings.

The Senate bill maintains loan authorizations at $1.4 billion through fiscal 1975, while the House bill expands them gradually to $2.4 billion by 1976.

The Administration had sought to have Sallie Mae finance defense loans as well as subsidized loans, but neither chamber bought this proposal. Mrs. Green protested that it would kill defense loans if Sallie Mae does not work properly.

Both bills raise the annual ceiling on subsidized loans from $1,500 to $2,500.

In addition, the House bill removes the $15,000 adjusted family-income ceiling for students to qualify for subsidized loans and opens them up to anyone who demonstrates need—another break for the middle-income students.

OTHER ISSUES

Institutional aid and student aid are almost sure to be the hottest higher education issues before the conference committee. Behind them is a raft of important but less controversial questions on which the Senate and House versions differ.

Innovation: Foremost among these is the establishment of two new agencies proposed by the Ad-

AN EDUCATIONAL CHRISTMAS TREE:
BUSING, INDIANS AND OTHER RIDERS

On the floor of the House of Representatives in the late night hours last Nov. 4, the debate on the higher education bill was reaching its oratorical climax. Rep. William S. Broomfield, R-Mich., had just offered an amendment that would postpone court-ordered busing of public school children until all appeals are exhausted.

Rep. Hale Boggs, D-La., objected that busing had nothing to do with higher education.

"Is there any higher educational institution in this country that has any busing problems?" Boggs asked. "I do not know of one. . . . This is a higher education bill."

It was not strictly a higher education bill for long. The Broomfield amendment and two others on the same subject were ruled germane, and what had been a higher education bill quickly became a combination higher education and busing bill.

Later that night an amendment to give $1.5 billion to school districts to help them desegregate was tacked on.

The Senate responded by adding antibusing and desegregation aid provisions of its own to the higher education bill. It also attached measures on youth camp safety, Indian education and ethnic studies.

The result is a bill in which some extremely important higher education issues are threatened with obscurity when a conference committee sits down to try to make one bill out of the widely differing Senate and House versions.

Busing: There is little doubt that busing, which has become the most potent domestic political issue of the year, also will be the most heated issue in conference. Conferees will have to reconcile strong House antibusing provisions with much milder Senate language—and House conferees are under orders from the full House not to compromise.

In addition to the Broomfield amendment, the House bill includes the so-called Ashbrook-Green amendment.

Rep. John M. Ashbrook, R-Ohio, added language prohibiting school districts from using federal money for busing. Rep. Edith Green, D-Ore., chairman of the House Special Education Subcommittee, which handled the higher education bill, amended Ashbrook's proposal to include a provision barring the HEW Department and other federal agencies from forcing school districts to bus.

The House passed the antibusing provisions by margins of about 2 to 1.

Mrs. Green said on the House floor that she "would have done

354

almost anything possible" to keep busing separate from higher education. After the two issues were joined, she tried to convince leaders of the Education Committees in both houses to separate them again.

But a House Special Education Subcommittee aide said Sen. Claiborne Fell, D-R.I., chairman of the Senate Education Subcommittee, did not want to face separate conferences on busing and higher education because he will be busy this year fighting an uphill battle to win re-election.

"We weren't able to unscramble the omelette that was scrambled in the House," was Pell's only comment. Any attempt to separate the issues also would have met resistance from House antibusing forces which want to hold the higher education provisions hostage to their strong antibusing language.

The Senate brought the higher education bill back to the floor to add antibusing language of its own, and by just one vote, it rejected amendments that would have met resistance from House antibusing forces which want to hold the higher education provisions hostage to their strong antibusing language.

Then the Senate adopted a milder amendment of Sens. Mike Mansfield, D-Mont., and Hugh Scott, R-Pa., the majority and minority leaders.

The Mansfield-Scott amendment postpones court busing orders involving two or more school districts until appeals are exhausted. It permits federal funds to be used for busing only "on the express written request of appropriate local school officials," and it prohibits HEW and other agencies from requiring school districts to bus "unless constitutionally required."

The delicate task of reconciling the House and Senate language may have been made even more difficult when the full House, on March 8, voted 272 to 139 to instruct its conferees to hold firm on the House's antibusing amendments.

House Minority Leader Gerald R. Ford, R-Mich., pointed out that of the 20 House conferees, only three had supported the Green amendment and four had supported the Ashbrook amendment.

Rep. Carl D. Perkins, D-Ky., chairman of the Education and Labor Committee, argued that the House conferees should have maximum flexibility, but to no avail. Rep. John N. Erlenborn, R-Ill., himself one of the conferees, said:

"I can understand the frustration that the Members of the House must feel when they see conferees from the Committee on Education and Labor being appointed to go to conference, and nine times out of ten they go there already committed to sell out the position of the House."

Desegregation Aid: A second rider that the House attached to the higher education bill is the Nixon Administration's measure to provide $1.5 billion over two years to school districts to help them desegregate.

ministration to promote educational improvement. The Senate bill provides for both:

The National Institute of Education, which is to do research and development at all levels of education. The authorization is $25 million in fiscal 1973.

The National Foundation for Postsecondary Education, which provides money to institutions and even individuals who propose promising experiments in higher education. The 15-member foundation would function much like the National Science Foundation, and would be authorized at $250 million in fiscal 1973.

Pell hopes that the institute and the foundation would join OE in a new Education Division within HEW, which he envisions as the forerunner of a new Cabinet department.

The House bill also includes the institute, which Brademas helped develop, as an agency independent of OE and responsible directly to the HEW secretary. But the House measure does not include the foundation because Democrats on the Education and Labor Committee were united in opposition to the idea.

The Senate and Republicans on the House committee want the foundation because they believe higher education is in sore need of reform. The House Democrats do not question the need for reform, but they believe the foundation is the wrong way to get it.

Mrs. Green said during House hearings that the foundation imposes "the judgment of a small group of people as to what higher education in the years to come should be like in this country."

Dellenback, a leader of the pro-foundation Republicans in the House, called this argument "specious," arguing that the foundation would merely coordinate proposals from the local level.

Brademas said the foundation's role as an innovator should not be isolated from the research and development of the institute. "The educational bureaucracy is big enough already, and if there is to be a foundation for any level of education, preschool education should come first," he said.

Women's Rights: Both bills contain limited provisions against sex discrimination in their admissions policies.

The Senate bill would withhold federal aid to any school from kindergarten to the university level that practice sex discrimination in employment and services.

It forbids sex discrimination in the admissions policies of all public undergraduate schools (with the exception of four women's colleges), all graduate schools and all professional and vocational schools. It exempts military schools and religious institutions such as monasteries.

It also provides a seven-year exemption for public undergraduate schools that switch from single-sex to coeducational.

The House bill was tougher when it was reported from the Education and Labor Committee, but its sex discrimination provisions were substantially amended Nov. 4 on the floor.

The committee bill would have required private as well as public undergraduate schools to adopt a sex-neutral admissions policy, unless their student bodies currently

Rep. Roman C. Pucinski, D-Ill., became the floor manager of this provision after it was amended to include a prohibition against using the $1.5 billion for busing.

"I wanted to pay for quality education, not for tires and gasoline," said Pucinski.

The measure had to be attached to the higher education bill to get it to the House floor, Pucinski added, because the Rules Committee had refused to release it as a separate bill.

Mrs. Green tried unsuccessfully to replace desegregation aid with a formula of unrestricted aid for all school districts.

"I don't want to give the Secretary of HEW a billion and a half dollars to play with," she said in an interview.

The Senate approved a similar measure, but without the anti-busing language. "It's very questionable whether we ought to put so much money into an effort that would be so hobbled at the outset," said Sen. Jacob K. Javits of New York, ranking Republican on the Labor and Public Welfare Committee.

The Senate's measure also reserves 15 percent of the $1.5 billion for bilingual education and educational television.

Senate Riders: The Senate has been busy attaching riders of its own to the higher education bill. They may run into the House's germaneness rule, which says that House conferees may not accept provisions that are not already included in some form in the bill approved by the House.

Indian Education—Sen. Edward M. Kennedy, D-Mass., succeeded in attaching his Indian education bill—a $131-million-a-year item—to the higher education bill.

His bill authorizes federal grants to school districts with heavy concentrations of Indian children. The grants may be big enough to double the amount of money the districts spend on their Indian pupils, and they must be used to improve Indian education.

The House has just begun to hold hearings on Indian education, and House conferees do not want to accept a bill until they have had more time for study.

Youth Camp Safety—The Senate also attached a youth camp safety program authorizing the HEW Secretary to establish national safety criteria for youth camps. Camps must satisfy these criteria to get grants under the bill, which would authorize $3 million a year.

The House Education and Labor Committee reported out a similar provision in the higher education bill, but it was eliminated on the floor Nov. 4.

Ethnic Studies—Another measure included in the Senate bill but defeated on the House floor is one that authorizes $10 million to establish "ethnic heritage studies centers," which would develop curriculum materials on American ethnic groups and train teachers to use them.

Pucinski says he will work to restore the program in conference.

"It's about time we quit teaching our children that America is a melting pot," Pucinski said. "I resent being called a piece of beef being boiled into a common stew."

were 90 percent or more of one sex. Ivy League and other private colleges, which are moving gradually to admit more women, protested that this would force them to radically alter their admissions policies in too short a period of time (seven years under the bill).

The House adopted a floor amendment proposed by Rep. John N. Erlenborn, R-Ill., exempting all undergraduate schools, public and private, from all prohibitions against sex discrimination.

Erlenborn said he feared that federal sex admissions quotas might follow from the committee bill, and that he was trying to "preserve the swiftly eroding rights of the colleges and universities of America."

Mrs. Green denied that there would be admissions quotas. "Any amendment that says we are going to end discrimination and then excepts 95 percent of the institutions in this country is pure fraud," she charged.

Erlenborn's proposal barely passed, 194-189. Of those who will sit on the conference committee, 13 opposed it and only six voted for it.

One effect of Erlenborn's amendment was to mandate that federal funds be withheld from single-sex elementary and high schools. Erlenborn admitted later that this result was unintentional, and he said he would work to eliminate it in conference.

The Senate language, proposed by Sen. Birch Bayh, D-Ind., after

consultation with Mrs. Green, does not include this defect.

Bayh said he was willing to study further the question of sex-neutral admissions policies for private undergraduate schools, which are exempt under this language.

"My view is that many of these exemptions will not be supportable after further study and discussion," he said.

Student Power: The Senate bill grants new rights not only to women but also to students.

By a vote of 66 to 28, the Senate accepted an amendment by Sen. Fred R. Harris, D-Okla., that urges every college and university governing board to include a voting student member selected by the student body.

Harris said a single student member will not revolutionize the performance of his governing board, but he "may bring about better communication and understanding."

He said he would have required student members on governing boards if he thought such a proposal would be accepted.

The House has no corresponding provision, and House conferees may invoke the House germaneness rule, which states that the bill approved in conference may not include provisions not yet considered by the full House.

Job training: The House bill provides $100 million in fiscal 1973 for occupational education, and the Senate bill authorizes $50 million for two-year colleges.

The two items overlap because community colleges provide many of higher education's occupational programs, and they are likely to compete in the conference on the bill.

If they do, Sen. Harrison A. Williams Jr., D-N.J., chairman of the Labor and Public Welfare Committee and author of the community college program, will be matched against Quie, ranking Republican on the House Education and Labor Committee and chief backer of the occupational education title.

Quie said the community college bill does not satisfy him, because more than 100 four-year colleges have occupational education programs leading to less than a bachelor's degree that would not benefit from Williams' bill.

Extensions: Finally, both bills extend a variety of programs, most of them first enacted in the Higher Education Act of 1965 (79 Stat 1219), which now are authorized only through the end of June.

Disadvantaged Aid — Both bills consolidate three programs (Talent Search, Upward Bound and Services for Disadvantaged Students) designed to help disadvantaged students get into college and to offer them counseling and tutoring on campus.

The Senate bill authorizes $100 million a year; the House authorization is open-ended.

Developing Institutions — Both bills extend federal aid to newly developing colleges and universities, many of them black. The Senate bill authorizes $100 million; the House bill, $120 million.

Construction—The Senate bill

authorizes $936 million for construction of undergraduate buildings, $60 million for graduate buildings and $50 million for community colleges. The House authorization is open-ended. Only $78 million was appropriated in fiscal 1972.

Libraries—Both bills extend federal aid for purchase of books and training of librarians. The Senate bill authorizes $130 million; the House version is open-ended.

Community Service—The Senate bill authorizes $60 million to help schools operate programs for their local communities; the House bill is open-ended.

Teacher Training—Both bills extend programs including Teacher Corps to recruit and train teachers. The Senate bill authorizes $600 million; the House authorization is open-ended.

Others—In addition, both bills extend authorizations for Networks for Knowledge, Law School Clinical Experience, equipment grants, cooperative education grants and an assortment of programs to improve graduate and undergraduate education.

OUTLOOK

Beyond November: The programs in the higher-education bill are, however, only a fraction of all federal expenditures for higher education. Other programs whose authorizations already have been extended through fiscal 1973, including the G.I. Bill and research grants, bring federal higher-education spending in fiscal 1972 to $7.4 billion.

Even if authorizations multiply, actual spending may not, at a time when all segments of education are crying out for more federal help and 48 percent of federal aid to education already is spent on higher education.

There is great pressure on Congress to provide more aid for public elementary and secondary education, especially since judges in six states have ruled that the local property tax is an unconstitutional means of paying for public schools.

The Nixon Administration is considering a value-added tax as a possible source of revenue for public education, but few expect such a tax increase in an election year.

Many school superintendents, as well as university presidents, are looking beyond the November elections to a time when they hope the Administration and Congress will be more inclined to find the money they say their schools need.

THE ENVIRONMENT

The past few years have seen a dramatic rise in public interest in the fields of environmental protection and controls. These pressures resulted in the enactment of the National Environmental Policy Act of 1970. Passage of legislation, however, does not by itself either solve the problems or resolve the conflicts that surround the legislative phase of the policy-making process. The following article dealing with efforts to implement environmental protection legislation demonstrates the continuing nature of political struggles once a bill has left the halls of Congress. The battle over how environmental legislation will be implemented is particularly effective in providing insight into the relationship between administrative agencies, congressional committees, regulatory commissions, the courts, pressure groups and private individuals.

White House seeks to restrict scope of environment law

Claude E. Barfield and Richard Corrigan

The Nixon Administration is trying to shorten the long reach of the National Environmental Policy Act.

Signed into law to the accompaniment of a ringing Presidential declaration just two years ago, the act has had impact far beyond what anyone then anticipated.

Through a series of court cases pressed by lawyers in the environmental movement, the law has stymied development projects from the Arctic Coast of Alaska to the Gulf of Mexico.

And now it has been employed to upset the Administration's own prized pollution-control program, an elaborate system requiring federal permits for industrial discharges into the nation's waters.

Banking on a questionable interpretation of the act's legislative history, the Administration had assumed that the permit program would be exempt from NEPA's provisions.

The Administration's chief authority in arriving at this interpretation was none other than Sen. Edmund S. Muskie, D-Maine, author of many anti-pollution bills.

Now, stung by a U.S. District Court decision that has negated the permit system, the Administration has three choices. It can prepare many thousands of detailed environmental-impact statements, try to overturn the court ruling on appeal or gain legislative relief.

The Administration views the first choice as an unacceptable burden on the bureaucracy, the second as a course it is pursuing

---

NEPA's BROAD MANDATE

The purposes of this Act are: To declare a national policy which will encourage productive and enjoyable harmony between man and his environment; to promote efforts which will prevent or eliminate damage to the environment and biosphere and stimulate the health and welfare of man; to enrich the understanding of the ecological systems and natural resources important to the Nation; and to establish a Council on Environmental Policy.

National Environmental Policy Act, 83 Stat 852, Jan. 1, 1970

---

with scant optimism and the third as a political nightmare.

Unsigned Letter: The Administration's first stab at suggesting legislative relief already has backfired in an embarrassing fashion following a quirky chain of events.

A nine-page, singled-spaced letter was carried to Capitol Hill on Feb. 1 bearing the printed names of Russell E. Train, chairman of the White House Council on Environmental Quality, and Administrator William D. Ruckelshaus of the Environmental Protection Agency. The letter described the problems caused by the court decision and suggested ways of resolving the situation; it was appended with several pages of proposed statutory changes.

But Ruckelshaus, whose agency administers most federal pollution-control programs, had never signed or even seen the letter, did not subscribe to its recommendations and had previously objected to the changes that the letter outlined. Nor had any other EPA

official approved the proposed changes.

Moreover, the staff of the House Public Works Committee—the committee to which the letter was primarily addressed—recoiled at the Administration's proposals.

Besides being asked to amend a law which carries an aura of environmental cleanliness, the committee—which is now grappling with a highly controversial omnibus water-pollution bill—was being asked to amend legislation that had originated in another committee.

But before CEQ general counsel Timothy B. Atkeson could retrieve copies of the letter—drafted after a meeting at which EPA was not represented—its supposedly confidential contents were circulating on Capitol Hill.

"It's about as confidential as me standing on second base at RFK Stadium and doing a jig," said Richard J. Sullivan, chief counsel of the House Public Works Committee.

Reps. John D. Dingell, D-

Mich., and Henry S. Reuss, D-Wis., both of whom have been deeply involved in NEPA's development, promptly assailed the Administration for tampering with the act.

Train, who said he signed the letter in the mistaken belief that Ruckelshaus concurred in its recommendations, said there was no intention to "gut" the act.

"It never entered my head, and so far as I know it was never in anybody's head around here," he said.

"We were not trying to gut NEPA," said Richard Fairbanks, the White House aide who chaired the meeting at which the substance of the letter was agreed upon. "If we were going to gut NEPA we would never have done this in so heavy-handed a way."

Ruckelshaus said of the letter, "That is not the Administration's official position."

But, as talks between Administration and congressional aides continue, the Administration still is seeking legislative relief of a yet-to-be-defined form.

"Where are we?" Ruckelshaus said. "I don't know."

Train said, "I think what we need to know is what the hell the Congress wants done in this area."

Two-edged Sword: Meanwhile, some industrial interests are starting to turn the National Environmental Policy Act on Ruckelshaus' agency by demanding that EPA analyze the impact of its own actions to control corporate pollution.

And if that effort succeeds, said John R. Quarles Jr., EPA's top legal officer, "it would substantially slow down the establishment of stringent requirements for environmental protection."

The potential use of NEPA as a two-edged sword—to be used by industrial as well as environmental interests—is cited by Administration officials as justification for clarifying NEPA's intent.

"I told Dingell that he and we are allies in keeping NEPA viable," said Atkeson of CEQ. "We may in the long run have a result which neither of us will welcome."

But Dingell does not seem impressed by arguments that if NEPA is not amended now it will come under heavy attack or misuse in the future.

ADMINISTRATION UNDER FIRE

"I have a feeling that the Administration wants very much to get the NEPA statements on environmental regulatory actions very restricted," Dingell said.

"The minute you take away" the NEPA requirements, he said, "you make it possible for them to close doors and make political decisions and it's almost impossible to catch the bastards."

Environmental Groups — Banded together in an ad hoc "Save NEPA" coalition—express fears that an effort is under way to open up the act to substantial changes.

They question whether any federal agency should be exempted from the requirements of NEPA—even if that agency's function is solely to protect the environment. And they also say the Administration's proposal was so loosely worded that it could result in wholesale exemptions throughout the federal bureaucracy.

A First Retreat?: Any successful attempt to roll back portions of NEPA would constitute the first significant reversal of the trend to stronger and stronger environmental legislation. It can be argued that congressional approval of NEPA in late 1969 was the opening salvo in a barrage of strong anti-pollution actions the federal government has undertaken during the Nixon Administration. Since then, EPA has been established under a reorganization plan assented to by Congress, a tough new air-pollution law has been enacted and a stringent water-quality bill has come close to enactment.

One attempt to amend the act seemed certain to succeed. Both the House and the Senate versions of the massive 1972 water quality bill (S 2770)—which still was in conference at the end of June—contain a provision that would relieve the Atomic Energy Commission of all NEPA requirements insofar as the water-pollution effects of nuclear power plants are concerned. The amendment was originally accepted by Muskie, who chairs the Air and Water Pollution Subcommittee of the Senate Public Works Committee.

Moreover, even some of the act's strongest defenders in Congress, notably including Dingell, have come to the view that limited exemptions to NEPA must be granted in emergency situations, in order to stave off broader attempts to change the law. Thus in March, two Administration-supported bills were introduced that would: exempt temporarily the water pollution permit program from NEPA's requirements; and give the

362 Atomic Energy Commission temporary authority to issue interim operating licenses to about a dozen nuclear power plants, to meet anticipated power demand in the summer of 1972 and the winter of 1972-73, before these plants had fully met the requirements of NEPA.

These measures had not been enacted as of the end of June, although the AEC had sought and received legislative relief from requirements of other laws that had impeded interim licensing of the nuclear plants.

EXPANSION OF NEPA

President Nixon signed the National Environmental Policy Act on New Year's Day of 1970 and, from the Western White House at San Clemente, Calif., declared in a statement that the 1970s "absolutely must be the years when America pays its debt to the past by reclaiming the purity of its air, its waters and our living environment. It is literally now or never."

The legislation, which laid out a general policy promoting environmental enhancement and authorized the formation of CEQ, did not appear to pack much power.

But the act contained a sleeper known as Section 102.

Section 102 has proved to be a powerful weapon for environmental attorneys.

Among the public and private projects delayed thus far by Section 102 are: the trans-Alaska pipeline, a $2-billion-plus joint venture of leading oil companies; the Tennessee-Tombigbee waterway, a massive navigation development of the Army Corps of Engineers;

offshore oil and natural gas leasing in the Gulf of Mexico expected to draw $400 million in bids; construction and operation permits for many nuclear-powered generating stations, and the Cross-Florida Barge Canal, first halted by a federal court and then cancelled by order of President Nixon.

Section 102: This section says that "all agencies of the federal government" shall, "to the fullest extent possible," include "in every recommendation or report on proposals for legislation and other major federal actions significantly affecting the quality of the human environment," a "detailed statement" on environmental impact.

The statement is supposed to deal with "any adverse environmental effects which cannot be avoided should the project be implemented," "alternatives to the proposed action" and other such factors.

CEQ's guidelines say that the impact statements, in dealing with alternative options to proposed actions, should include "a rigorous exploration and objective evaluation of alternative actions ... in order not to foreclose prematurely options which might have less detrimental effects."

Legislative History: The provision for environmental-impact statements was never the subject of public hearings.

The House bill, in fact, did not include any such provision. HR 12549, Dingell's bill, merely called for the formation of a Council on Environmental Quality and the issuance of an annual report on the state of the environment.

Jackson's bill, S 1075, a product of the Senate Interior and Insular

Affairs Committee, did not include the environmental-impact provision at the time that the one public hearing on the bill was held.

But on that day—April 16, 1969—Committee Chairman Jackson and witness Lynton K. Caldwell, professor of government at the University of Indiana and a consultant to the committee, discussed the merits of an "action-forcing" provision that would help fulfill the purpose of the legislation.

At Jackson's direction, committee counsel William J. Van Ness Jr. and staff member Daniel A. Dreyfus drafted the first version of Section 102.

"We came away from that hearing with the problem of figuring out a mechanism that would get everybody's attention," said Dreyfus.

Noting the current nationwide effect of the law, he said, "I guess we succeeded."

Dreyfus said "there wasn't much wrangling in the committee" over the proposed new section and that Jackson and the staff tried without success to generate public interest in the amendment.

"We tried our damndest to get people's attention, but everybody thought it was rhetorical and meaningless," he said. "There was a gross lack of appreciation for the significance of that language."

Senate Passage—Jackson introduced amendments to the bill, including the new section. The committee met in executive session on June 18 and ordered the measure reported.

The Nixon Administration, in comments on the bill, voiced no objections to the substance of Section 102—while opposing formation of CEQ.

On July 10, Jackson brought the bill to the floor under a unanimous-consent procedure and it was approved by voice vote without extended debate and with few Senators on the floor.

House Action—In the House, Dingell's bill had been ordered reported by a unanimous vote of the Merchant Marine and Fisheries Committee. It reached the floor on Sept. 23. An effort was made to add Section 102 in a floor amendment but it was blocked by a point of order raised by House Interior Committee Chairman Wayne N. Aspinall, D-Colo.

The House then passed the Dingell bill by a roll-call vote of 372 to 15.

Senate Compromise—Muskie was sponsoring a bill (S 7) somewhat comparable to Jackson's, and after the Jackson bill passed the Senate, he and the staff of his subcommittee became concerned about the language of Section 102 and other provisions.

Muskie viewed the Jackson bill as potentially granting governmental agencies that might degrade the environment—the dam-building Bureau of Reclamation, for example—the right to justify their own actions, by issuing their own "findings" on environmental impact.

The subcommittee staff and the staff of Jackson's committee worked on language intended to resolve this question and other overlapping aspects of both bills.

On Oct. 8 during Senate consideration of Muskie's bill, the Environmental Quality Improvement Act, a compromise agreement, was made public.

Under the compromise, federal agencies would be required under the Jackson bill to prepare a statement—not a "finding"—on the environmental impact of proposed actions, and to consult with federal, state and local agencies with relevant environmental responsibilities.

Conference Report—After three meetings of a conference committee, agreement was reached on the final form of NEPA. The conference report (HRept 91-765) was filed Dec. 17.

On Dec. 20, when the Senate took up the conference report, Jackson hailed the legislation as "the most important and far-reaching environmental and conservation measure ever enacted by the Congress."

Muskie had not been a member of the conference committee on the bill, but during Senate discussion of the report he made remarks upon which the Administration now leans heavily in its interpretation of the intent of Congress in passing NEPA.

Muskie spoke again of his concern that the original legislation might have impinged upon the operations of existing pollution-control agencies, and he said that documents inserted into the *Congressional Record* by Jackson made clear that "the agencies having authority in the environmental improvement field will continue to operate under their legislative mandates as previously established, and that those legislative mandates are not changed in any way by Section 102."

Muskie said further, in response to a question from Sen. J. Caleb Boggs, R-Del., ranking minority

member of the Muskie subcommittee, that Section 102 was designed to "apply strong pressures on those agencies that have an impact on the environment—the Bureau of Public Roads, for example, the Atomic Energy Commission, and others . . . (but) with regard to the environmental improvement agencies such as the Federal Water Improvement (*sic*) Administration and the Air Quality Administration (*sic*), it is clearly understood that those agencies will operate on the basis of the legislative charter that has been created and is not modified in any way by S 1075."

(The Federal Water Quality Administration and the National Air Pollution Control Administration, later brought into the new EPA, were then within the Departments of the Interior and Health, Education and Welfare, respectively.)

The Senate then adopted the conference report by voice vote.

On Dec. 22, the House took up the conference report. Dingell, as manager of the bill, inserted a statement that Section 102 was not designed to "result in any change in the manner in which (environmental-control agencies) carry out their environmental protection authority."

Aspinall had been a member of the conference committee, and during meetings of the group had evidenced concern about Section 102's effect on agency programs. He had inserted language designed to refine the law's scope, according to Dreyfus of the Senate committee staff. "Aspinall was the first guy I saw who appreciated the significance of that language, and he didn't like it," Dreyfus said.

In light of later developments in implementation of NEPA, Aspinall's concern was well-founded, but his additions in conference were insufficient to stop the consequences which had concerned him.

Harsha's Warning—One House Member who predicted the great impact that Section 102 might have was Rep. William H. Harsha, R-Ohio.

During debate on the conference report, Harsha, ranking minority member of the Public Works Committee, sounded a first public warning of what the law might mean.

Harsha, while clearly worried about such parochial questions as congressional committee jurisdiction, also said:

"The impact of S 1075, if it becomes law, I am convinced would be so wide-sweeping as to involve every branch of the government, every committee of Congress, every agency, and every program of the nation. This is such an important matter that I am convinced that we here should consider it very, very carefully and make a clear record as to exactly the direction in which we wish the various elements of our government to move.

"I regret that so important a matter is being handled in so light a manner. I realize the Members' desire to adjourn for Christmas. . . ."

Shortly after, the House approved the conference report by voice vote.

The legislation then was sent to San Clemente for presidential signature.

Court Actions: In its brief history, the National Environmental Policy Act has produced several significant court decisions.

Court interpretations of the statute have extended its meaning "beyond anybody's wildest dreams," said Dreyfus of the Senate interior committee staff, who helped draft Section 102.

"The trouble is," said Dreyfus, "when you say, 'What was the congressional intent?', no one of the 535 Members of Congress has more right than any other to say what it meant."

Dreyfus said that since he has no vote, his opinion counts for even less. But he said he had expected the environmental-impact statements of federal agencies to be brief, general statements averaging about two pages in length.

According to Rep. Nicholas J. Begich, D-Alaska, who has monitored the Department of the Interior's preparation of a final impact statement for the Alaska pipeline, the printing of documents for the statement kept two presses running round the clock for a week. The 4,000-page statement was finally issued on March 20, in nine volumes weighing 25 pounds.

AEC Cases—In a landmark case challenging construction of an atomic power plant at Calvert Cliffs, Md.—*Calvert Cliffs Coordinating Committee, et al v. U.S. Atomic Energy Commission, et al*—the U.S. Circuit Court of Appeals for the District of Columbia on July 23, 1971, delivered a blistering rebuke to the AEC, saying it had made a "mockery" of the act.

Judge J. Skelly Wright, who wrote the court's opinion, ordered drastic changes in the AEC's licensing process. One of the most far-reaching orders directed the agency to assess independently all relevant environmental factors even if other state or federal agencies already had certified that a nuclear facility met existing state or federal standards. In practical, administrative terms, the most important new assessment forced upon the commission concerned water-quality standards and thermal pollution.

Wright ruled that the AEC's decision to defer to other state or federal agencies on water-quality issues "is in fundamental conflict with the basic purpose of the act."

"NEPA mandates a case-by-case balancing judgment on the part of federal agencies. In each individual case, the particular economic and technical benefits of planned action must be assessed and then weighed against environmental costs . . . . Certification by another agency that its own environmental standards are satisfied involves an entirely different kind of judgment. Such agencies, without over-all responsibility for the particular federal action in question, attend to only one aspect of the problem. . . .

"The Water Quality Improvement Act of 1970 (84 Stat 91) does not preclude the commission from demanding water-pollution controls from its licensees which are *more strict* than those demanded by the applicable water-quality standards of the certifying agency."

The AEC had argued that it did not have to duplicate the independent reviews of water-quality factors by other agencies. But after the Calvert Cliffs decision it undertook to review for a second time some 63 licensing applications involving 106 nuclear power reactors which are slated to generate more than one-quarter of the nation's electricity. The review has caused substantial delays in the anticipated start-up schedules of the generating plants.

In an effort to get some of the generating capacity on line, the AEC in the fall began issuing licenses allowing plants completed or nearing completion (of which there are about a dozen) to operate on a partial-capacity basis—thus reducing the environmental impact of the plants—pending completion of full NEPA reviews.

But that effort was set back on Dec. 14, when the U.S. District Court for the District of Columbia ruled, in the case of *Izaak Walton League v. Schlesinger* that no partial-power license could be issued without a full environmental impact statement. The decision has become known as the Quad Cities case, after the name of a power generating station built by Commonwealth Edison Co. and Iowa-Illinois Gas & Electric Co. in Illinois.

Permit Program Case—Perhaps the most resounding decision so far, at least in its impact on the Nixon Administration, was handed down last Dec. 21 by Judge Aubrey E. Robinson Jr. of the U.S. District Court for the District of Columbia.

In the case of *Kalur v. Resor,* Judge Robinson upset the one antipollution program that had been put together not by the Democratic-controlled Congress but by the Nixon Administration itself.

The Administration had been prodded by several Members of Congress, most notably Reuss, to activate the long-dormant 1899 Refuse Act (33 USC 407). But the program nevertheless was the product of a Presidential order, not a congressional directive.

The suit is named for Jerome S. Kalur, a Cleveland attorney and Sierra Club member who challenged the government's right to issue permits for the dumping of chemical companies' pollutants into the nearby Grand River, where Kalur goes canoeing.

In the Kalur decision, Judge Robinson said the Refuse Act absolutely prohibits the dumping of refuse into non-navigable waters, and that no permits can be issued for dumping in those waters. Robinson held that dumping in navigable waters is allowed under the act if a permit is issued, but that permits would have to be accompanied by environmental-impact statements.

"There can be no remorse for those companies who have since 1899 violated the criminal law and who now find themselves in the position of being unable to comply with the law," the decision said of firms discharging wastes into non-navigable waters.

The decision prohibited the government from issuing permits "that shield polluters and potential polluters where Congress has specifically prohibited such activity."

Robinson found no merit in the government's claim that environmental-impact statements should not be required for the issuance of pollution control permits covering navigable waters, saying the Corps of Engineers must conduct the obligatory (Section 102) analysis under the prescribed procedures of NEPA.

Offshore Leasing—Another recent case of major dimensions involved the Administration's plan to accelerate leasing for offshore oil and gas tracts in the Gulf of Mexico.

In the case of *Natural Resources Defense Council, Inc., v. Morton,* the U.S. Court of Appeals for the District of Columbia ruled Jan. 13 that federal agencies, in dealing with alternative courses of action, must in some instances consider alternatives outside their immediate jurisdiction, such as alternatives that would require new legislation, and the environmental effects of these options.

"The impact statement is not only for the exposition of the thinking of the agency," the court said, "but also for the guidance of these ultimate decision-makers (Congress and the President), and must provide them with the environmental effects of both the proposal and the alternatives, for their consideration along with the various other elements of the public interest."

The Circuit Court decision upheld a ruling by the U.S. District Court for the District of Columbia that caused cancellation of the leasing—a program for which the Nixon Administration already had budgeted some $400 million in fiscal 1972 revenue from anticipated bids.

Bureaucratic Complaints: Court interpretations of NEPA have necessitated an unexpected degree of effort throughout the federal bureaucracy to gain compliance with the act.

Offices, some with no previous interest in environmental affairs—including such regulatory bodies

MAJOR COURT DECISIONS UNDER ENVIRONMENTAL POLICY ACT

The National Environmental Policy Act has proved to be a most effective tool for lawyers seeking to hold up development projects they believe would harm the environment.

Since its enactment on Jan. 1, 1970, the act has been the subject of 15 decisions by the U.S. Courts of Appeals, 14 opinions by U.S. District Courts and three discussions in dissenting opinions by members of the Supreme Court.

The law does not allow a project to be attacked on its substantive merits or demerits. Nonetheless, many projects—from highways to dams to the mammoth trans-Alaska pipeline—have encountered long delays because the federal agencies sponsoring them have failed to comply with the procedural requirements of the act.

The chief requirement, under Section 102 of NEPA, is to file an extensive statement weighing the environmental impact of proposed projects and the alternatives that might be considered. Courts have interpreted this provision very stringently, as demonstrated in the following sampling of major cases:

Calvert Cliffs (7-23-71): In *Calvert Cliffs' Coordinating Committee v. Atomic Energy Commission,* the U.S. Circuit Court of Appeals for the District of Columbia found the AEC's standards for complying with NEPA in the licensing of nuclear power plants invalid for the following reasons: 1) In cases where construction permits had been issued prior to the effective date of NEPA, AEC failed to provide environmental re-

view; 2) hearing boards to weigh environmental factors were not required by AEC unless regulatory staff or outside parties raised the issue; 3) in all cases where the date of hearings preceded March 4, 1971, AEC failed to include nonradiological environmental issues; 4) AEC accepted the state of Maryland's certification that the plant complied with water-quality standards and did not conduct its own assessment of the water-quality impact as required by NEPA. The court ordered revisions in AEC licensing procedures.

Gillham Dam (7-19-71): The Environmental Defense Fund Inc. and several other environmental groups (Ozark Society Inc., Arkansas Audubon Society Inc. and Arkansas Ecology Center) obtained a permanent injunction against further construction of the Gillham Dam across Arkansas' Cossatot River until the Army Corps of Engineers could meet the requirements of NEPA. Even though two environmental-impact statements had been submitted by the corps, the U.S. District Court for the Eastern District of Arkansas ruled the statements "legally inadequate" and said NEPA must be implemented even though the dam was authorized in 1958.

Cross-Florida Barge Canal (1-27-71): In a similar case involving another Corps of Engineers project, the U.S. District Court for the District of Columbia granted a preliminary injunction against further construction of the Cross-Florida Barge Canal. The court ruled in behalf of the Environmen-

tal Defense Fund that the law's requirements were applicable to the project even though it was begun before Jan. 1, 1970, the effective date of NEPA.

Tennessee-Tombigbee (9-21-71): In *Environmental Defense Fund v. Corps of Engineers,* the U.S. District Court for the District of Columbia found that the corps had shown in the "planning, design and development" of the waterway insufficient compliance with NEPA. The court temporarily enjoined further construction of the waterway.

Quad Cities Reactor (12-13-71): The Izaak Walton League of America obtained a preliminary injunction against AEC's issuance of a partial operating license for the Quad Cities nuclear power station at Cordova, Ill., before final NEPA review of the application for a full operating license was completed. The U.S. District Court for the District of Columbia found that issuance of the partial license constituted "final agency action" requiring compliance with Section 102 of NEPA.

Refuse Act (12-21-71): In the case of *Kalur v. Resor,* two citizens, Jerome S. Kalur and Donald W. Large, challenged the authority of Stanley R. Resor, Secretary of the Army, William D. Ruckelshaus, Administrator of EPA and Lt. General Frederick J. Clarke, Chief of the Corps of Engineers in the issuance of permits under the 1899 Refuse Act for discharges into nonnavigable waters. Additionally, the plaintiffs alleged that the corps' failure to require environmental impact statements rendered the permit program invalid. The U.S. District Court for the District of Columbia upheld Kalur's standing and enjoined further issuance of permits.

Interstate Highway (11-22-71):
Morningside-Lenox Park Association, a civic organization, obtained a preliminary injunction against further construction of Interstate 485, a federally funded highway through the city of Atlanta. The U.S. District Court for the Northern District of Georgia ruled that implementation of NEPA's Section 102 was required even though the location of the highway was approved prior to Jan. 1, 1970.

Offshore Leasing (12-16-71):
Three conservation groups (Natural Resources Defense Council Inc., Friends of the Earth and the Sierra Club) obtained a preliminary injunction against the proposed sale of oil and gas leases off the eastern Louisiana coast. The U.S. District Court for the District of Columbia held that the Interior Department failed to present detailed alternatives to the lease sales as required by Section 102.

The U.S. Circuit Court of Appeals for the District of Columbia upheld the lower court decision on Jan. 13, 1972.

Trans-Alaska Pipeline (4-23-70):
In *Wilderness Society v. Morton,* the U.S. District Court for the District of Columbia enjoined the Secretary of the Interior from issuing a road permit to cross public lands in Alaska from Prudhoe Bay to the Yukon River. The court ruled in favor of the three environmental groups (Wilderness Society, Friends of the Earth and Environmental Defense Fund) by finding that the department did not comply with Section 102 because it failed to prepare an environmental impact statement concerning both the road and the associated pipeline project.

---

as the Securities and Exchange Commission and the Interstate Commerce Commission—have had to restructure their operations to satisfy both the courts and the CEQ guidelines.

The bureaucracy's response has not always been wholehearted.

EPA Administrator Ruckelshaus said: "I don't think the top agency people are reacting that much against NEPA. I find that their attitude is generally quite positive. The real difficulty is with the middle-level bureaucrats—the twenty-year men who have been building dams all their lives, for instance. They have a kind of religious fervor about the development mission of their agencies—and suddenly someone has started questioning their very life work. Naturally they resent the exercise of having to explain and defend the basis of their careers."

Ellis L. Armstrong, commissioner of the Interior Department's Bureau of Reclamation, said in a speech last June 16 to the American Waterworks Association in Denver, "I somehow get the feeling that the Environmental Protection (*sic*) Act is being utilized in some quarters to build up a curtain of blind and unthinking opposition which could swamp the agencies charged with responsibility for specific functions in natural resources management and bring orderly programs to a halt.

"Certainly this negativism bears little relationship to a key phrase in the National Environmental Protection Act in which Congress declares that 'it is the continuing policy of the government . . . to create and maintain conditions under which man and nature can exist in productive harmony.'"

In a speech to the National Petroleum Council on Feb. 10, Secretary of Interior Rogers C. B. Morton said, "I am deeply—bitterly—disappointed" by the court decisions in the Gulf of Mexico leasing case.

"I am concerned," Morton told his audience of top executives from the energy industry, "that the legislative and management responsibilities of the Congress and of the executive branch of our government are being transferred to the judiciary, where the criteria and understanding prerequisite for fundamental resource decisions do not exist.

"We are in the testing phase of the National Environmental Policy Act. The intent of the law is being established over specific issues."

Morton said the department would try to comply with court rulings on NEPA, which he said "will delay every action we have programmed for developing our natural resources."

The decisions were cited by the department as necessitating at least two more months of work on the pending Alaska pipeline im-

368 pact statement.

At a Feb. 15 press conference, Morton said he hopes to see NEPA's scope defined by the Supreme Court and suggested that the Alaska pipeline suit could be the test case.

BAKER AMENDMENT

The vehicle first seized upon by the Administration in its attempt to amend NEPA was the pending water-quality legislation, which passed the Senate in November and the House in late March.

The Feb. 1 letter bearing the names of Ruckelshaus and Train asked for attachment of an amendment to the water bill that would have a broad effect on the implementation of NEPA by a number of federal agencies. While that request was doomed to failure, the bill already contained a Senate amendment that would lighten the AEC's workload in considering water-quality effects of nuclear power plants.

Joint Atomic Energy Committee: The AEC has suffered more than any other agency from the impact of judicial decisions on NEPA, and some members of the Joint Atomic Energy Committee are fearful that, without relief, the AEC's licensing process for nuclear power plants would grind to a halt.

Holifield—One of those most deeply disturbed is Rep. Chet Holifield, D-Calif., former chairman (1961-70) of the committee and still its most influential single member.

Holifield, who is now chairman of the Government Operations Committee, says that the "laudable purposes of NEPA have been thwarted by unreasonable interpretations of it by the courts and by agency overreaction to these interpretations." The result, he says, has been creation of "a procedural paradise" for "intervenors who wish to delay progress in the name of environmental protection."

Holifield and other joint committee members have pressed for an amendment to the water-quality bill that would relieve the AEC of the responsibility for independently establishing water-quality standards for nuclear power plants.

Baker: Sen. Howard H. Baker Jr., R-Tenn., a member of both the Joint Atomic Energy Committee and the Senate Public Works Committee, took the lead in persuading Muskie to accept an amendment spelling out the relationship between NEPA and the water-quality act.

Explaining the history of his amendment, Baker said in an interview: "There's no secret about the origin of this. After the Calvert Cliffs decision, several joint committee members approached me about the problem and then I began discussing possible wording with the joint committee staff."

Muskie and the staff of his Air and Water Pollution Subcommittee initially were reluctant to attack the difficult NEPA problem in a water-quality bill already loaded with complicated provisions.

Baker continued to press the issue, however, and Muskie finally agreed to the addition of a NEPA amendment to the Senate bill. The agreement was consummated in an exchange of letters between the two Senators in late October.

On Nov. 2, just before the bill passed the Senate, Baker introduced and Muskie accepted an amendment providing that NEPA requirements as to water-quality considerations would be satisfied by certification under the existing Refuse Act permit system or under the new water-quality permit system that Congress is creating this year. The AEC would benefit most from the amendment, but other agencies also would be affected.

Floor Statement—However, to the consternation of some joint committee members and staff, Baker simultaneously delivered a floor statement that seemed to them to wipe out much of the relief they thought his amendment afforded.

He strongly endorsed that portion of Judge Wright's decision which mandated a "case-by-case balancing judgment on the part of federal agencies in each individual case," stating that "my amendment should not in any way be construed to mean that water-quality considerations do not play a role in such a 'balancing judgment.'"

"On the contrary," he continued, "where pertinent, water-quality considerations must be considered by any agency when it decides, under the NEPA mandate, whether it is in the public interest to grant a license or permit and, if so, under what conditions and stipulations."

Baker Explanation—Baker explains the intent of his amendment this way: "In the first place as a matter of sound administrative policy, I think that the EPA or the state water-quality agencies—where the EPA has okayed their programs—should have the sole authority to make determinations on water-quality standards.

"What I wanted to end was the responsibility of the AEC to build up a separate expertise in the water-quality field that would go behind EPA or state agency and duplicate their decision-making process on water-quality considerations.

"However, I did not intend to overturn the Calvert Cliffs decision so far as the final NEPA balancing by the AEC on nuclear power plants was concerned—and frankly, I don't think the amendment would have passed the Senate had the wording been construed that way."

Supporters: Some of those supporting Baker's amendment do not agree with the Senator's own interpretation of his handiwork.

Holifield—Rep. Holifield believes that on water-quality issues certification by EPA or a state agency should be "dispositive"—that is, water-quality considerations should not be factored into the AEC's final balancing of environmental costs and benefits because they have already been analyzed by EPA or the state agency.

Under this interpretation, according to a member of the Joint Atomic Energy Committee staff, water-quality standards would become a "constant" in the final balancing.

It is Holifield's view that the Baker amendment—in contradiction to the Baker floor statement—accomplishes this purpose. However, because he is worried that Baker's floor interpretation might

prevail in future court cases, Holifield twice wrote to Rep. John A. Blatnik, D-Minn., chairman of the House Public Works Committee to express his concern. In a Jan. 13 letter, he suggested wording for the Public Works Committee's report to unequivocally back his interpretation of the amendment. But the report, issued in mid-March, merely quoted Baker's floor statement.

AEC—The AEC commissioners were not of one mind on the Baker amendment.

One point of division involved the question of whether the AEC should actively seek legislative relief from the Calvert Cliffs decision. Officially, the commission has never asked Congress to act, and William O. Doub, an AEC commissioner, says that "until the Quad Cities decision I thought that we could live with the additional workload the court had imposed; and I still think that if we can get around that roadblock things should begin to move more smoothly over the next few months."

Commissioner James T. Ramey, on the other hand, said he has feared from the outset that legislative relief from Calvert Cliffs would be needed if the AEC was to keep its licensing process for nuclear power plants functioning efficiently.

A second point of division involves the meaning of the amendment. Ramey agrees with Holifield's reading, and this position also was adopted by the AEC as a whole in a December memorandum to the Office of Management and Budget.

But during Jan. 26 hearings be-

fore the joint committee, AEC Chairman James R. Schlesinger suddenly announced that he supported Baker's own interpretation of his amendment—at which point Ramey interrupted to point out to the chairman that his remarks were at variance with the AEC's statement to OMB. The commission subsequently took a position close to Baker's.

Utilities—The electric utility industry "has been following the progress of the Baker amendment quite closely," says David R. Toll, general counsel of the National Association of Electric Companies, lobbying arm of the industry.

"We had originally thought that it meant the AEC would go back to the pre-Calvert Cliffs situation and get out of the water-quality evaluation business entirely," he said, "but now we're not so certain."

Power industry lobbyists, Toll said, also had hoped that the amendment foreclosed not only the NEPA balancing for water quality but also all AEC cost/benefit obligations under the act.

The AEC and the utilities have been at odds on the nature and contents of the NEPA statements required on nuclear power plants. At a Dec. 9 meeting called to elicit comments on the commission's draft guidelines for utility cost/benefit analyses, utility and nuclear equipment manufacturing representatives were severely critical.

James Wright, head of the Westinghouse Electric Corp.'s division of environmental systems, labeled the draft guidelines a "gross combination of arithmetic and science fiction" and the requirements for thermal-pollution impact analysis "balderdash, hogwash and unsupportable by any piece of scientific evidence that has been gathered."

Environmentalists: At House Public Works Committee hearings in December, the National Wildlife Federation and the Sierra Club strongly criticized the Baker amendment.

Louis S. Clapper, director of conservation for the Wildlife Federation, told the House committee that the Baker amendment "mocks" NEPA, which he said "requires a single federal agency to weigh the cost of the entire facility against its benefits. Air pollution, water quality, aesthetics, land-use preemption are all figured in the cost side; the benefits on the other. But what about water-quality costs now? Under this section they are factored out! Under this section they *never* come into the balance."

The foremost legal expert on NEPA and the AEC licensing procedure is Anthony Z. Roisman, the 32-year-old environmental lawyer who wrote the brief for the plaintiffs in the Calvert Cliffs case.

In explaining why he thought both Muskie and Baker "were sitting on a time bomb" with the Baker amendment, Roisman said: "I know this hasn't got much attention and Congressmen haven't received any mail. But if this amendment passes, there are citizens groups and environmental organizations all over the country who are going to wake up to the fact that just when they had won the right to a full environmental hearing on nuclear power plants, Congress suddenly has taken the guts out of the AEC licensing hearings.

"And when they start looking for culprits, the evidence will point directly to Muskie and Baker.

"The fact is that the Baker amendment subverts the clear purpose of NEPA which was to vest in the mission agency the ultimate power to make decisions and the obligation to look for every possible way to minimize the environmental impact."

Although the House Public Works Committee and the full House approved the Baker amendment without change, Roisman has worked hard to secure modifications in the provisions during the long House-Senate conference on the water bill. Roisman's most important objective has been to provide procedural safeguards protecting the rights of intervenors in AEC licensing hearings.

"The most vital element" during these proceedings "is the right to cross-examine the experts and challenge hypotheses and conclusions," Roisman said. "Under the Baker amendment, we would lose this right for water-quality considerations in the hearings—we would just have to accept water-quality certification as given. ... At a minimum, intervenors ought to retain the right to introduce new evidence on the thermal pollution where such evidence was not considered by EPA or the state certifying agency."

Roisman's suggestions received a cool reception from the staff of the Senate Air and Water Pollution Subcommittee, but found sympathy from Baker, who said that he would "welcome any suggestions for procedural amendment or clarifications that will insure more orderly and complete hearings and that will allow both environmentalists and industry representatives full access to the record of the process by which final decisions are made. The final NEPA balancing on nuclear power plants should encompass all relevant factors and information."

QUAD CITIES BILLS

The concern about procedural safeguards expressed by Roisman and Baker was to surface more dramatically in connection with legislation sought by the AEC to relieve it of the effects of the Quad Cities case—the decision that had stymied the commission's plans to grant interim licenses to about a dozen atomic generating stations. Again, Baker played a key role.

By early March, the AEC had concluded that two forms of legislative relief were needed to avert power shortages it claimed could result if the dozen nuclear plants did not start up this year.

The first bill proposed by the commission was to amend the basic AEC authorizing legislation, the Atomic Energy Act of 1954 (68 Stat 919), so as to specifically provide that interim operating licenses could be granted. No such authority was conferred by the existing law, and furthermore, the AEC wanted to be relieved of some of the red tape that existing law imposed upon the granting of any operating license. This legislation, first introduced by members of the Joint Atomic Energy Commission in March, was quickly passed and was signed into law on June 2 (HR 14655, 86 Stat 191). But its meaning is still much in dispute.

The second bill backed by the

AEC would relieve it of the need to file Section 102 statements on interim licenses. Although the Quad Cities case had been settled out of court, and no final ruling on the NEPA issue was handed down, the commission felt that the legislation was needed in case future litigation under NEPA ahould delay operations at the nuclear plants scheduled to come on line in the coming months.

Joint Committee Action—At the March 16-17 hearings before the Joint Atomic Energy Committee, bills to amend the Atomic Energy Act received the endorsement of Ruckelshaus, Train and AEC Chairman James R. Schlesinger.

On March 23, Rep. Chet Holifield, D-Calif., introduced a clean bill (HR 14065) incorporating some of the suggestions made by the Administration witnesses.

The bill authorized the AEC to issue temporary licenses to those facilities for which application for a full operating license had been filed on or before Sept. 9, 1971—with no cut-off date for the temporary license authority.

The utility's application for a temporary license could be filed only after the AEC had received and evaluated a safety report on the plant. In deciding whether or not to grant the temporary license the AEC had to find that health and safety requirements had been satisfied, that no significant damage to the environment would result and that operation of the plant was needed to meet the energy requirements of the public.

The most controversial section of the bill exempted the commission from important requirements of the Administrative Procedures Act (5 USC 551). The AEC was relieved of the necessity of holding a full adjudicatory hearing with provision for discovery of new evidence and cross-examination by intervenors against a power plant. It could make its final decision on a temporary license merely on the basis of affidavits filed by interested parties.

ENVIRONMENTALISTS

Environmental groups objected to the Holifield bill on a number of grounds, but they were particularly incensed by the waiver of the Administrative Procedures Act requirements which, they argued, would allow the AEC to ignore completely charges they have made that existing nuclear power plants as well as those being constructed are not safe.

That argument produced a crucial split in the joint committee.

The environmentalists' allegations stem from public rule-making hearings on reactor-safety issues convened by the AEC in January.

Major questions have emerged during the proceedings concerning adequacy of the emergency core-cooling systems (ECCS) that are intended to prevent a catastrophic accident should a reactor lose its primary cooling water through a ruptured pipe. Documentary evidence and direct testimony show that industry safety experts as well as AEC regulatory staff members have substantive reservations about the fail-safe system.

Some 60 environmental organizations around the country have banded together to form a coalition—the National Intervenors—to represent environmentalist interests in the issue. Myron M. Cherry, a Chicago-based environmental lawyer who often represents intervenors against nuclear power plants, is leading National Intervenors at the hearings, which are scheduled to continue through the summer.

Cherry charges that the Holifield bill represented a "blatant attempt by old-guard elements of the joint committee to silence nuclear-safety critics and allow the AEC to make decisions behind closed doors."

Specifically, he said the bills would have permitted the commission to "ignore the Administrative Procedures Act and issue a temporary license while intervenors are contesting the safety of a plant. We would have had no opportunity to challenge the commission's views or cross-examine the utility representatives."

AEC Rejoinder—AEC officials emphatically denied that a public airing of safety questions would have been abandoned under any of the interim licensing bills they supported.

"Our opinion throughout all of this discussion," said Commissioner William O. Doub, "has been that the safety and licensing boards will have to provide a full and complete public record whenever substantial questions arise regarding either a temporary or a full license."

Baker—A key role in resolving the impasse was played by Baker. A stickler for citizens' procedural rights in government adjudications, Baker refused to accept the exemptions the legislation proposed to give from Administrative Procedures Act requirements.

After four long executive sessions in April—one of which, on April 25, was attended by three AEC commissioners accompanied by general counsel Hoffman—a compromise was reached that conformed closely to Baker's desires: all reference to the APA was dropped and the clean bill reported out (HR 14655) directed the AEC to hold a hearing on issuance of a temporary license without saying what the nature of the hearing should be. No temporary license could be issued after Oct. 30, 1973.

Legislative Record: On May 3, the House passed HR 14655 by voice vote; legislation by an 80-0 vote. President Nixon signed the measure into law (86 Stat 191) on June 2.

Although the legislation was passed without opposition on the floor of both chambers, there remains much doubt and controversy about what it actually requires of the AEC. The division of opinion on that issue, Members of Congress with widely varying views tried to establish a legislative record that would guide the commission, and the courts in case of challenging litigation, in implementing the law.

On one side of the issue, Rep. Hosmer argued on May 3 that no "adjudicatory or trial-type hearing" would be required prior to issuance of a temporary operating license by the AEC, saying the whole point of the legislation was to provide the commission "procedural flexibility needed. ... to be responsive to emergency situations."

On the opposite side of the question, Baker and others, some in floor statements written by Roisman and Cherry, argued that a full adjudicatory hearing would have to be conducted in every instance where a controversy between parties to the case could not otherwise be resolved.

Baker argued that the AEC could "design its rules and regulations" to preserve "the right to discovery and cross-examination" and also to "prevent abuse of those rights."

(Holifield says that if this interpretation is upheld, "we might as well have not passed the bill; it won't mean a damned thing.")

Sen. John O. Pastore, D-R.I., chairman of the joint committee, along with vice chairman Rep. Melvin Price, D-Ill., and others tried to stake out a position midway between Baker and Hosmer.

Pastore argued on the Senate floor that the legislation would give the AEC the authority to decide whether to hold an adjudicatory hearing when issues between a utility applying for a temporary operating license and intervenors in the case were unresolved. Such hearings could be held, Pastore said, "in rare instances" where a "substantial issue of material fact. ... must be resolved for purposes of the temporary operating license findings."

AEC Regulations: On May 29, the AEC issued draft regulations pursuant to HR 14655, and Commissioner James T. Ramey said they adhere to "the middle position espoused by Sen. Pastore and what we took to be the majority of the joint committee."

The regulations will leave the AEC the discretion to decide what is material, what questions are of major substance and what kind of hearing should be held given the facts of the case.

Cherry, on May 31, just after he had first read the draft regulations, characterized them as "incredibly bad. These guys never seem to learn. They've written regulations that fit the old bills rather than the bill Congress passed."

Dingell Bill: The new AEC legislation does not exempt the commission from the obligation to comply with NEPA in its decisions on the temporary operating permits for nuclear plants.

But this would be done under legislation (HR 13752) introduced by Dingell on March 13.

That a principal author and protector of NEPA would himself propose to grant such a significant exception to its requirements is a reflection of growing pressures to grant other, broader exemptions.

In discussing NEPA's future, Dingell seems a driven and harried man. He said he is fearful that "the enemies of NEPA are gathering round" and that he worries that environmentalists may not have the strength to repel them. "I think they overrate their strength because of their success up until now," Dingell said. "But hell, we haven't seen anything yet—none of the real jackals have come out of their lairs."

Congress, Dingell continued, "is literally dripping with amendments and bills that would gut the act." He mentioned a closed meeting of the House Public Works Committee held early in February—whose minutes were leaked to the press—during which committee members seriously discussed steps that could be taken to exempt highway and waterway development projects from NEPA's requirements.

Strategy—Dingell's strategy over the last few months has aimed at:

protecting NEPA from major amendments stemming from the charge that it is causing wholesale economic and social disruptions, by accepting what he terms non-substantive amendments to deal with emergency situations;

establishing the principle that any amendment to NEPA must pass through his subcommittee.

Both of these factors lay behind the introduction of his bill to ease temporarily NEPA's rules for certain power plants.

The Bill: HR 13752, a companion bill to the joint committee's HR 14655, applies only to applications for operating licenses that were filed before Sept. 9, 1971, and also only to plants whose applications for construction permits were filed before Jan. 1, 1970.

For these plants the AEC may grant a temporary operating license even though a final environmental-impact statement has not been completed.

The commission must, however, make a determination that no significant adverse impact on the environment will result and that the plant is needed to help in an energy emergency. The authority for the temporary NEPA suspension extends only until Oct. 30, 1973.

Explanation: Dingell says of HR 13752: "It is carefully worded, exquisitely narrow piece of legislation. It makes no substantive

changes in NEPA; it gives only more leeway in time."

Dingell acknowledges that environmentalists have made a strong case that only one or two nuclear plants ready to come on line this summer or next winter would need to employ his legislation, but he said: "They could give me no assurance that we could defend NEPA against an all-out, irrational attack if any brownouts or blackouts occur.... We can't outshout the utility lobby; it is one of the best financed in the country and capable of unlimited distortion."

Rep. Henry S. Reuss, D-Wis., who also has been deeply involved in the development of NEPA, supports Dingell's position on the Quad Cities bill, saying, "I think we can better defend the act against attack later if we introduce some flexibility for emergencies now."

Campaign in Senate: On April 17, the Dingell bill passed the House by a vote of 285-78.

Only six days earlier, the "Save NEPA" campaign had been launched by leaders of the environmental coalition that formed its backbone.

For a variety of reasons, the Senate Interior Committee did not move quickly on the House-passed Dingell bill, and the delay gave the environmentalists time to lobby committee members.

Committee Chairman Jackson held a hearing on the bill on April 28, and, according to the committee's chief counsel, William J. van Ness, "A number of members didn't feel the Administration made a very strong case that day."

Sens. Frank E. Moss, D-Utah,

Lee Metcalf, D-Mont., and James L. Buckley, Con-R-N.Y., among others, were skeptical of the need for the bill, and their feelings were reinforced by vigorous lobbying on the part of the environmentalists.

On May 19, at a session planned to report out the bill, the committee decided to delay action, probably through the summer.

Assessments: The environmentalists' strongest argument against the Dingell bill was that the AEC did not need it.

The commission could have met NEPA's requirements to the satisfaction of the court in the Quad Cities case, said Roisman, if only it had made a minimal effort to follow procedures for filing an environmental-impact statement.

Further, Roisman and his allies argued that only two of the 13 nuclear plants identified by the Federal Power Commission last winter as needed in the coming months would actually be ready to go on line this summer, and these, they said, could be licensed under the recently enacted AEC bill.

The environmentalists note that in the case of other plants the AEC has said that final environmental-impact statements would be ready well in advance of scheduled operation.

AEC—AEC officials appear hopeful that the interim-licensing bill will carry them through, but evince worries about the lack of a clearcut congressional mandate to temper NEPA in an emergency.

Commissioner Ramey said the commission expects to produce impact statements well before nuclear plants are supposed to start up, but that "we may miscalculate and so the bill would be useful as insurance."

Though also expressing hope that the commission was out of the woods, AEC General Counsel Hoffman is much more sensitive to its continuing legal vulnerability to a challenge on the basis of non-compliance with NEPA, especially in interim licensing cases.

Hoffman dismisses as illegal and unworkable Roisman's and Cherry's proposal that the AEC amend its administrative rules to build shortcuts in the NEPA statement process.

"Those guys know damned well that such a course is of extremely doubtful legality. The courts have continually struck down agency actions that did not live up to NEPA's strict procedural requirements."

Some AEC officials also express the fear that environmentalists will launch a new series of interventions once the danger of amendment to NEPA appears to have passed.

CEQ, EPA—Top officials at CEQ and EPA testified in favor of both the joint committee bill and the Dingell bill, although EPA General Counsel John Quarles admitted that his agency made no independent assessment of the need for the legislation. The agency "had to rely on the experts—the FPC and the AEC" for data on the "power emergency," Quarles said, although "at the hearings, we've tried to disclaim responsibility for the data."

CEQ member MacDonald said: "Like Dingell, I am worried about the short-term viability of the act if it gets tagged for power failures. I see these interim-licensing bills as

a form of self-protection."

Utilities—Utility spokesmen are hopeful but not overly optimistic that the joint committee's interim-licensing bill will speed up the regulatory process.

John J. Kearney, vice-president of the Edison Electric Institute, the trade association of the privately owned utilities, said: "Unfortunately, Congress dawdled so long that the legislation won't really help us through the summer crunch. And then, my legal people tell me that if Baker's interpretation of the bill prevails, we'll end up back where we started—bogged down in endless procedural detail and delay."

Robert C. Dolan, a lobbyist for the National Association of Electric Companies, said that "much will depend on the shape of the final regulations the AEC writes pursuant to HR 14655. If they're really tough and force an expedited hearing, we should be in better shape."

Dolan said he is worried, however, about the failure of Congress to enact the companion Dingell bill. He said: "The AEC has been continually over optimistic about its ability to get out environmental impact statements on time. The fact is they have failed to get any of them out on time, and I think some plants may get caught by this."

PERMIT PROGRAM

Although the Nixon Administration lent its support to AEC-proposed steps to secure legislative relief from the Calvert Cliffs and Quad Cities decisions, it was most upset by another court ruling under NEPA—the Kalur decision

which stopped the industrial water pollution permit program dead.

It was in the wake of that ruling, in the beginning of January, that the comedy of errors involving the ill-fated letter began.

John C. Whitaker, deputy assistant to the President for natural resources and chief White House aide on environmental matters called a meeting on the Kalur issue. It was attended by Train and Ruckelshaus, as well as representatives from the Justice Department, the Corps of Engineers and OMB. Ruckelshaus said that a decision was made to seek legislative relief as well as to appeal Judge Robinson's decision.

He said he doubted that an appeal would be fully successful since there are "some pretty close questions involved."

White House Letter: CEQ's Atkeson was placed in charge of a working group to draft a letter outlining suggested legislative action.

A first draft was circulated for comment. Its language was too sweeping, Ruckelshaus said, since it suggested exemption of all federal regulatory actions on environmental matters from NEPA requirements. "When we saw that we said, 'Well, that's just too broad,'" Ruckelshaus said.

The second draft was generally restricted to the permit program, Ruckelshaus said, and EPA concurred in its recommendations.

Then a meeting was held at which EPA was not represented. This meeting was chaired by Fairbanks, Whitaker's assistant; in attendance were Atkeson and James F. C. Hyde Jr., OMB's coordinator on natural-resource legislation.

As a result of this meeting, a third draft letter was prepared. This version was written on "Executive Office of the President—Council on Environmental Quality" stationery. It was close to the original letter to which EPA had objected, since it suggested broad exemptions from the requirements of NEPA.

Train and Atkeson said the draft was sent to EPA for comment with a 48-hour deadline. When no response was heard from EPA, they said, they assumed EPA had no objections.

On the question of why EPA had not been invited to the meeting, Train said, "There's so goddamned many meetings. ... I call up and scream sometimes" when meetings are called without his notice.

"When I signed it, it was with the understanding that it was cleared all around," Train said. There was, he said, "not the slightest intention of shoving something down EPA's throat."

However, through some mishap that has yet to be explained, the letter never was reviewed by top EPA officials.

Ruckelshaus said, "I don't believe anybody is trying to do us in," and attributed the language of the third letter to "just plain lack of communication."

But, he said, "I was mad as hell, frankly," because EPA had not been involved in the drafting of the final letter.

On Feb. 1, Atkeson and Gary A. Baise, EPA's new director of congressional liaison, visited the staff of the House Public Works Committee to discuss the Kalur decision, the pending water pollu-

tion legislation and the proposed amendments.

Baise, a longtime personal assistant to Ruckelshaus, had been in the liaison job for only one day and had not seen the letter.

Atkeson distributed unsigned copies of the letter at the meeting and sought to convince the committee staff of the merits of the suggested amendments. But the reaction was not favorable.

Baise said that at the conclusion of the meeting, Atkeson realized the committee staff had "serious reservations" about the suggested amendments and that Atkeson then collected the copies of the draft letter.

But copies already had been circulated on Capitol Hill.

Baise said that on Feb. 2, before he had had a chance to show the letter to Ruckelshaus, Atkeson requested that the letters be returned.

Charles F. Lettow, an assistant to Atkeson, said of the letter, "It was not intended to be a specific legislative suggestion" but merely a reflection of the Administration's then-current thoughts on the issues.

Atkeson said the real issue is not whether EPA concurred in the letter's recommendations but that "the Administration sees a problem in the Kalur decision" and merely was proposing possible remedies.

Ruckelshaus said, however: "I don't blame anybody for looking at that letter and thinking that was the official position of the Administration."

Issues—In its draft letter, the Administration asked the House Public Works Committee to con-

sider an amendment that would exempt the Refuse Act permit program from the requirement for environmental impact statements, and similarly exempt the new permit program being created by the water quality legislation.

It also asked that "specified environmentally protective regulatory actions" in addition to the permit program be exempted from NEPA requirements. CEQ was to be given authority to define what kinds of actions would be included.

Describing the substantive legislative goals of the Administration regarding NEPA, CEQ's Lettow said: "Basically, we had two things in mind: to solve the major problems for the Refuse Act permit program created by the Kalur decision, and then at the same time to write into legislation the long-standing interpretations of NEPA that the CEQ had already published in its guidelines concerning the act." Lettow added that CEQ was very worried that it would not "be able to hold the lid on NEPA."

"What some environmentalists don't seem to understand," he said, "is that we're fighting a rearguard action on NEPA to stave off really drastic amendments and changes. Decisions like Kalur and Quad Cities are creating enormous counter-pressures against NEPA."

Reaction—Environmentalists were opposed to exempting the permit program from NEPA, but they were particularly horrified by the proposal to exempt "environmentally protective regulatory actions."

Said J.Gustave Speth, an attorney with the Natural Resources

Defense Council, "That kind of broad language might very well include regulatory actions of the AEC, FPC, the Corps and God knows what other agencies. . . . It's bad news all around."

Lettow vehemently denied that this was the correct interpretation, saying that "the phrase applies to the EPA and several other agencies—like the Coast Guard—that have a specific environmental mandate. It does not apply to the mission agencies." White House aide Fairbanks supported Lettow and said: "We thought about listing the agencies included, but decided against that because as conditions change the list might vary."

Despite Lettow's assertion, Speth's fears were echoed by EPA Administrator Ruckelshaus, who said that his agency opposes the draft letter "because we are not sure what the phrase 'environmentally protective regulatory actions' means—it might well exempt all federal regulatory agencies. We felt it was far too broad in its implications."

The House Public Works Committee staff also reacted negatively to the Administration's suggestions. Incorporating the proposed amendments in the water quality bill would have required new hearings and new executive sessions, staff members told CEQ and EPA. They also said the committee would be extremely reluctant to amend a law that had originated in another committee of the House.

New Attempt: Rebuffed by the Public Works Committee, the Administration lowered its sights in February and proposed to exempt only the permit program from the requirement for environmental impact statements.

Ruckelshaus supported this more limited goal, saying, "I am not certain we can keep the permit system viable if the Kalur decision is upheld."

But the committee reiterated its earlier objections, and did not include the suggested amendment. The water quality bill was passed by the House on March 29 and went to conference with the Senate with no NEPA exemptions for the permit program. Although the White House in early June still was expressing hope that the issue would be dealt with during the lengthy House-Senate negotiations, that prospect was viewed as highly unlikely by those close to the conference committee.

New Bill: Not until Feb. 3, two months after the Kalur decision was handed down, did the Administration appeal the case to the Federal Court of Appeals for the District of Columbia. The government's plea for an expedited decision on the case was denied by the court, and it may be well into 1973 before a further judicial determination is reached.

Meanwhile, the very heart of the water-pollution abatement program has been cut out."

In March, with no prospect of quick action either from the Public Works Committee or from the court, the Administration EPA turned to Dingell, asking him for temporary legislative relief.

Dingell on March 23 introduced a bill (HR 14103) to provide that relief and his subcommittee held two days of hearings on the measure, May 2-3.

HR 14103 would exempt EPA until Dec. 31, 1975 from the re-

quirement to publish environmental-impact statements on water-quality permits issued pursuant to the Refuse Act and to the new permit program being created by the pending water pollution legislation. The exemption applies only to plants on which construction commenced before April 1, 1972, and any permit issued under the NEPA exemption would not remain in effect beyond Dec. 31, 1977.

Though Dingell introduced HR 14103, he said he "is by no means certain it is necessary or wise as yet. I wanted to open up the question for discussion, but I am keeping my options open."

Dingell states emphatically that EPA has a legal obligation under the environmental policy act to issue impact statements on its own regulatory actions. "My bill doesn't change that: it just gives EPA more time," he said.

Environmental lobbyists have pressed Dingell not to go further with his bill until he sees what the House-Senate conference on the water pollution bill does regarding the new federal permit program.

They have also borne down hard on the argument—as they have with the Quad Cities bill— that EPA can get around the Kalur decision by administrative means.

After several recent discussions with Roisman, Rauch and Lahn, Dingell has drafted a letter to Quarles requesting EPA to explore the possibility of interim shortcuts to its NEPA obligations such as temporary mini-review statements or comprehensive statements on entire river basins or individual industries.

EPA Arguments: Gary H.

Baise, EPA's legislative director, argues that the environmentalists' campaign to stop all amendments to NEPA is a mindless approach. "The trouble is," he said, "they will save NEPA but at a very real expense to the environment."

Quarles said: "I know their motives are the purest, but I cannot understand how they fail to see that to force us to prepare thousands of impact statements will only delay the water-pollution abatement program and frustrate the very pruposes of NEPA . . . .
We are in a unique position and giving us an exemption will not serve as a precedent for other agencies to make the same demands."

Extent of Delay—The Corps of Engineers has received over 20,000 requests for permits under the Refuse Act. Quarles notes that EPA may not have to prepare impact statements for all 20,000—that will depend on how many constitute a "major federal action" as defined by NEPA.

But he said, "Even if we have to do statements for only the largest 2,500 polluters this will cause inordinate difficulties and delays. Each permit, we figure, takes us half a man-year's work, and for some plants—steel companies for instance—a typical discharge will have over 20 different components and may even take much more work."

Like Hoffman of the AEC, Quarles is doubtful that the courts would accept the shortcuts suggested by environmental lawyers.

New Permit Program—EPA believes it is in a stronger position to defend the new permit program to be created under the House and Senate water bills against the necessity of time-consuming environmental-impact statements.

In a May 23 letter to Sen. Baker, Ruckelshaus advanced two reasons why "the rationale for excluding the new permit program from the scope of NEPA is substantially stronger . . . than the rationale for excluding the Refuse Act permit program."

Ruckelshaus said first that NEPA's legislative history would seem to exempt EPA-run water quality programs.

More broadly, he contended that the provisions of the new water bill—as well as those of the Clean Air Act of 1970 (84 Stat 1676)—were incompatible with the "balancing judgment" required in NEPA statements.

The new water bill, he said, specifies that technology-based control requirements ("best practical technology") be imposed on each industrial discharger; the Clean Air Act requires EPA to establish ambient air quality standards at a level necessary to protect the public health. On the other hand, a meaningful NEPA balancing judgment, might well require standards to be set at levels different from those specified in the two enabling statutes. EPA would have to violate one act or the other, a situation clearly not intended by Congress, said Ruckelshaus.

But Quarles still is clearly worried about NEPA's potential impact on the new program.

Ultimately, under both the House and Senate water bills, the permit programs would revert to state control. Quarles never has made any secret of EPA's desire to issue very strict federal permits to the nation's largest water polluters before relinquishing control. "But," he said, "what worries me is that we'll be tied up in litigation right up until the deadline for turning the permit program back to the states—and the big polluters will escape."

SAVE NEPA

Evidence had grown during 1971 and early 1972, Roisman said, "of an ominous linkage of private interest groups with Congressmen and federal agencies to destroy NEPA one way or the other.

"But it all struck home when Dingell introduced the Quad Cities bill. We protested, but he said he had no choice. Our answer to that was the 'Save NEPA' campaign."

The central core of organizations in the "Save NEPA" coalition includes the Sierra Club, Friends of the Earth, Environmental Action Inc. and the Environmental Policy Center, a newly-formed environmental organization with headquarters on Capitol Hill. All the groups are registered to lobby.

The "Save NEPA" campaign works out of the offices of Roisman's law firm—Berlin, Roisman and Kessler—in a townhouse just off Connecticut Avenue in northwest Washington.

Though not formally a part of the loosely-organized coalition, other powerful organizations are lending significant support, including the League of Women Voters of the U.S., the National Wildlife Federation and the Izaak Walton League of America.

Lawyers' Leadership: The courts are the chief battleground on which the controversies surrounding the environmental policy act have been fought out. And the current legislative discussions regarding NEPA amendments require expert opinion on close and complicated questions regarding agency administrative regulations and likely court interpretations of amendments to the act.

Inevitably, environmental organizations have turned increasingly to a small group of young environmental lawyers who have been deeply involved in these legal and administrative issues since enactment of NEPA in January 1970.

Roisman—Much of the intellectual force and basic strategy behind the "Save NEPA" campaign has come from Anthony Roisman. Roisman, 34, first came to national attention as the successful lawyer for the plaintiffs in the Calvert Cliffs case.

Over the past year, environmental leaders have turned to him again and again for advice on matters pertaining to the environmental policy act, and he thus gradually has become a key not only to litigation in defense of NEPA but also to legislative strategy.

Myron M. Cherry, the Chicago-based lawyer who represents many intervenors against nuclear power plants around the country, also has been consulted, as have two members of the Natural Resources Defense Council Inc., J. Gustave Speth and Edward Strohbehn; and Joseph V. Karaganis, who argued the Quad Cities case for the Izaak Walton League.

Campaign: The coalition has contacted several hundred local and state environmental groups around the country with a newsletter urging them to begin a grassroots effort to oppose all amendment to the act.

"We've had a very good response," said Richard M. Lahn of the Sierra Club. "The issue is simple, and it's clear that NEPA has become a real symbol to environmentalists all over the country."

One quick result was a May 2 editorial in *The New York Times* blasting the "mounting offensive" against NEPA and criticizing moves to amend the act.

Roisman, when he appeared before the Senate Interior Committee on April 28 to oppose the Quad Cities bill, was able to produce over 100 telegrams from environmentalist organizations supporting the coalition's position.

Environmentalists' Case: The environmentalists' case against HR 13752 is based on several general and two specific contentions.

Coming of Age—In the first place, said Roisman, "NEPA as a law is just coming of age. The litigation of the last two years has gradually given shape and meaning to the act ... There is finally some hope that federal agencies will start to devote more time to complying with NEPA rather than finding ways to get around it."

"But," he said, "as long as you hold out the hope for amendments to get them off the hook—as the Quad Cities and Kalur bills do—then they'll never change."

Opening the Floodgates—In reply to the fears of Dingell and others that the environmentalists may be overextending themselves by attempting to dam up all amendments to the act, Roisman says: "We just don't have the resources to watch for 10 or a 100 bills, so we have to adopt almost a knee-jerk reaction, and establish immediately that we will oppose all tradeoffs involving NEPA."

The "Save NEPA" leaders often raise the fear that one amendment will lead to many others. Said Rauch: "Today, it's the energy crisis; tomorrow, the need for new highways; and then dams, housing projects, canals—industries and Congressmen will be inundating us with demands for relief."

Administrative Solution—Lawyers in the environmental movement have argued since the Quad Cities and Kalur decisions were handed down that the AEC and EPA could satisfy the courts merely with changes in their administrative procedures; that legislative relief is not needed.

"The trouble is that the AEC, like a number of federal agencies, is trying to portray NEPA as an inflexible act with rigid procedures," said Roisman. "They have persistently ignored suggestions on how to get around the Quad Cities decision."

The AEC, say environmental lawyers, lost the cases on two mistakes it could easily rectify; it provided for no public participation in its abbreviated NEPA review process and it did not circulate, even on a restricted time basis, a draft statement to other government agencies.

The Calvert Cliffs decision and several other cases clearly indicate, environmentalists say, that the courts are willing to allow flexibility where an emergency exists and that as the language of the act states agencies merely must live up to its provisions "to the fullest extent possible."

In the case of the permit program, the environmental lawyers have argued that EPA probably could satisfy the courts without providing detailed impact statements for each permit—by drawing up statements for entire river basins, for example.

Many environmentalists also feel strongly that the Kalur bill would set a highly significant and undesirable precedent. Testifying on May 3 against the bill, Robert Rauch of Friends of the Earth said the bill "represents a particularly serious threat to NEPA. ... The reason is that other agencies wishing to seek exemption for their programs will point to EPA and argue that if the nation's environmental agency cannot operate under the act, why should they be made to comply?"

INDUSTRY REACTION

The growing restiveness of some federal agencies over the delays and stoppages caused by the Environmental Policy Act has been matched by an increasing number of industries.

Electric Utilities: The electric utilities have been the hardest hit by NEPA, and they have made dire predictions about the act's potential consequences.

In Nov. 3 testimony before the Senate Interior and Insular Affairs Committee, a spokesman for the "Edison Electric Institute, the trade association of the investor-owned electric utilities, warned that as a result of the Calvert Cliffs decision "critical power supply situations may affect many parts of the country during the next several years" and that "power rationing in one form or another will almost inevitably be necessary. ... "

The EEI spokesman recommended that Congress provide "guidance" on NEPA through committee reports, joint resolutions or even outright amendment of the act.

During the first week in February, the National Electric Reliability Council, an industry group, warned that more recent court decisions involving NEPA would result in a 12-month delay in operation of all new nuclear and fossil-fired generating plants, with "disastrous" consequences for power supply.

Oil Industry: In like manner, the oil industry has bitterly commented on the history of the act's implementation.

A Feb. 7 editorial in the *Oil and Gas Journal* stated: "Life under the National Environmental Policy Act has approached chaos. In two short years under NEPA a series of events have combined to make a story that doesn't reflect credit on any of the participants—Congress which wrote the law, the Council on Environmental Quality which wrote the guidelines ... so-called citizens groups which have brought lawsuits challenging government actions ... and the courts which have interpreted the law as if it were the only one on the books."

"As things stand now," the magazine concluded, "the environment is running the government."

Clyde R. Hampton, chairman of the American Petroleum Institute's advisory committee on environmental law, said of NEPA's impact, "We have several areas in which we have decided we would like to see some kind of action."

Hampton, a Continental Oil Co. executive, said the committee has "not yet" drafted suggested amendments to NEPA. Asked whether court appeals or legislative action appeared to be the most likely avenue by which NEPA might be changed, he said, "I feel confident both routes will be utilized."

Hampton said the committee believes that the preparation of a single wide-ranging impact statement for an agency program should suffice, rather than requiring such statements for individual program actions. He also said CEQ should defer to the agencies in decisions as to what constitutes an action requiring an impact statement.

Furthermore, Hampton said his committee supports EPA's contention that its environmental regulatory actions should be exempt from impact statements. He indicated that petroleum companies would be saddled with a heavy burden if they were required to furnish EPA with detailed data needed for the preparation of impact statements on individual permits.

BLACKOUTS ON THE HORIZON?

In addition to such major cases as the trans-Alaska pipeline suit and the halting of offshore leasing in the Gulf of Mexico, petroleum and mining firms have been affected by NEPA in other instances.

For example, the Interior Department's Geological Survey has proposed new procedures, effective April 1, governing the issuance of drilling and exploration permits on public lands. Permits will not be issued until after at least a 30-day waiting period and environmental impact statements could be required for some permits.

Both the American Petroleum Institute and the Independent Petroleum Association of America have entered strong protests to the new regulations, which were established in light of court decisions regarding NEPA.

Robert A. Buschman, president of the Texas Mid-Continent Oil and Gas Association, is quoted by *Oil Daily* as saying: "This proposal provides a convenient instrument of sabotage for all who want to obstruct the development of energy reserves in this country."

Similarly, the American Mining Congress told the Geological Survey that the new procedures would be "totally unnecessary" and could "bring the (survey's) administrative processes. . . . to a halt."

Water Developers: "We're being hashed by neo-ecologists and pseudo-environmentalists," says Dale Miller, president of the Water Resources Congress, an association of waterway developers and users. "This environmental spree is just getting out of hand."

Miller says the organization plans to "marshal our forces" to counter the environmental groups that have tied up various water projects with court challenges.

"I certainly think it needs to be modified," he said of the Environmental Policy Act. "I don't think at all that it's impossible" but "it

certainly will be difficult," he said.

NIPCC: Thus far, industry has failed to utilize one frequently used rallying point within the government against environmental actions: the Commerce Department's National Industrial Pollution Control Council.

Walter A. Hamilton, deputy assistant secretary of Commerce, who serves as the council's executive director, said: "I guess this proves we are neither as ubiquitous nor as iniquitous as some people claim—but so far as I know, a groundswell against NEPA over here has not got beyond casual conversations."

Hamilton noted, however, that he detected a "rising concern" about the act among industry executives who serve on the council and that the recent Kalur and Quad Cities decisions had "perplexed and worried" a number of businessmen.

Counterattack: Ironically, one industry line of counterattack may well utilize the Environmental Policy Act itself as a weapon.

Within the past few months, some industry officials and corporate law firms have awakened to the fact that NEPA is a two-edged sword which possibly can be turned against the EPA and the environmental standards and regulations the agency is promulgating.

Legal Challenges—On Jan. 24, four operating companies of the American Electric Power System asked the U.S. Circuit Court of Appeals for the District of Columbia to review EPA's emission standards for new sources of air pollution. The brief for the companies will argue, according to the lawyer handling the case, the EPA

violated the environmental policy act when it did not formulate and publish an impact statement on its new standards.

Getty Oil Co. is making the same argument in a case against EPA's sulfur dioxide standards (*Getty Oil Co. v. Ruckelshaus*). The case is being heard on an expedited basis by the U.S. Circuit Court of Appeals for the district of New Jersey, Pennsylvania and Delaware, and a decision will come soon.

On May 31, EPA announced the acceptance or rejection of a series of state air quality programs pursuant to the Clean Air Act. On May 25, a week before the announcement, eight electric power companies from the state of Pennsylvania wrote EPA demanding an environmental impact statement before the agency put into effect the plan for that state. The companies maintained that implementation of the state-submitted plan would be more harmful to society than beneficial to the environment. The same day, the Baltimore Gas and Electric Co. wrote EPA requesting the same action with regards to Maryland's program.

Said Robert Zener, EPA associate general counsel: "The handwriting is on the wall; those guys are coming after us."

OUTLOOK

Environmentalists emerged from the winter and spring of 1972 with what they considered an impressive record of protecting NEPA from substantive amendment.

From the Joint Atomic Energy Committee, they had secured a bill they believe leaves them with the dominant hand.

More importantly, by claiming that the joint committee bill is sufficient to expedite the operation of new nuclear power plants, they managed to halt, at least for a time, the drive to directly amend NEPA with Dingell's nuclear power bill.

And action on the Kalur bill was forestalled, as Dingell tentatively decided to await the results of conference action on the water quality bill. Administration officials still hope the conference will act on the Kalur issue, but that prospect appeared unlikely in late June.

Behind the Kalur decision looms the larger question of the EPA responsibilities under the environmental policy act.

Court decisions arising from challenges demanding that EPA issue impact statements on its own environmental regulations may well go against the agency. Should this happen, within the next year EPA may be leading the pack in requests for NEPA exemptions.

A

Abel, I. W., 75, 78
Abrahams, Albert E., 314
Accounting Office, General, 44
Ackley, Gardner, 93
Adams, John Quincy, 34
Administration on Aging, 222-224
Administrative process, the, 195-239
Advertising & Sales Promotion, 92
AFL-CIO, 33, 46, 49
    Committee on Political Education, 15
    Conference on Jobs, 75
    and free-trade, 71
    Industrial Union Dept., 73
    and trade and investment legislation, 72
Agnew, Spiro T., 3, 17
    and broadcasters, 335, 336
Aiken, George, 108
Ailes, Roger E., 12
Ailes, Stephen, 322
Albert, Carl, 17, 97
alcoholism, control of, 212
Aldrich, Winthrop W., 93
Alexander, Herbert E., 26, 43
Alfultis, Richard J., 308
Alger, Mark W., 253
Allott, Gordon, 112
Alm, Alvin L., 206
American Airlines Inc., 45
    chart, 39
American Association for Public Opinion
    Research, 30
American Bankers Association, 61
American Bar Association, 90, 239, 271-289
    and busing, 284
    and Congress, 272
    and consumer protection, 278, 279
    and criminal law, 284, 285
    and Eisenhower administration, 275
    and environment, 279, 280
    ideology of, 283, 284
    image crisis of, 271
    Journal of, 274
    and judicial appointments, 275
    legal services of, 280
    lobbying by, 271
    membership of, 283, 284
    and Nixon, Richard M., 285
    organization of, 273
    and presidential disability, 282
    and Senate Judiciary Committee, 276
    staff of, 273
    and Truman Administration, 275

American Broadcasting Co., 46
American Council on Education, 348
American Importers Association, 82
American Telephone and Telegraph Co., 45
American Medical Political Action Committee (AMPAC), 33
American Motors and emission control, 65
American Trial Lawyers Association, 274
American Scholar, on Senate Finance Committee, 141
Anderson, Clinton P., 140
Anderson, John, 8, 41
Andrews, Mark N., 252
Antidumping Act (1921), 74
Antitrust Division of the Justice Department, suits initiated by, 57
appropriations bill (1971), and Congress, 207
Arlen Properties Inc., 88
Armendaris, Alex M., 10
Armstrong, Ellis L., 367
Armstrong, Frank, 69
Arner, Fredrick B., 130
Ashbrook, John M., 5, 6, 353
Ash Council, The, 262
Ashew, Reubin, 18
Aspinall, Wayne N., 363
Atkeson, Timothy B., 360
Atomic Energy Commission, 362
auto insurance, 273, 274
auto leasing on Capitol Hill, 69
automobile, as a health hazard, 62
Automobile Manufacturing Association, 54, 56, 62, 64, 65
Automotive Engineers, Society of, 64
Ayres, Robert U., 64

B

Bailey, John M., 16
Baise, Gary A., 375
Baker, Charles D., 323
Baker, Howard H., 66, 368
Baker, Robert G. (Bobby), 108, 114, 154, 155
balance of payments, U. S., 71
Ball Four, 172
Ball, George W., 294
ballots, absentee, 7, 17
Barabba, Vincent P., 33, 37
Barcella, Ernest L., 52
Barfield, Claude E., 360
barge industry, 319
Baring, Walter S., 256

Barkan, Alexander E., 15
Barkley, Alben W., 117
Bowditch, Fred W., 65
Bayh, Birch E., 16, 32, 66, 97, 287, 356
Beck, Lowell R., 90, 95, 272
Beckler, David, 208
Bechtle, Louis C., 267
Beebe, Norman, 328
Beggs, James M., 179, 318
Beidler, John H., 78
Bell and Howell Company, 80
Benham, Thomas W., 33
Bennett, Wallace F., 115, 142, 146
Bentsen, Lloyd M., 142, 298
Berrigan, Daniel, 252
Berrigan, Phillip, 252
Betts, Jackson, 126
Bickel, Alexander M., 303
Biddle, Francis, 243, 257
Bingham, Jonathan B., 301
Billings, Leon, 61
Black, Hugo L., 276
Black militants, and Common Cause, 100
Black vote, 12
Blackmun, Harry A., 276
Blackman, Herbert N., 130
Blakey, Robert G., 285
Boggs, Hale, 97, 127, 241, 353
Boggs, J. Caleb, 66
Boldt, George H., 306
Bonafede, Dom, 159, 169, 183, 197
Bonaparte, Charles J., 248
Bon Vivant Soups Inc., 225, 226
Bourland, Albert D., 56, 57
Bow, Frank T., 251
Bower, Robert T., 31
Boyd, Alan S., 318
Brademas, John, 214, 223, 345, 347
Brannon, Gerard M., 151
Brennan Jr., William J., 275
Bresnahan, William A., 319
Bricker, John W., 301
Briggs, Richard E., 329
Brinkley, David, 336
Bristol, George, 23
broadcast news censorship, 335
broadcasters, censorship by, 332
Broadcasters, National Association of, 45, 332
broadcasting, regulation of, 336
Broadcasting and Television Digest, 340
Broderick, Raymond J., 64
Brookings Institution on education, 351
Broomfield, William S., 353
Brown, Clarence J., 232
Brown, Robert J., 12

Browne, Secor D., 44
Brownell, Herbert, 93
Brownlow, Louis, 200
Brunner, Thomas J., 73
Buchanan, Patrick J., 162
Buckley, James L., 373
Buckner, Helen W., 88
budget assistants, 198
budget drafting, 199-204
budget:
    assistants, 198
    and cabinet officers, 197
    drafting, 199-204
    historic process of the, 200, 201
    making of the, 197-211
    terminology, 205
Bull, Stephen, 161
Burch, Dean, 336
Bureau of National Affairs Daily Executive Report, 57
Bureau of Social Science Research, 31
Burger, Warren E., 276
Burke, James A., 71, 74, 79, 123
Burns, Arthur M., 199
Buschman, Robert A., 380
busing, 353-356
Butler, Lewis, 215
Butterfield, Alexander P., 161
Butz, Earl L., 309
Byrd, Harry F., 139, 143
    and independent status, 106
    and Senate Finance Committee, 144
Byrd, Robert C., 103, 108
Byrnes, John W., 132

C

Cahn, Robert, 206
Caldwell, Lynton K., 362
Califano Jr., Joseph A., 93, 94, 231, 334
Callahan, Nicholas P., 253
Cambodia, 116
    Haldeman on, 160
Cambridge Opinion Studies Inc., 29
campaign spending, and Common Cause, 94, 95
candidates, as credit risks, 45
    dark-horse, 33
Cantril, Albert H., 37
Caplan, Marvin, 97
Cardwell, James B., 215
Carlucci, Frank C., 204
Carnegie Commission on Higher Education, 346
Carnegie-Mellon Foundations, 99
Carrow, Milton M., 287
Carson, Robert T., 252
Carswell, Harold G., 98, 276

Case, Clifford P., on access to the President, 168, 303
Cater Jr., S. Douglass, 231
Caterpillar Tractor Co., 71
Celebrezze, Anthony J., 222
Celler, Emanuel, 254
Central Surveys Inc., 36
Chamber of Commerce (U.S.), 20, 79
    and the Task Force on the Multinational Enterprise, 81
Chandler, John, 84
Chaney, Neale, 14
Channell, Donald E., 271
Chapin, Dwight L., 161
Chapman, William C., 51, 55, 57
Chase Park-Plaza Hotel, 20
Cheit, Earl F., 348
Chenea, Paul F., 63
Cherington, Paul T., 34
Cherry, Myron M., 371, 378
Childs, Kenneth D., 154
Chicago Tribune, 27
Chicago, University of, 55
Chiles, Lawton, 97
Chilton Research Services, 27, 29, 36, 37
Chotiner, Murray M., 5, 7, 9, 11
Church, Frank, 224, 294
Civil Aeronautics Board, 39, 43, 44
Civil Service Commission, 210
Clark, Ramsey, 93, 243, 249, 258, 270
Clayman, Jacob, 78
Clean Air Act amendments (1970), 206
Cleveland, Grover, 3
Clifford, Clark M., 187
Cohen, David, 87, 91
Cohen, Wilbur J., 86, 140, 222
Cole, Edward N., 52, 58, 64
Cole, Kenneth R., on John Erlichman, 170
colleges, aid for, 348
    Ivy League, and women, 356
    and job training funds, 356
    small, 346
colleges and universities, financial difficulties of, 348
Collins, Cyrus S., 45
Collins, George, 79
Colmer, William M., 94
Colson, Charles W., 9, 163, 256
Columbia Broadcasting System, 46
Columbia University, 81
Commerce Department, 83
Commerce, Secretary of, 44
Common Cause (citizen's lobby), 49, 50, 85-100
    and anti-war issue in house, 95
    and Black militants, 100

campaign, 85
    on congressional reform, 94, 95
    contributors (major) to, 88
    credibility of, 92
    and Equal Employment Opportunities, 94, 95
    finances of, 88
    and fund raising, 90
    membership of, 86, 91
    and presidential election (1972) campaign, 85
    and S. S. T., 94
    target areas of, 100
    and tax rules, 95
    and Vietnam war, 95
    and voting rights, 95
    and welfare reform, 95
Communications Company of Washington, D. C., 30
Community Change, Center for, 90
community development, 230, 231
Community Development Department, 234
computer system (AFL-CIO), 78
Congress, 101-155
    and access to the President, 168
    and appropriations bill (1971), 209
    and automobile recall, 70
    and General Motors, 68
    and the higher education bill, 353-356
    and Indochina, 103, 104
    and Nader investigation, 329
    Richard M. Nixon's relationship with, 5
    and presidents, 101
    pressure for aid to secondary and elementary education, 357
    Senate majority leadership (92nd Congress), 106
    standing committee system of, 101
Congress, the Sapless Branch, 144
Congressional Delegation Steering Committee, 77
Congressional Government, 117
Congressional Party: A Case Study, 115
Congressional Quarterly, 57
Congressional Record, 39, 57, 75, 76
congressional reform, and Common Cause, 94, 95
Conable Jr., Barber B., 126
Commanger, Henry Steele, 93
Connally, John, 8, 31, 229, 306
Connecticut, University of, 81
Connor, James E., 311
Constitution, U. S., First Amendment to, 50
Consumer Federation of America, 327
convention delegation, balance of, 10

conventions, description of, 21
Conway, Jack T., 90
Cook, Richard K., 230
Coolidge, Calvin, 3, 248
Cooper, David, 21
Cooper, John Sherman, 294
    on relations with the White House
        since 1970, 168
COPE and 1970 campaign, 73
Corcoran, Thomas G., 93
Coris, John, 45
Corrigan, Richard, 360
Corrupt Practices Act, 41, 42
Cost of Living Council:
    background of, 307, 308
    goals of, 315
    operations of, 306, 307
    staff of, 308
Crabill, Donald E., 206
Cranston, Alan, 109
credit, regulation of unsecured, 43
crime, fighters against organized, 260
    organized, 270
    profile report on, 265-267
Crime Control Act of 1970, Organized,
    256
"Crime in America," 243
Crime, National Council on Organized,
    262
    a profile of, 264
Crispi, Irving, 31
Cronin, Thomas E., 3
Cronkite, Walter, 335
Cross, Christopher T., 349
Crossley, Archibald M., 31, 34
Culhane, Charles, 71
Curtin, John T., 262
Curtis, Pamela, 95
Curtis, Thomas B., 125
Customs, Bureau of, 260
Cutler, Lloyd, 56, 63, 93, 94

D

Dailey, Peter H., 12
Daley, Richard J., 10, 30, 98, 126
Dallas, Texas, 20
Darman, Richard G., 223
Datamatics Inc., 37
David, Edward E., 207
David, Oksner and Mitchneck, Inc., 47
Davies III, J. Clarence, 206
Davis, Benjamin O., 203
Davis, Kenneth, 43
Dean, Alan L., 232, 235
Dean III, John Wesley, 163
Decision Making Information Inc., 29, 33
Dallenback, John, 347

DeLorean, John Z., 58
DeLorenzo, Anthony G., 52
Democratic Committee of St. Louis, 20
Democratic convention (1968):
    in Chicago, 18
Democratic Legislative Review Commit-
    tee, membership of, 106
Democratic National Committee, 43, 332
    and Common Cause, 95
    debts of, 32
Democratic Party, 1, 3
Democratic Policy Council, 23
democrats,
    and reorganization, 231
Dingell, John D., 360
Denison, Ray, 73
Dent, Harry S., 3, 5, 6, 9, 11, 163
Detroit Market Opinion Research, 35
Dewey, Thomas E., 34
dissent, 3
District of Columbia, 40
Doar, John, 246
Dodd, Thomas J., 143
Dodds, William, 47
Dogole, S. Harrison, 40
Dolan, Robert C., 374
Dole, Robert, 8, 92
dollar, the, devaluation of, 72
Domestic Council:
    membership of (listing), 178
    staff chiefs of (biographical sketch),
        180
    success of, 182
Dominick, Peter, 347
Donaldson, Lee A., 277
Donaldson, Lufkin and Jennerette, Inc.,
    27
Dore, Ann, 12
Douglas, Helen Gahagan, 7
Douglas, Paul H., 139
Douglas, Stephen A., 105
Dowdy, John, 252
Drayne, Richard C., 32
Drew, Russell D., 202, 208
Dreyfus, Daniel A., 362
DRIVE (Teamsters's political action or-
    ganization), 48
Drown, Joseph W., 88
Drucker, Peter, 51
drug abuse prevention program, 212
Duffey, Joseph D., 87
Dulles, Allen W., 247
Dulles, John F., 301
Dyer Act, The (1919), 245

E

Eagleton, Thomas F., 66, 223, 224, 298

Eastern Air Lines, Inc. (chart), 39
Eastland, James O., 113
economic issues 1972, Ehrlichman on,
    181
economic policy, 3
education:
    aid, distribution of by income level
        (chart), 352
    and busing, 354
    and community service, 357
    and congress, 343
    and desegregation aid, 354
    and developing institutions, 356
    ethnic studies, 355
    federal funding, 343
    for Indians, 355
    and libraries, 357
    lobby for, 348
    and Nixon Administration, 347, 348
    Office of, 349
    and pressure groups, 348
    and special interest groups, 351, 352
    and state governors, 348
    and teacher training, 357
Education Act of 1965, Higher, exten-
    sion of, 356
Education, National Foundation for Post
    Secondary, 354
Education, The New Depression in High-
    er, 348
Educational Opportunity Grant, The, 349
Edwards, Charles C., 226
Edwards, H. Lynn, 286
Ehrlichman, John D., 8, 157, 169-182,
    202
    Sherman Adams, as compared to, 169
    biographical sketch of, 171-173
    Califano, as compared to, 169
    Neustadt, on importance of, 169
    normal working day of, 174
    relationship to the president, 169
    Sorensen, as compared to, 169
    staff functions of, 176, 177
Eisenhower, Dwight D., 3, 39, 102
    staff style of, 177
Eisenhower, Julie Nixon, 6
Eisenman, Nathaniel J., 207
election, 1960, 7
election fraud:
    in Illinois, 7
    in Texas, 7
Election Research Center of the Govern-
    mental Affairs Institute, 31
electorate, 1
Elliff, John T., 253
Elson, Roy, 335
Embrey, Claude G., 322
Emerson, J. Terry, 296

Emerson, Thomas I., 255
engine, gas turbine, 64
English, John F., 16
environment, the, 359-381
    and Atomic Energy Commission, 362, 368
    and Army Corps of Engineers, 362
    Calvert Cliffs case, 366
    and court cases, 360
    and Cross-Florida barge canal, 362
    and electric utilities, 369
    Gillham Dame case, 366
    and major court decisions, report on, 366, 367
    and interstate highways, 367
    and offshore leasing, 365
    Quad Cities case, 365
    Refuse Act case, 366
    Senate compromise on, 363
    and Tennessee-Tombigbee waterway, 362
    and trans-Alaska pipeline, 362
Environmental Policy Act, National, 359, 362
    and court actions, 364
environmental groups, 361
Environmental Quality, Council on, 65, 66
Equal Employment Opportunities Commission, and Common Cause, 94
equal-time requirement, 46
Erlenborn, John N., 354, 356
Erwin, Sam J., 256, 337
ethnic studies, 355
Executive branch, the, 195
exports, capital, 74
exports and jobs, 72
Export-Import Bank, 75
Eve of the Storm, The, 141

F

Fact, 22
Fairbanks, Richard, 361
family planning program, 212
Farm Journal, 34
Fasser, Harold C., 319
Fowlkes, Frank V., 51
Federal Bureau of Investigation, 239-257
    before J. Edgar Hoover era, 248
    and Central Intelligence Agency, 241
    and Congress, 242, 256
    criticism of, 241
    and Victor Navasky, 248, 249
    news policy of, 244
    and organized crime, 249, 250
    profile report on, 246, 247
    reform proposals for, 255, 256
    and surveillance, 241

Federal Communications Commission:
    an *Inquiry Toward Evaluation,* 338-340
    the courts on, 333-334
    fairness doctrine of, 332
    and media access, 334
    special report on, 335-337
Federal Election Campaign Act, 42
federal emission standards (automobiles), 63
Federal Highway Administration, 69, 234, 235
Federal Register, The, 57
Federal Water Quality Administration, 206
Fellmuth, Robert C., 320, 328
Felt, T. Mark, 246
Fensterwald Jr., Bernard, 252
Ferber, Mel, 23
Ferris, Charles, 112
Fetter, Louis B., 280
Field, Mervin, 30
Field, Thomas F., 124
Financing the 1968 Election, 26, 43
Finch, Robert H., 5, 215, 348
Finch, Stanley W., 248
Fisher, Ben C., 278
Fishwick, John P., 318
Flanigan, Peter M., 11, 325
Flatow, Samuel, 62
Flemming, Arthur, 223
Flemming, Harry S., 10
Flood, Daniel J., 225
Florida primary election (1972), 4, 5
Florida, University of, 81
Food and Drug Administration, 225, 226
Fong, Hiram L., 252
Forbush, Wilford, 219
Ford, Gerald R., 223, 354
Ford, Henry, 58
Ford II, Henry, 59
Ford Motor Co., 51, 88
Foreign Investors Tax Act (1966), 152
foreign policy (U.S.):
    and J. W. Fullbright on, 299
    Nixon Doctrine, The, 297
    Tonkin Gulf Resolution, 294, 296
    and Vietnam War, 292
Foreign Trade and Investment Act, 74, 75, 76, 77
Fortune, 34, 51
Fowlkes, Frank V., 120
Fox, Lawrence, 130
Frank, Richard S., 240, 258, 271
Frankel, Emil, 236
Fraser, Donald M., 301
Frenkil, Victor J., and Russell Long, 143
Friday, Herschel, 276

Friendly, Fred W., 336
Friends of the Earth, 97, 334
Fredreick, Glenn D., 216
Freeman, Orville, 233
fund raising, 23, 24
fund raisers, political, 40
Fullbright, J. W., 298
Furness, Betty, 86

G

Galbraith, John K., 187
Gallamore, Robert E., 91
Gallup, George H., 27, 31, 34, 35
Gallup Poll (April 10, 1972), 13
Gallup Poll, The, 27, 40
Garcia, Raymond, 80
Gardner, Allan D., 47
Gardner, John W., 85, 115
    and Richard Nixon, 93
    special biographical report on, 98
Garment, Leonard, 93
Gechas, Olga B., 24
General Motors Corp., 49, 51
    and political campaign contributions, 67
General Motors Institute, 58
George, Walter F., 153
Gerstenberg, Richard C., 52, 59
Gibbons, Sam, 123
Gilbert, Carl J., 130
Gillers, Stephen, 257
G. I. Bill, 357
Gifford, William L., 199
Girard, Thomas E., 12
Glass, Andrew J., 26, 85, 103, 306
Goldfinger, Nathaniel, 72, 78
Goldwater, Barry M., 55, 295
    on declaration of war, 296, 297
Goode, Mark, 161
Goodman, Julian, 46
Gore, Albert, 118, 140, 141
    and opposition to R. Long, 143
    and tax reform bill (1969), 150
Government Operations Committee, 232
Government Operations Subcommittee on Executive Reorganization, 60
Graham, Donald E., 327
Grand Rapids Junior College, 58
Gray III, L. Patrick, 239
Grayson, C. Jackson, 309, 328
Great Treasury Raid, The, 121
Green, Edith, 345, 353
Griegg, Stanley L., 14
Gridiron Club of Washington, 52
Griffin, Robert P., 66, 142
Griner, John, 210

Gross, H. R., 137
Gross National Product, 305
Grundy, Richard, 64

H

Haas Jr., Walter A., 86, 88
Haig Jr., Alexander M., 295
Haldeman, H. R., 6, 26, 157, 159-161
    on Richard Nixon, 166, 167
    staff of (listing and biographical
        sketch on each), 164, 165
    White House role of, 160
Hall, Jay G., 51, 55, 57, 66
Hamilton, Alexander, and George Wash-
    ington's speeches, 185
Hamilton, William R., 30, 33
Hamilton interviewers, 32
Hampson, Robert J., 59
Hampton, Robert E., 211
Harlan, John M., 276
Harlow, Bryce N., 159
    on Presidential Aides, 170
Harper, Edwin L., 199
Harris, Fred R., 16, 19, 33, 329, 356
    and Congressional reform, 104
Harris, Louis, 27, 30, 35
Harris, Survey, The, 27
Harris, Thomas E., 47
Harrison, Benjamin, 3
Harsha, William H., 364
Hart, Gary W., 32
Hart, Philip A., 66, 275
Hartke-Burke Bill, 71
Hartke, Vance, 70, 71, 74, 79, 320
Harvard University, 59
    and Joint Center for Urban Studies,
        70
Harvey, James, 68, 70
Hatfield, Mark, 294
Hathaway, William D., 73
Hauser, Rita E., 12
Haveman, Joel, 344
Havens, Harry S., 207
Hawkins, Augustus, 347
Hayakawa, S. I., 93
Hayes, Maureen, on Mike Mansfield's
    education, 107
Haynsworth Jr., Clement F., 276
Hays, Alfred, 111
Health, Education and Welfare, Depart-
    ment of, 195, 212-228, 343-358
    Administration on Aging, 222-224
    budget of, 212
    and Congress, 213
    education division of, 354
    philosophy of, 213, 216
    strategy of, 212

Hearnes, Warren E., 20
Heineman, Ben W., 98, 231
Heiskel, Andrew, 90
Hemenway, Russell D., 41
Hertzberg, Stuart E., 67
Hickel, Walter J., 165
Highway Safety Bureau, 56, 59
Hillenbrand, Bernard F., 237
Hirschberg, Vera, 318
Hodgson, James D., 309
Holifield, Chet, 200, 210, 229, 232, 368
Hollabough, Marcus, 56
Hollander Jr., Sidney, 31
Holman, M. Carl, 85, 91, 100
Holman, Frank E., 301
Hopes and Fears of the American People,
    37
Hoover, Herbert C., 3
Hoover, J. Edgar, 7, 239, 248-254
    on Berrigan brothers, 252
    on drug addicts, 250
    on the federal strike force, 268, 269
    on wire tapping, 250
Horton, Frank, 231
Houghton Jr., Arthur A., 88
House Administration Committee, 31
House clerk, 44
House Foreign Affairs Committee, 77
House Interstate and Foreign Commerce
    Committee, 63
House of Representatives (1824), 34
House Special Education Subcommittee,
    346
House Ways and Means Committee, 73,
    77, 84, 120
    executive activity of, 128
    and lobbyists, 135
    and medicare, 135
    membership of, 123
    report on, 129-130
    success of achieving objectives, 102
    and tax legislation, 136
    and textile quotas, 136
Houthakker, Hendrik, 326
Hruska, Roman L., 336
Hughes, Emmet John, 187
Hughes, Harold E., 16, 119
Huitt, Ralph K., 114
Human Events, on John Gardner and
    Common Cause, 98
Humphrey, Hubert, 8, 9, 15, 16, 25, 28,
    32, 40, 106, 143, 168
    speech at Los Angeles (1968), 179
Hundley, William G., 249
Hutar, Patricia G., 12
Huntsman, John Meade, 161
Hyde Jr., James F. C., 374
Hymel, Gary G., 97

I

Iacocca, Lee A., 59, 66
Iglehart, John K., 212
Ikard, Frank N., 123
Immigration and Naturalization Service,
    260
Importers Association, American, 79
In Brief Authority, 243
Independence, Missouri, 19
Independent Research Associates Inc., 30
Indian health programs, 212
Indiana University, 55
Indochina, 103, 104
Industrial Union Dept. (AFL-CIO), 76,
    78
Inouye, Daniel K., 116
Internal Revenue Service, 260
Internal Revenue Code, 74
International Brotherhood of Teamsters,
    47
International Development, Agency for,
    75
International Research and Technology
    Corp., 64
International Telephone and Telegraph
    Corp., 3, 11
Interstate Commerce Act, 323
Interstate Commerce Commission, 43,
    44, 328, 329
Ioanes, Raymond A., 130
"Irish Mafia" (Kennedy Aides), 170
issues, how determined, 4, 32
Izaak Walton League v. Schlessinger case,
    365

J

Jackson, Andrew, 34
Jackson, Henry M., 16, 25, 33, 40, 104,
    301, 362
Jager, Elizabeth R., 75
Javits, Jacob K., 34, 38, 95, 237, 293,
    301, 344, 355
Jaworski, Leon, 271, 283
    interview with, 274
Jellema, William W., 348
Jencks, Richard W., 46, 335
Jennings, Paul, 75
job creation, and Common Cause, 94
job opportunities, in the U.S., 84
Joe, Tom, 226
Johnson, A. E., 236
Johnson, Felton M. (Skeeter), 113
Johnson, James D., 46
Johnson, Lyndon B., 3, 94, 107
    and Central Intelligence Agency to
        Mississippi, 247

and Federal Bureau of Investigation, 247
and government reorganization, 229
on Mike Mansfield, 141
and Senate Finance Committee, 141
as Senate Majority Leader, 103, 118
and use of power as a Senator, 101
Johnson, Wallace H., 256
Johnstone, Bruce, 348
Jones, Paul R., 10
Jordan Jr., Vernon E., 87
Justice Department, 62, 63
structure of, 260

K

Kaiser, Edgar F., 98
Kalur, Jerome S., 365
Kapenstein, Ira, 14
Katzenbach, Nicholas deB., 298
Kauper, Thomas E., 347
Kayser, Paul W., 10
Kearney, John J., 374
Keefe, Robert J., 32
Kelly, James F., 215
Kennedy, David M., 199
Kennedy, Edward M., 9, 16, 25, 32, 86, 97, 111, 142, 222, 242
and challenge of Russell Long, 143
and Indian education, 355
Kennedy, John F., 7, 20, 43, 108, 137
campaign of (1960), 30
use of Frost poetry in speeches, 193
use of polls, 28
staff style of, 177
Kennedy, Robert F., 263
as Attorney General, 243
relations with Charles Ferris, 112
Kendall, Donald M., 81
Kerr, Robert S., 143, 154
Krushchev Remembers, 172
Killy, Edward V., 324
Kimmitt, J. S. (Stan), 114
King, John J., 73
Kissinger, Henry A., 9, 162, 215, 295
role of, in Nixon Administration, 159
Kitzmiller, Howard L., 44
Klein, Herbert G., 5, 9, 165
Kleindienst, Richard G., 270, 277
Kliman, Albert J., 207
Kline, Richard A., 40
Knauer, Virginia H., 309
Knowland, William F., 301
Knudson, Simon, 58
Kofron, John H., 27
Kosatka, Arden P., 22
Kosters, Marvin, 310
Kostopulos, Nick, 19

Kraft, Fran Farrell, 36
Kraft, John F., 32, 36
Knoppers, Antonie T., 80
Kurrus, Richard W., 241

L

Labor Department, 260
labor leaders, and political participation, 46
labor, organized, legislation efforts by, 71
and multinationals (corporations), 71
Labor, Secretary of, 44
Labor Statistics, Bureau of, 75, 84
Lagomarcino, John, 91
Laird, Barbara, 93
Laird, Melvin R., and presidential access of, 165
Laitin, Joseph, 209
Lamontagune, Raymond A., 86
Landrum, Phil M., 123
Larson, Clif, 14
Latrobe Steel Co., 79
"law and order", 3
as a political issue, 239
law, disclosure, 43
law firm, Arnold and Porter, 86
law, political spending, 39
Leach, Daniel E., 112
Lee, Lorenzo M., 108
legislation, domestic, 3
Legislative Reorganization Act of 1970, 39
Lehigh University, 59, 81
Lenhart Jr., Harry, 120
Lewis, David L., 52, 67
Liberal Party, 34
licenses, 75
Lillie, Mildred, 276
Lilly, William E., 208, 209, 229
Lincoln, Abraham, and speechwriting, 185
Lincoln, George A., 309
Lindsay, John V., 9, 98
Linowitz, Sol M., 93
Literary Digest, straw polls of the, 34
lobbies, 230
Lobbying Act (1946), Federal regulation of, 85
lobbyists (see pressure groups), 55
credibility of, 61
dairy, 62
effectiveness of, 59
for General Motors, 70
local government, 237, 238
Lockheed Aircraft Corp., 345
loan guarantee for, 328
Leevinger, Lee, 340

Landon, Alfred M., 34
Long, Huey Pierce, 144
Long, Rose McConnell, 144
Long, Russell B., 77, 116, 120
biographical sketch of, 143, 144
and campaign contributions proposals, 143
and defense of Thomas Dodd, 143
and sugar interests, 138
Longman, William M., 36
Louisiana Tech University, 56
Low, George M., 202
Lucas, Scott W., 118
Lugar, Richard G., 237
Lundin, Oscar A., 52
Lynch, William, 263
Lynn, Laurence E., 212
descriptive profile of 215-218

M

MacDonald, Dr. Gordon J. F., 66
MacGregor, Clark, 9, 168, 295
MacKenzie, John R., 56
Magill, Robert R., 52, 61, 65
Magnuson, Warren G., 225, 275, 278, 301
Magruder, Job S., 3, 10
Making of the President, The, 1968, 164
Malaga, Joseph E., 208
Malek, Frederic V., 9, 163, 256
Malone, Ross, 63
Management and Budget, Office of, and H.E.W., 219
Manhattan Leasing, 69
Manley, John F., 138
Mann, Thomas C., 54, 56, 66
Mansfield, Mike, 17, 294, 354
career of, 107
and character, 107
and copper mining interests, 108
on Lyndon Johnson as Majority Leader, 114, 115
personality profile report on, 107-109
Marcantonio, Vito, 7
Mardian, Robert C., 12, 242
Market Opinion Research, 26
Market Opinion Research of Detroit, 29
Market Opinion Research, Inc., 12
Markley, Rodney W., 53
Marland, Sidney P., 220
Marshall, Burke, 255
Martin, Edwin W., 220
Martin, John M., 129
Maryland, University of, 56
Mathews, Tom, 90, 100
Mathias, Charles M. C., 104
Mays, Robert F., 198

McCarthy, Eugene J., 35, 44, 87, 141
McCarthy, Joseph R., on presidential
    aides, 170
McCoy, Thomas, 44
McClellan, John L., 254, 255, 285
McCloskey, Paul N., 6
McCormack, John W., 109
McCracken, Paul W., 199
McCulloch, William N., 272
McDaniel, Paul R., 150
McDonald, Gene E., 79
McDonald, Jack, 33
McDowell, John R., 207
McFarland, Ernest W., 118
McGovern, George S., 9, 16, 32, 41, 241,
    294
McKeon, Thomas J., 258
McKinley, William, 3
McMillan, John L., 94
McMillan, Robert K., 36
McNamara, Robert S., 58, 93
Meany, George, 72, 98, 306
Media, use of, 5
    spending, limits on, 47
Medicare, 123
Meeds, Lloyd, 281
"Meet the Press," 40
Meier, Robert, 88, 91
mental health centers program, 212
Merchant Marine and Fisheries Commit-
    tee, 363
Merck and Company, Inc., 80
Meserve, Robert W., 279, 283
Meserve, William, 70
Metcalf, Lee, 373
Metzger, Eugene, 58
Meyer, Andre, 88
Meyers, G. C., 66
Meyers, Robert J., 130
Miami Beach Convention Center, 18
    Democratic Convention in, 14
Miami, University of, 18
Michigan's Graduate School of Business
    Administration, University of, 52
Michigan, University of, 59
Middleton, Dr. John T., 65
Miller, Arjay, 58, 60
Millikin, Eugene D., 153
Mills, Wilbur D., 33, 77, 84, 101, 120
    biographical report on, 124-126
Mitchell, John N., 1, 3, 7, 10, 27, 241,
    258, 276
    and annual report to the President,
        270
    and Carswell rejection, 160
    and Presidential access of, 165
Massachusetts Institute of Technology,
    Joint Center for Urban Studies, 70

Mohbat, Joseph E., 14, 17, 19
Mohr, John P., 253
Monagan, John S., 254
Monday (Republican National Commit-
    tee newspaper), on non-partisanship of
    Common Cause, 92
Moos, Malcolm C., 187
Morgan, Edward L., on John Erlichman,
    170
Morgan, Lee L., 71
Morgan, Thomas E., 77, 301
Moriarty, G. Marshall, 225
Morris, James, 53, 55, 57, 70
Morse, John F., 348
Morton, Rogers C. B., 367
Mosher, Charles A., 95
Moss, Frank, 278, 373
Moss, John E., 201
Moss, Robert E., 15
Moynihan, Daniel Patrick, 70, 211
Muchmore, Don M., 36
"Multinational Corporation: The Issue
    and Policy Alternatives," 80
    and the Chamber of Commerce, 81
Mundis, James M., 45
Mundt, John C., 152
Munro, S. Sterling, 17, 33, 40
Murphy, George, 20
Murphy, James J., 223
Murphy, Richard, 18
Musch, Donald J., 81
Muskie, Edmund S., 6, 9, 16, 20, 30, 40,
    65, 97, 241, 360
My Years With General Motors, 51

N

Nader, Ralph, 60, 64, 69
    and Research Group, 328
Napca, 63, 64
Narcotics and Dangerous Drugs, Bureau
    of, 260
Nathan, Richard P., 198, 205
National Aeronautics and Space Admin-
    istration, and the budget, 207
National Air Pollution Control Adminis-
    tration, 59, 63, 65, 206
National Associated Businessmen Inc.,
    126
National Association of Counties, 230
National Association of Manufacturers,
    71, 79, 81
National Broadcasting Company, 46
National Commission on Individual
    Rights, 256
National Council of Farmer Cooperatives,
    327
National Council on Public Polls, 31

National Defense Student Loan Program,
    352, 353
National Democrat, 22
National Foreign Trade Council Inc., 84
National Heart and Lung Institute, 224
National Highway Safety Bureau, 51, 68
National Institute of Health, 221, 224,
    225
National Journal, 33, 35, 52, 53, 54, 57,
    58, 59, 61, 62, 68
    on political polls, 26
    interview with: Robert U. Ayres, 64
                Wallace F. Bennett,
                    140
                Gerald M. Brannon,
                    131
                broadcasters, 340,
                    341
                James Corman, 125
                Thomas B. Curtis,
                    122
                Russell Drew, 208
                John Ehrlichman,
                    181
                John W. Gardner, 89
                Chet Holifield, 175
                General Motors em-
                    ployees, 67
                Sam Gibbons, 125
                John Griner, 210
                Philip A. Hart, 104,
                    110, 118
                House Ways and
                    Means Committee
                    members, 124
                William E. Lilly, 209
                Russell Long, 140,
                    142, 153
                Harold McClure, 67
                Mike Mansfield, 103,
                    105, 109, 114
                Wilbur Mills, 123
                Walter Mondale, 113
                Richard P. Nathan,
                    198
                Donald Rumsfeld,
                    206, 310, 311
                Senate Policy Com-
                    mittee members,
                    112
                George P. Schultz,
                    199, 208
                a "Southern Demo-
                    crat," 115
                Stuart Symington,
                    118
                Francis R. Valeo,
                    110

a White House Aide on revenue sharing, 144
 Laurence N. Woodworth, 128
National Political climate, 4
National Republican Congressional (Campaign) Committee, 37
National Science Foundation, 354
National Wildlife Federation, 370
Natural Resources Defense Council Inc., v. *Morton,* case of, 365
Naval Academy, U.S., 55
Navarro, Anna, 30
Navasky, Victor S., 245, 248
Nedzi, Lucien N., 31, 95
Nehmer, Stanley, 130
Nelson, Gaylord, 65, 116, 142, 256
Neustadt, Richard E., 94
New England, declining jobs in, 75
Newman, Edward, 227
Newman, Frank, 348
New York Daily News, 38
New York's Off Track Betting Corp., 42
New York Times, The, 38, 57
New York Times Magazine, The, 70
Nichols, Lou, 7
Nixon Administration:
 and Common Cause, 95, 96
 and debt ceiling, 288
 Domestic Council, 172
 foreign policy concerns, 295, 296, 297
 and inflation, 72
 and multinationals, 71
 and Presidential access, 165, 166
 and relations with Senate majority leader, 104
 speechwriters, 183-195
Nixon Era, coinage of words during, 188
Nixon, Richard M., 1, 2, 3, 4, 5, 7, 20, 26, 39, 43, 77, 85
 and American Bar Association, 283, 285
 and AOA budget, 222
 and campaign contributions (1972), 41
 and Cost of Living Council, 306, 307
 and organized crime, 262
 and decentralization, 235, 236
 Democratic National Committee complaints against, 332
 and economic policy, 83, 326
 and education, 347, 348, 351
 and farm administration, 236
 and Federal Strike Force, 259, 260
 and government reorganization, 229
 on J. Edgar Hoover and F.B.I., 241, 244

and imports surcharge, 82
on ITT, 11
and judiciary nominations, 277
leadership style of, 158
and media access, 334
musical preferences of, 163
and National Environmental Policy Act, 360, 362
and transportation industry, 318
and value-added tax, 357
and war powers, 292, 293
a Washington workday of, 162, 163
and welfare, 214
on wiretapping, 250
Nobleman, Eli E., 139
Nofziger, Lyn, 8
Noise Abatement and Control Office, 206
North Atlantic Treaty Organization, strength of (1971), 294
"November Group," 12

O

O'Brien, Lawrence F., 1, 8, 14, 19, 21, 33
O'Dwyer, Paul, 38
Odle Jr., Robert C., 10
Odell Jr., Robert P., 43
Office of Economic Opportunity, 214
 and Common Cause, 94
Office of Management and Budget (OMB), 195
Ogilvie, Richard B., 348
O'Hara, James G., 139
Oil and Gas Journal report, 379
Okun, Arthur M., 111
Older Americans Act, 224
O'Mahony, Joseph E., 83
One Heartbeat Away, 282
O'Neill, Paul H., 207
O'Neill Jr., Thomas P., 95, 97
"Operation Eagle Eye," 7
Opinion Research, 33
 of California, 36
 of Princeton, N.J., 29
Orban, Kurt, 82
Oregon, primary election, 32
Ottina, John R., 216

P

Packard, David, 93, 203
Paine, Thomas O., 202
Palevsky, Max, 88
Parker, Barrington J., 94
Pastore, John O., 372
patents, 75

Patman, Wright, 132, 314
Pearce, Jack, 325
Pell, Claiborne, 354, 346
Pellerzi, Leo M., 253
Peloquin, Robert D., 259
Pepper, Claude, 241, 250
Pepsi Company Inc., 81
Percy, Charles H., 97, 142, 223, 232
Perkins, Carl D., 223, 354
Pertschuck, Michael, 60, 70
Peterson, Elly M., 86
Peterson, Peter G., 72, 93, 309
Philadelphia, Pa., Democratic mayoral primary in, 31
Philadelphia Plan, 93
Pilzys, Matthew, 206
Plesser, Tully, 33, 38
Plessner, William, 205
Poage, W. R., 94
Poff, Richard H., 276
Political Education, Committee on, (COPE), 33
political parties, 1-48
 effect on congressional policy making, 101
political polls, Ehrlicman on, 181
Political Surveys and Analysis Inc., 36
politics, divisive, 3
Politics of Finance, The, 138
polling:
 Truth-in-Polling Act, 31
 and research, cost of on state level, 35
polls, 26-38
 and field interviews, 31
 and public opinion, 2, 22
 rise of the, 34
 and sample methods, 36
 scientific, 34
Polls, Television and the New Politics, 31
Pollert, William R., 79, 81
pollution, air, 62
 control technology, 62
 1965 Clean Air Act Amendments, 63
Pomerance, Rocky, 18
poor people, money for, 212
Porter, Herbert L., 10
Postal Service, U.S., 260
poverty negotiations, 204-206
Powell, Lewis F., 277
Powers, George B., 274
Presidency, the, 157-195
 isolation of, 166
presidential, aides, 170
 campaign, expense of, 22, 39
 elections: 1948, 35, 36; 1968, 3, 4, 6; 1972, 4, 8
 relations, Ehrlicman on, 181

speechwriters, 183-195
President's Council on International
    Economic Policy, 82
President's Daily News Summary (sample of), 194
pressure groups, 49-101
Price, David, 138
Price, Melvin, 372
Price, Raymond K., 163
primary (1972), California, 6
Princeton University, 59
Proxmire, William, 105, 141, 143, 314
Prussian guards (Nixon aides), 170
Public Opinion Quarterly, 30
public policy, 291-304
Public Works Committee, 64
publications, political, 22
Pucinski, Roman C., 126, 355
Purcell, Joe, 14
Purdy, Allan W., 351

Q

Quarles, John R., 361, 374
Quayle III, Oliver A., 26, 32
Quie, Albert H., 350

R

Railpax, 204
railroads, 326
    abandonment of, 320
    Penn Central, 320
    and property taxes, 320
    regulation of, 320
    strike plan of, 204
Railroad Passenger Corp., National,
    (AMTRAK), 319
Ramey, James T., 372
Rand Corp. and HEW evaluation, 220
Randolph, Jennings, 64
Rathbun, Georgianna F., 91
Ray, James Earl, 244
Reagan, Ronald, 5, 8
Reardon, John T., 274
"Red and the Black, The," 348
Reedy, George, 167, 303
Reese, Mate, and Associates, 92
Rehnquist, William H., 242, 277
ReElector, The, 12
Reorganization Act of 1946, 121
Report from Washington, 92
Republican governors, 5
Republican National Committee, 5, 41
    and polls, 29
Republican National Leadership Conference, 3
Republican party, 3

Republican Policy Committee, 112
Reuss, Henry S., 361, 373
Reuther, Walter P., 90
Rhode, Earl D., 308
Ribicoff, Abraham A., 60, 140, 229
Riccardo, John J., 66
Rice, Donald B., 198
Richardson, Elliot L., 65, 93, 198, 212,
    222, 345
Rietz, Kenneth C., 12
Ritzinger, G. E. (Gene), 56, 57
Rivlin, Alice M., 351
Robb, John D., 280
Roberts, John A., on John Erlichman,
    171
Roche, James M., 52, 58, 98
Rockefeller, David, 98, 111
Rockefeller, Nelson A., 5, 35, 42, 93
Rockefeller III, John D., 86, 88, 93
Rogers, Paul, 53
Rogers, William P., 6, 165, 295
Roisman, Anthony Z., 370
Roll Jr., Charles W., 36, 37
Romnes, H. I., 98
Romney, George W., 93, 94, 207, 209,
    309
    presidential access of, 165
Rooney, John J., 251
Roosevelt, Franklin D., 3, 19, 34, 200
Roosevelt, Theodore, 3
Roper, Burns W., 34
Roper, Elmo, 33, 34
Rosenman, Samuel J., 192
Rouse, Andrew W., 233
Rowan, Michael, 26
Ruckelshaus, William D., 204, 360
Rumsfeld, Donald, 205, 306, 309
    biographical report on, 312, 313
Russell, Madeleine Haas, 88
Russell, Richard B., death of, 112
Ruttenberg, Stanley H., and Associates, 73

S

Safire, William, 165
Salk, Jonas, 94
Samuels, Howard J., 41, 42
Sanchez, Manola, 162
San Diego, Cal., convention bureau of, 11
Santarelli, Donald E., 286
Sargent, Francis W., 93
Sasaki, Wesley, 206
Saxbe, William B., 109
Sayler, John P., 64
Scammon, Richard M., 31
Scheuer, James H., 245
Schirra, Walter M., 329
Schleede, Glenn, 206

Schlesinger Jr., Arthur M., 294
    on war, 302
Schlesinger, James R., 198
Schorr, Daniel, 244
Schroeder, H. Kenneth, 262
Schultze, Charles L., 111
Schweiker, Richard S., 109, 277
    on relations with the White House,
    168
Scott, Hugh, 39, 43, 44, 63, 107, 207,
    295, 354
Secret Service, 260
Securities and Exchange Commission, 260
Segal, Bernard, 283
Seidl, John M., 227
Selling of the Pentagon, The, 335
Semer, Milton P., 234
Senate, U. S.:
    campaign (1950), 7
    Commerce Committee, 60
    Democratic Policy Committee, membership of (92nd Congress), 106
    Democratic Steering Committee
        (92nd Congress), membership of,
        106
    Ethics Committee and Thomas Dodd
        case, 143
    Finance Committee, 77, 120, 137,
        138, 139, 141, 142, 144; and
        Robert (Bobby) Baker, 154, 155
    Foreign Relations Committee, membership of, 298
    Judiciary Subcommittee on constitutional rights, 333
    leadership in twentieth century, 117,
        118
    majority leader, role of, 103-119
    and presidential power to make war,
        293, 294
    Public Works Committee, 61, 361
Senate Secretary, 44
Sessions, Clifton, 257
sex discrimination in education, 355
Shafer, Raymond P., 277
Shapeley, Willis H., 208
Sharp, Dean E., 275
Shelley & Co. Inc., E. F., 78
Sheraton-Jefferson Hotel, 20
Shultz, George, 93, 197, 202, 309
Shumway, DeVan L., 6
Sidey, Hugh S., 5
Sierra Club, 370
Simon, Norton, 88
sky marshall plan, 203
Sloan, Alfred P., 51
Smathers, George A., 319, 323
Smith, H. Allen, 44
Smith, Margaret Chase, 115

Smith, Neal, 252
Smith, Robert W., 53
Smith, William K., 325
Smith, Sylvester C., 272
Smithy, Wayne L., 53
Social Science Research Council, 34
Social Security Act of 1935, 120
Sofaer, Abraham D., 303
Sorensen, Theodore C., on Agnew
    speeches, 190
        on Kennedy style, 189
        memories of "New Frontier," 189-
            192
        on speechwriting for J. F. K., 184,
            188
South Florida Hotel and Motel Associa-
    tion, 18
South Texas College of Law, 56
Southern Caucus, 112
Southern Methodist University, 20
"southern strategy," 6
Spann Jr., William B., 283
Sparkman, John, 116
Spaulding, Josiah A., 86
speechwriters, presidential, 183-195
    staff line-up (listing), 184
    volume of work, 183
Spellerberg, Shirley, 5
Spencer-Roberts and Associates, 37
Speth, G. Gustave, 375
Springer, William L., 337
Springrose, James V., 325
Squier, Robert D., 30
Stafford, George, 324, 328
Staggers, Harley O., 70
Stam, Colin F., 128
Stans, Maurice H., 10
Stanton, Frank, 335, 336
Statistical Policy and Management Infor-
    mation Systems, 202
Stefan, Karl, 254
Stein, Herbert, 309
Steinem, Gloria, 93
Steinbeck, John, 187
Steinberg, David J., 135
Stennis, John, 104, 106, 298
Stern Community Law Firm, 332
Stern, Herbert J., 267
Stern, Phillip M., 121
Stevenson, Robert, 59
Stewart, John G., 14, 20
St. Louis, Mo., 20
Stone, Harlan F., 243, 248
Strauss, Robert S., 14, 43
strike force, federal, 258
student aid, 349, 350
Student Loan Marketing Association
    (SLMA), 352

student power, 356
Sullivan, Richard J., 360
Sulzberger, Iphigene Ochs, 88
Summers, John B., 332, 336
Sundquist, James S., 234
supersonic transport (SST), and Common
    Cause, 94
Surrey, Stanley, 111, 128, 140, 286, 287
surrogates, use of in campaign, 5
Swinford, T. William, 44
Symington, Stuart S., 21, 110

T

Tabor, Ralph, 230, 238
Taft Jr., Robert, 298
Taft, William Howard, 3
Talmadge, Herman E., 106, 112
    and veteran's interests, 138
Tames, George, 17
tariff code, 75
Tariff Commission, U.S., 74
Taylor, Eldon, 206
Tax Reform Act of 1969, 121, 140
tax rules, and Common Cause, 95
teacher training, 357
Teeter, Robert M., 12, 26
television, use of, 23
    advertising on, 47
    power of, 42
"Texas Rangers" (Johnson aides), 170
Texas Schoolbook Depository Building,
    20
Texas, senatorial contest in 1970, 33
Theis, Paul A., 37
Thompson Agency, J. Walter, 12
Thompson, Clark, 123
Thompson, David M., 99
Thompson, Frank, 345
Thompson, L. Fred, 45
Thompson, William D., 56, 57
Thorp, Bruce E., 332
Thurmond, Strom, 6
Tilman, Benjamin, 105
Tilton v. Richardson, 347
Todd, Webster B., 10
Tolson, Clyde A., 253
Toms, Douglas W., 69
Tonkin Gulf Resolution, 294
Tracey, John P., 281
Trade, Emergency Committee for Ameri-
    can, 79, 80
Trade Expansion Act (1962), escape
    clause of the, 74
trade, international, and legislative pro-
    posals, 72
Traffic Safety Act (1966), 60, 69
Train, Russell E., 65, 360

Transportation, Department of, 22, 317
    Committee on Modern Efficient
        Transportation (COMET), 325
    and Nixon administration, 318
Transportation (Surface) Act of 1971,
    318, 327
Trans World Airlines Inc., (chart), 39,
    45
Treasury Department, 83
    organization of, 260
Treleaven Jr., Harry, 12, 165
Trice, J. Mark, 113
Troop, Glen S., 154
truckers, 319
Truman, Bess (Mrs. Harry S.), 19
Truman, David, 115
Truman, Harry S., 19, 34, 250, 275
Truth-in-Polling Act, 31
Tunney, John V., 20
Turner, Francis C., 69, 236
Twilight of the Presidency, The, 167

U

United Auto Workers Union (UAW), 46,
    47, 78
Udall, Morris K., 44
Udall, Stewart L., 93
Ullman, Al, 127
unemployment, 71
Union of Electrical, Radio and Machine
    Workers, International, 75
unions, 61
United Airlines Inc., (chart), 39
United Nations International Children's
    Emergency Fund, 24
United States, and job opportunities, 84
    and results of foreign imports, 75
United Steelworkers of America, 75
Urban Coalition, 90
Urban Mass Transportation Administra-
    tion, 237
urban revewal and the federal budget, 206

V

Vail, Thomas L. C., 138
Valenti, Jack J., 94
Vandenberg, Arthur H., 295
Vander Jagt, Guy A., 68
Van Dusen, Richard C., 207, 237
Vanik, Charles A., 123
Van Ness Jr., William, 362
Vietnam war, 292
    and Common Cause, 95
    offensive in, 3
Veneman, John G., 65, 217, 226
Vinson, Carl, 133

392

Vinson Jr., Fred M., 259
violence, 3
Volker, Paul A., 130
Volpe, John A., 69, 319
    and presidential access, 165
voter registration drive in Janesville, Wis.,
    48
voters, young (1972), 36
voting machines, security of, 7
voting rights, and Common Cause, 95

W

Waddy, Joseph C., 70
Wade, George M., 303
wage-price freeze, 20
Walker, Charles E., 83, 306
Wallace, George C., 4, 8, 9, 35
Wallace, Harold E., 108
Wall Street Journal, 56, 57, 65
Walsh, Lawrence E., 275
Ward, Joe H., 151
Washington Post, 57
    on Common Cause, 98
Wasilewski, Vincent T., 45
Watergate Office Building, 16
Watts, John C., 127
Watson Jr., Thomas J., 93
Webb, James E., 202

Weber, Arnold, 202
Weinberg, Nat, 61
Weinberger, Caspar W., 66, 198, 201,
    213, 309
welfare reform and Common Cause, 95
Welfare Rights Organization, National,
    91, 150
Welsh, William B., 14
Wertheimer, Fred M., 95
Western, Tracy A., 332, 334
Wexler, Mrs. Ann, 87
Whalen Jr., Charles W., 95
Whitaker, John C., 206, 374
White, Harry Dexter, 250
Whitehead, Clay T., 337
White House, The, 1
    Conference on Aging, 222
    Conference on Children, 81
    reporting structure of, 165, 166
    staff of, 8
White, Theodore, 164
Wicker, Tom, on Russell Long, 143
Wiley, George A., 100
Williams, Harrison A., 356
Williams, John J., and opposition to
    Russell Long, 143
    on majority leaders, 109
Wilson, Charles H., 256
Wilson, Charles E., 58

Wilson, John O., 204
Wilson, Woodrow, 3, 117
    and speechwriting, 185
Wisconsin, primary election, 32
Wolkomir, Nathan, 210
women's rights, 355
Wood, Richardson K., 34
Woodcock, Leonard, 78, 87
Woods, Rose Mary, 163
Woodworth, L. N., 130
Working With Roosevelt, 192
World Affairs Council, 84
Wright, Edward L., 281, 285
Wright, James, 369
Wright, J. Skelly, 334, 364

Y

Yale University, 59
Yeutter, Clayton K., 10
Yoltan, Guy, 91
young people, Ehrlicman on, 181
youth vote, 11

Z

Zablocki, Clement J., 300
Ziegler, Ronald L., 9, 162